PHILOSOPHY IN THE HELLENISTIC AND ROMAN WORLDS

PETER ADAMSON

PHILOSOPHY IN THE HELLENISTIC AND ROMAN WORLDS

a history of philosophy without any gaps

volume 2

OXFORD
UNIVERSITY PRESS

OXFORD
UNIVERSITY PRESS

Great Clarendon Street, Oxford, OX2 6DP,
United Kingdom

Oxford University Press is a department of the University of Oxford.
It furthers the University's objective of excellence in research, scholarship,
and education by publishing worldwide. Oxford is a registered trade mark of
Oxford University Press in the UK and in certain other countries

First Edition published in 2015

Impression: 3

Published in the United States of America by Oxford University Press
198 Madison Avenue, New York, NY 10016, United States of America

British Library Cataloguing in Publication Data

Data available

Library of Congress Control Number: 2013956024

ISBN 978-0-19-872802-3

Printed in Great Britain by
Clays Ltd, St Ives plc

For my brother Glenn Adamson

CONTENTS

Part II. Pagan Philosophy in the Roman Empire

CONTENTS

Part III. Christian Philosophy in the Roman Empire

PREFACE

Like a particularly devoted tribute band, this series of books aims to cover not just philosophy's greatest hits, but the complete back catalogue. The project is born out of a conviction that we will understand the history of philosophy only by telling it as a continuous narrative, rather than jumping from one highlight to the next. It also allows me to discuss the many fascinating ideas and arguments that are found in less celebrated authors. I began applying this "without any gaps" manifesto in the first volume of this series, entitled *Classical Philosophy*. You don't need to have read it before turning to this book, but it wouldn't hurt. (I refer back to it occasionally in the notes.) *Classical Philosophy* devoted chapters to somewhat out-of-the-way topics like the Hippocratic corpus and the students of Plato and Aristotle. Nonetheless, much of that volume was spent discussing two giants, Plato and Aristotle, who are fixtures of undergraduate reading lists around the world. This book, by contrast, spends most of its time filling gaps.

It is divided into three sections, each more in danger of being unfamiliar than the last: Hellenistic philosophy, late antique philosophy among pagans, and ancient Christian philosophy. It is only relatively recently that the Hellenistic schools—the Cynics, Cyrenaics, Stoics, Skeptics, and Epicureans—became the object of serious interest among professional historians of philosophy. By now they are pretty well covered in secondary literature. Even so, one could easily get through a philosophy degree at most universities without being required to learn anything about the Hellenistic period. Still less frequently do philosophy departments offer courses on Neoplatonism, the dominant tradition of later pagan philosophy. As for the third section of this book, even specialists in ancient philosophy may be slightly surprised to see how much space I've devoted to the Christian thinkers. But it's my hope, and even my expectation, that ancient Christian thought will increasingly be included in our conception of ancient philosophy over the coming decades, just as Hellenistic philosophy and Neoplatonism have been incorporated into the field. One thing about historians is they are always looking for new texts to think about, and the texts of the Christians represent the last unexplored frontier in antique philosophy.

Don't get the wrong idea, though. The figures covered in this volume may be less famous than Plato and Aristotle, but some of them aren't *much* less famous. There are at least two giants in this volume too, namely Plotinus, usually credited with founding Neoplatonism, and Augustine, who I suppose needs no introduction. Because of their importance I have devoted numerous chapters to various aspects of their thought. Within the Hellenistic traditions we find a few more household names (though I guess it depends on the household), with Epicurus and the so-called "Roman Stoics": Seneca, Epictetus, and Marcus Aurelius. They are rightly cherished by a wide audience of readers for their intimate writing style and compelling ethical teachings. Another Roman whose celebrity still shines is Cicero, although his lasting fame has more to do with his unsuccessful attempts to preserve the Roman Republic than with the philosophical ideas covered in this book.

We will understand all these major figures far better once we know something about the (supposedly) minor thinkers who influenced, interpreted, and interacted with them. I can't claim to have devoted a full discussion to every worthwhile philosopher between Alexander the Great and the fall of the Roman Empire in the West, which is roughly the time-span covered here. Just to beat uncharitable reviewers to the punch, I could have honored Posidonius, Philodemus, or Marius Victorinus with their own chapters, instead of mentioning them only in passing. Still, I am confident that this volume offers a more detailed look at the period than any other book aimed at the general reader. My hope is that this level of detail will also make the book interesting to readers who already know a good deal about later ancient philosophy. There won't be many who come to it already familiar with every character we're going to encounter. I certainly wasn't before I started writing it, despite the fact that late antique philosophy is one of my main research interests.

Before we start to meet the cast of characters, though, let me say something about the philosophical themes that will recur throughout our story, lest the woods be lost for the trees. The most appropriate place to start is ethics. As I explain in the first chapter, the Hellenistic schools followed Socrates in believing that philosophy is about learning how to live. Many of the thinkers we'll examine thought that the right kind of life should be one that is wholly within our own power, invulnerable to misfortune. This applies even to hedonists like the Epicureans and Cyrenaics. In later antiquity so rigorous a moral thinker as Aristotle was frequently seen as weak-minded for admitting that happiness might involve having a happy family, good friends, and some money, in addition to the possession of virtue. When the ideal of indomitable individual perfection was finally questioned, it was not because ethicists were softening their stance. Rather, it happened for theological reasons. Augustine judged the Hellenic philosophers as prideful for daring to think that they could attain perfect virtue without outside assistance. The helping hand needed to come not from family, friends, or fortune, but from God.

The relationship between the human and the divine is another leitmotif of the book. It goes without saying that this was a core issue for our Christian philosophers. It was also an abiding concern of the Stoics, the Neoplatonists, and even the Epicureans—although in the latter case their goal was to show that there was no relationship to speak of (or worry about) between us and the gods. All of these groups tried to reconcile Hellenic religious belief with philosophical doctrines. But that challenge was a very different proposition depending whether you were, say, an early Stoic, as opposed to a late Neoplatonist. This is because the metaphysical world-views of these schools were themselves opposed. Broadly speaking, the Hellenistic period was a time of physicalism, with both the Stoics and Epicureans denying the reality of immaterial entities. It is an unusually dramatic shift within the history of philosophy, as if Alexander the Great sent out a memo to all philosophers telling them that incorporeal substances were no longer welcome. The down-to-earth consensus started to break down already around the time that Cicero and his allies failed to prevent the fall of the Roman Republic. In the first centuries BC and AD Platonism started to make a comeback. Before long, all philosophers were wholly convinced that there are incorporeal beings.

The Platonists' and Christians' commitment to the existence of things that cannot be seen or touched raises an obvious difficulty: how can we possibly know about such things? Earlier Greek philosophers had often sought to ground knowledge in sense-experience. Aristotle was one example, and the point was emphasized even more forcefully by Epicurus. But for Neoplatonists and Christian philosopher-theologians, the most important things of all were things inaccessible to the senses. These thinkers were thus led to contemplate the nature of contemplation itself, in an attempt to show that humans are capable of a sort of knowledge superior to that derived from sensation. Yet they recognized the limits of even this higher knowledge. The highest principle—whether the unknowable One of Plotinus, the even more unknowable Ineffable of Damascius, or the creator God of the Jews and Christians—was frequently seen as eluding our understanding. This was a more theological version of a problem that had long been troubling philosophers. One of the main Hellenistic schools was known by a name that more or less speaks for itself: the Skeptics. They worked to undermine the confident knowledge-claims of their rivals, the Stoics and Epicureans. Skeptical strategies and habits of mind survived in the works of authors that the Skeptics themselves would certainly have seen as "dogmatists," not least Plotinus and Augustine.

Later ancient philosophy is thus characterized by the question "What can we know, and how do we know it?" just as much as by question "How should we live?" A preoccupation with the extent and sources of our knowledge turns up in the scientific disciplines too, especially in the case of medicine. In the last volume, as mentioned above, I covered the philosophical contribution of the Hippocratic corpus. In this volume, to paraphrase Lucy from the Peanuts comic strip, the doctors are still in. I will discuss not only the medical schools and their epistemological debates, but also the greatest doctor of antiquity, Galen. We'll also observe the science of the stars, focusing on its greatest exponent, Ptolemy. I include these topics as part of the "without any gaps" approach. The ancient histories of philosophy and science are closely intertwined, to the point that a complete perusal of either one must include at least glancing at the other. In the case of medicine, astronomy, and astrology, this is particularly easy to document, as Galen and Ptolemy draw expressly on philosophical sources like Plato, Aristotle, and the Stoics.

In this book, then, we'll find contributions to the three most central areas of philosophy: ethics, metaphysics, and epistemology. There will also be forays into such branches as logic, philosophy of language, and the theory of mind. And philosophers of religion will of course find many resonances with the issues that concern them. As for political philosophy, though the book in general is based on the scripts of my History of Philosophy podcast series, I have added a chapter on late antique political thought, focusing on a parallel often drawn in antiquity between the household and the state.[1] This gives me a chance to talk about women and slaves, two groups of people we often forget when thinking about philosophy in the ancient world. Apart from this general discussion about philosophers' attitudes towards women, you'll also find a number of female figures discussed in the book you are about to read. It would, sadly, be a wild exaggeration to say that women played a major role in any phase of ancient philosophy. For that we really need to wait for the greater opportunities afforded to them in early modern Europe. But we will be meeting the Cynic Hipparchia, the pagan martyr Hypatia, and a number of Christian women, like the Cappadocian Macrina and Augustine's formidable mother Monica.

No matter how complete our historical and thematic approach, there is no getting around the fact that the historical record for the period we will be discussing is far from gapless. With the early Stoics and Skeptics we are back to sifting through fragments and biased reports found in later authors, as with the Pre-Socratics. Things do improve considerably with the Roman Stoics and in late antiquity. But apart from Plotinus, no author discussed in this volume left behind a significant body of work that is preserved in its entirety. On the other hand, writers like Galen and Augustine are so voluminously represented in surviving texts that one can hardly complain. Our situation is like that of Diogenes the Cynic presented with a big hunk of raw meat: there is plenty for us to get our teeth into. So without further ado, let's move on to Volume 2 of the History of Philosophy, without any gaps.

ACKNOWLEDGEMENTS

Just as you can't make an omelette without breaking a few eggs, you can't write a book about later ancient philosophy without being egged on by supportive colleagues, friends, and family. Among my colleagues and friends I would particularly like to thank my fellow ancient enthusiasts in London and Munich, especially Verity Harte, Fiona Leigh, M. M. McCabe, Oliver Primavesi, Christof Rapp, Sir (!) Richard Sorabji, and Raphael Woolf. The last two of these also kindly agreed to be interviewed for the podcasts on later ancient philosophy, as did many other wonderful scholars: George Boys-Stones, Sarah Byers, Charles Brittain, Serafina Cuomo, Jim Hankinson, Tony Long, John Marenbon, Dominic O'Meara, Jan Opsomer, David Sedley, John Sellars, Anne Sheppard, James Warren, and James Wilberding. For the production of the podcast I was ably assisted by Fay Edwards, who edited the episodes on later ancient philosophy, and Julian Rimmer, who created and maintains the podcast website. Thanks too to Stefan Hagel for allowing me to use his wonderful music in the podcast, and to Fedor Benevich for his work on the volume index.

I received very useful comments on the podcast scripts and book version from Dirk Baltzly, Marc Delcogliano, and Brad Inwood, as well as from listeners who wrote in with suggestions and corrections. I wouldn't be surprised if all this advice has not prevented me from making mistakes along the way. Indeed, I've read enough about ancient Skepticism to be sure that I must have. (Unless of course I didn't; but sadly, in that case the previous sentence is a mistake, so I made one after all.)

Of course my greatest debt of gratitude is owed to my family. I would especially like to mention my grandfather Arthur Adamson, whose amazingly productive and inventive life came to an end while I was revising this book. I think even an ancient Stoic would have recognized Arthur as a virtuous man. The love and support I have received from my parents have as always been unflagging. I have dedicated this book to my twin brother Glenn Adamson, in thanks for his enthusiasm for the podcast, among other things. And finally, of course, I would like to thank my wife Ursula and our children Johanna and Sophia. The three of them are living proof that Aristotle was right and Epicurus wrong: the most happy life is lived with family.

A NOTE ON REFERENCES

The only general abbreviation used for citations is LS, which stands for this invaluable reader: A. A. Long and D. N. Sedley, *The Hellenistic Philosophers* (Cambridge, 1987). Otherwise references to primary texts are keyed to sources identified in the notes, always at the first mention of a given text. Typically these point the reader to English translations, rather than Greek or Latin editions. As for secondary literature, in *Classical Philosophy* I focused on providing references for especially controversial or often-discussed topics. That approach especially made sense for Plato and Aristotle, about whom there is a vast secondary literature with long-running disputes on certain aspects of their thought. For this volume, where the figures and themes are somewhat less familiar, I have reverted to a more standard approach of recommending key secondary sources as I go along. There is also an extensive bibliography of further reading at the end of the book.

A NOTE ON REFERENCES

DATES

The abbreviation "fl." stands for *floruit*, "flourished," i.e. probably wrote at about that time, while "ca." stands for *circa*, "approximately," and "r." stands for "reigned."

Philosophers and other authors		Selected historical events	
BC		BC	
		Mythical date of the founding of Rome	753/2
		Destruction of the Temple in Jerusalem	586
		Building of second Temple in Jerusalem	515
		Death of Alexander the Great	323
		Peace treaty establishes tripartition	
		of Alexander's empire	311
		Founding of the Library of Alexandria	290s
Crates	d. ca.285	Death of Ptolemy I	283/2
Epicurus	342–271	Death of Lysimachos, king	
		of Macedonia; death of Seleukos	281
Pyrrho	d. ca. 275–270	First Carthaginian War begins	264
Zeno of Citium	344–262		
Euclid	fl. 300		
Arcesilaus	ca. 316–241		
Cleanthes	d. 232		
Timon of Philus	ca. 320–230		
Erasistratus	fl. first half 3rd cent.		
Herophilus	3rd cent.		
Archimedes	ca. 287–212	Second Carthaginian War begins	219
Chrysippus	d. ca. 206		
Carneades	ca. 214–129	First Macedonian War begins	214
		Second Macedonian War begins	201
		Death of Hannibal	183
		Third Macedonian War begins	171
		Judas Maccabaeus purifies the Temple	164
Philo of Larissa	158–83	Embassy of philosophers to Rome	155
		Destruction of Carthage by the Romans	146

Antiochus of Ascalon	ca. 130–69	First Mithridatic War	88
		Sack of Athens by Roman general Sulla	86
		Second Mithridatic War	82
		Pompey takes Syria for Rome	64
		First Triumvirate in Rome (Caesar, Crassus, Pompey)	60
Lucretius	d. ca. 50	Julius Caesar in Egypt	48
Philodemus of Gadara	1st cent.	Assassination of Caesar	44
Cicero	106–43	Battle of Actium: Octavian defeats Mark Anthony and Cleopatra	31
Aenesidemus	1st cent.	Death of Cleopatra VII, ending Ptolemaic rule	30
Agrippa	1st cent.		
Andronicus	1st cent.		
Boethus of Sidon	second half 1st cent.		
Eudorus	fl. ca. 25	Senate declares Octavian as Augustus	27
		Birth of Jesus	ca. 7

AD		AD	
Philo of Alexandria	first half 1st cent.	Death of emperor Gaius "Caligula"	41
Thrasyllus	d. 36	Letters of St Paul	50–64
Seneca	d. 65	Death of emperor Nero	69
Quintillian	ca. 35–100	Destruction of Second Temple	70
Plutarch	ca. 50–120	Jewish revolts in northern Africa	115–17
Epictetus	ca. 55–135		
Calvenus Taurus	first half 2nd cent.		
Aspasius	ca. 100–50		
Justin Martyr	ca. 100–65	War between Rome and Parthia	161–6
Ptolemy	ca. 100–70		
Marcus Aurelius	121–80 (r. 161–80)	Marcus Aurelius founds chairs of philosophy in Rome	176
Irenaeus of Lyons	ca. 130–200	Death of emperor Commodus	192
Sextus Empiricus	fl. ca. 200		
Clement of Alexandria	ca. 150–215		
Tertullian	155–ca. 220		
Galen	129–ca. 216	Death of emperor Septimus Severus	211
Alexander of Aphrodisias	fl. ca. 200		
Numenius	mid-2nd cent.		
Apuleius	mid-2nd cent.		
Alcinous	2nd cent.		

Origen	185–253		
Plotinus	205–70	Plotinus on campaign with Gordian	243
Porphyry	234–ca. 305	Invasion by the Sasanians	251
Iamblichus	ca. 245–ca. 320	Death of emperor Aurelian	275
Calcidius	fl. 320s	Death of emperor Diocletian	305
Arius	ca. 260–336	Constantine proclaimed Caesar	306
Lactantius	ca. 260–340	Constantine victorious at battle of the Milvian Bridge	312
		First Council of Nicaea	325
Anthony the Great	d. 356	Death of emperor Constantine	337
Victorinus	fl. 353–62	Altar of Victory removed at Rome (later restored by Julian, then removed again in 384)	357
Julian ("the Apostate")	331–63 (r. 361–3)		
Athanasius	295–373		
Basil of Caesarea	330–79	Julian's failed Persian campaign	363
Macrina	d. 379	Gothic army defeats Romans in battle of Adrianople	
Themistius	ca. 317–88		378
Gregory of Nazianzus	ca. 328–ca. 390		
Gregory of Nyssa	ca. 331–ca. 395		
Ambrose	ca. 340–97		
Evagrius	ca. 345–99	Vandals cross the Rhine	406
Rufinus	ca. 345–410	Withdrawal of Roman army from Britain	410
Hypatia	d. 415	Sack of Rome by Alaric's Visigoths	410
Jerome	d. 420		
Martianus Capella	fl. early 5th c.		
Macrobius	fl. early 5th c.		
Hierocles of Alexandria	first half 5th cent.		
Augustine	354–430		
Plutarch of Athens	d. 432		
Syrianus	d. 437		
Cyril of Alexandria	ca. 378–444		
Nestorius	ca. 381–ca. 451	Death of Attila the Hun	453
Proclus	412–85	Sack of Rome by the Vandals	455
Pseudo-Dionysus	fl. ca. 500	Production of Justinian's law-code	527–33
Boethius	ca. 480–524 or 525	Death of Theodoric, king of the Ostrogoths	526
Ammonius son of Hermeias	ca. 435/45–517/26		
Damascius	ca. 462–after 538		
Simplicius	ca. 480–560	Death of emperor Justinian	565

Olympiodorus	d. after 565		
John Philoponus	ca. 490–570s		
Maximus the Confessor	580–662	Death of emperor Maurice	602
		Persians sack Jerusalem	614
		Death of the Prophet Muhammad	632
		Arabs defeat Byzantines at the battle of Yarmuk	636

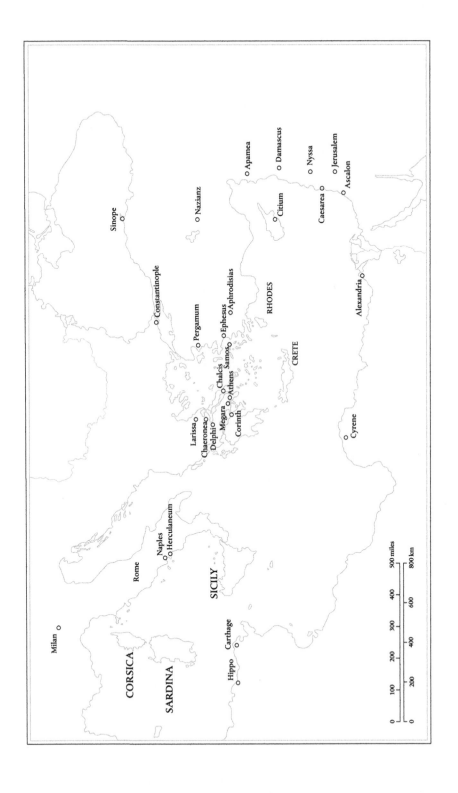

Milan

CORSICA

SARDINA

Hippo

Carthage

SICILY

Rome

Naples
Herculaneum

CRETE

RHODES

Sinope

Nazianz

Constantinople

Pergamum
Ephesus
Aphrodisias
Chalcis
Samos
Athens
Megara
Corinth
Larissa
Chaeronea
Delphi

Apamea
Damascus
Nyssa
Jerusalem
Ascalon
Citium
Caesarea

Alexandria

Cyrene

0   100   200   300   400   500 miles

0   200   400   600   800 km

PART I

HELLENISTIC PHILOSOPHY

1

FIGHTING OVER SOCRATES
THE HELLENISTIC SCHOOLS

S ocrates has a strong claim to be the most influential philosopher who never wrote anything.[1] It was not only Plato who wrote "Socratic" literature, using Socrates as a character and depicting his combative inquiries into ethical topics. There was also Plato's contemporary, the soldier and historian Xenophon, who wrote stylized reminiscences of Socrates and his conversations. But neither Plato nor Xenophon qualify as "Socratic" in the stronger sense of living a lifestyle inspired by the gadfly of Athens. That would have meant going barefoot, hanging around in the marketplace, accosting passers-by, and demanding that they account for their claims to knowledge. Plato and Xenophon were certainly inspired by Socrates, but they did not seek to imitate him. Indeed, writing about Socrates was itself a way of failing to imitate him, given that Socrates didn't write anything.

But perhaps this is a rather superficial idea of what it would mean to follow Socrates' example. Surely Socrates wasn't just asking us to throw away our shoes and be rude to pedestrians. He wanted us to reflect seriously on the most important matters, such as virtue. And this is certainly something Plato and Xenophon did. We might further ask, though, whether Plato, Xenophon, or Aristotle for that matter, arrived at distinctively Socratic *conclusions* regarding these most important matters. To be truly Socratic was not merely to choose poverty, nor to ask certain types of questions, but to give certain answers to those questions—that virtue is knowledge, for instance, or that all value derives from virtue and wisdom. Thus being "Socratic" could mean different things to different admirers. There was the lifestyle, with its defiant exhibition of self-sufficiency; there was the relentless questioning; and then there was the sheer fact that Socrates seemed to have achieved happiness, and done so by philosophizing. But it was not obvious how to follow the Socratic path to happiness. Should one endorse his characteristic "doctrines"? Or to the contrary, adopt his pose of Socratic ignorance, and admit knowing only that one knows nothing?

So it's no surprise that, as we turn our attention to ancient philosophy after Plato, Aristotle, and their immediate associates, we find that Socrates had followers of many types. There were some men who, as far as we know, were content simply to spend time with Socrates—faithful companions, if not disciples, like Critobulus or Apollodorus. These men have left no trace of independent philosophical ideas. But at least they showed up at Socrates' execution, which is more than we can say for Plato, who tells us in the *Phaedo* that he was ill. Of greater interest to us was a movement, which imitated the Socratic lifestyle, and also reflected on the meaning of this lifestyle. These were the Cynics, perhaps the most outrageous group of philosophers to emerge in the ancient world. They did choose poverty and make cutting remarks to the townspeople, accusing them of hypocrisy and insufficient interest in virtue. No doubt the good citizens of Athens and other ancient cities regretted this particular form of allegiance to Socrates. Having gone to the trouble of putting the man to death, it must have been annoying to find a whole movement dedicated to keeping the man's habits alive. But the Cynics were devoted to Socrates' philosophical ideals, not only his habits. They were convinced, in part by Socrates' arguments and in part by the example he set in his own life, that virtue is not only its own reward but the only reward worth having.

A similar outlook was adopted by the Stoics. They were a more successful school than the Cynics, in terms of their historical impact and dominance of the philo-sophical scene. But the early Stoics were influenced by the Cynics, and followed them by seeing Socrates as an ethical exemplar, and insisting on the primacy of virtue and wisdom. As we'll see in due course, they admitted that some things other than virtue, like physical health and safety, possess a lesser kind of value. But for them, the goal of the philosophical life—indeed the only rational goal for anyone's life—was virtue and wisdom alone. On the other hand, the Stoics did not follow the Cynics in adopting Socrates' way of life. If Stoicism had required voluntary poverty and anti-social behavior, it would hardly have been possible for a Stoic philosopher to be emperor of the Roman Empire.

Another group of philosophers in the period following Plato and Aristotle fastened onto yet a different aspect of Socrates: his incessant questioning. These philosophers, whom we call the Skeptics, adopted a permanent pose of, well, skepticism, greeting the claims of other philosophers with deft counter-arguments, without proposing positive views of their own. Some Skeptics went so far as to adopt what you might call *negative* views of their own. Where Socrates admitted to know only that he knew nothing, these radical Skeptics claimed to know only that *nobody* can know anything. Other Skeptics—the more interesting ones, for my money—followed Socrates' example more closely by remaining open to argument, always willing in principle to be shown that some philosophical claim is well grounded, but always able to pick holes in each positive argument as it came along.

A final philosophical tradition that arose at about the same time has, like Stoicism, become a household name: Epicureanism. Unlike the other groups I've just been discussing, the Epicureans do not seem particularly Socratic. With their atomism, which harks back to Pre-Socratic theories such as those expressed by Democritus and Leucippus, and their hedonism—that is, their view that pleasure is the good—they in fact seem almost deliberately anti-Socratic. But this may be misleading. On one occasion, even Plato has Socrates propose that things are good just in case they are pleasant, and bad just in case they are painful (*Protagoras* 351c).[2] Epicurean hedonism is a careful consideration of what Socrates suggests in that dialogue, namely, that if pleasure is the good, then wisdom will be paramount, since it will give us the ability to measure and calculate what will provide us with the most pleasure over our lives (*Protagoras* 357b).

These four schools—the Cynics, the Stoics, the Skeptics, and the Epicureans—are the main philosophical traditions of what we call the Hellenistic period. This is often defined as the time beginning with the death of Alexander the Great, in 323 BC, and ending wherever the historian you're talking to decides it should end, one popular choice being the death of Cleopatra in 30 BC. By that time we enter the period in which the Mediterranean basin, and beyond, is completely dominated by the Roman Empire, first under Augustus Caesar, and then under a series of emperors, some good, some bad, and one a Stoic philosopher. With the slow collapse of the Roman hegemony in the fifth and sixth centuries AD will come the end of what is usually thought of as ancient philosophy. It's worth dwelling on that chronology for a moment. Plato and Aristotle wrote in the fourth century BC. When Aristotle died in 322, ancient philosophy had been going for a couple of centuries. He was already able to refer to early Pre-Socratic thinkers like the Milesians as "the ancients." And yet ancient philosophy was only just beginning. The better part of a millennium would pass before ancient philosophy drew to a close, and late antique philosophy was passed on to medieval thinkers in the Christian, Muslim, and Jewish traditions. But let's not get ahead of ourselves. It will take us the rest of this volume to look at the Hellenistic schools and philosophical developments down to the fall of the Western Roman Empire. In the rest of this chapter I'll first sketch a bit of the historical context in which those schools operated. Then I'll say something about why I am calling them "schools." Finally, I'll return to the question of the Hellenistic response to Socrates, to his student Plato, and to his student's student, Aristotle.

First, then, the historical context. I just said that the Hellenistic period is traditionally dated from the death of Alexander. And with good reason, given the shattering sequence of events leading from his death. From his base in Macedonia

Alexander had conquered mainland Greece, and then pushed east through Asia Minor, Persia, and all the way to modern-day India. He and his armies left the indelible marks of Greek culture wherever they went. But even if Alexander's personality and military prowess could have served to unify such a vast terrain as a single, lasting empire, his untimely demise at a young age ended that possibility. After a contentious face-off between several of his lieutenants, his domain was fractured into three more-or-less stable units, which continued for a few centuries until the Romans became a new, almost unchallenged power.

These units were, first, the remnants of Macedonian power, which continued to dominate mainland Greece and the Balkans; second, the Ptolemaic dynasty in the fertile and rich land of Egypt; and third, the eastern power of the Seleucids, named for Seleukos, a commander in Alexander's army who was able to consolidate power in the eastern provinces following Alexander's death. During the Hellenistic period the dynasty of Seleukos ruled over a vast territory stretching eastwards from modern-day Iraq through Persia and central Asia. I have to say that I'm rather glad that these books are devoted to the history of philosophy, and not plain old history, because the Hellenistic dynasties can be a bit confusing.[3] Particularly annoying is that almost all the rulers of Egypt were named Ptolemy, unless they were women, in which case there was a good chance they'd be named Cleopatra. (The famous Cleopatra was in fact Cleopatra VII.) Similarly confusing patterns of dynastic naming held sway in the Macedonian and Seleucid empires too. The names of these rulers are recognizably Greek. One important outcome of Alexander's conquests was indeed the spreading of Greek language and culture throughout the areas he had conquered. For instance, the Ptolemaic rulers of Egypt spoke Greek, not Egyptian, and the famous Library they founded at Alexandria was principally intended for storing Greek works and doing research in Greek.

In the last days of the Hellenistic period, as the Roman Republic was about to complete its transition to a vast empire ruled by a single man rather than a Senate, the great lawyer, rhetorician, and philosopher Cicero visited Greece. For him this meant traveling to a place that retained dominance culturally, despite its loss of political relevance. Cicero knew Greek, and it was this that allowed him to learn and write about Hellenistic philosophy. In his own writings he often refers to the fact that he is having to find Latin expressions to correspond to Greek technical terms (see Chapter 17). Admittedly Lucretius, the greatest Epicurean apart from Epicurus, was a poet who wrote in Latin. But the greatest Skeptic, Sextus Empiricus, wrote in Greek. In due course Neoplatonism would become the main philosophical school in late antiquity. It was founded by Plotinus, a man who hailed from Egypt, and lived in Rome...but wrote in Greek.

So Hellenistic philosophical schools spanned cultural, political, and linguistic divides. Yet each of them, even as its characteristic doctrines developed, retained a reasonable degree of unity and continuity. Hellenistic philosophers were willing, indeed eager, to identify themselves as card-carrying Stoics, Epicureans, and so on. This is why I take the liberty of calling these groups "schools." The schools built allegiance over generations in part by devoting themselves to the authority of their founders.[4] In the case of the Stoics this meant giving an authoritative position to Zeno of Citium. For the Skeptics, the founding father was Pyrrho; Sextus Empiricus calls himself not a "Skeptic," but a "Pyrrhonist." The Cynics looked back to Diogenes of Sinope, while in the case of the Epicureans it was, of course, Epicurus.

Representatives of the Hellenistic schools always honored the memory and teachings of their founders. Even though the greatest early Stoic was certainly Chrysippus, not Zeno, and even though it was Chrysippus who systematized the teachings that all Stoics would defend for centuries, it was Zeno who was admired as the school founder. Thus all self-proclaimed Stoics had at least to pay lip service to the truth of his pronouncements. Unfortunately, though, we do not have any of Zeno's works. Nor do we have any extant writings of Chrysippus, though not for lack of effort on his part, since he wrote hundreds of them. Indeed, if Socrates is the most influential ancient thinker who wrote nothing, Chrysippus is surely the most important ancient philosopher for whom we have no surviving writings. I tend to think, in fact, that if a sizeable number of his works had survived he would be a household name, studied in philosophy departments around the world and seen as one of the top four ancient philosophers along with Plato, Aristotle, and Plotinus. As it is, with the early Stoics we do not have the luxury of referring to extensive surviving writings, as is possible with the great names I just mentioned. Instead, we have to consult later authors who report on their views. This means that with Hellenistic philosophy we are to some extent returning to the situation we faced with the Pre-Socratics. Our knowledge is indirect, often fragmentary or in the form of summaries or testimonies about what these philosophers thought.

On the bright side, that information is more extensive than in the case of the Pre-Socratics. This is due in no small part to a man I've already mentioned: Cicero. He wrote a series of treatises, in Latin of course, where he set out the positions of the various Hellenistic schools (that is, the Skeptics, Stoics, and Epicureans—he didn't see the Cynics as worthy of this sort of attention). He himself tended towards the Skeptical persuasion, but this didn't stop him from providing elaborate accounts of how Stoics and Epicureans might defend their doctrines. Many authors who lived under the Roman Empire also preserve evidence about the Hellenistic schools. This includes Christians who refuted Stoic ideas or adapted them for their own purposes. From the same period, we even have important original works of Stoic philosophy. These were composed by the so-called Roman Stoics: not only Seneca and Marcus Aurelius, but also Epictetus, perhaps the greatest Stoic apart from Chrysippus, who has left a significant body of writings (in Greek) thanks to one of his students.

For the Epicureans, we not only have the great poem *On the Nature of Things* by Lucretius, which expounds and defends the school doctrines in Latin verse. (This was written before the fall of the Republic.) We also have several extant works and sayings of Epicurus himself. We owe these to the biographer Diogenes Laertius, who saw fit to quote entire letters of Epicurus in his *Lives of the Philosophers*. For early Skepticism things are much as with early Stoics: we know the tradition solely through fragments and testimonies. But many of these are found in the works of the greatest representative of the Skeptic school, Sextus Empiricus. He lived well after the end of the Hellenistic period, in the second century AD, when Aristotelianism and Platonism are already returning to become dominant forces. Still, between Sextus, Cicero, and some other authors we're well served with information about the development of the Skeptical philosophy.

What about Plato and Aristotle, though? I just mentioned that they managed a resurgence by the second century AD, and in fact this process began at least a century earlier. But what was going on in the intervening 300 or so years? After all, Aristotle had been the teacher of Alexander, so you'd think that Aristotelian philosophy would have been ruling the roost following Alexander's conquests. But in fact Aristotle was not in vogue during the Hellenistic period. An ancient tale claims that his works were essentially lost at this time, literally buried underground until being rediscovered. This is surely an exaggeration, as I'll discuss later on (Chapter 25). And Aristotle may have exerted influence on specific points of doctrine among the Hellenistic schools. But this influence was minor—for the first few hundred years there was no sign that philosophy would, in due course, become nearly synonymous with the teachings of Aristotle, something that occurred only in late antiquity and, even more so, the medieval period.

With Plato, things were a bit different. The Stoics responded thoughtfully to the dialogues, and especially to Plato's *Timaeus*, which was a major influence on them. More obviously, the Platonic Academy itself continued as a force in the Hellenistic period. But the brief burst of Pythagorean theory among Plato's immediate successors was a false dawn for metaphysical Platonism. In the Hellenistic period "academic" philosophy turns out to mean Skepticism. Around AD 400 St Augustine could still attack Skepticism in a work entitled *Against the Academicians*. That may seem odd: we don't normally think of Plato as a skeptic. But imagine if you restricted your reading of Plato to the dialogues now considered early, also called the "Socratic" dialogues. These invariably pose a philosophical question, usually about the nature of some virtue like piety or courage, and then reach an inconclusive impasse at the end. The Skeptics looked to these Socratic dialogues when they made their negative brand of philosophy into the school position of the Platonic Academy. They were happy to embrace Socrates as a model philosopher. Always questioning, admitting to know nothing, he could plausibly be seen as a skeptic before there was such a thing as Skepticism.

As these Hellenistic schools competed to be the true heirs of Socrates, they adopted a broadly Socratic stance on the fundamental purpose of philosophy. We do find these thinkers speculating about logic, the universe, and the divine. But for all of them, philosophy centrally concerned the question of how to live. Ethics became a central preoccupation in the Hellenistic period, as it had been for Socrates. The Hellenistic schools also shared a devotion to Socrates' ideal of self-control and self-sufficiency. They had bitter disagreements too, though. The Stoics cared nothing for pleasure, where the Epicureans put it at the core of their ethics. The Skeptics, of course, were always out to undermine the teachings of all other schools. Yet all the schools, even the Skeptics, promised that their adherents would achieve what was called *ataraxia*, or "freedom from disturbance." Other philosophical questions were often explicitly marked as worthy of consideration only insofar as they would help lead to that ethical goal. The schools shared the conviction that *ataraxia* goes hand-in-hand with *eudaimonia*. Or, to say that in English, the notion that happiness requires freedom from disturbance.

Among the Hellenistic schools, none went so far in the pursuit of self-sufficiency and imitation of Socrates as the Cynics. Famous for their shocking behavior, whether it was living in wine jars or having sex in public, the Cynics were social critics who stood outside the society they criticized, and heirs to the Socratic practice of pestering their fellow citizens into philosophical reflection. Plato supposedly remarked that the greatest of the Cynics, Diogenes, was like a "Socrates gone mad."[5] The counter-cultural exploits and barbed remarks of Diogenes make him one of the most entertaining figures in ancient philosophy. At least, at this distance—a direct encounter with him in the marketplace would have been far from entertaining. But was there more to Diogenes than just a series of amusing and titillating anecdotes? Did Cynicism have any plausible claim to carry on the legacy of Socrates? Let's find out.

BEWARE OF THE PHILOSOPHER
THE CYNICS

I n 1967 a philosophical manifesto was put before the American public. It exhorted them to focus on the bare necessities. The simple bare necessities. To forget about their worries, their strife. Rather they should make do with the bare necessities—mother nature's recipes, which, this philosopher promised, would bring the bare necessities of life. The philosopher was, of course, Baloo the Bear, and his musical advice appeared in Disney's animated film *The Jungle Book*. I don't know whether Baloo studied ancient philosophy. If so, he probably did not put much effort into it, given his general approach to life. But if he did, he must have recognized a kindred spirit when he got to Diogenes of Sinope.

Diogenes was not a bear, though—he was a dog. The Greek word for dog is *kuon*, and Diogenes and his philosophers were called the "Cynics" in honor of this animal, not an admired beast in the Greek world. Then, of course, Diogenes wasn't seeking anyone's admiration. He lived the life of, well, a stray dog, choosing to beg for scraps and bark at anyone who he thought might deserve it. This most canine of thinkers set forth a teaching that has much in common with Baloo's song. The Cynics too taught that one should make do with bare necessities, and live in accordance with nature. In their case this meant not plucking fruit from the jungle trees but subsisting on a modest diet of lentils, owning nothing but a staff and leather pouch, and living in an improvised shelter, like Diogenes' famous earthen jar. This drop-out lifestyle served the goal also recommended by Baloo: to be without worry or strife. In common with other Hellenistic schools, the Cynics' highest aim was freedom from disturbance and imperturbability, in Greek *ataraxia* and *apatheia*.

The Cynics' radical methods for avoiding disturbance made some suspect that they might well be disturbed. Plato's supposed remark that Diogenes was "Socrates gone mad" is a hint that Diogenes was not, strictly speaking, a Hellenistic figure. He was already a noted personality, if not in Plato's day then at the latest in Aristotle's day—Aristotle refers to Diogenes and even calls him "the dog." The Cynics should be seen not as a post-Aristotelian phenomenon, but as a post-Socratic movement.

Even before Diogenes, there was Antisthenes. He began his career by studying with the sophist Gorgias, but he gave up rhetoric and burned his own writings upon encountering Socrates. He features as a kind of Socratic extremist in the writings of Xenophon and Diogenes Laertius—the author of the biographical compilation *Lives of the Philosophers*, and not to be confused with Diogenes the Cynic.

Antisthenes was not just a Socratic, he was a proto-Cynic. He wore his poverty like a badge of honor, claiming it was true wealth. He said it is better to be insane than to feel pleasure. The rejection of wealth and pleasure is a hallmark of Cynicism. Antisthenes also pioneered the Cynic practice of mocking the pretentions of his society. Sneering at the Athenians' boast to descend from men who were born from the earth, he said that the same is true of snails and insects (6.1).[1] He also suggested they should meet in their democratic assembly and pass a resolution declaring that donkeys are horses—after all, they are not afraid to declare fools wise enough to serve as generals (6.8). According to Diogenes Laertius, he already sported the classic Cynic outfit, carrying nothing but a staff and small bag, and wearing nothing but an unkempt beard and a thin cloak, which he would simply fold over for an extra layer of warmth in the winter (6.11). On this and other points, one has to wonder to what extent the stories and details of Diogenes the Cynic, and the Cynics in general, are being applied retrospectively to Antisthenes. But our stories about Diogenes come from the same sources and are no doubt largely fictional, so it's hard to be sure. In fact we can't even be sure where the name "Cynics" comes from. It may refer not to dog-like habits, but to Antisthenes' use of the gymnasium in Athens reserved for non-citizens, which was called the Kynosarges.

However large a role Antisthenes had in inspiring the philosophy and name of the Cynics, it is Diogenes of Sinope who embodied Cynicism in the ancient imagination. I won't be able to pack all the wonderful anecdotes about him into this chapter, but I'll mention the highlights, and talk about their philosophical meaning. We may as well start with the most famous. It seems that Alexander the Great heard of this famous philosopher Diogenes, and sought him out. He found the Cynic sage sunning himself on the wine jar that was his home. Standing over him, Alexander said, "What favor can I offer you?" Diogenes replied, "Get out of my sun" (6.38). According to another tale, Alexander said that if he were not Alexander, he would be Diogenes (6.32). In combination, these two legends speak volumes about Diogenes. He is indigent and has nothing, yet he is completely self-sufficient. The greatest ruler of the ancient world can offer him nothing, because nature—in this case, sunlight—is all he needs. His wisdom consists precisely in not wanting what he doesn't need. Alexander's supposed admiration of Diogenes is equally telling. Even wealthy, powerful men could admire the Cynics, because they enjoyed a kind of independence, freedom, and self-mastery that could otherwise be achieved only through great effort, if at all. As one Stoic philosopher remarked, Cynicism is a "short-cut to virtue." Hence the timeless appeal of Diogenes and his followers, which reaches as far as Friedrich Nietzsche, who remarked that Cynicism is "the only form in which base souls approach honesty."[2]

By late antiquity Diogenes had already become more fiction than fact. A whole tradition of Cynic literature developed, with him in the starring role. Even in Arabic medieval literature there were compilations of edifying and amusing anecdotes about this philosopher who lived in a jar—although, through a historical confusion, it was often Socrates who featured in these tales.[3] As for the real Diogenes, we cannot say much for sure about his biography. He was certainly from Sinope on the coast of the Black Sea, and his father apparently worked minting coins for the city. For obscure reasons, Diogenes' father defaced the coins. In another version of the tale it is Diogenes himself who ruined the coins. This became a symbol for the Cynic movement: "defacing the currency," that is, attacking social convention. It helps here that in Greek, the word for coins, *nomisma*, sounds like the word for custom, *nomos*. Rather amazingly, by the way, archeologists have in fact found defaced coins from Sinope dated to the mid-fourth century.

In any case, Diogenes was forced to leave his home city. He didn't regret this, saying, "exile made me a philosopher." A probably fanciful, but typically entertaining story has him being enslaved on his travels. He was put on the block to be auctioned, and said he should be sold to someone who needed a master (6.29). It's hard to pinpoint Diogenes' geographical movements, but several stories, including the encounter with Alexander the Great, put him in Corinth. Others put him in Athens, where he would have taken up the challenge to live like Socrates, much as Antisthenes had done. Predictably, ancient sources make Diogenes a student of Antisthenes, as usual making every famous philosopher the student of another famous philosopher. Wherever he lived, Diogenes became a law unto himself. He asserted the right to behave, and speak, however he liked. He called freedom of speech the greatest possession of man, and used this freedom to rail against the hypocrisy of his fellow Greeks. A famous story has him turning up at the market in broad daylight with a lantern, explaining that he was looking for a human being (6.41). In case the townsfolk weren't sufficiently offended, when asked where in Greece one could find good men, he replied, "Men nowhere, but boys in Laconia" (6.27), the region of the Spartans. (It's pleasing to notice that Diogenes' remark is itself rather laconic.)

What was it about his fellow Greeks that provoked Diogenes' disdain? One answer is that they failed to embrace poverty, and the total freedom and self-sufficiency that paradoxically came with it. If exile made him a philosopher, it was because exile gave him the priceless gift of poverty. Diogenes Laertius quotes Theophrastus, saying that Diogenes the Cynic embraced his lifestyle upon observing a mouse, and realizing that this humble creature makes do with nothing (6.22). A similar story has him already living as a Cynic, owning little more than his pouch, stick, and a cup for drinking. Seeing a little boy drinking from cupped hands, he threw away the cup, so as not to be outdone in frugality by a child (6.37). Diogenes applied these severe attitudes to others, as well as himself. Once he was invited into a rich man's fabulous house. He looked around at the opulent furnishings, and then spat in the owner's face. He then explained to the shocked man that everything else in the house was too nice to spit on (6.32).

There are plenty of other anecdotes about Diogenes' scorn for literal, as well as metaphorical, currency. He said that gold is a pale color because it is afraid—so many men are plotting against it (6.51). He also said that the love of money is the mother city of evils, anticipating a famous passage in the Gospels. Like Antisthenes, he regarded himself as wealthy in his poverty. All of which raises a question: why didn't Antisthenes and Diogenes die of starvation? Abusing rich citizens is fun, but it is pretty low in calories. So how did they make a living? The answer, at least in Diogenes' case, seems to be that he begged. This may seem more than a little hypocritical, given the Cynic claims of self-sufficiency. But Diogenes defended his right to other people's property with a satirical syllogism: all things belong to the gods; the wise are friends of the gods; friends share everything; so all things belong to the wise (6.72). His life as a beggar, of course, gave rise to some further choice anecdotes. Harassing a man who was slow to give him any money, he said, "I'm asking for a handout, not funeral expenses" (6.56). And here's one I really like: he was seen begging from statues, and explained that he was just practicing being rejected (6.49).

This being ancient Greece, those statues would have been religious in nature, which brings us to another feature of the Cynics' anti-social attitudes. Nothing was closer to the heart of Greek society than religion, and the Cynics followed in the footsteps of thinkers like Xenophanes and Plato by criticizing popular religious beliefs. Antisthenes met a priest who bragged that religious initiates like himself would be rewarded splendidly in the afterlife. Antisthenes acidly replied, "Why don't you die, then?" (6.4). Diogenes observed a temple thief that had been caught by the temple's officers, and said, "Big thieves carrying off a little thief" (6.45). Seeing offerings at another temple, left in thanks by people who had survived storms at sea, he pointed out that there would be many more offerings if they'd instead been left by the ones who *didn't* survive (6.59). None of this is necessarily to say, though, that the Cynics were atheists. The satirical syllogism I mentioned implies the gods exist, and it seems more in keeping with the Cynic approach to say that they rejected false conceptions of the divine but not the divine itself, just as they rejected false conceptions of freedom and wealth, but not true freedom or true wealth.

So far we've seen the Cynics putting forward ideas in a radical way. But how radical were the ideas themselves? Other philosophers wouldn't be shocked to hear that wealth is worthless. Aristotle allows a place for wealth in the good life, but only as an instrument for virtue,[4] and Socrates had already lived a life that combined virtue with poverty. I just pointed out that other philosophers had already distanced themselves from popular religion, too. The Cynics seem more genuinely radical, though, when it comes to the topic of pleasure. While Plato and Aristotle were not hedonists, they stopped short of denying the goodness of pleasure altogether. A philosophy that demands we give up all pleasure seemed to them too demanding. The trick was to show that although pleasure is not the good, the best life is nonetheless pleasant, because it contains the pleasures of virtue or contemplation.

The Cynics were having none of this. About the closest we find to an endorsement of pleasure is the observation, ascribed to Diogenes, that refraining from pleasure is itself pleasant. That's just a standard Cynic paradox, you might think, but he seems to have practiced what he preached. Finding a sweet amidst his humble breakfast, Diogenes tossed it away crying, "Steer clear of tyrants!" (6.55). And we've already seen that Antisthenes said that madness is preferable to pleasure. In place of pleasure, the Cynics promoted a life of toil—what in Greek is called *ponos*. This does not seem to mean actual physical work. Diogenes lived by begging, not by doing manual labor. Rather, it means deliberately choosing a hard life—for instance, wearing only that thin cloak and going barefoot in winter. So are the Cynics telling us that pleasure is not merely different from the good, but actually *bad*? That would be going further even than other anti-hedonistic philosophers like the Stoics, who considered pleasure neither good nor bad in itself. And it would put them in the surprising company of some students of Plato who excluded pleasure from the good life altogether.[5]

But the Cynic ethical stance is not best understood in terms of what it rejected. Yes, they mocked social norms, they refused to seek pleasure, and I suspect they weren't too keen on good old-fashioned personal hygiene either. But this was all in the service of a positive idea about what is valuable in life, which can be summed up in one word: nature. It's interesting here to compare the Cynics to Aristotle. For Aristotle, the good life for humans was also determined by nature. But he thought that we perfect our nature only through extraordinary excellence, through the exploitation of our full potential. The Cynics disagreed. They saw society as unnatural and acted accordingly, by flouting social norms. They equated virtue with a natural existence like that lived by dogs. Wealth, or even adequate clothing, would be a barrier to this natural lifestyle. We're told that Diogenes even attempted to eat raw meat, in an attempt to get in touch with his inner dog (6.34).

This explains an otherwise paradoxical feature of the Cynic lifestyle: while disdaining pleasure, they satisfied natural urges whenever and wherever they felt like it. For instance, when Diogenes was asked why he was eating in the middle of the marketplace, he said, "That's where I got hungry" (6.58). Notoriously, he also gratified himself sexually in public, and when challenged, replied with the immortal line, "I only wish I could get rid of hunger by rubbing my belly" (6.69). Or, think back to the famous encounter between Alexander and Diogenes. What Diogenes is doing there is not, for instance, slamming his head into his wine jar to make sure his life is as unpleasant as possible. Rather, he's enjoying the lovely sunshine. So it seems the Cynics weren't against pleasure as such; they were against pleasures that are not provided by nature. If pleasure can be had with no effort, then go right ahead, just as dogs do. But don't make your happiness dependent on pleasures that are more difficult to acquire.

This brings us back to the Cynics' quest to avoid disturbance. By refusing to desire anything that nature cannot provide, the Cynics made themselves effectively invulnerable, or as close as any human can be to that ideal. Thus Diogenes proclaimed that philosophy prepares you for any turn of fortune and makes you rich despite possessing no money. Many contemporaries no doubt collected and read tales of the Cynics because they were titillating and entertaining. But those who took Cynicism seriously enough to convert to the lifestyle, walking the barefoot walk as well as talking the bare-faced talk, were attracted not just by the humor but by the promise of self-sufficiency. An excellent example is the Cynic who comes along just after Diogenes, Crates. Though most of the best lines are ascribed to Antisthenes and Diogenes, there is no better summary of the Cynic creed than the one provided by Crates: "Philosophy is a quart of beans and to care for nothing" (6.86). In pursuit of this ideal, he gave away his property, living a life of ostentatious poverty and asceticism like Diogenes before him. On the subject of sex, he had this to say: "Hunger puts an end to lust; if not, time does; but if you can't use these, use a rope" (6.86). That's what I call tough love. But Crates' toughness didn't prevent him from finding love—in a relationship much celebrated in the ancient literature, a well-born woman named Hipparchia married him and joined in the Cynic lifestyle. Her brother Metrocles also joined the Cynic cause. As usual with ancient women philosophers, we know far less about Hipparchia than we would like. There are no writings by her, though there is a report of her justification for living as a philosopher instead of spending her time on feminine pursuits like weaving. Then we have letters supposedly addressed to her by Crates, on predictably household-related topics like childbearing and child-rearing.[6] Also predictably, this female philosopher is reduced to an object of sexual interest by the later tradition, which breathlessly reports that Crates and Hipparchia followed Diogenes' example of public self-pleasuring by having sex right out in the open.

If you're thinking that the debauched Greeks wouldn't have been shocked by this, think again: they were shocked. And that was the point. Where Socrates tried to convert people to virtue by arguing with them, the Cynics led by example, giving up on wealth and coming up with ever more outrageous ways to critique the society around them. Eventually, though, Cynics turned to written works in an effort to spread their message. Diogenes may not have written anything, just as Socrates had not. But Crates probably did put pen to paper; one title ascribed to him is *In Praise of Lentil Soup*, the Cynics' favorite humble meal. As we move forward into the third century BC, we find writers composing Cynic diatribes, trying to capture the savage wit of Diogenes in works that were called "serio-comic." Two major figures here were Bion and Menippus, whose satirical style was influential on Roman literature.

Indeed, one thing Cynicism has in common with the other Hellenistic schools we'll be considering in the first part of this book is that it passed from Greek into Roman society, and survived well into the Imperial age. Many Roman authors complained that the self-styled Cynics of their day were hypocrites. In Roman society Cynicism apparently became a kind of fashionable (or anti-fashionable) stance, rather than a living philosophical tradition. Nonetheless, we know that there were self-identified Cynic philosophers brave and principled enough to speak truth to power. The philosopher Demetrius refused a gift from that most ungifted of emperors, Caligula. And when the emperor Nero established an opulent bathhouse, Demetrius quipped that those who bathed there were making themselves dirty.

Among other philosophers in the Roman era, attitudes towards the Cynics were mixed. Cicero found their shameful behavior appalling, but Epictetus, Seneca, and other Stoics offered the Cynics at least grudging respect. Many forgave the Cynics their drop-out lifestyle and their shocking exhibitionism, because they at least had the good grace to disdain pleasure. The Epicureans had a far more socially accept-able lifestyle, and were much more philosophically sophisticated. Yet few represen-tatives of other schools showed anything but scorn for them, in part because they were hedonists. Pleasure was rarely far from the center of attention in the Hellenistic period. And it was sometimes put at the center of the good life, as well as the center of attention. The most famous hedonists were, of course, the Epicureans, but they were not the only ones.

3

INSTANT GRATIFICATION
THE CYRENAICS

About 200 years before the birth of Christ, a historian named Hippobotus sat down at his desk to write about the nine philosophical schools he considered most important. He included the usual suspects: Platonists, Aristotelians, Stoics, Epicureans. But at least three of the nine names are rather unfamiliar today: the Cyrenaics, the Annicerians, and the Theodorans. Don't panic, I won't have to devote the next three chapters to these obscure groups. Because, as it turns out, the Annicerians and Theodorans were simply developments within the larger tradition known as the Cyrenaics. Not that this tradition was very large. The Cyrenaics had already fizzled out by the time of Hippobotus, and they would be on nobody's list of the most influential ancient philosophical movements. But they're worth discussing, nonetheless. Along with the Cynics, they present us with a helpful introduction to the main debates of Hellenistic philosophy. They took up rather extreme positions within those debates, and did what philosophers tend to do when they're defending extreme positions: came up with innovative and provocative ways of defending their corner.

And there's one other reason I want to cover them: so that next time someone asks you what your favorite Hellenistic philosophical school is, you can impress the heck out of them by saying, "Oh, I've always had a soft spot for the Cyrenaics." Of course, a crowd will soon gather round and hang on your every word, as you explain the ideas of the Cyrenaics. Unfortunately, it's not so easy to say what those ideas were. As with the Cynics, our evidence for the Cyrenaics consists of reports and anecdotes rather than preserved philosophical treatises. Indeed, the comparison with the Cynics is an apt one. The Cyrenaics were committed hedonists, whereas the Cynics chose a life of deliberate hardship. But they shared the same goal, namely total freedom, and the same road to that goal, namely following nature. They even have a good deal in common historically. Ancient sources have Cyrenaics and Cynics engaging with one another,[1] and like the Cynics, the Cyrenaics could trace their lineage to an associate of Socrates. With the Cyrenaics, we see yet another variation on the theme of Socratic ethics. Where the Cynics could look back to the

Socratic follower Antisthenes, the Cyrenaics claimed to carry on the ideas of another Socratic: Aristippus.

If you're starting to get annoyed by the fact that all these names—Cynics and Cyrenaics, Antisthenes and Aristippus—sound rather alike, then I have bad news for you. It turns out that this follower of Socrates named Aristippus is the grandfather of the man who really developed Cyrenaic philosophy in all its glory. The name of this grandson? Aristippus. So, we need to distinguish between the grandfather, Aristippus the Older, who was a companion of Socrates, and the grandson, Aristippus the Younger, who was really the brains of the family firm. The reason we call them "Cyrenaics" is that Aristippus the Older hailed originally from a town in modern-day Libya called Cyrene. He was known as an associate of Socrates, and is already mentioned by Xenophon as a character in his Socratic *Memoirs*.[2] Xenophon presents Aristippus the Older as defending his hedonistic lifestyle, as Socrates urges him to adopt a life of greater self-control.

In due course Aristippus the Older became famous for his hedonism, or perhaps I should say infamous. Just as many tales were inspired by the poverty and wisecracking of Diogenes the Cynic, so Aristippus is the hero of plentiful one-sentence short stories, each of which could be titled: "Pleasure is my business." These anecdotes typically feature Aristippus at a feast or visiting prostitutes. For instance, we hear of him telling a student that the problem with visiting a whore-house isn't going in, but being unable to come back out (2.69). In another tale, a woman of loose morals accuses him of getting her pregnant. He tells her, "You're like someone who walks through a thicket and blames one particular thorn for scratching her" (2.81). Other stories have him demanding money from his students, in stark contrast to Socrates, who was well known for asking nothing but friendship. For example, a father brought his son to be taught by Aristippus, who said that the price of instruction was 500 drachmas. The father said, "For that much money, I could buy a slave!" and Aristippus replied, "Go ahead, then you'll have two" (2.72).

At first blush, Aristippus may seem to be not so much a philosopher as a debauched jerk, who recycles B material from the better-known act of Diogenes the Cynic. Certainly the ancient sources do give us that impression—in fact, they sometimes even credit the same one-liners to both Aristippus and Diogenes. But reading more carefully, we can see that Aristippus the Older put some thought into his hedonism. We're told that he practiced self-discipline, of a kind. He did grab any pleasure that came by, but by the same token, he was able to find pleasure in any circumstance. That story with the whorehouse—where he tells the student, "You need to be able to come back out"—shows that he valued a limited kind of self-control. He emphasized the need to be satisfied with the pleasures one can have *right now*, and claimed that this life would be easiest, most pleasant, and most free. So there is indeed a lot Aristippus the Older has in common with Diogenes and the other Cynics. He was clearly more interested than the Cynics in luxurious pleasure and wealth, unless we discount these aspects of the evidence as scurrilous rumors. And he put pleasure front and center in his theory of the best life, which the Cynics certainly didn't do. But like them, he accepted the satisfaction of momentary desire as a natural way to live, and strove to live free and unencumbered by social convention.

To be honest, though, Aristippus the Older by himself would not really merit a chapter in our history of philosophy. It's Aristippus the Younger who devised the signature philosophical theories we know as Cyrenaicism. Still central to his philosophical outlook is hedonism: the claim that pleasure is the good. He also inherits from his grandfather the idea that we should be interested in *present* pleasures. This forms a contrast to the Epicureans, hedonists who valued long-term planning. For them, pleasure-seeking is not a spontaneous, spur-of-the-moment thing, but a strategic way of life which involves careful training, forgoing present pleasures for the sake of future ones and to avoid future pains, and also the enjoyment of remembering past pleasure and anticipating future pleasure. None of that for Aristippus the Younger. For him, your life is as only as good as what you are experiencing in the present moment.

This brings us to something unusual and surprising about Aristippus the Younger. Almost all ancient philosophers follow the lead of Plato and Aristotle in trying to identify the best life as the happy life. As I said in the last volume when discussing Aristotle,[3] they center their ethics on the goal of happiness, or *eudaimonia*. For the Stoics and Plato, at least in some of his moods, wisdom and virtue guarantee happiness. So for them, wisdom and virtue are the good, at least as far as ethics are concerned. Aristotle is a bit harder to pin down—he makes virtue central to happiness, but leaves room for other goods, like friends, family, and even material comfort, and winds up endorsing a life of contemplation. But all agree that when we do ethics, we are trying to figure out what will make us happy. Of course, a hedonist can think this too. The Epicureans were hedonists precisely because they thought the life with the most pleasure is the happy and good life.

The Cyrenaics are the odd men out. They aren't particularly interested in the happy life. They focus on happiness in the here and now, rather than on what would be best on the whole in the long term.[4] Why does Aristippus the Younger take this unusual view? We have to speculate, but my guess is that he saw the pressure a hedonist would feel if he started to admit the need for planning and calculation. In his dialogue the *Protagoras* (357a–b), Plato has Socrates point out that a successful hedonist will need what he calls an "art of measurement" for deciding what will give him the most pleasure. This looks like a step on the slippery slope towards identifying the good with wisdom and rationality, and ultimately whatever reason commends to us—virtue, for instance. Aristippus, though, wants to stick to the idea that the good is whatever feels good.

Alternatively, perhaps Aristippus worried that it was simply impossible to achieve the goal of maximal pleasure over a whole life.[5] This might be because the goal is too indefinite (one can always add one more almond croissant), or because it is just the human condition to experience more suffering than pleasure over a whole lifetime (this point will be made explicitly by another Cyrenaic named Hegesias). So we should focus instead on what we can in fact achieve, namely pleasure in the here and now. To press home the point that memories of past pleasures and anticipations of future ones are not the goal of his philosophy, Aristippus observes that such pleasures don't even exist for us right now. What exists for us is whatever is affecting us at the present moment. Aristippus talks about this as a kind of motion: pleasure he defines as a "smooth" motion, and pain as a "rough" motion. In one of the many nautical metaphors that are scattered throughout ancient philosophy, he compares pain to a storm at sea, pleasure to a favoring wind, and the absence of both pain and pleasure to complete calm.[6]

But why does Aristippus identify pleasure with the good in the first place? It's as if he started out knowing he was going to defend a hedonism of present pleasures, and dispensed with anything that would get in the way—happiness, wisdom, memory, hope. In philosophy, holding to a position at all costs like this is not usually considered good form. So is this just misplaced filial devotion to granddad? Or does the Younger Aristippus have an argument to give on the Older's behalf? He does, and it's an interesting one, not least because it was used by a range of hedonistic philosophers around this time—and also by their opponents. Sometimes called the "cradle argument," the line of thought goes that, from earliest childhood, all humans seek pleasure.[7] Eudoxus, a mathematician noted for his work in astronomy, was a member of Plato's Academy who embraced hedonism. Apparently, he gave a version of the cradle argument, invoking the fact that all animals strive constantly after pleasure.[8] We'll see it used again in defense of pleasure soon, when we get to Epicurus, and later we'll see the Stoics use the idea that ethics can be grounded in the instinctive, natural responses of children.

You might think that the cradle argument is one even a child could see through. Just because animals and human infants seek pleasure no matter what doesn't mean that we mature adult humans should do it. You might even think that it's a sign of maturity to forgo pleasure for the sake of nobler ideals. But the cradle argument has more force if you admit, as many ancient philosophers did, that nature determines what is best for humans. Just think back to Aristotle's function argument, for example.[9] Even today, many people assume that if something is "unnatural," it must be unacceptable. The link between nature and ethical goodness is clearly an intuition that runs deep. And there's more. The Cyrenaics' emphasis on present pleasure helps them secure a goal they share not only with the Cynics but with other Hellenistic schools: *ataraxia*, the lack of disturbance. They take their cue from Aristippus the Older, who announced that he sought the easiest and most pleasant life. The man who has pleasure right now and is satisfied by that has no anxiety about the future and no regrets about the past.

Aristippus the Younger supported this radical idea about the supreme importance of present pleasures, by putting forward equally radical ideas about human knowledge. He started from the apparently innocent observation that I can only experience the way I am being affected by the things around me. So, for instance, if I see something white, that thing affects me by making me feel like I'm seeing white. Aristippus emphasized the passivity of this process by saying that if I seem to see something white, then I am being "whitened."[10] The later author Plutarch makes fun of this by suggesting that, for the Cyrenaics, if I seem to see a wall or a horse then I am "walled" or "horsed."[11] But probably Aristippus spoke only of simpler experiences, like seeing a color or tasting sweetness or sourness. This is a side issue, though. The main point is that our experience consists in nothing but being affected in various ways; and of course, things might affect you in one way and me in another way. For instance, if you are ill, everything may taste bitter to you. In that case, honey will, so to speak, "embitter" you, whereas it will "sweeten" me because I am healthy.

Of course, common sense would say that if honey tastes sweet to me and bitter to you, then that is because my tasting ability is working properly and yours isn't. After all, honey really is sweet. If you think it's bitter, then that's your fault, not the honey's fault and certainly not my fault. But the Cyrenaics think common sense needs some correction. Aristippus will remind us that we only experience the various ways the honey is affecting each of us. Those experiences are not something we can share. I can never take part in your experience of the honey, any more than I can genuinely feel your pain when someone hits you in the face. All this is bound to remind us of the position Plato ascribes to the sophist Protagoras in the dialogue called *Theaetetus*.[12] Protagoras says that there is no absolute truth about, for instance, whether a certain wind is cold or warm. If it feels cold to you, it is cold for you, and if it feels warm to me, it is warm for me. In general, all truths are true only relative to the way things seem to somebody or other.

Perhaps there's no more than a family resemblance between Protagoras' relativism and the theory of the Cyrenaics. The Cyrenaics seem to have focused exclusively on basic sensory experiences, like whether something is sweet or white, whereas Protagoras, as Plato presents him, was at least as interested in judgments about things like justice and the beneficial. But as with Protagoras, modern readers can't help seeing the Cyrenaic position as an exciting premonition of later, radical views. Were they adopting a skeptical view about knowledge in general? Were they, like Descartes, raising a doubt even about whether there are any external objects out there in the world we seem to see around us? Well, I don't think so. Certainly there is a skeptical flavor to their view, since they suspend judgment about whether the honey is in itself really sweet or bitter, and so on. But there's no suggestion that they suspended judgment about whether the honey exists at all. What they're after is rather an ethical point, namely that nothing is, or could be, important for me apart from the way things seem to me.

This, of course, goes hand in hand with their hedonism. If my awareness of life, the universe, and everything boils down to how things seem to me *right now*, then it only stands to reason that present pleasure and pain are going to be of paramount importance. Now you might argue that things right now can seem unjust, or unfair, or beautiful to us—that would give us a lot of other things to care about apart from present pleasure. But Aristippus may have added one more piece to the puzzle. He may have said that all the experiences we have are in fact pleasures or pains. So if something tastes sweet, that is a kind of pleasure; if bitter, that is a kind of pain. If it is not even slightly pleasant or slightly painful, we will have no experience at all—it will be like something so bland that it has no taste. This would explain why the Cyrenaics compare the state in which there is neither pleasure nor pain to a calm sea, where there is no wind at all.

Let's take stock. We've been looking at the views of Aristippus the Younger, and we've seen that, for him, what exists for me is what I am experiencing right now—which is, perhaps, nothing apart from various pleasures and pains. No wonder that the only good to be had in life is the pleasure I can have right now, while the only bad thing is pain I am having now. This picture is consistent and uncompromising, but it wasn't a huge success. The philosophy of Epicurus pushed the Cyrenaics into a distant second place in the competition to be the most influential hedonistic school. Still, Aristippus the Younger did have his followers, which is why that historian I mentioned at the beginning of this chapter lists several branches of the Cyrenaic school. These branches developed Aristippus' ideas in three different directions.

An obvious way to defend the Cyrenaic theory was to make limited concessions, so as to render it more plausible. This seems to have been the strategy of one

Anniceris, who still insisted that pleasure is the good, but took a broader view of pleasure.[13] Whereas Aristippus, both Older and Younger, seem to have concentrated on basic physical pleasure, Anniceris pointed out that honor and friendship are also pleasant. This more user-friendly version of the theory is in stark contrast to a second development at the hands of a thinker named Theodorus. He had no time for Anniceris' socially domesticated version of Aristippus' ideas, yet he also thought little of physical pleasure. This is surprising, from a man who is associated with the Cyrenaic school, but he held on to another central theme of their thought, namely self-reliance and self-sufficiency. Thus he rejected the need for friendship and social ties with our fellow citizens. We seem to be heading in a fairly depressing direction here, and that impression is confirmed by a third strand of the tradition: a philosopher named Hegesias accepted the hedonism and skeptical epistemology of Aristippus the Younger. But like an obscure Greek version of Schopenhauer, Hegesias taught that we cannot expect life to be more pleasant than painful. The best we can do is to avoid pain as much as possible. This crushingly pessimistic outlook won Hegesias the memorable nickname "death-persuader." This was a philosopher who could literally drive you to suicide. With that, Cyrenaicism itself seems to have died out, and perhaps deservedly so—a theory which puts pleasure at the heart of the good life really shouldn't be this unpleasant. Still, the Cyrenaics are an unusually fascinating footnote in the history of philosophy, remarkable especially for their innovative ideas about human experience, and for the contrast they offer with their great rivals, the Epicureans.

THE CONSTANT GARDENER
THE PRINCIPLES OF EPICURUS

D o you like a nice garden? Do you enjoy the company of friends? Do you believe the world is made of tiny particles, which you call atoms? Do you trust the evidence of your senses? Do you find politics tiresome, and raise a skeptical eyebrow at those who live in fear of God? If your answer to these questions is "yes," then you might want to consider becoming an Epicurean. Membership has its advantages. This is a philosophy which is devoted to pleasure, though to be honest, you might be disappointed about that bit when you read the fine print. And while I'm being honest, I should warn you that it won't all be garden parties. There will be a regime of memorization and training to carry out. Oh, and if you do decide to sign up, then you'll want to clear a date each year to celebrate the birthday of your school's founder: Epicurus.

Among the founders of the Hellenistic schools, Epicurus is the man we know best. We have only fragments and anecdotes to tell us about the founder of Stoicism, Zeno, and the first Skeptic, Pyrrho. But for Epicurus we have several extant writings, as well as a collection of memorable sayings intended to summarize his key teachings. We can thank our old friend Diogenes Laertius for preserving three letters of Epicurus, which deal respectively with his ideas about physics, cosmology, and ethics.[1] Four more letters, including one addressed to Epicurus' mother, and some further sayings have been preserved by another Diogenes. I'm well aware that along with Diogenes the Cynic, this makes three men named Diogenes that I've mentioned so far in this book, and we're only in Chapter 4! Sorry about that. This latest entry in our ever-expanding Diogenes collection is Diogenes of Oinoanda, who like Diogenes Laertius lived a good half-millennium after Epicurus. Diogenes of Oinoanda was himself an Epicurean, who paid to have teachings and texts of the school written up as a stone inscription, which has been discovered in modern-day Turkey.[2]

That shows something about the longevity of Epicurus' teachings. In letters to his friends and in pithy aphorisms, he encapsulated his doctrines in a way that was easy to study and memorize, and he explicitly encouraged his adherents to take advantage. This did the trick: unlike his fellow hedonist Aristippus the Younger, Epicurus launched a philosophical school that would still be alive and well in the Roman Empire. The first century BC, the period which saw the fall of Rome's Republic, was also graced by Lucretius, whose magisterial poem *On the Nature of Things* set Epicureanism into verse. Maybe this was Aristippus' problem: he didn't have a good enough poet working for him. We'll look at Lucretius in a bit. For now, I want to concentrate on Epicurus himself and try to understand how his philosophy fits together.

Like Plato and Aristotle, Epicurus had a sophisticated project, which had something to say on just about every area of philosophy, ranging from ethics to physics to the gods. Again like Plato and Aristotle, Epicurus set forth his system in Athens. This was not his home city—in 341 BC, six years after Plato died, he was born on the island of Samos. And yes, that's the same Samos that produced Pythagoras. If you're still not impressed, the same island was the home of Aristarchus, a younger contemporary of Epicurus who was the first to propose that the earth goes around the sun, instead of the other way around. (This paragraph has been brought to you by the Samos tourist board.) Epicurus moved to Athens in about 307 BC. Here he acquired a garden, which he could use as a base for his school. Significantly, this was located outside the city walls of Athens, which seems like a geographical shorthand for the Epicureans' lack of interest in political engagement. The Aristotelian ideal of practical, even heroic action was not a flower tended in Epicurus' garden. Instead, this school was going to devote itself to a pleasant life of quiet philosophical discussion.

That may give a false impression, though, because the Epicureans could be tenacious in defense of both the theories and the memory of their founder. The school would not have survived and prospered for hundreds of years had it not been willing to engage in polemics against other schools, and to foster loyalty by treating Epicurus himself as a literally divine figure. This is why they celebrated his birthday every year. The success of Epicureanism as a social enterprise is shown by that expensive inscription sponsored by Diogenes of Oinoanda. Not many philosophers have people paying to have letters they wrote to Mom carved painstakingly into rock, several centuries after they died. The success of Epicureanism as a philosophical enterprise, meanwhile, is shown by the fact that modern-day historians of philosophy find it worth dissecting every sentence of the precious remaining writings of Epicurus. So let's start to look at those writings, beginning with one of the letters preserved by Diogenes Laertius in his biographical collection, the *Lives of the Philosophers*. This letter is addressed to one of Epicurus' disciples, a man named Herodotus—same name, but not the same man, as the famous historian. (These

Greeks clearly didn't have enough names to go around.) Epicurus uses this letter to set out his physical theory, which harks back to the atomism of the Pre-Socratic Democritus but introduces some significant differences. In expounding this theory Epicurus incidentally touches on another theme, which is where I want to begin: his ideas about human knowledge.

Epicurus is an empiricist. He believes that sensation is the ground and source of all our knowledge. One of his collected sayings tells us that if we do not trust in sensation, we will have no standard against which to judge our beliefs. Epicurus is here raising for the first time a question that will dominate Hellenistic philosophy: what is the criterion of knowledge, which he calls the *kanon* or "measuring stick"? His answer to the question is that all our knowledge ultimately derives from sensation and must be measured against it. This isn't to say that Epicurus is unwilling to go beyond the senses. After all, you can't see individual atoms, yet he confidently puts forth an atomist physical theory. But he insists that claims about what is unclear to the senses need to be checked against sensation. He also uses analogies drawn from sensation for things that are not evident to the senses.

But why should we put our trust in the senses? The answer is simple, according to Epicurus: they cannot be wrong (LS 16A). Your senses are infallible guides to the way that the external world is interacting with your body. Of course, this doesn't guarantee that you can avoid false beliefs. A classic Epicurean example is a square tower that looks round from a distance (LS 16E). Gazing at the tower, you might well form the belief that the tower is round. You'd be wrong, but this isn't the fault of sensation: that really is how square towers look from far away. If you see the world through rose-colored glasses, everything will look rosy. Again, sensation is not failing here. Rather, your experience shows you exactly what it should show you, given that you are wearing those glasses. Epicurus insists on this point, worrying that if the senses are allowed to be false in some cases, there will be no end to our uncertainty. The upshot would be a pervasive skepticism, something Epicurus rejects out of hand: "If you fight against all sensations, you will not have a standard against which to judge even those of them you say are mistaken" (LS 16D). If they are always true, by contrast, the senses can provide that yardstick against which we test all our beliefs. So we can discover that some beliefs are false—for instance, by walking closer to the tower and seeing that it is in fact square—but there is no falsehood in the sensation itself, which gives rise to the belief.

Sensation also gives rise to something more basic than belief. This is what Epicurus calls a "preconception"—the Greek word is *prolepsis*, one of the many technical terms Epicurus coins for expounding his theories. His idea is that sense-experience gives us a range of rough-and-ready notions we can apply to the world.[3] Our preconception of a giraffe might be, "animal that lives on the savannah, with spots and a long neck." This isn't a definition of giraffe, but it's enough to help you identify giraffes and start thinking about them more carefully. Preconceptions can form both a basis for doing philosophy, and a kind of check on the philosophical theories we develop. If we wind up giving a theory which violates our preconceptions, that will cast doubt on the theory. Even more important is what Epicurus calls a "common conception." This is a preconception that just about everyone shares, for instance, that the gods are happy (LS 17E, 23C). These common conceptions are important because everyone will agree to them. They provide not just a starting-point for philosophy, but an uncontroversial starting-point.

With his theory of preconceptions, Epicurus seems to respond to the problem Plato identified in his dialogue the *Meno*. Meno's Paradox shows that inquiry is impossible, because we either know about the object of our search, or we don't (*Meno* 80d–e).[4] If we already know, there will be no point in inquiring. But if we do not, then how should we start trying to inquire? Epicurus' solution is not to invoke forgotten knowledge, which is already in us when we are born, as Plato has Socrates suggest in the dialogues *Meno* and *Phaedo*. Instead, he proposes that by remembering our sense-experiences we build up preconceptions (LS 17E). These won't qualify as rock-solid knowledge, of the kind Plato was seeking. But they are good enough to get us going. Like Plato's category of true belief, they offer a kind of halfway house between certain knowledge and total ignorance. When we begin to inquire, we need not start from nothing.

We can see these epistemological ideas put into practice in Epicurus' *Letter to Herodotus*, as he defends his new version of the atomic theory. In setting out the theory, he's venturing into the territory of what he calls the "unclear" or "non-evident." So he needs to make sure that he stays true to sensation. First, he observes that nothing can be absolutely destroyed or generated (LS 4A–C). He agrees with Parmenides and his Eleatic followers that there is no such thing as a passage from being to non-being, or vice versa. If being could be reduced to absolute non-being, then being would disappear bit by bit until it is all gone—but look around, and you'll see that the world is still very much here. The basic building-blocks of the world, then, cannot be utterly destroyed or made from nothing. On the other hand, Epicurus insists against Parmenides that the world does involve change. Again, look around: we see that there are bodies and that they are changing and moving all the time. To explain how this can happen, Epicurus makes a far-reaching theoretical point, which also seems to be grounded in sense-experience. If a body moves, then it must move into an empty space, a place where there is no body (LS 6A).[5] So we need to say that the world includes both body and empty space. This will be void, already a feature of Democritean atomism, albeit defended with a more careful methodology.

We can imagine Aristotle turning in his fairly fresh grave, complaining that Epicurus' careful methodology hasn't stopped him from assuming what he should be proving. Aristotle rejected the idea of void. He thought instead that the world is, as it were, "full." Every time something moves, something else has to get out of the way—I push air out the way as I walk, and it must flow around me and occupy the space I was just in so that no space is left empty (*Physics* 214a). Epicurus disagrees. He thinks that if the world were really full, nothing would be able to move. The whole universe would be like a tin packed full of sardines, where no sardine has any wiggle-room. A world without void would therefore be like the one Parmenides envisioned, static and unchanging, but this is not the world of our experience. So there must be void. The line of argument may sound convincing, but it looks like Epicurus is assuming something Aristotle would not grant, namely that bodies must be unyielding. We could capture the disagreement by saying that Aristotle's conception of body allows it to be rather fluid, so that it can shift around to accommodate motions, whereas Epicurus assumes that all body must be equally solid and resistant, unlike void, which puts up no resistance and is intangible.

Notice that we are still talking only about *bodies* and void, without claiming that bodies are made of atoms. But that's going to change now, which will annoy our ghostly Aristotle further, since he was a severe critic of atomism. For Aristotle, it is at least in theory possible to divide any body, and divide again, as many times as you like. This is what we sometimes call a theory of body as "continuous"—no part of the body is too small to be cut. To be an atomist, at least in the ancient sense, is just to reject this idea that body is continuous. The Greek word *atomon* means "uncuttable," so atoms are simply parts of bodies that cannot be physically divided.[6] Epicurus arrives at his atoms by considering something like Zeno's dichotomy paradox. If we allow every body to be infinitely divisible, every body will be made of infinitely many parts. But each bodily part must still have some size, so every body will be infinitely big.

To prevent this absurd consequence, Epicurus embraces atomism. But this is going to be an improved atomism, which benefits from being able to respond to anti-atomist criticisms like those presented by Aristotle. One challenge is to explain atomic motion. How can an atom be indivisible, critics could argue, if it is to move? Imagine an atom crossing a line. As it is doing so, the front part of the atom will be past the line, while the back part is not yet past the line. So it looks like the indivisible atom is divisible after all. Or if you don't like that argument, how about this one? Imagine an atom being touched on either side, perhaps by two other atoms. Then it is being touched on its right part, and on its left part. So it has two parts, and can thus be divided.

Not so fast, says Epicurus. I didn't say that atoms are conceptually indivisible, only that they are physically indivisible. Atoms themselves are made of parts, just like bodies, but these parts can't be physically separated from one another. He calls them "minima," or "minimal parts" (LS 9A–C).[7] These literally sub-atomic parts are quite simply the smallest possible size that there is. You can't conceive of anything smaller. They do not have a left half and a right half, for instance. Also, when an atom moves, this will always mean that at least one minimal part has moved completely. You will never have a minimal part being only halfway over a line: either the part is all the way over or it hasn't crossed the line. Just think how much goal-mouth controversy they could avoid if they used minimal parts as soccer balls! Again, in support of his idea Epicurus resorts to sensation. Having been born before the invention of soccer balls, he refers instead to the minimum body that we can see (LS 9C). Something like a tiny particle of dust has no visible parts, yet if enough dust-motes come together you have a pile of dust. In the same way, minimum parts have no sides or further sub-parts, but they can come together in some special way to form whole atoms.

And come together they do, forming atoms of many shapes and sizes. How many shapes and sizes, you ask? Inconceivably many, says Epicurus. He doesn't admit what Democritus may have, namely that there are single atoms big enough to see. But there are all sorts of configurations of atoms, and as Democritus taught us, an infinite number of atoms. These come together to form larger bodies when they get caught in clusters, vibrating as they bounce back and forth, since atoms never stop moving in the void, but only change direction when they collide into one another. These complex bodies come together to form a whole cosmos; in fact this happens many times. There will be inconceivably many worlds, with all sorts of configurations, scattered through the void, which is also infinite in all directions (LS 10A–B; 13A, D).

This, then, is Epicurus' universe: an inconceivably large void, which lasts for infinite time, and has infinitely many atoms moving and colliding within it, forming bodies and whole cosmic systems scattered through unending emptiness. It's a breathtaking conception, albeit one largely familiar from his atomist predecessors. But Epicurus, unlike those predecessors, is fastidious about objections drawn from sensation. One objection is quite basic: when you drop something, why does it fall? Aristotle had explained this by saying that the heavy elements, earth and water, naturally seek a place towards the center of the universe. But Epicurus' universe has no center. So instead, he again improves upon Democritus by proposing that all atoms have weight (LS 10C; 11E, H; 12D).[8] Left to their own devices, they fall—the universe has an up and a down, even though it has no center. This seems to suggest that when things are dropped in Australia, they should fall towards the sky. As far as I know that doesn't happen, but Australian readers can get in touch to correct me if I'm wrong. I guess it would explain how kangaroos jump so well.

Leaving that aside, though, let's consider another objection. This one is from Aristotle (*Physics* 215a–216a). He observed that when things move, they go slower if they are moving through a denser medium. For instance, you move faster through air than water, and through water faster than mud. So if you were moving through void, which has no density, you should move infinitely fast! But this is clearly absurd. Epicurus responds by holding simply that atoms all move at the same speed—you'll never guess how fast. Yes, "inconceivably fast." Lucretius argues that this speed must be even faster than sunlight (LS 11B). After all, sunlight should be slowed down by collisions with the atoms that make up the air it is shining through, whereas an uninterrupted atomic motion will encounter nothing at all.

The way Epicurus anticipates and responds to such objections shows how he is using sense-experience to build his theory. He not only takes sensation as his starting-point, he also uses sensation to check his theory, as he promised. If your theory can't explain why things fall, then your theory needs work. On the other hand, Epicurus is happy to stick with a theory so long as it is consistent with sensation, in the sense of not being disproven. We want to believe things that are supported by sensation, and avoid believing what is "counter-witnessed," as he puts it (LS 18A). For instance, we might go up to the round-looking tower and realize that it is in fact square. Epicurus is not really in the Platonic and Aristotelian game of seeking certainty. Some degree of support, and the absence of any "counter-witnessing" experience, is enough for him. He sometimes makes this explicit, especially when discussing less crucial points than the fundamentals of atomic theory. For instance, he allows several alternative theories to stand as being equally acceptable in cosmological contexts (LS 18C, D). This is not because he's lazy. It's because certainty about physics is not the goal of Epicurean philosophy. Rather, his goal is an ethical one: happiness, which he identifies with the absence of disturbance, and which we'll examine more closely next.

5

AM I BOTHERED?
EPICUREAN ETHICS

ynics, Stoics, Skeptics, and Epicureans. We all talk about them, whether or not we are interested in the history of philosophy. The names have entered into our everyday language. A politician can "cynically" manipulate an election result, then show "stoic" resolve when she loses anyway, because she was skeptical about whether she'd enjoy holding office. If she'd rather enjoy the good things in life, in particular fine food and drink, then we might describe her as an "epicurean." For us, an epicurean is not just someone who enjoys pleasure—after all, who doesn't?—but someone who has refined taste in their pleasures. The modern use of the word "epicureanism," though, is not a good guide to the philosophy of Epicurus. Epicurus would have been nonplussed—though not upset, since he let nothing upset him—to discover his name being associated with the life of a gourmet. In fact he encourages us to be ready to enjoy the simple delights of plain bread and water, and his philosophy certainly did not center around the search for refined pleasure.

Yet it's true enough that he was a hedonist. This is another word that might confuse us. It comes from the ancient Greek word for pleasure, *hedone*. Nowadays, we use "hedonist" to refer to someone who is unrestrained in their pursuit of pleasure. Although Epicurus was a hedonist, he certainly did not recommend the *unrestrained* pursuit of pleasure. Rather, he was a hedonist in the sense of someone who believes that pleasure is the good, the sole criterion we should use in determining the right way to live, the right choices to make, the right actions to perform. As we navigate our way through life, pleasure is the only star we need to steer by. But this does not imply lack of restraint, or a thoughtless embrace of every pleasure that comes our way. On the contrary, Epicurus teaches that the most pleasant life is a life of moderation, discipline, and careful planning. In this, Epicureanism makes a contrast with the Cyrenaic teaching of Aristippus the Younger. The Epicureans and Cyrenaics shared a commitment to hedonism, so of course they were bitter rivals. There's nothing worse than an opponent who is uncomfortably close to agreeing with you. As we saw, the Cyrenaics valued only present pleasures. By contrast,

Epicurus thought that the memory of past pleasure and anticipation of future pleasure can make the wise man happy even when he is undergoing extreme pain.[1] There is no more vivid example than Epicurus himself. We know of a letter he wrote to a friend from his deathbed, as he is suffering agonizing pain from the illness that killed him. He writes that this is the happiest day of his life, because he thinks back on pleasant conversations he has had in the past with his friend (LS 24D).

This may sound too good to be true, but it is nothing less than what Epicurus would expect of himself, and of us. His ethical teaching is not just a theory; it is a proposed way of life, which is intended to make us all but invulnerable to changes of circumstance. The goal of his philosophy is to show us how we can avoid disturbance even in the face of, say, an excruciating illness. Of course this was the objective of the Cynic and Cyrenaics schools too: the sort of self-sufficiency that would make us all-but invulnerable to turns of fortune. We'll see later that the same goal motivated Stoic ethics, and that even Skeptics claimed that their agnostic philosophy leads to lack of disturbance. But if this is the common destination, the Hellenistic schools travel different roads to get there. For the Epicureans, the recommended path was to memorize and internalize a teaching that maximized pleasure over a whole life, rather than at the present moment. On his deathbed, Epicurus showed how a thorough training in these precepts could allow him to overcome even great physical torment. This was a possibility the Cyrenaics denied on the basis that present physical pain would be far stronger than any memory or hope. Perhaps, as Epicurus lay dying, he allowed himself to take a bit of added pleasure in proving his opponents wrong once and for all.

Invulnerability like this doesn't come cheap. It requires discipline, and Epicureans would claim to be more disciplined than their fellow hedonists the Cyrenaics. Aristippus and the other Cyrenaics demand of us that we be satisfied with whatever pleasure we feel right now. The main strategy they offer for the future is imagining possible sufferings before we undergo them, so that we can steel ourselves against them. The Epicureans dismissed this as ineffective, and offered more demanding instructions for how to be happy over a whole life. We are not just trying to enjoy our current situation, like the Cyrenaics. So we should often forgo a current pleasure, because of the pain it will bring later (LS 21A–B, G, J). Obvious examples include over-eating and getting drunk. These might be fun here and now—in fact, let's face it, they *are* fun here and now—but we will regret it later when we have stomach-aches and hangovers. Epicurus also cautions us against indulging in sex, at least in part because, however pleasant sex might be, having children leads to more than enough worry and trouble to overwhelm that pleasure. The hedonistic calculation favors chastity over family life, as far as Epicurus is concerned.

For the same reason, Epicureans avoided engagement in day-to-day political life when possible, because the anxiety involved would outweigh the pleasure politics can provide. Of course, these same Epicureans might be willing to seek office to prevent personal disruption and worry. If the city of Athens had suddenly tried to evict Epicurus and his friends from their Garden, they would presumably have been willing to confront this threat in the political arena. But in general, politics is a fool's game, being a source of anxiety rather than pleasure. It may *seem* to offer great pleasure. The successful politician may be acclaimed by the crowd, or see statues raised in his honor, and get pleasure as a result. But the Epicureans discourage us from pursuing such pleasures, labeling them as unnatural. Unnatural pleasures are poisoned chalices, guaranteed to yield more pain than pleasure in the long run (LS 22C, L).

Instead, Epicurus tells us, we should look to nature itself to learn which pleasures are worth pursuing. This is another point of agreement with the Cynics and Cyrenaics. In fact, in a work comparing the various Hellenistic schools, Cicero tells us that Epicurus deployed an argument also used by the Cyrenaics in support of hedonism.[2] According to this argument, even animals and children seek pleasant feelings. The instinct is so deeply rooted in our nature that we cannot conceive of any good apart from pleasant feeling. Epicurus can improve on the Cyrenaics' use of this argument, in light of his epistemology. Given that sensation is for him the measuring-stick of all belief, he sees no need to argue for the goodness of pleasure. Any creature endowed with sensation, the capacity to have feelings, will seek out pleasure. The example of small children and animals is intended to illustrate this point, that nature itself calls us to identify pleasure with the good. But nature does not call us to seek statues or cheering crowds, the way it tells us to eat when we are hungry, to drink when we are thirsty. It is only these natural desires that we ought to satisfy. Fulfilling natural desires, and being satisfied with that degree of fulfillment, is the surest road to lack of disturbance. As Epicurus says, again echoing Cynic and Cyrenaic ideas, natural pleasure is easy to obtain since it is always ready to hand (LS 21B). Furthermore, these pleasures can be as intense as any others. When we are genuinely in need of food and drink, plain bread and water are so thoroughly enjoyable that nothing could improve upon them.

Epicurus' praise of natural and necessary pleasures—the pleasures we really need if we are to avoid pain—has led many to believe that he is that most paradoxical of philosophers, an ascetic hedonist. In his letter on ethics, written to a friend named Menoeceus, Epicurus memorably says that when he encourages us to pursue pleasure, he does not mean the pleasure of boys, women, and fish—that is, pederasty, sex, and fine food (LS 21B). Such passages encourage the idea that Epicurus wants us to avoid luxurious pleasures at all costs, steering clear of anything nicer than the most basic necessities. After all, he might say, luxury is always going to be more trouble than it's worth. But this seems wrong. Epicurus is not Diogenes the Cynic, after all. He is deeply convinced that pleasure is good, indeed *the* good. It would be inconsistent for him to avoid a pleasure if he could have it without incurring a pain that would outweigh that pleasure.

A preferable interpretation, to my mind, is that Epicurus wants us to train ourselves to be happy with a moderate, even minimal, array of pleasures.[3] We need to be ready to live happily on bread and water, in case circumstances offer us nothing more. Furthermore, we should not undergo great stress or exert ourselves painfully to get luxuries. That would be counter-productive. Nonetheless, the Epicurean will still enjoy luxuries if they come along and are easy to procure. Consider the following example: if an Epicurean were getting on a plane, and the airline offered to bump him up to first class, would he accept? The answer is yes. First class is more pleasant than economy, and in this case will cost him nothing in terms of worry or pain. The only exception would be if the Epicurean knew that it would pain him on future flights to sit in economy, having tasted the delights of first class. But a well-trained Epicurean would not have this problem, since he has many times rehearsed the teachings which remind him that natural and necessary pleasure is enough.

So a critic of Epicurus will need to do better than just insult him for being a debauched and mindless pleasure-seeker. To that accusation, Epicurus will say, "I believe you have Aristippus the Younger in mind. My hedonism is thoughtful and requires me to resist pleasure just as often as I partake in it." Can the critic do better? Yes, if she has read her Plato. In several dialogues, Plato has his characters mount an anti-hedonistic argument that goes something like this (*Gorgias* 495e–497b, *Republic* 585a–b). Imagine that you're thirsty. This, clearly, is painful, which we can agree is a bad thing. Fortunately there's a solution: go drink something. Drinking is pleasant, precisely because it restores the body to its balanced state. But as soon as the painful condition of thirst is gone, so is the pleasure. It's not nice to keep drinking when you aren't thirsty anymore. If all pleasure is like this, the hedonist is in trouble. The best we can do is break even, with the pain of thirst being balanced out by the pleasure of drinking. When we are done experiencing pain, the pleasure will be gone too—and soon enough the pain will start anew, as we grow thirsty again. So a life devoted to this sort of pleasure is doomed to failure, because you can never come out ahead, like someone who can't save money because they only earn enough to pay off the debts they are constantly accruing. In the *Gorgias* (493b), Plato memorably compares someone in this situation to a man continually trying to fill a leaky jar.

Epicurus answers this critique of the hedonist life, but in doing so he is forced to make a rather bold claim. Firstly, he thinks that when I am having pleasure, that precludes feeling pain—so I am not still pained by thirst as I am drinking. This isn't enough, though, if it turns out that every pleasure I have is balanced out by a prior or future pain. What he needs to do is show that I can do better than break even. Here comes the bold part: Epicurus claims that when I am no longer in pain, that will in itself constitute the greatest possible pleasure. As he says in one of the pithy remarks he offered for his students' self-training, the "cry of the flesh" is to be neither hungry, nor thirsty, nor cold. Someone who is without these, and expects to be free of them in the future, rivals the god Zeus for happiness (LS 21G).

Later authors tell us that Epicurus developed some newfangled terminology in explaining this idea. The terms don't appear in his extant works, but Epicurus did have a fondness for coining technical expressions, and they are well attested in later sources. He distinguished, we are told, between two kinds of pleasure, "kinetic" and "static" (LS 21R). The difference is that a kinetic pleasure involves some kind of change or process—the word "kinetic" comes from the Greek *kinesis*, which means motion or change. A static pleasure, by contrast, is stable and does not involve any process of transition. Paradigmatic examples of kinetic pleasure would be things like eating, drinking, and sex. These are, of course, the pleasures that, according to Plato's anti-hedonistic argument, are mere restorations of the body. Epicurus outflanks Plato by insisting that the state in which pain has been eliminated is not merely neutral, a brief and bland respite before the next round of pain and kinetic pleasure begins. Instead, this pain-free state is pleasant, indeed so pleasant that nothing could improve on it.

This does answer Plato, and significantly fleshes out our picture of the ideal Epicurean life. It is a life of moderation, intended to minimize the fluctuations of pain and kinetic pleasure and to maximize the time we spend in the serene, static pleasure that comes with the elimination of all suffering. This helps explain why we should only value natural and necessary pleasures. If we allow the absence of fine dining or honor to upset us even slightly, we risk missing out on supreme pleasure, which is the complete lack of pain. It also enables Epicurus to combine his two preferred answers to the question of what constitutes the happy life: on the one hand there is pleasure, on the other, there is *ataraxia*, the lack of disturbance. It turns out that these are actually one and the same, since lack of pain and disturbance just is static pleasure, the best pleasure there is.

This is a brilliant move on Epicurus' part. Unfortunately, it is at best controversial, and at worst obviously false. Later critics, such as Cicero, point out the implausibility of saying that the mere absence of pain is the best pleasure we can have.[4]

To some extent this comes down to a clash of differing intuitions. Plato assumes that the absence of pain is compatible with the absence of pleasure, and that someone who is merely free of pain may feel nothing at all, whether good or bad. By contrast, Epicurus thinks the same state would be one of utter bliss. Is there any way to decide the issue? For what it's worth, I find it plausible that pain-free existence could be deeply satisfying. Being aware that I have no unfulfilled needs and no pain is indeed a kind of awareness, not a blank state of unconsciousness. One might describe this positive state as one of tranquillity. What more could you want, than to be aware that you want for nothing? On the other hand, an opponent might argue that even someone who is free of pain would have reason to seek out additional kinetic pleasure. This would prove that absence of pleasure is not the best we can do. For instance, if I am in a wholly pain-free state and someone offers me an almond croissant, I may well say yes, even without being hungry, just because they taste good. Epicurus doesn't deny this, but insists that when I eat the croissant I am not actually making my life more pleasant. I am simply adding variety. Someone who managed to go through life without pain, but without almond croissants, would still be as happy as Zeus. But as with luxuries in general, I might have reason to eat the almond croissant even if it doesn't increase my share of happiness.

From what I've said so far, you might think that the right lifestyle for the Epicurean would be one of isolated moderation, minimizing contact with other people and their projects—we already saw that family life is a potential source of disturbance. But what about these friends who were the recipients of Epicurus' letters? Okay, one of his letters was to his mother, and he was pretty much stuck with her, and vice versa. (Fortunately for him, his advice to avoid having children came too late to help her.) But what about the other friends, and those who spent time with Epicurus in his garden? Aren't such engagements a potential source of pain, to be avoided at all costs? Far from it. Epicurus in fact claims that there is quite literally nothing that can safeguard our happiness so well as friendship (LS 22E–F, O). For one thing, friendship and companionable conversation is itself one of the greatest pleasures we can have—it's no accident that it was a memory of this kind of pleasure that consoled Epicurus on his deathbed.

Also, Epicurus realizes that even someone who is neither hungry, nor thirsty, nor cold might still worry about where their next meal is coming from, or how they will stay warm when winter comes. Remember, to attain a life like that of Zeus, we also need to expect that we will avoid pain in the future—the reverse of the Cyrenaic idea of rehearsing the likelihood of future suffering. Friends are the greatest boon we can have in this respect, the ultimate insurance policy. Friends do each other good and know that they can call upon each other for help in the future. If I have many friends, I know I will never need to go hungry, because if it comes to it I can get a meal at a friend's house. Thus friendship, says Epicurus, has its roots in mutual benefit. This means not so much the actual benefits we give one another, as our confidence that more benefit is available later on if we need it. So friendship is, on two counts, crucial for the happy life: it is itself a great source of pleasure, and it helps protect us against disturbance, including the disturbance of worrying about tomorrow.

This seems to make Epicurus vulnerable to an objection one can also raise against Aristotle's theory of friendship. Shouldn't we value our friends for a reason other than our own happiness? Epicurus has made it sound like my friends are mere instruments for avoiding disturbance. He might be able to explain why I would undergo pains for the sake of friends, in order to build up mutual confidence of future beneficial behavior. But this all ultimately boils down to "I'll scratch your back if you scratch mine." It looks to be a depressingly selfish view of friendship. Some interpreters find grounds for optimism, though.[5] They suggest that there is a two-level strategy here: in general I want to have friends because it benefits me, but in order to achieve that I must genuinely cherish some individual people as friends. All well and good, you might say. But ultimately, there is at least one threat that no friends, and no amount of moderate living, can protect me from. No matter how much you are enjoying this book, your enjoyment is diminished by the knowledge that you will finish reading it. And so it is with life: I can never truly be free of anxiety and disturbance, because I am going to die some day. This, you might think, is the real problem with not being Zeus: he gets to be immortal, and we don't. And speaking of Zeus, shouldn't I also worry that the gods might inflict all kinds of torment on me in the afterlife? If you thought all that hunger and thirst was bad, wait until you get to Tartarus! Good thing for us, then, that Epicurus devised not only the outlines of a sound hedonism, but also a few arguments that may help us sleep soundly at night.

NOTHING TO FEAR
EPICUREANS ON DEATH AND
THE GODS

"It's not that I'm afraid to die, I just don't want to be there when it happens." So says Woody Allen.[1] But I don't believe him about not being afraid to die. For one thing, this is the same guy who said, "I don't want to achieve immortality through my work, I want to achieve it through not dying." That's pretty much how I feel too. I can remember being about 15 years old and having a sudden, crushing realization in English class, that one day I would cease to exist. An intimation of utter nothingness—not black emptiness, but genuine nothingness, non-existence. Then the bell rang and we went to lunch. Some day, of course, the bell will really ring for me, for you, for everyone. We hope to go peacefully in our sleep, at an advanced age, but one way or another, we will all go, to find out whether Socrates was right to argue in the *Phaedo* that death is mere separation of the soul from the body, or rather total oblivion. Either way, I'm not looking forward to it.

Epicurus would see me, and probably Woody Allen, as needing a crash course in his philosophy. He believed that the purpose of philosophy in general was to relieve human suffering—he remarked, in fact, that a philosopher who provides no therapy against this is just wasting words (LS 25B–C). As a hedonist, he naturally took physical pain to be an important form of suffering, and offered advice on how to avoid it. But mental pain is worse than physical pain, just as the pleasure that lies in the absence of all pain is better than the volatile physical pleasures of sex, food, and drink. If Epicureanism has a chief aim, it is to dispel mental anguish, anxiety, and fear. Thus the Epicureans summarize their teacher's message as follows: "The gods are not to be feared, nor is death; pleasure is ready to hand, and pain readily endured." This is the so-called *tetrapharmikon*, or "fourfold remedy," quoted by authors like the first-century AD Epicurean author, Philodemus.[2] It's significant that it is described as a *remedy*. For Epicurus, ethics is like a medical regime, but for the soul rather than the body.

And it is the soul we need to discuss, if we're to understand Epicurus' arguments against fearing the gods and death. The importance of these two sources of anxiety is clear from the fact that they make up the first half of the *tetrapharmikon*. We've already seen how Epicurus would defend the other two bits of reassurance, that we can always find pleasure and always overcome pain. Just think again of his ability to master agony on his deathbed, by thinking of pleasant times spent with friends. But death and god? Those are harder nuts to crack, and the theory of pleasure won't suffice by itself. Instead, as I say, we'll need to look at what Epicurus has to say about the soul. If you were to guess what he might say, you'd have a good chance of getting it right on the first try. You already know that Epicurus is a materialist, who believes that the world consists entirely of atoms and void. So you won't be surprised to discover that he thinks the soul is a material thing, made of atoms.

But not just any atoms. Epicurus, like other philosophers, including Aristotle and the Stoics, believes that the soul is like warm air. Sometimes soul is associated with *pneuma*, which is Greek for "breath"—this is, of course, where we get words like "pneumatic." This makes a certain amount of sense: we need to keep breathing to live, and so long as we live, we are warm. Epicurus, of course, puts an atomic spin on the theory. He says in one of his letters that the soul is made of atoms that resemble hot air or wind (LS 14A). It also contains other atoms of a very special sort, even finer than the atoms of wind. This makes the soul uniquely capable of producing sensation. Because this complex of warm, windy, and special atoms is so fine and subtle, it can be dispersed into every part of the body, which is why every part of us is able to feel pain, pleasure, and other physical sensations. But for the same reason, the soul cannot survive outside the body—Epicurus believes that such a fine network of atoms would simply disperse if extracted from the body.

Equally important for Epicurus' purposes is that even if the soul could survive apart from the body, it would not be able to have any sensory experience. Sensation requires not just a soul, not just a body, but a mingling of the two—our soul and body are, Epicurus says, affected along with one another (LS 14A, C, D). The reason this is important is that it helps to show why we should not fear death. We'll come back to this in a moment, but for now I'll just mention the main upshot of the theory, which is that upon death, my soul will cease to exist. Even if my soul could survive, it would be unable to experience pain or anything else anyway. Thus it is doubly pointless to fear painful experiences after death. Woody Allen can rest easy: as it turns out, he *won't* be there once he dies.

Unfortunately, this will only comfort Woody Allen if he believes that his soul is really made of fine atoms distributed throughout his body. But what if the Socrates of the *Phaedo* was right? What if we each have an immortal, perhaps immaterial, soul, which will allow us go to Tartarus, or wherever evil souls are sent to be punished for their sins? Clearly, this is ruled out by Epicurus' atomic theory. But as he points out, the theory does include something immaterial or incorporeal: void. Epicurus understands void not just as empty space, but as that which cannot physically interact with other things. There's an important lesson there. If something is not material, it cannot affect or be affected by anything else. So the Platonists' immaterial soul would no more be able to have bad experiences than a patch of empty space—it is causally cut off from everything, including anything that could hurt it.

I sense, though, that you're still nervous about this whole death thing. Perhaps I can, with Epicurus' help, offer you further reassurance. Let's think a bit more about what it means to have a sensory experience. It must be some kind of physical interaction. That much is clear from the fact that we need to touch or be placed near things in order to sense them. Plus, as we just saw, without physical interaction nothing can be affected, and having sensation is surely a way of being affected. Consider vision, for instance. What must be happening here is that visual images are coming to our eyes from the things we see. These images—the Greek word is *eidola*—must be made of atoms because, well, everything is made of atoms. When the images strike our eyes the presence of soul atoms in the eyes allows us to register that impact as a visual experience (LS 15A). And so on with the other senses. This analysis can be extended to cover apparently non-sensory experiences, like when we imagine something. This too must have some physical cause. Lucretius suggests that if we imagine a centaur, for instance, it will be because an image of a horse has gotten tangled together with one of a man (LS 15D). We are able to receive these tangled images too. A similar explanation can be provided for dreams. In short, all our experiences, even imaginary ones, are somehow grounded in a physical interaction with the atomic world around us.

You may find some of the details there unconvincing. But you have to admit that this particular dose of Epicurus' medicine does do what it says on the label. It is a theory of sensation, and experience in general, that makes it impossible for a disembodied or immaterial soul to experience anything, whether painful or otherwise. In fact, this theory of soul and sensation looks like it was designed precisely with that outcome in mind. It is a theory designed to dispel the fear of death, not a theory designed to settle once and for all the nature of the soul. As far as Epicurus is concerned, so long as his theory is consistent with experience, and so long as it achieves the aim of removing fear, he can say "mission accomplished." His mission is to remove fear, after all. So one can consider his whole psychological theory as just an elaborate argument against the fear of death.

The Epicureans didn't stop there, though. Lucretius devoted the entire third book of his poem *On the Nature of Things* to arguments against fearing death. It's been counted that he offers thirty-three of them—enough to supply you with an argument a day for a whole month, with a couple left over if you're feeling particularly nervous.[3] The most fundamental point, however, is that we will no longer exist after death. Why should you be afraid of a situation where you will no longer be present? Lucretius presents a powerful version of this idea, often called his "symmetry argument" (LS 24E). It asks you to compare the time after your death to the time before your birth. In one case, you will no longer exist, in the other, you did not yet exist. But the two situations are the same insofar as you aren't there. You see nothing fearful, and remember nothing awful, about the time before you were born. So neither should you fear or expect anything awful in the time after death. Lucretius admits that, in theory, the atoms that make up your soul could one day re-form to make another soul, especially given the infinity of future time available. But by the same token, they could have formed a soul in the distant past. Yet we remember nothing of that. So I should, he says, assume that there will be no continuity of experience between me and a possible future person who has the same soul atoms. Even if my soul is there, I won't be there.

Convinced? Well, there's a pretty obvious objection to be made: it is not really painful experiences or torment after death that I fear. As I said, when I was 15 what really got to me was the sheer idea of not existing anymore. And isn't that worth fearing? The Epicureans say no, for the same reason that it isn't worth looking forward to. If it is neither painful nor pleasant, it is to be neither feared nor hoped for. The only possible reason to fear it is that I will miss out on the pleasures I could have if I were to live longer. But this too can give us no basis for anxiety. Not only is it self-defeating—I shouldn't ruin the time I do have by worrying about how long it will last. It is also to misunderstand the nature of pleasure. Epicurus thinks that the painless state, which he calls "static" pleasure, is already the most blissful condition for man. Someone who has achieved this state needs no improvement, whether by stuffing more kinetic pleasures into his life or by prolonging that life. The whole point of static pleasure is that one wants for nothing, and that includes not wanting things you can't have, like immortality. As Epicurus puts it, when it comes to death we all live in a city with no defensive walls (LS 24B). The only way to defeat this enemy is not to fear it at all.

Let's suppose that we've come this far with Epicurus. We've signed up to the atomism. We've trained ourselves to be content with modest pleasures, though we'll be glad to partake of luxurious pleasures should they come along. We've made good friends to give us security against bad fortune. And we've stopped fearing death.

Serenity beckons, as we sit in the garden chatting and memorizing the master's precepts. Unfortunately, there's one last thing to worry about: the gods. If there are gods, and they are anywhere near as temperamental as Homer makes them seem in the *Iliad*, we in fact have a great deal to worry about. These are mighty, terrifying beings, who need to be propitiated, lest they should ... well, do really bad stuff to us. In this life, they might bring it about that we and our friends are subjected to all manner of torment. If I may allude briefly to a different ancient culture, I refer you to the Book of Job, which shows what a god with a vivid imagination can inflict on us if he really sets his mind to it.[4] And that's nothing compared to what the gods might do to us in the afterlife. All that stuff about atoms and sensation is well and good, but I'm off to the temple to sacrifice to Athena just in case.

As it turns out, Epicurus would not discourage us from going off to make those sacrifices. Epicureans generally did not avoid participating in traditional religious ritual. But this was not because they feared what the gods might do if they failed to participate. Epicurus teaches that the gods are no more to be feared than death. He asks us to consider what he calls our "preconception" of a god (LS 23B, C). Again, preconceptions are rough-and-ready notions that we derive from sensation and memory. In this case, our basic idea of a god is a being who is supremely blessed and everlasting. Everyone, or at least just about everyone Epicurus knew about, accepts the existence of gods, so there is no point denying their existence. And yet most people have ridiculous ideas about the gods, ideas incompatible with the basic preconception of what it is to be divine. For instance, they think the gods fight with one another, get angry, and so on. This is incompatible with their blessedness, especially from Epicurus' point of view—remember he thinks that blessedness consists in being entirely untroubled.

Clearly, then, the gods will not be bothered about whether we sacrifice to them. Indeed, they will not be troubled about us at all. They will show us neither favor nor displeasure, since even paying attention to the petty actions of humans would compromise their exalted and beatific calm. Epicurus also points out that the world is full of evils, which is hardly compatible with the idea that the gods are exercising providence over us (LS 13F, G). Rather than blaming evils on these blessed divinities, we should simply accept that the gods are not getting their hands dirty by trying to arrange the world around us. Epicurus seems to be radicalizing the theological critique delivered by Plato, and before him by the Pre-Socratic Xenophanes. Both of them complained that traditional ideas about gods were degrading to the majesty of the divine. Epicurus agrees. But he goes further by effectively removing them from any interaction with us or the world we live in.[5]

But if the gods are this remote, why should we even believe that they exist? At first blush, Epicurus' answer is a simple one. We should believe in them because we have a preconception about them. But how can we have a preconception of them, if we've never had direct experience of a god? My preconception of giraffes is meant to arise from seeing giraffes, whereas I don't recall ever seeing a god. Remember, though, that Epicurus extends his account of sensation to include things like the images we encounter in imagination and dreams. In the same way, he supposes that our preconception of the gods arises from images we have received. He allows us to picture them as outsized humans, very much like us, because this would be the most dignified form to assign to them. The later Epicurean Philodemus even suggests that the gods must speak Greek.[6]

This account has led some to suspect that, in his heart of hearts, Epicurus was indeed an atheist. This image of god as a big human who has all the best features I can think of sounds dangerously like a fiction. It might arise through the same sort of process that gives me images of centaurs. I've seen big things like giraffes and I've seen humans, so I can combine the concepts to get the idea of god as a big human, as we do with horse and man to imagine a centaur. Perhaps, then, gods are no more real than centaurs. Neither Epicurus nor his followers come out and say that they are atheists, but you'd hardly expect them to. As it was, their opponents were already accusing them of adopting a view that might as well be atheistic, since the Epicurean gods are utterly uninvolved with us. Without trying to settle the issue, I will just remind you that the point of his theology is the same as that of his psychology: to dispel anxiety. The really pressing question is not whether there are gods, but whether we should be afraid of them. They might be fictional, or real and unconcerned with us; either way, there is nothing to fear.

Epicurus has another reason to hold on to the preconception of the divine, which is that the gods represent an ethical ideal to which we can aspire. Remember his provocative statement that someone who lacks all pain and expects to stay that way lives a life like that of Zeus. This shows how useful it is to have a conception of god. It is the conception of a being that is utterly free of anxiety and suffering. In other words, Epicurus agrees with Plato's famous remark that our goal should be "likeness to god, insofar as is possible" (Plato, *Theaetetus* 176b). As a rule, the possibility is unfortunately rather remote. Humans do by nature seek the good, namely pleasure. That much is crucial to the Epicurean "cradle argument" we looked at before. But we show little wisdom in the way we pursue pleasure, often bringing pain upon ourselves even while seeking pleasure, for instance, by overeating, or dating exciting people we know will break our hearts in the end.

Worse still is our tendency to dwell on upsetting fears, thus ruining our chances of attaining and keeping the godlike state of static pleasure. This is why Epicurus offers therapy for those fears, trying to argue us out of our anxieties. Admirable though this may be, it might be thought a waste of time. Sure, sometimes a false belief can make me afraid. But that isn't always how it works. I, for instance, am not crazy about flying, whether or not I am in first class (actually I've never flown first class, but having read some Epicurus I try not to let that bother me). I know perfectly well that the plane is exceedingly unlikely to crash, that the car ride to the airport was probably more dangerous than the flight, and so on. Yet my palms still sweat at the slightest sign of turbulence. It's no good trying to convince me the plane is almost certainly not going to crash: I already know that, but I'm scared nonetheless. So it is with fear more generally. Even if I came to accept the Epicurean arguments against fearing death and the gods, I might still be afraid. To their credit, the Epicureans understood the difficulty of extinguishing fear. Epicurus himself did not merely write down arguments, he encouraged his followers to repeat them and think of them daily. Later Epicureans came up with their own ways of delivering the master's message in ever-more effective ways—notably by setting the theories into Latin verse.

7

REAPING THE HARVEST
LUCRETIUS

It began in the early afternoon, in August. From far away it was visible as a towering cloud of smoke, which resembled an enormous spreading pine tree. Closer observers were almost instantly buried in ash and battered by falling stones—killed almost without warning. That was in the nearest city, Pompeii. A bit further away, in Herculaneum, they had time to evacuate. But they did not run far enough. That night a blast of hot wind tore through their city, killing anyone left in it and many hundreds who had taken shelter along the coast. The year was AD 79, and the cause of death was the eruption of Mount Vesuvius. Pliny the Younger was an eyewitness. He was further away still than Herculaneum, and lived to write letters about the event to the historian Tacitus. In them he describes the darkness falling—not, as he says, the darkness of a moonless night, but utter blackness, as in a shut room where the lights are snuffed out. Ash and fragments of stone fell like rain, as everyone near him panicked, some clinging to the hope that the gods would save them, but most abandoning their faith and despairing in the face of this apocalypse.

It would have been no consolation to the victims to learn that there is, for historians of philosophy, a significant silver lining to this particular dark cloud. Like any respectable Roman town, Herculaneum had respectable citizens who lived in respectable villas. In one of these was a library, containing roll upon roll of papyrus. These books were charred into solid blocks and left buried under meters of ash and rock, where they would be discovered almost two thousand years later. In the eighteenth century archeologists dug out the papyrus rolls and began to peel them apart. Now they can be read with advanced scanners, without damaging them physically. The most sensational find among these Herculaneum papyri was a collection of books on Epicureanism. It seems to have been assembled by an Epicurean philosopher named Philodemus. So, thanks to Vesuvius, we have the charred remains of many works by Philodemus, and even more excitingly, the otherwise lost work *On Nature* by Epicurus himself.

If you'll pardon the pun, this find speaks volumes about the influence of Epicureanism. Of course the texts, fragmentary though they may be after their ordeal, are a rich source of information about Epicurean thought. But their mere presence in an aristocratic library of a Roman town is itself telling. We've already seen that as late as the second century AD the Epicurean enthusiast Diogenes of Oinoanda had letters of Epicurus and other teachings of the school inscribed in stone in modern-day Turkey. Herculaneum shows us that Epicureanism had already made incursions into the upper crust of Roman society by the first century BC. This is confirmed by Cicero, who lived in the same century. As we'll see later in this book, Cicero was no Epicurean, but he wrote philosophical dialogues pitting the teachings of various schools against one another. For him, Epicureanism deserved a place among the main traditions, one to be set against the Stoics and Skeptics.

Indeed, all the leading Hellenistic schools managed the transition from Greek to Latin philosophical literature. This is especially true of the Stoics, who had a kind of rebirth in the world of the Roman Empire. Epicureanism had its greatest flourishing earlier, here in the first century BC, around the time that Rome itself made a transition from a republic, controlled by the aristocratic Senate, to an empire. This is the age of Caesar, of Cleopatra, and of Cicero himself—no mean player on the political stage. In addition to the extensive information Cicero provides in his dialogues about Epicurean teaching in his day, he also alludes in one letter to a man who we must recognize, with all due respect to Philodemus, as the greatest representative of Epicureanism after Epicurus himself: the poet Lucretius. In 54 BC Cicero writes in approving terms of Lucretius' poetry, and a few decades later the poet Virgil works a verse of praise for Lucretius into his *Georgics*.[1] So Lucretius was known to his contemporaries. Sadly, as a historical figure at least, he is barely known to us.

We do know that he wrote one of the great works of Latin literature, and one of the greatest attempts to render philosophy into verse. This is *De rerum natura: On the Nature of Things*.[2] It does what its title says. Lucretius expounds the nature of things, from the atomic structure of the universe to the mechanics of lightning and magnetism, from the fear of death to sexual ethics. The poem seems to be based closely on Epicurus' work *On Nature*, as we can see by comparison with the burnt remains of that work found in Herculaneum. But Lucretius did not just write an expanded, poetic version of Epicurus' Greek treatise on physics. He wrote an expanded, poetic version of this Greek treatise *in Latin*. Like his contemporary Cicero, Lucretius works directly with Greek texts and attempts to convey ideas from those texts in a new tongue. Both he and Cicero apologize more than once for their inability to render Greek philosophical terms perfectly in Latin.[3] The Epicurean

Philodemus and Cicero both made the pilgrimage to Athens, the home of philosophy, and studied with masters there. To be a lover of wisdom in Roman society was, at least in this period, to be a lover of things Greek.

In particular, the Greek who Lucretius loves is Epicurus. Of the six books in *On the Nature of Things*, four start with extravagant praise for Epicurus, who is hymned quite literally as a god (5.8). Never mind that in this very poem Lucretius says that the gods have nothing to do with us, but rather exist far away from us in the infinite void. Lucretius is entirely open about the fact that he is following Epicurus and setting his ideas down in Latin verse. The six books of the poem take us through the highpoints of the Epicurean theory, including atomism, the centrality of pleasure, and the absurdity of fearing death or the gods. Lucretius says that his poem aims to present this teaching in a more pleasing way—like smearing honey on the rim of a cup full of medicine before giving it to a child (1.936–8). His avowed aim is to convert the reader to the received wisdom of Epicurus, the reader being, in the first instance, an aristocrat named Memmius, the addressee of the poem.

Does Lucretius bring anything to Epicureanism beyond his ability to put it into difficult but beautiful Latin hexameter verse? He does indeed, and I would insist that the literary achievement is inseparable from the philosophical achievement. Perhaps Lucretius' greatest strength is the ability to conjure powerful and plausible images for Epicurus' ideas. He compares the quick-moving atoms of the soul to poppy seeds (2.453), the constantly moving atoms within an apparently unmoving body to the mad fracas of a battlefield seen from a distance as an unmoving blur (2.308–16). In one of my favorite passages, he is trying to persuade us that atoms have many, subtly different shapes. To illustrate, he mentions a slaughtered calf whose mother cow is forlorn in her grief. She is described in loving detail, searching for her lost offspring, scanning the ground for its beloved hoof prints, caring nothing for other calves, though they all look the same to us humans (2.352–66). In the same way, atoms with different shapes seem interchangeable until we carefully consider the point. As it happens, Lucretius is going to go on to say that every shape of atom occurs an infinite number of times in the universe, which pretty much undercuts his point. But when the point is made with that much style, one hardly cares. Similarly powerful is the end of the poem. Lucretius is trying to explain the causes of disease. He unleashes a terrifying description of the classical plague of Athens, inspired by the historian Thucydides. Here Lucretius seems to want us to see what Pliny says the victims of Mount Vesuvius realized, as they thought they would die: the gods do not care about us. We are on our own.

Now, this is all well and good, but are there any new *ideas* here? Yes and no. Some ideas absent from the remaining writings of Epicurus do turn up. But it is usually assumed that whatever is unprecedented in Lucretius is taken from the lost parts of Epicurus' writings. One example would be the account Lucretius offers for magnetism. Invoking the atomic theory, he suggests that the magnet sends out a powerful stream of particles towards nearby metal. These push aside the air between the magnet and the metal, creating a space dominated by void. But air is pressing on the magnet and metal from all other directions, so they lurch towards each other into the space between them, which provides less resistance (6.1002–89). More philosophically central is the distinction he introduces within the Epicurean theory of soul. He draws a contrast between two aspects of soul. With his newfangled Latin, he calls these two aspects *animus*, sometimes translated as "mind," and *anima*, sometimes translated as "spirit" (3.94, 117). The ruling part of the soul is the mind or *animus*, and is seated in the chest, as Aristotle and the Stoics taught. The spirit or *anima* is dispersed through the whole body. You can keep living without parts of your spirit—as we can see from the fact that people survive when limbs are amputated. But your life literally depends on the continued presence of the mind. It is our commanding faculty, and initiates our motions. Still, it should be noted that Lucretius' *animus* is not really a mind in our sense, or indeed in Aristotle's sense. Lucretius illustrates its powers mostly through examples of emotion rather than, say, intellectual activity or consciousness.

This brings us to a fundamental issue, one already discussed by Epicurus and a running theme of Hellenistic philosophy as a whole. Lucretius is one of the first to give the issue a technical name: *libera voluntas*, meaning "free volition" or "free will." He draws our attention to a fundamental difference between creatures that can exercise free volition, and other things like inanimate objects. With his flair for vivid examples, he describes what happens at the start of a horse-race. When the horses are allowed to charge ahead, there is the briefest of moments before they move—we might think instead of the few hundredths of a second between the starting-gun and the sprinter's leaping out of the blocks (2.263–5). This is unlike, say, one rock hitting another. The rock that gets hit doesn't pause before reacting, it just moves. That is because it is not moving itself, it is being moved by something else.

Plato and Aristotle already drew attention to the capacity of animate beings to move themselves. But the Epicureans may have been the first to worry about the conditions under which this was possible. In particular, they worried that if everything in the universe happens as a matter of necessity, the world unfolding inevitably from the past to the present, then nothing would have a power of free volition. And they were right to worry. After all, their physics describes the world as the result of atomic collisions, each of which seems to be like one rock hitting another. This suggests that the difference between the horse and the rock is only apparent.

Perhaps it takes a while for the chain reaction to produce a visible result in the horse but it is still just a bunch of collisions, an inevitable chain of cause and effect. To put it another way, given the immutable laws of physics, the distribution and motion of atoms right now will make everything in the future utterly inevitable and necessary.

It was apparently to avoid this that the Epicureans posited what they called a *clinamen*, or "swerve." The idea is not found in our extant evidence for Epicurus, though it does seem to be his idea; Lucretius discusses it in some detail (2.216–93). According to this notorious doctrine, atoms do not in fact always fall straight down. That's mostly what happens. But occasionally an atom will, apparently randomly, shift slightly sideways. Lucretius gives two reasons for thinking this. One is that if all atoms only fell down then the world would never arise, because the atoms would never start to collide with one another. They would be like raindrops hurtling next to each other in the void, all at the same speed. But this is probably not the real reason. After all, the Epicurean world is eternal, so there need never have been a moment where the atoms were not already colliding and moving in all directions. Thus they don't need to *start* colliding. The real motivation for the swerve is probably the second reason: avoiding the consequence that everything is necessary.

Now, one needs to be careful here. The mere presence of randomness in a physical system doesn't really help explain the power of choice. If what I am worried about is whether I am in control of my own actions, or whether my actions are instead induced by atomic motions of which I am not even aware, then the swerve is no comfort at all. It will just turn out that the atomic motions that determine my action are sometimes random rather than deterministic. But who cares about that? The point is to put me in control, not to have my actions ultimately traced back to random things out of my control. For this reason, it would be nice if the Epicureans weren't saying, for instance, that each choice I make actually involves a swerving atom. Instead, they are just saying that the universe contains indeterminism. This is intended to show that human actions are not necessary and inevitable events, since there are no necessary and inevitable events in an indeterministic world. One reading of Lucretius on the swerve would support this: he doesn't seem to say that choices are swerves, or vice versa. Rather, he draws an analogy. Just as atoms can move by themselves, when they swerve, so we can move by ourselves, when we make choices.

Nonetheless, it seems clear that any choice I make, any action I perform, must involve atomic motions, whether swerving or not. After all, there is nothing in the world apart from atoms moving in a void. This might lead us to say that choices, along with anything else you might care to name, are not real, except insofar as they are identical with atoms and their motions. That may be a consequence that the Pre-Socratic Democritus drew from his atomism. He said, "by convention sweet, by convention bitter... by convention color, but really atoms and void."[4] According to this fragment, Democritus apparently wanted to eliminate the properties we actually experience, like taste and color, or at least treat them as merely conventional. An adequate scientific account of the universe could dispense with talk of such properties. You might think the Epicureans would follow suit, being atomists themselves. But instead they stoutly resist Democritus' sentiment, insisting that all these properties are absolutely real, though they may depend on atomic motions. This will go for human choices just as much as for colors and tastes.

In another area of their philosophy, though, the Epicureans were happy to embrace a different kind of conventionalism. They did so in order to explain human society and language, a theme Lucretius takes up in the fifth book of his poem. With characteristically vibrant images, Lucretius gives a wholly naturalistic account of the origins of human political arrangements. Earlier in the book he has already explained how animals arose, giving a theory reminiscent of the Pre-Socratic philosopher Empedocles. As with Empedocles, Lucretius is often given credit for anticipating Darwinian evolutionary theory. He explains that animals first arose through random atomic entanglements, and propagated insofar as they were fit to survive. For instance, animals with no generative organs could not produce children and died after one generation. In much the same way, human society grows out of a long and painful process. In the beginning, as Lucretius vividly describes, humans were in a kind of state of nature. Only once they developed the rudiments of trust and cooperation could they advance beyond the most primitive condition in which each man fights for his own survival (5.958–1027).

It was at this time that humans first developed language. This too was simply a conventional advance on natural tendencies. Primitive man would naturally have communicated by grunts and gestures, something Lucretius illustrates by pointing out that children too young to talk articulately just point at what they want (5.1031–2). Animals too can communicate with rudimentary noises; just think of the different noises made by dogs when they are angry, frightened, or caring for their pups. Words are simply a more refined use of the same capacity. So far so good, but next Lucretius qualifies the optimistic account of progress he's been giving so far. Once language and human cooperation were on the scene, the next step was the development of cities, of political rule, and of money. This was the breeding ground for the unnecessary desires against which the wise Epicurus warned. In the struggle to satisfy these desires, society began to slide back into violence. A kind of second social contract was needed to restore order, and this explains the imposition of the laws that govern our society today (5.1146). One wonders what Lucretius might have made of the civil wars that tore apart Roman society in this first century BC. A sign, perhaps, that society was preparing to backslide, having failed to heed Epicurus' warning that honor and power are poisoned chalices.

It's almost a cliché to note that Epicureanism appeared in Greek society, and then reappeared in Roman society, at times of great upheaval. The post-Aristotelian Hellenistic schools emerged just after Alexander the Great achieved domination over Greece. The confident independence of city-states like Athens and Sparta, so recently centers of empire, was upset for good. From this point on, the political situation of the Greek cities was usually just a matter of which foreign power was calling the shots—the Macedonians? The Romans? Either way, an intelligent aristocrat was bound to seek out a philosophy of reassurance, both against the uncertainty of his circumstances and against his new-found impotence. Likewise, in the first century BC the Roman Republic fell, tearing power, if not wealth and noble lineage, from the hands of the senatorial class. Was Epicureanism successful because it could offer reassurance in times of upheaval? If so, it's appropriate that Lucretius' poem caused some upheaval of its own when it was rediscovered in the early fifteenth century, after going unread and nearly being lost in late antiquity and the middle ages.[5] Once unearthed, On the Nature of Things inspired such heavyweights as Machiavelli, who copied it out by hand, Gassendi, who adopted many of its doctrines, and Montaigne, who quotes it frequently in his Essays. Nor was Lucretius the only Hellenistic thinker to influence ideas in early modern Europe. In that period philosophy was also shaped by ancient skepticism (David Hume is a good example) and by the most successful of the philosophical movements that arose in the wake of Plato and Aristotle: the Stoics.

WALKING ON EGGSHELLS
STOIC LOGIC

When they invent time travel, I bet the first thing they will do is go back to ancient Athens to meet Socrates and tour the Acropolis. I also bet they will be disappointed. They'll probably forget to bring someone who can speak ancient Greek, so they won't get much out of Socrates. As for the sculptures and buildings, they will be surprised and a bit appalled to find that these things were all painted in bright, even gaudy colors. For us classical sculpture is pristine and white—marble made flesh. But that's just because the paint has worn off. Downtown, they'll find more paintings, in a space adjoining the *agora* or marketplace. It was a long, covered, colonnaded place for walking to and fro, called the *stoa poikile*, the "painted porch," for the murals that decorated it. If the time-travelers get their coordinates slightly wrong, and arrive a few decades after the death of Socrates, they'll still get to meet some philosophers if they venture to this public porch. Because the *stoa* was not only a porch, it was also the name of a philosophical school, named after its favorite hangout.

The early *Stoa*—better known to us as the Stoics—sought to follow Socrates' example in many things, including his habit of doing philosophy in the middle of urban life. Their Porch makes a striking contrast to the Garden, Academy, and Lyceum. Whereas Epicurus, Plato, and Aristotle set up shop on the fringes of Athens, the Stoics planted themselves next to the marketplace. Like Socrates, they wanted to engage with their fellow citizens, and make demands of them. Epicurus' philosophy is an invitation, a seduction, a promise. Pursue a moderate life of pleasure, he says, and learn to escape all disturbance. In the hands of the Stoics philosophy is instead an accusation, a gauntlet thrown down. Those who fail to seek and obtain wisdom are not just missing out on a great good—they are irrational. They are, the Stoics went so far as to say, insane. Of course Epicurus too disapproved of the way most other Greeks lived, but he was willing to meet them halfway. In pursuing pleasure they had the right basic idea, it was just that their strategy for getting pleasure was all wrong. The Stoics were far more radical. Pleasure, along with honor and all the other things non-philosophers value, are actually valueless. Socrates had it right: seek wisdom, or live a life of folly, a life befitting slaves.

This, of course, is an attitude towards philosophy, and a way of imitating Socrates, that we've already seen with the Cynics. And indeed, the founder of the Stoic school, Zeno of Citium, supposedly studied with the Cynic philosopher Crates—the one who joined with Hipparchia in a Cynic marriage. To study with Crates, Zeno first had to make the journey from Citium, in Cyprus, to Athens. I mentioned in the last chapter that first-century BC philosophers like Cicero and Philodemus the Epicurean were still making the pilgrimage to Athens, and the city remained a center of philosophy for centuries after that. In the ancient world, Athens was to philosophy what Las Vegas is to gambling. The phenomenon was already well entrenched in the early Hellenistic period, with all the main Stoics turning up in Athens even though they were born elsewhere.

The ancient sources tell us that Zeno started his philosophical career as an admirer of Socrates and a follower of Crates. We get the usual round-up of anecdotes about him, some of them describing how Crates tried to school him in the Cynic lifestyle, for instance by making him carry a pot of lentils with him wherever he went. There is some independent evidence for this link to Cynicism. Zeno wrote a work called the *Republic*, known only through later reports.[1] Despite its Platonic title, Zeno's *Republic* apparently defended a broadly Cynic political program. It proposed abolishing many of the social conventions Diogenes the Cynic had rejected. Currency was to be not merely defaced but eliminated; no temples were to be built to the gods; traditional education was deemed worthless; and all other men should be taken as our fellows, joining in a community on the basis of virtue rather than kinship (LS 67A–B).

Zeno's utopian ideas were not retained as a core of the Stoic manifesto, but his uncompromising ethical stance certainly was. However, this is only one aspect of Stoicism, and doesn't come close to capturing the full breadth of its philosophical vision. The Stoics were pioneers in just about every area of philosophy, and married their ethical absolutism to careful technical analysis. Because he was the school founder, Zeno's authority and status as a moral exemplar was unquestioned by all card-carrying Stoics. Many of their signature doctrines can be traced to him. But it was only with Zeno's successors that Stoicism matured into the system that would dominate ancient philosophy well into the age of the Roman Empire. After Zeno's death, in 262 BC, the headship of the school was taken over by a man named Cleanthes. Thirty years later he was succeeded by Chrysippus, who served as school head from 232 until his death in 206. It is to Chrysippus that we owe the subtle and rigorous systematization of Stoicism, without which it would never have become the greatest of the Hellenistic schools.

Unfortunately, not a single one of Chrysippus' works—and he wrote well over a hundred of them—has survived to us today. Instead, the reports of his ideas are often found in hostile authors like Galen, early Christian authors, and members of rival schools. Nor is it always easy to pry apart the specifically Chrysippan material from general reports about Stoic doctrine. Still, the evidence at our disposal shows that Chrysippus was probably the most sophisticated and influential ancient philosopher to work between Aristotle and Plotinus. (Sorry, Epicurus.) He excelled in the cut and thrust of inter-school debate, and for this sake sharpened Stoic doctrines and techniques of argument. Until we reach the predominantly ethical approach of "Roman Stoics" like Epictetus, Stoicism centers around the teachings of Chrysippus. Nonetheless, the Stoics were admirably willing to make adjustments to their doctrines in response to internal and external debate.

To understand the technical proficiency that Chrysippus brought to Stoicism, we need to consider a further historical influence from the age of Zeno. This, remember, was the generation or two after Aristotle, roughly the same time that Epicurus was putting forth his hedonistic ideas in competition with the more unrestrained pleasure principle of the Cyrenaics. At this time Cynicism too was a going concern—an influence on young Zeno, as we just saw. The Platonic Academy and Aristotle's followers were also active. So it was a time of great intellectual ferment, with the early schools all engaging with one another in mutual criticism and polemic. A minor player in this period, but one important for our story, is Diodorus Cronos. Ancient sources make Diodorus the lead thinker of the "Dialectical school"—specialists in logic and technical arguments. On several issues, it would seem that Diodorus and his followers goaded the Stoics, and especially Chrysippus, into careful reflection on argument forms, fallacies, and so on. The Stoics were thus provoked to develop some of their most subtle philosophical ideas, much as the sophists had provoked Plato and Aristotle.

It was in part thanks to fruitful competition with the Dialectical school that the Stoics achieved so much in logic. The Stoics placed great value on logic, considering it to be one of the three main parts of philosophy, along with physics and ethics (LS 26A–D).[2] Taking their lead from Zeno, who was always good for a vivid metaphor, the Stoics compared the three parts of philosophy to an egg: logic is the shell, physics the egg-white, and ethics the egg-yolk. (Another version switches physics and ethics around, but logic is still the shell.) There are other metaphors given too: logic is a wall around a field, the trees in the field are physics, and the fruit is ethics. This threefold division might seem to leave some things out, like philosophy of mind and metaphysics. But the tripartite scheme is as much a declaration of what the Stoics *don't* do as a statement of what they do. The omission of any metaphysics distinct from physics is deliberate: the Stoics are materialists. Their theory of mind too is to be found in their physics.

Part of the point of the metaphors is that the three parts of philosophy are closely connected. Thus, they also compare philosophy to a living body—logic is the bones, ethics the flesh, and physics the soul. Later on, Aristotelians insisted that philosophical disciplines had to be taken in a strict order, and that one should start with logic—meaning, of course, Aristotle's logical works. The Stoics disagreed: for them philosophy was an organic unity, and a question raised in ethics could lead you to physics or logic, and vice versa. Ultimately, wisdom consists in mastery of all three parts. Expertise in only one would not merely be inadequate, it would be impossible, because the three are so closely intertwined.

The Aristotelians also objected to the very claim that logic is a "part" of philosophy. For them, logic is something a bit less exalted than a part of philosophy. It is, rather, an instrument. This is why they called those logical works of Aristotle the *organon*, meaning "tool" or "instrument." To refute the Stoic view, they pointed out that a logical argument form is empty until it is, so to speak, filled out with specific terms. The logician tells you that it is valid to argue: "All A is B, all B is C, therefore all A is C." But you aren't doing philosophy until you substitute some words for letters. Throw in "giraffe" for A, "ruminant" for B, and "plant-eaters" for C and then you're in business. To be specific, the business of biology: you've just given a demonstration explaining why giraffes eat plants. More generally, we can say that for the Aristotelians logic was not yet a part of philosophy because it could not, on its own, give us knowledge. It only gives us an understanding of the argument forms, which can be *used* to obtain knowledge.

Now, the Stoics were certainly no slouches when it came to considering argument schemes. But their understanding of logic included much more than this. For them logic embraced analysis of language and rhetoric. They also realized that logical points are not always philosophically innocent, as the Aristotelians pretend. For instance, their understanding of the logical notion of possibility is intimately connected with their physics. In fact, the Aristotelians had a similarly wide-ranging conception of logic—they too wound up counting rhetoric as part of the logical curriculum, and Aristotle's *Posterior Analytics*, a work on philosophy of science or epistemology, was seen by them as the capstone of the *organon*. In light of this, I tend to think the Stoics had the better of this particular debate.

The disagreement between Stoic and Aristotelian logic is deeper than this, though. When the Stoics actually start doing logic proper, they take a very different approach to what we find in Aristotle's *Prior Analytics*.[3] Aristotle's logic is a theory of predication. It examines the relationships we can draw between claims like "A is B" and "some B is not C." The Stoics, by contrast, tend to give examples involving claims like "it is day" or "this man walks." They call these "simple" assertions, and say that they are "complete" because they can be either true or false. An incomplete assertion would be, for instance, "this man..."; you have to add something further, like "walks," or "is named Peter," or "is devastatingly handsome," to get something that can be true (or, you know, false). The next step is to think about how simple assertions can combine into more complex assertions. There are basically three ways to connect them: "if," "or," and "and."

You wouldn't think that these little words would cause controversy, but they do. The troublemaker is that word "if." Suppose I link two irrelevant statements with "if" and "then." For instance: "if giraffes are animals, then Socrates died of hemlock." Is that true? Or I might include a false statement, like this: "if giraffes fly, then Socrates died of hemlock." Not so obvious what to think about these inferences, is it? Today's logicians, and some ancient ones, tend to think that "if... then" statements are true just so long as they don't infer something false from something true. Suppose I say "if Socrates died of hemlock, then giraffes fly." That has to be wrong. After all, Socrates did die of hemlock, but giraffes don't fly, any more than pigs do. But the other way around looks fine, or at least harmless: since giraffes never fly, there's no harm in saying that if they did, Socrates would die of hemlock, or for that matter not die of hemlock.

But this wasn't satisfactory to some ancient logicians, for instance, our new friend Diodorus Cronus. And one is tempted to agree with him. Surely the point of asserting "if X, then Y" is to claim that X and Y have some kind of connection. Diodorus gets closer to this by adding another requirement: it can *never* be the case that X is true and Y is false. This helps him rule out the truth of assertions like, "if chickens are birds, then Socrates died of hemlock," because there was a time when chickens were birds but Socrates had not yet died of hemlock. Chrysippus basically agrees with Diodorus, but goes further: he and other Stoics speak of a "coherence" between the two parts of an "if... then" statement (LS 35B). I am only allowed to infer Y from X if the truth of X somehow *rules out* the falsehood of Y. For instance, suppose it is always true that penguins are birds, and that giraffes are ruminants. Still it is *not* true to say, "if penguins are birds, then giraffes are ruminants," because the fact that penguins are birds has nothing to do with giraffes. Here we catch a glimpse of how Chrysippus sees logic as connecting to physics. The relation Chrysippus is describing sounds like a causal relation: given the cause, the effect must follow.

Once we sort out these issues about complex assertions, we're ready to build some arguments. These will involve at least two assertions, and of those at least one will need to be complex. So a standard Stoic argument might be "if it is day then it is light; it is day; so it is light." Just as Aristotle itemized syllogistic forms and considered whether or not they count as valid, so Chrysippus identified five argument forms which he called "indemonstrable"—in other words, they are obviously valid arguments (LS 36A). The example I just gave, the one about daylight, would be the first indemonstrable, which has the form, "if the first, then the second, but the first, so the second." This looks a bit like what we find in Aristotle. Logic is the study of arguments. So you begin by considering parts of assertions, like "this man" or "walks"; then you see how they combine into complete assertions, like "this man walks"; finally you work on combining the assertions into argument forms, like "if this man walks, then he moves; this man walks; therefore he moves."

But the differences with Aristotle are more striking. The Stoics don't lay particular stress on predication, and in fact they are downright uncomfortable with the kind of predication that Aristotle considered most important: universal predication, like "all giraffes are ruminants." The Stoics would be happier to put this differently, and say, "if something is a giraffe, then it is a ruminant." In this case, with their rephrasing the Stoics are registering their unwillingness to countenance universal entities. For them, everything that exists is material. So there is no such thing as a universal form or species, *giraffe*, there are just individual giraffes. Again, we see that logical points can have serious philosophical consequences. The Stoic view puts clear water between them and Plato, with his theory of Forms, and also Aristotle, who tends to think that universal features of the world have some degree of reality.

In addition to building a logical system, the Stoics spent a fair amount of effort on the solution of logical puzzles. These were a favorite topic for Chrysippus, who wrote entire books about single paradoxes and puzzles, including the famous Liar and Sorites paradoxes. We'll see how he dealt with these in the next chapter. To get us warmed up for thinking about those, I'll consider another logical puzzle he confronted, which introduces a major topic in Stoicism: "modality," in other words, the concepts of necessity, possibility, and impossibility. Again, Diodorus Cronus provided the provocation, with something called the Ruling or Master Argument (LS 38A). The idea seems to have been this: let's suppose I never get to be a ruler, for instance, the president of a country. It seems like I *could* be a president, even if I never am a president. But Diodorus argues otherwise. He exploits the fact that everything about the past seems to be necessary. After all it's too late to do anything about the past. We can't, for instance, change the fact that Socrates died of hemlock. So Socrates' having died of hemlock is necessary. Now if, as we supposed, I will never rule, then it must have been true already in the past that I will never rule. But then this must be a necessary truth. After all, everything about the past is necessary. So if it was already true yesterday or one hundred years ago that I will never rule, then the ship has already sailed: it is impossible for me to rule.

This argument, and other arguments from the Dialectical school, yield an unnerving result, namely that if something will never happen, then it *cannot* happen. Other deterministic arguments tried to show something even stronger, namely that each thing must happen at the time that it happens. Aristotle already confronted this prospect in his famous sea-battle argument.[4] He also addressed the issue in a passage from his *Metaphysics* (1046b). It discusses a group he calls the Megarians, who claimed that everything that actually happens must happen. Chrysippus, like Aristotle, found these consequences troubling. So he proposed a novel conception of possibility and necessity. For Chrysippus, something is possible so long as it is not in itself impossible and furthermore is not prevented from happening (LS 38E–F). Thus, many things that could happen don't happen. I don't speak Chinese, but it is possible that I speak Chinese, because it is (just about) within my capacity to learn to speak it and nothing has intervened from the outside to stop me from learning it. Other sorts of things that never happen are impossible. Firstly, things that are in themselves impossible, like me lifting a skyscraper. Secondly, things that could occur in themselves, but are prevented from occurring. The classic example is a piece of wood at the bottom of the ocean, which in itself could burn, but is hindered from burning by being permanently underwater.

Chrysippus' interest in puzzles like the Liar, Sorites, and Master Arguments was not mere idle speculation. We already saw that the dispute over conditional assertions connects to Stoic physics, because causation is a conditional relation—*if* I watch a Buster Keaton movie, *then* I will laugh. The same goes for the dispute over modality. Chrysippus and other Stoics were causal determinists: they thought that true causes inevitably give rise to their effects and that all things arise in this way. But they were not logical determinists or fatalists: they still wanted to distinguish between possible and necessary truths. We'll see why shortly. As for the Liar and the Sorites, Chrysippus needed to solve these too. This results from his epistemology, which envisions the possibility of an infallible sage who always knows the right answer, or knows that there is no right answer. This would be a kind of super-philosopher, who never makes mistakes. It's among the most ambitious and sophisticated epistemological theories of the ancient world, and the topic of our next chapter.

9

NOBODY'S PERFECT
THE STOICS ON KNOWLEDGE

How, then, did Chrysippus deal with the twin threats of the Sorites paradox and the Liar paradox? And why were these paradoxes of such interest to him? First, let's consider the paradoxes themselves, starting with the Sorites.[1] The title comes from the Greek word *soros*, which means "heap." It's best understood as a kind of dialectical game, where I ask you whether one grain of sand constitutes a heap. Well, obviously not. How about two grains? Presumably you'll still say that this is not a heap of sand. But I keep going: three grains? Four? How about five?...until you admit that we now have a heap. As soon as you do that, I say, "you're telling me adding one grain of sand turns it into a heap?" It's absurd to suppose that adding or subtracting only one grain would make a decisive difference. Yet at some point, a heap must come into existence. So where do you draw the line? A variation, which touches on a sensitive spot for me personally, asks you to imagine plucking hairs off a man's head one at a time until he becomes bald. It's absurd to suppose that one hair could make the difference, yet he surely becomes bald at some point. It's a cute little paradox. But does it rise to the exalted level of being philosophy?

As it turns out, this puzzle and others like it provoke a lot of excitement among philosophers nowadays. They raise the issue of vagueness. There are certain concepts which seem to have no sharp boundaries, like "bald" and "heap," as the puzzle illustrates. Those are, if you'll pardon the expression, particularly clear cases of vagueness. But they are far from the only ones. Think, for instance, about evolution: apes turn slowly into humans, generation by generation. Is it any easier to say which generation separates ape from human than it is to say which strand of hair separates hirsute from bald? Probably not. So "human" seems to be a "vague" term, and presumably all our other biological concepts are too. Concepts of man-made things, like tables and airplanes, look even more obviously vague. Likewise for colors, and other qualities like thin and fat. The more you think about it, the vaguer the world seems. Philosophers can hardly avoid being interested in this once they've noticed it, and have tried to develop more precise notions of vagueness. Hence the fascination of the Sorites paradox.

Chrysippus was apparently the first to feel this fascination. He wrote entire treatises on the paradox, and thus has some claim to be the first philosopher to deal with the topic of vagueness. Sadly, these works are lost. We know only from later reports that his way out of the paradox was this: simply fall silent before it becomes unclear whether the sand is a heap (LS 37H). If things start being unclear around about twenty-five grains, then when you are asked about the twentieth grain of sand, just say nothing at all—refuse to be drawn on the issue. Now, this does not seem to constitute a solution to the Sorites paradox. It's only a strategy for approaching the dialectical game the paradox envisions: in order to avoid falling into an absurdity, Chrysippus advises you to just keep your mouth shut. As Cicero says in reporting the strategy, you will be like a chariot-driver pulling up his horses before running off a cliff (LS 37H). Notice that Chrysippus tells us not to be silent the first time we are unsure, but *before* we start to be unsure. His goal is purely defensive. He just wants to help us avoid saying something false or something absurd, for instance, that twenty-four grains of sand isn't a heap, but twenty-five grains is a heap. This may strike us as a bit disappointing. We were hoping to learn something about the problem of vagueness, but Chrysippus' advice seems to be simply, "don't go there."

As for the Liar paradox, this involves a statement along the following lines: "What I'm now saying is false." If it's true it's false, if it's false it's true. This problem is at the heart of all logical paradoxes, which always produce a self-contradiction. Again, Chrysippus devoted a whole series of lost treatises to it. And again, his aim was apparently to prevent any contradiction or absurdity from arising in the first place— to find a defensive strategy. As far as we can tell, his diagnosis of the paradox was that a statement like "What I'm now saying is false" is not a genuine proposition. It only *appears* to be one. It's just not the sort of thing that can be true or false.

Why, then, should Chrysippus have devoted so much energy to these paradoxes? Surely the puzzles appealed to his natural gift for logical analysis. But just as surely, he had a broader philosophical project in mind. He inherited from Zeno, the founder of the Stoics, an ambitious theory of knowledge. This theory envisioned the possibility of a perfect sage who would never make a mistake. That's not to say that Zeno himself was such a sage, or that he knew where to find one. The Stoics sought only to defend the theoretical possibility of the sage. They weren't committed to the idea that there actually are or have ever been any. Their point was a philosophical one, namely that without the possibility of faultless rationality, there is no standard against which we can measure ourselves.

One of the main dramas of Hellenistic philosophy was the opposition between the Stoics' extreme optimism and ancient Skepticism. The ancient Skeptics argued that all candidates for knowledge seem to involve some uncertainty. The battle-lines were drawn: the Stoics claimed that certainty is possible, the Skeptics that it is not, or more modestly, that as far as we can tell it is never achieved. Here we need to be careful, though. The Stoics were not saying that we can be certain about everything, or that the sage would know everything. Rather, they were saying that the sage would have certain knowledge in some cases, and that he would be able to tell the difference between certainty and doubt. In cases of doubt, he would refrain from making any judgment at all (LS 40D, I). This explains Chrysippus' answer to the Sorites paradox, namely to fall silent, to avoid committing oneself. The fact that this option is available means that a perfect sage can avoid saying anything he is unsure about, even when confronted by cases of vagueness. The idea of suspending judgment is also at the heart of the Skeptical project. Indeed, we can sum up the difference between the two schools by saying that the Stoics thought we should suspend judgment when we are not certain. The Skeptics agreed, but added that as far as we can tell certainty is never available, so we should always suspend judgment.

Stoic epistemology, then, revolves around the task of showing that we can have certainty. In this, the Stoics were returning to a project dear to the hearts of Plato and Aristotle. They wanted to distinguish between true knowledge or understanding, and mere opinion. The Stoics laid it on pretty thick when it came to making this distinction. They thought that people who have opinion and not knowledge only get at the truth by being lucky—after all, they lack certainty, so they could just as well have been wrong. In fact the Stoics go further, and compare them to insane people, since the insane likewise can get things right by luck (LS 40E). Or perhaps I should say, the Stoics compare us, and themselves—anyone who is not a sage—to insane people. This may itself sound a bit crazy. But the Stoics were uncompromising on the point, apart from one concession: some non-sages are better than others. Those who, like the Stoics themselves, are at least trying to achieve certainty are better than those who let their beliefs run out of control, endorsing any thought that comes to mind.

Where, then, is our certainty going to come from? Like the Epicureans, the Stoics point to sensation. All our knowledge is ultimately grounded in our sensory experiences, since it is the senses that give us access to the physical world around us (LS 39D–E). This is unsurprising given that, again like the Epicureans, the Stoics believe that only physical bodies exist. They call the sensory impact of bodies on us "impressions." An impression would be the way things seem to be to you. For instance, if you walk into the kitchen and smell coffee, you're having an impression that coffee has been brewed. The Epicureans express total confidence in such sensory experiences. They think that all sensations are true, even if we put the wrong interpretation on those sensations.

The Stoics are more skeptical, if you'll pardon the term. They would say that some impressions are true, but some are false. Perhaps the kitchen smells that way because someone spilled coffee grounds on the floor. Part of the debate here concerns the question of what sensation is telling us. For the Stoics, your experience makes it seem to you true that coffee has been brewed. For the Epicureans, it presents only the smell of coffee. It is you who adds the delightful, but possibly false, inference that coffee actually awaits you. Of course, the Stoics are not saying that you—and much less the sage—are forced by your senses to believe there is coffee in the pot. But they analyze the mistake differently. For them, you have from your sense of smell the impression that there is coffee, but it is up to you whether to *assent* to that impression (LS 39G). You could reject the impression, for instance because you also see spilled coffee grounds on the floor. Or you could do what the sage does, by suspending judgment until you are absolutely sure, for instance because you have actually tasted the coffee.

But if some sensory impressions are false, then how can sensation provide certainty? The answer is simple. Though some impressions are false, some are true, and some are so obviously true that they could not be false. The Stoics call these special experiences "cognitive impressions" (LS 40A–C, E, K). These are the impressions in which we securely "grasp" something—that metaphor of "grasping" lies behind the Greek used by the first Stoics: *phantasia kataleptike*. This "grasping" word *katalepsis* was translated into Latin by Cicero using the word *cognitio*, which is why scholars writing about Stoicism in English usually call them "cognitive impressions." I mention this in part because ancient languages are cool, and in part because the word "cognitive" might otherwise mislead you. The point is not that other impressions have nothing to do with thinking or cognition, but that other impressions are such that they might be false. A cognitive impression is rock-solid, and can serve as the basis for certain knowledge more generally.

Zeno gave a vivid analogy to illustrate this theory (LS 41A). He held out his open palm and said that this represents the mere impression—the way things seem to you. Then he put his fingertips together and said that this is assent—it is agreeing that things really are that way. Next, he formed his fingers into a fist and said that this was the cognitive impression—the fist indicates that one has a firm grasp, so that one is assenting to something that must be true. Finally, he placed his other hand over his fist, and said that this represents knowledge. Notice that the cognitive impression is not yet knowledge. It is, rather, the *basis* for knowledge. We achieve knowledge only when we are systematic, when we combine together many rational impressions into a global understanding of the world.

To understand that understanding, we need to retrace our steps. Go back to the most basic stage, the impression. Our entire experience is made up of impressions. The exact manner in which we receive them was a matter of debate among the early Stoics. Taking a leaf from Plato's *Theaetetus*, the earliest heads of the school, Zeno and Cleanthes, argued that the impressions are like imprints made in wax. Chrysippus disagreed, pointing out that we can receive and retain many impressions all at the same time, something impossible in the case of wax (LS 39A). Still, all the Stoics were committed to the idea that impressions have some physical realization—after all, according to them, nothing non-physical exists. Next is the stage of assent. The Stoics believe that this capacity for assent is already a great gift, something that differentiates us from animals and small children. It is, you might say, the core of rationality. A beast can experience that the world seems a certain way. But only a mature human can take a critical stance regarding the world, and say to himself, "well, things may seem this way, but I'm not so sure."

Ideally, the human will remain self-consciously unsure unless there is certainty, which arises only through a cognitive impression. It is not only sages who can have such impressions. According to the Stoics, even children have such impressions. Your impression that you're reading about the Stoics right now might count as such an impression—there's no way you could be wrong about this. Or, if you don't like that example because it involves no caffeine, then consider your impression that the coffee you're drinking is warm. You just can't be wrong about that. However, it is possible to improve oneself in this respect. The Stoics speak of the cognitive impression as being "technical" or "artistic," by which they mean that our knowledge and beliefs inform the way we have experience (LS 39A). I look at someone and see that they have a yellowish complexion; the doctor looks at the same person and sees someone who has jaundice and quite likely a liver disease.

Thus we can expect that with increasing wisdom comes an increase in the extent and detail of our cognitive impressions. By the same token, knowledge helps us relate cognitive impressions to one another. Or we might even say that knowledge just *is* grasping the interrelation of cognitive impressions. To achieve this, one makes use of what the Stoics call "preconceptions" (LS 39E, 40A, T). Whereas for the Epicureans this word meant rough-and-ready concepts, for the Stoics it means the reliable beliefs that arise for all humans through careful observation of the world. This allows us to put our impressions within a more general framework. The sage, of course, is the one whose framework is beyond reproach. He has maximized his opportunity for having cognitive impressions informed by expertise, and is always careful not to leap to conclusions in cases of even slight uncertainty.

It's a nice theory. But the ancient Skeptics pointed out its potentially fatal flaw. A house is only as strong as its foundations, and for the Stoics knowledge is built upon the foundation of cognitive impressions. The Skeptics showed up with the dynamite for exploding that foundation. They pointed out that any impression, no matter how apparently reliable, will be indistinguishable from some possible misleading impression (LS 41C). Suppose you see your best friend standing before you, in good lighting conditions. You will have no hesitation in assenting to the impression that your friend stands before you. But isn't it just possible that your friend has an identical twin? Your friend has kept this twin a secret from you; or they were separated at birth, so your friend doesn't even know this twin exists. Okay, the possibility is remote, but it can't be totally ruled out. So there is some possibility that you are seeing, not your friend, but your friend's twin. The Skeptics say that this problem is general and inescapable. There is no impression so convincing that it eliminates all possibility of error.

Faced with this, the Stoics could have gone two ways. One would be to say that cognitive impressions do lead us to the truth, so that we are guaranteed to be correct in assenting to them—but that perhaps we do not know which impressions are cognitive. This would be, to put it in modern jargon, an "externalist" solution. From outside the situation of the person judging, we would say the person did have knowledge, because they were assenting to an impression that couldn't be wrong. But the Stoics seem to have been what are nowadays called "internalists." They insisted that the person judging must not only be free from the possibility of error, but must *know* that they are free of the possibility of error. So against the Skeptics, they claimed that cognitive impressions are "distinct," having a special quality that marks them out as utterly reliable for the person who is sufficiently expert to have the impression.[2]

It's clear why they must insist on this: they want to preserve the possibility of the ideal sage, who never makes a mistake. It shouldn't be just a matter of luck that the sage always gets things right. Rather, he gets things right because he knows that he is assenting only to cognitive impressions, which are always reliable. In other cases the sage will play it safe, and "suspend judgment." He will, that is, avoid assenting to impressions where there is room for doubt. Of course the Skeptics say that this will mean never assenting to any impressions, since there is always room for doubt. A lovely, though no doubt apocryphal, story about a Stoic named Sphaerus illustrates the difficulty facing the Stoics (LS 40F). While the guest of a royal court, Sphaerus was presented with very realistic wax pomegranates as a practical joke. When he tried to eat one, the king mocked him for assenting to a false impression. But Sphaerus replied he had assented only to the impression that it was *reasonable to suppose* that these were pomegranates.

64

It would also be reasonable to touch on one last question regarding Stoic views about belief and assertion, which for them counts as an issue within logic but for us will also be a good way to warm up for a discussion of their understanding of the physical world. (Warming up for this is not a bad idea, since they think the physical world is pervaded by fire.) Suppose I say, "this giraffe is a majestic beast." How do we account for the fact that this string of English words, or any string of words, connects with the world around us? It's the most fundamental issue in the philosophy of language, and the Stoics were sufficiently worried about it to devise one of their most original doctrines: the idea of *lekta*, or "sayables" (LS 33).[3] Remember, the Stoics were materialists: they thought that nothing really exists, apart from bodies. When I say "this giraffe is a majestic beast," the only relevant body here seems to be the giraffe. But clearly, my sentence doesn't say, or mean, the giraffe itself. I can touch a giraffe, but I can't say it. Rather, the Stoics suggest, there is something called a *lekton*, the "sayable," which I have latched onto with my utterance. The sayables form a kind of bridge between language and the world, between the noises coming out of my mouth and the giraffe herself.

It would be easy to suppose that sayables are something like thoughts in my mind, but this seems not to be the case. After all, there are many sayable things that neither I, nor anyone else, has said or will say. So the sayables would seem to be part of the furniture of the world, as it were. But how can this be, given the Stoics' rigorous commitment to materialism? Sayables are not bodies, after all. The Stoics realize this, and see a similar problem in other cases, for instance, time and void. These things seem to be required for any complete philosophical understanding of the world, yet they are not bodies. Thus the Stoics admit that sayables, time, and void, are "somethings," but not that they are really real (LS 27D, 33C). Or, as they put it with a further bit of technical terminology, they "subsist," without actually existing. Given the Stoics' materialist credentials, this may seem a surprising concession, regarding entities that they themselves refer to as "incorporeals." After all, they make a big deal of rejecting such immaterial entities as Platonic Forms, which for them absolutely don't exist. The difference is that sayables, time, and void are needed to make sense of the physical world around us, whereas Forms could never help with this task. They are meant to be causes, but as the Stoics stress, nothing can be a cause for bodies without itself being corporeal. To see what sorts of causes they do accept, we'll need to examine their understanding of the cosmos and of our place within it.

WE DIDN'T START THE FIRE
THE STOICS ON NATURE

"Most majestic of immortals, many-titled, ever omnipotent Zeus, prime mover of nature, who with your law steer all things, hail to you. For it is proper for any mortal to address you: we are your offspring, and alone of all mortal creatures which are alive and tread the earth we bear a likeness to god. Therefore I shall hymn you and sing forever of your might. All this cosmos, as it spins around the earth, obeys you, whichever way you lead, and willingly submits to your sway. Such is the double-edged fiery ever-living thunderbolt which you hold at the ready in your unvanquished hands. For under its strokes all the works of nature are accomplished. With it you direct the universal reason which runs through all things and intermingles with the lights of heaven both great and small."

This is the beginning of a Hymn to Zeus written by the Stoic Cleanthes.[1] Cleanthes, as mentioned above, was the successor of Zeno, the founder of Stoicism, and the predecessor of the great Chrysippus. It shows us that a pious attitude towards the divine was at the heart of early Stoicism. This may come as a surprise, given that they were materialists. They insisted that what really exists is what can act on something, or be acted upon by something else (LS 45A, C). And this, for them, means bodies. Thus they agreed with Aristotle in dismissing Platonic Forms as a fantasy: how could something like the Form of Large actually make anything large? You make things large by, for instance, inflating them with air or stretching them. And so for any feature of the world around us: it is caused by the interaction of bodies. Aristotle had also complained that Plato's Forms could not accomplish anything, but the Stoics are going further than he did. After all, Aristotle did invoke an immaterial god as the primary cause of his cosmos.[2]

Yet the Stoics too included God in their vision of the cosmos. In fact, they quite literally *included* God in the cosmos, seeing him as a physical being that pervades all things. Here they again mention their idea—which incidentally, and ironically, is borrowed from Plato—that what exists is what can act or be acted upon. In general they see God as the active cause in the universe, and speak of "matter" as the passive cause that is acted upon (LS 44B). But this is, to some extent, just a conceptual distinction, because in fact God is never apart from matter. The cause is never apart from what it acts upon. Instead, God and matter are both physical principles, which, in their permanent and mutual interaction, form the body of the cosmos. Thus the Stoics are willing to call their god "nature," rather than seeing the divine as something supernatural, as might be suggested by Aristotle. Indeed, later in the history of philosophy there will be a long tradition of seeing the title of Aristotle's *Metaphysics* as appropriate precisely because it studies that which is "after" or "beyond" nature, namely God.

So the Stoic god is immanent, physically interwoven through all bodily things and hence through everything that exists. But if he is physical, what kind of physical thing is he? Here, the Stoics reach back into the Pre-Socratic past for inspiration, making common cause with, of all people, Heraclitus. He had portrayed God as a fire or as a "thunderbolt that steers all things," an idea that appears in our quote from Cleanthes' Hymn. Following Heraclitus, Stoics too describe god as having a fiery nature, although god is not to be imagined simply as a flame such as you see rising from the wick of a candle. The sense in which god is fire is more that he is physically subtle and active. He is also unlike earthly fire, in that his activity is not blind or mindless. To the contrary. The Stoics call god a "designing fire," and also a craftsman or "demiurge," echoing the name given to god in Plato's *Timaeus* (LS 46A–B). He does not just pervade the cosmos, but wisely and artfully builds it from within, as if the carpenter's designing skill were inside wood and able to make it into a table.

For this reason, the Stoics point to the apparent design of the world around us as a proof of god's existence.[3] This kind of proof, often called a "design argument," was certainly on the table (if you'll pardon the expression) in Plato's *Timaeus* and in the works of Aristotle. But the Stoics make it very explicit, claiming that it is just obvious that there is a pervading principle of wisdom in the world. To deny this, Zeno said, in a weird and striking image, would be like encountering a tree that grows flutes that play tunes, and then denying that there is a principle of music in that tree (LS 54G). The Stoics see every feature of the cosmos as the result of divine wisdom and purpose, claiming that all things are as good as they could possibly be, and devoted to the fulfillment of god's plan. Often god's plan coincides with our own. My favorite detail from Stoic design arguments comes when they claim that pigs are clearly designed by providence to be food for man, because their flesh is naturally salty, which keeps it from rotting![4]

The Stoic god, then, is a principle of order and activity, and yet immanent within the body of the cosmos. Doesn't this sound less like a god, and more like a soul? Doesn't it, in fact, sound a bit like the so-called "World Soul" of Plato's *Timaeus*? In fact this is no coincidence: although Plato's World Soul is immaterial, in other respects it is indeed comparable to the Stoic god, which is likewise woven together with the body of the cosmos. In fact, one could see Stoic theology as a weaving together of a different kind, taking both the World Soul and the divine craftsman or Demiurge of Plato's *Timaeus*, and combining them into one single principle. It would seem that this is not a coincidence. The early Stoics were carefully reacting to Plato, borrowing from him even as they rejected some of his ideas, not least the Ideas or Forms themselves. That was incompatible with their materialism, but the comparison of god to a craftsman, the analogy between the cosmos and a living thing, the notion that providence and wisdom are visible in the design of the universe, all these things were taken over from the *Timaeus* and given a distinctively Stoic, materialist spin.[5]

Cleanthes says in his Hymn that we alone among earthly beings bear a likeness to god, which looks like another Platonic allusion, to the dialogue *Theaetetus* and its suggestion that mankind's purpose is to achieve likeness to god (176a–c). Of course, as materialists, when the Stoics say this they must mean that the soul too is a bodily thing, which somehow resembles the divine nature that physically pervades all things.[6] Our souls can be thought of as portions of this divine nature, and they give to our body what god gives the world: order and a principle of activity. The human soul is also, like god, fiery. Starting with Chrysippus, it is identified with a kind of warm breath, in Greek, *pneuma*. Thanks to this breath, living animals possess a "vital heat" that spreads along with the soul through the body, just as god, the designing fire, spreads through the cosmos (LS 54I). The Stoics naturally locate the center of the soul where we find the center of heat, namely (as Aristotle too had said) the heart. It is here, not in the brain, that we find the soul's so-called *hegemonikon*, or commanding-faculty (LS 53D, G). Later on in this book we'll see that claim being thunderously refuted by the great doctor Galen.

Of course, the Stoics knew that their materialist understanding of soul would be no less contentious than their materialist portrayal of god. So they argued for it. One proof was the fact that children resemble their parents in character as well as in appearance (LS 53C). Parents produce their children through a physical process. So how could our character dispositions be inherited, if the soul were not somehow physical? They also describe the way that the soul physically acts upon, and within, the body. Taking their cue from respiration, they imagine the soul as a kind of breath that is moving both inward and outward in the body, holding the body together in a balanced state of tension. Actually, something like this is true even for lifeless things such as rocks, which also have a so-called "tenor" (LS 47P). This is what holds a rock together as a single thing, and makes it distinct from the other objects around it. But humans have a much more exalted sort of unity, which gives them the godlike capacity for reason and intelligence.

Here the Stoics run into a problem. They are saying that god and the soul are physical things, which spread all the way through other physical things, namely the cosmos and the ensouled body. But how is this possible? It seems to presuppose something absurd, namely that two physical objects can be in the same place at the same time. If only this were true, it would solve all our housing problems. But unfortunately, each physical object seems jealously to guard its own space. Some kind of force is needed to push it out of its place to make room for something else. When I pour wine into a glass, for instance, the air in the glass is pushed out of the way. So it seems that god cannot be everywhere in the cosmos, because there is no room: the cosmos would have to get out of the way. But the Stoics can now ask, what happens when wine is poured into water? In that case, the wine does not push the water aside. Rather, it mixes together with the water, so that the two are both together in the same place. Similarly, the Stoics want to say, god is thoroughly mixed together with the body of the cosmos, and your soul is mixed together with your body (LS 48C).

This theory of mixture provoked a good deal of discussion, and derision, in the ancient world. Of course some philosophers, like the atomists, thought that there is no total mixture—only the juxtaposition of particles, jumbled together the way that pebbles or beans might be. Chrysippus, author of the Stoic view on this issue, did of course agree that mixture can happen by juxtaposition. But he insisted that two things can be in the same place at the same time, if they are suitable for this more thorough kind of mixture, like wine and water. Opponents retorted that, in that case, a body could be stretched to be coextensive with another body, no matter how large. A drop of wine could be mixed into the entire ocean, and would be stretched across the whole ocean, a little bit of that drop in every drop of water. A gorier version, suggested by the Skeptic Arcesilaus, pointed out that if Chrysippus were right, a single leg that rotted in the ocean could become big enough for two fleets of ships to fight in, since the decomposed leg would spread throughout the entire sea (LS 48E). If this was supposed to scare Chrysippus, it didn't work: he insisted that a drop of wine can in principle exist throughout the sea (LS 48E). His opponents, of course, continued to feel that he didn't have a leg to stand on.

The Stoic god, then, is not only a source of all order and activity, which steers all things like Heraclitus' thunderbolt, but it is also present within all things. He could hardly be more unlike the Epicurean gods, who are envisioned as uninvolved, remote entities living in detached bliss. The Stoic god, by contrast, is about as involved as he could be. Indeed, Stoic physics in general is diametrically opposed to that of Epicurus. Instead of unmixed atoms colliding at random, we have divisible and intermixing bodies woven together by a providential rationality. A more subtle contrast for the Stoics would be Aristotle. Of course his god, like a Platonic Form, is an immaterial cause, something the Stoics reject out of hand. But the Stoics agree with Aristotle, and most other ancient philosophers, in thinking of the cosmos as spherical, with the more divine heavens surrounding an earthly realm. They accept a system of four elements, air, earth, fire, and water. And like Aristotle, they assume that these are "continuous," in other words, that they can be divided, and divided again, ad infinitum, without ever reaching indivisible parts (like the atoms of Democritus and Epicurus).

Thus, the Stoics find much to agree with in Aristotle's physics. Regarding the past and future, though, they do not see eye to eye. Aristotle believes that the cosmos is eternal, and has always been organized more or less as we see now. For the Stoics, though, the world-order we experience is only one chapter in an ongoing story. Long ago the cosmos consisted of nothing but divine fire—a pure fusion of god with matter, in which all was wisdom and there was no evil. Our world emerged from this state when the fire condensed into the other elements and, as in many a Pre-Socratic cosmology, transformed into the earth below and heavens above. Also familiar from Pre-Socratic philosophy—even if it is an idea that turns up too in some Platonic dialogues—is the idea that our world undergoes cycles. The Stoics believe the cosmos will revert to its original state in a so-called "conflagration," when it will be consumed in fire and be reduced, or rather increased, to nothing but fire (LS 46E–F, I, K).

I say "increased" because the Stoic theory takes account of the fact that the elements vary in density. When fire transforms into water or earth, it takes up much less space, and the reverse of course is also true. This means that when the cosmos is in a state of conflagration, it will take up vastly more room than it does when it has partially condensed into its current form. To make this possible, the Stoics posit that our cosmos is surrounded by an infinite emptiness—a void. Here again, it's useful to compare them to the Epicureans and to Aristotle. Aristotle rejects the possibility of void entirely. For him, the cosmos is a finite sphere, surrounded by nothing at all, not even empty void. Epicurus instead goes for an infinite void, the emptiness in which atoms can move and collide, combining into indefinitely many worlds. Like Aristotle, the Stoics recognize only one world, our world. But they say it is able to expand in volume because there is plenty of room around it, since they also recognize infinite void, like the Epicureans. Against Aristotle and whoever else doubts that the cosmos is surrounded by void, the Stoics ask what will happen if someone standing at the very edge extends his arm (LS 49F).

If he can stretch his arm out past the edge of the cosmos, there is empty space. But if he can't, there must be something outside the cosmos blocking his motion. So if the cosmos really does have an edge, with nothing beyond it, that nothing must be conceived as void.

When the Stoics combine their cosmic cycle with their respect for divine providence, they come to an unnerving conclusion. God designs the whole world with maximal wisdom. Presumably, then, when the world has been consumed in fire and reborn, we can expect god to make the same choices again. Every cosmic cycle, in other words, will be exactly the same (LS 46O). This is the idea of eternal recurrence, also famously discussed by Nietzsche. It is not merely an idle cosmological speculation, but is intended to make us weigh up each choice as if it will be repeated infinitely many times. Nietzsche saw great ethical significance in this idea, seeing it as the ultimate affirmation of life in this world, as opposed to the supposed afterlife of Judeo-Christianity.[7] Marcus Aurelius (also no friend of Christianity) saw it as ethically important too, but for a rather different reason: it puts things in a great deal of perspective.[8] For instance, why should I be afraid to choose an honorable death over cowardly safety, if my life will be repeated an infinity of times, so that I will live forever either way?

To draw this sort of moral, of course, Marcus and other Stoics need to believe that it will literally be *me* who exists again and again, in cycle after cycle of the world. Some Stoics denied this under pressure from their critics (LS 52E–F, H). But it seems that the original Stoic view here was that the very same Socrates will exist in every world-cycle, will drink hemlock in every cycle, and so on. It has even been suggested that time, for the Stoics, is therefore circular.[9] If this is right, the Stoics see the future not as an infinite series of repeated events that are exactly alike, but as a loop of literally identical events happening over and over again. This may be captured in the image of time as an unwinding rope, which Cicero uses to describe the Stoic theory (LS 55O).

But how, we might now ask, can Marcus Aurelius or any other Stoic speak of choosing, whether or not we choose with eternal recurrence in mind? If god so orders the world as to achieve the best and most rational results, and if our actions too fall within that ordering, then can we really be said to "choose" our actions? Are we not rather puppets of divine causation? The Stoics might, like later philosophers, have sought to reconcile divine providence with the idea that our actions are uncaused by god, or by anything else. But they went in the other direction. They embraced the notion that all things are caused, including human actions. They were, in a word, determinists, convinced that all events, including human choices and actions, arise out of unbreakable chains of prior events, a web of cause and effect that is inescapable, and the product of divine wisdom.

The Stoics saw all parts of philosophy as interconnected, and we've here arrived at a connection between physics and ethics. In fact, we already saw that the physical doctrine of eternal recurrence had a practical significance. Determinism, though, has further-reaching consequences for ethics. The thought that all things are fated to occur as they do by divine providence might fill us with a deep peace, leading us to accept even the most horrifying events with equanimity. We might, that is, take what we have come to call a "stoic" attitude towards misfortune and suffering: what happens is inevitable, so there is no point getting upset about it. Moreover, it is preordained by god, and getting upset would just be to show our all-too-human incomprehension of his greater plan. On the other hand, this same thought might itself strike us as pretty upsetting. It seems to depict us as mere pawns moved by irresistible divine will in a cosmic chess-game, albeit a game of chess that happens over and over, with a big fire breaking out at the end. So is nothing, to put it as the Stoics and other philosophers of the period put it, "up to us"? It's up to you to turn the page and find out.

11

LIKE A ROLLING STONE
STOIC ETHICS

Imagine that you're walking along a railway line. You're just out for a stroll, musing on the finer points of ancient philosophy. Suddenly, your blood runs cold. You see an innocent child playing on the rails, and a train bearing down at great speed—too fast to slow down in time. Without a thought for your own safety, you rush forward instinctively, snatch the child in your arms, and leap aside just in time to save both your lives. The train hurtles obliviously onward, but onlookers have witnessed your brave act. You are hailed as a hero in the local community, and use the brief weeks of fame to encourage your admiring public to buy this great philosophy book you've been reading lately.

It's a story with a happy ending. But does it have an unhappily confused middle section? We spoke of your bravery, the heroism of your split-second decision to save the child. Yet we also said you acted instinctively, without pausing to weigh up the costs and benefits of your perilous undertaking. If this is right, why should you get any credit for what you have done? You acted, we might say, automatically, and your dash towards the child was no less inevitable than the oncoming rush of the train. You are, it would seem, just the kind of person who reacts that way in these child-threatened-by-train situations. Sure, it's lucky for the child that you happened to be there. But it's not as if you had any choice in the matter. You didn't pause to choose, and if you had had time to pause, you wouldn't seriously have considered letting the child be crushed anyway. How can we reasonably praise you and write admiring newspaper articles about your bravery, given that in the situation that confronted you, you quite literally could not have done otherwise?

In this book I've been trying not to derail things by introducing too many technical terms—all those words ending in "-ism." But in this case, the train of our thought will have trouble leaving the station without a couple of terms like these in our trunk. So, two -isms: "determinism" and "compatibilism." Determinism is the idea that everything that happens is...wait for it...determined. All things are unavoidable, or to put it another way, everything that can happen does happen. Why would anyone think that? Well, there are various reasons. One kind of determinism has it that nothing can be true without being necessary, as the so-called "Master Argument" or Aristotle's famous "sea-battle" argument would show.[1] Another kind is what you might call "causal" determinism, the view that everything that happens has a cause, and that causes necessitate their effects. If this is true, then there is an unbreakable chain of cause and effect stretching back into the past, which guarantees both that the present could not have been otherwise, and that there is only one possible future. This is the Stoic view.

Determinism deepens the problem of your heroics and the train. We said that, if it was impossible for you to do anything other than what you did, then it's hard to see how you should get any credit for it. Similarly, if I cannot help, say, pushing you in front of an oncoming train—if I literally cannot do anything else—then how can I really be blamed? In short, if determinism is true, how can anyone be morally responsible for anything? That brings us to our second -ism: compatibilism. This is simply the view that freedom, or moral responsibility, or something along these lines, is after all compatible with determinism.[2] In other words, a compatibilist thinks that, even in a deterministic world, people should still be praised and blamed for what they do—not as a convenient fiction, but because, as the Stoics put it, their actions really are "up to them." This second -ism is also accepted by the Stoics. The early Stoic Chrysippus, in particular, devoted careful attention to the question of how actions can be "up to us," even if those actions are fated to happen by inevitable chains of cause and effect, which are carrying out the irresistible providence of God.

It's worth emphasizing that Chrysippus and the other Stoics were really serious about this. You cannot escape fate, in even the tiniest detail. So the idea is not simply that, for instance, whatever Oedipus does, he will wind up killing his father and marrying his mother, just as the prophecy says. The idea is that even the actions Oedipus takes to avoid his fate are also fated. Fate determines not only Oedipus' patricide, his excessive mother-love, and his poking out his own eyes, but also which eye he will poke out first, which clothes-pin he will use to do it, and what he will have had for breakfast on the fateful day. For the Stoics, every day, and every action, no matter how trivial, is fateful. And yet they insist that Oedipus' actions are up to him. It is up to him what to have for breakfast, to murder the man at the crossroads, to take out his eyes.

This might seem to you a paradox, but it's worth exploring how the Stoics defended their position, not least because many philosophers nowadays also endorse compatibilism. Chrysippus should probably be credited with the first sophisticated defense of this -ism. In essence, he argued that it will be up to an agent how to act so long as the action flows from the desires and character of that agent. If you push a cylinder, he said, it will roll in a straight line; if you push a cone, it will roll in a circle (LS 62C). Similarly, the same situation will provoke different reactions in different men. Oedipus' murder of his father was in large part due to the pride and temper of Oedipus himself. A meeker man would not have committed murder at the crossroads. It is in precisely this sense that it was up to Oedipus whether or not to kill, and the same goes for all the actions for which we are morally responsible.

If an event is not up to us in this way, we are not responsible for it. If I threw Chrysippus out of a window and he landed on a man and killed him, Chrysippus would insist that this murder was *not* up to him, and that he should not be blamed for it. He would also insist that the actions that are up to us are not strictly speaking necessary. As we saw in Chapter 8, Chrysippus held that possibility is a matter of what a thing is capable of, and that possibility can be removed by external forces. For instance, it's possible for a piece of wood to burn, even if it doesn't ever burn. But if the wood is at the bottom of the sea, the water eliminates this possibility. We can now see what he was after. With this definition in hand, Chrysippus can say that it is "possible" for me to perform an action or not, so long as it is something I am physically capable of. Normally it is possible for me to walk or refrain from walking. But if I am tied to my chair, then it is no longer up to me whether I walk or not, and no one can blame me for not going to put out the garbage.

This nifty interweaving of logic and ethics is entirely characteristic of Chrysippus, and of the Stoics generally. It means that they can have their cake and eat it, holding on to both determinism and contingency in the world. But make no mistake: everything you do is still necessary in a different sense, in that it is made inevitable by the causal chains of fate. The later Platonist author Plotinus complained that the Stoic view makes humans out to be little more than stones being rolled along[3]— rather ironic, in light of Chrysippus' analogy of the cylinder and cone. Though the Stoics would admit that we are guaranteed to do whatever divine fate decrees for us, they insist that part of what is fated is our own internal attitude and character, which in itself helps to explain the things we do. As the Stoics put it, we are like a dog tied to a rolling cart: it is up to us whether to go along with the dictates of fate cheerfully or with much whining and resistance, but we will go along either way.[4]

The sage is the man who always goes along cheerfully. As you'll remember, the sage is an ideal figure, who never makes any mistakes, so perfect is his wisdom. This is as true in the ethical sphere as in the sphere of non-ethical judgments. In fact, it is ethical judgments the Stoics had especially in mind when they argued for the possibility of this perfect sage. Whatever the world throws at the Stoic sage, he will react appropriately, in terms of both belief and action. Only the sage is truly virtuous, according to the Stoics, because true virtue means being not just fairly reliable, but infallible, in acting well. Furthermore, the Stoics follow Socrates in claiming that nothing but wisdom and virtue is truly valuable. They adopt the Socratic point that things like wealth, health, and political power are just as capable of aiding evil as furthering goodness. In fact, they seem to go even further than Socrates did. Socrates, at least as Plato presents him, said that wealth, health, and so on are indeed good, but only when used wisely. The Stoics, in a slight but crucial change, insist that wealth, health, and so on always remain "indifferent"—neither good nor bad. Any good that attaches to them is derived only from virtue, so they have no value in themselves (LS 58A, B).

Here we can detect a family resemblance between Stoicism and Cynicism. The Cynic philosopher's faith in himself as utterly self-reliant, clothed only in virtue, finds an echo in this Stoic idea that all is indifferent, save for virtue itself. But in that case, why weren't the Stoics living in wine-jars and living like dogs, like the Cynics did? Well, the Stoics agree with the Cynics that everything apart from virtue and wisdom is indifferent, having no genuine intrinsic value. Yet for them, all indifferents are not created equal. Some are to be preferred, others not (LS 58B, C). Health is a good example. It is not intrinsically good, because it fails the test Plato applied to causes in his *Phaedo*: a really good thing would not give rise to what is bad. And health clearly can help cause bad things, as for instance when health belongs to a tyrant. Nonetheless, the Stoics argue, it is still eminently reasonable to prefer health to illness, all else being equal. So the sage will choose health—he will "prefer" it—unless this choice would run afoul of the demands of virtue.

This position led to a rupture within early Stoicism. Chrysippus held to the theory of preferred indifferents, and this would become the standard Stoic position. But his contemporary Aristo of Chios insisted that an indifferent should really be indifferent (LS 58F). If health is not good, then one cannot reasonably prefer it. Chrysippus, according to Aristo, was smuggling in a lesser kind of intrinsic value for health: it is indeed good, it's just that its goodness can be trumped by the goodness of virtue. That sounds like a powerful objection. But before we become dissident Stoics like Aristo, we should reflect that Chrysippus has an equally powerful counter-argument. He can say that something is only really good if it is required for our happiness. And health simply isn't required. How could it be, if we will sometimes be happier by deliberately avoiding health, as when we volunteer for a suicidal military expedition to save our city? If you'd prefer a more up-to-date example, but not *too* up-to-date, consider yourself going to a silent-film festival. You'd prefer to see a Buster Keaton movie, but none is playing. Still, you won't let this ruin the festival for you. You'll be content to see a Charlie Chaplin picture, and equally happy with the festival as a whole.

The Stoic sage is able to retain this implacable attachment to happiness because he understands that all is for the best, since it is ruled by providence, and because he unerringly knows what he should do in each situation. But now we might worry that the Stoics are telling us very little about what the sage would in fact do. They've told us he will prefer some indifferent things, like health, but we can't be exactly sure when he would give up on these preferred items. If the Stoics' advice boils down to: "Do whatever the ideal sage would do," that will be pretty disappointing, given that none of us have ever met an ideal sage, nor are we likely to. But wait, there's more. Remember that for the Stoics, nature is in some sense identical to god. It is not so surprising, then, to discover that the Stoics find another point of agreement with the Cynics, saying that the good and happy life is the life lived in accordance with nature (LS 63A–C).[5]

In a more rare moment of agreement with the Epicureans, the Stoics make reference to the behavior of animals and small children in explaining this idea (LS 57B). Even such irrational beings, they say, have a sense of what is appropriate for them. The Greek word for "appropriate" is *oikeion*, and relates to the Greek word for "home." When a baby nuzzles after milk, or a lion tears into its prey, it is, we might say, "right at home," looking to acquire what is appropriate for it. We go astray by turning away from what is natural and appropriate, for instance by desiring that statues be built in our honor. Of course, if this is to be a basis for ethics, we will need to inquire more deeply into our natures. But at least we can now understand how it is that the sage achieves such perfect ethical judgment. He knows his own nature and the nature of other things, of the cosmos itself. His beliefs, his desires, are thus aligned with the providential divine order.

There's more than a hint of Aristotle here, insofar as the Stoics ground their understanding of ethics in nature. A healthy dose of Plato can be detected as well— the Stoics seem to have appropriated the providential ordering deity of the *Timaeus*.[6] But something else divides the Stoics from Aristotle, and from Plato (at least in some of his moods). This is their insistence that only the ideal sage is virtuous. They pull no punches here, claiming that a non-sage can perform no virtuous actions (LS 61I, T). But this lands them with yet another problem. Being a sage requires total perfection, immunity to falsehood in belief and weakness in action. That doesn't really look like an attainable goal. If the world is divided into fools and sages, it looks as if I'm bound to remain a fool. In which case, I may as well have a good time. I can't have virtue, so perhaps I should settle for good old-fashioned pleasure. Pass the wine and call in the flute-girls! Or, if I hesitate to become a debauched libertine, I could seek a more refined type of hedonism by leaving the Stoic porch and calling in at Epicurus' garden.

Clearly, then, the Stoics need to say something to explain why some fools are better than others, and how I could make progress towards sagehood. For this reason they developed the notion of "befitting" actions, in Greek, *kathekonta* (LS 59B, C). Respecting one's parents, for instance, or paying a debt is befitting. In general, a person who performs such actions is better than one who doesn't, even if they are not sages and do not perform the actions out of genuine virtue. That doesn't mean you should do these actions in every circumstance. To borrow an example from Plato,[7] if someone lends me a weapon and then goes insane, I shouldn't repay my debt by returning the weapon. But in general, the strategy of choosing befitting actions allows us to achieve a kind of second-best virtue: not the unerring perfection of the sage, but the dutiful and occasionally misplaced rectitude of the upstanding citizen. In a further bit of good news, pursuit of those things that are indifferent to virtue but still rationally preferable, like health, could also count as befitting. So again, we see that the Stoics can encourage us to pursue such things as we are working towards genuine virtue.

In fact, as Stoicism developed, increasing attention was also paid to the question of how we can improve ourselves, even if becoming sages is a distant prospect at best. Panaetius, a Stoic of the second century BC, seems to have been especially interested in this issue. Seneca quotes him responding to the question of whether a sage would ever fall in love (LS 66C). The answer given by Panaetius is, in effect: "Who knows? But for non-sages like you and me, it's probably not such a great idea." Panaetius urges you to reflect on your own character and seek out a walk of life that will suit you. This already seems a big step away from the nearly Cynic attitudes of early Stoics like Zeno and Chrysippus, for whom the main point seemed to be that ethics is an all-or-nothing game. But a more tolerant attitude towards those who are merely making progress fits well with Chrysippus' stance in his argument with Aristo, who thought that the unique value of virtue meant that nothing else was even worth valuing. When Chrysippus sided with what looks like common sense, and allowed us to prefer things like health over things like illness, he vindicated a judgment even we fools can share. With these obvious and undeniable preferences, all of us seem to have some instinctual awareness of what is natural—an instinct that, as the Stoics emphasized, we can observe even in animals and children.

Another beautiful example of later Stoic reflection on the question of moral progress comes from Hierocles, who lived in the second to first centuries BC, and who incidentally laid great emphasis on the fact that animals do seem to understand what is appropriate to them. For instance, he pointed out that horned animals instinctively understand how to use these natural weapons (LS 57C). But the best bit of Hierocles is the one where he explains to us how we can make ourselves better people. Everyone, he says, naturally places value on himself. Imagine yourself, then, within a small circle, and then extend it, to encompass your friends and family—drawing them within the circle of value. Even better would be to draw your circle around your fellow citizens. But best of all is to draw it around all humans, out to the furthest foreigner (LS 57G). This arresting image of moral development leaves it slightly unclear whether we are meant to see ourselves as actually united with others in some way, or simply to include them within our sphere of affections.[8]

But whatever the point, Hierocles is showing how Stoic ideas about nature and appropriateness can be the basis for a powerful, even uplifting, ethical attitude. In this, Hierocles was setting a trend that would continue into the Roman Empire. The development of Stoicism sees the school turning ever more towards ethical concerns, ethical development, and concrete reflection on what Stoicism means for us in our everyday lives. The so-called "Roman Stoics" show that this is a philosophy with something to say to all of us, whether slave or emperor.

ANGER MANAGEMENT
SENECA

G naeus Calpurnius Piso was a powerful man. He was born into the senatorial
class of Roman society, and in the year 7 BC served as consul with his friend, the
future emperor Tiberius. He also had a really bad temper. Two soldiers under his
command were given leave, and one returned without the other; Piso leapt to the
conclusion that the missing man had been murdered by the one who returned, and
ordered his execution. A centurion was tasked to carry out the grim deed, but at the
last moment the absent soldier turned up, and the execution was halted. When Piso
learned of this, he was not relieved, but furious. His rash judgment had been exposed,
his order countermanded without his authority. He announced that there would now
be three executions: the first soldier would still die as planned, as would the centurion
for failing to kill him, and also the soldier who was late in returning, since the whole
thing was his fault.

If only Piso had lived a couple of generations later, he could have found some
good advice on curbing that temper in the works of Seneca.[1] Seneca was born in
Roman-controlled Spain between 4 and 1 BC, not long after Piso's consulship and
right in the middle of the long rule of Augustus Caesar. Seneca came too late to meet
such figures as Cato, Julius Caesar, and Cicero, but he tells stories about them in his
works. In the writings of Seneca we can see that the Roman aristocracy was still
digesting the seismic shift from a republic controlled by the Senate, to an empire
controlled by a single man—first Augustus, then his successor emperors Tiberius,
Caligula, Claudius, and of course, Nero. Nero is of particular importance for our
story, because Seneca served as an advisor to the young emperor. One of his
philosophical works, *On Mercy*, stands as a written record of his attempts to
moderate Nero's immoderate tendencies. That project was ultimately a failure, and
Seneca paid for this failure with his life.

Though Seneca remains an admired philosopher, his legacy is inevitably tarnished
by his association with Nero. Before he moved on to fiddling while Rome burned,
Nero had his own mother, Agrippina, assassinated in AD 59. Presumably Seneca, being
a paragon of unyielding virtue and valuing his life far less than his integrity, risked

certain death by publicly denouncing Nero? Sadly, no. What he actually did was write a speech for the emperor to help him recover from this public-relations disaster. Clearly, this was not Seneca's finest hour. If he was motivated by the desire to exert some degree of beneficial influence on Nero, then his plan failed: in AD 65 Nero accused Seneca of conspiring to assassinate him, and ordered him to commit suicide. This fatal command was not, incidentally, Seneca's first experience of the harsh realities of Roman politics. In AD 41, in the reign of Claudius, he had been exiled to Corsica. A philosophical work of consolation addressed to Seneca's mother Helvia advises her on how to cope with this setback.

Thus Seneca was very much a "philosopher in politics," to borrow the title of one of the more important studies of the man.[2] In fact his legacy goes beyond politics and philosophy. His philosophical writings are themselves a major landmark of Latin literature, and he also wrote dramas, of which eight tragedies survive. But as philosophers, what interests us is Seneca's Stoicism.[3] He is the first of three great figures to work in the imperial period, known collectively as the "Roman Stoics": Seneca, Epictetus, and Marcus Aurelius. They will be occupying our attention in the next several chapters. Of the three, Seneca was the only one to write philosophy in Latin, and it has been well remarked that Seneca thinks in Latin,[4] even if he is heir to ideas from the Greek tradition. Nonetheless, his philosophical works—especially a series of letters and so-called "dialogues"—display tendencies shared by all three Roman Stoics. He largely turns his back on the logical and metaphysical questions that fascinated the much earlier Chrysippus, and focuses relentlessly on the question of how to live. Seneca is at his most powerful when he dissects human weakness and advises us on how to rise above that weakness. His philosophical works are almost always addressed to a real recipient, whether it be his mother or one of his aristocratic friends. Yet reading him, we ourselves are cajoled, chastised, and exhorted to take up a life of virtue—if not the perfect virtue of the ideal Stoic sage, then at least a life better than the one we are leading now.

This is not to say that Seneca has abandoned more technical aspects of the Stoic system. The claim that an ideal sage is possible was itself a rather sophisticated notion, which presupposes the possibility of perfect and unfailing knowledge. Perhaps because he was not subject to constant harassment by Skeptical philosophers, as Chrysippus and other early Stoics were, Seneca says little by way of defending the possibility of a perfect sage. But he does presuppose it. Still, there is a change of emphasis in Seneca, if not a change of doctrine. Chrysippus had worried about, for instance, how the sage would preserve his infallibility when confronted with paradoxes and illusions. Seneca is more interested in how real people who are not sages can improve themselves. Similarly, he alludes to Stoic determinism, but not in order to tinker with Chrysippus' theory of possibility and necessity. Instead, he urges us to reflect on the ethical significance of the Stoic idea that we live in a world where all things are fated, steered by a providential god (*On Providence* V.8). We can see even his most non-ethical philosophical work, the *Natural Questions*, in this light. On the face of it a lengthy study of such phenomena as earthquakes and comets, this text is also an exploration of the divine forces that shape the cosmos, and of humans' relatively modest place within that cosmos.[5]

It's not earth-shattering to discover that Seneca's views on ethics have had more staying power than his account of earthquakes. Much of the advice he gives is genuinely useful, even for those of us who are not card-carrying Stoics. If you want to read a powerful discussion of how to make the most of your limited lifespan, you can hardly do better than Seneca's dialogue *On the Shortness of Life*. He reminds us that everything we do is a use of a scarce resource, namely time, and argues that even the briefest life will have been worth living if the time was used well. His writing is powerful because of his rhetorically charged style, his eye for vivid detail and memorable anecdote. For instance, in this work *On the Shortness of Life* he mentions a virtuous man named Julius Canus, condemned to death by Caligula. When they came to his prison to execute him he was found playing a game with his guard, and as they dragged him off he said to the centurion, "You're my witness that I was ahead by one piece."[6] If he could face his immediate and certain execution with such tranquility, why should we be bothered by the prospect that we will die some day?

In this passage, and many others, Seneca tries to help us make progress towards total freedom from disturbance. This is the goal of Roman Stoicism, just as it had been for earlier Stoics. One of Seneca's most important philosophical contributions is his analysis of the chief threat to our tranquility: emotion. The Stoics had always argued that we should strive to avoid being controlled by our emotions. They used the Greek word *pathos* for emotion and related experiences, a word that emphasizes the passivity of emotion. To get angry or sad or frightened is to be somehow "affected." The corresponding Latin term used by Seneca, *adfectus*, preserves this connotation. Seneca follows the traditional Stoic view, holding that emotion means surrendering one's self-determination, and being controlled by what is outside us. No emotion fits this pattern better than anger, which is perhaps why Seneca devoted a lengthy and fascinating dialogue to the topic.

In *On Anger*, Seneca offers up a particularly memorable range of anecdotes to illustrate his point, including the tale of Piso mentioned above. Caligula figures here and in other works as the vicious man par excellence, a kind of anti-sage. We hear of him inviting a man to dinner and then complaining loudly that the man's wife is lousy in bed (*On Firmness* 18). On another occasion, Caligula leads a man to think that he is being forced to drink the blood of his own son (*On Anger* 2.33). At the other end of the spectrum are Seneca's heroes. Among the Romans, he has greatest admiration for Cato the Younger, whose noble suicide ended a noble life. He killed himself when Julius Caesar overthrew the Roman Republic, which prompts Seneca to a typically graceful aphorism: "freedom did not live after Cato, nor Cato after freedom" (*On Firmness* 2). Seneca praises him as the closest thing we know to a perfect sage, comparing him favorably to Hercules and Ulysses. Plato appears in a similarly glowing light. Seneca relates that Plato once began to strike a slave in anger, but mastered himself just in time. He let the slave go untouched but stayed still, his hand remaining in the air poised to strike. Hours later a student of Plato's came upon him, and was amazed to find him still in this awkward position. Plato explained that he was punishing an angry man, namely himself. Seneca adds a second tale with a similar moral, in which Plato tells Speusippus to whip a disobedient slave, because Plato is angry and one should never punish while angry (*On Anger* 3.12).

But doesn't anger often lead us to punish those who *ought* to be punished? And isn't it right to get angry some of the time? Suppose a tyrant comes and unjustly murders my family. Would it really be virtuous to react to this without a trace of anger? Seneca confronts these objections squarely. Like the other Senecan works called "dialogues," *On Anger* is addressed to a specific recipient, and Seneca repeatedly imagines this recipient posing objections. Seneca's own view emerges as he replies to these objections. Of course, in *On Anger* the most pressing objection is that anger can be appropriate and beneficial. If this is right, the virtuous man will get angry. As Aristotle would put it, he will get angry on the right occasions, for the right reasons, and in the right way. Seneca indeed refers to Aristotle here, as well as Aristotle's colleague Theophrastus (*On Anger* 1.9, 1.12). He quotes them as believing that anger is an inevitable part of human life, and that we should aim for moderation in anger, as in all things.

Seneca responds by painting a vivid picture of what it is like when we get angry. He points out to us the physical symptoms—flushed cheeks, rapid breathing, contorted facial expressions. These outward signs betray the violence of the inner emotional state. Anger, by its very nature, causes us to lose control over ourselves. Seneca compares the loss of one's temper to running off a cliff: once you do lose control, it's too late to turn back. The idea of moderate anger is a contradiction in terms. That would mean anger under the restraining influence of reason, but anger is precisely a state in which reason is no longer exercising restraint. Hence another Senecan aphorism: "other vices impel the mind, anger overthrows it" (*On Anger* 3.1). To the objection that anger sometimes leads us to punish those who should be punished, Seneca replies that one should punish out of a desire to do justice, not for the sake of retaliation or revenge. If justice motivates us, we will have every chance of imposing just punishments, whereas if anger is our motive, we will wind up acting like Piso.

Aristotle would no doubt complain that Seneca's view sounds almost inhuman. He could insist that the tendency to become angry is natural, and that everything natural has some purpose. Certainly Aristotle would see a man who never grew angry for any reason as cold or impassive. Such a man would fall short of moderation, just as the easily angered man exceeds it. Neither man would be virtuous. To some extent Seneca can avoid this result by insisting that anger is in itself excessive, because it is a loss of reason. On his behalf, I'd add that the way we talk about anger supports his view: we say things like, "I totally lost it." But what about the point that anger is in some sense natural? Seneca can handle this objection too, by offering an interesting modification of previous Stoic views on the emotions.

To see his point, it may help to consider a perfect sage confronted with some outrage. Perhaps he is slapped suddenly in the street; perhaps the tyrant murders his family; perhaps someone says within his earshot that Buster Keaton's films are not all they are cracked up to be. We know that the sage will not actually be disturbed by this. His reason will remain in control and prevent him from lashing out in an undisciplined way. But that does not mean that he can avoid a natural, all-too-human initial reaction: he may flush, for instance, or his heart may start to beat more quickly. The story of Plato raising his hand to strike a slave, and then stopping himself, is a vivid example, though Seneca would probably say that a true sage would not even get as far as raising his hand or curling his fingers into a fist. Instead, he may simply twitch. Such instinctive, natural, and unavoidable reactions are called by Seneca "first motions" (*On Anger* 2.4).

Such motions accompany the initial impression we receive from our surroundings, for instance, that we have just been insulted, or even worse, that Buster Keaton has been insulted. The sage cannot avoid them, but he will stop himself from endorsing these impressions in a second motion, an act of reason which judges that the impression is in fact true. This may then give rise to a third motion, in which reason loses control and we give in to anger. Here Seneca is adhering to a long-standing Stoic idea about emotions, which is that they are ultimately grounded in reason. Emotional reactions, contrary to appearances, are judgments. Just as we might look at honey and get the impression that we see something sweet, so we might hear a man belittling the silent films of Buster Keaton and get the impression that, if the man likes sound so much, we should give him a sound beating. But we have the ability to withhold our consent to these impressions. We might realize that the jar seems to contain honey, but actually could contain vinegar; we might see that the right thing to do would be to instruct the uncultured buffoon by giving him a ticket to an open-air screening of Keaton's masterpiece, *The General*.

What Seneca adds to this picture is a sensitivity to the involuntary reactions we initially have along with the impression—the twitching, the flushing cheeks—and also a vivid portrait of what it is like when reason loses control. There has been some discussion of how Seneca's view relates to that of an earlier Stoic named Posidonius.[7] According to some evidence, found mostly in Galen, Posidonius adopted a complex psychology according to which the soul has both a rational and an irrational aspect. This evidence has been questioned, but if Galen presents Posidonius accurately, he must have been taking his cue from Plato. Plato's *Republic* too posited both a rational and irrational soul, and taught that justice in the soul is mastering the irrational part with the rational part.[8] Some have suspected that Seneca has a similar idea, but I agree with those who see him as sticking to the traditional Stoic view. The soul is rational through and through, so our emotional reactions must involve some kind of judgment, an assent to the way things seem to us. It is precisely for this reason that it feels so alienating when our reason does judge that we should retaliate or exact revenge. Then anger takes over, and we lose control.

This loss of control is what Seneca always wants us to avoid, whether it is occasioned by anger, pleasure, luxury, or grief. He exhorts us to face not only insult, but all turns of fortune, with as much serenity as we can manage. While the goal may seem modest, Seneca presents it as downright heroic. As he says at one point, in facing misfortune bravely we perform a deed that even god cannot manage, since god never undergoes misfortune. He adds a good deal of practical advice. For instance, he would approve of the widespread strategy of counting to ten when we get angry, since he too recommends waiting to act when we feel the flush of rage upon us. As for more general lifestyle advice, Seneca has told us that peace and tranquility are the highest possible achievement, so it is unsurprising to find that he's sympathetic to the idea of withdrawing from public life. It's clear that, for Seneca, the best life is a life of quiet study, and not a life of money-making or political achievement. In the moving work addressed to his mother on the occasion of his exile, he advises her to find comfort in this kind of life.[9] At the same time, Seneca's own life shows us that he was willing to become politically involved—indeed, sometimes too willing. Seneca was pulled in two directions, towards the duty to engage with his fellow humans and the drive to seek wisdom through private contemplation. Here he's in good company. Plato too wrestled with the question of why the philosopher would return to the cave after beholding the real things in the sunlight outside, and the most famous tension in Aristotle is that between the life of practical virtue and the life of contemplation. Seneca concludes that it is fine to retreat from the pressures and stresses of public life, so long as the retreat is an orderly one.

But in a sense, Seneca's virtuous man will be engaged in a kind of retreat no matter what he does. He achieves lack of disturbance and total self-mastery by exercising his reason, and yielding to nothing else, whether it is emotion, misfortune, or temptation. This is the hallmark of Roman Stoicism: not just an interest in ethics, but a relentless focus on our interior life, our reason and judgment. The power of Seneca's teaching lies in the promise that, with patience and practice, we can reshape ourselves so that we are really under our own control. But this requires us to renounce our obsessions with things that are not under our control. A final Senecan aphorism sums it up: we should not try to arrange what is up to fortune, while neglecting what is up to us. This sentiment brings us to our next Roman Stoic, whose philosophy pivots around this notion that our interior life, and nothing else, is truly "up to us."

13

YOU CAN CHAIN MY LEG
EPICTETUS

"Man is condemned to be free." So said Jean-Paul Sartre, the French existentialist.[1] And perhaps only a French existentialist could think we are *condemned* to be free. It's the kind of thing that would occur to you as you sit in a Parisian café on a rainy afternoon, smoking unfiltered cigarettes and feeling the enormity of existence settle upon your shoulders, as you gaze in ineffable, inexplicable horror at the glass of beer sitting on the table in front of you. But didn't Sartre have a point? If we are truly free—free even in chains, as the saying goes—then we are also responsible for what we do. This was Sartre's point, or part of his point. We are irreducibly, unavoidably free, and thus cannot escape responsibility, cannot blame anyone or anything else for our failings, our impure thoughts, our misguided intentions. We are, in this sense, always on our own. It's a terrifying thought, and one that can, paradoxically, be paralyzing. Towards the end of his enticingly titled novel *Nausea*, Sartre has his main character stop in the street, alone, contemplating the infinity of choices available to him. He realizes that his life until now does not determine his next action, and this radical freedom strikes him as being like death. It's the sort of thought that can make you sick to your stomach.

Of course, Sartre was not the first philosopher to worry about freedom of the will. It's one of the oldest philosophical topics, so much so that we tend to assume it goes back before the dawn of philosophy. Surely, humankind has always felt itself free, and speculated about the nature of this freedom? Perhaps this is true in some sense, but in fact the notion of "free will" is a fairly late arrival in the philosophical record. We saw it briefly in Lucretius, but it emerges with clarity only in late antiquity, in part because talking about free will requires first having the idea, and vocabulary, of having a will in the first place. A favorite game of scholars is to look for the first philosopher who asserts that we do have a will—whatever that might mean, exactly—and that this will is free—whatever that might mean, exactly.[2] A favorite answer in this game is the greatest of the Roman Stoics, a man who knew what it meant to be in chains: Epictetus.

Though we call him one of the "Roman" Stoics, Epictetus was not born in Rome, nor did he conduct his teaching there. He was born into slavery in AD 55, in Phrygia. This region, in modern-day Turkey, was under Roman domination. But as in much of the eastern part of the empire, the local language was Greek. From there he did go to Rome, in the service of a master named Epaphroditus, who was associated with the emperor Nero. During his time there Epictetus encountered a Stoic teacher named Musonius Rufus, an influential figure whose works are unfortunately lost to us. Rufus was one of the few men to impress Epictetus during his lifetime. For the most part, he reserved his admiration for his two favorite role-models, Diogenes the Cynic and, inevitably, Socrates. Epictetus modeled his teaching style on that of Socrates, posing provocative questions in lively exchanges that are preserved with remarkable vividness in his writings.[3] Epictetus also followed Socrates in not writing anything himself. What we have instead are records of conversations and diatribes that took place in Epictetus' school, which he set up in Nikopolis in Western Greece after he was freed from slavery.

For these texts we must thank a student of Epictetus, who was also a historian: Arrian.[4] He compiled the so-called *Discourses*, an extensive collection of Epictetus' conversations, in which his aggressive but intoxicatingly persuasive philosophical style is on full display. A much briefer second work is called the *Handbook*—in Greek *Enchiridion*, meaning something that fits comfortably into one's hand. It is more like a greatest-hits collection, often in the form of aphorisms or short paragraphs that can be easily remembered and reviewed for the purposes of ethical training. Indeed, it is ethics that occupies center-stage in these records of the thought of Epictetus, and his philosophy focuses on ethics more than the other areas of Stoic doctrine, logic and physics. It's clear from the *Discourses* themselves that Epictetus did teach logic at his school, and that many of his students came to him expecting to learn the ideas and technical tools associated with the greatest of the early Stoics, Chrysippus. But Epictetus has mixed feelings about this. On the one hand, he believes that one should indeed study logic. He even gives a brief proof of this, to the effect that anyone who contends that logic is useless will need to argue for its uselessness; but arguing successfully for this, or any other, claim means arguing logically (2.25).

Usually, though, Epictetus brings up technical issues like logic in order to chastise his students for concentrating on these things, instead of seeking to become better men (1.4). In one typical passage, he advises a student who wants to learn about Chrysippus' solution to the Liar paradox that he should go hang himself, unless he also wants to become good (2.17). This isn't the only passage where he suggests that one of his listeners should go kill himself. He also constantly addresses his students as "slaves"—an ironic allusion to his own lowly origins, and a pointed reminder that until the students achieve virtue, they are the true slaves. Epictetus makes the same point by lamenting that his students are not really interested in being Stoics, never mind Cynics, a vocation that Epictetus describes as nearly unattainable for most men. A true Stoic or Cynic is a philosopher with complete self-control, who values what is really valuable, who chooses in accordance with reason and nothing else. Given that even the people who have sought out Epictetus are, by his estimation, enslaved to their base desires, vain ambitions, and prideful self-delusions, the learning curve is bound to be a steep one.

This brings us back to Epictetus' most important contribution to the history of Stoicism, indeed to the history of philosophy in general: his conception of choice or the will. For this he uses the Greek word *prohairesis*, which means deliberately choosing or preferring something. It's a word that had already been used by Aristotle in his account of voluntary action (*Nicomachean Ethics* 1111b). Epictetus makes *prohairesis* the core of his ethical theory. Though this theory is definitely innovative, it is built on foundations laid by earlier Stoics. The Stoics described most of the things people value and esteem as being in fact indifferent. Such things as pleasure, reputation, wealth, and even health lack any intrinsic value. Only virtue, which guides the correct use of such things, is genuinely good and worth pursuing in itself. Epictetus adapts the theory by arguing that our virtue really consists in the right use of *prohairesis*—that is, choosing rightly (1.30). For example, money is in itself without value, but it acquires value when we choose to use it correctly.

Epictetus has a powerful argument for this point, which again relates to earlier Stoic ideas. The Stoics had always rejected certain things as valueless because of their vulnerability: wealth can be lost, beauty fades, family members and friends die. But virtue and knowledge are stable and invulnerable once achieved, and within our power to pursue and attain. These things are, as the Stoics had always said, "up to us." Epictetus goes further, by pointing out that it is really our power of choice, and *only* our power of choice, that is up to us. For instance, I can choose to go to the zoo to visit the giraffes, and that choice is up to me. But it is not up to me whether I succeed in reaching the zoo and seeing the giraffes—there may be too much traffic, the giraffes may have tragically succumbed to a virus, or a giraffe-hating tyrant may send his thugs to imprison me before I get there. Ultimately, I can completely control only the choices I make, the intentions I form. The situations to which I respond, and my degree of success in responding to them, can never be fully up to me.

Of course, I may have all kinds of reasons, or apparent reasons, to choose one thing rather than another. A tyrant may attempt to compel me to obey him by imprisoning me, or saying he will execute me. In one of the most celebrated passages of his *Discourses*, Epictetus imagines precisely this case. He envisions the tyrant threatening to chain us up—and says we may respond, "You can chain my leg, but you cannot chain my power of choice" (1.1, 1.18). Even my body is, on this way of thinking, a dispensable, external thing. If the tyrant says he will throw me in prison, I can say, "No, you will throw only my body in prison." If he says he will cut off my head, I can shrug and say, "Who ever said that my head cannot be cut off?" The true philosopher is the one who values nothing that is not up to him; and it is not up to me whether my body is in prison, whether I am decapitated. What is up to me is my choice. Nothing, whether the allure of the giraffe enclosure or the command of a tyrant, the promise of pleasure or the threat of pain, can force me to choose. Epictetus draws a parallel here, between our power of choice and our power of assent. Just as no power on earth can force me to believe something that seems to me false, so no power can compel my choice.

But there is a problem here. Epictetus has told us that our choices are up to us, and that the value of our lives consists only in using this power of choice well. He hasn't, though, told us what it means to use choice well. This seems especially puzzling if everything other than choice is indifferent.[5] If it is really a matter of complete indifference whether I am rich or poor, healthy or sick, slave or emperor, then what difference does it make what I choose? In fact, how am I to avoid the despair of one of Sartre's existential heroes? If nothing outside of my power of choice is worth pursuing, then life itself begins to look meaningless. Fortunately, Epictetus does give us some further guidance. Like other Stoics, he endorses the goal of living in accordance with nature, and believes that we can use our reason to discern what is natural and what unnatural. In a passage I can't help admiring, he complains about men who shave their beards, since they are going against nature (1.16). The point is not as trivial as it sounds: in the ancient world a beard was often the symbol of a philosopher. This, incidentally, is why the emperor Hadrian, a great fan of Greek culture, decided to start going unshaven, to the alarm of his fellow Roman aristocrats.

Epictetus also speaks of what he calls "primary duties"—the natural duties that fall to us in virtue of our family relationships, for instance. Two memorable passages in the *Discourses* concern the attitude a father should take towards his children. In one, a father has come to Epictetus and told how he fled from his own house out of dismay when his child was sick (1.11). Epictetus firmly instructs the man that this was an unnatural act, even if it seems to have been a manifestation of his paternal love. On the other hand, in what may be the most chilling single passage in all of ancient philosophy, Epictetus asks what harm it could do to whisper while kissing your child, "tomorrow you will die" (3.24). In so doing, you remind yourself that the child is not given to you forever, and you prepare yourself for the child's possible death.

The two passages together capture the rigorous ethics of Epictetus: we must never shirk from our duty, but neither should we allow ourselves to place value on things in an unreasonable way. If a child dies, we should be prepared to reflect that all humans die—just as no one ever told you that your head cannot be cut off, no one ever said your child is immortal. Besides, if it is the will of god that your child dies sooner rather than later, then it would be impious and irrational to object.

Epictetus gives plenty of other concrete advice, much of which can speak to us today, though some is more redolent of specifically Roman social practices. For instance, it was common for less-wealthy Romans to become clients of rich citizens and to visit their houses daily, to shake them down for money in exchange for support. When asked whether this is appropriate behavior, Epictetus responds that it depends: if you are the kind of person who begs for money, then it is appropriate (3.24). You have to choose whether you are that kind of person. Everyone must know at what price they sell their self-respect (1.2). This is typical Epictetus, reminding his listeners of what they already know deep down. Notice, incidentally, that in this, and many other cases, we do not need to add anything to the theory of choice in order to know what is the right choice. Debasing oneself to get money is something we can learn to avoid simply by reflecting that money, unlike choice, is indifferent.

We can sum up Epictetus' view, then, by saying that what is external to our choice is indifferent, but the way we *use* these external things is not. Rather, it makes all the difference. Just as I must, as the Stoics put it, "make good use of impressions" by knowing when to assent to the way things seem, and when to suspect I am being misled, so I must use my power of choice to make good use of external things. It might seem paradoxical that it could matter so much how I use things that have no intrinsic value. Epictetus does not shy away from this paradox. He compares our lives to a ball-game (2.5). There is nothing more to being a good player than knowing how to use the ball skillfully, even though it doesn't actually matter whether the ball winds up in the goal or not. Another way of thinking about this is one borrowed from Socrates: although money, health, and so on have no intrinsic value, they gain value in relation to choice so long as the choice is virtuous. In a wonderful passage, Epictetus compares virtue to the magic wand of Hermes (3.20). This is a wand that can turn everything to gold. In the same way, virtue changes everything it touches into something good.

In common with many other ancient philosophers, Epictetus has an ethical theory so rigorous that it is hard to imagine how one might ever live up to it. But if anything characterizes Roman Stoicism, it is attention to the problem of how we make progress towards the goal of perfect virtue. Epictetus does, like the early Stoics, emphasize the gulf separating vice from virtue. But he is not satisfied with the early Stoics' pessimistic claim that everyone who lacks perfect virtue is wholly ignorant and may as well be insane. For one thing, he expresses a remarkably tolerant attitude towards those who are not even trying to attain virtue. He suggests that those who cannot be converted to philosophy should be treated the way we treat children—we humor them, cheerfully clapping along with them when they celebrate and patting them on the head when they are upset. As usual, Socrates is his exemplar: Epictetus alludes to the end of Plato's *Phaedo*, where Socrates first chastises his philosophical companions for lamenting his death, then expresses apparently sincere gratitude for the guard who is nobly weeping over the execution (1.31).

In a way, Epictetus is even tolerant of wrongdoers. He sees them not as targets for vengeance but objects of pity. Again following Socrates, he assumes that wrong-doing comes from a kind of ignorance of the true good. An evil man is just an ignorant man, and putting an ignorant man to death is akin to executing someone for being blind and deaf. Besides, if you find yourself angered by wrongdoing, it is often because you share the values of the wrongdoer. Suppose someone steals your money. If you cannot face this with calm composure, it can only be because, like the thief, you think the money is well worth having (1.18). Instead, you should remember that the money was never yours in the first place—only your choice is truly yours, because it is the only thing that cannot be taken from you. Thus Epictetus reserves his harsh judgments for those who say they want to become good. They are the only people who have any chance of benefiting from his tough love. And because the ethical teaching he offers is so rigorous, only the most rigorous of regimes has any chance of succeeding. He also tells us to be on guard against cultivating a show of virtue so that we can show off how virtuous we are. As an example of the kind of training that might work, he likes the following suggestion: on a hot day, when you are extremely thirsty, take a mouthful of cold water...then spit it out, and tell no one what you have done (3.12).

As you might expect, not everyone who comes to Epictetus for help is able to benefit from this sort of advice. Several times in the *Discourses* he's shown refusing to engage with his listeners because he thinks they will be unable to benefit. At one point he imagines a frustrated visitor to his philosophical school going away and complaining, "I met Epictetus, and it was like talking to a stone" (3.9). This may itself be a cunning strategy. Epictetus mentions that his own teacher, Rufus, was in the habit of harshly sending people away, simply to test their determination to learn from him (3.6). When would-be students fail to learn from Rufus or Epictetus, the blame does not rest with the teachers.

But let's suppose that you, being a better sort of person, have gone to see Epictetus, or have read the *Discourses*, or failing that, have read to the end of this chapter. You're now persuaded that you should value nothing but your own power of choice, and accept the will of god, always ready to give back immediately whatever has been given to you, whether it is wealth, family, or life itself. Will you instantly become a perfectly wise sage? Of course not. Like the Epicureans, the Stoics, and especially the Roman Stoics, put great stress on therapeutic training—a lifelong journey of self-discipline. Epictetus is recorded in the *Discourses* as advising his students to review their Stoic principles daily. That his words did not fall entirely on deaf ears is shown by the next great Roman Stoic, a man who wrote down ideas influenced by Epictetus in a daily ritual of self-examination. Yet in terms of his biography, our next thinker could hardly have been more different from Epictetus. Epictetus was a slave, whereas this philosopher was quite literally master of everything he surveyed. He was, in fact, the most politically powerful philosopher who has ever walked the earth.

THE PHILOSOPHER KING
MARCUS AURELIUS

A few years back, a book was published with the title *If Aristotle Ran General Motors*.[1] It's a cute title, isn't it? But I have a question that blows it out of the water: what if a Stoic philosopher ran the Roman Empire? I mean, with all due respect to General Motors, they only make cars, whereas the Roman Empire was the Roman Empire. Also, my scenario has a significant advantage, namely that it isn't hypothetical. A Stoic philosopher *did* run the Roman Empire. He reigned, first jointly and then on his own, for twenty years. He was praised by contemporaries and later Roman historians for his moderate lifestyle and justice, and considered the last of the so-called "five good emperors." He faced numerous threats to the empire, including a massive plague and wars with the Parthians and with German tribes. He also had to cope with the death of most of his children. His name was Marcus Aurelius.

Marcus was born during the reign of the third good emperor, Hadrian, of wall-building fame. He was not in a direct line of succession to the imperial throne, but then, neither was anyone else. Hadrian adopted as his official heir the future emperor Antoninus Pius, who in turn adopted Marcus at Hadrian's request. This, by the way, was something of a pattern among the five good emperors. The first of them, Nerva, had adopted his successor Trajan, of column-building fame, and Trajan in turn adopted Hadrian. The success of these good emperors was no coincidence: each was hand-picked, in a far more meritocratic system than would hold sway in the declining years of the Roman Empire. Some would argue that that decline began because of Marcus' one big mistake. Instead of choosing and adopting a talented man as heir, he allowed his natural son to succeed him. That son was Commodus, and if people talked about the five bad emperors, Commodus would definitely be on the list. He was bad enough that in the movie *Gladiator* the happy ending consists in Commodus getting killed by Russell Crowe.

But apart from his megalomaniac son, Marcus had plenty to crow about. He ascended to the throne in AD 161. He immediately displayed both confidence and intelligence. Anticipating the later realization that multiple emperors would be needed to rule over a territory as vast as the empire, he nominated a man named Lucius Verus to rule with him as co-emperor. Marcus would be sole emperor only as of 169, when Verus died, probably from the so-called Antonine Plague. This disease, which may have been smallpox, was only one of several existential threats to menace the empire during the reign of Marcus. Like many emperors, he spent his years on the throne rushing from one military engagement to another. He waged war against the Parthians—these were the successors to the Persians, who posed an almost constant danger to the east of the Romans, just as the Persians had posed a threat to the ancient Greeks. Marcus also campaigned against numerous groups of Germanic barbarians along the Danube river. These wars were still going on when Marcus died in 180.

It was here on the frontier that Marcus supposedly composed a set of notes to himself, appropriately entitled simply *To Himself*, and commonly referred to as *The Meditations*.[2] It is a work of great power and influence, a literary legacy that just about makes up for the political legacy of bequeathing the purple robes of imperial power to Commodus. A note attached to the end of the first book informs us that the *Meditations* were written "among the Quadi," a Germanic tribe. If we believe this note, as opposed to dismissing it as a later scribal invention, then we must imagine Marcus late in life, retiring each night from his military endeavors, sitting down to collect his thoughts, and writing a series of admonitions aimed squarely at his own soul. He used Stoic ideas to combat his own fears, vanity, and irritability. No doubt the *Meditations* were also intended for a wider readership, but they are more than plausible as a work of self-examination and philosophical therapy.

Some would doubt that anything much was personally at stake for Marcus when he wrote the *Meditations*. The historian Mary Beard has commented that if we "scour the Meditations for signs of Marcus' inner conflicts, [we] might as well be looking for the evidence of psychic turmoil in the essay of a modern philosophy under-graduate".[3] No doubt, the *Meditations* does fit into a genre of ancient writing in which philosophical themes were woven into an ostentatious display of self-conscious virtue. If we wish to read a radical re-imagining of this genre, we should turn not to these *Meditations* but to the *Confessions* of St Augustine. (In fact we'll be turning to it later in this book.) Yet there are signs that Marcus is speaking genuinely for himself and to himself, not just trying to impress a learned readership with his erudition and integrity. He makes frequent reference to the stresses and annoyances of life at the top. At one point he writes, "never let anyone hear you complaining about court life again . . . including yourself" (8.9). At another point he compares the court to his stepmother, and casts philosophy in the role of mother (6.12). Contemporary reports of Marcus' character lend some credence to the idea that he was more a lover of books than a lover of power, and he was described even in the ancient world as a "philosopher king." No less an observer than Julian the Apostate—the other philosopher-emperor of late antiquity—admired Marcus greatly. So, while we should not necessarily look to Marcus for innovations in Stoic doctrine, I think we may take the *Meditations* as a deeply felt application of that doctrine to an extraordinary life.

The *Meditations* are divided into twelve books, the first of which could easily have been entitled "How I got to be such a great guy." Not that Marcus would ever allow such an immodest thought to go unchallenged in his own mind. He gives the credit for such virtue and wisdom as he possesses to a long list of teachers and relations. His adoptive father and predecessor as emperor, Antoninus Pius, receives particular praise for his comprehensive virtue, praise which culminates by comparing Antoninus to no less a figure than Socrates (1.16). But most of Marcus' influences were teachers. Nothing but the best would do for the young emperor-to-be, and the leading intellectuals of Rome were brought into his aristocratic home to school him in grammar, rhetoric, and, of course, philosophy. One of these was the Stoic Rusticus, who exposed Marcus to the work of Epictetus. For this alone we should join Marcus in being grateful to Rusticus. Bringing Epictetus to the attention of the future emperor was akin to giving Charlie Parker his first saxophone. The various teachers in Marcus' formative years taught him various lessons, but the *Meditations* is above all a set of variations on themes found in Epictetus.

Of course, Epictetus himself had drawn on the earlier Stoic tradition, so that Marcus is also the inheritor of the ethics of Chrysippus and other early Stoics. Thus, his main theme, to which he returns again and again, is the importance of controlling his own judgments and desires. By putting Marcus on the throne, fate has presented him with wealth and access to limitless pleasures, but also with plentiful enemies. Marcus thus faced an unusually challenging set of temptations and opportunities for anger. Yet his fundamental advice to himself could be applied by anyone: when the world provokes you into a reaction, think first whether the reaction is the right one. Does a man offend your pride? Remember that he will be dead soon, as will you. Are you wrapped in the purple robes of unchallenged power? Remember that they are just rags dyed in ink. Are you consumed with desire for a woman? Do not pray that god will give her to you; pray rather to be relieved of your lust. In one of my favorite passages, he recommends a method for confronting misfortune. Do not lament the misfortune. Instead, rejoice that you are the sort of man who can undergo misfortune without letting it upset you (4.49).

Marcus describes this process of self-discipline and rational reflection as an "art of living." It is an art, he says, more akin to wrestling than to dancing, because it requires that we always be on our guard (7.61). Now, I know what you're thinking: this advice could be inspired by practically any ancient ethical theory. Plato wanted us to subordinate desire to reason; Aristotle thought virtue is in large part a matter of using reason to steer our desires; and even the Epicureans thought intelligent hedonism means using reason to choose carefully between the pleasures that present themselves. The Stoics had no monopoly on the view that reason should rule over desire. And in fact, Marcus sometimes sounds almost like a Platonist when he considers the role of reason in our lives. He describes the body as an "instrument" of the soul (10.38), which is the true man, and compares our rational capacity to the pilot of a ship (11.20)—an image which recalls passages in both Plato's *Republic* and Aristotle's *De Anima*.

Yet Marcus' Stoic allegiances are clear, and not only from the fact that the philosophy teachers he mentions in his intellectual autobiography were Stoics. For one thing, his picture of rationality is very Stoic. It's not just a matter of having the right beliefs and acting on them, but a matter of controlling our assent to the impressions the world presents to us. Marcus doesn't put the point in these technical terms, but it is certainly his picture of ethical action. Tellingly, he claims that banishing the belief that you have been treated wrongly is sufficient to banish the anger that would follow from such treatment (4.7). Thus we have a fairly standard Stoic picture of human ethical life: an impression presents itself, we assent to it or refrain from assenting, and our emotional reactions proceed accordingly. Another Stoic thread woven into the cloth of the *Meditations* is the idea of fate. Indeed, Marcus compares his own life to a thread in fate's web, and reminds himself that his thread will unspool in a way that is for the best, since it is part of that divine web that is woven through the universe (4.40, 7.57).

When Marcus considers his own little patch of that web, he often emphasizes the fleeting, ephemeral nature of his life and everything it contains. His remedy against feeling insulted is to remember the imminent death of everyone concerned, and that's a typical thought. He applies it to fame and honor: why seek the approval of others, when they will soon enough be dead? He applies it to misfortunes and suffering: everything we undergo will be over soon, seen from the perspective of eternity. Of course, it takes a certain kind of person to take that amount of perspective on their own situation. Perhaps only a Stoic sage could go through life thinking of his own affairs as a mere speck in the great scheme of things. But Marcus reflects also on the more positive aspects of any upheaval we may face.

Everything natural, he tells himself, depends upon change. For instance, we could gain no nourishment from food without its changing (7.18).

When he compares the world to a flowing river (5.23), it's hard to escape the thought that Marcus is thinking not of the stable, providential universe of Stoicism, but the unstable, flux-ridden cosmos of Heraclitus. Or rather, of Heraclitus as portrayed by Plato. Remember, though, that from its earliest days Stoicism had claimed Heraclitus as an intellectual ancestor.[4] Although Marcus emphasizes the theme of constant change more than your average Stoic, it is an emphasis that fits into the school's philosophical lineage. Much the same could be said for Marcus' attitude towards Socrates. Many Stoics, especially Epictetus, seem to have taken Socrates as a primary inspiration. This tendency is somewhat less prominent in Marcus, but it is evident nonetheless. In one passage, he remarks that Alexander, Caesar, and Pompey—perhaps the three greatest political heroes Marcus could have named—led lives inferior to those of Socrates, Heraclitus, and Diogenes the Cynic (8.3). But elsewhere, with typical focus on inner life rather than outward seeming, Marcus reserves judgment about Socrates. We know only Socrates' words and actions, not the state of his soul: he was famous for facing his death without fear, but Socrates alone could know whether there was fear in his heart after all (7.66).

So Marcus has his philosophical heroes, and they are more or less the usual Stoic suspects. Yet he also quotes Plato with approval several times in the Meditations. Indeed, some entries consist of nothing but quotations from Plato and other authors. Clearly these were passages Marcus found particularly helpful or powerful. The closest thing to a criticism of Plato is when this philosopher king tells himself that he can be satisfied with small successes, rather than expecting to achieve perfection as envisioned in Plato's Republic (9.29). But even this seems more like a characteristic acceptance of cirumstances than a deep objection to Plato's idealism. More generally, the way Marcus uses philosophical authorities seems to be of a piece with his ethical outlook: he takes each authority in turn, accepts what he finds reasonable, and doesn't worry too much about points of disagreement.

The best example of this is his handling of the Epicureans. One would think that Marcus, being a Stoic, would find little to value in this school. And indeed, one of his favorite motifs is an anti-Epicurean one. He reminds himself numerous times that the world must be either a random jumble of atoms, as Epicurus claimed, or providentially ordered (e.g. 4.3). Since Marcus finds the Epicurean alternative absurd, this leaves him only with the remaining hypothesis, that the world is indeed guided by a sure divine hand. Yet aside from this, Marcus usually mentions Epicurus and his school in order to agree with them. He apparently finds only one topic where he can agree with them, but it's a big one: the fear of death. Or rather, the topic of not fearing death. He gives apparently unalloyed praise to Epicurus for the brave way that he met his end, and he also repeats the Epicurean argument that death is nothing to us, because when we cease to exist we will no longer have any sensation (11.41, 8.59).

Marcus constantly returns to this topic of death, which is one of the things that makes him distinctive in the Stoic tradition. It's as if he is trying to show that Stoicism can rise to this challenge, just as Lucretius and other Epicureans had done. Perhaps there were also personal considerations in play here. They say that nothing is certain but death and taxes. But as emperor, Marcus didn't have to pay any taxes, which left only death to worry about. And if it's true that the *Meditations* were written during his final campaigns along the Danube, Marcus was not far from death himself as he wrote them. In any case, he was plagued by poor health throughout his life, and saw four of his children die. So he would have plenty of reason to reflect on his own death and on death in general. Of course, the considerations he uses to combat anxiety and grief in other areas of life apply here too. Thus, he points out that if all natural things are fleeting, it would be irrational to object to our own end. Or, that death too is part of the divine plan that governs the universe wisely. Or, that in the great scheme of things it matters little whether we die today or decades from now (4.47).

Marcus also urges us to see death, along with aging and other apparently regrettable aspects of life, as part of a natural cycle. He does think that all things change, but also that they change in ever-repeating ways. At the most global level, there is the Stoic idea that all events in the universe will recur in future world-cycles. Marcus alludes once to this notion (9.28, also mentioned above in Chapter 10), but usually he has a more humble idea of cycles in mind, for instance, the stages of life from youth to old age (9.21). He even applies this to his own situation as emperor, reflecting that his own court will be like a repeat performance of a play staged earlier in the courts of Alexander, Hadrian, and other rulers (10.27). It's characteristic of Marcus to show awareness of a technical Stoic notion like world-cycles, but constantly to draw attention back to the ethical situation that he faces himself. For instance, he mentions that his soul is nothing but a vapor exhaled from the blood, not because he wants to set out some theory of human nature, but to remind himself not to take praise too seriously (5.33).

His suggestion that he is merely acting out the part of emperor, a part played by others before him, is equally characteristic. This gets us to what, for my money, is the heart of Marcus' achievement as a philosopher. If Marcus anticipates Shakespeare in considering all the world to be a stage, he also anticipates Shakespeare's greatest character, Hamlet, by withdrawing into a rich inner, mental life that is no longer fully identified with the role that he plays. This interiority did not paralyze Marcus, as it does Hamlet. The Parthians and others could testify to this, having suffered the slings and arrows of Marcus' legions. But Marcus would agree with Hamlet that there's nothing either good nor bad but thinking makes it so. He was a man of action who did not identify himself with his actions, but rather with his thoughts. In theory, at least, Marcus considers it a matter of no importance that he plays out the role of emperor rather than the role of a farmer. Marcus himself is not the character he plays outwardly, but is the soul that lives inwardly. Just as much as the emperor, the farmer has a soul that can make peace with divine fate or wage futile combat against it.

This is why the *Meditations* is a work that can speak to anyone, even if it was written by an emperor for his own benefit. What Marcus offers us is a crash course in therapy for the soul, and this therapy asks us to take withdraw into an invulnerable, detached self—what Marcus calls his inner "citadel" (8.48). The philosophical basis for this is already present in Epictetus. But Marcus articulates the interiority of Roman Stoicism with unmatched directness, and usually with stylish charm, rather than the withering wit of Epictetus. It is appropriate that Marcus should offer such effective medicine for the soul, given that he employed the greatest doctor of his age, indeed, of just about any age: Galen. A towering figure in the history of medicine, and no midget in the history of philosophy, Galen was employed as doctor to Marcus and to his son Commodus. I mention this simply because we'll soon be taking a look at Galen and the relation between ancient medicine and ancient philosophy. But first there is a final major Hellenistic school to look at, in fact, one whose greatest representative was a doctor: the Skeptics.

15

BEYOND BELIEF
PYRRHO AND SKEPTICISM

There are a few philosophical issues that are so deep, so troubling, that they make movies about them. I don't mean intellectual European films, I mean proper movies, with special-effects budgets. Hollywood has made blockbusters about free will and future truth, for instance. I have in mind the Tom Cruise vehicle *Minority Report*, whose theme comes straight from the deterministic argument in Aristotle's *On Interpretation*. The nature of time itself is another obvious case. I need only mention *Back to the Future*, to say nothing of *Back to the Future, Part 2* and *Back to the Future, Part 3*. But maybe the most cinema-friendly topic in philosophy is skepticism. The skeptic asks how we can be sure that we know what we think we know. Perhaps we are prey to systematic falsehood in our beliefs, because we are... oh, I don't know, perhaps being used as living batteries in an energy farm built by intelligent machines, while our brains are, for reasons that remain poorly explained, entertained with a virtual reality called "the Matrix."

It's gotten to the point where it is obligatory, when discussing skepticism in philosophy classes, to mention this movie, *The Matrix*—though not so much *Matrix Parts 2* and *3*, because they were rubbish. It's a real time-saver, actually. If you're trying to give an argument for skepticism, you just have to point out that Keanu Reeves didn't know he was in the Matrix. And if he couldn't figure it out, then what chance do the rest of us have? Really though, any movie that features a dream sequence in which the characters or audience believe that the dream is real is touching on the theme of skepticism. This is one of the oldest tricks in the movie-making book. It goes back at least as far as Buster Keaton's wonderful silent movie *Sherlock Jr.*, in which a film-projectionist falls asleep and dreams of himself as a character in a movie. Keaton already realized that the question of what is real, and how we can know what is real, relates naturally to cinema because cinema is itself an alternate version of reality.

Now though, I want to discuss not so much an alternate version of reality as an alternate version of skepticism. The skepticism of the ancient world influenced modern skepticism, and continues to fascinate philosophers who work in this area. But it is not the same thing as modern skepticism. The father of modern skepticism was Descartes, who proposed radical doubt as a stepping-stone towards reaching conclusions that could not be doubted. In his *Meditations*, Descartes subjects all of his beliefs to skeptical attack—in fact, he raises the question of how he knows he isn't dreaming, and also proposes a scenario not unlike the Matrix, in which a malicious demon is filling him with false beliefs.[1] The reason Descartes does this is that he wants to see which beliefs, if any, are immune to doubt. After Descartes, skepticism has usually taken roughly this form: we consider beliefs of various kinds and ask whether they can be doubted, and if so, what that means about the status of those beliefs. For instance, it may seem to you that you are holding a book in your hands right now. But in fact you cannot know that you are holding a book since maybe, just maybe, you are in the Matrix, waiting to be freed from your confusion by Laurence Fishburne.

The ancient skeptics had a very different approach. We can see this already by considering the name "skeptics." As you won't be surprised to learn, this word comes from ancient Greek. *Skeptikos* means someone who is inquiring or searching. The ancient skeptic is not, then, testing his beliefs against some kind of radical, doubt-inducing scenario, like the Matrix or Descartes' evil demon. He is, rather, someone who is sharing in a process of philosophical inquiry. Nor is he raising radical or systematic doubt as a general issue. Rather, he is inquiring into the success of other believers, especially other philosophers like the Stoics. The Skeptic is struck by the objections that face each attempt to determine the truth of things. He finds that incompatible theories seem to have more or less equally good arguments on their side. He also finds that the theories of other philosophers fall short of the standards of proof suggested by those very same philosophers. In short, he always finds room for doubt. Nonetheless, he remains (in theory at least) committed to the positive enterprise of seeking truth. Upon finding that various proposals about the nature of things are doubtful, he does not give up the search. But given that the search has so far failed to turn up a victorious candidate for truth, he does suspend judgment.

This idea of "suspending judgment" is at the core of ancient skepticism, whereas it plays no role in Cartesian skepticism. The Greek word for the suspension of judgment, *epoche*, became something of a standard around which the skeptical tradition could rally. Which is not to say that only the Skeptics were interested in suspension of judgment. As we saw when looking at the Stoic theory of knowledge, early Stoics like Zeno and Chrysippus thought that the perfect wise man, or sage, would suspend judgment rather than assenting to impressions which were in any way doubtful. But the Skeptics pointed out that the Stoics' own standards for knowledge were set so high that they made knowledge unattainable: all impressions leave room for doubt (LS 1A, F; 71D, 72A–K). Thus the wise man would always suspend judgment.

Here we have another striking difference between ancient and modern skepticism. Since we now usually think of skepticism as a challenge to be overcome, if at all possible, we do not think about skepticism as a stable philosophical posture, a way of living one's life. But in common with the other Hellenistic schools, the Skeptics put forth a picture of the ideal sage, and of a life that would be free of disturbance. This is perhaps the most surprising feature of ancient skepticism: it was presented as a recipe for happiness. To some extent this is symptomatic of the competition between the Skeptics and other philosophical groups. Since rival schools like the Stoics and the Epicureans had an account of the sage and of the happy life, the Skeptics needed to say something on these same topics too. But it was not merely a dialectical afterthought, as we can see by turning to the man who is usually recognized as the first Skeptic: Pyrrho of Elis.

Pyrrho was born in the 360s BC and died in the 270s, making him roughly a generation younger than Aristotle and a generation older than Epicurus. He was an admired figure in his home of Elis, the north-west corner of the southern part of mainland Greece. Like Socrates and Diogenes the Cynic, he wrote nothing. Our understanding of him as a personality relies on the reports of his followers and other ancient recorders of the history of philosophy. Diogenes Laertius' *Lives of the Philosophers*, an important source for so many Hellenistic thinkers, preserves a report on Pyrrho. Apart from that, the most important information derives ultimately from Pyrrho's student Timon, who was a great supporter of Pyrrho and his skeptical approach to philosophy. That skepticism found an irreverent embodiment in a work of Timon's called the *Silloi*, or "parodies"—it was other philosophers who were the butt of the jokes. It's not entirely clear how much of the philosophical stance we associate with Pyrrho was in fact Pyrrho's and how much was invented by Timon. But it was Pyrrho, not Timon, who in due course was honored as the founder of a skeptical tradition. Beginning in the first century BC and carrying on into the period of the Roman Empire, there were Skeptics who proudly styled themselves as "Pyrrhonists."

Although Pyrrho is thus credited with beginning something new, his skeptical attitude did not come from nowhere. One hypothesis about his inspiration already excited ancient authors who wrote about Pyrrho. In the 320s BC Pyrrho participated in the military campaign of Alexander the Great, which meant traveling as far away as India. There, we are told, Pyrrho encountered Indian wise men, who may have been a source for skeptical ideas (LS 1A). This idea is not without merit, given that skepticism did play a role in classical Indian philosophy. On the other hand, there were antecedents for Pyrrho's views in Greek philosophy. Pyrrho himself seems to have acknowledged Democritus as an important predecessor (LS 1C). After setting forth his atomic theory Democritus drew skeptical conclusions from it, declaring that perceptible qualities like sweetness and color are merely conventions, since in reality there is nothing but atoms and void. In general, Pyrrho, or at least his faithful follower Timon, treated other philosophers with scorn, but Democritus was respected for his anticipation of skepticism.[2]

It must also be said that, possible influence from India notwithstanding, Pyrrho's image and way of life fits comfortably into the age of Diogenes the Cynic, Epicurus, and Zeno, the founder of Stoicism. Like them, and like Socrates, Pyrrho cultivated the persona of an imperturbable sage. He did not shrink from fearful situations like storms at sea, and was happy to stoop to performing menial tasks, like washing pigs. Nor did physical pain bother him—a typical legend has him undergoing the horrors of ancient surgery without so much as flinching. Supposedly, in describing his own way of life he used that most central technical term of Hellenistic ethics: *ataraxia*, or lack of disturbance (LS 1F, 2C, 71A). Thus Pyrrho claimed to have achieved the Holy Grail pursued by almost all the philosophers of his day. Like Diogenes the Cynic, he managed this without taking the trouble to devise a complex philosophical theory, such as Epicurus and Zeno offered. Far from it. Pyrrho's indifference to danger and pain was the supposed consequence of his lack of beliefs and commitments.

But why would a life without belief be a life of calm, a life free of trouble? One might just as easily suppose it would be a life consumed with worry. If I don't have firm beliefs about the world around me, won't I face each new situation in a state of ignorance and confusion? Aren't the Stoics right to think that it is knowledge and understanding that yield confidence and serenity? To be honest, I tend to side with the Stoics here, but there is something to be said for Pyrrho's side of the argument. Let's consider again those tales of Pyrrho's indifference to circumstances. For instance, his ability to undergo excruciating pain without registering any dismay could be explained by the fact that he does not believe pain is a bad thing. His cheerfulness about performing menial tasks would derive from the absence of beliefs about which activities are unworthy. Outwardly Pyrrho's life is in fact very like that of the Stoic sage. The Stoic sage too is immune to pain and conventional feelings of shame, because his positive commitments lie elsewhere: he believes that only virtue is worth having, and has a solid theory about the nature of virtue. Inwardly, of course, Pyrrho doesn't have those positive beliefs. But he doesn't need them. All he needs to do is avoid having beliefs that would give rise to disturbance, and of course, he has no such beliefs, since he has no beliefs at all.

If Pyrrho is to be anything other than one more example of an indomitable Hellenistic wise man, though, he needs to give us some kind of philosophical rationale for the skeptical attitude that yields *ataraxia*. For this, we have to rely principally on a single piece of evidence (LS 1F), which reaches us through a philological version of the children's game of "Telephone" or "Chinese Whispers." The report is found in the fourth-century AD Christian theologian Eusebius—hardly a promising place to find details about the ideas of a fourth-century BC Skeptic, but beggars can't be choosers. Eusebius is relating an account about Pyrrho preserved by an earlier Aristotelian philosopher, who in turn was taking his information from Pyrrho's follower Timon. And don't forget that what we can read would be manuscripts that are only copies, or copies of copies, of the text Eusebius himself wrote. Do you suppose that scholars just might have proposed emending the Greek text in such a way as fundamentally to change the logic of the whole passage? Why, of course they have.[3] Such are the delights of trying to reconstruct early Hellenistic philosophy.

Still, we have some reason to think that the passage tells us something fairly reliable about Pyrrho, or at least about Timon's understanding of Pyrrho, which is about as much as we can hope for. Plus, it's really interesting. So let's see what it says. The report tells us that things in themselves are neither one way nor another—they are indifferent, impossible to measure or to judge. Our perceptions and beliefs do not provide either truth or falsehood. Thus, we should remain without belief, inclining neither this way nor that, as a result of which we will avoid making any assertions and, finally, achieve *ataraxia*. Since Pyrrho himself attained this freedom, he is presumably a reliable guide to the method, and this at least claims to be his own description of the method. The passage is, in short, exactly what we were looking for. Unfortunately, it's not easy to understand.

We can start with the basic observation that Pyrrho is telling us to avoid opinion or belief. The word he uses, *doxa*, is the same word that Plato and Aristotle use to describe the state of mind in which one takes something to be true yet lacks knowledge in the proper sense. In Plato's classic formulation, belief lies between ignorance and knowledge (*Republic* 478d). Of course, Plato and Aristotle urge us to shun ignorance, and not to be satisfied with true belief. Rather, we should push on until we achieve knowledge and understanding of the way things are. But this, Pyrrho claims, is impossible: things in themselves are neither one way nor another. Unfortunately the passage contains no defense of this alarming statement, but we've seen the sentiment before. Think, for instance, of Protagoras in Plato's *Theaetetus*, saying that if the wind feels cold for you and warm for me, then there is no truth of the matter about whether the wind is warm or cold in itself. All truth is relative to an observer. Or think of Democritus again, saying that the perceptible features of things are only a matter of custom, because in reality they are atoms and void. Pyrrho's reference to perception, in addition to belief, suggests that he also had in mind examples like this.

The moral of the skeptical story is that Plato and Aristotle were wrong: belief is not inadequate because it falls short of knowledge; rather, it goes too far. To have a belief presupposes that we are able to determine the nature of things, but this is impossible. Does this mean that the skeptic is settling for ignorance, having given up on true belief, never mind full-scale knowledge? Well, it's obvious that the skeptic must be ignorant in a sense, at least if "ignorant" just means "lacking knowledge." The skeptic accepts that knowledge has not been attained, either by himself or by anyone else, as far as he can tell. Yet it's equally obvious that the skeptic's "ignorance" is special. It will not involve having false beliefs, of course, since he will have no beliefs at all. Rather, it is a mature, self-conscious, and blissful lack of knowledge, in which he suspends all belief, and in this way achieves peace of mind.

There are several difficulties that remain, though. I'll mention two of them. The first is that Pyrrho seems, in our passage, to be laying down a bold philosophical thesis, namely that the natures of things cannot be determined. Now, Pyrrho isn't doubting the existence of the things around us. He apparently didn't raise Descartes-style worries about whether there is a wind; he only suggested that there is no fact of the matter about whether the wind is warm or cold. But that's not the problem; in fact it's just another difference between ancient and modern skepticism. Ancient skeptics in general did not raise worries about whether external things are really out there; they only raised problems for attempts to determine the natures of those things.[4] The problem is rather that, at least on the interpretation I've just given, Pyrrho asserted confidently that the natures of things are unknowable.[5] He seems to be completely convinced that things cannot be determined, which is why we should refrain from belief. But this conviction is itself a belief! Later Skeptics will be more careful on this point, and say only that they suspend judgment about whether the natures of things might be knowable.

The second problem I want to mention is also one that confronted the later Skeptics. We've understood Pyrrho to be saying that he can do without any beliefs at all, in fact, to be saying that his freedom from disturbance is achieved by giving up on the whole enterprise of forming beliefs. This, he has discovered, is the happy life. But not only does this life sound less than happy, it doesn't even sound feasible. To give just one example, how am I supposed to avoid starving to death if I suspend judgment about which items in my environment are edible? This sort of worry infected the biographical reports about Pyrrho, so that we are told fanciful legends about his students following him around, stopping him at the last minute from walking in front of oncoming wagons and stepping off cliffs (LS 1A). The idea that Pyrrho actually behaved like the cartoon character Mr Magoo, blinded by his lack of beliefs rather than by real blindness, is clearly silly. But a serious point underlies the stories, namely that life without belief seems downright impossible, at least for humans. Perhaps Pyrrho agreed: in one anecdote he is frightened by a dog and reacts, betraying his belief that the dog is dangerous. After regaining his composure, he remarks that it is difficult to divest oneself of one's humanity.

But the evidence at our disposal concerning Pyrrho does not really allow us to say with confidence how he would have solved these problems, or indeed whether he tried to solve them. Fortunately, the Skeptical tradition is only just starting. Soon enough there will come a new group of thinkers who avoid commitment, belief, and assertion, and who respond to the two problems I've just raised: first, that skepticism is itself a kind of commitment; and second, that one cannot live without belief. These new Skeptics arise within Plato's Academy, of all places. One can easily imagine Plato, to say nothing of his immediate successors Speusippus and Xeno-crates, spinning in their graves at the thought of their Academy being run by Skeptics. But the Skeptics could claim Platonic legitimacy. They looked not to Democritus or Pyrrho. Rather—like so many other Hellenistic thinkers—their idol was Socrates. After all, Socrates did claim to know only that he knew nothing. The Skeptics of the New Academy are going to wonder if they know even that much.

THE KNOW-NOTHING PARTY
THE SKEPTICAL ACADEMY

Everybody loves a good rivalry. Ali vs. Foreman. The Montagues vs. the Capulets. Gryffindor vs. Slytherin. And the history of philosophy too has its rivalries. Think of Plato vs. the sophists, the Rationalists vs. the Empiricists, or Nietzsche vs. God. Few philosophical rivalries have been as central to their era as the rivalry between the Stoics and Skeptics, a dispute that ran for generations from the early Hellenistic period down to the time of the Roman Empire. Julius Caesar set Rome on the path towards empire by assuming the role of dictator in the middle of the first century BC. One of his critics was the great orator, lawyer, and intellectual Cicero. Cicero wrote works on philosophy throughout his career, especially during moments of enforced political inactivity, such as the one that resulted from Caesar's ascendancy. When Cicero looked back at the history of philosophy as it had developed since Plato, he saw this dispute between Skeptics and Stoics as one of primary importance, on a par with arguments about the nature of pleasure in the good life and the question of the nature of the gods. He wrote treatises on all of these subjects, devoting a work called the *Academica* to the topic of Skepticism. It is one of our main sources for Skepticism in the Hellenistic period.

But why would Cicero call a work on Skepticism "*Academica*"? The answer is simple, if surprising: in the generations leading up to Cicero's day, Plato's Academy in Athens had become synonymous with the Skeptical approach to philosophy. That certainly would have surprised the first heads of the Academy following Plato's death, Speusippus and Xenocrates. They were anything but Skeptics, instead promoting a bold interpretation of the cosmology and metaphysics of Plato.[1] The next scholarch, or head, of the Academy was a man named Polemo, who shifted things to the terrain of ethics but continued to set forth what he took to be Platonic doctrine. These successors to Plato would probably be broadly happy with the way Plato is usually taught in universities these days: the Platonic dialogues are presumed to contain certain doctrines, and the task of the faithful interpreter is to discover, and perhaps elaborate upon, those doctrines.

Then, in about 268 BC, everything changed. The headship of the Academy passed to a philosopher named Arcesilaus. Any doctrine-loving Platonists still frequenting the Academy would have felt like meat-lovers whose favorite restaurant is suddenly taken over by militant vegetarians. It was an end to the steady diet of arguments claiming to establish metaphysical and ethical truths. Arguments were certainly still on the menu at Arcesilaus' Academy. But this was, to borrow the ancient phrase, a 'New' Academy, and it had new arguments—arguments that aimed to destroy rather than build theories. This may seem a shocking direction for the Academy to take. But the Skeptics could point to Socrates for institutional legitimacy. They could remind us of Socrates' claims of ignorance, and also of the fact that Plato lets so many of his dialogues end in a kind of impasse or *aporia*—where the characters have failed to find the object of their search.

Still, it wasn't the doctrinal Platonism of the Old Academy, or the suggestions of positive doctrine in Plato himself, that were targeted by Arcesilaus. Rather, his great opponent and rival was Stoicism, or to make things personal, his contemporary Zeno of Citium, the founder of the Stoic tradition. Their rivalry was continued by the leading successors of both the Stoa and the Academy. On the doctrinal Stoic side was the great Chrysippus, who was well matched on the skeptical Academic side by Carneades. Amending the frequent remark that without Chrysippus there would be no Stoa, Carneades said, "without Chrysippus, there would be no me."[2] He was the Muhammad Ali to Chrysippus' George Foreman, and his aim was to deliver a knock-out blow to the Stoics' claim that certain knowledge is possible.

Skepticism and Stoicism could have been designed specifically as opposing philosophies, and in fact, to a large extent they were. Some of Chrysippus' improvements on Zeno were made directly in response to Skeptical attack, and the Skeptics of the Academy often seem to have had little more on their minds than undermining the Stoics. This is perhaps just what we'd expect, since the Skeptics professed no doctrines of their own. What they brought to the table was not a rival theory, like that of the Epicureans, but an arsenal of dialectical weaponry designed to undercut and cast doubt upon the Stoic position. They were willing to fight on any ground, from logic to physics to ethics. But at the core of the dispute, inevitably, was the nature of knowledge itself.

As discussed earlier in this book, Zeno, followed by Chrysippus and the other Stoics, claimed to have discovered the criterion of truth, a yardstick by which to sort possibly false beliefs from definitely true beliefs. With such beliefs in hand, we can work our way towards the systematic understanding that the Stoics honor with the name of *episteme*, "knowledge" or "understanding." A quick reminder: for the Stoics, the criterion of truth is what they call a cognitive impression, that is, an impression about how things are that corresponds to how things are, and that cannot be misleading. The Stoics add that a truly wise man will never assent to non-cognitive impressions, though he may accept that some such impressions are more reasonable than others and act accordingly. For instance, if it seems to the wise man that a tiger is leaping from a nearby tree to attack him, he will not wait to assess the lighting conditions and possibility of practical jokes, he will just take cover. Still, he will not necessarily form the positive belief that there is a tiger unless he's satisfied that the impression of the tiger is indeed cognitive. If circumstances leave room for doubt, he will suspend judgment.

It's perhaps already clear from this why the Stoics are ideal opponents for the Skeptics. For one thing, the Stoics are emphatic that certainty is possible and insist that wisdom requires certainty. In this respect the Epicureans, for instance, would make less satisfying enemies. We found that Epicurus was happy to accept theories so long as they were not ruled out by evidence, and so long as they led to freedom from disturbance. Although he did insist on the truth of all sensations—something the Skeptics could enjoy refuting—Epicurus was not really in the absolute-certainty business. For another thing, the Stoics themselves deploy the idea of suspending judgment, which happens to be the centerpiece of the skeptical strategy. The Stoics have very high standards for belief: if there is any doubt, they counsel us to suspend judgment and withhold our assent. The Stoics were almost asking for someone to come along and tell them that, according to these standards, no one should ever believe anything.

And this, of course, is precisely what Arcesilaus came along and told them. He argued, as we saw when discussing the Stoics, that in principle any impression, no matter how vivid and apparently unproblematic, could be indistinguishable from another impression that leads us into error (LS 40D). The possibility of error may be remote, but if it is present then the Stoics must admit that the impression in question is not cognitive. This highlights a difference between the skepticism of Arcesilaus and the skepticism we usually encounter in contemporary philosophy. Nowadays skeptics concentrate on the question of knowledge, and wonder whether we can even get to the state where we know something, and perhaps know that we know it. Arcesilaus is applying the brakes at a much earlier stage: he's raising a doubt as to whether we should ever even *believe* something, never mind take ourselves to *know* it. This is clearly a much more fundamental skeptical strategy: when Descartes worries that perhaps his beliefs are fed to him by an evil demon, that does not lead him to think he might need to stop having beliefs. He just worries that the beliefs he has and will continue having may not constitute knowledge.

This move on Arcesilaus' part gains most of its plausibility from the stringent requirements that the Stoics have placed on belief. It is the Stoics, not Arcesilaus, who proposed suspending judgment when the criterion of truth is not satisfied. This leads us into the central question about Arcesilaus, one that will also arise with his successor, Carneades. To what extent were their conclusions merely dialectical, that is, merely offered in the context of arguing against the Stoics? And to what extent were they, paradoxically, beliefs that the Skeptics themselves held? Consider Arcesilaus' argument against Zeno. It shows that the wise man will always suspend judgment. Exactly what a Skeptic should believe. But hang on, a Skeptic shouldn't believe *anything*, should he? And he certainly shouldn't believe that one should have no beliefs, since that would be a contradiction.

Here the dialectical reading can come to the rescue. On this reading, Arcesilaus is not endorsing the view that no one should ever have beliefs, he's only saying that, if we were to adopt the Stoic standard for belief, no one should ever have beliefs. Since he would not himself adopt that Stoic standard, neither would he lay down prohibition on belief as a belief he himself holds. Indeed, what Arcesilaus should do, to be consistent, is suspend judgment about whether the Stoic criterion of truth is the right one. In fact he should also suspend judgment about whether there are indeed cognitive impressions. He himself is not committed on any of these points. He's merely arguing that the Stoics are wrong to commit themselves, by defending such ambitious standards for belief and by insisting that there are cognitive impressions, when in fact all these things are unclear.

It's a matter of controversy whether this is the right way to understand Arcesilaus.[3] It doesn't help that neither he nor Carneades wrote any works, leaving us with only indirect evidence as to their oral teaching. But certainly some interpreters, including the greatest ancient Skeptic, Sextus Empiricus, did not adopt the dialectical reading. He in effect accused the New Academy of "dogmatism," that is, of holding a commitment or doctrine—this is the meaning of the Greek word *dogma*, often used in the context of political decisions or, later, tenets of theology. Of course, Arcesilaus would be a dogmatist of an unusual sort, a negative dogmatist, whose doctrine is precisely that one should have no doctrines. But this was still enough to damn him, in the eyes of Sextus, for being insufficiently skeptical. A thoroughgoing Skepticism would be skeptical even regarding the questions of whether one can have knowledge and whether one should have beliefs.

Of course, that is a difficult position to understand, and we'll have to do some work to wrap our minds around it when we get to Sextus. For now, though, let's look at another problem faced by Arcesilaus, aside from this charge of self-refutation and negative dogmatism. This is the so-called *apraxia*, or "inactivity," objection. According to the objection, the Skeptic cannot do anything at all if he lacks beliefs (LS 69A). Consider, for instance, the action of going to the zoo to see the giraffes.

To leave the house, get on environmentally friendly public transport, and reach the giraffes will require a whole series of beliefs, for instance, that this bus does go to the zoo, that the map does show the location of the giraffe enclosure, and so on. An utter lack of belief seems to doom us to an utter lack of visits to see the giraffes, a prospect none of us would wish to contemplate. And the same argument goes, of course, for any action you care to name.

Arcesilaus dealt with the objection by once again exploiting weapons unwittingly placed into his hands by the Stoics. As we saw with the attacking-tiger example, the Stoics think that the sage will on occasion follow impressions which strike him as reasonable, without necessarily giving these impressions his full assent. Now Arcesilaus himself can pounce, and say that what goes for avoiding tigers will work just as well for visiting giraffes. The Skeptic will take certain things as reasonable, and this will be enough to allow him to act, without ever forming settled beliefs (LS 69B). This response is typical of Arcesilaus, in that it works within the Stoic system he is attacking. Again, it is hard to tell whether he's being dialectical or giving us his own position. If it is his own position, though, it would give him an escape from the previous problem about self-refutation. He can say that he does not actually believe that one should never form beliefs; he's actually not sure about this. Still, given the arguments that undermine any possible criterion of truth, it does strike him as reasonable that one should never form beliefs, so he never does.

So what exactly is the difference between believing something and taking it to be reasonable? Of course that's a problem for Zeno's Stoics too. But it seems more pressing for Arcesilaus than for Zeno, since his whole stance is now turning on the distinction. So it's no surprise that the next head of the Skeptical Academy, Carneades, devoted considerable attention to this question of how the Skeptic's actions are guided. Using different terminology, he said that certain impressions strike us as *pithanon*—the word means "persuasive" or "plausible" (LS 69D).[4] Like Arcesilaus, he suggests that these impressions will be used as a practical guide by the Skeptic. But he went further, observing that the standards we use will differ depending on how high the stakes are. In the normal course of affairs one bit of evidence will suffice. For instance, if I'm looking for the giraffes, I'll just ask another zoo-visitor and follow their directions. But what if it is really important—if, say, I need to be at the giraffe enclosure in five minutes to pay a ransom to the giraffe-nappers who are demanding £1 million for the safe return of Hiawatha, who just happens to be my favorite giraffe? Then I will want to make extra sure.

Similarly, Carneades suggests that our caution will vary in accordance with the importance of the matter at hand, and that in really crucial situations I will not, for instance, merely look several times, but also consider the lighting conditions, whether anyone might be trying to deceive me, and so on. In short, when the chips are down I'll do all the things the Stoic sage would do to make sure he's having a cognitive impression. Only when these tests are passed will I pronounce myself "persuaded." But the arguments against the Stoic position are still taken as decisive. So even in these circumstances I will not take myself to be certain. I will not delude myself into believing that my impressions really are cognitive, meaning that they could not possibly be false. There is always room for doubt.

Carneades presents us with a conundrum. On the one hand, there is this Carneades I've just been describing, who seems happy to allow us to take ourselves to be pretty sure about things for all intents and purposes, even if the Stoic criterion of truth remains unsatisfied. On the other hand, there is the Carneades who showed up in Rome in 155 BC. He was one member of an embassy of philosophers to Rome, sent to plead for the lifting of a fine imposed on the Athenians by the Romans.[5] On that occasion Carneades scandalized his audience by arguing in favor of justice and then on the next day arguing just as persuasively against everything he'd said in the first speech (LS 68M). This kind of logical scorched-earth campaign hadn't been seen since the days of the Sophists. That sound you hear is Plato slapping his forehead with disbelief, as a head of his Academy shows that it is possible to argue with equal plausibility on both sides of the most important issues we face. The real question, of course, is what Carneades wanted the audience to learn from his display.

Even the most intimate associates of Carneades already felt the difficulty of determining his exact view. His follower Clitomachus, who took over as scholarch of the Academy in 127 BC, set forth a dialectical reading like the one we considered for Arcesilaus. Clitomachus frankly admitted that Carneades was impossible to understand fully. This was intended not as a criticism but as an expression of his admiration for Carneades, whose skepticism was of a depth that simply could not be fathomed. Nonetheless, he was confident that Carneades was a thoroughgoing Skeptic who argued for global suspension of belief, and who presented his practical criterion of plausibility only within the context of disputing with the Stoics (LS 69H). But other followers of Carneades, who had also studied at the feet of the master, disagreed. For them, Carneades had indeed been suggesting that we can allow ourselves belief of a sort, assenting to impressions which strike us as plausible, while of course stressing that this kind of belief is always fallible. The leading proponent of this reading was another student of Carneades, Philo of Larissa.[6]

For some Skeptics, Philo's stance was all too moderate. To mark the difference between the hard-headed Skepticism that dispensed with all belief, and the half-hearted Skepticism-lite of Philo, they took up a new figurehead. This new figurehead was also the oldest figurehead available: Pyrrho. Returning to this earliest of the

Skeptics, they rejected the Skeptical Academy as a fall from grace, and initiated the last phase of ancient Skepticism, calling it Pyrrhonism. It was this form of Skepticism that was embraced by Sextus Empiricus in the second century AD. He will finally supply us with a leading Skeptic who wrote extensively, and whose writings are preserved to this day. The subtle defense Sextus provides for the non-doctrine of Pyrrhonian Skepticism ranks among the great achievements of later ancient philosophy, and we'll be discussing it shortly.

But first, we need to stay in the first century BC, and with Philo of Larissa. His importance is to some extent a function of geography. Carneades had visited Rome, but Philo of Larissa actually moved there. He made a huge impression, not least on Cicero, whose own fairly mild-mannered brand of Academic Skepticism is derived chiefly from encountering Philo. Cicero also details for us one more heated rivalry, between Philo and his student Antiochus. Both of them claimed to be members of the Academy, but Antiochus broke with the New Academy and embraced dogmatism, setting out a kind of grand synthesis which found common ground between the Stoics, Plato, and even Aristotle. Antiochus was displeased when Philo, newly arrived in Rome, published books setting out his moderate Skepticism. His rebuttal of those books constituted nothing less than a contest for the soul of the Academy. It was these contentious events that set the stage for Cicero's composition of the *Academica*, and more generally for the philosophical contributions of this famous orator and politician.

RHETORICAL QUESTIONS
CICERO

J ulius Caesar was a man who was used to getting his own way. So when another man, Quintus Ligarius, took sides against Caesar in a war in Africa, he had him hauled into court so that Ligarius could be executed. This seemed a foregone conclusion: Caesar had already seized unchallenged power as "dictator for life" over the Romans. But Caesar had not reckoned with the defense counsel, who was a man of considerable eloquence. The defense counsel launched into a speech in exoneration of Ligarius, which we can still read today. The speech admitted that Ligarius was on the ground in Africa, but argued strenuously that he had done nothing to oppose Caesar's will. As the speech continued, Caesar began to shake with anger, outraged that the outcome was being thrown into doubt by this upstart lawyer. In the end, Ligarius was acquitted. As for Caesar, on this occasion he came, he saw, and he was conquered.[1]

The name of the upstart lawyer was, of course, Marcus Tullius Cicero. He was one of the greatest minds of Rome, in that or any age, and wielded one of its most silver tongues. Cicero was born in 106 BC near Rome, into the equestrian class, but his career was built more on talent than on any exalted family background. He served as both quaestor and consul, and well before his defense of Ligarius he had made a name for himself as the most brilliant legal orator Roman society had to offer. Perhaps the peak of his rhetorical achievements was a set of speeches denouncing a man named Catiline for conspiring to overthrow the Republic. These speeches, and the many other oratorical displays of Cicero that survive today, stand as a monument of good Latin style. For many readers, such as St Augustine, Ciceronian Latin has been more or less synonymous with good Latin. But Cicero was more than an orator and politician—otherwise we would hardly be devoting a chapter to him in this book. He was also a philosopher.

Indeed, without the philosophical writings of Cicero[2] this book would be a lot shorter. Along with Diogenes Laertius, Cicero is the most important source to preserve the ideas of the Stoics, the Epicureans, and the Skeptical Academy. He is also the chief source for several major thinkers of his own time. Cicero's own philosophical stance was the outcome of a critical reflection on the teachings of these thinkers. He tells us that only the weak-minded will adhere to a philosophical position out of devotion to a school, rather than out of this sort of independent reflection. Though his writings on philosophy show that Cicero found much to admire in Stoicism, it was the Skeptical position that won his heart. This is why I am discussing him here, as we continue to follow the developing story of ancient Skepticism.

Cicero lived at just the right time to think hard about the relative merits of the Hellenistic schools. The first century BC was a crucial period for the infusion of Greek ideas into Roman society. A series of wars gave Rome secure dominion over Greece, and during the upheaval of these years many well-educated Greeks sought refuge in the embrace of Rome. One of these was the leading Academic Skeptic, Philo of Larissa, and Cicero studied with him. Cicero was a broad-minded man, though, and also opened his house to a Stoic philosopher named Diodotus. If Rome offered a home away from home to such philosophers as Philo and Diodotus, Athens offered something equally compelling to such Romans as Cicero: it was the home of philosophy. Cicero made the pilgrimage there when he was in his twenties. At Athens he was able to study with Epicurean philosophers, but more crucial for Cicero's intellectual development was the opportunity to study at the feet of Antiochus of Ascalon. We're fortunate that Cicero had this opportunity, because Antiochus seems to have been one of the most interesting thinkers of the first century BC, and without Cicero's testimony we would know very little about him.[3] Antiochus, like Cicero himself, was a disciple of Philo of Larissa. But Cicero reports that Antiochus broke angrily with the teachings of Philo when Antiochus received a copy of books Philo had written in Rome (*Academica* 2.4). Upon reading them, he was stunned, and at first could hardly believe that Philo was really their author. But once he overcame his skepticism, he disowned Philo and challenged him with a diametrically opposed view on the main philosophical issues of the day, and on the history of philosophy itself.

We saw in the previous chapter that Philo was a member of the so-called "New" Academy, who seems to have softened the Skeptical teaching. He held the Academic line against the Stoics, insisting that we can never be sure that our impressions are true. But even if absolute certainty remains out of reach, one can still commit oneself, and follow plausible belief. This was a new kind of Skeptical attitude, which allowed its adherents to assent to their impressions. Philo may even have held that, when we assent to what is plausible and it turns out that we are right, this counts as knowledge, albeit a weaker kind of knowledge than the one envisioned by the Stoics. Suppose your friend asks you to name a kind of ruminant animal apart from the giraffe (your friend has been reading my books and is sick to death of giraffes). You answer, "goats." And you're right: goats are indeed ruminants. Even while being very confident about this, you might admit that you could be wrong—there was that embarrassing incident last month when you identified the spider monkey as an arachnid. Philo says we must be satisfied with such true judgments that leave open the possibility of error. That is as good as it gets, because no one can have total certainty about anything. Not even about whether goats share the exalted company of giraffes and other ruminants, by having four stomachs.

Antiochus was probably not upset by the fact that Philo had no stomach for defending a stronger Skeptical position. Antiochus wanted to adopt an even less Skeptical position. What really got his goat was Philo's claim about their shared philosophical heritage. For Philo, the whole tradition of the Academy was unified. Socrates and Plato had already adopted the stance recommended by the New Academy: embrace what seems most like the truth, while realizing that we lack total certainty. Socrates knew only that he knew nothing, as we know from Plato's dialogues. But this didn't stop him from assenting to many beliefs, for instance, that it is good to pursue wisdom and virtue. As Cicero puts it, "they call the [Skeptical] Academy New, but it seems old to me" (*Academica* 1.12). Against this, Antiochus defended an alternative history. For him, the New Academy had opened a schism in the fundamentally unified philosophy of the ancients.

Antiochus anticipated the direction Platonist philosophy would take in subsequent generations, by adopting a syncretic approach. What I mean by this is that he admired a range of philosophers and philosophical traditions, and carefully harmonized them in a single overall position. He traced his lineage above all to Plato and Aristotle, but also believed that the early Stoics were part of the family. When presenting Antiochus' position, Cicero says that, for him, the Stoics were basically just following the doctrines of the "Old" Platonic Academy and correcting details (*Academica* 1.12). For all of these thinkers, knowledge is possible; knowledge is needed in order to make virtue possible; and virtue guarantees happiness. Without knowledge of what is good, we cannot be good people, and good people are happy people. By focusing especially on these issues of knowledge and on ethical concerns, Antiochus makes a reasonable case for a historical claim that may strike us as preposterous. We certainly do not see Plato, Aristotle, and the Stoics as occupying the same philosophical position. But Antiochus was contrasting these admired figures to the New Academy, who think knowledge is impossible, and to the Epicureans, who think that happiness lies in pleasure and not virtue. By comparison, he saw the differences between Platonism, Aristotelianism, and Stoicism as relatively minor. For instance, he noted that Aristotle rejected the existence of Forms. But he thinks this pales in significance compared to Aristotle's loyalty on the questions of knowledge and virtue.

Now, this chapter is about Cicero, so why do I keep going on about Philo and Antiochus? It isn't only because Cicero is our primary source of information about the dispute. It's also because the dispute was crucial to Cicero's own philosophical viewpoint. After some ruminating of his own, Cicero decided that Philo had the better of the argument. In his own philosophical works he adopts the quintessentially skeptical practice of exploring arguments from all the philosophical schools. He's explicit about following this strategy, saying that he discusses philosophy *in utramque partem*, "on both sides" of every dispute.[4] For instance, Cicero's work *On the Nature of the Gods* pits an Epicurean spokesman and a Stoic spokesman against a New Academic critic, named Cotta. The adherents of the two dogmatic schools are given ample space to defend their respective theological views—indeed, one of the three books of the work is devoted entirely to the exposition of the Stoic theory. But then Cotta demolishes each position, leaving the reader where Cicero too finds himself: in a state of well-considered doubt.

Along the way, of course, we learn valuable information about the Hellenistic schools, and this work *On the Nature of the Gods* remains one of our most important sources for Stoic and Epicurean theology. But Cicero is more than just a source to be mined for information about other thinkers. Even when writing philosophy, Cicero is still a rhetorician, and he frequently insists that good philosophy should be stylistically appealing (as at *Tusculan Disputations* 3.3). He criticizes other contemporary thinkers for their poor style—he seems to have in mind especially Epicurean authors, which is ironic, given that he was a contemporary of the great Epicurean poet Lucretius. By contrast, Cicero greatly admires Plato and Aristotle, not only for their dialectical approach to philosophy but also for their rhetorical craft. Aristotle is praised for his inquiries into rhetoric, and Plato appears repeatedly as a master of language as well as thought. For Cicero, Plato is, as he has a Stoic spokesman put it, "almost a god of philosophers" (*On the Nature of the Gods* 2.12). This point is underscored even when Cicero is praising others, for instance when he says that Aristotle is the best philosopher, apart from the obvious exception of Plato, the greatest of all.

Cicero paid homage to his Greek exemplars not only by discussing their ideas, but also by translating them into Latin. He undertook a Latin translation of Plato's *Timaeus*, though he didn't manage to complete it. His own works are festooned with translations of passages from Greek, especially Plato. Cicero rightly prides himself not only on his facility with Latin, but also on his ability to render Greek accurately and in good style. He frequently draws attention to the difficulty of translating Greek technical terms, and briefly discusses the merits of alternative Latin versions—for instance, he suggests *perturbatio* ("disorder"), rather than a word meaning "disease," to capture the Stoic term *pathos* (*Tusculan Disputations* 4.5). In some cases Cicero's decisions have prevailed down to the current day. For instance, he translates the Greek *poiotetes* into Latin as *qualitates*, and we follow him in translating this word as "qualities" (*Academica* 1.7). Seneca claims that the Latin word *essentia*, the root of our English word "essence," was invented by Cicero to correspond to the Greek *ousia*.[5]

Cicero's love of Greek and his rhetorical prowess were not the only features of his personal history to make themselves felt in his histories of philosophy. In fact, the question of why Cicero wrote so much about philosophy can be answered only by looking a bit more at his life-story. I mentioned at the beginning of this chapter that he was no fan of Julius Caesar, and the feeling was mutual. He was forced to leave Rome under the First Triumvirate, when Rome was ruled by Caesar together with Crassus and Pompey. Cicero was able to return in 57 BC, but his renewed opposition meant that when Caesar assumed the dictatorship, Cicero was effectively excluded from politics. This left him with some time on his hands, for which we can be grateful. Most of Cicero's philosophical works were written in the mid-forties BC, while he was cast into the political wilderness. During this time he was also struck by personal tragedy: his beloved daughter died in childbirth in 45 BC. Thus a key theme of Hellenistic philosophy had a deep resonance for Cicero: can philosophy offer us consolation in the face of suffering?

Skeptical leanings notwithstanding, Cicero answers this question with a fairly resounding "yes" in one of his greatest philosophical writings, the *Tusculan Disputations*. Despite the title, this is not a set of arguments about elephants, but rather a dialogue set in Tusculum, where Cicero owned a villa. (It included two exercise areas, named the Academy and the Lyceum!) The dialogue is between two unnamed characters who are considering philosophical arguments on subjects like the fear of death, whether the sage would ever feel distress, and whether we should attempt to eliminate all emotions. Cicero repeats his officially Academic stance, declaring that he always follows what seems persuasive rather than seeking certainty. But aside from this caveat, he supports a strikingly Stoic viewpoint. Epicurus is praised for saying that all pain can be mastered, but the praise is damningly faint: Cicero adds that it is hard to see how a hedonist can consistently give such advice (*Tusculan Disputations* 2.19). This is typical of his attitude towards the Epicureans, and also the Aristotelians. Rather disappointingly, Cicero seems to follow the line of other Hellenistic schools in reducing Aristotelian ethics to the claim that external goods, like wealth and health, are intrinsically valuable. Cicero has little patience with this, seeing it as soft-minded.

It is unsurprising, then, that he prefers the Stoics, whom he sees as the most tough-minded philosophers and thus as the rightful heirs of the ethical teachings of Socrates and Plato. Like them, the Stoics insist that perfect virtue and wisdom guarantee happiness. Cicero finds this idea to be persuasive, if not certain, and also a potential source of great comfort. He thus agrees with the Stoics that philosophy is the art of healing the soul, as medicine is the art of healing the body (*Tusculan Disputations* 3.3). This isn't to say that he hesitates to borrow ideas from schools other than the Stoics. Even the Cyrenaics are commended for their useful advice about anticipating pain so that the pain is less hard to bear when it arrives (3.15). Nor are Cicero's favorite Hellenistic dogmatists, the Stoics, above criticism. He complains about their pedantry on more than one occasion, and finds the "all or nothing" ethical theory of the early Stoics too simplistic. In a wonderful rhetorical turn, he writes: "They claim that all fools are insane, just as all mud smells bad. But not always; stir it up, and you'll get a whiff. Likewise, the man given to anger is not always angry. Rile him, and you will see him in fury" (4.24). Nonetheless, in the *Tusculans* Cicero could often pass for a Stoic himself, as when he argues that emotions like anger have no place in the good life (4.19). In such passages, Cicero evokes the somewhat later Stoic Seneca, rather than earlier Academic Skeptics like Arcesilaus.

Cicero seems to take sides in other philosophical disputes too. I've already mentioned his work *On the Nature of the Gods*. It is pretty rude about the Epicureans, but ends with a qualified endorsement of Stoic theology: it "seems to be a closer likeness of truth" (3.40). Another Stoic-inspired work is called *De Officiis*—roughly, *On Befitting Actions*, since Cicero chose the Latin word *officium* to translate the Greek *kathekon*. As you'll remember, Stoics used this word to refer to befitting actions performed by non-sages. Cicero's treatise on the topic draws extensively on the teachings of the Stoic philosopher Panaetius, with whom he had a chance to study when he visited the city of Rhodes. So it was thanks to Cicero that these philosophical teachings from Rhodes led to Rome.

Yet another work that argues positively for various philosophical claims is an early treatise with the familiar-sounding title *De Re Publica*. Although there is clearly an allusion to Plato's *Republic* here, we should also not miss the resonance with the Roman Republic itself. Cicero was a lifelong advocate of the traditional Roman model, according to which power is placed in the hands of an aristocratic legislative body, the Senate. He followed Plato and Aristotle in distrusting democracy, because the people are not likely to deliberate effectively. But he was equally opposed to the sort of autocratic rule exercised by Caesar. For Cicero, a legitimate state gets its legitimacy from the fact that it rules in the interests of the people, who have transferred rights and freedom to the aristocratic legislatures for the sake of furthering these interests.[6] Incidentally, like Plato's *Republic*, Cicero's work ends with a kind of mythic narrative that integrates cosmology into the fabric of a treatise on politics. In Cicero's version, the famous Roman general Scipio Africanus appears to his grandson in a dream vision. This work was later the subject of an influential commentary by an author named Macrobius, whom we'll meet at the end of this book.

On the whole, then, Cicero sets forth a good deal of positive philosophical doctrine, which is not exactly what you'd expect from a self-confessed Academic. Though there have been suspicions that Cicero's devotion to the Academic viewpoint wavered, I think we should rather remember that he was a follower of Philo of Larissa. Philo encourages us to follow what is plausible or persuasive, and this is what Cicero does. He often says explicitly, when preferring one view to another, that it is being preferred only as more persuasive and not as definitely true. Hence that last, purposefully non-committal line of his work on the gods, which says not that the Stoic view is true, but that it seems to Cicero a closer *likeness* of truth.

Of course, Cicero was able to make persuasive doctrines even more persuasive by setting them forth in his highly crafted Latin. Indeed, if we had to name Cicero's chief philosophical contribution, it would be his role in ushering Greek philosophical ideas into Latin. He names this himself, remarking in the *Tusculan Disputations* (2.2) that in his works, philosophy is being born in the Latin tongue. Philo's brand of Academic Skepticism would not outlive Cicero, its most famous exponent. Cicero's welcoming of Greek philosophy into Latin prose was a far more lasting achievement. No less an author than Augustine will look back to Cicero as a major source, even discussing the topic of Skepticism in a title called *Contra Academicos*, that is, *Against the Academics*. We'll be getting to Augustine much later in this book. For now, we have one last Skeptic to consider—and in this case, I've saved the best for last.

HEALTHY SKEPTICISM
SEXTUS EMPIRICUS

People have a lot of respect for doctors. Along with philosophy professors, they rank among the most admired members of our society. We turn to them in our hour of need, seeking not just basic competence, but total commitment, confidence, and self-assurance. You do not want to find hesitancy and uncertainty lurking in the facial expression of your doctor, any more than you want to hear it in the voice of the pilot making announcements as your plane goes through turbulence. So it's ironic that the greatest of all the ancient skeptics was a doctor. He is known to us as Sextus Empiricus. The "Empiricus" part refers to his membership in the Empiricist school of medicine, a fact to which I will return at the end of this chapter.

Apart from that, we know little about him. Even his dates are, appropriately enough, uncertain, but he is thought to have lived in the second century AD. That puts him a couple of centuries later than the last representatives of Skepticism we've considered—the followers of Carneades, like Philo of Larissa, and of course Cicero, lived in the first century BC. Their age was one of transition. The center of philosophical activity was moving from war-torn Athens to Rome, the center of political power moving from the hands of the Senate to those of a single ruler— Julius Caesar as dictator, followed by Augustus as *princeps*, and a line of emperors after that, including, of course, Marcus Aurelius, who like Sextus lived in the second century. At this time Aristotelianism and Platonism are beginning to make a comeback. Soon they will supplant the Hellenistic schools, Neoplatonism will take center-stage, absorbing a lot of Aristotle, some Stoicism, not very much at all from Epicureanism, and little more from the Skeptics.

Thus Sextus was, no doubt unwittingly, writing the last chapter of Skepticism when he set out the arguments of his school. But he would not have let this bother him. For Sextus had mastered the art of not being bothered by anything. *Ataraxia* had been associated with Skepticism since Pyrrho. Pyrrho lived some 500 years before Sextus, but Sextus took him as a role-model and as the founder of the skeptical outlook, which he called "Pyrrhonism." His most frequently read work is a summary of the teaching, the *Outlines of Pyrrhonism*. We have several other treatises which approach specific philosophical and scientific topics from a skeptical point of view. These may all have belonged originally to a single treatise. Because the Skeptical approach more or less died out with Sextus, his writings were not very influential in subsequent centuries. Only when they were rediscovered in the sixteenth century did they cause a sensation, inspiring pro- and anti-skeptical philosophical discussions in early modern philosophers ranging from Gassendi to Hume.

Sextus did not originate the label of "Pyrrhonism." For that we need to go back to the first century BC. Philo of Larissa endorsed a moderate or mitigated skepticism, which recommended assenting to beliefs in the full realization that such assent is fallible. Like radicals forming a new political party after their colleagues have moved towards the center ground, some Skeptics found this moderate stance insufficiently, well, skeptical. The leading critic was Aenesidemus, who complained that disputes among members of the Academy boiled down to "Stoics fighting with Stoics" (LS 71C). The new party he founded was the Pyrrhonists, and its platform was the banishment of belief. The long-dead Pyrrho was taken as a namesake because he seemed to represent this more uncompromising sort of Skepticism. This was "back to basics" rhetoric, attempting to undo the softening concessions made by the Skeptical Academy.

Of course the Pyrrhonists, like the Skeptical Academy, would spend a good deal of effort trying to undermine dogmatic views like those of the Stoics. But Aenesidemus also went on the offensive, devising one of the most characteristic features of Pyrrhonian skepticism: the modes (LS 72).[1] A quick way to describe the modes would be to say that they are arguments to show that everything must remain unclear and uncertain. But that wouldn't be quite right. Sextus is clear that such a sweeping claim would in itself be a kind of doctrine, albeit a negative one, so it would count as dogmatism (1.14).[2] Rather, the modes are like a toolkit for raising doubts concerning some given belief, or a whole type of beliefs. I don't have time to go through all ten modes, but I'll look at a few to give you an idea.

The first mode refers to animals, and points out that since animals vary widely in terms of their physical makeup, they are likely to perceive things in very different ways. For instance, some kinds of insect find perfume repellent, which undermines the belief that it smells pleasant. While presenting this mode Sextus argues against rejecting the impressions of animals. He suggests that dogs, for instance, not only have sharper sense-perceptions than we do, but are also capable of reasoning (1.66)—an unusual idea in the context of ancient philosophy, but one we'll be meeting again later in this book when we get to Porphyry. Other modes turn on the variation between people—for instance, a healthy person may find honey sweet while an ill person will think it bitter—or between different groups of people. Sextus delights in mentioning foreign cultural attitudes as a way of undermining his readers' ethical beliefs. Memorably, he claims that in India people have sex in public (1.148).

Now of course, neither Aenesidemus nor Sextus was trying to show that perfume really is repellent, or that it is okay to have sex in public. Rather, the point is that with these modes one can raise a doubt concerning just about any belief. This step is crucial, because unless an initial doubt can be raised, the Skeptic's dogmatist opponents will say that there is no reason to suspend judgment. Now, just because a doubt is raised doesn't mean we will immediately suspend judgment. The ten modes are only an initial tool, which must be complemented by a further set of five modes, attributed by Diogenes Laertius to another Skeptic, named Agrippa (1.164–77).[3] These modes are worth looking at carefully, because they form a genuinely formidable challenge to the possibility of rational belief.

The five modes pick up where the ten modes left off: the first of the five is the mode of Dispute, meaning that we point out a disagreement about whatever belief we are considering. Bees don't like perfume, for instance, and we do. The Stoics think pleasure is valueless, the Epicureans see it as the good. Most of us think motion exists, but Parmenides denies it. To this we can add the fourth mode, of Relativity: that perceptions and judgments are relative to those who make them. These two modes basically do the same work as Aenesidemus' ten modes, by raising an initial doubt. The remaining three modes move in for the kill. Now that a doubt has been raised, how can either party to the dispute hope to settle it? Not by simply insisting that they are right. That would be begging the question, merely hypothesizing that their side of the argument is the correct one. This kind of arbitrary claim is eliminated by the so-called mode of Hypothesis. Suppose, for instance, that we are arguing over who is the greatest silent movie comedian, Buster Keaton or Charlie Chaplin. If you say Chaplin, but refuse to give me any reasons for your view, this mode shows why I should not be convinced.

But suppose you do give reasons. You might say, for instance, that Chaplin is more famous than Keaton. But why should I agree that being more famous means being greater? You might just insist without further rationale that fame decides the issue, but this too is debatable. So you might try to defend your appeal to Chaplin's fame on the basis of a further claim, for instance, that that many people can't be wrong. But the problem is already obvious: this new claim will also be open to dispute. As the mode of Regress says, there is no point appealing to an unending string of debatable points. At some point, to block off further debate, you'll have to just stop giving further reasons. At that point you'll just be insisting that you're right—which we already saw will not work. The only other option is to argue in a circle, which brings us to the final mode, the Reciprocal mode. If you say that Chaplin is greater because he's more famous, and more famous because he's greater, then you've made no case at all, you've just led me around in a circle.

The upshot of this is twofold. First, as far as we can tell, every belief is debatable. Second, all disputes seem to be balanced, with neither party able to strike a knockout blow against the other. Things are left in the condition Sextus calls *isotheneia*, in other words, a counterbalancing of views, which seems incapable of resolution (1.8). It's important to note that Sextus really means the dispute is *balanced*. It isn't that one side of the argument seems more persuasive yet there is some doubt remaining. That would leave open the moderate skeptical solution of endorsing the more persuasive side while being aware that one lacks certainty. Rather, the modes are meant to show that every conceivable topic of belief involves a dispute where neither side has an advantage over the other. We suspend judgment because of the stalemate that arises once one has applied the modes.

This skeptical strategy can be applied in a very general way or a very specific way. We can apply it not just to silent comedians or the taste of honey, but also sense-perceptions in general. That seems to be the drift of Aenesidemus' first mode, since it suggests that animals have systematically different sense-experiences. Sextus tries to get the same result by opposing the senses to the mind itself (1.170, 2.48–76). Previous philosophers, like Democritus and Epicurus, had worried about the possibility that sensation and the mind could disagree—for instance, if the mind tells us things are made of atoms and the senses do not. Sextus exploits this, pointing out that this fundamental dispute can immediately cast doubt on all our perceptions and all our thoughts. By way of example, he cites Anaxagoras (1.33), who said that the mind knows that snow is made of water. Since water is black, the senses are refuted by the mind, which realizes that snow is in fact black and not white.

It's at this point that *ataraxia* enters the picture. We began investigating because we were bothered by the status of some belief. We knew that it was disputable, and wanted to discover the truth of the matter. It bothered us, perhaps, not to be able to prove that snow is white, that perfume is pleasant, that having sex in public is very uncool. You might think that the result of the skeptical process would be further frustration. But the Pyrrhonists claim that, to the contrary, the suspension of judgment yields freedom from disturbance—the very goal we began with, achieved through means we did not expect. Sextus compares this to the case of a painter who was trying to render the foam on the mouth of an exhausted horse. The painter tried repeatedly to get the effect he wanted, failing each time. Finally he gave up and threw his sponge at the painting in despair. Lo and behold, the sponge left behind a perfect image of foam around the horse's mouth (1.28). It's a nice image, but in one respect misleading: whereas the painter has given up in frustration, the Skeptic, at least according to Sextus, has not given up investigating. Remember that the word "skeptic" means "inquirer." True to this etymology, Sextus says that whereas the Dogmatists have their doctrines, and the Skeptical Academy has decided that inquiry is fruitless, he and his fellow Pyrrhonists are the ones who are still searching (1.3). Their undisturbed state is a relaxation that follows upon suspension of judgment. Despite the modes, it most certainly does not result from the discovery that all disputes are irrevocably undecidable. Again, that would be a dogma, a settled belief or doctrine, an indulgence a Pyrrhonian will never allow himself.

This brings us to the most difficult aspect of Sextus' Skepticism: the question of whether he can really avoid having beliefs, and whether he really wishes to do so. As with Pyrrho and the Skeptical Academy, there are two reasons to think Sextus may need to accept some form of assent or belief. First, there is his commitment to Skepticism itself. Doesn't Sextus, for instance, believe that disputes are equally balanced, that it is right to suspend judgment, that *ataraxia* results from suspension of judgment? Second, there is the objection that the Skeptic will need beliefs just to get through life. Sextus solves both problems in the same way: he says that the Pyrrhonian Skeptic always suspends belief, but cannot help having things appear to him in a certain way. Thus, for instance, it seems to him that a given dispute is equally balanced, just as it seems to him that honey is sweet. The Skeptic does not commit himself to any truth regarding these matters. But he does follow appearances (1.13). This is why he spreads honey on his toast, finds a private room when he's feeling romantic, and suspends judgment after applying the modes.

Is that just moderate Skepticism by another name? What is the difference between following an appearance and forming a belief? Isn't Sextus recommending a weak form of assent, as Philo of Larissa had done? He would insist otherwise. For one thing, Sextus promises that the Skeptic remains genuinely open-minded about every issue he considers. He does not judge it more persuasive or convincing that the honey is sweet—he has absolutely no view on that matter whatsoever, because he has suspended judgment. If he spreads honey and not motor oil on his toast, this is done out of a passive surrender to the way things appear, rather than by actively forming a belief or actively assenting to the appearance. The Skeptic yields to the appearances, letting them guide him through the world. On the other hand, he remains detached from these appearances so far as their truth is concerned, refusing to commit himself even to the relative likelihood or plausibility of each appearance.

This applies also to the Skeptical arguments themselves. Sextus compares them to a purgative drug, which is evacuated from the body along with whatever the drug is meant to purge (2.188). Thus, for instance, the Skeptic is not committed to the claim that there is no criterion of truth, or that the modes of Agrippa show that no dispute can be resolved. Rather, the Skeptics' arguments merely make it appear to him that disputes are unresolved, and he acquiesces in this result. When the Skeptic says, for instance, that things seem to be no more one way than another way, Sextus describes this as an announcement or report of how things strike the Skeptic. It is not a statement of what is true about these things, but rather a kind of autobiographical observation: I looked into this matter, and things seemed to be unresolved.

At least on the interpretation I've just given, then, Sextus does try to avoid belief and assent entirely. I should admit that there are rival interpretations.[4] For instance, it has been suggested that Sextus must admit to having beliefs at least about how things seem to him. He would not believe that Buster Keaton is a genius or that honey is sweet, but would believe that Keaton *seems* to him to be a genius and that honey *appears* sweet. After all, Sextus himself must be an authoritative judge of how things seem to him; there's no room for doubt here. Another proposal would land Sextus with an even wider range of beliefs. On this interpretation, the Pyrrhonian Skeptic is not applying skepticism to all topics, but only the technical issues considered by other philosophers. Thus, for instance, he would believe that honey is sweet, but not believe that it is in the nature of honey to be sweet, since natures are something posited by philosophers rather than normal people.

I myself don't adopt that reading. I think it presupposes a sharp division between philosophical and everyday beliefs that is simply not recognized by Sextus—or, for that matter, by other ancient philosophers. Still, Sextus does present himself as being on the side of the common man. The Skeptic's passivity in the face of impressions means that he'll just go along with the way things seem, and thus lead an outwardly normal life. This will include, for instance, the prevailing cultural norms. If the Pyrrhonian lives in India, he'll cheerfully have sex in public; if in Greece, he'll go to the temple to sacrifice to the gods, even though of course he suspends judgment about whether gods exist. He will also follow appearances that arise by nature. For instance, he will eat when he feels hungry and something seems to him edible, and so on. And he will even follow the practices of technical skills, going through the motions of being a blacksmith or, indeed, a doctor, but always without belief.

At the beginning of this chapter I said that it was ironic that Sextus, the greatest of Skeptics, was a doctor, given that we look to doctors for certainty and confidence.

But here, in good Pyrrhonian spirit, is a countervailing thought. Medicine is an inexact art, and rarely provides certainty. This is true still today, but ancient medicine was of course an even more uncertain enterprise. Good doctors then knew their limits. They emphasized that medicine deals in probabilities, that its rules apply only inexactly to different patients with all their variety, and so on. From this point of view, it may seem appropriate that Sextus was a doctor. It's also appropriate that he presents Skepticism as a kind of therapy or cure. Like Epicureanism, Sextus' philosophy is a means of dispelling disturbance. Someone who is not bothered by a topic of inquiry has no need to embark upon the Skeptic path. Hence Sextus' comparison of the skeptical arguments to purgative drugs. Skeptics often pile up arguments on both sides of a dispute without any apparent regard to the strength of those arguments. The aim is to cure by leading the audience to suspend belief and achieve *ataraxia*. For some audiences, a bad argument can be just as effective as a good one, and the Skeptic chooses the effective arguments as a doctor would choose a drug for the patient before him.

Still, one can't help but find a tension between Sextus' philosophy and his medical profession. Medicine may deal in probabilities, but as we've seen, Sextus would not assent even to what seems probable. As Sextus himself notes, there was a school of ancient doctors who seemed fairly skeptical—they were called the Methodists, and their treatment followed a simple set of appearances. But Sextus was not a Methodist, he was an Empiricist, that is, a member of a medical tradition which laid great emphasis on past observation while shunning theories about underlying causes, like those devised by the so-called Rationalist school. Next, we'll turn to these schools and consider the philosophical interest of their medical theories. I won't, however, try to solve the puzzle of how Sextus could have been both an Empiricist doctor and a Skeptic—given that he himself says Empiricism does not quite fit with Skepticism (1.236). After all, what could be more appropriate than our ending this chapter in a state of puzzlement?

19

THE JOY OF SECTS
ANCIENT MEDICINE AND
PHILOSOPHY

The ancient Egyptian practice of mummification was a lengthy and complex one, which took many weeks. The first step in the process was, naturally, making extra sure the person to be mummified was dead. Then the process of embalming began, which meant removing the body's internal organs. The abdomen would be emptied through an incision, while the brain was extracted through the nose. Afterwards, these organs would be wrapped in bandages and popped into jars to be placed in the tomb with the mummified body. Yuck, right? The ancient Greeks would have said so too. In classical Greek civilization there was a firm taboo against the dissection of human bodies. Thus Aristotle, for instance, did not extend his program of anatomical investigations past fish and other animals to include humans. Of course, battlefield injuries and so on occasionally provided a glimpse into the secret recesses of human bodies, but Greek science included no systematic investigation of human anatomy.

Until, that is, the third century BC. At about 300 BC, Ptolemy I chose Alexandria as the site for an ambitious project: a Library, which would gather together all the writings that could be found on all topics, and a so-called "Museum." The name refers to the Muses, in whose honor and with whose guidance activities in the Museum would be conducted. Scholars and scientists would receive free lodging in the Museum, along with a place to do research, to collaborate and investigate. Alexandria thus became a center for intellectual inquiry, and it remained so until late antiquity. It was here, perhaps in the Museum itself, that the first anatomical dissections of human bodies were carried out. We have no texts reporting on these dissections at first hand, but from later authors we know that the two main anatomists were named Herophilus and Erasistratus. It's an interesting question why these two boldly cut where no one had cut before. Certainly the protection of the Ptolemies themselves was a factor, and it may be that organ removal in Egyptian funeral practices provided a precedent. If you can have your loved one's brain pulled out through their nostrils for the sake of a religious burial, it is perhaps less unthinkable to dismantle strangers in the name of science. But Herophilus and Erasistratus were culturally Hellenic, not Egyptian, and they would certainly not have been involved in any such local religious practices. Indeed, there is some ancient evidence that they left out that crucial first step in the mummification process: the part where you make extra sure the person is dead. Later authors tell us that these Alexandrian anatomists dissected criminals who had been condemned to death while they were still alive.[1]

Whether or not this is true, there's no doubt that the doctors of Alexandria took a great leap forward in the understanding of the human body, and of medicine as a whole.[2] Perhaps the most dramatic advance was the discovery of the nervous system, and realization that this system is distinct from the system of blood-vessels. This showed that there are two major networks spread through the human body, one branching from the brain and spinal cord, the other branching from the heart. And that raised questions of far-reaching, and indeed philosophical, importance: how do these systems relate to other phenomena, like breathing and the motion of the muscles? What did these discoveries mean for our conception of human nature itself? If we have an immaterial soul, could we now give a more detailed account relating soul to these physical structures? Or should the human body be understood as a bewilderingly complex machine? After all, it has parts that function like everyday instruments already used by the ancients. The lungs, as Erasistratus pointed out, could be compared to a blacksmith's bellows, while the liver and bladder seem to function like filters or strainers.[3]

The discoveries at Alexandria thus posed a challenge to philosophers, who would need to accommodate the new anatomy within the philosophical school traditions they followed. But of course, a conversation between medicine and philosophy had already been going on for centuries. Plato already mentions Hippocrates (at *Protagoras* 311b–c), whose supposed writings incidentally were probably gathered for the first time at the Library of Alexandria. Though they are often neglected by historians of philosophy, the Hippocratic works are themselves of great philosophical interest.[4] Plato and Aristotle may not have gone in for human dissection, but both had things to say about human anatomy and other medical topics. The influence went the other way also. Aristotle in particular made a great impact on medical authors. For instance, Diocles of Carystus was a near-contemporary of Aristotle who emphasized the importance of the four humors: blood, phlegm, bile, and black bile. Following on suggestions in the Hippocratic corpus, Diocles understood health as a balance of these humors.[5] While we don't find this elaborate humoral theory in Aristotle himself, he alludes to similar ideas, for example when he describes people of a certain character as "melancholic" (the word comes from the Greek for "black bile").

Another figure influenced by Aristotle was Praxagoras, who provides a link to our Alexandrian investigators because he was the teacher of Herophilus. He made an important, though incorrect, contribution to anatomy by defending a theory about the blood-vessels and how they relate to respiration. For Praxagoras, the veins are full of blood, but the arteries are filled with breath—in Greek, *pneuma*.[6] This is still the position we find in Erasistratus, and to some extent it goes back to Aristotle, who had emphasized *pneuma* as a kind of physical life-force that pervades and sustains the body. Even in later authors like Galen, who realize that the arteries contain blood just like the veins, *pneuma* remains a vital substance—in every sense of the word "vital." It becomes standard to assume that the nerves are allowing us to control our bodies through *pneuma* that passes along hollow channels within the nerves.

Of course, to get to that theory the Greeks needed to discover nerves in the first place. Particularly important in this story is Herophilus, whose bad record regarding the humane treatment of criminals is balanced by his contributions to medical research. How he stands overall is perhaps a question we should set aside for a few years, until we reach John Stuart Mill's utilitarianism in a future volume. It was he (Herophilus, not Mill) who distinguished between the sensory and motor nervous systems. His work survives in the very terminology of modern anatomy: for instance, he christened one part of our body the "pineal" gland because of its resemblance to a pine-cone.[7] Both he and his master Praxagoras also pioneered in medical diagnosis, by laying great emphasis on the pulse. Much later, in the Roman Empire, Galen still valued the pulse as one of the most important diagnostic indicators. Also important is the fact that Herophilus wrote on women's medicine, in a treatise describing what makes someone a good midwife. Ancient medicine is one of the richest traditions for classical discussions of women, and again, we see much later figures like Galen writing extensively on gynecology.

Of course, anatomy and gynecology were only two strands in the ancient medical tradition. In the Hellenistic period we also see authors contributing to pharmacology, by transmitting lists of naturally occuring substances and recipes. These form the basis for many centuries of writing about drugs. There's another connection here to the Aristotelians, since drugs were often made of plants, and Aristotle's student Theophrastus literally wrote the book on that subject. Also important throughout classical medicine was the idea that doctors should not only heal the sick and wounded, but help the healthy to stay healthy, by prescribing the right diet and exercise regime. All of which raises a pressing question: whether the goal is healing the sick or preserving health, how should doctors go about discovering the right therapies? This question provoked one of the most interesting ancient debates in the philosophy of science. Different doctors had very different ideas about how we make progress in our knowledge of medicine, and these ideas often interacted with and were inspired by more general philosophical discussions of knowledge.

We know about these debates largely thanks to a figure I've mentioned several times in this chapter: Galen. He lived in the second century AD, quite a bit later than the early scientists of Alexandria. But he provides us with at least one thing that figures like Erasistratus and Herophilus do not offer: extensively surviving writings about medicine. And when I say "extensive," I mean it. You could start reading Galen right now and not finish until you are ready to be mummified yourself. He is the ancient Greek writer for whom we have the largest surviving body of work, despite the fact that a number of his writings have been lost. He was astoundingly prolific, and is the source for most of what we know about pre-Galenic medicine. As with Aristotle, who is a similarly important source for the Pre-Socratics, this is something of a mixed blessing, in that both Galen and Aristotle hardly ever report earlier thinkers' ideas without trying to score some point of their own. This makes their testimony unreliable and biased, but no less valuable, given that it is sometimes the only information we have.

One of the debates that fascinated Galen was this one I have just mentioned, concerning what one might call "medical epistemology": how is it that doctors discover their treatments? In several works on this subject, Galen describes three major so-called "sects," the Rationalists, the Empiricists, and the Methodists.[8] We have already met one Empiricist in the shape of Sextus. He was roughly contemporary with Galen. But the Empiricist sect went back much further than either of them. It was founded in the mid-third century BC by a student of Herophilus named Philinus, who was followed by another doctor, Serapion. As their name implies, these Empiricists believed that the source of our medical knowledge is experience—in Greek, *empeiria*. Though it may seem obvious that experience should play an important role in developing medical theories, the Empiricists put the point in a way that was controversial indeed. They claimed that we need *only* use experience, and that in fact no theory is required (*On the Sects*, ch. 1).

Opposed to them were the so-called Rationalists, sometimes referred to as Dogmatists. They did not necessarily reject the importance of experience entirely, but insisted that any doctor worthy of the title would also have an understanding of the underlying causes of illness and health. The humoral account already mentioned would be a classic case of a Rationalist theory. As we'll see in the next chapter the disease melancholy would be explained by an excess of black bile, which could be treated by combating that imbalance. Since black bile is cold, one might apply warming drugs in hopes of a cure. At first blush, it seems that the Rationalists and Empiricists would thus have offered very different treatments. But Galen explicitly says that they did not. Rather, they would prescribe the same drugs and other treatments, recommend the same kind of diet, and so on (*On the Sects*, ch. 4). The disagreement rather concerns method and justification. The Empiricists would recommend the same drug as the Rationalists, not because it is warming and thus counterbalances the cold of black bile, but simply because in their experience people who presented these sorts of symptoms tended to recover after ingesting this drug.

So whereas the Rationalists point to "hidden" causes and underlying principles, the Empiricists stick to what is readily observable or, as they put it, "evident." They try to match symptoms that are evident to the senses with remedies that have been observed to relieve those symptoms in the past. The Rationalists complain that it is hard to see, in that case, how anyone could ever make any progress in medicine. In fact, there seems to be a paradox lurking here: we are just following what our predecessors did, but how did they arrive at the remedies they found effective? The Empiricists offered several answers to this question. For one thing, useful therapies can be discovered by good luck. Also, one may have a sudden inspiration or hunch about something that could work, and try it out. If it is successful, it can be tried again in the future and may ultimately prove itself a reliable therapy. Finally, the Empiricists speak of a method they call "transition to the similar" (*On the Sects*, ch. 2). For instance, we may happen to observe that it helps to apply cold to a thigh which is red and swollen, and then think to apply cold to a red and swollen arm.

The Empiricists' disdain for Rationalist theories may seem, from our perspective, rather well founded. After all, Rationalist explanations such as the humoral theory were not in fact true. On the other hand, the Empiricists rejected much of what we would recognize as good scientific practice. For instance, they denied the need for anatomical research, repeating their mantra that one should attend to what is evident—which does not include things hidden inside the body. Rather optimistically, they suggested that anything useful to be learned about anatomy had probably already been discovered.[9] We now think of natural sciences like medicine as "empirical," but this first group of thinkers to use the name "Empiricists" were not interested in discovering underlying causes, as we assume science should do. Indeed, there's a family resemblance between medical Empiricism and ancient Skepticism— Galen compares the Empiricists to the original Skeptic Pyrrho, and I don't need to repeat yet again that Sextus was an Empiricist doctor. For the same reasons, the Empiricists stand in contrast to the pioneers of Alexandria. For instance, Erasistratus once weighed a bird, stopped feeding it for some time, then weighed it again along with the excrement it had produced in the meantime. He found that this total weight at the end was less than the bird's original weight, showing that some matter had been lost through invisible emanations from the bird's body.[10] This was careful observation, but in the service of a Rationalist theory about causes.

Galen agreed with Erasistratus and the Rationalists that a good doctor should understand the underlying causes of things. For Galen, this often meant attending to the purposes of nature. He followed Aristotle in believing that natural things like bodily organs have goal-directed functions. In a lengthy work called *On Natural Faculties*, Galen argued against Erasistratus that bodily organs do not work like mechanical parts—filters, bellows, and pumps—but have innate powers, for instance the power to digest food or expel waste. Another treatise, *On the Usefulness of the Parts*, extols the well-designed functioning of all bodily organs.[11] When we study the hidden causes of health and disease, Galen argued, we are uncovering the exquisite design of nature itself—for him, nature is itself a sort of craftsman, and in this respect is like the divine craftsman or "Demiurge" described by his hero Plato in the dialogue *Timaeus*. Galen also accepts other distinctively Rationalist ideas, for instance, the humoral theory, never missing a chance to remind us that this theory goes back to his other hero, Hippocrates.

On the other hand, Galen wants to emphasize that he is not simply a Rationalist. A good doctor must also pay close attention to experience, both the findings of others and what one can discover for oneself. Thus, he suggests that the best method is a kind of fusion of the Rationalist and Empiricist approaches. By contrast, he finds nothing to value in a third sect of doctors, the Methodists (*On the Sects*, ch. 6). We're particularly unfortunate in being so dependent on Galen for our knowledge of this sect. He can barely mention the Methodists without resorting immediately to mockery and invective, so his evidence is even more biased than usual. Still, it is clear that the method of the Methodists did make a difference with respect to their actual medical practice. To understand why, we need to turn to the grandfather of this third sect, Asclepiades. He came to Rome from his home Bithynia, in modern-day Turkey, in the late second century BC. Like Greek philosophers who turned up in Rome at about this time, he had a great impact. An admirer of Asclepiades was a court doctor under Augustus, for instance.[12] His medical theory is reminiscent of ancient atomism and resonates with Epicurean descriptions of the human body, such as we find in Lucretius. For Asclepiades, the body is made up of tiny particles. Disease results when corpuscles cluster in such a way as to block appropriate motions in the body, or scatter so that things flow too freely. Other authors followed Asclepiades in thinking that this theory was preferable to the four-humor idea of the Hippocratic and Aristotelian traditions. In particular, two figures of the first century BC, Themison and Thessalus, adopted the ideas of Asclepiades in a radically simplified form. This was Methodism.

According to the Methodists, all bodily disorders come about because of one of three conditions: either a blockage, a flux, or a mixture of blockage and flux. They identified a limited number of certain so-called "commonalities," specific types of blockages or fluxes that were revealed by evident signs, like inflammation or a leaking of fluid like pus or phlegm. Because the range of commonalities they recognized was relatively small, they thought it was easy to remember both them and the appropriate remedy in each case. Galen is outraged to report that the Methodists believed anyone can learn to be a doctor in just a few months. Reversing a famous Hippocratic aphorism, they declared that "life is long, but the art is short" (*On the Sects*, ch. 6). One of the things that most annoys Galen about Methodism is their refusal to offer medical therapies that were tailored to each patient. Galen was, after all, a doctor for the rich and powerful—I've mentioned previously that he attended Marcus Aurelius and his son—and part of his professional self-image was that his patients would receive a kind of bespoke treatment, one just right for their bodily condition, their location, the season of the year, and so on. This is another idea he finds in Hippocrates, in such texts as *Airs, Waters, Places*, which studies the effect of one's environment on one's health. This notion was embraced by the Rationalists and even the Empiricists, who would have taken account of a patient's circumstances in considering which previous experiences would be relevant to them. Only the Methodists had neither time for nor interest in such niceties.

Perhaps the everyday medicine dispensed on the streets and in the houses of Roman society was more like what the Methodists offered than what Galen could promise. But Galen would triumph as far as the future of medical literature was concerned. One reason his works are so voluminously preserved is that he was so cherished by later doctors. Galen was almost synonymous with medicine in the medieval Greek, Latin, and Arabic traditions, like Aristotle with philosophy. And for good reason. Galen not only fused together the methods of the various sects into a more sophisticated hybrid, but drew connections between medicine and philosophy in a way that was unprecedented. He was also a master of medical techniques such as pharmacology, surgery, and dissection. These skills enabled him to prove once and for all that the Stoics and Aristotelians were wrong: our soul's ruling faculty is not in the heart, but in the brain. So how did he do this, and where exactly does he fit in the ancient philosophical tradition? We'll find out in the next chapter.

THE BEST DOCTOR IS A PHILOSOPHER
GALEN

We've considered method, now let's turn to madness. In his voluminous writings, Galen has much to say about psychological disorders. He mentions, for instance, a man who believed he was made of pottery, and was afraid of touching other people lest he be shattered. Another sufferer obsessed about the prospect that Atlas might grow weary of holding the world and let it fall (*On the Affected Parts*, K 8.190).[1] Galen would explain such events in terms of the humoral theory of previous doctors like Diocles and (on Galen's interpretation) Hippocrates himself. In this case he blames the psychological problem on an imbalance of black bile in the body. Such an imbalance can lead to what ancient authors call "melancholy," from the Greek *melas* (black) and *khole* (bile). Galen also tells us what part of the body is especially relevant in such disturbances of reason: the head, and more specifically the brain. The delusions result when smoky exhalations rise to the head from the black bile building up in an inflamed stomach.

Galen was not the first author to hold that reason is above all seated in the brain. The idea was put forward explicitly in Plato's *Timaeus* (69c–e), and (again, on Galen's interpretation) by Hippocrates. These are the two authors Galen respected above all others, and he was at pains to emphasize the agreement between Plato and Hippocrates. He even devoted a lengthy treatise entitled *On the Views of Hippocrates and Plato* to proving the point.[2] However, Galen was also at pains to emphasize that he would never slavishly adopt the views of another author, no matter how authoritative. Instead, he sought to demonstrate his doctrines, preferably by means of empirical proofs. He was rather fastidious on the point: another Galenic work, *On Demonstration*, has been lost, but we know enough about it to see that it consisted largely of criticisms directed at previous authors (Aristotle, for instance) who in Galen's eyes had failed to rise to the level of proof in defending their theories.[3]

It was just this sort of proof Galen promised concerning the role of the brain. In one of the most brilliant, albeit rather cruel, series of experiments in the history of science, Galen drew on his formidable skills in anatomy and dissection. Following on the anatomical discoveries made in Alexandria by Herophilus and Erasistratus, Galen had a complex and sophisticated understanding of the human body. He also realized that there are close parallels between human anatomy and the anatomy of non-human animals. He thus undertook to demonstrate that the brain, and not the heart, as claimed by Aristotle and the Stoics, is the seat of the "ruling faculty" (hegemonikon). This could be accomplished by compressing different parts of an exposed brain in a living animal, with different impairments being observable as a result. Galen also showed in public dissections that tying off or cutting nerves branching from the brain could cause an animal to go lame in some of its limbs, or to become unable to use its voice. He remarks that this is particularly effective with a pig, since its screams prior to the cutting of the nerve are so loud, creating a more impressive effect when the animal is suddenly rendered mute (On Anatomical Procedures, K 2.663).[4]

Galen never tires of mocking the inadequate arguments offered by Aristotle and by the Stoics (especially Chrysippus) for their heart-centered theory. Their bad anatomy is the result of their bad methodology. Galen wrote his On Demonstration to show his readers how to avoid such errors. In a more positive vein, he encouraged all doctors to undertake the study of philosophy. He even wrote a little text on the subject, with the self-explanatory title The Best Doctor is also a Philosopher. Adopting the Stoic division of philosophy (see Chapter 8), he says that doctors can profit from all three branches of philosophy (K 1.60–1). Ethics will help him focus on the welfare of his patients, rather than the potential of his art for making money. Physics will help him understand the composition of the human body: the four elements, which lend their properties of hot, cold, dry, and moist to the humors, for instance. And logic will train the doctor in the rules of demonstration, ensuring that he accepts theories that are not merely plausible but actually well grounded.

As a corollary of this methodological rigor, Galen refuses to commit himself on matters that cannot be settled by solid proof. Cosmological questions tend to fall into this category. It might be fun to speculate about whether the universe had a beginning or not; whether it is surrounded by void, as the Stoics held, or by nothing at all (not even empty space) as Aristotle believed; and whether there may be more than one universe. But such questions cannot be answered on the basis of empirical evidence, so they are doomed to remain precisely that: a matter of speculation (On the Views of Hippocrates and Plato, K 5.766–7). This is not to say that Galen refused to be drawn on questions of natural philosophy. He becomes especially opinionated when natural philosophy has a bearing on medicine. A good example is one of the topics just mentioned, namely void.[5] We might not be able to say whether there is void outside the universe, given that we can hardly go and see for ourselves. But

Galen enthusiastically refutes his predecessor Erasistratus, who liked to invoke a sort of "void principle" in his anatomical theories.

For Erasistratus, such phenomena as respiration and the heart's (supposed) role in distributing breath around the body could be explained in terms of what he called "the filling of what is emptied." For instance, when the heart dilates it takes in air from the lungs to prevent a void from forming in the larger space created by the heart's expansion. Likewise, nutriment is drawn into the stomach, and urine into the kidneys, to stop voids from forming in these organs. Although Galen thinks that nature's tendency to prevent void from forming does explain some anatomical phenomena, he generally wants to resist Erasistratus' account. He prefers a different explanation that invokes "natural powers." The kidneys do not take in urine thanks to some sort of automatic physical mechanism, like bellows drawing in air. Rather, the kidneys have a "power of attraction" for urine (*On Natural Faculties*, K. 2.62–3). Galen's stance here is akin to that of Aristotle, who also understood plants, animals, and humans as having parts that fulfill certain specific functions.

Galen also sides with Aristotle against another theory that we might consider to be more mechanistic, namely atomism. We have seen that atomism lived on after the Pre-Socratic theorists Democritus and Leucippus in the Hellenistic school founded by Epicurus, and in the medical theory of authors like Asclepiades. Galen wrote a now-lost work critiquing Asclepiades' theories and also rejected atomism in the now-lost *On Demonstration*. Fortunately, there is plenty of Galen that still survives, and he was never afraid to repeat a good polemic. We can see how he thought atomism can be refuted by turning to his still-extant treatise *On the Elements According to Hippocrates*.[6] Here he complains that atoms are meant to be unalterable and to remain "unaffected." They can be moved around and bounce off each other, but they can never *feel* anything. Imagine pricking your skin with a needle (K 1.420–4). How would you feel the pain if your body were made of atoms? An atom will not feel a needle jabbing into it, since it cannot be affected. Nor does it matter how many atoms the needle strikes: the concussion of atoms will never yield the sensation of pain.

With his criticisms of the mechanistic theories offered by Erasistratus and the atomists, Galen was not out only to tear down polemical opponents—though there's no mistaking the relish he takes in this aspect of things. He was also trying to make space for a goal-oriented, or "teleological," understanding of nature. I've already said that there is an Aristotelian flavor to Galen's ideas on this topic, but more important in Galen's mind would be Plato. In agreement with Plato's *Timaeus*, Galen sees the entire universe as bearing the marks of intelligent design.[7] The outstanding example is, of course, the human body. A lengthy Galenic treatise

On Usefulness of the Parts describes the cunning way that our bodies have been fashioned. Even eyelashes are an optimal length: short enough not to impede vision, long enough to protect the eyes. He speaks passionately in defense of nature's providence in a so-called "hymn" in On Usefulness of the Parts (K 3.236–42). This is directed against anyone who dares to suggest that there would have been room for improvement; for instance, people who think that it would be nice if the anus were placed on the foot, so they could go to the toilet without getting out of bed in the night. (Now *that's* lazy.) Also in agreement with the *Timaeus*, Galen thinks that material possibility does place constraints on what nature can do.[8] He even talks about nature as exhibiting the providence of a divine craftsman or Demiurge. On the other hand, his self-imposed methodological constraints stop him from asserting anything much about the divine principle that is responsible for the providential design we see around us. He firmly believes in natural teleology, while remaining agnostic about its source.[9]

With all this providential design and oversight by nature, why is it that things nonetheless go wrong? Of course, if things never did go wrong Galen would be out of a job, and his medical writings naturally have much to say about illness as well as health. He defines health as that good condition which enables us to carry out all our activities as nature intends (On the Best Constitution of Our Bodies, K 4.739–40). As we saw with the case of melancholy, a standard explanation for illness would be that there is an imbalance of humors in the body or in one part of the body. A famous example would be Galen's story of how he discerned the cause of painful cramps that afflicted Marcus Aurelius. He did so by taking the emperor's pulse: the problem was not an illness, as the other doctors in attendance claimed, but only an excess of phlegm caused by an excess of food in the stomach (On Prognosis, K 14.660). The anecdote is a typical one for Galen, in that it shows him outdoing other supposed medical experts. In this case it is his long experience with the pulse that enabled him to make the diagnosis: he knew exactly how the pulse of a man of Marcus' age ought to be, and what it means when a pulse varies from this.

I mentioned in the last chapter that Galen presents his own medical method as a kind of compromise between the approaches of the rationalists and empiricists. The anecdote about Marcus shows us both sides. While the humoral theory plays a role (the buildup of phlegm), there is no substitute for experience. It renders the doctor sensitive and responsive to the almost infinite range of variables that may be relevant in diagnosing any particular patient: age, bodily temperament, gender, time of year, geographical location, and so on. This is one of the more appealing aspects of Galenic medicine, at least for those who like the idea that doctors should have a personalized approach, tailoring the treatment to the particular needs of the patient. Even the basic idea that humors should be in balance needs to be understood in light of what is appropriate for each person. Naively, one might suppose that the goal here is an exactly equal proportion of all four humors, or of their qualities like cold and dry (in fact Galen suggests this himself in *On Mixtures*, at K 1.555). But in fact older people are naturally colder than young people, and of course this is not something a doctor should try to rectify. Furthermore, within each person different organs have different ideal properties. If your brain is not colder than your heart, something is very wrong. Diagnosis, then, requires an individual approach which calls not only on theory but on long experience with a range of different patients seen in different circumstances, and an understanding of each particular part of the patient's body.

Once the doctor knows what ails you, it will be time for treatment. Like most ancient and medieval doctors, Galen takes a rather conservative approach here. Certainly, dramatic interventions are on the menu of options for the Galenic doctor: cauterizing wounds, administering purgative drugs, letting blood, or actually performing surgery. Such radical measures will be undertaken in light of anatomical and physiological theory. For instance, drugs are understood by Galen to work by manipulating the basic contraries of the body. They heat, cool, dry, and moisten, with different drugs having these effects to different degrees. But drugs, and even more so surgery, are measures of last resort. A lot can be accomplished by means of adjusting the patient's diet and overall "regimen," including the extent to which they take exercise, bathe, and so on. It would be an exaggeration to say that it is too late to call the doctor once illness has struck. But the prevention of disease through correct regimen is at least as important for Galen as the healing of disease. Inevitably, he therefore wrote a substantial work on the topic, called *On Regimen*.[10]

All of this applies not only to stomach cramps and the like, but also to psychological illnesses and even our ethical characteristics. This brings us to the Galenic work that is most obviously of philosophical interest. It has another fairly self-explanatory title: *That the Capacities of the Soul Depend on the Mixtures of the Body*.[11] Though Galen is going to argue forcefully for this claim, he does so while acknowledging his inability to say exactly what the soul is. He seems to tend towards the idea that the soul is nothing other than a bodily mixture or capacity, a view he ascribes to the Aristotelian philosopher Andronicus (K 4.782), on whom more in due course (see Chapter 25). But as far as Galen is concerned, no philosopher has yet given a demonstration of the soul's true nature, so he is going to suspend judgment on the question. Here he is well aware that Plato believed the soul can exist without the body (K 4.772–3), and that on this point he is refusing to follow one of his most esteemed predecessors. But of course, Galen's independence of mind allowed for such departures from Platonic authority.

On the other hand, Galen does find plenty to agree with in Plato. Drawing yet again on the *Timaeus*, and also on the *Laws* of Plato, Galen produces extensive evidence to show that Plato too thought that "the capacities of the soul depend on the mixtures of the body." The same view is asserted by Aristotle and the Stoics. The point clearly applies even to the functions of the rational soul, as we can see just by considering the effects of wine. Once he shows that Plato was well aware of this (K 4.810–12), Galen is in a position to accuse contemporary Platonists of betraying the authentic teachings of Plato, since they claim that the rational soul is unaffected by the body. He points out too that, on their theory, we can't even understand why the soul would separate from the body when someone, to take a not-so-random example, drinks hemlock (K 4.775). On this score at least, the Stoics do better. Their idea that the soul controls the body through a pervasive "breath" or *pneuma* is used extensively by Galen in his medical writings, and underlies his view that the nerves are conduits for "psychic *pneuma*." Indeed, one could be forgiven for thinking that, according to Galen, the soul is nothing other than the *pneuma*, even if he officially avoids making this or any other doctrinal claim about the nature of the soul.

The body's decisive influence on the body also explains why children differ so much in their dispositions from a very young age. This has to do simply with the child's bodily temperament or "mixture," one of the things that a good doctor must take into account in tailoring his treatment to the patient. On this point, Galen can even delight in once again claiming the agreement of Hippocrates. For one of the works of the Hippocratic Corpus, entitled *Airs, Waters, Places*, explains precisely the far-reaching effects of environment on humans. Obviously, these effects occur through the manipulation of the body's mixture (K 4.798). The same sort of mechanism would presumably be the explanation for the rather gnomic remark that ends the treatise: the Scythians have produced only one philosopher, while the Athenians have had many; in Abdera lots of people are stupid, while the Athenians are clever (K 4.821). (What about Democritus of Abdera? Well, he was stupid enough to be an atomist.)

The reason why the best ancient philosophers, unlike Galen's contemporaries, understood all this is that they followed the right method. That is, they based their theories on facts of experience (K 4.817). What could the contemporary philosophers do to improve themselves, apart from adopting this more rigorous, empiricist methodology? Well, Galen suggests, they could start by coming to him and letting him prescribe them a diet (K 4.808). This would make them less apt to argue and more apt to accept reasonable argument. This is Galen at his insulting and polemical best. But it is not *only* insult and polemic. The views he puts forth here about soul's relation to body form the basis for works that Galen wrote on the topic of ethics. One of these, *On Character Traits*, has survived only in an Arabic translation, in which version it had a great impact on ethical writings in the Islamic world (as we'll see in the next volume of this series). A work entitled *On Affections and Errors of the Soul* shows in greater detail that a doctor like Galen can, and indeed should, be able to diagnose and treat psychological problems as well as physical ailments.

Indeed, it would not be going too far to say that Galen considers ethical vices to be a kind of illness. They result from the imbalance of the parts of the soul (5.27–8), much as bodily illnesses result from an imbalance of humors. Here Galen is, of course, adopting the account found in Plato's *Republic* and *Timaeus* (that dialogue again), which sees the human soul as having three parts, namely reason, spirit, and desire. Like Plato, Galen thinks that virtue consists in training the lower parts of soul to be subservient to reason. This seems to be a precondition for the good functioning of reason, which is why Galen divides one of his ethical treatises into two sections, *On the Affections* and then *On the Errors of Soul*. Given the effect of the bodily constitution on the entire soul, and given the effect of diet on bodily constitution, it turns out to be genuine Galenic theory that eating the right things is a big step towards having the right, well-reasoned philosophical views. So I hope you had a healthy breakfast today before attempting to read this book.

Given the sheer size of the Galenic corpus, even a large breakfast has only enabled me to mention a few of the more philosophically relevant themes found in Galen's writings. Of course he was a doctor and is thus usually seen as a (if not *the*) major figure in the history of medicine, rather than the history of philosophy. Yet I would say he is one of the five ancient authors who were most influential on later philosophy, along with Plato, Aristotle, Plotinus, and Augustine. This is because so many philosophers, from the medieval period until relatively recently, have also been doctors. And until relatively recently medicine was mostly based on the works of Galen, just as philosophy was mostly based on the works of Aristotle. In fact, Galen's centrality in medicine outlasted that of Aristotle in philosophy. When authors as varied as the Muslim medieval thinker Avicenna and the French modern philosopher Descartes pondered the nature of humankind, they had to factor in the most up-to-date physiology and anatomy. In medieval and early modern times that meant factoring in the brain-centered, humoral, empirically based medicine of Galen.

PART II

PAGAN PHILOSOPHY IN THE ROMAN EMPIRE

21

CAESARIAN SECTION
PHILOSOPHY IN THE
ROMAN EMPIRE

R elatively wealthy societies have always been the fertile soil in which philosophy
has flourished. It's no accident that Pre-Socratic philosophy first emerged in the
affluent trading cities of Ionia, or that Athens became the center for philosophical
activity only after becoming the center of a Mediterranean empire. A bit of social
disruption may not be an insurmountable obstacle, and can even be helpfully
provocative—just think of Plato's engagement with the political events leading up
to the death of Socrates. But clearly some degree of stability is also needed, to ensure
that some members of the society can become not just literate but well-read, and have
the leisure to devote their lives to reflection and study. So you might expect that
philosophy did pretty well in the Roman Empire. By the time of Augustus Caesar,
who began his reign in 27 BC and died in AD 14, the Romans already held sway not only
over all of Italy but also modern-day France and Spain, parts of Germany, Greece, Asia
Minor, and the fertile lands of northern Africa. With some boundary changes—for
instance, the addition of a remote island the Romans called Britannia—the empire
was able first to thrive, and then at least to survive, for centuries to come.

While Athens remained strongly associated with philosophy, Rome itself played
host to many a philosopher, including those who spoke and wrote in Greek. We'll
find the most important late ancient philosopher to write in Greek, Plotinus, living
there in the third century AD. A third philosophical center was Alexandria on the
coast of Egypt, named after Alexander the Great and built up into a cultural hub
under the Ptolemies during the Hellenistic age. It was still important for philosophy
as late as the sixth century. Plotinus hailed from Egypt, a reminder that philosophers
who used Greek came from all over the empire and not only from mainland
Greece. In fact a good number of philosophers, such as the important Platonist
thinker Iamblichus, were from Syria. Philosophy would be still be a going concern in
Syria even after the fall of the Western Empire. As late as the ninth century, Muslim

patrons seeking translators to render Greek philosophical works into Arabic could draw on the expertise of Christians of Syrian extraction.

But I'm getting ahead of myself. Actually I was ahead of myself before even starting this chapter. Here I am introducing philosophy in the Roman Empire, yet we've already looked at several figures who wrote in the Imperial age, including most obviously the so-called Roman Stoics. It's hard to miss the fact that they lived after the fall of the Republic, given that one of them, Marcus Aurelius, was actually an emperor. Other Imperial age figures we've examined include Marcus' doctor, Galen, and the greatest of the Skeptics, Sextus Empiricus, who like Marcus and Galen lived in the second century AD. I have to admit that dates have never been my strong point, but in this case the chronological confusion is not really my fault. Splitting philosophy into historical periods is always a tricky and somewhat arbitrary business, and this case is no exception. The so-called "Hellenistic" schools survived very nicely until well after the Hellenistic period, pretty much however one chooses to define that period. Thus we have Stoics, Skeptics, and Epicureans still defending their schools' doctrines, or lack of doctrines, well into the time of the Roman Empire. Conversely, the most distinctive philosophical feature of late antiquity begins already in the first century BC: the renaissance, and ultimate fusion, of dogmatic Platonism and Aristotelianism.

During the Hellenistic period Aristotle had a few adherents, but he was not a dominant figure, while the Platonic Academy adopted their Skeptical bent. Once Aristotelianism and dogmatic Platonism came back into vogue, there was a kind of free-for-all in which five or even six distinct schools had some claim on the best minds of the early empire. From the first century BC to the second century AD Aristotle began a comeback that would eventually see him crowned as the chief philosopher by all medieval traditions. Platonism also emerged as a force to be reckoned with. At this time the philosopher, historian, and literary stylist Plutarch was able to declare himself a proud adherent of the "Academy." By this he certainly did not mean he was a Skeptic, but rather that he adopted the sort of Pythagoreanizing Platonism which had first been seen among Plato's immediate followers. Nonetheless, during this transitional period of the early empire, which is sometimes referred to as the "post-Hellenistic" age of philosophy, the Hellenistic schools were still going strong. I've already reminded you about proponents of Stoicism and Skepticism in these centuries, and can further remind you of Diogenes of Oinoanda the Epicurean. You may also recall that a sixth group, the Cynics, were still on hand to mock the pretensions of emperors like Nero and Caligula.

And as long as we're calling things to mind, cast your mind back to the 155 BC embassy of Greek philosophers to Rome.[1] They represented three separate schools:

Stoicism, Skepticism, and Aristotelianism. In a later echo of this idea that the schools could have official spokesmen, Marcus Aurelius established four chairs of philosophy in Athens. For him, the four chief schools were (of course) Stoicism, and then Platonism, Aristotelianism, and Epicureanism. Rich patrons and political rulers continued to influence the way philosophy was practiced right down to the last days of the Western Empire. We know that Plotinus benefitted from association with wealthy Roman aristocrats, for instance. These aristocrats typically sent their kids out to be educated, especially in grammar and rhetoric, a practice that influenced the development of philosophy. The case of Philo of Alexandria is illustrative. An aristocratic Hellenized Jew of the first century AD, Philo received an education that included the study of grammar, geometry, and the great Greek poets. St Augustine, growing up in the second half of the fourth century, underwent a Latin version of this curriculum and almost wound up as a rhetoric teacher himself. The Christian Neoplatonist John Philoponus was sneeringly called "the Grammarian" by his arch-enemy Simplicius, because he was a teacher of grammar.

This same school structure would serve philosophy well in the Imperial age. Like Plato, Aristotle, and Epictetus before him, Plotinus set up a philosophical school. Later there were important schools of Platonists in both Alexandria and Athens. But what the rich and powerful give, they can take away: the Christian emperor Justinian shut down the school of Athens in AD 529, an act which has come to symbolize the dying of pagan philosophy in the late empire. Because so much philosophy in the later ancient period was done in a school setting, we must always read the works of this period with pedagogy in mind. Some of Plotinus' treatises were written in direct response to issues raised by students in his school. In fact, the most voluminous body of philosophical writing in late antiquity had an explicit educational purpose. These were the commentaries devoted to the dialogues of Plato and the treatises of Aristotle, sometimes little more than records of school lectures expounding the texts of these two great masters. Here's a jaw-dropping statistic for you: by word-count, about half of the entire surviving corpus of Greek philosophical writings consists of late ancient commentaries on Plato and Aristotle.[2]

More generally, in terms of sheer quantity most surviving philosophical literature in Greek was written not in classical antiquity but in late antiquity—the period of the later Roman Empire. Some of these works were written about one thousand years after Plato and Aristotle. Those were one thousand years during which texts could disappear: the fate of the writings of the Pre-Socratics and of early Stoics like Chrysippus, for instance. This disappearance was not mere accident, a case of too many libraries going out of business or catching fire. Rather, it is a sign of evolving intellectual tastes. Until very recently the preservation of any writing was a costly and time-consuming business. Texts needed to be copied in order to be disseminated, and this was of particular importance when there were shifts in the technology of the book. In late antiquity there was a shift from the papyrus roll to the codex—much more like our modern-day book, with leaves of paper folded, sewn together, and placed between two covers. Plato never leafed through pages, he rolled and unrolled. But by the time the scribes of the Byzantine Empire were copying out the earliest manuscripts of Plato that have survived until today, scrolls were an outmoded technology. The codex was the only game in town. Styles of writing too underwent transitions, with a major shift in the ninth century AD from writing in uncials, which is like writing all in capital letters, to writing in minuscule, which is more like a lower-case cursive script.

Texts could easily be lost when these shifts in writing technology and practice occurred: a book written in an outdated script was like the vinyl records in your attic, supplanted first by cassette tapes and then by CDs. (Unless you are below the age of 30, in which case you may want to go find a middle-aged person and ask them what a vinyl record is.) With every change, someone needed to make a deliberate choice to copy a text out by hand in the new style. So as texts were passed down from generation to generation, implicit decisions were made about which works were worth copying. This means that the philosophical tastes of late antiquity and the Byzantine period were a filter through which Greek literature had to pass to reach us. (The same is true of medieval European tastes and ancient Latin literature.) So it's no accident that the works of Platonists and Aristotelians have survived better than the works of Stoics and Epicureans. After all, Aristotelian Platonists were the ones who decided what would survive.

Of course, this too needs explanation. We just saw that in the second century AD Stoicism and Epicureanism were honored with official chairs in Athens. Why did these two schools fade away, whereas Platonism and Aristotelianism rose into the ascendancy? As we'll see shortly, the works of both Plato and Aristotle were re-edited at about this time, which certainly helped. But why were the new editions read so avidly, and to the exclusion of other classical authors? If you were to give the credit, or blame, to just one man, it would have to be Plotinus. His Platonist system would become the dominant philosophy of late antiquity, and go on to be a pervasive influence on medieval philosophy, in both Arabic and Latin. Scholars distinguish this system from what came before by calling it "Neoplatonism." Not everyone likes the term,[3] but we're pretty much stuck with it. So I'm going to go ahead and speak freely of "Neoplatonism" and "Neoplatonists" in the rest of this book—but with the following caveats. First, it's important always to remember that ancient Platonists called themselves just that: "Platonists," and never "Neoplatonists," this term having been invented only in the modern age. Second, it's not as if Plotinus came out of nowhere. There was in fact a continuous development of dogmatic Platonism starting in the first century BC. Third, and along the same lines, it's not as if Neoplatonists after Plotinus just agreed with him about everything. Indeed, they often mention him only to disagree with him, and there are many differences between his thought and what we'd find in, say, a Neoplatonist commentator in sixth-century Alexandria.

Yet it remains the case that Neoplatonism, in all its variety, ruled the roost in late antiquity. To some extent it simply absorbed its rivals. There is a good deal of Stoic cosmology and ethics woven into the fabric of Neoplatonism. This co-opting strategy had been used already by Platonists before Plotinus, and he perfected it. Much the same can be said about Aristotelianism. Plotinus' attitude towards Aristotle is a matter of some controversy, but there's little doubt that he managed to integrate a number of Aristotelian ideas into his philosophy, even as he criticized Aristotle explicitly on other points. We'll have ample opportunity to observe Neoplatonists expressing these mixed emotions towards Aristotle. But it was always at least a love–hate relationship, and not infrequently a love–love relationship. For Neoplatonists, the usual goal was not to refute Aristotle but to show how Aristotle could be harmonized with Plato.

As for Epicureanism and Skepticism, these schools really did vanish from the scene in late antiquity. Neoplatonists found them useful only as opponents to be defeated, and often seemed to think that Epicureanism in particular was barely worth refuting. There are plausible historical explanations for this. With the dogmatic shift in Platonism, the Skeptics lacked a sufficient institutional basis such as the Academy. Their anti-belief program had in any case been compromised in the days of the early empire, provoking the backlash from more stringent "Pyrrhonist" Skeptics. But Pyrrhonism would not be influential again until the early modern period, when it appealed to authors of no less a standing than Montaigne and David Hume. Similarly, Epicureanism never regained the heights of devotion and articulacy we find in Lucretius, and it was universally rejected in the later Imperial age. This outcome was certainly unpredictable from the standpoint of the second century AD, when we have inscriptions of Epicurus being erected in Turkey and an endowed chair for the school in Athens. So what happened?

In the case of both Skepticism and Epicureanism, the answer may be that late antiquity was no time to be anti-religious. The Skeptics suspended belief about the nature of the gods, along with everything else. The Epicureans did admit the existence of the gods, but immediately added that these gods have nothing to do with us, so that we need not fear them. There was no place for such views in the religious ferment of the later empire, when paganism struggled to retain its cultural standing in the face of a new faith: Christianity. This new religion was promoted with a vehemence and sudden success that was disconcerting, and sometimes terrifying, to its opponents. Adherents of traditional religion could not help seeing the Christians as disruptive fanatics. Pagan religious beliefs had always allowed for a degree of ecumenical inclusivism. Egyptian and Greek gods were identified with the traditional gods of the Italian peninsula, or simply added to the pantheon. By contrast, Jews and Christians made claims to exclusive possession of the truth. And their God was not content to be one among fellow divinities. This led to violent conflict between Jews and Romans, and to even more violent conflict between Romans and Christians.

The Christians began, of course, as victims of persecution. But over a period of several centuries Christianity steadily gained power and influence, and then, finally, imperium. In the early fourth century Constantine changed the Roman Empire into a Christian empire, and his successors mostly adopted the new faith. (We'll be coming to an exception later on, with an emperor who was also a pagan Neoplatonist philosopher.) Of course, the traditional cults and beliefs did not die out overnight. In fact, many of the significant philosophers of late antiquity were still pagans. I have already mentioned that Christian hostility towards paganism could still affect the philosophical scene in AD 529, when Justinian closed the school in Athens. I've also mentioned the bitter dispute between John Philoponus and Simplicius, a dispute not unrelated to the fact that Philoponus was a Christian and Simplicius a pagan. In short, this was a period when philosophy was closely allied to religious belief. It was only to be expected that in such an environment Epicureanism and Skepticism would drift into near-oblivion.

Harder to expect was the success of Neoplatonism in co-opting, or rather being co-opted by, one last tradition: Christianity itself. Since before Plotinus, dogmatic Platonism had been a deeply religious enterprise. Plutarch devoted numerous works to philosophical discussions of religious topics, such as the nature of demons or oracles. Iamblichus, the Neoplatonist who hailed from Syria, put pagan religious belief at the very center of his philosophy, and was followed in this by generations of passionately religious Platonists. They modified the system pioneered by Plotinus, making room for the multiplicity of gods and semi-divine entities recognized in late antique paganism. So it would seem that any marriage between Neoplatonism and Christianity was bound to be a stormy one. Nonetheless, despite the occasional marital squabble, Christians found in Neoplatonism a partner worth loving and honoring, if not obeying.

This too cries out for an explanation. Part of the credit should again go to that man Plotinus. He was certainly no Christian, but his Neoplatonism was a fairly austere affair, metaphysically speaking. He posited a single first principle that bears a striking resemblance to the monotheistic God of the revealed religions. This resemblance made it possible for Neoplatonism to be purged of its more baroque pagan structures, yielding a metaphysical picture that would be found attractive in such disparate times and places as ninth-century Baghdad, eleventh-century Constantinople, and Renaissance Italy. Indeed, it was possible for the tradition of commentary on Aristotle to pass from pagans to Christians almost without skipping a beat. Pagan teachers taught Christian students, who passed on the Neoplatonic reading of Aristotle to subsequent generations. We find the same practices of teaching and commenting on Aristotle not only in the Greek-speaking Byzantine Empire, but also among Christians writing in Syriac and Arabic up until the time of Islam.

There is another reason why the monotheistic religions were able to absorb this strand of the ancient philosophical tradition: they had a lot of practice. Christians and Jews had been appropriating ideas from Greek philosophy since the time of Jesus of Nazareth. A somewhat older contemporary of Jesus, and like him a Jew, was Philo of Alexandria, who should be credited as the first representative of these faiths to engage seriously with Greek philosophy. Among Christians, the earliest Church Fathers were likewise deeply influenced by Platonism and Stoicism. Indeed, even St Paul seems to have been influenced by the philosophical ideas that penetrated the world-view of antiquity. For this reason, the rest of this book will need to trace two parallel, and intersecting, stories within the history of philosophy: not only the resurgence and triumph of Plato and Aristotle among pagan thinkers, but also the appropriation of the pagan intellectual heritage among Jews and Christians.

This leads us to a final difficulty, not unlike the problem of demarcating Hellenistic from later ancient philosophy. When does late ancient philosophy end and medieval philosophy begin? Nowadays, figures like Augustine and Boethius are frequently taught in the context of classes on medieval philosophy. But these were indisputably men of late antiquity. Augustine lived from the fourth to the fifth centuries, and Boethius from the fifth to the sixth. Their world-view was shaped not just by the Bible, by controversies over grace and the nature of the Trinity, but also by Plotinus and Aristotle. Thus, the history of philosophy in Western Europe is difficult to split into discrete periods, ancient as opposed to medieval. The same goes, of course, for the plain old history of Western Europe. Feudal structures of land-ownership started to emerge already in late antiquity, as a strong imperial center disintegrated amongst civil war and barbarian raids. Perhaps this instability was one more factor that contributed to the popularity of Neoplatonism. It is a philosophy that urges us to turn away from our bodily existence and towards a more perfect, stable realm.

But before we get to Neoplatonism, we need first to look at its roots in the earlier, so-called "Post-Hellenistic" period. As Rome made its transition from Republic to Empire, admirers of Plato turned their back on Skepticism. This meant a return to the Pythagorean obsession with number, and the confident metaphysical speculations, of the Old Academy.[4] This is not to say that the immediate followers of Plato, Xenocrates and Speusippus, were treated as unimpeachable authorities. For these early Imperial Platonists, only Plato was beyond criticism, and it was possible to heap scorn on Old Academic interpretations of the master. These thinkers are sometimes called the "Middle" Platonists, because they come after the ancient Platonic tradition of the Old Academy and before the Neoplatonism of Plotinus. But this somewhat dismissive label masks their pivotal role in ancient thought. For Middle Platonism paved the way for much of what would be new in "Neo"-Platonism.

22

MIDDLE MEN
THE PLATONIC REVIVAL

If your handwriting is anything like mine, then even you may not be able to read what you have written. Certain letters in particular may be easily confused. A lower-case B and a lower-case K, for instance. If I wrote out the name of my favorite silent film comedian in lower case, you might read it and wonder why you've never heard of this kuster beaton, if he's supposed to be so great. And I'm not alone. I just mentioned in the last chapter that Greek manuscripts made a transition from being written in capital letters to being written in minuscule letters, and in some types of minuscule script the Greek letter *Beta*, or b, looks similar to the *kappa*, or k. It turns out that a potential confusion between these two letters is at the heart of one of the niftiest philological controversies in ancient philosophy.[1]

At question is the name of the man who wrote a book called the *Didaskalikos*, or *Handbook*, a guide to the philosophy of Plato. He probably wrote it in the second century AD. As for his name, a ninth-century manuscript, the earliest that preserves this text, tells us that he was called Alcinous. Here's the nifty part: we know of no Platonist from this period called Alcinous, but we do know of a thinker named Albinus. So in 1879 it was ingeniously suggested that our "Alcinous (*Alkinoos*)" could be a scribe's mistaken version of "Albinus (*Albinos*)"—the Greek letter *kappa* replaced with the letter *beta*. The suggested correction would banish Alcinous from the scene, leaving the already familiar Albinus as the author of the *Didaskalikos*. But a century later, in the 1970s, it was pointed out that even in manuscripts that are written in minuscule, the heading with the title and author's name is written in nice bold capitals—and no one is going to confuse a capital K with a capital B. So it's now widely accepted that we are stuck with Alcinous.

Why, though, should we even care who wrote the *Didaskalikos*? Well, it is one of the few complete texts to survive from a philosophical movement in the early Roman Empire which re-established Platonism as a force to be reckoned with. Before them came the Skeptical Academy, after them the dominant tradition of Neoplatonism inaugurated by Plotinus—and these guys were in the middle. Thus, they have come to be called the "Middle Platonists." The very name shows the lack of esteem they have received from historians of philosophy. If the whole history of philosophy is footnotes to Plato, they can sometimes seem like a footnote to one of the footnotes, mere transitional figures whose ideas are often preserved only inadequately in fragments and testimonies found in later authors. But in this chapter I want to give a little love to the Middle Platonists. They set the basic agenda for the Platonism of later antiquity, defending doctrinal Platonism at a time when Skepticism was still a going concern, and when Stoics and Aristotelians provided serious competition.

This period of the Platonist tradition also gave us two figures who have left extensive surviving writings: Philo of Alexandria and Plutarch. We'll look at them in greater depth soon, but first I want to consider the movement as a whole. In terms of chronology, we're basically talking about the first and second centuries AD, the heyday of the Roman Empire. But the action begins earlier with two thinkers of the first century BC. We've looked at one of them already: Antiochus of Ascalon. When we discussed Cicero, we saw that Antiochus rejected the New Academy's skeptical reading of Socrates and Plato. For him, the Platonic dialogues were a rich source of positive doctrines, which he saw as being fundamentally in agreement with Aristotle and the Stoics. He also admired still-earlier figures, like Pythagoras. But he did not put Pythagoras front and center in his history of philosophy.

For that, we need to turn to a second, slightly later philosopher of the first century BC: Eudorus of Alexandria. He was apparently not the first dogmatic Pythagorean of this era. Cicero mentions a man with the rather wonderful name of Publius Nigidius Figulus, who would have been a generation older. Cicero credits Figulus with reviving the tradition of Pythagoreanism which had fallen into oblivion in its Italian homeland.[2] Sadly, we know nothing more than this about him. But further evidence of Pythagorean activity comes from texts that passed themselves off as writings by antique authorities. The most interesting of these pretends to be a treatise by Timaeus, the main character in Plato's dialogue of that name. It's not clear how early these Pythagorean texts were written. With Eudorus, at least we have a name, a place, and a rough time for his activity. But we know don't much about him either: none of his writings survive, and we have little information about his personality.

Eudorus adopted something like Antiochus' idea of a unified tradition centered on Plato's writings.[3] But unlike Antiochus, he did not claim that all non-skeptical philosophers were basically in agreement with one another. Rather than embracing Aristotle as a mostly faithful student of Plato, Eudorus criticized points in Aristotle's logical work, the Categories. He also differed from Antiochus in that he did not make Plato the fount of all philosophical wisdom. Instead, he saw Pythagoras as the primary figure. For instance, Plato's famous exhortation that mankind should seek "likeness to god" was said by Eudorus to be lifted straight from Pythagoras. Plato, supposedly, merely added the caveat that we should seek such assimilation only "insofar as is possible for mankind." In keeping with this, Eudorus had a rather selective approach to reading Plato's dialogues, emphasizing passages and themes that could be made to harmonize with Pythagoreanism as he understood it.

Particularly important was Eudorus' scheme of first principles. With some changes of detail, this scheme appears in nearly all the Middle Platonists, and it will be revised to become the core of Plotinus' metaphysics in the third century. To understand what Eudorus is after, we need to put ourselves in a Pythagorean frame of mind. This, of course, means thinking about numbers. For Pythagoras and his first followers, numbers were fundamental to reality as a whole.[4] This isn't a crazy thought: you don't need modern science to tell you that the physical world displays mathematical regularities, from the revolutions of the heavens to the fingers on our hands. And already in the ancient world, mathematics was taken as a paradigm of certain knowledge. For instance, Aristotle's *Posterior Analytics* often uses mathematical examples when explaining what is meant by demonstrative understanding (as at 85a–86a).

But there is a bit of a problem with numbers: there are an awful lot of them. I don't know if you've tried counting them, but if you have, I assume you gave up at some point or you would still be at it. Ancient philosophers, of course, realized that there are an infinity of numbers. Usually they regarded infinity as something that we *cannot* know—the infinite has no limit, and its indefiniteness threatens to elude human understanding. So, paradoxically, numbers appear in antiquity both as a paradigm object of knowledge and as something that is potentially unknowable. Eudorus and other Pythagoreans squared this circle by following Plato's immediate successors, the "Old Academy." They proposed that indefinitely many numbers can be derived from only two basic principles, the so-called Monad and Dyad. These are, respectively, the principles of unity and multiplicity. Picking up on terminology used by Plato himself, these two principles are also sometimes referred to as Limit and the Unlimited. Whatever they are called, the picture remains basically the same: we have a source of oneness, and a source of multiplicity. When these two principles come together, an ordered, but infinite, series is produced. The Monad or Limit bestows knowability and order, while the Dyad gives the series its unbounded multiplicity.

This is also how the Old Academy explained the mathematical structure of things. From the Monad and Dyad they generated not just numbers but Forms, geometrical figures, bodies—in short, everything. Their theory may seem obscure, but at its root is the fairly straightforward idea that the properties and determinations of things are produced by imposing a limit or order on something indefinite. Unity or limitation is furthermore seen as a source of goodness and beauty, since the goodness of each thing will consist in its having correct order and proper proportion. Take the very Pythagorean example of a string on a musical instrument, like a guitar or a Greek lyre. To produce notes you have to strike or pluck strings of specific lengths. One can apply the same idea to colors and even to three-dimensional shapes. A cube, for instance, is space enclosed by the limits that are its sides. And in Plato's *Timaeus* the fundamental elements are argued to consist of geometrical atoms. Earth, for instance, is made up of cubes at the atomic level. Examples like these show why Pythagorean Platonists, from the Old Academy onwards, portrayed the universe as an ordered ladder of mathematical structures and harmonies, in which all things are made, and made to be good, from a mating of unity with indefinite multiplicity.

Eudorus added a rung to this metaphysical ladder. Perhaps he was disturbed by the idea that an opposition between two principles should be fundamental. After all, the *Republic* envisions a single Form of the Good, which has no partner. So he insisted that, above the primordial generative couple, Monad and Dyad, there should be an even higher principle. Over the next centuries Platonists will call it by several names. In keeping with the religiosity of the age, this first principle is not only "the Good," but also "Father" and even "God." Most often it will take the name Eudorus gave it: the One.[5] This is a big step in the direction of Neoplatonism. Plotinus too will posit a single One above all things, a source of goodness, order, and unity for everything else. Other Neoplatonists will follow him in this, agreeing that the fundamental principle of unity is also the fundamental principle of goodness. In other words: the One is the Good.

Though Eudorus had a major role in the development of this idea, he was not Plotinus' most immediate source. That distinction instead goes to Numenius, a Platonist of the mid-second century AD.[6] The works of Numenius were read in Plotinus' school, and in fact Plotinus' critics claimed that he plagiarized his philosophy from Numenius.[7] Since we have far less evidence for Numenius than for Plotinus, it's hard to know how justified that accusation may have been. But certainly Numenius would have been a direct inspiration for the doctrine of a highest One or Good. He also anticipated Plotinus in writing about this One with a flair for evocative imagery, which was sorely lacking in most Middle Platonists, as far as we can tell. In one fragment Numenius compares the philosopher who fleetingly grasps the Good to a lookout who glimpses a one-man boat, floating far out upon the endless ocean.[8]

With Eudorus and Numenius we ourselves fleetingly glimpse a problem faced by Middle and Neoplatonists alike. If the principle of goodness is identical with the principle of unity, wouldn't it be better if no multiplicity was produced by the One? Why can't it just remain alone, serenely unproductive and perfect? This is arguably the central difficulty of late ancient Platonism. I raise it now because Eudorus and Numenius seem to have adopted the two obvious, but incompatible, solutions. For Eudorus, the highest One is the principle of all things, including the Monad and Dyad. It is thus a single, supreme cause for everything. Numenius doesn't like this idea—he doesn't see how a principle of multiplicity like the Dyad can come from a principle of unity. So he says that both Monad and Dyad are fundamental: his system reduces all things to an opposed pair, rather than a single source. This allows him to sidestep the problem of how one gives rise to many. But if God has an opposite, an enemy if you will, does that make the universe a kind of battleground in which unity struggles to overcome a source of multiplicity that is its equal? As we'll be seeing, that was precisely the view taken by a religious group called the Gnostics. Plotinus was occasionally tempted by this idea, but ultimately rejected it, and along with it the dualist elements found in Numenius and some other Middle Platonists.

With Numenius we've taken our story up to the second century AD, and that's where I want to stay for the rest of this chapter. This means returning to our friend Alcinous. His *Didaskalikos* was a guide to reading, or perhaps teaching, the works of Plato. It moves swiftly through the main features of Plato's philosophy, depending especially on the *Timaeus* but drawing on a range of dialogues. Alcinous takes it for granted that the dialogues are a source of positive doctrines, and has no time for the Skeptical approach to Plato or Socrates—indeed, he doesn't even mention it. Other Middle Platonists were not so tactful. Numenius, for instance, wrote a polemical work called *On the Divergence of the Academy from Plato*.[9] For Middle Platonists, as for Antiochus, Plato was what the Skeptics would have called a dogmatist.

In some cases, Middle Platonists also agreed with Antiochus in presenting all the non-skeptical classical philosophers as a unified tradition. Alcinous is an example. Of course he takes Plato to be the greatest of philosophers, and his greatness includes his having (supposedly) thought of Aristotle's and the Stoics' ideas before they had a chance to do so themselves. Alcinous would have us believe that all of Aristotelian and Stoic logic is already contained in the dialogues, a point he proves by the rather dubious expedient of pointing out that arguments presented by Platonic characters have various logical structures.[10] Of course, it's one thing to use an argument of the form "if A then B, but A, therefore B," and another thing entirely to do what the Stoics did, by isolating the argument form in its own right and calling it a hypothetical syllogism. Alcinous was willing, indeed eager, to overlook this distinction. Similarly, Alcinous casually ascribes to Plato some very Stoic-sounding ideas about the importance of resisting emotion.[11] All in all, his strategy is to kill the rival schools with kindness. Their best insights are quietly incorporated into a Platonist system and claimed to be the discoveries of Plato, while other features of their thought are quietly dropped.

This strategy, so reminiscent of Antiochus, was not universally adopted by the Middle Platonists. We already saw that Eudorus attacked Aristotle's *Categories*. This seems to have been something of a favorite pastime for Platonists in the early Roman Empire. Two obscure philosophers, named Lucius and Nicostratus, are known only for their criticisms of the *Categories*. They may have been Platonists attacking Aristotle out of school rivalry. A more important figure was Atticus, the leading Platonist in the city of Athens towards the end of the second century AD.[12] We have an extensive report of his withering criticisms of Aristotle, especially on ethical topics. The Stoics reacted harshly to Aristotle's admission that external goods like health and wealth might make some difference to our happiness. Atticus too seizes on the point. He complains that it makes our happiness due to chance rather than virtue, as if Aristotle had built his whole ethical theory around the importance of external goods. Of course, the divine Plato would never make such a mistake. For him, virtue guarantees happiness, and nothing else matters.

Although our Platonists tend to agree with the Stoics about virtue and happiness, they take exception to other features of Stoicism. It almost goes without saying that they reject Stoic materialism. As Platonists, they in fact see immaterial principles like Platonic Forms as being more real than physical objects. But actually, they have a bit of a problem here. Whatever one makes of the Forms, there are clearly going to be a lot of them. So how do they relate to the highest source of unity that sits at the top of their metaphysical hierarchy? Many Middle Platonists simply make the many Forms ideas in the mind of a single god—problem solved. More difficult for them is the question of what to do with the Stoic teaching on providence and fate. They enthusiastically agree with the Stoics that the physical world is governed by divine providence. But they find the Stoics' determinism repellent. They therefore develop a cunning theory, according to which divine providence is exercised over the physical world only by bestowing general laws and order on that world.[13] Individual events within the physical world, such as those due to human choice, are not caused by fate but they fall under its jurisdiction. What this means is that fate establishes laws of cause and effect that can be triggered by human choice. Consider good old Oedipus. The laws of fate do not force him to kill a king at the crossroads and marry the dead man's queen. But they do ensure that once Oedipus has taken these actions the rest of the story will unfold with its unstoppable logic, until Oedipus has discovered the horrible truth and taken his eyes out. At that point, Oedipus has quite literally met his fate.

Again, these features of Middle Platonism set the stage for Neoplatonism. Plotinus too deals with the rival schools—especially Aristotelians and Stoics—by criticizing them loudly while accepting many of their ideas quietly. He too attacks the *Categories* and Aristotle's stance on external goods, yet accepts important principles of Aristotelian metaphysics and psychology. Likewise, he absorbs Stoic ideas about universal providence but rejects their determinism. Above all, he simply assumes, as the Middle Platonists had assumed before him, that Plato is a dogmatic philosopher whose theories can be extracted from the dialogues. Though we do not know much about how Plato was read in Plotinus' school, we can already see that in Middle Platonism there was a trend towards organizing the Platonic material along doctrinal or pedagogical lines. The first attempt to arrange Plato's dialogues was made by a Platonist named Thrasyllus.[14] He grouped them into sets of four and, reasonably enough, he sometimes let himself be guided by their dramatic order. So he suggested starting with the four dialogues *Euthyphro, Apology, Crito*, and *Phaedo*, which tell the story of Socrates' trial, imprisonment, and execution. Our friend Albinus (with a B) found this superficial. He instead began with dialogues that would provide an ethical orientation for beginning students.

However the dialogues were organized, it's clear that for all these Platonists they were something akin to sacred texts. In late antiquity Plato's adherents often called him "divine," and they were not kidding—they believed that the dialogues contained inspired and superhuman truths. The same truths had been taught by Pythagoras, but Plato elaborated them in a substantial body of texts that could become the object of teaching and commentary. Of course, Plato's dialogues were not the only writings to be held in reverence in the ancient world. There were many pagan religious texts, and paganism was starting to get stiff competition from Judaism and Christianity. Sometimes the traditions mingled together. Already in the early first century AD we find Middle Platonist doctrines showing up in the rather unexpected context of Jewish philosophy and theology. This remarkable combination was the work of an equally remarkable man. Though he is often described as a Platonist, he wrote commentaries not on the dialogues but on the books of Moses. He will give us our first chance to see Greek philosophy interacting with the Abrahamic religions.

TO THE LIGHTHOUSE
PHILO OF ALEXANDRIA

Here's the story of a man named Noah, who was busy with three boys of his own. They were four men, living all together, but they were not alone. In fact they were surrounded by an extended family and two of every creature that crawls upon the earth and flies in the sky, having delivered them from certain destruction in an ark that had been built to precise specifications. After making landfall, Noah showed where his priorities lay by immediately planting vines, turning the grapes into wine, and getting drunk. The youngest of his sons saw him in this sorry state, and fetched the other two, who respectfully covered up their naked father. Once Noah sobered up and awoke, he was furious with the youngest son who had seen him so exposed. He cursed this son's son—his own grandson Canaan, condemning him and his descendants to servitude.

As you know, this rather sorry tale appears in the Bible, in fact almost at the very beginning of the Bible (Genesis 9). Whether you are a believer or not, you have to wonder what is it doing here? Why would the Bible tell us that Noah, savior of mankind and animalkind to boot, got senselessly drunk and was shamefully exposed in front of his sons? It's a problem not unlike one that had arisen in the pagan tradition. Some ancient readers were shocked by stories in which colorful misdeeds were ascribed to the Greek gods. Some, like Xenophanes and Plato, rejected these stories.[1] Others assumed that these myths had a less obvious, and more instructive, meaning. Giving the awkward bits a less awkward interpretation was sometimes called *therapeia muthon*, the "healing of myths."

By the time of the Middle Platonists, interpretive healing had frequently been applied to Homer and other revered texts of the Hellenic tradition. In the mid-first century AD an author named Cornutus set down a compilation of such readings.[2] He drew especially on the Stoics, who used allegory and etymology to uncover the messages that lay hidden in sacred tales of the gods. Even before the Stoics, in his dialogue the *Cratylus* Plato too used etymology to extract a philosophical meaning from the names of gods. Inspired partially by this Platonic precedent, later ancient Platonists were eager to see philosophical content in Homer and Hesiod, and would use any means necessary to find it. Nor did they ignore the Jewish Scriptures. We are told that one of the greatest Platonists of the early empire, Numenius, asked "what is Plato, but Moses speaking in Attic Greek?"[3] Later Platonists, like Porphyry, who had nothing but disdain and hostility for the Christians, showed considerable interest in Judaism, treating the ancient faith and its ancient Scriptures with respect.

But to see allegorical interpretation in full sail, being applied not only to the ark and to Noah's being four sheets to the wind, but to the Jewish Bible in general, we need to turn to Philo of Alexandria—not to be confused with the New Academic skeptic Philo of Larissa. Philo of Alexandria is sometimes called Philo Judaeus, because he was a Jew. His works consist mostly of exegesis of the first five books of the Bible, the Pentateuch or Torah, which were taken to be the writings of Moses himself. Philo's approach to this sacred text was inspired in part by philosophical allegories like the ones I've just mentioned, and in part by previous Jewish commentary. But Philo's handling of the Mosaic teaching is unprecedented. He was not out simply to "heal" the text by explaining away potentially embarrassing episodes. Nor was philosophy just a tool to be used occasionally in reading Scripture. Rather, he took Moses to be the source of all true philosophy. Pythagoras was a follower of Moses and Plato a follower of Pythagoras, so that Platonism was a key to unlock the message of Moses. This gave Philo license to go further than Stoic or Platonist interpreters had gone with Homer or any other text. He saw *every* passage in the Torah as conveying philosophical instruction, usually detectable only by means of allegory.[4] Philo's approach would live on as a powerful tool for doing philosophy within the context of revealed religion. The idea that a text like the Bible or Koran can implicitly contain philosophical teachings is common to the Jewish Philo, the Christian Augustine, and the Muslim Averroes. We're at the start of something big here.

But let's not get distracted from telling, if you will, the history of Philo without any gaps. He was born towards the end of the first century BC and died in approximately AD 45, making him a contemporary of Seneca and of Jesus. In Philo we find a marriage of Hellenistic philosophy and the Jewish faith, and there was no more appropriate place to hold the wedding than Alexandria. It boasted not only the library founded by the Ptolemies and a lighthouse that was literally a wonder of the ancient world, but also the largest Jewish population in Egypt. This community was part of the Hellenistic Diaspora, that is, the relocation of many Jews to lands other than Israel and within the Greek-speaking Mediterranean. To understand how Philo's community came to be here, we need to take a brief look at the history of the Jewish people.[5] The primary evidence for their early history is, of course, the Hebrew Bible itself. It tells us that Moses led the Jews out of persecution in Egypt, and that they settled in the land once promised to Abraham, around the city of King David—Jerusalem.

It was here that David's son Solomon built the first Temple in the mid-tenth century BC. The Temple was understood to be the house of God. Within this house was the Holy of Holies, a chamber that remained empty apart from the Ark containing the tablets upon which were inscribed God's covenant with the Jewish people. The Bible tells us of Moses, David, and Solomon, and then continues the story with the books of prophets like Isaiah, Jeremiah, and Ezekiel, who lived in the eighth to sixth centuries BC. They bring us up to the time of the earliest Pre-Socratic philosophers and also of a traumatic event in the history of Judaism: an invasion by the Babylonians, who deported many Jews and destroyed the first Temple of Jerusalem in 586 BC. The period of Judaism in which Philo lived is sometimes called "Second Temple Judaism." It is the age beginning with the rebuilding of the Temple in 515 BC and ending in AD 70, a generation after Philo's death, when it was destroyed by the Romans amidst a massacre of rebellious Jews. The Temple was the locus of sacrificial rites, the home of the high priest, and ultimately the house of God. It would not be too dramatic to describe it as the center of the Jewish world. Jews of the Diaspora, like Philo, faced the difficult question of what it meant to be a Jew in a foreign land, without access to the Temple. After the second Temple was destroyed all Jews would face the same question, no matter where they lived.

Even before then, the fortunes of the Temple, and the Jews more generally, were usually determined by more powerful political actors. The second Temple could only be built once the Persians defeated the Babylonians and ushered in an age of relative peace for the Jews living in and around Jerusalem. But this situation (along with pretty much every other situation) was changed by Alexander the Great. He conquered the Near East in 332 BC, ten years before his death. At first tossed back and forth between two of the empires that arose following Alexander's death, the region eventually fell under the sway of the Ptolemaic dynasty of Egypt. This meant that Jerusalem was governed by the same power as the city of Alexandria, a magnet for people of numerous cultures. Hence the large Jewish population in Philo's time, when control over Egypt had been seized by Rome. A dynamic of cultural confrontation and cooperation between Greeks, Jews, and Egyptians continued as before, except that now the political prize to be won was above all the favor of the Romans.

Philo is a perfect example: he tells us that he went on an embassy to plead the case of the Jews of Alexandria before the emperor Caligula in the late 30s AD (*Embassy to Gaius* 1).[6] The mission was a reaction to anti-Jewish violence that had erupted in the city among the Hellenic citizens who considered themselves to be true Alexandrians. We should not be misled by this. The Jewish community may have had strained relations with its Hellenic neighbors. But Philo himself wrote in Greek and even read his Bible in Greek. His version of the Bible is called the "seventy," in Latin *Septuagint*, an allusion to the seventy-two scholars who were held to have translated it into Greek. These scholars were said to be divinely inspired, so that Philo assumed his Greek Bible could be read as the word of God, and not a second-hand version of that word in a new language. Indeed, he invoked the inspiration of the translators in claiming that every passage had been translated with fidelity to the individual words, the surface meaning, *and* the inner meaning of the Hebrew text. If you've ever tried to translate from one language to another, you'll agree that divine intervention is the least that would be required to explain such a feat.

The Septuagint is in fact not quite the same as the Hebrew Bible, differing in order and including additional material. In fact it is closer to what the Christians would come to call the "Old Testament." But for Philo the Bible was, in any case, above all the five books of the Torah, and his philosophy is mostly presented as an exegesis of the revelation of Moses. He wrote three series of works expounding the Torah. One set out problems about the text, with suggested solutions; another provided a verse-by-verse commentary on Genesis, explaining both the superficial and allegorical meaning of each verse; a third expounded a more thematic "exposition of the law." At the head of this threefold series is one of his most philosophically interesting treatises, *On the Creation of the World*, which deals with the opening sections of Genesis. Here Philo takes on the task of squaring the Biblical creation story with Plato's *Timaeus*, the dialogue in which Plato sets out his own creation story.

To some extent, Philo's task is an easy one. When he sums up the principal doctrines underlying the Genesis account, his list could apply to Plato with equal plausibility. God exists; God is one; He created the world; this world too is only one; and God exercises providence over it (*Creation of the World*, §61). Plato says all these things explicitly in the *Timaeus*, although he describes the divine maker as a crafts-man or Demiurge, who employs helpers who also have the status of gods (*Timaeus* 40d). But a closer look reveals tensions in Philo's attempt to reconcile Plato with Moses. Like Plato's *Timaeus*, Philo compares the creator to a human designer—specifically, an architect who builds a city in accordance with pre-existing plans (§4). These plans are, of course, the Platonic Forms. But Plato says that the Demiurge "looks to" the Forms and builds the world as an image of those Forms. Philo draws a different message from the opening of Genesis. He takes it to refer to a creation of an intelligible world of Forms. This is the creation of the first day, with the physical world being fashioned only later in the Genesis story. As if he is aware that readers will suspect that philosophy is being sneakily imported into Scripture here, Philo remarks defensively, "this is the doctrine of Moses, not mine" (§6).

With this seemingly subtle shift, Philo has made a dramatic move in the direction of reconciling Plato with Judaism. Whereas Plato seems to suppose that the Demiurge is an eternal principle distinct from the Forms, Philo asserts the utter primacy of the single Creator and locates the Forms as ideas in this Creator's mind. We'll find a similar position in Plotinus, who explicitly rejected the idea that Forms are outside the divine intellect, and that this intellect looks towards them like a pre-existing cosmic blueprint. In another anticipation of later Platonic doctrine, Philo uses the Greek word *logos* to describe the Forms insofar as they serve as God's instruments in making the world (§8). *Logos* is one of the most difficult terms to translate in ancient Greek philosophy, but here it means something like "rational principle." Philo is taking a leaf not just from Plato, but from the Stoics, who likewise used the word *logos* for a divine, providential order that pervades the cosmos. The difference is that, for the Stoics, the *logos* was simply identical to God. For Philo, it is God's ideas, which God creates as a first step towards creating the physical universe that will exist by the end of the six days.

That mention of "six days" would make any self-respecting Middle Platonist sit up and take notice. We already know that Platonists of this era fused the teachings of the dialogues with the number theories of Pythagoreanism, and Philo is certainly no exception. He does not see the six days of creation as a literal reference to time; rather, the numbers assigned to each day have an allegorical or symbolic value (§3). For instance, animals are said to be created on the fifth day because sensation is the distinctive feature of animals, and there are five senses. The whole creation is said to take six days in order to convey the perfection of this creation. This is because six is a perfect number.[7] We might find it preposterous that this sort of numerology could be a key for understanding the Bible. Philo would respond that it would be truly preposterous to imagine God literally spending six days creating the universe— surely God created all things at once. Nonetheless, Philo did accept that the physical universe came into existence at some definite time. He wrote another treatise *On the Eternity of the World*, summarizing arguments for and against eternity in what may be an echo of the strategy the Academic Skeptics had used to reach suspension of judgment. In our version of the text only the pro-eternity arguments survive, which is ironic, given that Philo would have sided ultimately with the anti-eternity camp.

So in Genesis, Philo finds metaphysical doctrines about issues like God's creative act and the status of the Forms. Yet he places at least equal weight on questions of ethics. For him the Torah exhorts us to turn away from the pleasures of the body and towards virtue, which for Philo means faithfulness to God. Moses, as the source of all philosophy, was the greatest teacher of this message. But he was not its only teacher. Indeed, precisely because Moses was the source of all philosophy, Hellenic philosophers can be treated as collaborators in the task of interpreting Moses. In particular, Philo admires the Hellenic philosophers who champion rationality and virtue over pleasure. He would agree with Cicero and Antiochus that the heroes of Greek ethical thought are Plato and the thinkers taken to be his followers, namely Aristotle and the Stoics. Philo reproduces Stoic lists of the virtues, Aristotle's doctrine of the mean, even the imagery of Plato's *Phaedrus*, in which the soul must grow wings to return to its heavenly home.[8]

The difference is, of course, that Philo weaves these ideas into an exegesis of the Bible. The Paradise of Adam and Eve signifies virtue, and their Fall is surrender to pleasure, represented by the serpent. Philo understands Eve as symbolizing sensation or the irrational soul,[9] which is what leads reason (personified by Adam) to be seduced by pleasure—a somewhat reductive view of women that is partly compensated by more positive allegories of other women in the Pentateuch. Philo's focus on ethics continues past the stories of creation and the Garden of Eden, to include episodes such as Noah's drunkenness. Philo takes that passage as an opportunity to produce another set of arguments for and against a philosophical thesis, in this case the Stoic-sounding question of whether the wise man would ever get drunk. Predictably, he sees the story as a warning against indulging in the pleasures of the body. But he has a more arresting, and less Stoic, point to make—that there is a higher, intellectual kind of intoxication as well.[10] Those who attain wisdom and knowledge of God may seem drunk to the uninitiated, because they are transported out of themselves.

Although I've been talking as if metaphysics and ethics represent two distinct themes in Philo's exegetical works, in fact he would insist that they are intimately related. The Jewish law itself, which is imposed upon the people of God in order to bring them away from the lures of pleasure and to their Lord, is a kind of mirror-image of the providential law that governs the cosmos. For instance, the dietary laws of Judaism are intended to induce self-control—their aim is not just ritual purity, but also ethical purity. Our goal is to regain what was lost in the Fall from Paradise, namely, perfect participation in God's ideas. Philo's Platonism is again on display in his thinking about the Fall. The physical creation is by its very nature subject to change and flux, so that the Fall is seen as a metaphysical necessity (*Creation of the World*, §53). But as a Jew, he understands the Fall and journey towards redemption in a more historical context, with Moses showing his people the way back to God through his leadership of the Jews, and of course through the Torah itself.

Philo is, then, more than just another Platonist who happened to be Jewish. Certainly he gives us an invaluable insight into the way that Platonism was being practiced in Alexandria at this time. He fills out an otherwise sketchy picture based mostly on our indirect knowledge of Eudorus of Alexandria, who was only a little earlier than Philo. But Philo is no less significant for the history of Judaism, and even Christianity. His works were read enthusiastically by Christian Church Fathers, who preserved and engaged with Philo's allegorical expositions of the Bible. It is fitting that his ideas had such an ecumenical reception. He showed a way towards resolving the interpretive, metaphysical, and ethical dilemmas posed by every revealed text—whether Torah, Bible, or Koran. These dilemmas will become increasingly crucial as late antiquity wears on, and Christianity supplants traditional Greek and Roman religion. For now, though, we're only in the early days of the empire, and pagan Platonism still has a lot of life left in it. Next we'll look at an author who, like Philo, often presented his philosophy in the form of an interpretation of religious symbols and beliefs. But he was neither Jew nor Christian. In fact, he was a priest at the temple of Apollo at Delphi.

DELPHIC UTTERANCES
PLUTARCH

This chapter is brought to you by the letter E. We'll be discussing topics like Evil, Eternity, Eclecticism, and Ethics. But let's begin with the letter E itself, or rather the Greek letter Epsilon. It would seem that at the temple of Apollo in Delphi, the ancient Greeks had placed not only statues and inscriptions, such as the famous "Know thyself" and also "Nothing in excess." They also had models of the letter Epsilon, named *ei* in Greek, fashioned out of materials like wood and bronze, which they left to honor Apollo. Why, you might ask, would they do such a thing? By the period of the early Roman Empire the answer to this question was lost in the mists of time, and the Greeks themselves could only speculate about the origins of the practice. Among the enquiring minds was a man who had more reason than most to speculate. He was a priest at Delphi, by the name of Plutarch.

Plutarch hailed from Chaeronea, not far from Delphi, in Boeotia, a region in mainland Greece. His life spanned from AD 45 to 125, during which time he traveled widely in Greece and beyond, winning friends among the aristocracy of the Roman Empire and even, apparently, being granted Roman citizenship. But he retained a deep attachment to his home, where he was a man of considerable standing—he could trace his family to archaic heroes of Boeotia. Plutarch was more than an aristocratic priest, though. He was also the author of a huge body of writing. A mere list of the titles makes for interesting reading, and survives as a document called the *Lamprias Catalogue*. The *Catalogue* lists many works that are, like the motive for devoting the letter E to Apollo, lost to posterity. Still, plenty of Plutarch's output survives. He remains one of the most valuable ancient sources for Greek and Roman history. But for our purposes his philosophical writings are the main attraction. Many of these have a dialogue form, in imitation of Plutarch's most revered authority, Plato.

Plutarch's dialogues include a work called *On the E at Delphi*.[1] It presents a philosophical conversation set within a dramatic frame, where a character recounts a conversation he heard. The structure is like that of Plato's *Symposium*, where a similar frame-narrative introduces a series of speeches setting out different view-points on a common theme. Here the issue is not love, as it was in the *Symposium*, but those mysterious E's at Delphi. Various characters present different theories about the Epsilon, in what Plutarch would consider to be ascending order of insight. Thus we begin with a fairly banal, merely historical explanation premised on the fact that Epsilon was used in Greek to write the number five—being the fifth letter of the alphabet, just like E in English. According to this story, the Epsilon represents five wise men of Greece: the so-called "Seven Sages," minus two interlopers who should not have been included in this august company (385E). Before long, though, we are into more philosophical territory. A second speaker takes the Epsilon to mean the Greek word for "if," also pronounced *ei*. This speaker wants to highlight the importance of logic, which studies conditional statements of the form "*if* X, then Y." A third speaker takes us in a Pythagorean direction, preferring to interpret the Epsilon as the number five, and then waxing enthusiastic about its numerological significance (389F).

Just as Socrates provides the climax of the *Symposium* by telling of his philosophical instruction at the feet of Diotima, so here Plutarch gives the final word to his teacher Ammonius.[2] I should warn you that the name "Ammonius" is to late antique philosophy what the name "Diogenes" was to Hellenistic philosophy. The teacher of the great Plotinus was also an Ammonius, as was the head of a school of commentators in late ancient Alexandria. All three of these men were Platonists, all were teachers of more famous men, and all are known mostly indirectly through these more renowned students. Have I mentioned that ancient Platonists believed in reincarnation? Anyway, when this Ammonius, the teacher of Plutarch, gives his explanation of the Epsilon, he begins by distancing himself from the Pythagorean speech about the number five. Not because he doesn't approve of numerology—to the contrary, his worry is that this explanation would minimize the importance of a different number for Apollo, namely seven (391–2).

Instead, Ammonius reminds his listeners that the syllable *ei* in Greek can also be a verb: it means "you are." And this, he suggests, is the key to understanding the E at Delphi. It is an address to the god. It is appropriate to say "you are" to the god, because god exists at the level of *being*, whereas things in our physical realm are subject to *becoming*. This may remind us of the God in the Hebrew Bible saying "I am that I am," but the contrast between being and becoming is taken straight from the *Timaeus*. That Platonic dialogue may not be on every reading-list today, but Plutarch, and apparently his teacher Ammonius before him, saw the *Timaeus* as a particularly important Platonic work. As we'll see, Plutarch had controversial things to say about it. But all Platonists of this period would agree with Ammonius that the divine is unchanging and eternal, whereas bodily things are subject to constant flux (392). Since we are not gods, we dwell in this inferior, ever-changing region. Ammonius concludes, therefore, that the E at Delphi is a kind of partner to the famous Delphic inscription, "Know thyself" (394C). In saying *ei*—"you are"—we declare to the god that he is exalted beyond our realm, and when the inscription reminds us to know ourselves, it means we should never forget our more lowly station.

This combination of bold metaphysics and modesty about human nature and what it can achieve is entirely characteristic of Plutarch himself. He embodies the gradual transition from the skepticism of the Hellenistic Academy to Platonic dogmatism—that is, the embrace of positive philosophical doctrines. He is not shy in putting forth theories about the nature of the gods, the intelligible world, the cosmos, and the nature of man. As with other so-called "Middle" Platonists, Plutarch sees such theories as the doctrinal core of Plato's dialogues. Yet Plutarch will occasionally caution us that he is merely saying what he finds "probable," an echo of the Academic Skeptic Philo of Larissa. Plutarch's caution has a rather different, and more metaphysical, basis: if reality is divine and immaterial, then material creatures like us should not expect to understand it fully. I remarked earlier that, with the rise of dogmatic Platonism, the Skeptical approach of Philo, Sextus, and so on seems to have died out. That is basically right, but the epistemological modesty of the skeptics does live on in later Platonists, who frequently emphasize that humans cannot grasp divine realities completely.

Modesty notwithstanding, Plutarch had no hesitation in nailing his colors to the mast of Platonism. He attacked the theories of other schools, in a treatise *Against Colotes* (an Epicurean philosopher) and in another work called *On Stoic Contradictions*.[3] He is, in fact, a major source of information about these Hellenistic traditions. Here there's an obvious comparison to Cicero, who likewise preserved precious data about philosophical movements even as he criticized them. But, again like Cicero, Plutarch didn't let his school allegiances stop him from fraternizing with representatives of the other traditions. His own student Favorinus had Aristotelian leanings, and Plutarch also consorted with Stoics and Epicureans.[4] Nor is he above drawing on the ideas of Aristotle, especially in ethics. Plutarch's openness to various strands of Greek thought has led some interpreters to describe him as an "eclectic,"[5] but if this is so, it is only in the original sense of the word: someone who is deliberately choosing from a range of sources. Plutarch did draw on various sources, but he unambiguously saw the results as good Platonism.

Indeed, Plutarch waded into the question of the history of the Academy itself, which had sparked such controversy between Antiochus and Philo of Larissa. From the catalogue of his works we know that he wrote a treatise entitled *On the Difference*

Between the Pyrrhonists and New Academics. It is lost, but was presumably intended to show that the skeptical Academy had been within the fold of the Platonic tradition, whereas the more radical Pyrrhonists were no longer part of the family. This goes well with the qualified skeptical attitude Plutarch voices in his own works. But the most obviously Platonist feature of his written legacy is his explicit engagement with Plato's writings. We have a set of brief *Platonic Questions*, in which he resolves difficulties that arise in interpreting the dialogues. More interesting still is a work called *On the Generation of Soul in the "Timaeus"*.[6] With this text we arrive at core issues of late ancient Platonism—indeed, of Platonism in any age.

If you are a Platonist, then you believe that the physical world is only an image, an effect, of perfect, divine entities. But if this is so, you have to wonder why the world is so far short of perfect. In fact, without wishing to get too depressed about it, we can't help noticing that the world is full, not only of moral evil, but also of misfortune, deformation of natural things, death, and ugliness. How is it that perfect causes produce such imperfect results? Also, you might wonder how the causes relate to their results. Do they give rise to them automatically, or do they choose a first moment to start making the physical universe exist? These are questions that will disturb Platonists for many generations to come. In fact, they will still concern medieval thinkers whose relationship to Plato is a good deal more indirect than the one Plutarch could enjoy. So Plutarch was making some opening moves in what would be a long-running debate, moves that are grounded in a careful reading of Plato.

His first big claim concerns the question of the world's imperfection. He comes to that question indirectly, though, since his immediate ambition is to solve an apparent contradiction between two of Plato's dialogues (1013C–F). In the *Phaedrus* Plato gave a famous proof that the soul is ungenerated and eternal, on the basis that it is self-moving. But in the *Timaeus* Plato said explicitly that the soul of the entire cosmos is created by a craftsman god or Demiurge. So which is it: is the soul generated or not? Plutarch eliminates the difficulty by saying that Plato had in mind two different souls (1017B). There is one ungenerated, eternal soul, which is not fashioned by the Demiurge. Because it is not the product of a wise and perfect creator, it is irrational (1014B), associated with the disordered motions that dominate matter before the Demiurge comes along and fashions a well-ordered world. Part of this ordering process is the Demiurge's creation of another, rational soul for the entire universe. This is the soul that is said to be generated in the *Timaeus*. Problem solved.

In a roundabout way, Plutarch has answered our first question. The universe is imperfect because it is produced not only by a perfectly wise god, but also by a disorderly soul. It is a joint production, like a work of carpentry made by a master carpenter in cooperation with a particularly incompetent apprentice. Later Platonists will be nervous about the dualism this account ushers into our understanding of the soul: we would have not only the good, rational soul but also an irrational, perhaps even *evil*, soul. So we'll see them making alternative suggestions about the source of imperfection in the universe. Plutarch already anticipates one of these later ideas, which is to make matter itself the culprit. But he rejects this solution, because matter is purely passive (1014F–1015A, 1015D). Without an irrational soul causing trouble, it would give no more resistance to the Demiurge and rational soul than perfectly pliant wood would hinder a carpenter. Besides, Plutarch can point out that Plato himself was committed to a kind of dualism of the soul. Plato argued that the human soul has a highest, rational part and lower, irrational parts. For Plutarch, this duality in the human soul merely reflects the duality of soul in general. We share the imperfection of the universe we live in, yet we have the option of identifying ourselves chiefly with our rational part, and thus approaching the perfection of the gods.

Plutarch's second controversial point in his essay about the *Timaeus* is already implicit in what I've said: the physical universe has not been here forever. Again, Plutarch can point to evidence in Plato for this. At one point the *Timaeus* says that the universe is "generated" and has a "beginning." Plutarch, along with another philosopher named Atticus, whom we met briefly in Chapter 22, was notorious among later Platonists for taking this at face value as denying the eternity of the world. Both Plutarch and Atticus took Plato to say that the world was created out of pre-existing matter through the intervention of the Demiurge. Plutarch asserted this not only as the correct reading of Plato but also as the truth: if the world were eternal, we would lose one of the greatest proofs of the power and existence of the gods, namely, the divine creation of the universe (1013E). Yet Plutarch's position would turn out to be a minority one among late antique Platonists. Another Platonist, named Calvenus Taurus, somewhat later than Plutarch, pointed out that the word "generated" could mean a variety of things.[7] When Timaeus says the universe is generated, he might mean simply that it is subject to generation in the sense of constant change; or he might mean that it has a cause. Much later we find Neoplatonists like Proclus seizing gratefully on this point. It helped vindicate their reading of the *Timaeus* as upholding the eternity of the universe, and thus the orthodox Platonist understanding of how the gods relate to that universe.

It's a shame, in a way, that Plutarch came to be associated so strongly with the non-eternity of the world in the minds of Neoplatonists like Proclus. For he was a thinker very much to Proclus' taste, in that he devoted great effort to marrying pagan philosophical beliefs with Platonist philosophy. We've already seen one instance, the *E at Delphi*. Another fine example is his essay on the Egyptian myth of Isis and Osiris.[8] This fascinating text is among the earliest recountings of any such myth, valuable for the light it sheds on Egyptian religion and Greek attitudes towards that religion. He bears witness to the interpenetration of pagan belief systems in this period, with the deities of Greece, Rome, and Egypt being united in a common pantheon, or being identified one with another. As Plutarch himself puts it, the gods are common to all men, even if they have different names—just as the sun and moon are the same for all, but are named differently in different languages (377–8). Still, he brings a distinctively philosophical sensibility to the myth by seeing the main characters as representing cosmological and metaphysical principles.

The Egyptian myth recounted by Plutarch pits a wicked character named Typhon against two heroic lovers, Isis and Osiris. Osiris is torn to pieces, so that poor Isis is forced to try to reassemble his body. For Plutarch, these characters personify physical features of the cosmos—Osiris represents life-giving moisture, Isis is nature, and their child Horus is the world itself (363D). Typhon, meanwhile, stands for the drought that threatens life. At a higher level, Osiris can be taken to represent the Demiurge, with Typhon representing the irrational soul discussed in *On the Generation of Soul in the "Timaeus"* Plutarch is unapologetic about the dualist tendencies of his reading, but these would have appalled a thinker like Proclus, for whom all things must come from a single principle that is purely good. As Plutarch himself points out, his dualist view instead has something in common with earlier thinkers—Empedocles, with his dual principles of love and strife, and even the Zoroastrian tradition (369C–E).

I don't want you to go away with the impression that Plutarch spent all his time thinking about gods and metaphysics, though. In fact many of his writings are devoted to ethics, often on very specific points: there are entire works on talkativeness, on coping with exile, on undue curiosity, and on how to tell a flatterer from a friend.[9] This was not so much moral philosophy as moralizing, with the advice-columnist style of the works reminding us of similar works by Seneca (who also discussed the appropriate reaction to exile). Like Seneca, Plutarch writes for fellow aristocrats. Unlike Seneca, he is not too demanding: he does not set himself the task of replacing their value system with a new, more philosophical one. Rather, he aims to give useful advice and a bit of perspective on their everyday problems. Plutarch's Platonist psychology could have led him in radical directions, for instance, to an utter rejection of wealth and bodily health as valueless. But he tends to lean more towards the Aristotelians here, accepting that external goods do have their place in a happy life lived in accordance with nature.

Plutarch's most famous works are ethical writings of a different kind. These are his *Parallel Lives*, which recount the biographies of Greek and Roman figures. The project begins with Romulus and Theseus, the legendary founders of Rome and Athens, and goes on through other pairings, like Alexander and Julius Caesar. The importance of these works for our knowledge of ancient history is beyond dispute. But Plutarch intended them as studies of moral character, and used character to structure the *Lives*. For instance, one of Alexander's successors, Demetrius, is paired with Mark Antony—two famous hedonists. It wasn't only the ethical purpose underlying Plutarch's *Lives* that made them appealing for later readers—there was also his eye for the telling detail. Caesar is shown passing by a remote Alpine village, remarking that he'd rather be first in this backwater than second in Rome.[10] Occasionally Plutarch even shows a sense of humor. In one of his ethical treatises, when stressing the importance of looking on the bright side of things, he gives the following example: if you want to hit a dog with a stone, and hit your mother-in-law instead, this isn't so bad either.[11]

If the overt theme of the histories is an ethical one, its implicit theme is the relation of Greece to Rome. Plutarch wrote in old-fashioned Attic Greek, already a classicist though he lived in the classical world. He was a Hellenic patriot, and attacked the great historian Herodotus for daring to paint the Greeks in an unattractive light. For Plutarch, Athens was especially admirable, not only for its philosophy but also for its great military achievements. Yet his world was a thoroughly Roman one. The Romans were now the unchallenged rulers of Greece and the lands beyond, and for all his devotion to Plato and to pagan religion, Plutarch's cultural attitudes are more like those of Seneca than of any ancient Athenian. In the second century AD, men like Plutarch were already looking back to the glories of a Hellenic past. But Greek philosophy had plenty of life left in it yet. In fact, before we reach the third century and Plotinus, we need to look at other developments in and around the first and second centuries AD—above all, the rebirth of Aristotelianism.

LOST AND FOUND
ARISTOTELIANISM AFTER
ARISTOTLE

There seems to be a deep-seated human need to collect the things we like. A real James Joyce enthusiast will own not just a volume of Joyce's short stories and a copy of *Ulysses*, but also *Finnegans Wake*. Indeed, the enthusiast may even go so far as attempting to read *Finnegans Wake*! In music, the true fan is not the one who listens to a greatest-hits album over and over, but who owns a copy of every album the band released, perhaps on several formats. The more obscure output is treasured the most—the classical-music buff who can discourse on the fine points of obscure orchestral recordings from the 1950s, or the Led Zeppelin fan who insists that their greatest album is *Presence*, and who collects bootleg recordings of live performances. We even have a word for this sort of behavior: "completist." I myself suffer from this malady. I own not only all of Buster Keaton's silent movies, but also copies of some of the films he made after the advent of sound. I have been known on more than one occasion to explain to the uninitiated that the James Brown album you really want to get is the little-known *In the Jungle Groove*.

And I must also confess to a weakness for books about philosophy. I trace this tendency to a moment, shortly after I got my first academic position, when a student told me he could tell I was new at the university because my shelves were so empty. That stung, I can tell you. On the bright side, at least I am trying to collect philosophy books after the invention of printing. Before then, enthusiasts had to track down everything their favorite author wrote and pay to have copies written out by hand. The Renaissance marks the high-point of this sort of behavior, but it already existed in the ancient world, the most ostentatious example being the Library at Alexandria, where the Ptolemies of Egypt applied the completist principle to all of ancient literature. Of course, hand-made copies of texts nearly always contain errors made by scribes; many would also be damaged in some way. So ancient and medieval readers already did what classical scholars now do, getting hold of multiple manuscripts and comparing them to one another, in order to have the best chance of reading what the author originally wrote.

The procedure I've just described was challenging, but for ancients it represented the best-case scenario. In the worst-case scenario, the author's works would simply be lost. Surviving texts were often in a chaotic or error-strewn state and needed to be reorganized and corrected. All of which brings us to the works of Aristotle, and one of the most famous tales about ancient textual transmission. Strabo, who lived in the first centuries BC and AD and was author of a famous work on geography, tells us a complicated story about what happened to Aristotle's private collection of books after his death (2A).[1] Supposedly, Aristotle left his books to his follower Theophrastus. A student of the Aristotelian school named Neleus inherited the books along with the rest of Theophrastus' library. They passed to Neleus' family, who hid them in an underground trench to stop them being seized and placed in the library at Pergamum. In these harmful conditions the books were damaged, and when they were finally sold to another man, named Apellicon, he made matters worse by making copies that were full of errors. With Apellicon the books came to Athens, where they were seized after all by the Roman general Sulla, who conquered the city in 84 BC. The story's happy ending has the books coming back to Rome with Sulla.

This narrative is detailed and, for a story about a collection of books, pretty exciting, what with the underground trench and Sulla's wartime exploits. Indeed, it is one of the few philological stories that seem ripe for a Hollywood film adaptation. As Strabo implies, it would also explain what seems to us a puzzling feature of early Hellenistic philosophy. The early Stoics, Epicureans, and Skeptics failed to engage much with Aristotle's works, which we now see as a highpoint of Greek intellectual achievement. Yet Aristotle re-emerged as a force to be reckoned with in the first century BC. Indeed, the books' arrival in Rome did come shortly before a burst of activity centering on Aristotle. No wonder, Strabo would have us think: his thought had been lost, but now it was found. The story has, however, received a skeptical reaction from some modern scholars, especially Jonathan Barnes.[2] He pointed out that the temporary loss of Aristotle's own books would not explain much unless it was the only copy available, which seems a dubious assumption.

Barnes also doubted another long-held assumption. Once the Aristotelian works came to Rome, they had to be brought together and re-edited, especially if they were in such a bad state. On the traditional story, this was the work of the original Aristotle completist, a man named Andronicus. Andronicus hailed from Rhodes, but apparently worked in both Athens and Rome. Supposedly he got hold of these ancient texts of Aristotle and produced a ground-breaking edition, like a collected works. Some have supposed that Andronicus edited and organized the Aristotelian writings more or less in the form that we have them today. But Barnes pointed out problems with this assumption. For instance, later ancient authors rarely speak of Andronicus as an authority on textual questions concerning Aristotle. Admittedly, the Neoplatonist Porphyry compares his edition of the works of his master Plotinus (see Chapter 29) to the collection assembled by Andronicus. But Porphyry took major liberties with Plotinus' works, for instance, cutting a single treatise into multiple parts and scattering these parts out of order through his edition. So this parallel is not very encouraging. On the other hand, it lends plausibility to the idea that Andronicus would do something like, for instance, taking a pile of unrelated texts and putting them together as if they were a single work by Aristotle.

This is where philology can have serious philosophical implications. Of all the works of Aristotle, the one with the most controversial textual history is the *Metaphysics*.[3] Many experts today regard it as a mere stitching together of originally unrelated texts, some of which may not even be by Aristotle. In the late ancient and medieval world, though, the *Metaphysics* was seen very differently—as having a careful structure, which leads to a climax in the twelfth book, where Aristotle discusses God. Aristotle's whole philosophy will look very different if you think he intended this theological material to be read alongside the rest of the *Metaphysics*, where we find discussions of topics like the principle of non-contradiction and the nature of physical substances. So a lot is riding on the editorial work Andronicus may or may not have done. Indeed, one can go further. Although Aristotle never uses the word "metaphysics," this branch of philosophy has ever since antiquity been taken to include more or less what is covered in the Aristotelian work of that name. If it was Andronicus who assembled unrelated texts to create the *Metaphysics* as we have it today, then he should get much of the credit, or blame, for deciding what is and is not included in the discipline of metaphysics itself.

Whatever the extent of his editorial activity, Andronicus certainly represents a surge of interest in Aristotle in the first century BC. To the extent that he was read in the preceding centuries, it was often the so-called "exoteric" works that attracted attention. These were written by Aristotle for an audience beyond his students and colleagues. Ironically, these originally more widely circulated writings are lost today, apart from fragments. Supposedly they were models of elegant Greek composition, a fact that will amaze anyone who has spent time perusing the rather technical and difficult works we now have. These surviving writings are from among Aristotle's so-called "esoteric" treatises. The term means not that they were full of mystical or occult teachings, but only that they were intended to be read within his school, the Lyceum. It took a long while before they would reach a wider reading public, even after Andronicus and the resurgence of Aristotelianism. Seneca and Plutarch, in the first and second centuries AD, still don't seem to know these texts well.

Even admirers of Aristotle, like Cicero for instance, admitted that the esoteric treatises were very difficult. Aristotle's partisans sometimes claimed that he had purposely written in such an obscure way (2E), perhaps as a way of training the reader to think. (One might even draw a comparison between Aristotle's obscurity and Plato's use of the dialogue form, which forces the reader to reflect on what the characters are saying.) But whether their challenging nature was intentional or not, Aristotle's texts clearly called out for explanation and interpretation. Andronicus and others answered that call. He and other Aristotelians, also known as the Peripatetics, wrote commentaries elucidating the master's works. This would before long become one of the chief vehicles for philosophical reflection in antiquity. Pagan philosophers commented on Aristotle, on Plato, even on Hesiod and works of pagan religion like the Chaldean Oracles. Jews and Christians set forth their ideas in commentaries on the Bible.

Our earliest surviving commentary on Aristotle is by an author named Aspasius, who worked in the first half of the second century AD.[4] It covers parts of Aristotle's *Nicomachean Ethics*, which is slightly surprising, because the *Ethics* did not loom as large in ancient discussions of Aristotle as it does today. More than a century before Aspasius, heated debate already surrounded a different, much shorter and superficially less interesting text, the *Categories*. Here again, at least a bit of credit should go to Andronicus. Even if he didn't produce a complete edition of Aristotle's works, he at least authored a catalogue of those works. This implied an order of reading, and also involved his making decisions about which treatises were authentic. He argued that one logical work, *On Interpretation*, was not in fact by Aristotle (11A). This was because it contains a cross-reference to Aristotle's *On the Soul*, and Andronicus couldn't find anything in *On the Soul* that seemed relevant to the passage.

Later ancient authors found that reasoning rather flimsy. But they were greatly influenced by two other decisions made by Andronicus.[5] First, he defended the use of the title by which the treatise is known today: *Categories*, which means "predications." Second, he placed the *Categories* at the head of Aristotle's logical works. For centuries to come, the *Categories* would serve as an introduction to logic, and thus, given that logic was the first thing studied in late antiquity, an introduction to philosophy as a whole. Even as it assumed this prominent place, the *Categories* was causing controversy. The work sets out a division into ten classes: substance, quality, quantity, place, time, and so on. But it isn't clear what this division is meant to divide. The *Categories* begins with brief reflections on language, for instance, the phenomenon of words that are used equivocally—as when a person and a picture of a person are both called "man"—and the difference between simple expressions like "man" and compound expressions like "man runs." This suggests that the ten classes covered in the *Categories* are supposed to be a list of types of linguistic expressions.

Stoic critics pounced on this, complaining that the *Categories* is woefully inadequate compared to the sophisticated distinctions they had been making in their philosophy of language. The charge was answered by a student of Andronicus named Boethus of Sidon—not to be confused with the later, much more famous Christian philosopher Boethius. Boethus defused the Stoic challenge by lowering the stakes a bit. The *Categories*, he said, was never intended to be a complete analysis of language. Rather, the ten classes are only types of predicates, and divide linguistic expressions insofar as they relate to things out in the world (8F, 8H). Stoic distinctions, like the one between literal and metaphorical uses of language, would have no place here. So naturally Aristotle doesn't mention them. Rather, he distinguishes between substance-terms like "man" or "giraffe," quality-terms like "black" or "elegant," quantity-terms like "two cubits tall," and so on. Aristotle is interested only in terms that reveal the furniture of the world, so to speak—the substances that populate it, and the properties these substances possess. Andronicus himself had a similar outlook. For him, the terms that Aristotle was studying in the *Categories* "carve nature at the joints," to use a metaphor that goes back to Plato. The right division of words goes hand-in-hand with the right division of things out in the world.

This early defense of Aristotle was gratefully adopted by later commentators on the *Categories*, who also confronted another question that may already have been explored by Andronicus and Boethus. If the *Categories* classifies words insofar as they relate to things, then how does Aristotle think that this relationship works? The later commentators consider two possible views. The first is simple: terms refer directly to objects or their properties. Thus, the term "giraffe" would immediately signify such things as Hiawatha the giraffe, munching on hay in the zoo enclosure. The idea is simple, but it raises some puzzles. For instance, if I utter a word without knowing what it means, will the word still refer to the thing? This problem could be dealt with by a different proposal, inspired by Aristotle's remarks about language at the beginning of his *On Interpretation* (16a). On this suggestion, words refer to things only through the intermediary of thoughts. When I say "giraffe," this is meant to signify in the first instance my thought, which is a thought about giraffes; it is the thought that relates to the giraffe directly. Though the debate between these two positions is known to us from later commentators, it's likely that the positions go back to our early Peripatetics. The three-part theory, which makes thoughts an intermediary between words and things, is ascribed in some sources to Boethus. The two-part theory, meanwhile, would fit with what we know about Andronicus. After all, he didn't think that *On Interpretation* was even by Aristotle. So he may well have adopted a simpler theory of reference that didn't make use of its remarks about how thoughts relate to language.

Andronicus, Boethus, and other Peripatetics were no doubt interested in the *Categories* partly because questions of language and logic had received so much attention from other Hellenistic schools, especially the Stoics. In this age of philosophical allegiances, they had to show that their man could compete on territory that had been claimed by their rivals. This brings us back to the *Ethics*. Hellenistic philosophers frequently mention Aristotle only to dismiss his ethical theory as insufficiently rigorous. Authors of the first centuries BC and AD, like Cicero and Seneca, still tend to reduce Aristotle's subtle and elaborate ethical reflections to two fundamental ideas, both of which provide a contrast to Stoicism. First, the emotions should be moderated rather than eliminated, as the Stoics recommended. Second, external things like health and wealth do play a role in the good life, whereas the Stoics saw them as indifferent. This is obviously not an adequate summary of Aristotelian ethics. But the Aristotelians still needed to respond, especially on the issue of external goods. They did so by meeting the Stoics halfway: they admitted that virtue suffices for happiness, but said that the supremely happy man would be the man who has it all, both virtue and external goods (15A).

In the second century, Aspasius, author of that earliest surviving commentary, is still fighting this battle. He defends the idea that virtue involves moderating emotions like anger, and argues that external goods too are intimately related to virtue. Part of being virtuous is doing noble things. And, as he memorably remarks, someone whose father was a male prostitute is not going to have many opportunities to do noble things (18W). Here he resists the temptation to Stoicize Aristotle; elsewhere, he passes over a chance to Platonize him. Aristotle had said at the end of the *Ethics* that a life of contemplation is the highest possible for man. Platonists, who were fond of Aristotle, later seized on this to insist that Aristotle ultimately shared their conception of happiness as residing in nothing but intellectual fulfillment. But Aspasius firmly locates human happiness in a life that involves both virtuous practical action and intellectual contemplation: the battlefield and the senate, as well as the lecture room.

Here in Aspasius we can detect the prospect of an alliance between Peripatetics and Platonists. This will come to fruition eventually in Neoplatonism, above all thanks to Porphyry, who I mentioned above as the faithful student and editor of Plotinus. Porphyry was first and foremost a Platonist, so his approach to Aristotle was more friendly takeover than straightforward allegiance. But his was only the most influential answer to the long-running question whether Platonists and Aristotelians should be making common cause against other schools, or instead seeing each other as targets for refutation. The Platonists had taken a variety of approaches. In the wake of Antiochus' presentation of the ancient thinkers as one big happy family, some Platonists like Alcinous tried to show that Aristotle was just making explicit what was already implicit in Plato's dialogues. By contrast, Atticus issued scathing attacks on Aristotle's ethics, effectively erecting a big sign saying: "This way to happiness: no external goods or pleasure required; all copies of the *Nicomachean Ethics* to be left outside."

The Peripatetics too were unsure whether to engage in appropriation or polemic. Several summaries of Aristotelian doctrine derive from this period (for instance 3A, 15A), and they tend to fuse Aristotle's teachings with those of other schools, especially the Stoics. And I've just mentioned the irenic overtures we find in Aspasius. The earlier Boethus, though, seems to have been a strong critic of Plato. We have indirect evidence for a set of arguments he wrote against Plato's *Phaedo* and its defense of the soul's immortality.[6] Admittedly, these are difficult to interpret. It is not even clear whether they derive from the Peripatetic Boethus of Sidon or a Stoic thinker who, annoyingly, was also named Boethus, and who, even more annoyingly, also came from Sidon. Whichever Boethus wrote the arguments, he was no fool. For instance, he has a good objection to the crowning argument in the *Phaedo* that the soul is essentially alive and therefore not susceptible to death, the way that the number three is essentially odd and thus not susceptible to being even. Boethus says that the soul may well be essentially alive. But really we are worried that the soul will cease to exist completely, not that it will continue to exist and be dead. And if it does cease to exist, it will lose even its essential properties.

The philosophy of late antiquity will show that opposition to Plato was not essential to Aristotelianism—it could survive, even thrive, within a Platonist worldview. Thanks to Porphyry, the Platonists had their way with Aristotle, all the while promising to respect him in the morning. But before the dawn of this grand, harmonizing vision there was still time for the Peripatetics to enjoy one last shining moment. It came in the work of a man who certainly considered himself a faithful Peripatetic and not a Platonist, even if he borrowed from Plato now and again, and wound up serving as an indispensible guide for centuries of Platonists who wanted to understand Aristotle. An outstanding philosopher like Aristotle deserves an outstanding commentator, and with Alexander of Aphrodisias, he got just that.

26

NOT WRITTEN IN STONE
ALEXANDER OF APHRODISIAS

People like me tend to complain about how much of the culture of antiquity has been lost. But really we should be thankful that so many ancient Greek and Latin writings still exist. As I keep emphasizing, ancient texts reach us only through centuries of copying by later scholars. Only rarely can we read the actual documents the ancients themselves produced. There are exceptions, though. Papyrus rolls have been preserved by the dry sands of Egypt and by the odd volcanic explosion. And when the ancients really wanted their words to last, they quite literally wrote them in stone. Inscriptions on stone tablets were erected already by the ancient Greeks, to announce new laws or agreements between cities, as part of funeral rites, or in religious contexts. The Romans followed suit, as in the so-called *Res Gestae* or *Things Accomplished*, which detailed the achievements of Augustus Caesar, and which survives in copies in far-flung parts of the empire.

Surviving inscriptions are among the richest sources exploited by classical historians. Normally they don't play such a big role in the study of ancient philosophy. Although we did see Epicurean philosophy being preserved in the Diogenes of Oinoanda inscription of the second century AD, in general the cut and thrust of philosophical argument seems badly suited to the cut and thrust of chisel in stone. Yet occasionally an ancient inscription will provide us with a vivid glimpse into the lives of philosophers, if not their ideas. It happened in 2001, when they unearthed a tablet from the ancient city of Aphrodisias in modern-day Turkey.[1] Standing a bit more than a meter tall, it is a son's dedication for the statue of his father. Son and father have the same name, Aurelius Alexandros, and both are given the same epithet, *philosophos*. But the son claims an additional title: he also calls himself *diadochos*, which means "successor." This indicates that the younger Alexandros, known to us today as Alexander of Aphrodisias, was head of the Aristotelian philosophical school. The inscription thus confirms other evidence showing that Alexander held one of the chairs of philosophy set up in Athens by Marcus Aurelius.

That other evidence comes from another dedication, this one at the beginning of one of Alexander's philosophical writings, a diatribe against the Stoic teaching on fate. Alexander addresses the work to another father–son pair, the emperors Septimus Severus and Caracalla. This helpfully dates the work, and thus Alexander's career, to around AD 200. In attacking the Stoics, Alexander was of course engaging in the time-honored practice of inter-school debate. In this respect, he seems to have one foot still in the Hellenistic era, with its competing intellectual rivalries. But with his other foot Alexander was kick-starting another genre, one that will dominate the philosophical scene in the centuries to come: the commentary. Alexander was the greatest ancient commentator on Aristotle. He was recognized as such by his successors. Like Andronicus and Aspasius, Alexander was a confirmed Peripatetic, devoted to interpreting, analyzing, and expounding the thought of Aristotle. But this didn't stop Platonists from respecting Alexander and using his works. His writings were studied in the school of Plotinus, the founder of Neoplatonism, and Platonist commentators on Aristotle frequently quote Alexander's interpretations.

Alexander's standing as the foremost authority on Aristotle outlived late antiquity. He was still an important source for Byzantine philosophy, and in the Islamic world his works were translated into Arabic alongside Aristotle. Indeed, several of Alexander's writings are lost in Greek but preserved in Arabic. As late as the twelfth century, the greatest medieval commentator on Aristotle, the Muslim Averroes, would work Alexander's interpretations into the fabric of his own. Averroes' commentaries were then translated into Latin, and used by medieval Christian thinkers like Thomas Aquinas, who thus knew not only the name of Alexander but the details of Alexander's exegesis. For the Platonists of late antiquity and for medieval authors writing in Greek, Arabic, and Latin, philosophy frequently meant reading Aristotle. And reading Aristotle frequently meant reading Alexander of Aphrodisias, the most reliable guide to his thought.

Philosophy was carried on in commentary form for many centuries, but that form changed from time to time and author to author. The works being explained might be epitomized—summarized to make them briefer and (hopefully) clearer. They might be made the subject of a running paraphrase that could serve as a kind of explanatory guide through the text. Or the commentator might isolate certain puzzles or questions arising from Aristotle's teachings. We have a whole series of such treatments from Alexander's school, which pose and solve difficulties within the Peripatetic system.[2] But Alexander was above all known for his full commentaries, which would quote an entire treatise by Aristotle one bit at a time, with lengthy explanations of each bit. To help you impress your friends with your knowledge of late antique commentary practice, I'll tell you that each quoted bit of text is called a "lemma." As the commentators refined their approach they would often begin the interpretation of each lemma with a so-called *theoria*, meaning that they would explain the overall gist of Aristotle's remarks. They would then move on to the *lexis*, a phrase-by-phrase or word-by-word analysis of what Aristotle was saying. It also became standard to preface the entire commentary with a discussion of certain standard questions, for instance the meaning of the title of the Aristotelian work, any possible doubts about authenticity, its overall intention and topic, and so on.

Alexander's approach is not yet quite so elaborately standardized, but his commentaries—a number of which still survive, thanks to Byzantine copyists—were lemmatized. In other words, they quoted the entirety of Aristotle's text in chunks and interspersed extensive explanation between the quotations. The format is telling. Every sentence in Aristotle was treated with great care and attention. Platonist commentators might allow themselves the thought that Aristotle made an occasional mistake, especially when he dared to criticize Plato.[3] But Alexander's goal was to explain and justify Aristotle in lavish detail, raising difficulties only so that they could be solved. While this might sound more like apologetics than philosophy, sophistication and even creativity was required to make Aristotle's words come out true. Especially given a further assumption made by Alexander and later commentators, namely that Aristotle was always consistent, and never changed his mind. Commentators rarely strove to be original, but they usually managed it anyway, using great ingenuity to make Aristotle agree with himself and defend the results.

Of course, sometimes the best defense is a good offense. This is why we find Alexander writing the polemical treatise I mentioned above, *On Fate*.[4] Although it is not a commentary, it's a good chance to see how Alexander does philosophy. He promises only to present Aristotle's position on the topic of fate (§1), but winds up offering a theory of fate that certainly does not appear in Aristotle's original writings. He also turns the tools of Hellenistic philosophy to his own advantage. He begins by agreeing with the Stoics that fate does exist. This can hardly be doubted, he says, because all of us share a so-called "common conception" that some things are indeed fated (§2). The phrase "common conception" is Hellenistic rather than Aristotelian terminology, but Alexander does not hesitate to use it. Next, though, he reaches for a tried and trusted Aristotelian distinction: the four types of cause (§§3–4). Fate is, after all, a cause for the things that are fated, so what type of cause is it? Clearly not form or matter, nor is it a final cause, a purpose. That leaves only the agent or efficient cause. But there are different sorts of efficient cause, too. Whereas natural things like fire act automatically, human agents act through deliberation, choosing one course of action rather than another. Fate seems to be more like fire, in this respect—it brings about things inevitably and necessarily. Fate, then, must be a natural efficient cause. Indeed, Alexander concludes, fate should simply be identified with nature itself (§6). After all, Aristotle recognizes that nature provides for constancy in the universe. It is due to nature that mother giraffes produce baby giraffes, not baby monkeys. Nature also ensures that the existence of giraffes is, thank goodness, a necessary and permanent feature of the world around us. Fate is meant to be permanent, eternal, and necessary. What, then, could be more obvious than to identify fate with nature?

Another work of Alexander's, which survives only in Arabic, deals with the related topic of divine providence, and thus sheds further light on our problem.[5] Alexander claims that god's providential care over our world extends to causing the regularities of nature. This leaves plenty of room for things that god did not intend, like evil human actions and the occasional corruption of nature in the form of illness, deformity, and the like. To sum up: fate is nature, which acts generally in our world thanks to the gift of divine providence, but unlike the Stoics' version of fate, nature is subject to accidental exceptions. This account preserves both fate and providence and lets god off the hook for all the bad things that happen. Alexander 2, Stoics 0. And yet, doubts linger. The whole point of fate, we might think, is that it is universal in scope and includes everything.

Alexander simply rejects this idea. For him, many things occur without being determined by nature. Human actions are one example, as we've already seen. He also raises the issue of lucky or chance events (§8). Again following discussions of the topic in Aristotle, he explains that an event is lucky if it is the sort of thing someone might intend to happen, but it does not come about intentionally. For instance, if I go to dig in my garden to plant a pumpkin patch, and discover a buried treasure, then my discovery is lucky because it is accidental to the digging. Normally when I dig I don't strike it rich, and it wasn't actually my intention to find treasure. Whereas if I'd been following a treasure map and dug up a treasure, this would not count as lucky. In that case, getting treasure would be the expected result of digging rather than being accidental. The moral of this story is that nature, which produces its results in an expected and regular way, cannot include lucky chance events, any more than it can include freely chosen human actions. So neither of these is fated.

Although Alexander pays a good deal of attention to this topic of chance, it is the need to preserve human choice that is really decisive. He complains that the Stoics would give fate the responsibility for all things, and leave nothing "up to us." Taking his cue from Aristotle, as usual, he points out that no one deliberates about things they think are unavoidable (§11). So if everything is necessary, then deliberation is always pointless. Chrysippus and other Stoics had already given an answer to this objection, namely that deliberation is "co-fated" along with the action you will take (LS 55S). When you deliberate, this does affect the result, but the deliberation itself is fated; and the same is true if you fail to deliberate. Alexander would still claim an advantage here, though. As an Aristotelian, he has a nice, plausible account of what makes an action "up to us," namely that our rational deliberation chooses one thing while also having the power to choose the opposite thing (§12). Unlike the inscription he placed on his father's statue, our future actions are not written in stone. While we might find this position attractive, it seems Alexander has said little that would persuade a Stoic reader. Certainly they wouldn't agree that human actions and luck are exempt from the workings of fate. For them, god's designs for the universe are all-encompassing, and cannot be thwarted. To my mind, this raises the question of what Alexander is trying to achieve. I assume the idea is not just to irritate the Stoics, to see if he can get them to forget their Seneca and show some anger. More likely, he is addressing himself to the neutral reader. It's more a sales pitch for Aristotelianism than a sober critique of Stoicism.

On the other hand, Alexander has a problem the Stoics do not. Remember that Aristotle had put great emphasis on the role of ethical character. When virtuous people see an opportunity for virtue, they have the tendency, the ability, and the desire to take it. And similarly for vicious people and opportunities for vice. Doesn't this mean that character will determine our actions just as surely as Stoic fate does? Alexander sees the problem, but points out that even if a person is determined by his character to be virtuous, this doesn't settle which virtuous action he will perform (§29). One virtuous person might choose to erect a statue to honor his father, while another instead devotes his energies to, say, writing books about philosophy. Furthermore, we are responsible for our character itself, because our previous actions helped to form that character in the first place (§28). It was our choices earlier in life that made us generous or greedy, courageous or cowardly, sensitive or, like Buster Keaton and the statue of Alexander's father, stone-faced.

Alexander carved out his philosophical positions not only in response to opponents like the Stoics, but upon the platform laid by earlier Aristotelians. Without the work of predecessors like Andronicus, Boethus, and Aspasius we can hardly imagine Alexander's massive project of commentary. Still, he didn't hesitate to criticize his Peripatetic predecessors. An example would be Boethus of Sidon, who (probably) criticized Plato's arguments for the immortality of the soul. He seems to have been keen to avoid Platonism in other areas too. Where Plato had supposed that the Forms that give things their natures are separate and transcendent, Boethus proposed seeing all forms as mere qualities of the matter they inhabit.[6] The form of Hiawatha the giraffe, for instance, would be nothing more than Hiawatha's matter having a giraffe quality. This suggests that the form–matter relationship is a rather casual one, like the relationship between a wall and the color it happens to be painted.

For Alexander this was going too far. The form of giraffe doesn't relate to the giraffe's body in this casual or accidental way, as white is present in a wall. Rather, the form makes Hiawatha what she is, namely a giraffe. This sort of form is, as Aristotle himself had proposed in his *Metaphysics*, the "substance" of the animal. A qualitative form like white in a wall is a mere accident. In other words, the whiteness plays no role in making the wall a wall—this is why it remains a wall if it is painted green. Boethus' theory makes it impossible to distinguish between these two cases. Still, his heart was in the right place in rejecting Platonism. Alexander was no fan of Platonic Forms either, and would have said that the substantial forms recognized by Aristotle render Platonic Forms unnecessary. Since plant and animal species are eternal, forms like sunflower or giraffe are permanent features of the world, even though these forms only ever exist in particular flowers and particular giraffes. So these forms provide a basis for universal and necessary human knowledge.

All this relates back to what Alexander said about fate and divine providence. What really matters philosophically—and what really matters to god—is that natural kinds of things like sunflowers, giraffes, and so on are always present in the world. Fate ensures that this happens through the natural propagation of species. But the particular details don't matter—god wants there to be giraffes, but doesn't care or even notice what Hiawatha the giraffe has for lunch. As humans, we have a less lofty perspective, bound up as we are with the world of particulars. I mean, I don't know about you, but I certainly do care what I am going to have for lunch. This is why deliberation and rational choice is unique to humans. God doesn't need to deliberate because there is nothing for him to decide. There are necessarily and eternally giraffes, and this is guaranteed by god's necessarily and eternally causing the heavens to move. Heavenly motion indirectly brings about the production of giraffes, and of course all the other less impressive animals, like goats and indeed humans.

Like many philosophers, Alexander was even more interested in humans than he was in giraffes. He wrote several treatises addressing the topic of the soul, and unsurprisingly, the human soul was of particular importance.[7] His comments about the soul were disturbing to some later readers, because he made soul depend heavily on the composition of the body. Again there is an anti-Platonism here, which had been running through the Aristotelian tradition for generations. Galen claims that Andronicus simply identified the proportionate mixtures of the body with the soul. As with his reaction to Boethus on the topic of form, Alexander shows himself a bit more circumspect—and naturally so, given Aristotle's claim that the soul is the form of the body. In light of this, Alexander was bound to accept the substantiality of soul. The form of a giraffe is a substance, and the form of the giraffe is nothing other than its soul. But it's also consistent for him to depict this soul as heavily dependent on the body, a real substance that can only exist within matter. On Alexander's reading of Aristotle, there doesn't seem to be much prospect of life after the death of the body.

Nor was there much life in Peripateticism after the death of Alexander. Certainly the next generations—indeed, the next centuries—of philosophers will consider Aristotle a leading authority. But Alexander is the last significant thinker of antiquity to consider himself a Peripatetic and *not* a Platonist. Platonist commentators would use his expert analysis of the writings of Aristotle, but always within a broader Platonist project. The closest we get to an exception is a man who wrote more than a century later, in the mid-fourth century AD. He was not a philosopher of Alexander's stature, but he did focus on expounding Aristotle, with only occasional signs of a further allegiance to Plato. His name was Themistius. He'll give us a chance to discuss a question that was left hanging by what I've just said about soul. Although Aristotle says that the soul is the form of the body, he also claims that the human intellect needs no bodily organ. Might this offer the prospect of a more dualist take on Aristotle, perhaps even an afterlife that is more real than being immortalized in a statue? Themistius will also give us a window onto a broader cultural phenomenon, because he was a rhetorician as well as a philosopher. In late antiquity rhetoric was as closely intertwined with philosophy as mathematics or medicine. In the next chapter, then, we'll be turning to Themistius and considering not just the human soul but also the soul of wit.

SILVER TONGUES IN GOLDEN MOUTHS
RHETORIC AND ANCIENT PHILOSOPHY

It was December 1981, with New Year's Eve just around the corner, and Busy Bee Starski was at the microphone. He was enthusiastically laying down some rather simplistic rhymes over a beat. His main theme was that everyone should party. Then fellow hip-hop performer Kool Moe Dee leapt onto the stage. Kool Moe Dee proceeded to demolish poor Busy Bee with a torrent of rhyming, improvised invective, accusing him of lacking lyrical imagination, of stealing rhymes from other rappers, and of generally being really lame. A typical passage, which I quote mostly because of its unusual lack of obscenities, went like this: "In a battle like this you know you'd lose, between me and you, who do you think they'll choose? Well if you think it's you, I got bad news, 'cause when you hear your name, you're gonna hear some boos. " Ok, it's not T. S. Eliot. But Kool Moe Dee's tongue was quick and poisonous enough to make this a legendary humiliation for Busy Bee, and a pioneering moment in the development of freestyling "battle rap," in which MC's throw rhymed insults at one another. As Kool Moe Dee put it on one of his albums, he considered rapping "as a competitive sport." In the ancient world, too, there were performers who competed at improvised verbal pyrotechnics. They did not rap to a beat, but they could help defendants beat a rap: they were rhetoricians, and they were at home in the law-courts, as well as legislative bodies or even before the emperor himself.

The art of public persuasion already played a role in classical Greek philosophy, Plato contending with the sophists and Aristotle devoting a treatise to rhetoric. But it also helped to shape the philosophical scene in late antiquity. And no wonder: rhetoric was part of the standard educational curriculum for the young men, and occasionally women, who might go on to learn and write about philosophy. If your parents could afford to educate you at all, you would be packed off at an early age to learn to read and write. Many did not progress beyond this stage of basic literacy. Those who did would study grammar to become properly lettered. (The Greek word *grammata* in fact means "letters" or the alphabet.) For the ancients, this discipline included what we think of as grammar, but much more besides. It also meant learning to appreciate the classics of Greek or Latin literature. Young students would be taught to read aloud properly with poetic meter, about the historical allusions and difficult vocabulary used by Homer and other authors, about etymology, and so on. Again, some students would stop there, but those who progressed would study rhetoric. Studying grammar and then rhetoric, especially with the right teachers, was a way to climb the social ladder. Students paid handsomely to learn from well-respected and influential masters, who reciprocated by greasing the wheels of power to their students' advantage. Having learned at the feet of an outstanding teacher was a status symbol, even if one didn't exploit the connection for direct favors. In towns like Athens, teachers of rhetoric could draw well-paying students who flocked from all over the Roman world to sit at their feet.

An outstanding witness to the place of rhetoric in the educational affairs of the Roman Empire is Marcus Fabius Quintilianus, known to you and me as Quintilian. Born in AD 35, he was a rough contemporary of Seneca. In fact Quintilian, like Seneca, hailed from Spain, in the western reaches of the empire. He came to Rome, where eventually, in 88, he was appointed holder of the chair of Latin rhetoric, established by the emperor Vespasian. This chair was not unique. I have mentioned the chairs of philosophy established at Athens by Marcus Aurelius, and he also created chairs of rhetoric there. Such prestigious posts brought wealth and political influence. Quintilian profited greatly from his silver tongue, rising to the rank of consul under Domitian. But he did not present rhetoric as a pathway to wealth and power. Rather, he saw education as a path to moral excellence. A teacher of rhetoric needs not just mastery of his art but also mastery of his self, a paragon not only of persuasion but also of virtue.

Quintilian's enormous treatise *Institutio Oratoria* would become a classic treatment on both rhetoric and educational theory for later generations, down to the Renaissance.[1] In the fourteenth century the Italian humanist Petrarch wrote a letter to the long-dead Quintilian. It is not recorded whether Quintilian wrote back, but given his way with words you wouldn't put it past him. Of course most of Quintilian's *Institutio* deals with rhetoric itself: how to assemble material for a persuasive speech, the art of memory (indispensible to those living before the age of the teleprompter), the use of gesture, correct pronunciation, and so on. But tellingly, it begins with two books on the education of the youngsters who are to grow into perfect orators. He starts at the beginning, giving advice even on the selection of nurses for babes in arms—like a modern writer explaining how to improve a newborn child's chances of getting into a top university. Regarding grammar, he defends the practice of packing young men off to public school, where they can test themselves against their peers and be given public praise or corrective abuse. Marcus Aurelius would disagree: in his *Meditations* he expresses gratitude that he was home-schooled.

Quintilian and Marcus share something else though: a deep debt to the Greeks. Marcus wrote in Greek, and though Quintilian didn't go that far, his discussions of grammar and rhetoric show the extensive influence of Greek authors. He even draws on the great Stoic Chrysippus' lost work on pedagogy (1.1). Still, Quintilian speaks in terms of a canon of literary classics in Latin, featuring such authors as Livy and, above all, Cicero. Cicero too had written instructional works on rhetoric, and his style was seen by Quintilian as the best model for young men to learn to imitate. When Quintilian speaks about solecisms or the inappropriate use of foreign words (1.5), he bends over backwards to explain away passages where Cicero seems guilty of such lapses. Quintilian's own educational theory is rather appealing. He does want the student to learn by imitation, but only in order to achieve independence, like a bird leaving the nest (2.6). Ultimately, the teacher's goal is that the student should need no further teaching.

The type of education envisioned by Quintilian was remarkably durable throughout late antiquity. As emperors rose and fell, as barbarians invaded and were repulsed (or not), the children of the well-heeled and the upwardly mobile were put through their paces by grammarians and rhetoricians. Three hundred years after the time of Quintilian, Augustine speaks of his father scraping together money to send him for a first-rate education in Carthage.[2] There he received a training in rhetoric, as is evident on every page of his voluminous writings. What students learned was not only a set of skills, but a set of cultural references, which identified them as members of the educated classes. Then, as today, education could involve not only intellectual and ethical formation but also religious belief—after all, you can't read Homer carefully without thinking about the traditional Greek gods. Thus education became a weapon in the culture war between paganism and Christianity, a theme which will be occupying us later in this book. Nonetheless, the curriculum remained remarkably stable through the transition from paganism to Christianity.

Because grammar, rhetoric, and philosophy belonged to the same educational culture, it was inevitable that these disciplines would influence one another. Besides, grammar and rhetoric raise many philosophical issues. Perhaps that's clearer in the case of rhetoric. Its aim of instilling belief brings it into close contact with epistemology, the branch of philosophy that deals with justification and knowledge. It's no accident that when Plato wants an example of a group of people who believe something true without knowing it, he gives the case of a jury persuaded to convict a genuinely guilty man (*Theaetetus* 201a–c). Less obvious, at first glance, is the connection between grammar and philosophy. But given that we express our knowledge of the world in language, philosophers have always suspected that understanding language helps us understand the world. For instance, ancient authors compared Aristotle's idea of a species, like *giraffe*, to the grammarians' "common noun."[3] By this they meant a name that was shared by many things, in contrast to a proper noun like "Hiawatha" or "Socrates."

This topic of the parts of speech turns out to be an unexpectedly rich source of connections between ancient grammar, rhetoric, and philosophy. The ancient grammarians recognized numerous parts of speech: a typical list includes noun, verb, pronoun, adverb, preposition, conjunction, and article. That was problematic for philosophers, and especially for Platonists. Their man Plato had, in the *Sophist*, recognized only two parts of speech: noun and verb (261e–262e). In the second century we find Plutarch defending this on the basis that these are the only indispensable parts—the rest are just for stylistic variety, like seasoning on our food, as he puts it.[4] Centuries later the Christian philosopher and translator Boethius is still fighting what seems to us a losing battle, trying to show that all other parts of speech are somehow improper parts or can be reduced to noun and verb.[5]

It's interesting that even the more expansive list of the grammarians didn't include adjectives. The ancients needed some time to wrap their mind around the idea of an adjective. Even once the category was identified, the adjective was understood as a noun that needs another noun to complete it. This shows that their idea of a "noun" was rather different from ours. The relevant Greek word *onoma* can mean "name" as well as "noun," and it is natural to think of a word like "white" as the name of, say, the color of a piece of paper. Again, philosophical issues are looming: Aristotle uses this very example of whiteness to illustrate his idea of an accidental feature that subsists in a substance (*Categories* 1a). But rhetoric too influenced the theory of adjectives. It seems that the adjective, sometimes called a "quality" or "epithet," was made a distinct grammatical category in part to account for the terms of praise and blame that rhetoricians practiced applying in their speeches.[6] One Latin grammatical text tells us that a so-called "epithet" is simply a word used to praise or censure someone in terms of their soul, body, or their external circumstances. Not coincidentally, that threefold distinction of soul, body, and externals itself comes from Platonist discussions of the virtues.

It's no wonder that Plato and Platonism keep coming up in discussions of grammar and rhetoric. Plato was, after all, a literary classic. He was widely praised as a great stylist of Attic Greek, a dialect that was fetishized in the Imperial age, when the great rhetorician Aelius Aristides could praise Attic as the only type of Greek that possesses both dignity and charm.[7] Philosophers like Plutarch followed suit, cultivating an interest in antique Attic vocabulary and style. Even the doctor Galen, also in the second century, wrote philological works on the differences between Greek dialects in order better to understand the works of Hippocrates. Previously I've explained the victory of Platonism over the Hellenistic schools by mentioning how Platonism co-opted those schools and lent itself to religious belief. But another significant factor was that well-educated people considered Plato to be part of their canon. For the Romans, just as for us, effortlessly quoting authors like Homer or Plato was a way to establish one's breeding and refinement. A standard technique was to allude to what was already "ancient" Greek literature, but without identifying the source. The reader is flattered by the assumption that they too are in the know.

Another way to prove one's refinement was to go hear philosophers lecture. Hypocritical or superficial devotion to philosophy became an obvious target of satire. The star example is Lucian, a rhetorician of the second century AD who wrote stinging parodies of the philosophy of his day. In his work the *Nigrinus*, a philosophical tourist waxes enthusiastic about his recent visit abroad, where he sat at the feet of a Platonist master.[8] The comedy comes in part from the fact that the tourist's philosophical adventure has left his character entirely unchanged. For him, philosophy is nothing but an exquisite performance. It makes no demands on him to become more virtuous. Here Lucian has put his finger on a sore spot: cultivated Romans studied Greek literature in the context of an education that included philosophy. But when philosophy threatened to subvert the values of this cultivated elite, they were unmoved. Many an aristocrat swooned at stylish speeches showing that money and reputation are valueless—and then returned to the Forum in search of wealth and fame.

All these trends culminated at the highpoint of the Roman Empire, from the first century to the early third century AD. It was an age of sophists. The word "sophist" is familiar to us from fifth-century BC Athens, but it re-emerged in third century AD Athens, where a man named Philostratus devised the expression "Second Sophistic" to describe the movement covered in his treatise *The Lives of the Sophists*.[9] The rehabilitation of the term "sophist" went along with a rehabilitation of eloquence for its own sake. In this period rhetoricians devised showpiece speeches about historical topics, just as the sophists of classical antiquity had done. Gorgias had written a speech in defense of Helen; the great sophist Dio of Prusa went him one better, with a speech proving that, whatever Homer might say, Troy was never sacked in the Trojan War. This man Dio was also called "Chrystostom," meaning "Golden Mouth." Like modern-day hip-hop artists, sophists like Dio could wield the silver tongues in their golden mouths without preparation, speaking extemporaneously, often on a topic given to them by the audience. Ever ready to mock his peers, the satirist Lucian found humor in the reliance of rhetoricians on pre-prepared tropes, exaggerated gestures, and dramatic facial expressions. But notwithstanding Lucian's satire, such techniques did work. Ancient sources tell us of rhetoricians so admired that their adherents affected the same style of clothing, or could be reduced to violent weeping by the mere mention of the orator's name.[10]

The Second Sophistic is now taken seriously by classicists and historians, but it used to be seen as a sign of the decadence of the empire. Some contemporaries tended to agree. We already find Seneca, in the first century, complaining about those who value style over substance, and in the second century, the heyday of the Second Sophistic, Plutarch is banging the same drum. Such serious-minded men were bound be exasperated by the self-conscious playfulness of rhetoric in this period. My favorite example comes from somewhat later in antiquity: before he became a bishop, the fourth-fifth century author Synesius wrote a treatise In Praise of Baldness.[11] On behalf of the follicularly challenged, I extend my thanks to him. Nor was philosophy immune to the witty use of eloquence and self-aware appropriation. The sophists loved to rework themes from Plato, producing pastiches or retellings of the Ring of Gyges story from the Republic or the speeches on love in the Symposium.

But for a true fusion of philosophy and rhetoric, we need to turn to a man who lived in the fourth century, after the time of the Second Sophistic: Themistius. Like Quintilian, he rose to eminence thanks to his gift of gab. Eighteen surviving speeches document his relations with a series of emperors.[12] Some speeches were declaimed to the emperors in person; others were written when he served as an emissary. Despite being a pagan, Themistius received his first imperial patronage under the Christian emperor Constantius II, and he showed nimble political skills as well as a nimble tongue to retain an influential position under subsequent emperors, ultimately entering the Senate and helping to decide who else would be allowed to sit in this august, albeit now largely powerless, body. Ironically, the stridently pagan and philosophically minded emperor Julian was more cool towards Themistius, perhaps because he did not share the Christian emperors' need for a pagan court philosopher to demonstrate ecumenical and intellectual broad-mindedness. Themistius also argued for peaceful co-existence between pagans and Christians, something certainly not on the cards under Julian.[13]

In his speeches Themistius drew on sophists and rhetoricians, like Dio of the golden mouth and Aelius Aristides. But he also emphasized his philosophical credentials, pointedly wearing the simple cloak of a philosopher at court, and presenting himself as a man bound to tell truth to power, since philosophers always tell the truth (honest!). The credentials were genuine. He wrote numerous commentaries on the works of Aristotle, though actually, "commentaries" is perhaps too grand a word. They are more like running paraphrases, easier and clearer versions of difficult Aristotelian texts. Meanwhile Themistius quietly indicated points of harmony between Aristotle and Plato. In this he was typical of the philosophy of his age, when Neoplatonism was already harmonizing the thought of these two giants. But his overall philosophical outlook was closer to that of the great Peripatetic commentator Alexander of Aphrodisias than that of later Neoplatonist commentators.

Yet Themistius sometimes disagreed with Alexander's interpretations; the best example is his treatment of Aristotle's remarks on the intellect.[14] Themistius especially wanted to sort out one of the most contentious and tantalizing passages in all of Aristotle: the fifth chapter of the third book of On the Soul (430a). In the previous chapter Aristotle has explained that the human intellect is a kind of potentiality for receiving intelligible forms, just as eyesight is a potentiality for receiving visual forms. Now Aristotle says that if there is potential intellect there must also be an intellect that is always actual. This will be, as he says, a "maker intellect." It is comparable to light; it is always thinking; it alone is separate and eternal. The chapter has always fascinated and frustrated in equal measure. The only thing that is clear about the passage is that it's very important. Down to the present day there is no real agreement about the identity of the maker intellect Aristotle is describing.

In at least one work Alexander of Aphrodisias argued that it should be identified with god himself, given that god is always thinking, separate, and eternal. But Themistius was convinced that Aristotle must be describing an aspect of the human mind. For him, the universal maker intellect is, as he puts it, "what it is to be me." It facilitates the inception of my thoughts, which are actual forms in my mind—just as light makes it possible to see visible objects. The choice between these two interpretations is one of far-reaching importance. On Alexander's view, it looks as if the human mind is just another power belonging to the embodied person; there is little reason to expect that we will survive the death of our bodies. For Themistius, though, we each are above all to be identified with the maker intellect. When Aristotle says that this is eternal, he is promising us a shared immortality.

Themistius attained another kind of immortality too, because his paraphrases of Aristotle were valued for many centuries. His rhetorical gifts were likewise cherished; the Christian theologian Gregory Naziantius called him "the king of words."[15] In his own day, even emperors found it politically expedient to have a man of his pedigree around—a surviving letter from Constantius II to Themistius shows how keen the emperor was to present himself as a guardian of philosophy and the classical heritage more generally. But speeches and court intellectuals could only take an emperor so far; what they really needed was evidence of divine favor. A crushing military victory was always helpful. Failing that, though, a divine vote of confidence could be taken from another source: the stars.

28

SKY WRITING
ASTRONOMY, ASTROLOGY, AND PHILOSOPHY

What would it take for you to look at yourself in the mirror, and think that you really ought to be the most powerful person in the known world? Perhaps you are fired by civic duty, a desire to help the people. Perhaps you've got connections—your father was the most powerful person in the world, and one likes to keep these things in the family. Or maybe you're just a megalomaniac, who thinks untrammelled power over humankind is no less than you deserve. In the Roman era a large number of people were led by such reasons to think that they ought to don the purple and become emperor. To be fair, some more or less had power thrust upon them. But most seized it eagerly with both hands, and often with an army as well. Occasionally things got really out of control, as in AD 69, also known as the "year of the four emperors". This was a point in history when it didn't take much to make men see themselves as potential emperors. One of that year's four claimants, whose name was Otho, made a daring grab for power, which included the brutal murder of his predecessor, Galba. He lasted only three months, but he did have an excellent reason to see himself upon the throne: some astrologers told him he would be emperor. I guess they didn't mention the part about only lasting three months.

Now, if you opened your newspaper today, turned to your horoscope, and saw that this is a good week to declare yourself President of the United States, you presumably wouldn't drop everything and start writing your first State of the Union address. But the Romans took astrology more seriously than most people do nowadays. Astrology had already played a role in imperial politics before Otho's day. Consider the following tale of two friends who went to consult an astrologer. The first friend was named Agrippa, and the astrologer prophesized that he was destined for almost unimaginable greatness—a true prophecy, given that Agrippa went on to win the battle of Actium and serve as the most powerful lieutenant of the great Augustus Caesar. After this, Agrippa's friend was reluctant even to hear his own fortune, which could hardly be as auspicious. But when he finally gave his time of birth and the calculations had been done, the astrologer didn't even bother to utter a prediction. He simply fell at the man's feet. For this second man, named Octavian, would go on to be Augustus Caesar.

That story is a legend, of course, but Augustus really did use astrology as part of his imperial image. He had his horoscope made public, and his star-sign of Capricorn is found on surviving coins minted in his reign.[1] What astrology could help give, astrology could also threaten to take away. Emperors often worried that astrologers or other diviners would declare that someone else was destined for power, undermining their authority. Ancient historians tell numerous anecdotes in which someone receives the dubious benefit of such a prophecy, and shortly thereafter a death-sentence from the capital intended to thwart the prediction. Imperial edicts were sometimes passed against the use of astrology to predict death—not coincidentally, this occurred late in Augustus' reign—or against any use of astrology. Of course, there's not much point outlawing and censoring something no one takes seriously. Such laws are part of the abundant evidence that, along with magic and forms of divination, like reading the entrails of animals, astrology was a well-established part of the ancient world-view.

If you think about it, it would be a pretty poor philosopher who, living in a society where astrology was commonly accepted as genuinely efficacious, would just shrug and decide not to think about it. If the stars really do indicate future events, this stands in need of explanation. Thus, many ancient philosophers tried to explain astrology's supposed success. The topic was additionally interesting to them because, unlike magic or reading entrails, it was inextricably linked to a major branch of philosophy, namely cosmology. We have seen before that the heavenly bodies were a source of continuing fascination for ancient thinkers. This was true already with the Pre-Socratics—for instance with Heraclitus' claim that the sun and moon are bowls of fire[2]—and in Plato's *Timaeus*. Aristotle wrote an entire treatise called *On the Heavens*.

These philosophers pre-dated the widespread belief in astrology in the Mediter-ranean basin, which seems to have begun only after Alexander's conquests and the exchange of ideas between the Greek and Babylonian worlds. But by the second century AD it was possible, one might almost say inevitable, for the leading ancient expert in astronomical theory to write also about astrology. This was Claudius Ptolemy. His mathematically sophisticated presentation of the heavenly system lived on for centuries, especially in a work we call the *Almagest*. Its name contains a hint of its extraordinary historical influence. Originally called the *Mathematical Systematic Treatise*, it was often referred to in Greek simply as "*He Megiste*," meaning

The Great Treatise. This passed directly into Arabic as *al-Majusi,* and the beginning of the English title *Almagest* simply retains the definite article "*al-*" from the Arabic. A similar etymology, incidentally, underlies the word "alchemy." It comes from an Arabic transliteration of the Greek *chemia,* the same word that underlies our word "chemistry."

Ptolemy didn't write about alchemy, but he did compose an extensive work on astrology, called simply *The Four Books,* or *Tetrabiblos.* He thus embodies a more general ancient phenomenon, the intimate connection of practices we now usually consider disreputable with intellectual disciplines that live on in our universities. Alchemists availed themselves of Aristotelian chemistry, that is, the theories of elemental transformation he set forth in works like *On Generation and Corruption.* Magic could be explained using ideas from Stoic and Platonist physics, in particular the idea that the whole cosmos is like a single organism. The parts of the universe relate like parts of a body, so that they are capable of being "jointly affected"—in Greek, *sumpatheia,* another word that lives on in English as "sympathy." This same idea was used by the Stoics to explain astrology,[3] while authors like Ptolemy borrowed heavily from Aristotle's four-element theory and his cosmology.

We might expect that astrology would be a good match for Stoicism. After all, the Stoics were determinists, who believed that the natural order is an inevitable unfolding of divine providence. The possibility of foretelling future events fits nicely with this theory, and yet the Stoics were slow to embrace it with any enthusiasm. One passage in Cicero does suggest that the early Stoic Chrysippus accepted the following example of a conditional statement: "If someone is born at the rising of the Dog Star, he will not die at sea" (LS 38E). But again according to Cicero, Diogenes of Babylon, the Stoic representative in the famous embassy of philosophers to Rome in 155 BC, allowed only limited efficacy to astrology.[4] Things really got going only with Posidonius, a Stoic who was known to Cicero personally, and is mentioned in Cicero's work *On Divination.* Posidonius seems to have accepted astrology and other forms of divination as a welcome confirmation of the Stoic determinist theory. His interest in the topic may relate to his famous construction of a model of the heavens, an armillary sphere.

Despite this, it was the Aristotelian cosmic theory that appealed to the later Ptolemy and that would go on to be assumed by philosophically inclined astrologers (and astrologically inclined philosophers) even into the Arabic tradition. Aristotle assumed, as did nearly all ancient cosmologists, that the earth sits at the center of a spherical cosmos. At the edge of the cosmos is the sphere of the so-called "fixed" stars—since the earth is assumed to be unmoving, this sphere is taken to be revolving swiftly around the earth, once per day. Between this outermost sphere and our earthly world are more transparent spheres, in which the visible planets are embedded. From night to night they change their position against the revolving background of the fixed stars. Now in fact the earth is of course tilted on its axis, and it is not only spinning around once per day but also travelling around the sun once per year, give or take a leap-day now and again. This means that the sun seems, if you suppose the earth to be unmoving, also to be moving relative to the fixed stars, describing a motion along a circle that it is an angle to the celestial equator. This motion takes one full year to be completed, and the inclined path the sun travels is called the ecliptic. The angle of the ecliptic was credited with the change of seasons.

The sun's path does slip very slightly from year to year, a phenomenon called the "precession of the equinoxes"—this is in fact due to the wobble of the earth spinning on its axis. Ptolemy said the effect was only about 1 degree per century.[5] The fact that ancient astrologers were aware of such a subtle change shows how observations and measurements were being made over the course not only of years but of generations. A more obvious phenomenon, which can be seen even within a single year, is that the planets do not look like they travel in stately circles around the earth. Unbeknownst to the ancients, they are really moving in elliptical orbits around the sun, just as the earth is. This means that, from the point of view of the earth-bound observer, they sometimes appear to stop and go backwards. So it's patently obvious that the planets, including the sun and moon, are not moving in perfect circles around the earth. This was a problem for anyone who, like Aristotle, believed that the planets are seated upon rotating spheres. He had to introduce multiple movers for each sphere to explain the irregular motions of the planets (*Metaphysics* 1074a). A later expedient was the epicycle: the planet sits upon a much smaller rotating sphere embedded within the sphere rotating around the earth. Thus the planet is like a dot on a spinning marble, which is inside a big, rotating glass sphere. This lesser spinning motion explains why the planet sometimes appears to move backwards. Another device was the "eccentric sphere": a planet-bearing sphere could have a center other than the midpoint of the universe, something impossible to reconcile with the physical picture of nested celestial spheres.

As is clear from such attempted corrections, it was vital to Aristotle and Ptolemy that the heavens remain a world of perfect circles. The non-circular motions observed by the ancients had to be explained as the product of multiple, interacting circular motions. This provided a contrast between heavenly bodies on the one hand, and on the other hand the four elements in the world here below the heavens—air, earth, fire, and water. These have rectilinear motions. The light elements, air and fire, move up, and the heavy elements, water and earth, move down. In other words, the light elements move away from, the heavy elements towards, the midpoint of the universe. This gives Aristotle a basis for his claim that the heavens are made of an entirely different kind of substance, the so-called fifth element, which is eternal and indestructible.[6]

Ptolemy appreciates the exalted status this implies for the study of the stars. At the beginning of his *Almagest* he argues that there is no greater theoretical discipline.[7] He agrees with Aristotle that theology must study the ultimate mover of the heavens, which is divine. Sadly, a full understanding of this first cause of motion exceeds the grasp of humankind. Meanwhile natural philosophy, which considers the world of the four elements below the sphere of the moon, deals with things subject to constant change. So these disciplines are imperfect—theology, because no adequate comprehension is possible; physics, because there can be no stable understanding of unstable things. By contrast, when we consider the heavens on the basis of their motions, we are doing mathematics, a study that combines feasibility with perfectly stable objects of knowledge. As Goldilocks would say: not too ambitious, not too modest, but just right. Ptolemy strikes a Platonic note by adding that the study of the stars will bring our souls into a kind of order that imitates the perfect order of the heavens. The same point was made in that favorite dialogue of the late ancient world, the *Timaeus*.

But none of this gets us from the science explored in the *Almagest*, which we would call astronomy, to the much more ambitious and contentious practice of astrology. Astrologers used horoscopes to predict the fates of individuals, and they also pronounced on the outcomes of more particular events, advising on everything from the best time to take a journey, to the result of illnesses, to the winners of chariot races. How is this possible? Broadly speaking two kinds of answer were given, which have been dubbed "hard" and "soft" astrology.[8] Hard astrology claims that astral bodies actually cause things to happen down here in our world. Soft astrology says that the stars merely signify future events without causing them, making prediction possible for those who know how to read this sort of sky writing.

As we've seen (Chapter 26), the Aristotelian Alexander of Aphrodisias balked at the idea that the stars cause everything to happen down here. For the stars, with their perfect and eternal motions, partake of divinity. And let's face it, a lot of what happens down here is really unfortunate. The wrong people become emperors, children refuse to finish their supper, the giraffe enclosure just happens to be shut the day we visit the zoo. To put the blame for such things on the stars would be blasphemous. Astrology was criticized more directly by representatives of other philosophical schools.[9] The inscriptions of Diogenes of Oinoanda include an attack on astrology, unsurprising given the Epicureans' dislike of Stoic determinism. Sextus Empiricus and other skeptics likewise refuted astrology. They too were opposed to

Stoicism, and of course ancient skeptics were in the business of refuting pretty much everything anyway. An amusing anti-astrological argument was offered by the early Academic skeptic Carneades: if time of birth determined one's fate, then everyone who dies in a huge battle must have been born at the same time.

As Christianity came to dominate late antiquity, astrology itself became increasingly embattled. Authors of no less standing than Augustine tried to refute it. For instance, he used what was by his day a very old argument, not unlike that of Carneades: if the moment of birth decides one's fate, then identical twins should have the same fate, but this isn't true.[10] The much earlier Christian thinker Origen seems to have admitted "soft astrology"—the stars do signify future events without causing them. Having held out this concession to astrology, he snatched it away by denying that humans are able to read these signs. But even for Christians, things were not always so clear-cut. Origen thought he had to admit that stars serve as signs because of a passage in the Book of Genesis, and there were other religious reasons to allow that stars do serve as messengers from God. Just think of the star shining over Bethlehem at Jesus' birth, a story which has been seen as the Christian equivalent of Augustus using his horoscope to support his political legitimacy.[11]

Of course, philosophy could be used not only to critique astrology, but also to support it. A remarkable example is the poem called *Astronomica* by an otherwise unknown author named Manilius.[12] Taking inspiration from Lucretius, and perhaps from the Stoic Posidonius, Manilius put complex mathematical accounts of the heavens into torturously difficult Latin verse. This is the earliest complete theoretical work on astrology to survive from antiquity, and even it barely survived through the medieval period before being rediscovered in the Renaissance. Far more influential was our new friend Ptolemy, who not only adopted a broadly Aristotelian cosmology in the *Almagest*, but also called on the resources of Aristotelian physics in his astrological work the *Tetrabiblos*.[13]

Aristotelian cosmology had always faced the difficulty of explaining how the heavens exercise influence on the earthly realm. You don't have to believe in astrology to wonder about this. The sun and moon have evident effects on the seasons and tides, and in fact astrologers presented their theories as a mere extension of this kind of phenomenon. But Aristotle denied that the sun is hot—so how does it warm us? He flirted with the possibility of invoking friction, but this makes little sense, given that the sun's sphere is separated from our atmosphere by the impenetrable and presumably heat-proof sphere containing the moon. Ptolemy did not really solve this problem either, but simply associated various planets with certain elemental properties. The sun was, of course, heating, albeit not hot, while the moon causes moisture (hence the tides), and so on for other planets (1.4). Like other astrologers, he linked such properties to more obviously metaphorical ones, claiming, for instance, that the moon is feminine and the sun masculine (1.6). As standard in ancient astrology, he also made the effects of planets depend on their location in the zodiac, their relative positions to other planets, and so on. While all this might make Ptolemy sound like an unashamed hard astrologist, he hedges his bets by insisting that astrology deals only with probabilities. The stars do cause, but in so complex a way that we cannot be sure of our forecasts. Thus he compares astrology to medicine: both are beneficial to mankind, but neither offers absolute certainty (1.3).

We can find similarly nuanced views among critics of astrology. A century after Ptolemy, Plotinus took a great interest in astrology, devoting a treatise to the topic and discussing it at length in other treatises.[14] Like Alexander, Plotinus worries about making the divine stars causes of evils, and about the deterministic implications of astrology. So he sometimes seems to deny the stars any causal role at all, at one point sarcastically comparing this suggestion to the idea that birds make future events occur—an allusion to the ancient practice of divination based on the flight of birds.[15] On the other hand, he explicitly speaks of the stars as a kind of writing that signifies the future. This makes his view seem like a clear case of soft astrology. In fact though, his position is more nuanced than that. In one of many borrowings from Stoicism, Plotinus accepts that the universe is bound together by a kind of sympathy. This gives him a physical basis for allowing some causal influence from the stars upon our world. His considered view does allow this, but only to some extent. For instance, the positions of the stars at the time of our birth may influence our ethical dispositions, but they do not predetermine our actions. This is not only because the stars are only part of a more complex cosmic causal system, but also because our souls are immune to influence from mere bodies—even divine, heavenly bodies. All of which should make perfect sense, once we have turned our attention to more fundamental aspects of his philosophy.

A GOD IS MY CO-PILOT
THE LIFE AND WORKS OF
PLOTINUS

W e seem to expect that a great life should have a great ending. Hence the
fascination of famous last words: deathbed remarks that show wit or insight,
or seem to encapsulate the personality of the dying person. The best of them are
probably apocryphal, like the one attributed to Oscar Wilde: "Either that wallpaper
goes, or I do," and Goethe's supposed dying request for "More light" (a little too
good to be true, that one). But apparently the great physicist Richard Feynman really
did say, "I'd hate to die twice, it's so boring." As in so much else, the ancients set a
high standard for the rest of history with their last words. It's hard to see past Julius
Caesar's "*Et tu, Brute?*" for the top entry in this competition, but Socrates' "We owe a
cock to Asclepius" (Plato, *Phaedo* 118a) should get an honorable mention. And then
there's the dying remark of the greatest philosopher of late antiquity, Plotinus. He
said to a friend sitting with him, "Try to bring back the god in us to the god in the
universe" (*Life of Plotinus* 2).[1] As if that wasn't good enough, a snake appeared and
wriggled out through a hole in the wall just as Plotinus shuffled off his mortal coil.
The year of his death was AD 270, and the place was Campania, a region in Italy to the
south of Rome. Plotinus had come to Rome to open a philosophical school. Whether
he meant to or not, he also opened a new chapter in the history of philosophy.

A good case can be made for seeing Plotinus as the most influential Western
philosopher of all time, apart from Plato and Aristotle themselves. The case would go
like this: Plotinus is recognized as the founder of the tradition we call Neoplatonism.
He fused together the doctrines he claimed to find in Plato with many of Aristotle's
ideas, along with a healthy dose of Stoicism. The resulting mixture proved appealing,
to put it mildly. It would be embraced by pagans in the Roman Empire, by Christians
in Byzantium and Western Europe, and by Christians, Jews, and Muslims who
lived in the Islamic Empire and wrote in Syriac, Arabic, Persian, and Hebrew.
Within decades of Plotinus' death, Augustine drank deeply from the Neoplatonic
stream. A millennium after Plotinus lived, Thomas Aquinas would do the same.

Neoplatonism would become, if anything, even more dominant in the Renaissance, finally being chased away from center-stage in the early modern period. Western philosophy began about two-and-a-half thousand years ago, with the Pre-Socratics. And for about half that time, from the third to the fifteenth centuries AD, philosophy was to a significant extent dominated by Neoplatonism.

The achievement is so significant that it remains impressive even once we register a few caveats. For one thing, Plotinus never set out to create a new philosophical system. It's worth reiterating that he and other late ancient Platonists called themselves just that—Platonists, not Neoplatonists, a term devised by modern scholars and originally used in a rather dismissive fashion. We should also recognize that the new Platonism of Plotinus was not as "new" as is sometimes thought. The so-called "Middle" Platonists anticipated Plotinus' ideas to a great extent—indeed, to such an extent that Plotinus' detractors accused him of plagiarizing from the earlier Platonist Numenius (see Chapter 22). For these reasons, the Platonists who came after Plotinus did not see him as representing a break with the earlier tradition, any more than Plotinus saw himself this way. Neoplatonists like Iamblichus and Proclus respected Plotinus deeply. But they saw him as only one particularly significant link in a chain of Platonist authorities. Finally, we should bear in mind that, especially in the medieval period, Neoplatonism could travel without the original texts of Plotinus in tow. Most Latin medieval thinkers had no access to his writings. In Arabic his texts were only partly available in a translation that was incorrectly ascribed to Aristotle.

We ourselves are more fortunate: we can read everything Plotinus wrote. For this we must thank Plotinus' student Porphyry, who produced an edition of the writings. He gave the individual treatises titles, which they had lacked before, and called the entire thing *Enneads*, meaning "*Nines*." This is because he had grouped the treatises into six sets of nine. Porphyry was as much a sucker for numbers and their deeper symbolism as the next Platonist. So naturally the possibility of arranging his master's philosophy in this format was irresistible. In fact he cheated a bit to get the six-by-nine result, taking longer works and splitting them up into several treatises, in one case dividing a treatise in the middle of a sentence! The most striking example is a lengthy work by Plotinus known nowadays by the German nickname *Großschrift*, which sounds to English speakers like it might mean "disgusting treatise," but in fact just means "big treatise." Porphyry not only divided it into four separate pieces, but he separated them and put them out of order in various sections of the *Enneads* (treatises 3.8, 5.8, 5.5, and 2.9). The moral of this story is: if one of your students offers to edit your collected writings, ask to see the planned table of contents first.

Yet we should be grateful to Porphyry, not only because he preserved Plotinus' writings for posterity but also because he wrote a kind of introduction, which was attached to the editions and was transmitted in manuscripts of the *Enneads*. This introduction combined a biography of Plotinus with an explanation of how the *Enneads* were put together, along with a few tributes to Plotinus by contemporaries. This so-called *Life of Plotinus* is absolutely packed with memorable anecdotes and fascinating windows into the activities of Plotinus' school, and in its way is as invaluable a document for the birth of Neoplatonism as any of Plotinus' own treatises. In writing the *Life* Porphyry has two great themes. First, Plotinus was a really wonderful guy. Second, Porphyry is a pretty wonderful guy too. Porphyry rarely misses a chance to let the *Life* reflect well on himself. The scholar Gillian Clark has remarked that the phrase "I, Porphyry" recurs in the *Life* so often that it is unintentionally comic.[2] In particular, Porphyry wants to leave the reader with the strong impression that he, Porphyry, is Plotinus' most cherished and important disciple. For instance, he lets it drop that Plotinus' best works were those written after he, Porphyry, joined the school, and that some of these were written in direct response to probing questions raised by him, Porphyry (13).

He has some competition here from another disciple of Plotinus, named Amelius. This might explain why Porphyry starts the *Life* with the following anecdote (1). Amelius wanted to have Plotinus sit for a painted or sculpted portrait. Plotinus said: isn't it enough that I have to carry around the image that is my body, without making an image of that image? Amelius responded by inviting a painter to attend sessions at the school until he'd memorized Plotinus' face, and with further input from Amelius a portrait was made anyway. It's a good story and one that highlights Plotinus' consistency in adhering to Platonist principles. Also, it just happens to put Amelius in a slightly bad light. You can imagine Porphyry watching the whole thing unfold and thinking, "Oh man, if I ever write a biography of our master Plotinus, I'm definitely starting with this." He also mentions that a set of copies of Plotinus' works prepared by Amelius produced complaints (19–20), though Porphyry does excuse Amelius by saying that Plotinus' way of writing was just rather unusual—which is true enough, as anyone who has read him in Greek can attest. Compounding this difficulty, as he, Porphyry, tells us, was the fact that Plotinus had bad eyesight and therefore never read over what he had written. Again, the story evokes a slightly otherworldly Platonist sage—more acute in mind than in sensation—while incidentally excusing Porphyry for any deficiencies in his own edition.

But perhaps I'm putting Porphyry himself in an unfairly bad light. He does have nice things to say about Amelius too, and my hunch is that their relationship was more one of friendly competition than serious rivalry. For instance, we know

Plotinus was said to have plagiarized from Numenius because Porphyry quotes from Amelius' refutation of this accusation (17). Porphyry even tells a story that puts himself in a worse light than Amelius. When he first came to Plotinus' school he still adhered to doctrines he'd learned from his previous teacher, Longinus. Porphyry and Longinus were convinced that the Platonic Forms are outside the divine intellect, beheld as a kind of external blueprint in accordance with which god makes the world. Plotinus assigned to Amelius the task of converting Porphyry to the school's doctrine, namely that the Forms are rather ideas in a divine mind. After an exchange of written arguments with Amelius, Porphyry finally gave in and converted to Plotinus' teaching on the matter (18).

Porphyry's *Life of Plotinus* already raises several key themes of Plotinus' philosophy. For example, in his writings Plotinus frequently seems torn about the value of the physical world. His fundamental ethical teaching is that we should turn away from the things of the body and pursue the life of the mind, which means discovering one's true self. The point is made by numerous anecdotes, including the story about the painting. Elsewhere in the *Life* Porphyry tells how Plotinus was able to continue contemplating intelligible things even while having a conversation (8). Other anecdotes expound this spiritual perfection of Plotinus against the backdrop of late antique religious beliefs, reminding us that this was a time when astrology, magic, and the presence of the gods were everyday realities. In one story a magician hostile to Plotinus tries to cast a curse on him, but Plotinus' soul is so powerful that the spell rebounds and afflicts the magician instead (10). In another, Plotinus is invited by a friend to a summoning of his guardian spirit. When the spirit appears the priest announces that Plotinus' guardian is no mere minor demon, as expected, but a full-blown god. The god, however, disappears, because the friend is frightened or jealous and strangles the ritual birds he is holding (10).

From these anecdotes we get a strong sense of Plotinus as an otherworldly figure, who barely deigns to notice his own body and who dwells more with the gods than with the rest of us. But Porphyry tells us that Plotinus was a man of this world, as well as the divine world. He attracted students from all over the Mediterranean—Porphyry was from Tyre in modern-day Lebanon, and other students came from Egypt (like Plotinus himself), from Arabia, from Palestine. In Rome Plotinus moved in aristocratic circles, and was entrusted with guardianship over orphans from among these elite (9). Even the emperor Gallienus was a fan, and through his good offices Plotinus hatched a plan to found a new city called Platonopolis, which would be ruled in accordance with Plato's proposed legal system (12). This doesn't sound like a man with no time for the physical world around him. Some of Porphyry's more picturesque anecdotes would lead to the same conclusion. When he, Porphyry, fell into a bout of suicidal depression, Plotinus recommended that he should go abroad to a better climate, and this indeed cured him (19). On another occasion Plotinus was told of a theft in a rich household. He had all the slaves lined up, eyeballed them, and picked out the culprit on sight (11). I can't resist mentioning that a very similar scene occurs in Buster Keaton's wonderful film *Sherlock Jr.* Well, maybe I could have resisted. I don't know, because I didn't try.

Plotinus was clearly much better than I am at resisting temptation. He was abstemious and refused to consume animal products, even in medicines (2). He also paid heed to the welfare of the people around him, and even went out of his way to do so, as with the scheme for Platonopolis. Some interpreters have felt that Plotinus' philosophy gives us little or no reason to strive for practical virtue.[3] His way of life shows, however, that it gave him reason enough. Still, there's no doubt that Plotinus devoted his life to philosophy. We learn one startling detail about Plotinus' childhood from Porphyry—that he still wanted to be breast-fed at the age of eight (3)—but mostly the life-story concerns his philosophical development. He was from Egypt and came to Alexandria in search of a teacher; there he met Ammonius Saccas, about whom we unfortunately know little. If you're keeping count, this is the second of the three men named Ammonius I mentioned in Chapter 24. Even Plotinus' decision to join a military expedition led by the emperor Gordian is explained by Porphyry as stemming from Plotinus' desire to travel east, where he might encounter the wisdom of Persia and India (3). Whether he learned anything there that actually influenced his thought is an interesting question. The most careful examination I've seen suggests, somewhat disappointingly, that there is no evidence of detailed influence on Plotinus from Indian philosophy, even if he and Porphyry were intrigued by the notion of wisdom from the East.[4]

Plotinus had influences enough to deal with, of course. As I said, he brought together themes not only from Plato but also the Stoics and Aristotle. Porphyry tells us that Aristotle's *Metaphysics* is distilled in the *Enneads,* and that the works of Alexander of Aphrodisias were read in Plotinus' school (14). But obviously, Plotinus' main inheritance was from the Platonist tradition. Like the so-called "Middle" Platonists, Plotinus especially favored certain dialogues, and certain passages in those dialogues. For him, the crucial texts were metaphysically rich dialogues like the *Parmenides,* the *Timaeus,* and the middle part of the *Republic.* Certain bits of the *Philebus* and *Theaetetus* also made a big impression. By contrast, one could read the whole *Enneads* without being reminded of so-called "Socratic" dialogues, like the *Euthyphro.* Still, Plato was read carefully in Plotinus' circle, and a handful of treatises in the *Enneads* are little more than direct commentaries on a passage from Plato. On the basis of his favorite Platonic passages, and the interpretations of Plato that came to him from earlier Platonists like Numenius, Plotinus devised the system that would remain the core of pagan Neoplatonism for generations to come.

This system takes the form of a hierarchy, in which a highest principle gives rise to a second principle, which in turn gives rise to a third. All three of these principles transcend the physical world, yet Plotinus describes them with vivid analogies drawn from nature. They are like shining lights, overflowing fountains, burning flames, or in one fantastic passage, a sphere with many faces (6.7.15). At the top we have a first cause, which is more or less familiar from the Middle Platonists: the One, also called the Good. It is comparable to a brilliant light that gives rise to a secondary light, like a ray shines out of the sun. This secondary principle is called by Plotinus *nous*, or "Intellect." I mentioned that Porphyry at first was unconvinced by Plotinus' central insight about the Intellect, namely that it should be identified with the Forms, which are its own ideas. This Intellect is very like Aristotle's God, a pure mind that does nothing but think—although this Intellect is not the First Cause, but secondary to the One. After the Intellect comes soul, the principle of life and order for the physical cosmos. Its function is to bring images of the Forms into matter, which results in the making of physical things.

Customarily, nature or the physical world is treated as the fourth rung in Plotinus metaphysical ladder, giving us the sequence: One, intellect, soul, nature. But in fact Plotinus is reluctant to concede genuine being or existence to the things in the material or natural world. At one point he tells us that "everything matter says is a lie" (3.6.7), and as this suggests, bodies are for him more illusion than reality. Hence his remark to Amelius that his own body is only an image of his true self. He would disagree with Hamlet, who was frustrated that his too, too solid flesh refused to melt and resolve into a dew. For Plotinus our bodies are only seemingly solid, since they are in continual flux, making a constant retreat into non-being. At this level of reality, or apparent reality, Plotinus is a Heraclitean. So, to a considerable extent, Plotinus' metaphysical picture consists *only* of One, intellect, and soul. This will make it difficult for him to explain why there is matter, which receives the fleeting images of the Forms that yield bodies.

The consequences of all this are momentous, and not only for metaphysics. For example, in epistemology: even the sketch of the system I've just given shows that, for Plotinus, genuine knowledge must involve access to the Intellect and its Forms, rather than pertaining to the bodily world. Or in aesthetics: all order and beauty in our realm is a mere shadow of the true order and beauty in that realm of Forms. Or in ethics: it would seem that the attention we pay to the physical world is misguided, quite literally much ado about nothing (to continue the Shakespearean theme). What we ought to do is concern ourselves with the sources of value that transcend our image world, the Forms in *nous* and ultimately the Good itself, from which all things have emanated. It is also by turning away from our material world that we can hope to discover our true selves, since we are not our bodies but our souls. Indeed, we are only the highest, thinking part of our souls, the part that is furthest removed from bodies.

Now you can see why it might be difficult for Plotinus to explain why we should strive for practical virtue. Why wasn't the time he spent caring for orphans and planning cities just wasted, since it was a distraction from the really crucial task of contemplating the higher realities? Indeed, why even write the *Enneads* themselves, which are, after all, a way for Plotinus to reach out to the students and other readers around him, instead of reaching for the stars of his otherworldly heaven? This is a puzzle I'm going to defer solving until a future chapter. Because first I want to look at the even more fundamental puzzles that arise at the top of Plotinus' hierarchy. What was Plotinus' justification for positing a single, utterly simple principle as the source of all things? How, if at all, can we conceive of such an entity, and how should we understand it to relate to the other principles that come after it?

30

SIMPLICITY ITSELF
PLOTINUS ON THE ONE AND INTELLECT

Here's a trivia question you won't hear at any pub-quiz night: what do armies, houses, sunflowers, and giraffes have in common? Things painted by Van Gogh, perhaps? No. He inexplicably failed to capture the noble giraffe in any of his artworks, and I don't believe he was particularly keen on armies either. The right answer is that all these things are mentioned at the beginning of Plotinus' treatise *On the One* (6.9.1), which was placed at the very end of the *Enneads* by his student and editor Porphyry. Actually, he doesn't mention sunflowers or giraffes by name, speaking instead generally of plants and animals, but I think we all know at least which animal he had in mind. He mentions these things because of something else they have in common: they are all one. Without unity an army would just be a bunch of people standing around with an alarming amount of weaponry. And nothing can be a giraffe without being one giraffe. Indeed, to qualify as a thing of any kind is to be *one* thing—unity is a condition of being.

On the other hand, not everything possesses unity to the same degree. Though you might say that each army is one army just as much as each sunflower is one sunflower, armies clearly have less unity than sunflowers. Like all plants and animals, the bodies of sunflowers and giraffes are animated by an internal principle of life. This explains their ability to nourish themselves, to turn towards the sun, or lope gracefully towards tasty acacia leaves. By contrast, things like armies and houses have unity imposed upon them, by generals or house-builders. Aristotle would say that such things have their unity accidentally and from outside, whereas living organisms have an innate, essential unity. Plotinus would agree, and infer a general metaphysical principle: the more unity something has, the more reality it has, and vice versa. An army is a being to a lesser extent than a sunflower, even if it is considerably more dangerous than a sunflower.

Plotinus points out in this same passage that good conditions like health and beauty are also cases of unity (6.9.1). What is health, after all, other than the cooperative ordering of the body's parts, while illness is the result of these parts coming into conflict with one another? What is beauty but a kind of harmony? And what is harmony but a kind of unity? The same is true even for the human soul, at least according to Plato. It has parts, and the virtuous soul is the soul that achieves harmony and unity through the unchallenged mastery of its rational part.[1] Or consider, finally, the entire cosmos. Nowadays science has arguably exposed the physical universe as something of a chaotic mess, though some think that there is a divine plan behind the apparent chaos. But in antiquity almost everyone, with the notable exception of the Epicureans, considered the universe to be well ordered and unified. Plato compared it to a single animal (*Timaeus* 30b–d), and Aristotle finished his inquiry into how God moves the heavens by quoting Homer: "the rule of many is not one; let there be one ruler" (*Metaphysics* 1076a).

These considerations lead Plotinus to an inescapable conclusion: if we are looking for the source of all things, we should be looking for a source of unity that is itself maximally one. It will also be the source of goodness, beauty, harmony, and order. It will be that from which all else derives and towards which all things strive to return in whatever way they can. Plotinus calls it "the One" or "the Good." Of course, these ideas do not derive exclusively from Plotinus, the way all things are meant to derive from the One. Looking back as far as Parmenides, we have the idea of reducing reality to a principle of unity. Plato introduces a Form of the Good in the *Republic*, and makes it the source of intelligibility and value for all other Forms. We then come even closer to Plotinus' conception in the Old Academy and Middle Platonists, who try various ways of putting a principle of unity at the top of their metaphysical systems.[2]

Plotinus recognizes all these intellectual debts, especially the ones to Parmenides and Plato. It is telling, though, that he does not begin this treatise *On the One* by surveying previous opinions, as Aristotle might have done. Instead, he starts with armies and houses, sunflowers and giraffes. Similarly, he says in another treatise on the topic of the One that we should start our inquiry not with the ultimate principle, but by thinking about ourselves (6.8.1). This is part of what distinguishes Plotinus from his predecessors among the so-called "Middle Platonists"—at least, as far as we can tell, given how incompletely we know them. Plotinus does offer detailed expositions of Platonic dialogues, and he does occasionally save time by assuming the truth of Platonic metaphysics so he can focus on the finer points. But his natural mode is dialectical. He probes problems, seeking to persuade and carry the reader with him, not just to lay out preconceived doctrine. Even when he stretches his inquiry to the limit by trying to understand the One, he asks us to begin by reflecting on familiar things and on ourselves.

Unlike the familiar things of our world, the One must, of course, be incorporeal. Bodies have many parts, and also change over time—so they are multiple in at least two ways. The soul is immaterial and thus has a higher kind of unity. But it too has parts, as Plato already established by pointing to the all-too-familiar phenomenon of inward psychic conflict. Like bodies, it also changes over time. Even the soul's thinking involves change, as it passes from one idea to the next. Which appropriately enough leads us to the next thought: couldn't the first principle be a mind? Not the human soul, perhaps, but an immaterial intellect, that would grasp its knowledge all at once and never do anything else? The suggestion was certainly an option for Plotinus. After all, Aristotle's god is precisely this, a pure intellect that always thinks upon itself. More recently, Platonists like Philo of Alexandria had understood Platonic Forms to be ideas in the mind of God, the cause of all things (see Chapter 23). Plotinus thinks this proposal is on the right track. He agrees that Forms are ideas in a divine mind or Intellect—in Greek, *nous*. He just doesn't think that this Intellect is the first principle, because it falls short of total unity.

It's here that we start to see just how radical is Plotinus' understanding of the One. So radical, in fact, that it's not clear that he or anyone else *can* understand the One. After all, the Forms were always supposed to be the objects that ground all our knowledge. They just are what is knowable, what is intelligible. To make them ideas in a divine Intellect but then say that the One is beyond that Intellect seems to imply that the One cannot be known. For the most part, Plotinus accepts this conclusion. Occasionally he will try to push the boundaries of what language and philosophy can offer (especially in treatise 6.8), but his usual line is that the One is ineffable, that is, beyond anything we can say or think. To say or think anything about it would be to turn it into a multiplicity. For instance, although Plotinus treats this principle as both the One and the Good, if I say something like "the One is good," then I seem to be applying a property to something that has the property (6.9.6). So I'd have two things, the One and its goodness, which are at least conceptually distinct. But the whole point of the One is that it is beyond all multiplicity.

There remains the possibility that the One is accessible to us, but not through language or thought. If we are to reach the One, it would seem that we could only do so by achieving complete unity with it. Porphyry tells us in the biography of his master that Plotinus managed to do this only four times during their time together (23). In Plotinus' writings there are allusions to these experiences, which one can only call mystical. Perhaps the most evocative is the last sentence of one treatise, where Plotinus has asked how we are to reach this origin of all things. He answers his own question with the words *aphele panta*: "take away everything" (5.3.17). But the prospect of *henosis*, or unification with the One, does not play a central role in the *Enneads*, and tends, in my opinion, to loom larger than it should in discussions of his philosophy. His more important philosophical claim, and more important legacy for later thinkers, is that the One transcends Intellect and the Forms.

This result is paradoxical. Remember, we were looking for ever more intense examples of unity because we observed that unity is correlated with reality, intelligibility, and order. But we've ended by positing a principle beyond intelligibility and order. More paradoxically still, the One is in a sense even beyond reality. Plotinus understands Intellect to be the paradigm of being, and the Forms as the manifold expression of all the sorts of being that there are. The Form of Giraffe is just what it is to be a giraffe, and the Form of Sunflower is the being of sunflowers. Thus Plotinus frequently (for instance at 3.8.9) quotes one of his favorite lines from Plato, a remark Socrates makes about the Form of the Good: the Good is said to be "beyond being in majesty and power" (*Republic* 508b). Plotinus takes Plato to mean that the Good or One is in fact not a Form after all, but transcendent above the realm of Forms, and thus "beyond being."[3]

The extremes to which Plotinus has led us are apt to make us wonder whether we should have followed him this far. Perhaps we should have stopped with Intellect and its Forms, as Philo of Alexandria did? But that would be to overlook Plotinus' subtle analysis of how Intellect falls short of absolute unity. For one thing, even if it is thinking about all the Forms at once without ever passing from one Form to another, it will still be thinking about many Forms. Indeed, there are presumably an indefinitely large number of Forms—a result that will follow quickly if we accept that there are Forms of numbers.[4] So Intellect displays an indefinite multiplicity because of the objects of its thought. Plotinus also points out that if the Forms are internal to the Intellect, it will be thinking about itself when it thinks about them (5.5). It is, then, both that which is thinking and that which is being thought. As both subject and object of thought, it has a kind of duality that the truly first principle must lack. Plotinus sums up these findings by calling the Intellect a *hen kai polla*: a "one-and-many" (5.1.8, quoting Plato, *Parmenides* 144e). It has a very impressive degree of unity, being not only immaterial but unchanging and identical with the objects of its own thought. Indeed, it is the most unified thing that can be conceived. But the very fact that it can be conceived, and that it conceives itself, shows that it is not utterly one and is thus not first.

If you still wanted to resist this conclusion, you might offer the following alternative. What if the Forms were not inside the Intellect, as Plotinus is claiming, but distinct from it? Then it could be a simple mind that looks to Forms that are safely outside it, where they would not compromise its oneness. Plato actually says in the *Timaeus* that god "looks to the Forms" when designing the world (29a), and some Platonists had taken this to mean that the Forms are independent of the divine mind. In fact this was the view Porphyry held when he turned up at Plotinus' school. As we saw above, he'd been taught it from his earlier instructor, a man named Longinus, who was better known for his linguistic and textual expertise than his philosophical sophistication. Porphyry stuck to Longinus' position tenaciously and gave in to Plotinus' view only after a debate with his fellow student Amelius. We are not told what the decisive point in this debate may have been, but in his writings Plotinus offers a powerful reason to think that Intellect is identical with its objects, rather than looking to Forms that are external to it. His argument looks similar to one given by Sextus Empiricus, a rare borrowing from the Skeptical tradition.

The argument begins from the point that whatever grasps an external object has only a representation of that object (5.5.1). For instance, when we see a giraffe cantering across the savannah, the giraffe is not actually in our eye or our eyesight. Rather, we are getting a visual image of the giraffe. But when images are involved there is always a risk of error. A further principle is needed to provide some kind of guarantee, to come along and ratify that the image is accurate. Thus reason frequently corrects the images offered to it in sensation, judging perhaps that that shimmering object just behind the giraffe is not a pool of water, as it seems to be, but rather a mirage. It's no problem that sensation works like this, but at the level of Intellect it would be a disaster. After all, Intellect was supposed to be the paradigmatic case of knowledge. So how could it need yet a further principle to tell it that its intellection is true? We are in danger of infinite regress, with each kind of cognition needing another kind of cognition to reassure it that it is really getting things right. By insisting that the Forms are inside the Intellect Plotinus avoids this problem: Intellect knows that its knowledge is knowledge, because what it knows is nothing other than itself.

Now, doing philosophy is like taking care of small children. No sooner have you solved one problem than the next problem is looming into view (and we wouldn't have it any other way). In this case, Plotinus' success in proving the multiplicity of Intellect leaves us with the puzzle of how the One could possibly have produced something of this sort. The One is supposedly the source of all things. But if it is utterly and completely one, how does it generate something multiple? Later authors, wondering about this aspect of Neoplatonism, invoke the so-called *ex uno unum* principle: from one thing, you only get one thing. And although Plotinus doesn't explicitly endorse a principle along these lines, he clearly sees it as an important challenge to explain how multiplicity can arise from unity. Unlike Neil Armstrong, he doesn't try to accomplish this giant leap in just one step. Instead, the production of *nous* from the One is a two-stage process.

First, the simple One allows an equally simple second principle to go forth from itself. This second principle, which will become the Intellect, then turns back upon its source, like a child looking towards its father. In an almost tragic turn of events, it finds that it cannot grasp its father—that would compromise the One's transcendence. Instead it does the next best thing, grasping itself and making itself an image of the One. As it does so it generates the Forms as its ideas, in a single act of intellection that imitates the total simplicity of the One (5.1.7, 5.3.11, 5.4.2). The puzzling thing here, if there is only one puzzling thing, is why this should give rise to the Forms. Plotinus says at one point, "the One is all things, and no one of them" (5.2.1), which I take to mean that the One has the power to generate everything that comes after it, though it remains distinct from everything it generates. Only once Intellect begins to think about itself does it become clear what these things will be. One might further wonder why it is that we get just the Forms that emerge, and not some other Forms. Why is there a Form of Giraffe and no Form of Unicorn? Perhaps our questions are simply wrong-headed, though. Intellect knows whatever there is to know, and this does not include Unicorn, because there is no such thing as a unicorn. This is a matter of necessity. It's not as if Intellect is deciding to think about Giraffe, but giving Unicorn a miss even though it could have thought about that, too. At this level of the Plotinian universe everything that happens is inevitable.

That, of course, brings us to yet another problem. Even if we accept this rather mysterious story about how Intellect is produced by the One, we might be reluctant to accept the idea that it proceeds from the One necessarily. Plotinus uses a variety of metaphors to describe the way Intellect cascades forth from the One. The One is like an overflowing fountain or a shining light. He uses the same language of "emanation" to speak of the production of Soul from Intellect. Subsequently, many philosophers and theologians will complain that this makes the divine principles automatic causes. If the One gives rise to Intellect necessarily, then it is like fire mindlessly giving off heat. Anyone who conceives of the first principle as a generous God, who freely gives a gratuitous gift when He creates the universe, will find this conception disappointing, to say the least. In fact, doubly so. Not only does the One cause its effects necessarily, but it causes most of its effects indirectly. Strictly speaking, it gives rise only to the inchoate subject of thought that will become Intellect when it generates the Forms within itself. Soul is then produced by Intellect, not the One, and the One has only a very distant and mediated relationship to the physical universe. This looks to be a far cry from the voluntary creation of all things envisioned in the Bible and Koran.

And yet Plotinus devoted an ambitious treatise to the freedom of the first principle (6.8). He begins from the nature of human freedom, asking what it means for something to be—as the Stoics liked to put it—"up to us." He answers that our actions are up to us when we are masters of ourselves, rather than being pulled this way and that by external forces (6.8.1). Of course, he considers the desires and needs that derive from bodily existence to be forces external to our souls. The One, by contrast, has no such competing demands on its attention, and is influenced by nothing outside itself. Strictly speaking, we cannot say that it "masters itself," because that would introduce the same kind of duality as would arise if it were to think about itself (6.8.12). But we can still say that it is free in the negative sense that nothing is exercising compulsion upon it.

Ironically, then, Plotinus' conception of freedom does not look that far from what we find in the Stoics, despite their materialism—and in fact among philosophers nowadays with similar inclinations. For him, freedom is simply the power to do what one wishes without hindrance or compulsion exercised by anything else. Again, strictly speaking, we cannot say that the One "wishes" to do anything, but this treatise is notable for Plotinus' willingness to speak more positively about the One than usual, often adding the caveat *hoion*, meaning "so to speak" or "as if." Thus, we can say that the One is free because it is "as if" it can act by doing whatever it wants, "so to speak." We souls, existing at a much lower level of Plotinus' scheme, can only strive towards the same kind of untrammeled freedom of action. We achieve this above all by—what else?—doing philosophy. Indeed, although Plotinus is perhaps most famous for his ideas about the One, he devotes much more attention to the soul, investigating its powers, the dangers of its relation to the body, and its relationship to the higher principles of Intellect and the One.

ON THE HORIZON
PLOTINUS ON THE SOUL

Wouldn't it be fun to invite an assortment of ancient philosophers to a screening of the *Wizard of Oz*? Just picture the scene. The Stoics would be muttering critically about the Tin Man's deplorable desire to get in touch with his emotions, and pointing out that if the Scarecrow wants to be clever, he should wish for a heart and not a brain. Aristotle would be sitting at the back, taking notes on the winged monkeys for his zoological writings. Galen and the anatomists of Alexandria would tap their toes as the Cowardly Lion launched into their favorite tune, "If I Only Had the Nerve." Thales would feel vindicated by the fact that the heroes win the day by using a bucket of water. Meanwhile the Pythagoreans would be trying to get everyone to be quiet. And Plotinus? I think his favorite scene would come at the end, when Dorothy says: "If I ever go looking for my heart's desire again, I won't look any further than my own backyard. Because if it isn't there, I never really lost it to begin with."

Dorothy's observation might well remind Plotinus of something he says in one of his own treatises: "One might be unaware that one has something, holding onto it more powerfully than if one did know" (4.4.4). He is describing the way that the human soul relates to the things it has seen in the intelligible realm, the realm of the Forms. Following Plato, he believes that the soul is eternal and has seen the wondrous beauty and truth of this realm before it came to be in a body.[1] Yet the embodied soul retains a memory of these realities, and Plotinus here suggests that the deeply buried memory of the Forms is possessed more intensely than the soul's conscious experiences. Thanks to your soul's relationship to a body, it is aware of an almost unceasing stream of sensory phenomena—the whirlwind of colors, motions, and sounds that reach it through the eyes and the ears. It's easy for the soul to be distracted by these fleeting impressions. In its most debased condition, the soul may become so confused as actually to identify itself with the body. But Plotinus believes that even people in this condition have within them the power to remember what they have seen in the world of the intellect.

On this score Plotinus is more optimistic than almost any other late ancient Platonist. Not only does he believe that we can find traces of the intelligible within ourselves; he is convinced that we never depart completely from the intelligible world. The soul remains in part "undescended," in other words, still actively contemplating the Forms even while it is ensconced in a material body. He knows this idea is controversial and even paradoxical, at one point introducing it with the phrase, "if we may dare to present our own opinion" (4.8.8). After all, as later Platonists like Iamblichus and Proclus pointed out, it's hard to see how it could be that I am even now engaging in an intellectual vision of the Forms without my being aware of it. But Plotinus is, among other things, a pioneer in the philosophy of awareness. For him, the soul's challenge is not to achieve union or contact with the intelligible Forms. Rather, the soul needs to realize that it is *already* always in contact with those Forms, and to this extent not just a soul but an intellect. Characteristically, he offers an analogy drawn from everyday experience (1.4.10): when you are concentrating on reading a book, you are not aware that you are reading. Nor does the brave man fighting in battle consciously think that he is being courageous. (The surprisingly Plotinian *Wizard of Oz* incidentally makes the same point: the Cowardly Lion does not realize he is brave, nor is the Tin Man aware of his own compassion.)

Plotinus showed his own compassion by writing the *Enneads*. They are many things—a running engagement on themes and passages in Plato and later thinkers, a conversation with imaginary opponents and his own students, technical treatises suffused with powerful and even poetic imagery. But above all, they constitute an act of charity on Plotinus' part. He has already identified with his true intellectual self. Porphyry tells us that he could continue to commune with intellect even during a conversation (*Life of Plotinus* 8). So he already has his heart's desire, and stands to gain nothing personally from straining his bad eyesight to write the treatises collected as the *Enneads*. Much as the One and the intellect spontaneously give rise to the good things that come after them, Plotinus wrote anyway, as an exhortation for his students and readers. The soul is the only part of Plotinus' universe that could need such an exhortation. The One, of course, reigns in its supreme and silent singularity, while the intellect permanently thinks about the Forms that are its ideas. Below the soul there is the mindless indefiniteness of matter, something we'll discuss in the next chapter. But the soul, uniquely, is torn between two possibilities. As Plotinus says (4.4.3), it is "on the horizon" of the bodily and the intelligible. The point of philosophy is to turn our attention upwards, away from our bodies and towards the immaterial causes that are more real than any body. Plotinus wants to wake us up, to tell us that there's no place like home, and that we have never left it.

Plotinus was well aware of philosophical rivals who denied the reality of Forms or a world of intellect, who even denied the immateriality of the soul itself. He finds it hard to take the Epicureans seriously, so his main opponents here are the Stoics. Despite being cleverer than any Scarecrow, they were convinced that they, or their souls, were nothing but material objects. Plotinus is happy to set up Stoic materialism as a straw man to be knocked down, and also directs his fire at Aristotle's claim that the soul is the form of the body (4.3.20, 4.7.8, 6.7.4). Against such views, Plotinus argues in a variety of ways for soul's independence as an incorporeal substance. As so often, he focuses on unity. The body has separate parts, whereas the soul does not. For one thing, the soul can grasp immaterial objects of thought, and he fails to see how something with separate parts could grasp something that has no parts. He draws a similar conclusion from the soul's awareness of what is happening in the body. After all, it is not as if we have one soul in our finger to perceive things that happen to the finger, and another soul in some other part of the body (4.1.2). Rather, the soul is a unified locus of awareness for the entire body. He dismisses Stoic attempts to explain this via some kind of chain-reaction of physical signals through the body, to a so-called "ruling faculty" seated in the heart. If that were the case there would be only an indirect perception of what happens in the finger, whereas Plotinus wants to insist that the soul is wholly and immediately aware of each bodily experience. On the other hand, when he gives his own theory of perception he insists that the soul cannot actually be *affected* by anything that happens in the body (3.6.1).[2] Rather, the single soul makes a discrimination or judgment on the basis of material events that happen in the sense organs.

Rather ironically, given Plotinus' scorn for Stoic materialism, the philosopher who comes closest to anticipating his ideas about the self is probably the Stoic Epictetus. Stoics had long held that the rational part of each person stands in judgment over the impressions of sense-experience. And in Stoic ethics, especially Epictetus—who lived only a few generations before Plotinus—we found the idea that the true self is the reasoning aspect of the person, and that wisdom consists in valuing this true self rather than apparent bodily goods like wealth, food, pleasurable experience, or even physical health (see Chapter 13). Plotinus endorses these Stoic ideas, but draws more radical conclusions. In the treatise that Porphyry placed at the very beginning of the *Enneads* (1.1), Plotinus asks who "we" are, thus tackling the question of the self more directly than any philosopher had done before. As we would by now expect, he concludes that our true self is the higher aspect of soul that engages in intellection, and not the self of bodily experience.

In a remarkable final paragraph (1.1.13), though, Plotinus wonders who it is that is inquiring into the identity of the self. Is that really "us"? There is a paradox lurking here: if the real "me" is the "me" who is always contemplating the Forms, then whose attention needs to be turned to the Forms? Apparently, not my own attention, since I am really only my intellectual self, whether the lower, incidental part of me knows it or not. As usual in Plotinus, the solution lies in unity. I should be trying not just to figure out which part of me is the real me, but to make all of me into a single, self-aware being. That means continuing to have bodily experiences, but to recognize these experiences for the incidental, fleeting, valueless things that they are—and also to understand how they relate to my higher self. So Plotinus can also say that my "self" is that which becomes aware of both its higher and its lower nature. The goal is to integrate and unify these two aspects, by doing some philosophy and thus obeying the Delphic command, "Know thyself."

Does this mean that the soul has no nature of its own by which it is distinguished from both body and intellect? Or is it nothing but a center of attention that can look up or down? For all his talk of soul as existing on a horizon, Plotinus does think that some activities exist properly at the level of soul. Above all, the activity of discursive reasoning (in Greek, *dianoia*). He sharply distinguishes this kind of thinking from the intellection (*noesis*) that we find in the case of Intellect or *nous*. Whereas *nous* grasps all possible objects of knowledge all at once, it is characteristic of soul to think first about one thing then about something else. Those of us who find it hard to think about even one thing at a time may find this impressive enough, but for Plotinus the soul's reasoning activity is a mere image of the perfect thinking of Intellect. Still, we shouldn't be too discouraged. Soul does manage to think about the same things as Intellect, albeit in a more laborious and partial way. We can thus consider the soul's discursive thought to be a kind of unfolding or piecemeal spelling out of the undivided, complete knowledge possessed by Intellect.

The fact that soul re-enacts the activity of Intellect in a lesser, more divided way has far-reaching consequences in Plotinus' philosophy. For one thing, it allows him to give a novel theory of time and to explain how time relates to eternity (3.7). As so often in late ancient Platonism, the touchstone text here is Plato's *Timaeus*. There we learn that time comes about along with the orderly motions of the heavens in the physical cosmos, whereas eternity is appropriate to immaterial beings like the Forms and the divine craftsman. Plato also has Timaeus say that time is the "moving image of eternity" (37d). With his distinction between the all-at-once activity of Intellect and the one-thing-after-another activity of soul, Plotinus is able to explain Plato's remarks as follows. Eternity is the "life of Intellect" (3.7.3). It is simply a name for the way that Forms are all simultaneously and permanently grasped in the Intellect's contemplation. Time is correspondingly the "life of soul."

Since we are souls, we have an intimate experience of time as we go through our sequential thought processes. To say that our thinking is "discursive" is just to say that it happens in time—to think at one time about one thing, and then at another time about something else. Suppose you are following a philosophical argument. You consider each premise in turn and then see that a conclusion follows from these premises. Or consider the more homely example of reading this chapter. You aren't thinking about the ideas I'm trying to explain all at once, but one idea after another. First you pondered the *Wizard of Oz*, then you contemplated the undescended soul, and now you're wondering what to have for dinner, because your mind started wandering about two paragraphs ago. (Don't feel bad, it happens to all of us.) Because this discursive kind of thinking is an image or unfolding of the Intellect's comprehension, Plotinus can say that Plato was right. Time is indeed an image of eternity.

For Plotinus, then, eternity is not simply unending time. On his theory, if you pledge to love someone forever you aren't, strictly speaking, pledging to love them "eternally." You're only promising to love them at every moment of future time. Plotinian eternity, by contrast, doesn't mean "at every moment," whether past, present, or future. It means timelessness. Plotinus' theory itself achieved a kind of timelessness, being embraced by many generations of philosophers in Neoplatonism and beyond. Christian thinkers like Boethius and Aquinas, for instance, will gladly agree that God is beyond time and has His knowledge all at once (for Boethius see Chapter 53). Though Plotinus' idea of eternity was thus very influential, the way he tries to convey the idea can be puzzling. Though he will say that the notions of "before" and "after" do not apply to the eternal Intellect, he still applies words like "always" to it, and at one point even says that "it always was and always will be" (5.8.12). This sounds like he is applying temporal concepts to eternity after all, though he does immediately warn us that the words he is using are misleading.[3]

A further problem is that he thinks the soul and physical universe must be everlasting, that is, infinite in past and future time. He thinks this will make them the best possible image of eternity. But it's hard to see why that should be so. If eternity really means the *absence* of duration, why should infinite duration be a more faithful image of eternity than temporary duration? Indeed, how could any kind of duration be an image of something that totally lacks duration? And there's yet another puzzle here, regarding soul's relationship to intellect. He keeps telling us that, as souls, our goal is to realize our connection to intellect. But insofar as we are consciously thinking like the intellect, our thinking is eternal and timeless—how, then, does it get lost and regained? Perhaps for this reason, Plotinus de-emphasizes the Platonic theory of recollection.[4] Plato's idea, that when the soul grasps Forms it remembers something it used to have but has temporarily forgotten, doesn't fit very well with Plotinus' claim that an intellectual grasp of Forms must be timeless.

This brings us to a further consequence of Plotinus' contrast between Intellect and soul. Since Intellect is the realm of Forms, it must be recognized as an ultimate cause of the physical universe. But it does not relate to the universe directly. Rather, it uses the soul like an assistant, which is responsible for putting images of the Forms into material bodies. To understand how this works, we need to think about two closely connected contrasts that are central in Plotinus' system: internal and external activity, and procession and reversion. Plotinus illustrates the first contrast with the example of fire (5.4.2). A flame has its essential, internal activity of burning and being hot. But it also has an external activity—the influence it has on other things by warming them up. In just the same way, the soul has an internal and an external activity. Internally, it engages in its special kind of discursive thinking about the Forms. But externally, it bestows these very same Forms on physical objects, insofar as it is able. Plotinus does not understand these two activities as being in tension, as if the soul would be distracted from thinking about giraffes by the task of actually making physical giraffes. Rather, the external activity is an automatic result of the internal activity—and the result will always be weaker, just as fire causes a warmth that is weaker than its own heat.[5]

That brings us on to procession and reversion. Given the theory of double activity, each level in Plotinus' system is automatically going to give forth some kind of effect. In Neoplatonic jargon, this automatic causation is called "procession." Even the One, despite its transcendence, seems to obey this model. It remains simple and inviolate in itself, which is a kind of internal activity. But it also emanates an external effect, which becomes Intellect (5.2.1). When we were looking at that process in the last chapter, we said that Intellect generates the Forms when it turns back towards its source. This moment of turning back is "reversion." Everything in Plotinus' system reverts back to its cause, apart from the One itself, since it has no cause. Soul looks to its intellectual father, just as Intellect looks to the One. If procession is leaving home, reversion is coming back and asking Mom to do your laundry. But inevitably we wind up doing the laundry ourselves, and not as well either—we mix the dark and the light fabrics. Intellect doesn't quite get back to the One and has to perform an activity of its own, internally contemplating the many Forms and externally giving rise to soul. Similarly the soul reverts on Intellect, and the result is its internal discursive thinking and its external, processive ordering of the physical universe. In both cases the activities fall short of the higher perfection found at the level of their causes, and give rise to a lower external effect.

Now, when Plotinus talks about the soul ordering the physical universe, he doesn't primarily have in mind souls like yours or mine. Our souls are "partial" or "individual," and relate specifically to one body. Yet again following Plato's *Timaeus*, Plotinus believes that the entire cosmos has a single soul—the so-called World Soul. It is this soul that is responsible for arranging things that seem to have no soul, or barely any: things like plants and rocks. But Plotinus insists that even rocks are animated, observing that this is why minerals grow within the earth (6.7.11). The World Soul, in combination with the many partial souls present in humans and animals, ensures that the Forms in intellect are represented at the level of bodies. The details of this process are somewhat obscure. One of the thornier problems in Plotinus is whether individual humans, or any other kind of individual, exist at the level of *nous*. Does the Intellect contain a Form of Socrates and another Form of Buster Keaton, or only the Form of Man, which is imitated by many images in this world? Plotinus wrote a whole treatise on this question (5.7), but his considered opinion remains difficult to nail down.[6]

What is more certain is that when the Forms get their physical images, the result is far inferior to the original. The Form of Man is indivisible, eternal, and perfect, whereas even Buster Keaton was nothing of the sort, never mind the rest of us. This can in part be explained by the fact that the things we see in our world are mere images, made by a soul instead of being grasped through perfect intellectual contemplation. But this can't be the full explanation. Plotinus believes that the World Soul too is a sort of divinity, and that it exercises providence in arranging the universe. So how does it come about that the cosmos is so rife with evil, with suffering and ugliness? (The Wicked Witch of the West put it best: "What a world, what a world!") Plotinus rose to this challenge with an explanation of evil so powerful that it will echo down through later antiquity and medieval times.

32

A DECORATED CORPSE
PLOTINUS ON MATTER
AND EVIL

A re you a pessimistic sort of person? When you look at a glass that has been
filled to the halfway point with water, do you think, "Water? Is that the best
they can offer me?" When life gives you lemons, do you make lemonade, but then
refuse to drink it, realizing you would really have preferred the water after all?
Among the seven dwarfs in *Snow White*, do you most identify with Grumpy? Most of
the dwarfs seem to have no sophisticated views about the world, contenting themselves with sneezing or sleeping. Dopey more or less sets the tone. Happy is an
exception, but he is clearly deluding himself. At least Grumpy has the courage to face
the world as it is. It's a world of wicked stepmothers, of poisonous apples with worms
in them. Grumpy knows that life can be a nightmare, and that Prince Charming is
not coming to wake us up.

The undeniable fact that the world around us is full of suffering and evil has
always presented a challenge to philosophers of a more optimistic bent. In contemporary philosophy it is most familiar in the form of the so-called "problem of evil."[1]
Actually there are several problems of evil, only two of which really feature in
philosophy nowadays. The starker of these two is called the "logical" problem of
evil, and claims that there is a straightforward contradiction between the existence
of evil and the existence of a perfectly good, all-powerful, and all-knowing God.
The thought is that a God who was perfectly good would want to avoid any evil that
He knew about and could avoid. But the God we're considering knows everything
and can do anything, so there can't be any evil that escapes His notice or His power.
Yet we see that there is evil. Thus God, at least as described, doesn't exist. Since the
God of Judaism, Christianity, and Islam seems to fit the description—perfectly good,
omniscient, and omnipotent—the logical problem of evil accuses adherents of these
faiths of a rather fundamental error. They believe both that God exists and that evil
exists, which is simply a contradiction.

I tend to think that philosophers of religion have succeeded in answering this version of the problem of evil. Remember, this version of the problem states that there is *no possible* way that such a God and evil could coexist. But this seems wrong. God might well have reasons for tolerating the existence of evil, despite His perfect goodness. The standard reason offered is that if God wanted to give us free will He might allow evil to exist as a consequence of this freedom. That doesn't end the debate, of course. We might think that God, being all-knowing and all-powerful, could find a way to create free creatures without evil ever resulting. Here the philosophical issues get rather difficult,[2] but suffice it to say that with the logical version of the problem the burden lies on the anti-theist to show that the theist's beliefs are actually contradictory or impossible. That's quite a high standard to reach. Thus the anti-theist may be well advised to retrench to a second version, the so-called "evidential" problem of evil. On this version, we admit that God theoretically *might* allow evil to exist, but we say that the amount and type of evil we actually see in the world makes it vanishingly *unlikely* that there is a perfect God. The evidence at our disposal seems to include pointless evils that a perfect God would have eliminated. Here, the burden of argument between theist and anti-theist is much more evenly distributed.

These two versions of the problem of evil need to be distinguished from the problem that was of interest to Plotinus, and to the centuries of philosophers who followed in his wake. I would call it the "metaphysical" problem of evil. It goes like this. Plotinus, and many a thinker after him, believed that all things derive from a first principle, which is perfectly good. Indeed, he called his first principle not only "the One" but also "the Good": as the source of all things, it is the source of whatever is good and is thus to be identified with goodness itself. But how can anything evil derive from something that is purely Good? This would be as if the Form of Horse caused some things not to be horses, or if water made things dry. So Plotinus' problem of evil is really a problem about *causation*. We need to explain how evil effects can arise from good causes. Actually, even that's not quite right. Plotinus isn't exclusively, or for that matter mostly, concerned with moral evil. The Greek word he uses, *kakon*, means "bad" in a broader sense, and for Plotinus it describes any defective state, such as illness or deformity. In fact, his most common example of something bad is not moral evil, but ugliness. So what he really wants to explain is how there can be anything bad in a world derived from good causes. His basic answer, paradoxical though it may seem, is that this can't happen, and so there is nothing bad in the world.

This is in part because the causes of Plotinus' universe are not merely abstract causes, like Plato's Forms seem to be: they are benevolent, providential gods. One of his most powerful treatises, split into two by Porphyry (3.2–3) and placed at the beginning of the third *Ennead* along with a briefer work on fate (3.1), is devoted to the subject of providence. Here Plotinus develops the optimistic world-view of the Stoics, insisting that misfortunes and evils are beneficial and good when seen from the wider divine perspective. For instance, in one rather appalling passage Plotinus speculates that men who rape women will be reincarnated as women who are themselves raped (3.2.13). On the other hand, he rejects the Stoic conviction that all events are determined by an irresistible divine providence. When I was discussing Stoic determinism (in Chapter 10), I mentioned that Plotinus says that determinism makes humans like stones that have been set rolling. Plotinus thinks this mistake goes hand in hand with another Stoic error, namely their understanding of humans as entirely material beings.

For Plotinus, our ability to transcend determination by physical causes is due to the immateriality of our souls—since they cannot be affected by mere bodies, we are guaranteed independence and self-determination. So long, that as, as we do not fall under the sway of our bodies, succumbing to the lure of pleasure and bodily needs. Freedom, for Plotinus, means identifying ourselves with our immaterial and, ultimately, our intellectual selves. This may seem rather puzzling, insofar as Plotinus seems to be telling us that we will be free if, and only if, we make this choice and no other choice. But for Plotinus freedom is not about being able to choose between one thing rather than another. After all, he considers the One to be free, even though the One necessarily and eternally causes its effects, without selecting this from a menu of options. Rather, for Plotinus an action is "up to us" if we are the cause determining the action. The One can never be so determined, since no cause can affect it. We, by contrast, can be enslaved by the body, but only if we let it enslave us.

These Stoic-flavored meditations on providence and self-determination do little to persuade us that evil does not exist. At best, they show merely that evils are woven into the fabric of a cosmic tapestry that is, on the whole, good. But Plotinus has a more decisive card to play. Of course, he does admit that bad things happen. But there is no such *thing* as badness. Strictly speaking, it has no being (1.8, 2.4.16). Rather, badness (or if you prefer, "evil") is always a mere lack or deficiency, which is found within something that has a degree of goodness. To put it another way, badness is when something fails to be as good as it *ought* to be. But something that was not good in any way at all simply could not exist. The giraffe may be sick and cantankerous, and these are deficiencies—a healthy, playfully cooperative giraffe would be better. But the giraffe still has its life, its ability to move, to see. These capacities, however impaired they may be, remain good, and if they were all stripped away there would be no giraffe. And likewise for any case of imperfection you care to name, including moral evil. When the evil Queen tries to poison Snow White, this is a failure of her rationality or self-control (1.8.4). But without her crafty mind and her basic ability to act she could do nothing, evil or otherwise.

Evils are thus the holes in the Swiss cheese of the universe. They are not things in their own right that the divine causes have brought into being. Rather, they are precisely cases where the divine causes have *not* brought something into being, or rather, have brought less into being than we might have hoped. Thus there is no accusation to place at the doorstep of the gods. They have not made evils, because evils are not the sort of thing that can be made. This is, I would say, a breathtakingly clever and original solution to the *metaphysical* problem of evil. It was recognized as such by many subsequent philosophers, notably St Augustine (see Chapter 47). He adopted the Plotinian theory of evil and passed it on to the medieval tradition, where it became a standard part of the argumentation used to absolve God of responsibility for evil. Still, one might feel that Plotinus' theory is itself lacking something. Even if we grant that evils are not beings in their own right but mere deficiencies, isn't there still a puzzle as to why the effects of perfect causes should be imperfect and deficient at all?

Plotinus would admit that there is, but he has a final move to make, an explanation for why the images of Forms we find in this world are not as perfect as the Forms themselves. In a way, the answer is obvious. Since deficiency is found not in the intelligible world but only in the material world, the culprit must be matter (1.8.7, 13). Our sick giraffe is like a wobbly table, made by an expert carpenter working with poor-quality wood. This idea—that matter is somehow incapable of receiving form perfectly—has a certain plausibility. It's clear that a material object will differ from an intelligible paradigm in some ways. Even the best giraffe or table in our world will have parts, will occupy space, and be subject to change over time. None of these things apply to the Form of Giraffe or the Form of Table, and for Plotinus they already constitute a falling away from perfection. Remember that he sees a close connection between unity and goodness. So for him, just having parts and changing from one moment to the next is already a way of being worse than the Form.

Still, we might think it possible for each material object to be the best possible *material* version of its Form—all giraffes would be equally healthy and elegant, all tables equally well made, all humans equally virtuous. Why doesn't this happen? It looks like Plotinus' theory needs matter to be resistant to perfection, somehow recalcitrant and prone to undermining unity and proportion. That would be hard to understand from the perspective of someone like Aristotle, who thinks of matter as nothing but potentiality for form. For an Aristotelian, the whole point of matter is to become perfected in various ways. But Plotinus rejects this rather positive idea of matter, and goes so far as to describe matter as a sort of non-being (1.8.7, 2.5.5). This is the core of his solution, because it shows why matter is intimately involved with badness—also a kind of non-being. It also explains why a material universe must involve failures to receive form and being. Plotinus insists that matter cannot, as Aristotle claimed, be actualized or perfected. Rather, it remains inert and unaffected, even as higher causes try to give it form (3.6).

The result is a radical rethinking of the physical reality around us. Bodies may seem to us solid and real. But they are only a conjunction of matter, which is in itself nothing at all, with incorporeal images that are weak imitations of the Forms. Our worldly experience is of these mere images, flickering through the darkness of matter without actually turning the matter into anything real. Plotinus compares the images to reflections in a mirror or ghosts (3.6.7), and in a wonderful turn of phrase, describes matter as a "decorated corpse" (2.4.5). The images are often beautiful, because they are, after all, imitations of the perfect Forms in the intellect. Yet Plotinus compares the situation to a prisoner who has been bound in chains of gold (1.8.15). Thus, his theory is often summarized as the claim that matter and evil are the same thing. But it would be more accurate to say that matter is the *principle* of evils.[3] In itself matter is nothing at all, whereas any given case of evil is a specific deficiency that results when the death, darkness, and indeterminacy of matter undermines the reception of a specific form in a specific body.

All this seems to be aimed at explaining natural evils, like illness and deformation, rather than the evil found within us humans. In fact, you might suppose that Plotinus will have a hard time explaining moral evil. If humans are really immaterial souls, how can they be subject to the deficiency and imperfection caused by matter? The answer is: indirectly. Matter is still the cause of human weakness, because for a soul weakness is nothing but turning towards bodies and away from its true intelligible home. Again, this might look rather inadequate. Does Plotinus really have nothing to say about human evil and goodness, apart from telling us to stop paying attention to bodies? Remember that this is the man who took care of orphans and tried to found a city governed by Platonic theories of justice. Events in our world were clearly not a matter of indifference to him.

He can, I think, explain how and why humans can be practically virtuous in terms of the theory of matter and evil we've been discussing. Even though matter can never be redeemed by the imitations of Form that appear in it, it's obviously better for Form to be imitated as fully as possible. So, just as it's preferable that a giraffe be healthy rather than sick, it's preferable that we act virtuously rather than viciously. Indeed, the wise man's virtuous actions will be a natural result of his wisdom.

Because the wise man grasps the Form of Justice, for instance, he will seek to instantiate justice in the material realm. There still lurks a paradox here, in that wise people would really prefer to spend all their time contemplating the intelligible Forms. But Plotinus' view is that our embodied condition just doesn't allow that. In one of my favorite passages in the *Enneads* (6.8.5), he says that a man who fights bravely in a war is like Hippocrates healing a sick person. Hippocrates would prefer that the patient weren't ill in the first place, and the brave man would likewise prefer that his city didn't need to be defended. But given that there is illness, that the city is besieged by the enemy, the appropriate action follows naturally from the brave man's virtue or the doctor's skill.

We can't give Plotinus' theory of evil a clean bill of health just yet. He's done all this work to explain how matter undermines the reception of goodness, and seduces the soul away from its true calling. But now we seem forced to ask: where did matter come from? After all, if the chain of emanated principles had gone from the One to Intellect, then to Soul, and then just stopped, we wouldn't have all these problems. Of course, the question of where matter comes from is a slightly odd one, given that matter is non-being. Rather than saying that some cause brought about all this nothingness, Plotinus might (and sometimes does) just compare it to the way light must eventually give out, leaving darkness where the power of the light-source can no longer reach (1.8.4). But he also suggests that matter should somehow derive from higher principles. His considered view on this is a matter of debate. Some interpreters think that, for Plotinus, matter is the product of soul, simply the last in the chain of direct emanations. On this reading, the soul is too weak to originate anything with a causal power of its own, so it makes inert, dead matter instead. Another possibility is that matter emerges from the Intellect itself.[4]

But whatever the mechanism, it's clear what Plotinus absolutely wants to avoid: the idea that matter is an independent, evil principle that would counterbalance the first principle Plotinus calls the One or the Good. We already saw that Plutarch was tempted by this sort of dualist theory, which posits an evil principle that undermines all the good work done by the gods in our world. But when Plotinus thinks about dualism he has in mind another opponent: the Gnostics.[5] They were a religious sect with an elaborate, moralizing cosmological theory that could well be compared to that of Plotinus himself. We are fortunate in knowing a good deal about them, thanks especially to twentieth-century discoveries of manuscripts in Egypt. These texts, preserved in the Coptic language, tell us that the physical universe is the product of an ignorant and erring divinity, and that only an elite few souls are chosen to escape from cycles of rebirth in the prison of bodies.

We know that works by Gnostic authors were read in the circle of Plotinus, and Porphyry actually entitled one of the treatises in the *Enneads* "Against the Gnostics" (2.9, actually a part of the so-called *Großschrift*). A second title given to this treatise by Porphyry is revealing: "Against Those Who Say that the Maker of the Universe, and the Universe, are Evil." Here Porphyry understood well the teachings of his master. Plotinus may have made matter the principle of evil, but he was adamantly opposed to the idea that the physical cosmos as a whole is evil, or that it would be better if it did not exist. His praise of the divine providence that governs this cosmos was just as passionate as his insistence that we should identify ourselves with the highest, intellectual part of our souls. His conviction that we do have such a part—and that all of us do, not only an elect few, as the Gnostics claimed—is another sign of Plotinus' deep optimism. He saw the physical world as imperfect in its details but perfect as a whole, as a danger to souls, but a danger that we can defeat.

Before we move on to Porphyry himself, a final word about Plotinus. In recent decades he, and Neoplatonism in general, have increasingly been embraced by historians of philosophy. It was not always so, and in the popular imagination Neoplatonism may still be associated with mystical anti-philosophy and "the irrational." I hope the next several chapters will show that this would be an inaccurate assessment even of later Neoplatonism, and that the last several have shown that it certainly does not apply to Plotinus. He may often reach for metaphor and rhetorical gesture, and admit that human reason falls short of understanding the highest realities. But his writing is distinguished above all by restlessly probing argument, offered in careful engagement with his dialectical opponents, his students, and his readers. The best description of his approach may be the one he himself gives when he is contrasting himself to the Gnostics: "the kind of philosophy which we pursue, besides all its other excellences, displays simplicity and straightforwardness of character along with clear thinking, and aims at dignity, not rash arrogance, and combines its confident boldness with reason and much safeguarding and caution and a great deal of circumspection: you are to use philosophy of this kind as a standard of comparison for the rest" (2.9.14, Armstrong trans.).

KING OF ANIMALS
PORPHYRY

Never underestimate the importance of a good introduction. As you may have noticed, each chapter of this book has begun with an attention-grabbing example or anecdote, which may (let's face it) be of dubious relevance to the actual topic but highlights a central theme I want to discuss. This chapter will be no exception, as I begin by paying tribute to a man who made an entire career out of introductions. His name was Danny Ray. He performed a crucial role in one of the best stage-shows of all time. As the main act prepared to hit the stage, Danny Ray would warm up the audience by telling them they were about to witness an artist who would make their "liver quiver," their "bladder splatter," and their "knees freeze": "Godfather of Soul, King of Soul, Soul Brother Number One All Over the World—James Brown"! At the end of the show Danny would return to escort James Brown off the stage while draping a cape over his shoulders, which Brown would then cast aside repeatedly to return to the microphone for one last verse.

The Danny Ray of ancient philosophy was named Porphyry. Actually, this was a nickname. It means "purple" in Greek, and he was called after this royal color because his real name meant "king" (albeit not "King of Soul"). Not only did Porphyry write the *Life of Plotinus* as an introduction for his edition of Plotinus' writings, which he organized as the *Enneads*. He also wrote a little treatise with the wonderfully imaginative title *Introduction* (in Greek *Eisagoge*).[1] In due course it would become Porphyry's most influential and famous work, in fact, what I suppose was the single most frequently read philosophical treatise of late antiquity. In a few pages Porphyry deftly sketched some of the basics of Aristotle's logic as he understood it. He focused on the notions that came to be called the five Porphyrian "words" or "expressions": genus, species, specific difference, accident, and property. Drawing especially on Aristotle's *Topics*, Porphyry is here offering an alternative, and perhaps more general, classification of predicates than the one we find in Aristotle's *Categories*. In other words, every term we use to describe something will fall into one of these five types.

The most familiar are genus and species, and I suppose you will be disappointed if I don't illustrate with the contrast between animal and giraffe. What marks out a species from its genus is its specific difference (§3). For instance, if among animals humans, and humans alone, are rational—something Porphyry elsewhere questions, as we'll see shortly—then rationality can serve as a specific difference for the genus of animal. Of course every individual falls under a unique genus and species, and will have many of its features by virtue of belonging to that genus and species. Thus Hiawatha will be alive and capable of sensation because she is an animal, and be vegetarian and have a long neck because she's a giraffe. But individual members of the same species will also differ from one another. Aristotle calls the features that distinguish them "accidents," so Porphyry adds this to his list (§5). The fifth class is the "property" or "proper accident" (§4). This is a feature possessed by all members of a species and only found in that species.

Lurking just offstage, like James Brown during Danny Ray's introduction, are various metaphysical questions. Porphyry declines to investigate them in his *Introduction* (§0), precisely because it is meant to be introductory. Yet he does venture the suggestion that any individual is simply a unique collection of distinguishing features that fall under the five kinds of predicate (§2). Each of its features may be shared by many other individuals, but no individual will have all the same features. Thus, each individual can be understood as nothing more than the union of those features. Other questions are raised in the *Introduction*, without being answered: should universals like genera and species be counted among the things that really exist? If so, how do they exist? Are they immaterial? If so, are they independent and separate from the individuals that fall under the universal? This series of questions without answers was one reason for the popularity of the *Introduction*. Later authors who were commenting on it had a chance to give their own solutions to the so-called "problem of universals."

The *Introduction* was used to teach many generations of students, and was thus commented upon by later Platonists who wrote in Greek. Once it had been translated into Latin and Arabic it received new commentaries in those languages. I explained earlier (Chapter 26) that Alexander of Aphrodisias was used for centuries as a guide to Aristotle. But Porphyry went him one better. His *Introduction* was actually incorporated into the group of Aristotle's logical writings, the so-called *Organon* (meaning "instrument"). Ironically, then, nearly all late ancient and medieval students of Aristotle began to study him by reading something written by a Platonist. Porphyry himself would probably have been bemused to learn that his vast body of other writings—which included numerous commentaries on Plato and Aristotle (including two on the *Categories*), Homeric exegesis, ethical treatises, and works on religion and the history of philosophy—would be overshadowed by the little *Introduction* he devoted to Aristotle's logic. Still, he would have been quite pleased to play such a central role in the integration of Platonism and Aristotelianism. If the *Introduction* was his most influential work, his most influential idea was that Plato and Aristotle are fundamentally in harmony.[2]

Actually this idea goes back earlier, even to the so-called "Middle" Platonists before Plotinus. Generations after Porphyry, a Platonist by the name of Hierocles claimed that the harmony idea should above all be credited to Plotinus' teacher Ammonius Saccas.[3] And Porphyry himself says, in his *Life of Plotinus*, that his master's writings are full of Aristotelian ideas, which is true enough. Still, Porphyry played a crucial role in adopting Aristotle on behalf of the Platonist family. He was the first Platonist to write commentaries on Aristotle,[4] and proposed a way of reconciling these two greatest philosophical authorities. For Porphyry, Plato was the more advanced thinker, a philosopher who teaches about divinity and the highest causes. Aristotle, by contrast, tells us mostly about the world of nature, about living things, about bodies at rest and in motion, and about human thought and language as it relates to this physical realm. By demoting Aristotle himself to a relatively "introductory" level, Porphyry made his works safe for Platonists to study. And study them they did, to the point that they wound up producing more commentaries on Aristotle than on the more exalted Platonic dialogues. Porphyry's own extensive commentaries on both Plato and Aristotle are mostly lost. But we know a fair amount about them, because they were used and quoted—sometimes without attribution—in other surviving Greek commentaries. For Boethius, a Christian philosopher who wrote in Latin and served as a conduit for ancient ideas to the medieval world (see Chapter 53), Porphyry was the most important source for understanding Aristotle's logic, even more important than Alexander.

There is another irony here, namely that Porphyry was also known for his critique of the religion which he considered the greatest abomination of his age: Christianity. He was not the first pagan philosopher to attack the Christians. In the second century an author named Celsus had raised objections that are preserved in a refutation by the Church Father Origen. (We'll return to this in Chapter 41.) Like Celsus' anti-Christian writing, Porphyry's criticisms of Christianity are known only in the form of quotations, especially amongst Christians like Augustine who were stung into a response.[5] It isn't even clear whether Porphyry wrote a large single work called *Against the Christians*, or whether later authors are quoting from a range of texts in which Porphyry complained about what he saw as a new and irrational faith. Porphyry turned the interpretive skills he had sharpened by reading Plato and Aristotle against the Bible. He complained about the implausibilities of the supposed revelation—for instance, Jonah's survival in the belly of a whale—and the forced allegorical readings offered by Christians. Ironically, given that the Jewish Philo of Alexandria was a great pioneer of this sort of interpretation, Porphyry shows himself much more respectful towards Judaism, which he respects as a venerable faith. What bothers him about the Christians is not just their lack of ancient pedigree. It is also the unjustified nature of their beliefs—which he calls *alogos*, meaning "irrational."

Speaking of rationality, human and non-human reason takes center-stage in Porphyry's most fascinating work: *On Abstinence from Animal Food.*[6] It is a lengthy and impassioned plea for vegetarianism, addressed to a colleague named Firmus Castricius. Firmus was a wealthy admirer of Plotinus, mentioned in Porphyry's *Life of Plotinus.* Given the good taste Firmus showed in attaching himself to this Platonist group, Porphyry is distraught and disappointed that Firmus has given up on vegetarianism and acquired another taste, for meat (1.1). *On Abstinence* is intended to show Firmus the error of his new, meat-eating ways, and of course to convert other readers to abstinence. Porphyry is not, in fact, the first ancient philosopher to recommend vegetarianism. This diet had long been associated with Pythagoreans and the Pre-Socratic thinker Empedocles, both of whom are mentioned by Porphyry (1.3). He also draws extensively on a work about animals by the more recent Plutarch. We know from Porphyry himself that Plotinus too was a vegetarian (*Life of Plotinus* 2). But there is no other surviving ancient treatise that explores the topic so fully. Porphyry not only argues for vegetarianism, but also presents the anti-vegetarian arguments of Epicureans, Stoics, and Aristotelians, before going on to refute them.

Porphyry's main reason for not eating meat is that it tastes good. Following his master Plotinus, he believes that our true selves are our intellectual souls. Anything that ties the soul to the body is counter-productive, since it hinders our ability to focus on the things of the mind (1.47). And nothing ties the soul to the body more powerfully than pleasure. It is, as Porphyry says, like a nail that attaches us to our bodies (1.57),[7] which he compares to mere garments made of skin (1.31, 2.46). And by the way, it isn't only the pleasure that is problematic. Procuring meat, he says, is difficult and often expensive—a point that held rather more weight in the ancient world than it would today. Far better is to partake of light and simple foods, whatever comes easily to hand, and to eat just enough to keep ourselves alive and in good health. (For all his disdain for the body, Porphyry considers it wrong to kill oneself (1.38), though we know, again from the *Life of Plotinus*, that he was once tempted to do so.)

Because this is Porphyry's main argument against eating meat, he recommends vegetarianism only for those people who are actually trying to concentrate on intellectual activity rather than their embodied lives. At one point he explicitly says that he is addressing his arguments only to "philosophers," and not to soldiers, craftsmen, or politicians (1.27). Such people are not trying to free their soul from the distractions of the body so that they can concentrate on intellectual contemplation. So why should they restrict themselves to eating plants? That may make Porphyry's treatise seem disappointing for modern-day vegetarians, who typically want as many people as possible to abstain from eating animals, not just an intellectual elite. It's also worth noting that, so far, Porphyry's reasons for vegetarianism would also rule out, say, driving out of one's way to pick up a tub of organic, artisanal hummus. Food that is hard to procure and dangerously tasty can be vegetarian, after all, and Porphyry would think that putting effort into obtaining and enjoying such foods would be another way of tying oneself to one's body. From what we have seen, he seems to be focusing on meat especially because it was such a luxury item in the ancient world.

But to eat meat, of course, you have to kill a sentient being. Although this does not seem to be Porphyry's primary reason for vegetarianism, it is something he discusses at length in his responses to other philosophers. His main opponents here are the Stoics, who argued that it cannot be unjust to kill animals, because they simply do not figure into considerations of justice. Why not? Well, on the Stoic theory, rational beings like us can have a relationship involving justice only with other rational beings. But animals are not rational, which means that they are too much unlike us for them to fall within the scope of justice (3.1). Porphyry responds by arguing that animals are rational just like humans, albeit not to the same extent. Porphyry admits that in animals reason is imperfect or "blurred" (3.18, 3.23). But they are capable of some kind of reasoning, which on the Stoic theory means we *do* have obligations of justice to them.

Porphyry follows Stoic ideas about rationality when trying to prove this. In fact, he may not really believe that animals are rational in any sense a Platonist would recognize. Rather, this whole discussion of animal rationality is simply a way of undermining the Stoics by using their own philosophical principles against them. The Stoic view of reason turns on that difficult Greek word *logos*. It can mean word, account, reason, and several other things. The Stoics thus say that what they call the "outer *logos*" is a sign of the so-called "inner *logos*." The inner *logos* is the process of reasoning that goes on in the soul, while outer *logos* is spoken speech. The fact that humans use language is proof that they are rational. To defeat the Stoics, then, Porphyry need only argue that non-human animals also have language. He rises to this task with great gusto, relating numerous fabulous tales. These include the case of a Pythagorean sage who understood the chirping of a swallow, when it told its fellow birds about a load of grain that had been spilled outside of town (3.3). Porphyry himself finds this story difficult to swallow, but is able to tell of a language-using partridge that he owned himself (3.4). Besides, it's quite obvious that animals like dogs can understand what humans say, and they seem to communicate well enough with one another too. If we cannot understand what they are saying, remarks Porphyry, then so what? We don't understand the Persians or Scythians either (3.5), but we don't go around eating them! Porphyry then goes on to argue that whether or not animals have language, the outer *logos*, they clearly have inner *logos*. This is proven by the clever things they do, like building nests and avoiding traps, and also by the fact that even sense-perception is useless if one cannot use reason to interpret it. This claim is proven by the observation, borrowed from the Aristotelian philosopher Strato, that we may be unaware of what we are seeing or hearing if we are too lost in thought (3.21). Since animals quite obviously use their senses, they must also be using reason.

All of this gives Porphyry a problem that doesn't worry too many vegetarians nowadays: if we aren't going to eat meat, how will we sacrifice to the gods? Here I need to explain that it was a standard pagan religious ritual to sacrifice an animal on an altar, roast it for the gods, and then feast upon it. This practice is already described in the *Iliad*, in fact. But Porphyry argues that in the grand scheme of things it is a relatively newfangled religious practice. Originally the gods were offered not animals but the first fruits of crops (2.5), and people began to sacrifice animals only when a famine or a war made this impossible. He draws on his Platonist conception of the divine to argue that the highest gods would not want animal sacrifice anyway (2.37). For one thing, the gods are perfectly just, and so they would be appalled by any offering that involved unjustly killing something. But in any case, the whole idea is misconceived, since the gods are immaterial and beyond the reach of physical offerings. What we should give them is not the life of an animal or even the fruits of our crops, but rather philosophical thoughts. If there are supernatural entities that enjoy the ritual, they must be evil, vaporous demons who fatten themselves on the smoke of the roasting flesh (2.42). Porphyry furthermore points out that even if we did need to sacrifice animals to the gods, there would be no need to go on to *eat* the animals (2.44). He reminds us that in some cultures people engage in human sacrifice, without necessarily eating the victims.

Porphyry's entreaty to his friend Firmus blends these sorts of religious reflections with arguments that would be at home in any argument over vegetarianism today. At the core of his diatribe with the Stoics is the question of what animals share with us, and whether the common ground is enough to mean that they deserve our moral concern. Porphyry's vegetarianism may be motivated chiefly by his distaste for bodily things, which seems extreme even for a late ancient Platonist. But he should still get credit for exposing the weakness of ancient attempts to draw a clear line between humans, who deserve justice, and animals, which are served for dinner. Whether or not we are vegetarians, we will probably agree that Porphyry was on the right track in seeking to blur this line. Unfortunately, *On Abstinence* had nothing like the historical influence of Porphyry's *Introduction* to Aristotle's logic, and it is only recently that it has come to receive its due acclaim. A more immediate reaction was provoked by Porphyry's coolly rational attitude towards antique religious belief. We just saw that he dismissed the need for sacrificing animals to the gods. This was not his only critical discussion of pagan ritual. He also wrote in rather skeptical terms about the religious practice of theurgy, in which pagans used physical objects to contact the gods. Porphyry's disdain for bodily things seems to have made him wonder how such practices could possibly be efficacious. The answer came from his own student, a man who would go in the other direction from the highly rationalist Plotinus and Porphyry by integrating pagan belief fully into Platonism, and in so doing, set the tone for the rest of late ancient pagan philosophy.

34

PYTHAGOREAN THEOREMS IAMBLICHUS

Before he became the last pagan ruler of the Roman Empire, Julian the Apostate was a philosophy student. (So don't ever let anyone tell you that studying philosophy isn't a good career move.) One of Julian's teachers particularly impressed him with the following anecdote. It seems that a philosopher named Maximus invited this teacher to attend a ritual at the temple of the goddess Hecate. Incense was burned, a hymn was chanted. As Maximus performed these rites, the statue of the goddess that presided over the temple seemed to come to life—it smiled, and then laughed. At Maximus' command, torches held in the statue's hands burst spontaneously into flame. Julian's teacher regarded all this as mere trickery, but Julian himself reacted differently. He left town to travel to the city of Ephesus, where he might sit at the feet of this wonder-working philosopher.[1] About a decade later Julian would take the purple, and for a brief time the religious and philosophical ideas of pagans like Maximus would become the basis for imperial policy. It was a last chance for Christians to experience hostility from a Roman emperor, and for the old gods to be venerated as the patrons of Rome.

However much he may have impressed Julian, Maximus was a mere footnote in the history of pagan Neoplatonism. His ideas, to the extent that we know about them, closely followed those of a far more influential thinker who was also much admired by Julian: Iamblichus. By the time of his death in 325, a few years before the birth of Julian, Iamblichus had set the tone for all subsequent pagan Platonists. It was the spirit of Iamblichus, more than Plotinus, that presided in both Athens and in Alexandria, the two main centers of Platonist philosophy in late antiquity. His philosophy was resolutely pagan. He introduced complex modifications to the simpler system of Plotinus, in order to make room for the many divinities recognized in pagan worship. He argued for the efficacy, indeed the absolute necessity, of the practice of theurgy—ritual activities that allow the gods and goddesses to reveal themselves in our world, as Hecate did at the behest of Maximus. Soon the flame of pagan philosophy would be extinguished by the new wind of Christianity that was blowing with ever greater force across the Mediterranean. But for a couple of centuries it sputtered on, fed mostly by the fuel of Iamblichus' particularly pious brand of pagan Platonism.

Iamblichus hailed from Syria, and the city now called Qinnasrin. He was well-born, and could supposedly trace his family back to royal forebears. Syria would have been a place of upheaval during his childhood. When he was born it was Roman territory, but the Persians invaded and rampaged through the area in the year 256. Any trauma he may have experienced has left no traces in his writings, though we have seen that Neoplatonic philosophy offered an escape from the uncertain world of late antiquity—and it doesn't get much more uncertain than having Persians suddenly invade your country. Iamblichus eventually set up a school in Apamea, also in Syria, so that he is strongly associated with this eastern province of the empire. However, he may have traveled abroad to study with his fellow Syrian, Porphyry. Just as Socrates had taught Plato and Plato Aristotle, so Plotinus taught Porphyry and Porphyry Iamblichus. And just like Aristotle, Iamblichus reacted critically to the writings of his teacher, and of his teacher's teacher.

I've said already that the idea that Plotinus founded a new tradition called Neoplatonism is itself built on rather shaky foundations. He reacted, often critically, to previous Platonists, without seeing himself as initiating a new philosophical movement. To the extent that something new did start with Plotinus, we have another beginning with Iamblichus, who changed Platonism just as much as Plotinus had done. One of his most influential legacies was a curriculum for studying Plato. Iamblichus laid down an order of reading that included twelve dialogues, beginning with those he took to focus on ethics: the *Alcibiades*, as a kind of introduction to Plato, and then the *Gorgias* and *Phaedo*. The student should then graduate to theoretical philosophy, covering philosophy of language with the *Cratylus*, theory of knowledge with the *Theaetetus*, and so on. The last dialogues to be studied were the *Timaeus* and *Parmenides*, which, for Iamblichus, contained the whole of Plato's thought—the *Timaeus* teaching us about nature, and the *Parmenides* about theology. But all the dialogues could be mined for insights about the gods.

The Middle Platonists, Plotinus, and Porphyry were certainly pagan believers, who referred to their metaphysical principles not only as "Intellect" or "the One" but also as gods. And they would have agreed with Iamblichus that the dialogues taught their readers about theology. But with Iamblichus we have something new. No longer is pagan religion simplified and rationalized as a philosophical system. Rather, there is a perfect fit between the systematic and the sacred. Iamblichus multiplies transcendent entities by invoking complex rules of causation. What was a single level in Plotinus, like Intellect, will be divided and then subdivided into many intellective gods that play different metaphysical roles. This results especially from Iamblichus' principle that between two causes that have different natures we must postulate another cause that shares features of both. For instance, he assumes that if we have immaterial gods who transcend the cosmos, and also the physical cosmos itself, there must be a kind of entity which shares aspects of both. These will be the stars, or "heavenly gods," which share in both the divine nature of the immaterial gods and the physical nature of bodies. For Iamblichus, this provides a philosophical rationale for ascribing divinity to the heavens, a welcome result, given that pagan religion involved worshipping the planets and stars.

Iamblichus refers to these additional, mediating entities as "means," the way that 3 is the mean term between 1 and 5. The use of mathematical language is no accident. Taking a leaf from the Middle Platonists, Iamblichus sees Plato as a venerable branch growing from even more ancient roots. Like Plutarch and others, he assumes that a primordial wisdom has been passed down not only in Greek culture but also in Egypt and further east. Within Hellenic literature he sees Pythagoras as the foremost figure, and as a forerunner of Plato's teachings. Thus, Iamblichus would describe himself as a Pythagorean as much as a Platonist. Iamblichus so esteemed Pythagoras that he wrote an enormous series of Pythagorean books, including the surviving *Life of Pythagoras*, and treatises on the philosophical significance of mathematics.[2] Being a Pythagorean, Iamblichus believed that mathematics, no less than the Platonic dialogues, could be mined for insight about transcendent divinities.

In keeping with his idea of an ancient wisdom received by many cultures, he also looked beyond Plato and Pythagoras. As we saw when looking at Plutarch (in Chapter 24), Hellenic pagans were happy to absorb Egyptian gods into their pantheon, and even to identify certain Egyptian gods with certain Greco-Roman divinities. So naturally Iamblichus identified Egypt as a source of great insight. This particular tributary of the stream of antique knowledge flowed above all through the body of works ascribed to "thrice-great Hermes" (Hermes Trismegistus), a divinity who was both the Greek god Hermes and the Egyptian god Thoth.[3] They record Hermes' own education from a character named Poemandres, and the lessons he gives to his own disciples, including the god Asclepius. The text reads more like a sacred or mystical work than a philosophical treatise, but it resonates strongly with Platonist philosophical doctrine. For instance, the opening passage of the first book tells of an intellective first god who gives rise to a *logos*—a word or reason. We've already seen this idea in Platonists like Philo of Alexandria.

That's no coincidence, since the text emerged contemporaneously with Middle Platonism. What Iamblichus saw as an inspired and ancient source of Platonic truths was in fact itself derived from the Platonist tradition. The same goes for an equally important source used by Iamblichus: the *Chaldean Oracles*, named for their supposed origin in the eastern land of Chaldea.[4] Produced in the second or third centuries AD, the *Oracles* present a visionary description of the universe and its causes. In this system, the transcendent causes of Platonist metaphysics are personified as divine characters. A first mind and a secondary intellect are referred to as Father gods, with the soul being associated with Hecate—the same goddess who obligingly smiled and laughed for the philosopher Maximus. Of course, Iamblichus could have found this kind of metaphysical system, with or without the mythical trappings, in any number of Platonist texts. The reason he constantly alludes to the *Oracles* and the works of Hermes is that their supposed pedigree proved the venerable and sacred roots of Pythagorean and Platonic teaching. Later Neoplatonists will invoke the antiquity of pagan belief, and its supposed appearance in Egyptian and eastern culture, as a proof of its superiority over the far younger faith of the Christians. Furthermore, these texts provided the pagans with scriptures that could compete with the Bible. But Iamblichus, unlike his master Porphyry, was not unduly concerned by the Christians. He worried more about newfangled innovations among his fellow pagans. They should turn to texts like the *Oracles*, to learn the authentic ritual practices.

Even when Iamblichus gave his attention to more mundane philosophical topics, he kept his eyes turned towards the gods. As a student of Porphyry, he knew better than to neglect his Aristotle, and like Porphyry, he was particularly interested in the logical works. He wrote a commentary on Aristotle's *Categories*, now lost but known indirectly through later commentators. His ideas here make an interesting contrast to both Porphyry and Plotinus. For Porphyry, the *Categories* was relevant only to physical things, and analyzed certain terms in our language insofar as they applied to such things—a useful, if limited ambition. Plotinus, by contrast, had extensively attacked the *Categories*, trying to expose them as an inadequate attempt to classify reality. Plotinus preferred the set of concepts called the "greatest kinds," in Plato's dialogue the *Sophist*.[5] These five kinds—being, rest, motion, sameness, and difference—are the true anatomy of reality, used by Plotinus to describe the intelligible world of intellect.

In a characteristically bold move, Iamblichus instead gave a so-called "intellectual interpretation" of Aristotle's *Categories*. Rejecting Porphyry's peacemaking suggestion that the *Categories* were limited to the humble things of the physical cosmos, he insisted that all ten categories could be applied also to the intelligible and divine world.[6] I'll mention just one example of how this worked. In discussing the category of substance, Aristotle said that substances alone can change in their properties— for instance, a giraffe can go from being hungry to being not-hungry—whereas non-substantial properties, like the giraffe's hunger, are incapable of this. Iamblichus has no quarrel with Aristotle's claim. But as always, he wants us to raise our minds to a higher level. Intelligible substance, he says, is like this too. The difference is that it can have two contrary properties *at the same time.* Ironically, he gives the very example Plotinus had used: intellect partakes of the "greatest kinds" of the *Sophist*, so that it is both moving and at rest, and both the same as and different from itself. Iamblichus goes on to make a similar case for each of the categories. All apply to physical things in one way, to the intelligible in another, more exalted way.

Iamblichus' critical attitude towards Plotinus is even more obvious when he turns to one of his illustrious predecessor's most distinctive doctrines, the undescended soul. Plotinus believed that every soul remains connected to the intelligible realm at all times (see Chapter 31). Even now, as you read this, some part of you is communing with the Forms. Iamblichus is having none of this, and subsequent Platonists unanimously side with him against Plotinus.[7] He raises obvious objections, for instance, that if we are already connected to intellect all the time, and if intellectual contemplation is the ultimate fulfillment and happiness for mankind, then we are all always fulfilled and happy, whether we know it or not. That sounds rather weird, even by the standards of Neoplatonism. It also means that there is no reason for us to try to improve ourselves through philosophy—after all, we're already perfectly happy. Iamblichus makes other objections that are more distinctively, well, Iamblichean. Because he has populated his metaphysical hierarchy with many more kinds of entity than Plotinus, he does not believe that the human soul is continuous with pure intellect. There are not only lower divinities, like the heavenly gods we've already mentioned, but also lesser supernatural beings, like daemons and heroes—better than humans, but worse than gods. Again, Iamblichus postulates these beings to ensure that philosophical doctrine and pagan religious belief match perfectly. But he also has a more principled reason. Heroes and daemons are possible kinds of beings, and if they didn't exist then their absence would leave a kind of gap in the metaphysical scheme. Iamblichus' mean terms provide continuity between different levels of the scheme, a point that also applies to the soul itself. It is quintessentially a mean between the bodily and the immaterial. Whereas Plotinus often seems to make the soul nothing but a subject of attention, turned either up towards intellect or down towards body, Iamblichus emphatically gives soul its own distinctive nature. His verdict is that Plotinus' optimism led him to violate this nature by putting the soul beyond its proper station.

This leaves us with a problem: if we are not always already in touch with intellect, how can we make contact? The problem is especially pressing for Iamblichus, since he is so insistent that the intelligible things are not just Forms, but gods. If we cannot access the intelligible, there will be not just philosophical frustration but dire religious consequences. Iamblichus' answer is that we can reach the gods through the ritual practices described in the *Chaldean Oracles* and admired by Julian: the practices of theurgy.[8] Literally, "theurgy" means "god-making." It applies to a wide range of exercises and undertakings, including the animation of statues described at the beginning of this chapter. Divination of various kinds was also theurgic, as were such religious customs as the chanting of hymns and superficially meaningless words of power, the sacrifice of animals, the use of objects like sacred stones, and so on. Iamblichus was forced to defend the efficacy and integrity of theurgy, and hence of religion as he understood it, against questions posed by his own master, Porphyry.

We saw in the last chapter how Porphyry was led by his inquisitive and somewhat skeptical instincts to reject animal sacrifice. He also wrote a more general work questioning the tenets of theurgy. Adopting a tone rather like that of Plato criticizing the Homeric myths, Porphyry complained that many theurgic practices seem inappropriate to the gods—in some rituals, for instance, one would utter obscenities or display effigies of the male genital organs. At other times the theurgist might aim commands or threats at the gods. Above all, Porphyry could not see how the physical actions of theurgy could affect the transcendent and immaterial gods. In reply, Iamblichus composed a work usually called *On Mysteries*—the title given to the treatise by the Renaissance philosopher Marsilio Ficino, who also translated it into Latin.[9] In *On Mysteries* Iamblichus responds to Porphyry that we are not *forcing* the gods to do anything with our theurgic practices. Rather, the gods are present everywhere at all times in the cosmos. The ritual just allows their presence and influence to become manifest. The apparently obscene and repellent practices noted by Porphyry are merely symbolic, and when interpreted rightly need offend nobody (1.11). Animal sacrifice is indeed inappropriate to the highest, purely immaterial gods, but it is effective for communing with the gods within the cosmos—those heavenly divinities again (5.14, 5.19). In addition to fending off these objections, Iamblichus makes a spirited case (pun intended) on behalf of the religious practices. It is theurgy, and theurgy alone, that allows us to communicate with the intelligible gods. When Porphyry objects that the theurgist seems to be trying to pull the gods down to his own physical level, Iamblichus replies: no, the theurgist is trying to purify his own soul, and the souls of others, so that they may rise up to the gods (4.2).

This is a shocking claim. Platonists, beginning with Plato himself, had always been trying to achieve "likeness to god" (to borrow the famous phrase used in Plato's *Theaetetus*). But from Aristotle down to Plotinus, it had always been understood that the path to this goal was philosophy. Iamblichus was the first Platonist who seriously questioned this rather smug philosophical claim. At one point we find the sarcastic remark that Porphyry is "slipping away into philosophy" (9.8), which makes philosophy sound distinctly second-rate in comparison to the sacred activities of the theurgist. This aspect of *On Mysteries* has alarmed some readers. The great scholar of antiquity E. R. Dodds called the work "a manifesto of irrationalism."[10] Even some historians of philosophy who have great respect for Plotinus get impatient with the religious and ritualistic proclivities of Iamblichus and subsequent pagan Neoplatonists.

But we should note that Iamblichus' argument for the necessity of theurgy is itself philosophical. He bases himself ultimately on an idea familiar even from Aristotle: that every possible kind of being must be expressed in reality. It is anything but irrational for Iamblichus to follow this to its logical conclusion, by positing mean terms between different kinds of entities, so that the entire fullness of being will be realized. One consequence is that human souls must occupy a much lower rank than the exalted gods of the intellectual realm, and have a distinctive activity that falls far short of divine intellectual activity (whatever Plotinus might think). Iamblichus seems to make an exception for certain so-called "pure" souls (5.18). They occupy yet another mean, between normal human souls and the gods. These pure souls belong to men like Pythagoras and Plato, who have been granted a direct insight into the gods. For the rest of us theurgy is indispensible. It is the only way for a soul to transcend its own limitations by availing itself of divine assistance. Thus the real goals of theurgy are purification and ascent, not making statues smile or divining the future. If Iamblichus did use theurgy to predict future events, he may have discovered the good news that he had managed to set the agenda for the last generations of pagan philosophers in antiquity. The bad news was that these would indeed be the *last* generations. Christianity was on the rise, and pagan thinkers would be increasingly embattled.

35

DOMESTIC GODDESSES AND PHILOSOPHER QUEENS
THE HOUSEHOLD
AND THE STATE

A t the risk of sounding like an old fogey, I'd like to say how much I regret the fact that no one really writes letters anymore. I believe the historians of the future will agree with me on this. Scholars who work on the American Civil War, say, can examine the handwritten letters sent back from the front, redolent of the experiences of common soldiers. What will scholars interested in the early twenty-first century be able to read? Probably nothing, since all the emails and text messages will by then be deleted, or stored on obsolete hardware. Even if they do survive, such electronic missives don't have the literal or figurative weight of the handwritten letter, with its suggestion that the author's words are being recorded for posterity. If you aren't convinced, consider the following question: if you had some exciting philosophical ideas to share with the world, would you commit them to an email? Probably not. By contrast, throughout the history of philosophy it has been common to write philosophy in the form of letters, though we often dignify such writings with the more exalted term of "epistles."

Many of the authors we're meeting in this volume wrote such letters, which at least in theory were intended for a specific recipient, but have survived until today—suggesting that the epistle format was an excuse to disseminate a text more widely. For instance, we have letters on philosophical themes by Epicurus, Cicero, Seneca, Plutarch, Porphyry, and Augustine. Such letters could have personal significance as well as broader philosophical import, as we see from epistles sent for the sake of consolation, which form a kind of genre all on their own.[1] They could also offer a chance for the author to let his or her hair down, addressing topics not usually touched upon in lengthier or more formal works. A good example here is Iamblichus. Twenty of his letters can be found in an anthology by the later author Stobaeus.[2] These are mostly ethical in theme, and rather down-to-earth (not to say

244

conventional) in comparison to the high-flown metaphysical and religious content that characterizes most of Iamblichus' writings.

Neoplatonists like Iamblichus, no less than the Epicureans and Stoics, wanted to tell their readers how to attain happiness and fulfillment. Yet the Neoplatonic recipe for happiness usually involved disdain for the things of the physical world, an otherworldly attitude which has given rise to the perception that these late ancient pagan thinkers had barely any interest in practical philosophy at all. But Iamblichus' letters give a different impression. In them he has a good deal to say about virtue, and in an epistle addressed to one Asphalius he makes a general comment which is a helpful key to unlocking the Neoplatonic understanding of practical human affairs. Wisdom, says Iamblichus, allows us to arrange our mutual relations in the best way. It shows us how to "refer cities and households and the private life of each individual to a divine model, portraying them in likeness to what is best," and in so doing makes the wise person like a god.

That last phrase is, of course, another reminiscence of Plato's injunction to become like a god insofar as this is possible. But the first bit strikes a more Aristotelian note. The Aristotelians routinely divided practical philosophy into three parts, dealing respectively with the individual, the household, and the city. The three sub-disciplines devoted to these topics were ethics, "economics" (from the Greek word for household, *oikos*), and political philosophy. So what Iamblichus is saying is that the wise man will be able to arrange his own individual soul, his household, and his city in light of divine principles. Iamblichus' idea has a sound basis in Plato, especially when it comes to the parallel between the soul and the city, a central theme in no less a Platonic dialogue than the *Republic*. Plato's *Timaeus* suggests a further analogy between the well-ordered city and the well-ordered cosmos, whose arrangement displays wise divine governance. So in fact later Platonists tended to see a fourfold parallel between individual virtue, good order in the household, the best arrangement of a city, and the providential design of the universe as a whole.

How seriously should we take this? After all, the everyday tasks involved in running a house or governing a city don't look to have much in common with exercise of divine providence—the gods don't have to go shopping or set up recycling schemes. Yet the Platonists did spell out the parallel in considerable detail. A good example is their handling of fate. I mentioned earlier (Chapter 22) that the Middle Platonists treated fate as having the character of a law. The gods ensure that evil actions will be recompensed with the appropriate penalties through the working of fate. This idea was taken up by the Neoplatonist Hierocles of Alexandria, who wrote a whole treatise on providence, trying to show that the gods are not to blame for bad things that befall humans.[3] For Hierocles, fate is to be identified with the laws governing the cosmos as a whole. These laws even oversee the fortunes of non-human animals. For humans, they play the role of administering justice or punishment (the Greek word *dike* can mean both). If you escape punishment for your evil deeds in this life, don't sigh with relief on your deathbed. Hierocles promises that you will pay for it next time around. Plotinus' repugnant remark that rape victims are reincarnated rapists is an application of the same idea (see Chapter 32). So the Neoplatonists really did see the gods as governors or legislators. How, then, are humans meant to imitate the gods in our practical affairs? We've already devoted a lot of attention in this book to ethics, so let's concentrate for this chapter on the household and the city. Of the three spheres of practical philosophy, the household is the least frequently discussed in later antiquity, but there are notable exceptions. In another work on the subject of providence, this one by Alexander of Aphrodisias, we find an extended parallel between the divine rule of the cosmos and the wise man's rule of his household.[4] Alexander uses the analogy to make his point that the gods do not attend to particular events, but oversee the stability of nature and the eternal survival of natural species. This is not unlike the Middle Platonic idea echoed by Hierocles, that the gods simply lay down laws that guarantee punishment for evildoers, without having to intervene directly to bring about such punishment. Alexander thinks the well-run house is the same. The householder does not worry about every little detail, exercising oversight over the mice and ants scurrying around the place, but sets down general rules for all the other members of the household to follow.

Alexander has a certain kind of householder in mind here: a well-to-do man. The other members of his household should include a wife, children, and slaves. (The mice and ants are optional.) Naturally Alexander doesn't go into the niceties of the domestic arrangements in his treatise on providence, but we can get a good sense of the Roman intellectual's understanding of household affairs from a work by a somewhat earlier author, named Bryson.[5] He probably lived in the first century AD and was a philosopher of the Neo-Pythagorean persuasion, though this rarely comes out in his treatise on household management. Bryson is out to give his reader practical advice, some of which runs towards the moralizing end of the spectrum. He has much to say about moneymaking, since no master of a Roman estate could avoid seeing his domestic situation in financial terms. The costs of running the household had to be offset by the gains to be made by selling its products.

Bryson takes a dim view of lying and cheating for gain (25), but is otherwise, to borrow a phrase, intensely relaxed about people getting filthy rich. He even recommends setting aside money for capital investment, something Bryson compares to the natural growth of the body (34). This may come as a surprise, since we tend to imagine philosophers of the Roman era as considering wealth to be beneath their notice. But in fact thinkers of the various Hellenistic schools had a tolerant attitude towards the whole business of, well, business.[6] The Epicurean Philodemus said that the ideal philosopher or sage would be good at making money, since it would be to his benefit to acquire wealth and use it well. Likewise, while the Stoics regarded wealth as making no difference to our virtue, they allowed that it is a *preferred* indifferent. This is not to say that the later ancient philosophers offered anything like "economic" theory in the modern sense of that term. Cicero duly remarked that one can learn more about money from Rome's bankers than from philosophers.[7]

More alarming to us, but perfectly conventional for Bryson's readers, are his remarks about slavery. Like Aristotle before him,[8] Bryson simply assumes that slavery is a basic fact of life. It is obvious for him that the successful householder will need to own slaves. He repeats Aristotle's idea that some people are "natural slaves," noting that this is the sort of slave the householder really wants to own (57). Such slaves are just clever enough to carry out the master's commands, without being intelligent enough to master themselves. Bryson recognizes two other kinds of slaves: those who just wind up being slaves (an example might be those enslaved through war, a common event in antiquity) and those who are slavish in their desires, this latter group being good for nothing. Much as Aristotle described slaves as living tools, Bryson sees them as being akin to the limbs of a master's body (61), which means that the master should take care of them just as he would take care of his own limbs. Bryson even encourages the master to imagine himself in the slave's position. The slave too is a human being, with the same kinds of thought and desire as the master, and dwelling on this shared humanity should persuade the intelligent master to show kindness (62). But Bryson does not make what, to modern eyes, would be the obvious inference. It doesn't occur to him that this very shared humanity provides grounds for rejecting the whole institution of slavery. In fact, showing kindness to slaves is really just the best way to get them to work effectively.[9]

Bryson was not the only ancient author to recommend empathy for slaves without questioning the legitimacy of owning them. We can find another example by turning again to the genre of the philosophical epistle, one of the great exponents of which was Seneca. Among his surviving letters is a short missive which advises the recipient to treat slaves respectfully, for instance, by dining together with them.[10] The epistle opens with a passage that could well have been written by an abolitionist: "They are slaves—no, they are humans. They are slaves—no, they are companions. They are slaves—no they are humble friends. They are slaves—no, they are fellow slaves (*conservi*)," subject to the whims of fortune just as we are. Later in the letter Seneca reminds the recipient that the slave was "born from the same seed," breathes, lives, and dies just like the master. Seneca also points out that people fall into and out of slavery, mentioning a man who found the door shut to him when he came as a supplicant to the house of his erstwhile slave, who was now rich. For all you know, Seneca warns the reader, you too may be a slave some day.

Despite all this, Seneca is no more inclined to reject the institution of slavery than Bryson is.[11] His remark that we are all slaves to fortune is telling, as is the former slave Epictetus' habit of addressing his interlocutors as "slave." The Stoics did not make slavery an object of political critique, but used it as a metaphor and as an example in ethical argument. We should reflect on the fact that anyone can be unlucky and fall into slavery, not to stoke outrage at such injustice, but to remind ourselves that adversity can be visited upon us all. The slave's plight calls for sympathy, even empathy. That should give a Stoic a reason to treat his own slaves well, and maybe even set them free, but it does not move the Stoic to propose abolition. This attitude was passed on to philosophers of different school allegiance. In a treatise which shows how influenced he was by Stoic ethics, Plotinus alludes to enslavement as a misfortune, but not one that can really take away autonomy. One always has the option of suicide, after all. If our daughters are dragged away too, then it's not as if we didn't know such things were possible (1.4.7).

What about that other indispensable figure in the household, the householder's wife? The ancients are not, to put it mildly, known for their feminism, so you might expect the treatment of the wife to be not much better than that of the slave. Yet Bryson gives women a great degree of responsibility and even autonomy in helping to run the estate. Her presence is needed not just for the bearing of children, but also to manage the household (88). Bryson is also unusual among ancient authors in emphasizing the emotional bond between man and wife, which may connect to his even more unusual (among non-Christian authors) absolute ban on sex outside of marriage.[12] Having said that, the wife is to some degree in the same position as the slave, in that her role is to be obedient to the man and serve him, rather than pursuing her own good (82). The wife must share the virtues and good character of the husband (91), but this is to ensure that she manages the household well, not because it will make her a more perfect or fulfilled human.

The Stoics too claimed that women can be virtuous. We already find Zeno, the founder of the Stoic school, taking over some of the radical ideas about women found in Plato's *Republic*. In his own *Republic* Zeno agreed that women should be shared in common among men, and said that they would dress alike. It has thus been commented that "Zeno's city was no more a men's club than Plato's."[13] But, one might add, also no less. Plato thought that women have no special sphere of activity, because they share in the same human nature as men. But he also thought that they were generally inferior to men.[14] This might have been the view of the early Stoics too, for instance Cleanthes, who wrote a now-lost work called *On the Thesis that the Same Virtue Belongs to a Man and a Woman*.

The suspicion that, for the Stoics, women have the same kind of virtue as men but less of it, is borne out by surviving fragments from the Roman Stoic Musonius Rufus.[15] He went so far as to argue that women ought to do philosophy, precisely on the basis that female and male humans have the same virtues. Nor were these empty words. As we'll see later in this book, there were indeed female philosophers in late antiquity, notably Hypatia. Yet Musonius also says loudly and clearly that men are superior to women and should oversee them, and he compares the husband's relationship to the wife to that between the ruler and the ruled (again, we see the parallel between the household and the state).[16] Like Bryson, Musonius says that women must be virtuous in order to fulfill their role in the household as well as possible—which, by the way, includes managing the slaves! Virtue and philosophy may make us like the gods, but the virtuous woman must be satisfied with being a domestic goddess.

What about that other point made by Plato, that women in the ideal city would not just stay in the house, but also take part in ruling the city? This notion ran very much against the grain of Greek and Roman society, and in general the Stoics do not seem to have insisted on political engagement for women. Platonists could not so easily sidestep the issue, given Plato's explicit recommendation in the *Republic*. On the other hand, a second major dialogue on political affairs, Plato's *Laws*, gave women a lower place than men in the running of cities. The Neoplatonist Proclus explained that the *Laws* envisions a less idealistic scenario than the *Republic*. Giving women some civic role, but a more limited one than men, is all that can realistically be achieved in a community that would evolve out of our current, imperfect cities.[17]

So the Platonists envisioned an ideal ruler who was a philosopher king, not a philosopher queen. The ideal ruler should oversee the state just as god providentially governs the universe and the householder his estate. To this extent the philosophers could endorse the actual arrangements in the Roman Empire, with all power in the hands of a sole ruler—though at least some emperors may have been, in their eyes, unjust tyrants rather than wise kings. The Platonists would also, at least in principle, have admired the centrality of law in Roman political affairs. Another letter of Iamblichus is devoted to this topic.[18] It describes the ruler as the "preserver and guardian of the laws," while the law itself is "king of all," because good laws induce virtue in those who are subject to them. So the perfect ruler applies his philosophical understanding primarily by setting down and maintaining laws that produce good order, in each of the citizens and in the society as a whole. This resonates with Alexander of Aphrodisias' comparison of the gods to the wise householder. Whether on the estate, in the city, or in the universe, good rule is general, not a matter of making good ad hoc decisions about particular cases.

For late ancient Platonists, the good oversight exercised by the ruler would have included religious functions.[19] As emperor, Julian saw it as his duty to preserve and defend the ancient religious rites, and he also appointed high priests. This was a last attempt to perpetuate paganism as a genuinely civic religion, with the weight of political authority behind it. Christian emperors were no less ready to involve themselves in religious affairs. Already Constantine called church councils in an attempt to resolve theological disputes, setting an example that would later be followed by rulers in medieval Europe and the Byzantine Empire. The Christian emperors also took over the philosopher-king ideal from the classical philosophical tradition, something we can see in a speech of praise for Constantine written by the scholar Eusebius. The ideal of a ruler who quite literally wields godlike power had not changed, even if Constantine was portrayed by Eusebius as an image of the Christian God, rather than the demiurge of Plato's *Timaeus*. It's just one example of the way that late antique Christian culture appropriated pagan ideas, allowing ideas from Plato and others to live on in a new religious context. Which, of course, would have been at best cold comfort to staunch pagans like the man we are about to meet: Proclus.

36

THE PLATONIC SUCCESSOR
PROCLUS

In Athens, at the foot of the Acropolis, lies an archeological site that was discovered at the end of the nineteenth century. It was a villa from late antiquity, near the holy sites of Dionysus and the healing god Asclepius. The ruins contain, among other things, a statue of the goddess Isis and the remains of a sacrificed piglet. In the 1950s it was suggested that the site could be none other than the house of Proclus.[1] Born in Constantinople in the year AD 412, Proclus came to Athens, distinguished himself as a great philosopher and practitioner of pagan ritual, and ultimately became head of the Platonic school. He was thus known as the Platonic "successor," one of the last thinkers in the golden chain that expounded and defended Platonism in late antique Athens. I don't know if Proclus and his colleagues made the sacrificial piglets into sausage, but they were determined to forge new links in this golden chain.

We know more about Proclus than we have any right to, thanks to a surviving biography of the great man by Proclus' own successor, Marinus. Marinus' *Life of Proclus* is more hagiography than biography—a portrait of not just a philosopher but a sage, a man of deep piety and uncompromising virtue.[2] Or rather, virtues. Marinus organizes the story of Proclus' life in accordance with the levels of virtue recognized by the Platonists, namely physical, ethical, political, purificatory, theoretical, and theurgic. Thus we are told first of Proclus' handsome features and robust constitution—he was sick only twice in a life of seventy-five years—then of his ethical excellence, and so on. It's telling that Marinus relates the peak of his virtue to theurgy. Proclus agreed with Iamblichus that perfection in this art of communicating with the gods brings a happiness even greater than the happiness reached through philosophical wisdom. Marinus gives us many examples of Proclus' remarkable gift in this direction, telling, for instance, of how he brought about a miraculous cure by praying to Asclepius, and how he was able to foretell the future.

Most scholars, though, have valued Proclus more for what he tells us about the past. We certainly do not have all of Proclus' works, but those that survive are packed with information about his own Platonic heritage. Much of what I was able to tell you about the so-called "Middle" Platonists, and even later thinkers like Iamblichus, is taken from reports found in Proclus. This means that Proclus suffers from the same syndrome that afflicts Cicero, and will afflict the somewhat later commentator Simplicius: he has been valued as a treasure-trove of data about other thinkers, but not treasured much himself. Even those who do take an interest in Proclus' own philosophy must admit that his ideas seem to be drawn largely from his immediate predecessors. Proclus was taught by Plutarch of Athens, who is not to be confused with the earlier Plutarch discussed in Chapter 24. This second Plutarch used the wealth of his family to resurrect the Platonic Academy in Athens.

A second teacher seems to have had an even greater impact: this was Syrianus, Proclus' predecessor as the head of the school. His relationship to Proclus was so close that Proclus arranged to be buried next to his master in a shared tomb. Proclus' philosophy, especially in his commentaries on Plato, was based closely on that of Syrianus. To some extent, the sophisticated systematization of Platonic thought we find in Proclus is really the work of his teacher. The details of Proclus' reliance on Syrianus are obscure, given that Syrianus' own works are mostly lost. We do have numerous reports of his views in Proclus and others, as well as a surviving commentary on parts of Aristotle's *Metaphysics*.[3] Here, Syrianus dispenses with the idea we've seen in Platonists like Porphyry: that Aristotle and Plato are basically in harmony. Syrianus concentrates all his attention on places in the *Metaphysics* where Aristotle criticizes Plato. He admires Aristotle, but when Aristotle criticizes Platonic and Pythagorean ideas, Syrianus responds with sarcasm and refutation.

Mostly, though, we must turn to Proclus to see what sort of Platonism was embraced in this revived Athenian school. Pride of place must go to the works dealing directly with Plato, and especially Proclus' vast, though incomplete, commentaries on the *Timaeus* and *Parmenides*.[4] Another commentary was devoted to the *Alcibiades*, today an obscure dialogue whose authenticity is uncertain, but for Proclus (and before him Iamblichus) the ideal introduction for beginning students because of its ethical orientation.[5] Proclus also wrote a set of essays on the *Republic* and a commentary on Plato's exploration of names, the *Cratylus*.[6] Another enormous treatise on Plato is not a commentary: this is the *Platonic Theology*, which interprets the dialogues as a monument of pagan religious belief.[7] Another commentary by Proclus is devoted to Euclid's *Elements*, and he found time to compose a group of treatises on the theme of divine providence, and several hymns to the gods.[8] There are some further works besides, but I'll just mention the *Elements of Theology*, which imitates the axiomatic structure of Euclid's *Elements*, laying down principles and building up a systematic exploration of Proclus' metaphysics.[9]

Because of its relative brevity and clear expository style, Proclus' *Elements* has always been his most popular text. This is a bit unfortunate, given that Proclus himself would no doubt have seen his commentaries on Plato as a greater philosophical contribution. Still, the *Elements* does helpfully set out the principles according to which Proclus' system is organized.[10] Perhaps the most important of these is a rule he shares with this series of books: there should be no gaps. He has taken over the idea that goes back through Plotinus to the Platonists of the early empire: all of reality arises from a simple principle, the One, whose effects become more and more multiple as they unfold (11). Broadly speaking, he also accepts Plotinus' scheme according to which the One is followed by a world of intellect and Platonic Forms. This is followed by soul, and finally the physical universe. Proclus, however, would say that this description paints with the broadest of strokes. He seeks to ensure continuity between the levels of the hierarchy.

For that, we need more rules, and Proclus provides them. Most notoriously, he uses triadic or threefold structures to introduce complexity at every level. (To use a joke that is not original with me: Proclus demands that Forms be filled out in triplicate.) This is an idea that goes back to Iamblichus, but it is only in the works of Proclus that we see the system presented in all its glory. Let's take as an example the world of mind or intellect. Proclus, of course, follows Plotinus, and for that matter Aristotle, in thinking that intellect is something divine. He also agrees with Plotinus that intellect cannot be the first principle, because it is not simple (20). Even if it is thinking about itself, it will be in a sense two, because it is both the thing that is thinking and the thing that is being thought. But for Proclus, this means we cannot speak only of one divine intellect. Rather, what is doing the thinking—the intellect—should be distinguished from what is being thought about—the intelligible. And there should be many gods of each kind. So Proclus says that there are two orders of gods: the intelligible gods, which are higher than the other order, the intellective gods (163).

But this still isn't enough, because it seems to leave a gap or discontinuity between the intelligible and the intellective—as if Plotinus' single intellect had been divided in half, and each half populated by many divinities. Proclus solves the problem by saying that there is a third rank of gods in between, the gods that are both intelligible *and* intellective; they form a kind of link between the two other ranks of gods (181). Together, the three ranks of gods form a triadic structure, with two extremes and a linking term in the middle. Such structures are found all over his system. Thus Proclus not only provides a philosophical system that is admirably without any gaps, but also establishes the existence of a great many divine principles. And he's going to need these. He associates the levels of his rather baroque philosophical system with a bewildering range of traditional Greek gods, demigods, heroes, and demons.

Because Proclus is so keen to avoid gaps, he is bound to worry about the generation of intelligible and intellective things from the One. A perennial difficulty for Neoplatonism was the question of how many things derive from an utterly simple first principle. Actually, I hate to say this, but don't we really *want* a gap here? If the first principle is to be truly transcendent, it should have nothing in common with what comes after it, and thus, we might worry, not even a causal connection with these things. After all, causes seem to share features with their effects: it is because fire is hot that it heats things up. For this reason, Proclus admits that causation would compromise the lofty majesty of the One. So he suggests that there should be a principle of unity lower than the highest One, which gets its hands dirty, so to speak, by bestowing oneness on everything else. This second One is called Limit, and it has a partner, which naturally enough is called the Unlimited (90). This terminology is taken from Plato's *Philebus* (16d), but the two principles are also clearly related to the Monad and Dyad of the Pythagorean tradition, and already played a role in Iamblichus' rethinking of the Neoplatonic hierarchy. Proclus' idea is that Limit and Unlimited cooperate at every level of reality. For instance, the unity of a soul, or a body, can be traced ultimately to the influence of Limit. But the multiplicity of the same things—such as the fact that they have parts, or are subject to time rather than being timeless—is explained ultimately by the Unlimited. Meanwhile, the One itself is above even Limit and Unlimited, serenely untouched by any causal relationships.

We humans find ourselves at some distance from the exalted realms of unity and divinity I've just been describing. Proclus believes that our attitude towards those principles should be one of reverence and worship, not just philosophical analysis. Still, it's clear that philosophical analysis is relevant. He thinks that one can establish the existence of things like, say, gods that are both intellective and intelligible, by appealing to laws of reason. The identification of these divinities with Greek gods, however, is possible only because of the revealed and inspired teachings found in holy texts. These include Plato's dialogues, but also the writings so cherished by Iamblichus, such as the *Chaldean Oracles*. Reading Proclus, one may easily be unsure as to whether he was a faithful devotee of a revealed religion or a rigorous reasoner. The truth is that he was both: he saw a perfect marriage between the dictates of thought and the dictates of traditional pagan religion.

Proclus thinks that religious teachings are necessary for us, in part because of the limitations on what human souls can know. Like Iamblichus, he rejects Plotinus' idea that some part of our soul is "undescended," permanently connected to the divine intellect. At best, our soul sometimes receives an illumination from above— to be specific, from the intellective gods, the lowest of the three ranks in the divine realm of mind (182–3). But the normal workings of the human soul, even at its best, are not like the workings of divine intellects. We think in time, and discursively, making distinctions and grasping simple ideas by means of complicated proofs. Rather unexpectedly, Proclus' clearest explanation of this process appears in his commentary on Euclid's *Elements*.[11] Given the context, he focuses especially on geometry, but some of what he says would hold for the soul's knowledge more generally.

If you cast your mind back to Plato, you'll remember that in some dialogues he makes our knowledge depend on a so-called "recollection" of things the soul already knows but has forgotten it knows. Proclus builds this into a sophisticated theory, according to which the soul always has within it images of the Forms in the divine intellectual world. When we think, for instance by doing a geometrical proof, we are unfolding these images that are innate within us. He calls this process "projection," and gives as an example the use of the imagination to build diagrams in geometrical proofs. For instance, all our knowledge of triangles is ultimately derived from the simple Form of triangle understood by the intellective gods. Unfortunately, we can't just think really hard and instantly grasp everything there is to know about triangles—this is why, unlike Zeus, we have to take geometry classes. But when we sit in class proving the Pythagorean theorem, we are not, as Plotinus might have it, drawing on a permanent, direct connection to the mind of Zeus or any other divine intellect. Rather, we are coming to understand explicitly what is already inborn within us. So when the oracle at Delphi tells you, "Know thyself," this means in part that you should have paid more attention in seventh-grade math class.

The fact that the Forms are in us illustrates yet another general rule of Proclus' metaphysics. Modifying Anaxagoras' famous proclamation that everything is in everything, Proclus says that "all things are in all things, but appropriately" (103). For instance, the Forms are in our souls, but in a way appropriate for souls. This rule comes with a caveat, though. The higher a principle is, the further down the chain of beings it will reach (25). Thus Limit and Unlimited, being at the very top of the hierarchy, exert their influence all the way to physical bodies. Since the divine intellects are lower in the chain, they don't reach as far. Their influence is seen in souls, but not in mere physical objects. This explains why souls can think but rocks cannot (so that clears *that* up).

But if the world around us is suffused with divinity and governed by providence—as it must be, since the highest gods are in this world, but appropriately—then why does the world seem to leave so much room for improvement? The working of providence seems amply proven by the existence of creatures as exquisite and well designed as giraffes, to take a completely random example.

But what should we say about the suffering of a giraffe caught in a brush-fire and burned to death, or about an illness that strikes down an entire herd? Plotinus had an answer to such questions (see Chapter 32). He pointed to matter as the culprit, identifying it as the principle of evil and also as utter non-being, so that specific cases of evil are understood as mere privations or instances of non-being—like holes in Swiss cheese. We also saw that in giving this solution Plotinus came dangerously close to the position of the Gnostics, who saw matter as an independent entity opposed to the Good. Proclus, in fact, thinks Plotinus' Swiss-cheese solution plunges him into the bubbling fondue of Gnostic dualism, so he rejects the idea that matter is a principle of evils. Where, then, do evils come from, given the rule of providence over our cosmos?

Proclus addresses this problem in three treatises, two on the subject of providence and one called *On the Existence of Evils*.[12] The title is a good clue to his conviction that evils do exist, and cannot be understood merely as privations of goodness. But he denies that there is just one source of evil. Matter is certainly not the principle of evil, as Plotinus claimed, because it derives from good principles—indeed, from the Good itself. We can also see that matter participates in goodness, from the fact that it provides the potential for good things to come about. The cosmos as a whole is not only good but divine, and it is made from matter. Instead, evils arise from a whole range of sources. They result from the fact that physical things are able to come into conflict, something that cannot occur in the more unified, simpler intelligible realm populated by immaterial gods. In fact, evil depends on good things, and the pursuit of good things, in order to exist. For instance, fire is a good thing, an indispensible source of warmth and light, and giraffes are obviously good things. Yet it is precisely when these two good things come together in the same place in the savannah that an evil arises: the poor giraffe is caught in a raging inferno.

Thus Proclus says that evil has *parupostasis*, a "parasitic existence," an existence alongside and dependent on things that are good. Though this is a new suggestion for how evil might fit into a Platonist metaphysics, Proclus also depends on traditional arguments found in the Stoics and in Plotinus, to hold that from the cosmic perspective all things are for the best. And no wonder: the physical universe is full of divinity. But divinity does not emerge equally at all places and all times. This is why we need to pray, and perform other rituals that invite the divine to make itself more fully manifest in our world. For Proclus, as for Iamblichus, theurgy is in fact a higher means of access to the divine than philosophy. This is because philosophy will, at its best, elevate us only to an understanding of the Forms in the lowest rank of gods, the intellective gods. The more exalted divinities are beyond the reach of soul, which means that if we want to make contact with them we must beseech them to come to us. We have a written record of how Proclus did so, in the form of numerous hymns he wrote to gods like Athena. The writing of such hymns was connected to his eager participation in pagan rites, and aimed at purifying himself for a union with god higher than anything philosophical argument can offer. Marinus tells us that the gods did come to Proclus. After Christians removed the statue of Athena from the Parthenon, she appeared to him in a dream and asked him to prepare his house, for she wished to dwell with him. This anecdote fits nicely with what has been discovered in the house that may have belonged to Proclus—including the sacrificed piglet.

Proclus wove together many threads of the Greek tradition. He brought out the underlying logic of the metaphysical system embraced by his master Syrianus and by Iamblichus, providing the most explicit and elaborate account of late ancient Platonism that survives today. He also claimed to be the heir to a much more ancient philosophical tradition. Like Iamblichus, he saw Pythagoras and Plato as singing from the same hymn-sheet. According to the biography of Marinus, Proclus announced that he was himself the reincarnation of an earlier Pythagorean philosopher and mathematician, Nicomachus of Gerasa. But Proclus' deepest commitment was to the pagan religious beliefs that were so threatened by the increasingly confident and powerful Christians. This was an age when temples were being converted into churches, when statues were being ripped from their sacred homes. The last pagan philosophers of antiquity faced the bleak prospect that their faith might die out altogether.

A TALE OF TWO CITIES
THE LAST PAGAN
PHILOSOPHERS

I'm going to go out on a limb, and guess that you have never sacrificed an animal to Zeus. If I'm right that you haven't, some of the credit should go to an anonymous Persian infantryman. In the year AD 363 this unknown soldier thrust a spear through the unarmored abdomen of the emperor Julian. As so often in history, if things had gone differently the consequences could have been enormous. Had Julian not ventured into a rash campaign against the Persians, had he not rushed into battle without pulling on his armor, he might have lived. And had he lived, he might have gotten further with his project of weakening Christianity's hold on the Roman Empire, of resurrecting the pagan rituals and re-dedicating the temples. But as always in history, things did not go differently: Julian was mortally wounded, and died some time later. He was 32 years old, and had ruled the empire for less than two years.[1]

Julian was, like Marcus Aurelius before him, a philosopher as well as an emperor. But Julian was no Stoic. He was a Platonist, and his philosophy went hand in hand with belief in the existence and power of the traditional gods. Julian was a great admirer of Iamblichus and a great believer in the pagan ritual practices known as theurgy. Above all, he was a great opponent of Christianity. After surviving a political massacre of most of his close family, Julian was raised a Christian. But he converted to the path of paganism. Hence his nickname "the Apostate," applied by Christian authors who condemned him for renouncing the true faith. Julian was a scholar by temperament, and even while emperor wrote philosophically informed works justifying his pagan world-view. This world-view influenced the decisions he made during his short reign. Most notorious was his declaration that Christians would be banned from teaching throughout the empire. This was intended to block the Christians' access to the educational institutions that were so fundamental to the lifestyle of the late antique elite classes. But Julian could offer a plausible rationale, too: how could Christians teach the great works of antiquity, such as Homer and

Hesiod, if they rejected the gods named in those texts? Julian also employed less obvious ways of undermining the Christians, for instance by making it easier for sectarian disputes to fester within the new faith.

The emperor's death put an end to this short-lived experiment in pagan traditionalism. Julian was not the last ancient admirer of Iamblichus. But he was the last man who could hope singlehandedly to restore Iamblichus' gods to their position of undisputed honor. From now on it would be the Christians who wielded imperial authority. The story of how that authority was used against Platonist philosophers is a tale of two cities: Athens and Alexandria. Both had long been centers of intellectual activity. Athens had gone through rough times in the Roman era, but its prestige as the home of Plato and Aristotle could still attract intellectual tourists, including Julian himself. As for Alexandria, it was not only the home of the famous Library but had been a center of Platonism in the early Roman Empire. So it's no surprise that these were the cities that boasted the two most important philosophical schools of late antiquity.

It has been argued that the two schools had distinct intellectual identities, with the school of Athens upholding the fervently religious Platonism of Iamblichus, and Alexandria concentrating on Aristotle and adopting a style of Platonism that reached back to the Middle Platonists. But this distinction has come in for some searching criticism. The two schools were bound by student–teacher relationships and even family ties, and if the Alexandrians failed to embrace Iamblichus' pagan enthusiasm very loudly, this was likely for political reasons. There was cause for caution in both places, but the group in Athens paid too little heed to the warning-signs. The founder of the Athenian school, Plutarch of Athens (again, don't confuse him with the Middle Platonist Plutarch), had enough wealth and social standing to put the school on a firm footing, and it fared well through several generations. Proclus and his beloved master Syrianus were heads of the school during this time. But the institution was closed down by imperial edict in the year 529, when the head was a man named Damascius. He and his associates were forced to seek asylum in the Persian Empire, though they did return after a short stay there. The "golden chain" of Platonist teachers and students had been broken, and it would not be re-forged in the city of Athens.

The closing of the school was a blow aimed directly at the philosophy inspired by Iamblichus and taught by men like Proclus and Damascius. In fact, Damascius thought Proclus insufficiently loyal to Iamblichus, and frequently criticized him. But the Christians who appealed to the emperor Justinian to close the school would not have been interested in pagan disputes over fine points of metaphysics. Justinian was persuaded by Christian informers that the Platonists were illegally practicing divination, which became the excuse for shutting the school down.[2] It did not come without warning. A century earlier the other city of Platonists, Alexandria, had seen the most famous act of Christian violence against a pagan philosopher: the brutal murder of Hypatia, in 415. We saw in the first volume of this series that women played a part in the history of ancient philosophy almost since its beginnings.[3] In late antiquity aristocratic women continued to have limited but real opportunities to do philosophy. We've already seen that Plotinus' circle of patrons and friends included women, and that Stoics like Musonius Rufus exhorted women to study philosophy, even if they did not abandon traditional conceptions of women's role in society. When we get to the ancient Christians, we'll see women again changing the course of philosophy. Monica, the mother of St Augustine, and Macrina, sister of the Cappadocian Fathers, participated in intellectual discussions and appear as characters in philosophical dialogues written by their male family members, like Christian versions of Socrates' teacher Diotima from Plato's *Symposium*.

But whereas women like Monica exercised their influence within private Christian communities, Hypatia actually taught at a philosophical school.[4] Both she and her father, Theon, were specialists in mathematics. In fact Damascius, writing about Hypatia, sniffed that she was not only a woman rather than a man, but more a mathematician than a philosopher.[5] This unattractive comment has some truth in it, because her real interest was probably in astronomy rather than Platonist philosophy.[6] This would fit well with the fact that her father, Theon, wrote commentaries on the works of Ptolemy, and with the content of letters written to her by her student, the Christian Synesius. Synesius would not have been Hypatia's only student who was a Christian, and in fact it seems that Hypatia was far from being an anti-Christian pagan figure like Julian the Apostate. Her death was mostly a matter of being in the wrong city at the wrong time. She was accused of witchcraft and then slain by a mob made up of partisans of the bishop, Cyril of Alexandria.

Hypatia's treatment was not the only case of violence against a pagan Platonist of Alexandria. Hierocles, whom we met briefly in Chapter 35, was active there in the middle of the fifth century. In addition to his thoughts on the topic of providence, we have from him a commentary on a collection of Pythagorean sayings called the *Golden Verses*.[7] Hierocles was summoned before a Christian court, perhaps because he practiced theurgy. He was beaten bloody, but had the courage to scoop up some of his own blood and flick it at the judge, along with a choice quote from Homer's *Odyssey*: "Here Cyclops, drink this wine now that you have eaten human flesh." This story, the closure of the school of Athens, and the death of Hypatia suggest a context of unrelieved suppression and even savagery against pagans. But it's been suggested that Hypatia's shocking murder actually made it easier for a pagan school to arise in the following century, because many citizens were appalled by this killing of an innocent woman.[8]

When it did arise, the school was gathered around a man with a name that will sound familiar: Ammonius. This third entry in our ever-expanding collection of ancient Platonists named Ammonius followed the lead of Hypatia in having both Christian and pagan students. In fact, Damascius bitterly criticized Ammonius for making a deal with the local Christian authorities, which may explain the absence of references to theurgy and other typically Iamblichean themes in the works of his school. His prudent approach was continued by the last pagan head of the Alexandrian school, whose name was Olympiodorus. He was clearly seeking peaceful coexistence with the Christians when, in his commentaries, he suggested that his audience might prefer to interpret the various divine entities of the Neoplatonic system as attributes of a single God.[9] Mostly steering clear of more controversial subjects, the school concentrated on something both pagans and Christians could appreciate: Aristotle's logic.

This may seem surprising, given that Ammonius and his students were committed Platonists. But the pedagogical setting of their work is crucial. Following Porphyry, they saw Aristotle as being fundamentally in harmony with Plato. And as Platonists, they assumed that the works of Aristotle were more appropriate as an introduction to philosophy. The dialogues of the divine Plato were reserved for more advanced study. Thus, their school commentaries tend to focus on Aristotle, since it was his texts that were above all being taught in lectures for students. Just as there are more books printed every year on basic geometry than on advanced topology, so the ancients wrote more commentaries on Aristotle than on Plato, and more on the introductory subject of logic than advanced disciplines like metaphysics. If this also helped the pagan teachers to avoid alienating Christian students and angering Christian bishops, so much the better.

This also meant that the activities of the school could be carried on much as before by Christian Platonists. After Olympiodorus, the tradition of commentary on Aristotle was continued by his Christian students, one of whom sported the wonderful name "David the Invincible." By this time Christianity itself was invincible. There was no need to shut down the school of Alexandria by imperial edict, as had been done in Athens. In the fifth century the Christians had beaten pagans like Hierocles; in the sixth century they simply joined them. Olympiodorus' Christian students did not hesitate to write down his ideas about Plato's dialogues, just as Ammonius' students had recorded his lectures. These student notes are the commentaries that survive today. Both Damascius and Olympiodorus taught Plato by following the instructions of Iamblichus, and beginning with dialogues they saw as introductory and ethical. But even these supposedly introductory, more ethical dialogues were quietly given a religious interpretation by the Neoplatonists. For instance, the *Phaedo*, the dialogue that depicts Socrates' death and his final conversation about the soul's immortality, was taken to concern not just immortality but the purification of our souls. Damascius and Olympiodorus took seriously this dialogue's remark that philosophy can be understood as a kind of preparation for death.

We're lucky enough to have commentaries, or at least sets of notes, on the *Phaedo* by both Damascius and Olympiodorus.[10] Their approaches are strikingly different. Where Olympiodorus faithfully follows earlier Platonists, especially Proclus, Damascius rarely misses an opportunity to strike off in new directions. Indeed, he goes out of his way to reject the interpretations of Proclus and Iamblichus—which, by the way, are known to us mostly because they are quoted in these later commentaries. Yet the goal of all these Neoplatonists is the same: not only to interpret Plato, but also to vindicate him. They are still aware of attacks by long-dead opponents of Plato, such as the Aristotelian philosopher Strato. They quote these criticisms and rebut them forcefully. But ironically, they often use Aristotelian concepts in doing so.

A good example is Damascius' handling of one rather unpersuasive argument in the *Phaedo* (103c–105e). The argument is that everything comes in cycles from its opposite. For instance, justice comes from what is unjust, and vice versa. That means that what goes from life to death should come back to life again. Thus, the death that befalls us at the end of our present life is only a temporary condition, which will be followed by another life in the future. Damascius does two things to show that this argument might be better than it looks. First, he readily admits that the argument is too weak to prove the soul's immortality all by itself, as Iamblichus had claimed with his characteristic enthusiasm. For Damascius, Socrates' goal is only to show that the soul will go through many lifetimes, while admitting that it may run out of steam eventually. That possibility will be ruled out by different arguments, which are found elsewhere in the *Phaedo*.

A second way that Damascius lowers the stakes is to claim that Socrates is simply assuming that "death" is a condition the soul can be in, rather than sheer non-existence for the soul. For soul to be "dead," on this assumption, is merely for it to be separate from body. Damascius remarks that the soul is thus a "substance" that acquires the "accidents" of being alive and dead—that is, connected to and then separate from the body. I think we should give Damascius some credit here. He's right that in the *Phaedo* Socrates just assumes that soul and body are two different things, and that death is nothing more than the separation of soul and body. He may also be right when he says that the argument from opposites is merely supposed to persuade us that what gets separated is liable to be joined again. Perhaps soul will not get the very same body back, but it will be connected again to some body or other, just as what is hot is liable to get cold and vice versa. We should also admire, or at least notice, how Damascius effortlessly draws on Aristotle in defending Plato. The idea of a substance that survives through the alternation of accidents is pure Aristotelianism, after all. The novelty resides in his applying that idea to the soul, and using it to explain the limited goals of Plato's argument.

Damascius' most famous work is not this commentary on the *Phaedo*, but a long and complex treatise called *Problems and Solutions Concerning First Principles*.[11] Here Damascius grapples with the system handed down to him from Iamblichus and Proclus. He does not follow them slavishly, but rather raises and then resolves problems that arise within this late Neoplatonic system. His most important contribution comes towards the beginning of the work, when he tackles the difficult problem of the First Principle itself. For centuries Platonists had been arguing that all things come from a transcendent source of unity, the One. It is meant to be utterly transcendent above the things it produces, a divinity beyond all other divinities. And yet it is still supposedly producing these things, is somehow a cause for them. Damascius asks how can this be. In general, causes are related to their effects and share characteristics with them, as we saw with the example of fire giving its heat to the things it affects. But if this First Principle relates to and shares characteristics with the things it produces, then won't this compromise its transcendence? Even though Proclus had raised the same worry, Damascius accuses him and other Neoplatonic predecessors of trying to have their cake and eat it too. They insist that the One is completely removed from all things and above all description, because it is so exalted, but in the next breath they add that the One is intimately connected to all things because it is the ultimate source of unity.

Damascius decides to blow out the candles on this cake, and let darkness fall. If we are going to have a transcendent First Principle, we should accept that it really is beyond all description. Drawing inspiration from Iamblichus, Damascius calls it simply "the Ineffable," cautioning us that even this name is misleading because the First Principle cannot even be said to be ineffable. He distinguishes this Ineffable from the One, which we can describe to some extent, simply by calling it "one." However, even this One should not come into relation with anything else by giving it unity. Damascius thus envisions, following the Ineffable, a highest One that is aloof from all things, remaining secluded in its utter unity, and only then a second, lower One that actually bestows unity on everything. Thus, where Proclus had a single First Principle called the One, Damascius winds up with three: the Ineffable, the highest One, and the lower One from which unity streams forth to other things.

Even fans of Neoplatonism may feel that things have gotten out of hand here. Surely the whole point of the One is that there is, well, only one of them. But cast your mind back to the Middle Platonists (Chapter 22). We saw that, before Plotinus, figures like Numenius suggested that there should be two versions of the first principle, already called the One. The point of this was precisely that there should be a completely unified, transcendent principle, and then another god who would carry out the role of the divine craftsman of Plato's *Timaeus*. This would be the one who gets his hands dirty by actually relating to the rest of the universe. Plotinus reacted by identifying the lower one with a universal intellect. Damascius, following Iamblichus, has effectively undone Plotinus' good work and re-established the Middle Platonic distinction between types of principle: one that is exalted, one that condescends to cause other things. But he goes the Middle Platonists *one* better by positing the Ineffable even beyond the more exalted One.

It would have been interesting to see the next move in this metaphysical chess-game. But there was no next move, because paganism itself was swept off the board, leaving only the bishops. Damascius was the last author to engage in the extravagant metaphysical speculation of late Neoplatonism. This is not to say that Neoplatonism itself died after Damascius—far from it. But after him, Neoplatonism was domesticated within the revealed monotheistic religions. No longer would conceptual distinctions be drawn ever more sharply so as to accommodate the various divinities of traditional Greek religion. The pagans were now on the run, in the most literal of senses. This is shown poignantly by the career of a man who studied with Damascius in Athens, and with Ammonius in Alexandria. His name was Simplicius.[12] He fled to Persia in the entourage of Damascius, and his works allude to the difficult situation facing pagan philosophy in Athens. Some of his commentaries on Aristotle may even have been written in Persian exile.

Wherever they were written, we should be thankful to Simplicius for his labors. These were commentaries unprecedented in their size and detail. He used them as an opportunity to record not only the ideas of previous commentators, especially Alexander of Aphrodisias, but also texts of early Greek thinkers mentioned by Aristotle. To provide context for Aristotle's discussion, Simplicius went to the trouble of copying these out in his commentary, often verbatim. Without Simplicius we would know much less of Parmenides, for instance, and also lack many fragments from other Pre-Socratic philosophers. This was not mere pedantic completism on Simplicius' part. His commentaries, scholarly and dry though they may be, are haunted by his sense that the pagan heritage is being obliterated by the rising tide of Christianity. Simplicius reacts by constantly seeking to show the unity and power of pagan Greek thought. He is thus one of the foremost defenders of the idea that

Plato and Aristotle were fundamentally in agreement on all significant points of doctrine. He goes further, by insisting that the Pre-Socratics too were in harmony with these doctrines. Even Stoic philosophers could be embraced within the pagan philosophical family. Simplicius devoted a commentary to the *Handbook* of Epictetus, portraying it as a useful text for introductory ethics.[13] Though he would have had no sympathy with Stoic materialism, his Neoplatonism gave him good reasons to value the *Handbook*. After all, we saw how Epictetus drew a strong opposition between the will, which is internal to each of us and under our control, and the external things beyond our control. That's a good match for the strong metaphysical distinction that late ancient Platonists drew between the soul and the things of the bodily world. It has also been suggested that Epictetus' advice on greeting tyranny with fortitude struck a chord with Simplicius, living under the shadow of the Christian emperor Justinian.[14] Whether or not this is true, Simplicius' writings were clearly motivated by the hope of keeping alive the unified tradition of pagan philosophy.

Naturally then, Simplicius was horrified when a fellow student of Ammonius, a Christian named John Philoponus, had the temerity to criticize a fundamental tenet of Aristotelian philosophy. So horrified was he that he took the trouble to quote Philoponus' arguments at great length, much as he'd done with the texts of Pre-Socratics and others. In this case, he wrote down the arguments not to preserve them, but to expose their stupidity. This turns out to have been a mistake. Philoponus' arguments are far from stupid; in fact, they stand among the cleverest bits of philosophy in late antiquity. This has led modern scholars to read Simplicius' quotations of Philoponus with great interest, while usually ignoring Simplicius' sarcastic and hostile rebuttal. Let this be a lesson to you: if ever you should find yourself attacking someone in print, don't do them the favor of carefully recording everything they say.

38

FOR A LIMITED TIME ONLY
JOHN PHILOPONUS

Modern-day scientists estimate that the age of the universe is 13.7 billion years. That's a very long time. If I'd started just after the Big Bang, I could already have finished writing this series of books on the history of philosophy, and still had about 13.6999999 billion years to kill. And yet, as staggeringly large as this amount of time may be, it is as nothing compared to the age of the universe according to Aristotle. You could double it, triple it, or for that matter multiply it by one billion, and get no closer. For Aristotle, the universe has already existed for an infinitely long time, and will never stop existing. Moreover, the universe has always been pretty much the way it is now. It has always been spherical, with an outer sphere of fixed stars at the edge, containing more nested spheres with planets seated upon them, and at the center the region of air, earth, fire, and water inhabited by humans, plants, and animals, all of which are likewise eternal in species.

Aristotle's commitment to an eternal universe was so emphatic that no ancient philosopher seriously questioned it. Convenient doubts about Aristotle's confidence would be raised only later by medieval thinkers like Maimonides and Thomas Aquinas. With Plato, however, things were not so clear. Some Middle Platonists, notably Plutarch and Atticus, read Plato's dialogue *Timaeus* as endorsing a beginning in time for the universe, and were happy to say that on this point Plato was right and Aristotle wrong. But from Plotinus onwards, Platonists took this to be a misreading of Plato. Some, like Porphyry and other commentators on Aristotle, might have been motivated by their desire to make Aristotle agree with Plato whenever possible. But they had other reasons too. If the physical universe is a necessary effect of transcendent causes, which give rise to it like shining lights or overflowing fountains, how could the universe be anything other than eternal? Thus, all the figures we call Neoplatonists accepted its eternity, and believed that in doing so they were in agreement with both Plato and Aristotle.

Until, that is, the year 529 (or starting from the big bang, the year 13700000529, give or take), when a Neoplatonist named John Philoponus wrote a massive work arguing that the universe is *not* eternal, and that Plato knew it. The treatise was called

Against Proclus, reasonably enough, given that it demolished a series of pro-eternity arguments collected by Proclus. The arguments given by Proclus drew not only on Aristotle's physical theories but also on Platonist interpretations of Plato's *Timaeus*. For instance, Proclus argued that the world results from its creator's goodness or generosity—something implied in the *Timaeus*, which says that the divine crafts-man is not "envious." Since the creator is permanently generous, the results of his generosity must likewise be permanent. Otherwise the creator would change, suddenly acquiring the necessary generosity or ability to create, which had previ-ously been lacking. This was only the first of eighteen arguments, which Philoponus refuted at immense length. Each of Proclus' arguments is set out in about a page or two, whereas the English translation of Philoponus' *Against Proclus* runs to four volumes.[1]

In a further treatise,[2] Philoponus tore into the arguments for eternity found in Aristotle's works the *Physics* and *On the Heavens*. The original version is lost, but extensively preserved by the commentator Simplicius, who did to Philoponus what Philoponus had done to Proclus, quoting his opponent in order to refute him. Simplicius was not well pleased about Philoponus' temerity in attacking the great Aristotle. He compares his own labors to the task of Hercules, who had to clean horse-manure out of the largest stables in Greece. He uses various terms of abuse for Philoponus, but especially delights in calling him "the grammarian." This is probably meant to call attention to the fact that Philoponus never headed a philosophical school, and pursued a career on a lower rung of the educational curriculum. Yet this grammarian is now recognized as one of the most innovative philosophers of his era. His critique of Aristotle takes much of its power from his expertise in the texts he is attacking. Philoponus, like Simplicius himself, had studied at the feet of Ammonius in the city of Alexandria—though apparently not at the same time, since Simplicius claims never to have met his antagonist in person.[3] And like Simplicius, Philoponus wrote a number of commentaries on Aristotle. Of these, some are apparently faithful recordings of the lectures of Ammonius. Others report on these lectures while occasionally weaving in Philoponus' own innovative ideas. In fact Philoponus continued to comment on Aristotle after he began his campaign against the eternity of the universe.

What was his motivation? Certainly, he insists that Plato rejected the world's eternity. For many Platonists, that might have been reason enough to disagree with Aristotle. But not for Philoponus. In *Against Proclus* (9.1) he says that, although Plato happens have to been right on this point, it is the truth that matters and not Plato's authority. He then provocatively lists a whole series of claims found in Plato that are just plain wrong; for some of these Philoponus draws on his expertise in another field, medicine. Philoponus did not reject eternity because he was a Platonist, then; he rejected it because he was a Christian. Indeed, this may be the explanation of his nickname, "Philoponus." It means "lover of work," and given its length, *Against Proclus* alone would earn him that title. James Brown may have been the hardest-working man in show business, but Philoponus was definitely the hardest-working man in the eternity business. Still, the nickname probably has a quite different explanation: the term *philoponoi* referred to certain Christians who had no clerical role, but supported the cause of the faith and often agitated against the pagans in Alexandria. Our John Philoponus may have been a member of this group.

We saw in the last chapter that pagan teachers like Ammonius frequently had Christian students, and that this relationship was fraught but often respectful. In Alexandria especially, pagans went out of their way to find common ground with Christians. To the examples mentioned above we can add Ammonius himself, who wrote a whole work to show that, for Aristotle, God was a cause not just of motion but of the very being of the universe, a thesis that was, of course, also dear to the Christians.[4] It is likely no coincidence that Philoponus chose to break ranks in 529, the very year in which the Platonist school of Athens was closed down by an imperial edict. Perhaps he was bidding for the headship of Alexandria. If so, Philoponus failed—he was passed over for the pagan Olympiodorus. But Philoponus didn't need to be the head of the school to know his Aristotle thoroughly. This is the difference between Philoponus and other Christians who attacked the Neoplatonists on this same issue. In particular, two Christians from the city of Gaza, named Aeneas and Zacharias, had already written about the eternity debate.[5] Particularly fascinating is Zacharias' work, a dialogue featuring as one of the main characters none other than Ammonius. In the dialogue Ammonius is reduced to silence by a series of anti-eternity arguments. But in fact, though both of these Gazan thinkers had been taught by Neoplatonists, the arguments they mount fall far short of Philoponus' sophistication.

Because the pagans offered numerous arguments for eternity, Philoponus has to fight on many fronts. Some pagan arguments for eternity relied on features of the universe we see around us. Although Proclus does use arguments of this kind, they are mostly drawn from Aristotle. For instance, he had argued for eternity on the basis that the heavenly bodies must be made out of an ungenerated and incorruptible substance. The pagans also thought they could show that divine principles must give rise to an eternal universe. We already saw one such argument—Proclus' first proof, which invokes God's generosity—and in general Proclus is the main opponent when it comes to metaphysical or theological arguments for eternity. Aristotle, by contrast, is the main target when it comes to physics and the nature of the heavens.

First then, let's see how Philoponus takes on Aristotle's physical arguments for the world's eternity. As I say, these invoked the unique characteristics of the heavenly bodies, to show that these are bodies that can be neither generated nor destroyed. Aristotle thought this could be proved from the fact that the heavens move in a circle, unlike air, fire, earth, and water, which move in straight lines— either away from or towards the midpoint of the universe. The thing about circular motion, Aristotle observed, is that it has no contrary (*On the Heavens* 269a, 271a). For one motion is contrary to another if it begins where the other motion stops, and stops where the other begins. But a circular motion starts and stops in the same place—if you walk in a circle, no matter how big or how small, you will always wind up where you started, something familiar to anyone who has ever gotten lost in a forest. Furthermore, things are always destroyed by their contraries. Thus, if the heavens move in circles, as they evidently do, they have no contraries and thus cannot be destroyed.

This is clever, albeit perhaps not the most convincing bit of philosophy ever to flow from Aristotle's pen. Philoponus makes short work of it, pointing out that the contrary we are interested in here is not a motion in a contrary direction, but the complete *absence* of motion (*Against Aristotle* 4.65). What we are asking, in other words, is not whether the heavens can move a different way, like fire being forced to move down instead of up, but whether the heavens can come from, and be reduced to, non-existence. And here we get to the real core of Philoponus' disagreement with Aristotle. Aristotle wrestled with the question of how to explain change without saying that things pop into existence from nothing, or get destroyed into nothing.[6] He agreed with Pre-Socratics like Parmenides that such absolute change is impossible. Instead, he offered his analysis of matter and form: in any change a surviving subject, the matter, gains or loses some feature, the form. If, for instance, a stone becomes hot, nothing comes suddenly into existence or vanishes. A previously existing stone simply gains a new property, namely heat. Philoponus wants instead to insist that God *can* create something from nothing. He adds that even in the kinds of change recognized by Aristotle, something does come into being from nothing, namely the new property that is gained (6.116). That is, even if a hot stone comes to be from something else, namely a cold stone, the heat that appears in the stone comes to exist after not existing.

But Philoponus is only getting warmed up. So far, he's questioned a long-standing assumption of Greek philosophy that nothing comes to be from nothing. Now he wants to question a newer assumption of Neoplatonists, that Plato and Aristotle pretty much agree about everything. He points out that, according to Plato's *Timaeus*, the heavens are *not* made of a special fifth kind of matter, but out of pure versions of the elements we find down in our world—predominantly fire. This brings us back to his other refutation, *Against Proclus*. There, Philoponus spends a lot of time on interpretive questions concerning Plato's dialogues, especially the *Timaeus*. He wants to show that Proclus was wrong not only about the world's eternity, but also in his interpretation of Plato. Proclus insisted that a divine cause like the Demiurge or the Forms cannot begin to produce its effects after not doing so. Philoponus retorts that this would make the causes somehow dependent on their own effects (*Against Proclus* 2.3). Proclus, after all, seems to be saying that the causes are incapable of existing without producing those effects.

And now, we've come to the real core of his disagreement with Proclus. Philoponus objects to the idea that God is forced to create a universe at all, that he produces what comes after him necessarily, as Neoplatonists have been saying since Plotinus. This explains Philoponus' relentless attention to the eternity question: he is trying to safeguard the idea that God freely bestows existence on a universe that would otherwise not exist. That idea underlies another typically clever move, where he turns to his own advantage a passage in Plato that at first looks better for Proclus. Plato has the divine craftsman promise that the universe will never pass out of existence once it has been made. So the universe is eternal after all, in at least in the future. But now Philoponus pounces: if the universe must exist at all times, past, present, and future, what is the point of having God promise not to destroy it? Rather, the fact that the universe *could* be destroyed shows that it is also subject to generation. The passage therefore confirms that, for Plato, it is up to God how long the universe will exist.[7]

But in that case, mightn't God have decided, perhaps for reasons beyond our grasp, to create an eternal cosmos rather than one that begins to exist? To put it another way, if God can do anything, it looks like the universe might be eternal or it might not; it was up to God. Here though, Philoponus points out that God cannot do anything impossible. And it is indeed impossible that the universe has already existed eternally. His chief argument for this claim is as powerful as it is simple: if the universe were eternal, it would already have existed for an infinite time. But an infinite time cannot ever finish elapsing, so we could never have reached the present moment (*Against Proclus* 1.3). Here he can yet again turn his enemies' weapons against them, because Aristotle himself said that infinity cannot be traversed or completed. This is why Aristotle was worried about Zeno's dichotomy paradox.[8] Zeno suggested that every motion in fact consists of an infinity of submotions. To this Aristotle replied that a motion, or a distance, or a time, is only *potentially* divisible into infinity: you can cut it up as fine as you want, but you will never actually get an infinity of parts. Philoponus thus needs only to say that an eternal past time would give us an *actual* infinity, and not only a potential one. Even worse, it would be an actual infinity that is getting bigger all the time: the world has already existed for an infinite number of years, and each January that infinite number grows by one. Since Aristotle rejected the possibility of actual infinities, or the idea that infinity could be increased, these look like devastating objections. Simplicius, however, responds that past eternity is in fact only *potentially* infinite. An actual infinity is one that is simultaneously present in its entirety, for instance, an infinite number of divisions that are actually made in a motion or a line. But past eternity is not like this, since the times and things of the past no longer exist.

This debate, appropriately, is going to go on and on, finding echoes especially among philosophers in the Islamic world, some of whom adopt Philoponus' arguments, with others repeating Simplicius' replies. As for Philoponus, by the time he was done with the eternity debate he had thoroughly undermined Aristotle's system of natural philosophy. This led him to make other adjustments to that system, of which I'm going to mention just the most momentous.[9] In fact it concerns the issue of momentum: what causes a moving object, like a thrown javelin, to continue moving? When you are in the act of throwing the javelin, and your hand is still in contact with it, obviously your hand is causing the javelin to move. But once it leaves your hand it seems to be moving without being caused to move, at least until it lands on the ground some distance away.

To avoid admitting that the javelin's motion is indeed uncaused, Aristotle devised the following ingenious, albeit totally false, theory. As it leaves your hand, the javelin is pushing air out of the way. The air needs to go somewhere, so it pushes back around the javelin, until it winds up pushing the javelin from behind. After all, as the javelin continues flying forward, the space just behind it is available for the displaced air to rush in. Weirdly, then, the javelin powers its own motion by shoving air back around itself and using this air as a kind of engine. The only reason the javelin can't continue flying indefinitely in this way is that the air resists being moved around. Hence the javelin will fall back to the ground after a certain distance. In a related argument, Aristotle observed that the less resistance a moving thing encounters, the more easily and faster it will move. If this is right, then in a void, which offers no resistance at all, every motion should be infinitely fast! From this Aristotle concludes that void is impossible. Philoponus is not impressed by these arguments, and offers a new theory, which has been compared to the modern theory of impetus. In fact Galileo will mention him by name in his own writings on motion.

For Philoponus, things do not move because of any displaced air—he mocks Aristotle's theory by asking why armies don't launch javelins at their enemies using bellows to create gusts of wind. Rather, when you throw a javelin you impress into the javelin a certain amount of power for moving. The javelin will move until the power runs out. All that air can do is get in the way. This means that motion could in fact occur in a void: if you threw a javelin in a void, it would go further than it does in air because there is no resistance. But (and here is a difference from the modern way of thinking about things) it would still stop, because you have not imparted to it an infinite power to move. This is not to say that Philoponus thinks that void really exists. In fact he denies that it does. He just wants to insist that void is theoretically possible and that motion would work just fine, in fact better, in a void than through mediums that offer resistance.

Philoponus' innovative theory of impetus turns out to relate to his views on eternity. Since he rejects Aristotle's idea that the elements and heavens eternally move in straight lines and circles by nature, he needs to explain how it is that they do move. His answer is that God Himself imparts to these bodies whatever power they have. Thus he makes all motion depend on God, as Aristotle had done, but in a much more direct way: God gives each thing its motion by giving it existence and a certain power to move. Though the universe has not always existed, Philoponus probably agrees with Plato that it will exist forever into the future. This is not because it has the natural capacity to be eternal, as Aristotle claims, but to the contrary, because God overrides the physical universe's natural tendency to corrupt. He gives it an unnatural, infinite power to continue existing and moving. Philoponus' position here is a characteristic one. It is an innovation motivated by Christian belief, yet results from his deep engagement with the pagan philosophical tradition. This is why I have placed him here. He both rounds off our examination of pagan thought in late antiquity, and gives us new impetus to examine the topic that will occupy us for the rest of this book: philosophy among Christians.[10]

CHRISTIAN PHILOSOPHY
IN THE ROMAN EMPIRE

CHRISTIAN PHILOSOPHY
IN THE ROMAN EMPIRE

39

FATHER FIGURES
ANCIENT CHRISTIAN PHILOSOPHY

As a historian of philosophy it's somewhat embarrassing for me to admit this, but I'm pretty bad with dates. I don't mean the dried fruits, or romantic encounters, though to be honest neither of those was ever my strong point either. I mean when things happened, when famous people were born, and for that matter, birthdays and anniversaries. So I'm always grateful when a historical figure has a really memorable birth- or death-date. The best example has to be al-Ghazālī, the great Muslim philosopher and theologian, who did people like me the favor of dying in the year 1111. You might say he should get no credit for this noble service, since this is the date of the Christian calendar; but in the Muslim calendar he passed away in the almost equally memorable year 505. What a professional! Of course, if we do stick with the Christian calendar, no one has a more memorable year of birth than Jesus of Nazareth himself, namely 1. As for the precise day of birth, even I can remember that Christ was born on Christmas.

Sadly, scholars reckon that the historical Jesus was probably not, in fact, born on Christmas Day in AD 1. Rather, he was born in the last few years BC, which last time I checked was supposed to stand for "Before Christ." Nor was Christ's birth a sudden turning-point in the history of philosophy. Some of the developments we've already examined spanned the first centuries BC and AD, such as the emergence of Middle Platonism and the rebirth of Aristotelianism. The Roman Stoics come along beginning in the following decades—Seneca, for example, lived in the first half of the first century AD. The birth of Jesus, and of a faith which accepted him as a Messiah, had no immediate impact on the history of philosophy. But in due course it would have an impact exceeded by no other single historical development. This impact already began in the ancient world.

When we think of Christianity in relation to philosophy, we are likely first to think of medieval philosophy in Europe, and then perhaps modern-day philosophy of religion. Antique Christian philosophy does offer one household name though:

Augustine. He was exceptional in his genius and his influence, but far from the only philosophically sophisticated Christian author. Even a casual study of Christianity in this period will acquaint you with great theologians like Tertullian, Origen, Gregory of Nyssa, the Pseudo-Dionysius, and Maximus the Confessor. The earliest Christian thinkers are collectively called "Church Fathers." (I use the phrase in a broad sense, without necessarily implying that the "Fathers" I mention are considered orthodox.) Most were educated in the ancient rhetorical curriculum described in Chapter 27. This is clear from every page of their writing. It's just as clear that they were steeped in the Hellenic philosophical tradition. They knew their Plato, their Aristotelian logic, and the Stoics' teachings. Some living in later antiquity even knew their Proclus. Those who wrote in Latin also responded to authors like Lucretius, and especially Cicero, a major influence on Augustine. There's no real room for doubt, then, that the Church Fathers made extensive use of philosophical ideas. But I suspect some may be skeptical as to whether they made any *contributions* to philosophy. Did they have ideas of their own, of philosophical and not just religious and historical interest? In the rest of this book I hope to convince you that they did.

Let's first look briefly at the historical context. By the end of antiquity Christianity will be consumed by refined and complex theological debates. But the very earliest Christians would have been nonplussed, if not stunned, to learn of the disputes that lay ahead. In the first century AD we do not yet find bishops gathering in cities to dispute the technicalities of the Trinity, or Platonic and Stoic doctrine being used to refute heretics. Some even detect echoes of the philosophical tradition in the Bible itself—even in the teachings of Jesus, who since antiquity has been compared to Socrates. Ancient Christians preferred to detect an influence in the other direction. Unlike me, they were very good with dates, and pointed out that Moses came long before the Hellenic philosophers. Thus he could be recognized as an influence on their thought. Still, early Christian groups were not philosophical schools, like the later Neoplatonist enclaves of Athens and Alexandria. Nor were they committed to the passionate defense of dogma. They were bound together by the practices of sharing bread and wine in the Eucharist, baptism, and group prayer, not by the intense scrutiny of sacred texts. They anticipated an imminent final reckoning with God, and lived in hope, thanks to the mediation offered in the person of Jesus Christ.

Though the new faith was not yet associated with Greek philosophy, it was associated with the Greek language. Of course, the books of the New Testament are in Greek, not Hebrew, and the religion was spread around the empire by Greek-speaking missionaries like Paul. Even in Rome, many early Christians were Greek-speakers. This helps to explain why philosophy was later able to penetrate into Christianity, and vice versa. Much ink has been spilled over the question of

Christianity's Hellenic nature and its contrast to the Jewish culture out of which this new faith grew.[1] It has been a controversial issue since antiquity, given that the boundary between Judaism and Christianity was at first rather blurry. One key point of differentiation was that Christians did not demand circumcision. It has been suggested that for them baptism occupied the role played by this ritual in Judaism.[2] Christian writers of antiquity instead speak of circumcision as a metaphor, symbolizing, for instance, the way the faithful should renounce the things of the body. Before long, Christian theologians began to accuse their opponents of "Judaizing."

If the line between Jew and Christian was blurry, the divide between Christian and pagan was clear to see. Christians were distinguished by their ethical beliefs, especially their praise of chastity. Romans had traditionally admired moderation and self-control, but without renouncing such basic human functions as sexuality. Like the Jews, the Christians were also distinguished by their refusal to accept the traditional pantheon of Greco-Roman gods. We've seen that the traditional pantheon was rather porous and flexible, able to accommodate divinities from Egypt and other cultures. So the Judeo-Christian insistence on a single true God struck pagans as not just wrong-headed but bizarre and needlessly provocative. They duly accused Christians of being "atheists." This sounds rather strange to our ears, but the great Church Father Justin Martyr admitted that he and his co-religionists were indeed atheists, as far as the gods of Rome were concerned.[3]

Justin's name is a clue to another major feature of ancient Christian life. His honorific title "Martyr" refers to his death at the hands of the Romans, in AD 165. The reigning emperor? The philosopher, Marcus Aurelius. Marcus' fabled Stoic restraint didn't extend to putting up with Christians, and he was far from unique among emperors in this respect. Some were more tolerant towards Christians than others, but for two centuries the new faith faced the constant threat of persecution, even if actual persecution was more occasional and sporadic than we tend to believe. Some Christian writers seemed almost to revel in the danger of their precarious position. The Church Father Ignatius promised he would be glad to serve as wheat to be ground up by the teeth of wild animals, yielding flour for the bread of Christ.[4] Origen, the greatest of the early Greek Fathers, wrote a letter to a friend urging him to greet his probable impending martyrdom with eagerness rather than reluctance. (You can see why he wrote a letter: they don't make greetings-cards for occasions like this.) Some felt it necessary to caution their fellow Christians against deliberately inviting martyrdom. There's a fine line between dying in the name of faith and using faith as an excuse for suicide.

The Romans had what they considered to be good reason for the persecutions. When not throwing the Christians to the lions, they threw various accusations at the

ANCIENT CHRISTIAN PHILOSOPHY

Christians. They at least pretended to think that the Christians' gatherings concluded with sexual orgies, and called the Christians cannibals because their ritual involved eating the body of Christ. But the above-mentioned charge of atheism was the key complaint. The survival of the empire was believed to depend on the favor of the gods, and here were people who not only refused to sacrifice at the temples, but who rejected the gods' very existence! As antiquity wore on, the emperors themselves were credited with being gods. Christians, naturally, denied this also, which was reason enough for the persecutions. The repression and violence against adherents of the new faith would end only once the emperors themselves became Christians. The first to do so was, of course, Constantine.

Which brings us to another date worth remembering, AD 306—the year that Constantine became emperor in the West of the empire. In 305 the emperor Diocletian had relinquished power, after a reign that saw particularly enthusiastic persecution of Christians. Famously, Constantine consolidated his rule over the empire at the battle of the Milvian Bridge—in 312, since you ask. Just as famously, he supposedly had a vision before the battle which encouraged him to support the Christians. Whether this vision actually occurred, what he might have seen, what (if any) role it played in his benevolence towards Christianity, and when exactly he himself converted are all matters debated by historians. We historians of philosophy we can leave these issues aside though, and simply note that, after Constantine, the empire would be ruled by Christians, with the notable exception of Julian the Apostate. This made it possible for Christianity to thrive, to grow from an oppressed community to a major institutional force within the empire.

Free of persecution by pagans, the Christians wasted little time in turning upon one another, as they engaged in doctrinal disputes with increasing fervor. In the second century AD figures like Justin were using their rhetorical and philosophical skills to uphold what they took to be orthodoxy, and to refute what they took to be heresy. But the institutionalization of Christianity provided a new context and new impetus for such disputes. Already within the reign of Constantine, doctrinal clashes were causing headaches for the emperor. He was the first, but far from the last, emperor to attempt a peaceful resolution of the heated theological debates. In due course disagreements over such issues as the Trinity and the Incarnation would lead to street violence, would inspire insurrection against emperors of the East, and would provoke the leading intellectuals of the empire to write massive works of mutual refutation.

Which brings us back to philosophy. There is plenty of evidence that the Church Fathers were influenced by the Hellenic philosophical tradition. Here one need look no further than Augustine, who before his conversion took a large step towards

278

Christianity thanks to his reading of what he calls "the books of the Platonists," by which he probably meant Latin versions of Plotinus and Porphyry.[5] They showed him how he could understand God to be an immaterial cause, something he had previously found hard to accept. Of course Augustine was an exceptional man, but in this respect not all that exceptional. Clement of Alexandria and Origen, two great Church Fathers who wrote in Greek, were steeped in Hellenic culture generally and Hellenic philosophy in particular. This is not to say that all Christian thinkers clasped philosophy in a warm embrace. All three of the theologians I've just mentioned criticize the pagan philosophers in various ways. Other theologians, like the Latin Church Father Tertullian, were actively hostile, as they exalted the Gospel over the works of Plato and Aristotle.

Despite this, Christian writings should be seen as being part of the ancient philosophical tradition. To be honest, this is not a widely shared view. Rarely would you find papers on the Church Fathers in ancient philosophy periodicals, and they are not usually taught in university philosophy courses. Instead, the study of the Fathers, often called "Patristics," usually falls within the purview of Theology or Religious Studies departments. Even Augustine, one of the greatest philosophers who has ever lived, receives attention from historians of philosophy mostly in connection with the study of medieval thought—despite having died in 430. Yet scholars of ancient philosophy are showing increasing interest in the Church Fathers, attracted by the sophistication of these texts and the opportunity for finding new topics to investigate. Let me give you a few reasons why they would be right to do so.

First, there is the attitude of the ancient Christians themselves. Admittedly some, like Tertullian, did complain bitterly about pagan philosophy and even identify it as a source of heresy within Christianity. But others sought to appropriate the word "philosophy" for the new religion. We'll see Justin speaking of Christianity as the true philosophy, and Clement treating philosophy as a stepping-stone towards the truth of the Gospels. We've already seen how it served this purpose in Augustine's case. It would in fact be surprising if the Fathers had not attempted to appropriate philosophy for their own purposes. The Fathers were well educated and wrote for a well-educated audience. They wanted to show this audience that their faith was equal, or rather superior, to intellectually refined pagan systems like Stoicism and Platonism. Their pagan opponents understood the danger of allowing Christianity to draw on classical education. This is why the pagan emperor Julian banned Christians from teaching rhetoric. As for the Christians, they were not slow to point out that "philosophy" means "the love of wisdom" and depends on reason, in Greek, logos. If Jesus was quite literally the incarnation of divine wisdom and logos, what could be more "philosophical" than Christianity? There is more to this point than mere word-play. The Christians recognized that philosophers had always been pursuing truth, and sometimes praised them for this. But the philosophers were doomed to fail, at least in part, since perfect truth is given to man only in the Bible and in the person of Christ. Divine revelation opens a path to the wisdom that philosophers had been trying to achieve with the power of human reason alone.

Does this mean, though, that our theologians were not philosophers after all, given that they prefer revelation to rational argument? Well, consider Origen's *On Principles*, perhaps the greatest work of Christian philosophy in antiquity outside the works of Augustine. At the very beginning he lists several doctrinal points that are not up for serious debate, because they are established beyond doubt by Scripture. These include the existence and oneness of God, the begetting of the Son by the Father, the incarnation of the Son in Christ, and so on. But Origen immediately goes on to emphasize how much still remains *open* for debate. What is the nature of the soul and how does it relate to the body? What exactly does it mean to say that the Father begets the Son? What, if anything, existed before God created the world? These are just a few of the questions Origen goes on to investigate. In doing so, he usually proceeds by giving philosophical arguments, which are only afterward shown to be consonant with the Scriptures. Often, it must be said, the supposed demonstration of agreement between his conclusions and Scriptural authority is the least convincing part of Origen's presentation.

It's natural that the Church Fathers should have proceeded in this way. The Scriptures were, apart from the odd textual dispute, common ground between them and their theological opponents. Certainly, theologians did not hesitate to hurl biblical proof texts at one another, but those texts were already well known to the other side, who could reply by quoting their own favorite passages. So it was common in such debates to appeal to the neutral ground of rational argument, sometimes including explicit use of logic and other tools of Hellenic philosophy. Philosophy was thus a weapon that could be used to combat heresy and to defeat rival theological theories. Especially in the hands of more adventurous and exploratory authors, like Origen and Augustine, philosophy could be an instrument for solving difficulties not settled unambiguously by Scripture. As a result of all this, we can indeed find innovative philosophical ideas in ancient Christian texts, ideas that should be of interest even to the most confirmed atheist. I will mention three.

First, there is the issue of causation. The most hotly debated theological issue of late antiquity was the interrelation of the Trinitarian persons. All agreed that the Father begets the Son. But how to understand this divine relation of begetting? Presumably, it should have *something* in common with the case where a human father begets a human son. This calls for a careful analysis of the causal relationship between human fathers and human sons, and an equally careful consideration of how the divine case might differ from the human case. Nor would even that be enough. After all, the Christians believe that God causes the world to exist, but they are at pains to deny that God relates to the created world the way that the Father relates to the Son. So any satisfactory position on the Trinity needed to compare and contrast three causal relations: between God and world, between divine Father and divine Son, and between human father and human son. It is no wonder that Church Fathers offer some of the most sophisticated discussions of causation to be found in antiquity.

Then there is the special kind of causation involved in freely chosen action. We have seen that ancient philosophers, including Stoics and Platonists, thought carefully about the sense in which human actions are free. Christian authors respond to these discussions, above all to the notion of an autonomous will or power of choice, such as we find it in the Stoic Epictetus. But they take this notion much further, exploring the conditions under which a will may be said to be free. They also discuss how moral responsibility attaches to the will. Again, the context of this discussion is usually theological debate. For instance, Augustine's teaching on the will is developed partly in order to show that humans cannot merit salvation without divine grace. But the Christians' ideas about freedom and the will lived on even once those debates had faded into history. Today even non-Christians find themselves with powerful intuitions about freedom and moral responsibility that resonate more with Augustine than, say, Aristotle or Plato.[6]

Thirdly, ancient Christians were fascinated by language—by both its power and its limitations. The need to interpret Scripture forced them to reflect on the way that language both conveys and conceals meaning. Sometimes implicitly and often explicitly, they set forth new ideas about what we would call "hermeneutics," the interpretation of texts. This topic had been explored by pagan philosophers, and by grammarians and rhetoricians who were commenting on Homer and other classical authors. But Christians recognized with new force the possibility that a given text may be subject to an indefinite range of interpretations. They were, of course, thinking primarily of the divinely revealed text of Scripture, but the interpretive theories developed by Augustine and others are applicable to language more generally. Ancient Christians also worried about how language could describe God, including passages in Scripture that describe Him in terms that clearly could not be taken in their literal or surface sense.

This is by no means an exhaustive list of areas where Church Fathers say things of novel philosophical interest. One could easily add more examples, such as the nature of the soul or the metaphysical relation of parts to wholes, another issue that arose in the Trinitarian debate. Also central to their writings was the problem of whether God's knowledge of the future leads to determinism, a version of a problem that appeared in Aristotle's logic.[7] Philosophically, then, we have good reason to spend a while in the company of the ancient Christians. Historically, their importance is even more obvious. One cannot understand medieval philosophy without looking first at ancient Christianity. That goes not just for the medieval age in Europe, but also for the Byzantine tradition, and even philosophy in the Islamic world. In all three spheres we see engagement with late ancient Christians, and the theological controversies that started in late antiquity continued to make themselves felt throughout the history of philosophy.

40

PLEASE ACCEPT
OUR APOLOGIES
THE GREEK CHURCH FATHERS

A boy sits cross-legged on the ground. It is the last night of October, and a chill seeps up from the ground through a layer of snaking vines. He does not notice, so keen is his sense of anticipation. He has chosen this place carefully, for its sincerity. If he has chosen well and his expectations are fulfilled, he will be rewarded with gifts, as will all other good children in the world. But he will be alone to witness the appearance of the figure who will rise up out of the vines, and prove once and for all that his faith is justified. He will be the first to behold... the Great Pumpkin. The boy, of course, is Linus from the *Peanuts* comic strip, who each Halloween tries to convince Charlie Brown and the other children to await this Santa Claus-style figure. Every year he is disappointed, but he does not renounce his faith.

Now, pumpkins are not the most philosophical of vegetables. That distinction surely belongs to the tomato, because everyone thinks it is a vegetable, but actually it is a fruit. Nonetheless, the humble pumpkin has played an occasional role in the writings of philosophers. Seneca wrote a satirical attack on the emperor Claudius called the *Apocolokyntosis*, which means something like "pumpkinification." (The title is a pun on the term "apotheosis," applied to emperors when they become gods.) More recently, the philosopher of religion Alvin Plantinga imagined an objection to his own views regarding the rationality of religious belief.[1] Plantinga claimed that a Christian can rationally accept the existence of God without having proved it—the Christian could simply take this belief to be basic, the way you believe you ate dinner last night without needing any proof for that. (Bonus points if you believe you had pumpkin pie for dessert.) But if this is right, then couldn't someone like Linus rationally believe in the existence of the Great Pumpkin, without giving any good reason for that belief?

In fact, a careful reading of the *Peanuts* comic shows that Linus' belief is not a "religious" one. In one strip he says: "There are three things I have learned never to discuss with people: religion, politics, and the Great Pumpkin." Pumpkinology, then, is distinct from religion, albeit equally controversial. If we go back closer to the time of Seneca, though, we do find pumpkins invoked in a religious controversy. The context is the *Refutation of Heresies* by the Church Father Irenaeus, who wrote in the late second century.[2] His targets are the so-called Gnostics, a group of thinkers who claimed to follow Christ but were, as far as Irenaeus was concerned, no Christians at all. Various Gnostics adopted various cosmologies—indeed, Irenaeus was happy to emphasize the differences between them, like a Skeptic pointing out disagreements among dogmatic philosophers. But all the Gnostics postulated a highest God who presides over a range of lower divine beings, who receive names like Silence, Unity, Truth, Wisdom, and Life. In an uncharacteristically amusing passage, Irenaeus sarcastically suggests that they may as well believe in a divinity called *Kolokunthe*, the Greek word for "pumpkin" (1.11).

Some surviving Gnostic texts were discovered in Egypt, near the town of Nag Hammadi, in the mid-twentieth century. But we would know far less about them than we do without the refutations of Irenaeus and the works of other Church Fathers who are sometimes called "Apologists," because of their indefatigable defense of the new faith.[3] As the Fathers present them, the Gnostic theories indeed seem about as reasonable as Linus' faith in the Great Pumpkin. Yet the Gnostics were taken seriously enough to provoke such refutations. They were also read by philosophers, notably in the next century in the school of Plotinus (see Chapter 32). In both cases, this may be because Gnostic views seemed too close for comfort. They drew inspiration not just from the Gospels but also from the philosophical tradition, their distinctive teachings echoing Middle Platonic ideas. They believed that the cosmos was created not by the highest God but by a more ignorant, lower deity. This explains why we don't live in a perfect world, free of suffering and evil. Accordingly, they disdained the material world and held that redemption lies in a purely spiritual life defined by certain knowledge. So far, so Platonist. A less familiar note was struck when they claimed that this life is available only to a select few. Jesus came for the sake of this elite group, and brought to them a new message about the highest God. The Old Testament or Hebrew Bible had, according to them, spoken only of the ignorant creator deity.

We saw that Plotinus was provoked by the Gnostics into defending the beauty and goodness of the physical realm, despite thinking that matter is the principle of evils. The Church Fathers were likewise provoked. But why? Charlie Brown didn't believe in the Great Pumpkin, but he reacted to Linus with amused toleration, not the lengthy abuse offered by Irenaeus and other Church Fathers. Irenaeus would like us to think that he is motivated by moral indignation. He particularly resents the Gnostic claim to be an elite above the rest of the material world—they compare themselves to gold immersed in filth (1.6). Already chosen by God for salvation, they have no need to perform good works to merit God's favor, as Christians like Irenaeus struggle to do. Instead they feel free to indulge in scandalous behavior, seducing young women with promises of initiation.

But, sorry Irenaeus—I'm not buying it. No amount of sexual misbehavior could explain the detailed exposition and refutation of Gnostic theory presented by Irenaeus. I suspect that he attacked the Gnostics because he feared they might appeal to his own audience. They were that most dangerous of opponents: the enemy who agrees with you just enough to seduce your friends. They were also a convenient opponent, in that Irenaeus' own views on God, creation, and mankind were brought into sharp relief by the contrasting views of the Gnostics. Refuting the Gnostics was an opportunity to defend the one true God, conceived not as a remote first principle followed by other principles, but a single Creator who reigns supreme. So Irenaeus does not just rename the Gnostics' principles after vegetables. He hopes that, by rooting out their heresy, he will plant the seeds of truth in his readers' minds.

For instance, he points out that if there are inferior divinities that act contrary to God's will, as the Gnostics claim, then these divinities must be more powerful than God (2.2). How else could they defy his will? Instead, we should say that all things are subject to God's volition. Again, if the ignorant principles came from God, then God too must be ignorant (2.17). For causes share their natures with their effects. So we must reject the idea of an ignorant creating god. Yet again, regarding Gnostic dualism—the idea that there is a source of evil outside of God's power—he points out that if God is to be separate from the lower, evil principle, there must be some third power in between them, keeping them apart (2.1). Indeed, once we abandon the idea of a single God, there is no reason to stop at two. We will wind up with an indefinite multiplicity of divinities filling gaps between other divinities. Here Irenaeus is remarkably prescient, describing in advance the sort of opulent metaphysical scheme espoused by the pagan philosopher Proclus several centuries later.

This is appropriate, because for Irenaeus the vine of heresy is rooted in pagan philosophy. He is happy to use philosophical premises in his invective against the Gnostics. For instance, we just saw him deploying the Platonist principle that causes and effects share a nature. But philosophy usually appears as the raw material that has been woven into the fabric of Gnosticism. Indeed, he compares the heresy to a garment sewn together from the old rags of Greek philosophy (2.14). He finds parallels between the Gnostics and the Hellenic schools: their shameless behavior is reminiscent of the Cynics, the number symbolism they associate with their principles sounds suspiciously Pythagorean, and so on. Even Plato has been hijacked for their nefarious ends. They present lower principles as images of higher ones, borrowing the Platonic understanding of particular things as images of Forms. Irenaeus seems to be objecting to this in part because he admires Plato, at least to some extent. Certainly Plato is far preferable to the Gnostics (3.25), even if he did make the occasional error, for instance, by believing that after death human souls pass into the bodies of animals (2.33).

Something else divides Irenaeus from both the Gnostics and the philosophers. They are confident that humans can, in principle, attain perfect knowledge. We know that this possibility was a fundamental commitment of the Stoics, and the idea is fundamental to the Gnostics' elitism. By contrast, Irenaeus denies that men can know everything, and gives examples of questions that lie beyond our ken (2.28). We can make only plausible guesses as to what makes the Nile rise, or what causes rain and other kinds of weather. At a more exalted level, how can humans know what God was doing before He created the world? Later, Augustine will raise this same question and be unable to resist quoting a joke answer he's heard: God was preparing hells for people who ask impertinent questions like this one.[4] Irenaeus agrees with the spirit of that joke, going so far as to say that anything unexplained in Scripture should be left to God.

One might assume that all the Church Fathers shared Irenaeus' attitude, and at best saw philosophy as a weapon to be used in refuting opponents. But that assumption is itself refuted by another second-century figure, the apologist Clement of Alexandria. The "of Alexandria" part of his name already helps to explain his enthusiasm for Hellenic philosophy. Whereas Irenaeus came from the eastern edge of the Roman Empire, in Asia Minor, and wound up in the West as bishop of Lyons, Clement resided in the intellectual center of the empire. Alexandria housed the greatest library and research institute of the ancient world, and was the headquarters of Middle Platonism in the generations leading up to Clement's lifetime. Notably, Philo of Alexandria, one of Clement's major influences, had lived there around the time of Jesus. Later Plotinus will study there, and it will be the home of the last school of Neoplatonists. As for Clement himself, he served as the instructor of Christian converts in this sophisticated city. It's no wonder that he sought to show how the ancient educational curriculum, from grammar to rhetoric and, especially, philosophy, could be a faithful friend to Christianity.

Clement's pedagogical outlook is indicated by the title of one of his works, the *Paedagogus* or *Teacher*—the title is a reference to Christ, who is here portrayed as a teacher who cures his students of sin. Another work is called *Stromateis*, meaning a patchwork of fabric.[5] This recalls Irenaeus' dismissive description of Gnostic doctrines as a ragbag of philosophical influences. But Clement's quilt is, as he tells us, stitched together from the best parts of Hellenic philosophy, and will help the reader to reach an understanding of Christian truths. Certainly, he admits that some pagan thinkers traded in falsehoods—he gives obvious examples, like Epicurean atheism and Stoic materialism (1.50–1). But truth too can be found in the Hellenic philosophers, especially Plato. Just as a coin retains its value no matter who handles it, so truth can be used to procure happiness even if it is unearthed in pagan soil (1.98). In fact, Clement says that for him the very term "philosophy" means not everything the Hellenic thinkers have said, but only the true part of what they said, like a nut extracted from its shell (1.18, 1.37). This kernel of philosophy is sent by God, first to help pagans to live better than they otherwise would have—and now for Christians, to prepare the way for salvation.

Clement claims that he is not just taking truth from the philosophers, he is taking it *back*. He provides a detailed chronology to show that Moses lived many generations before even the earliest Hellenic philosophers (1.101–7). This lends historical plausibility to his claim that Plato's political ideas, for instance, derive ultimately from the Old Testament. Indeed, Moses handed down truth in all the major departments of philosophy: politics, ethics, physics, and metaphysics. As a whole, Scripture instructs us in that most philosophical of skills, dialectic, by which Clement means the ability to extract the true from the false. So it turns out that the best bits of philosophy, the snippets worth bringing to Clement's Christian quilting bee, come ultimately from the Bible. Of course, this is something of a back-handed compliment. Clement is telling us that the Greeks stole what wisdom they possessed, but at least had the good sense to steal from the best. In that case, though, why not dispense with philosophy and follow the advice of Irenaeus: seek the answers to all our questions in Scripture, and if we do not find them, reconcile ourselves to ignorance?

Clement's answer will be repeated by Christian, Jewish, and Muslim philosophers for the next millenium and more. We use philosophy to prepare ourselves for faith, to understand more fully what we believe by faith, and to defend the faith against its enemies. Those who proceed straightaway to faith without study are like those who want to harvest pumpkins without first caring for the patch, if I may adapt an agricultural image used by Clement. This may sound strange to the modern ear, since nowadays we tend to think of religious faith and philosophical or rational argument as mutually exclusive paths. Faith, surely, is nothing other than belief that takes no heed or feels no need of reason? Well, not for Clement. He carefully analyzes the Greek term *pistis* (2.14), which can be rendered into English as "faith," but also as "trust" or "conviction," translations which might be less misleading in the present context. Clement does use the word *pistis* to describe religious belief in the absence of philosophical reflection. But he also uses it for the attitude one takes towards the very things that are demonstrated in a philosophical argument—for instance, the conclusion of an Aristotelian syllogism. Furthermore, *pistis* describes the belief we have in the case of first principles, the undemonstrated foundations of philosophical knowledge, according to Aristotle.

What do these three kinds of belief have in common? Clearly, *pistis* or faith is not applied specifically to religious, as opposed to secular, beliefs. Nor does it pick out things believed immediately, without giving any rationale for the belief. That would apply to unreflective religion and first principles, but not to demonstrated conclusions. Rather, *pistis* is distinctive because of one's level of commitment. When we have faith, we believe with confidence, even certainty. Thus Clement contrasts faith to mere opinion, where one's belief is still open to doubt. He adds, though, that faith is not just what we helplessly find ourselves believing. To have faith involves an act of the will, so that we are responsible for what we believe (2.28). Here Clement seems to be drawing on the Stoics. Remember that Stoic thinkers like Epictetus likewise insisted that our assent is under our control, and our control alone. Clement combines this with Aristotelian ideas about belief and knowledge to forge a new notion of *pistis* suitable for use by Christianity.

When we have this sort of secure belief in God (comparable to the knowledge achieved by Stoic sages), then we have attained what Clement pointedly calls *gnosis*. This word means "knowledge," which is why the thinkers attacked by Irenaeus were known as "Gnostics." Clement is reclaiming the word *gnosis* for the true faith, just as he is reclaiming philosophy from the pagans. Actually, some scholars have claimed to find common ground between Clement and the Gnostics, because he too portrays human fulfillment in a highly intellectual way.[6] Also reminiscent of Gnosticism is his conviction that the Scriptures are symbolic texts that need to be decoded through the use of philosophy. On both scores, though, his real model is not the hated Gnostics but Philo of Alexandria. Clement follows Philo in pursuing philosophical exegesis of the Bible, and even quotes some of Philo's allegorical readings. Gnosticism's role in forming Clement's approach is that of a competitor, not an inspiration. He seeks to show that orthodox Christianity too can make use of traditional learning, and match Gnosticism in its sophistication.

Clement and Irenaeus were struggling both to defend orthodoxy and to define it. In this era orthodox Christian belief had several rivals: not just pagans and Gnostics, but also Jews. In the first century after Christ the boundaries between Christianity and Judaism had been contentious. Now, in the second century, Clement could point to the Hebrew Bible as the root of all that is good in philosophy, and draw gratefully on the Jewish thinker Philo. Yet Christians also needed to differentiate their religion from Judaism, and explain why it should be preferred. No text sums up this problematic relationship so well as the *Dialogue with Trypho*, written by another apologist, Justin Martyr.[7] Like a Platonic dialogue, it dramatically presents an encounter between a sage and an interlocutor. The sage, Justin's mouthpiece, describes himself as a philosopher who dresses in a philosopher's distinctive garments. He debates with Trypho, a possibly fictitious Jew, trying to convert him to Christianity. The speaker himself, presumably describing Justin's own conversion, tells how he was originally trained in philosophy, only to encounter a Christian who showed him the incoherence of various philosophical teachings. For instance, he at first accepted Plato's doctrine of the immortal soul, but was then persuaded that something subject to change and moral failure, like the soul, cannot possibly be ungenerated—that can apply to God alone (5). Soul is not, then, essentially alive, as Plato had argued in the *Phaedo*. Rather, God creates the soul and bestows life upon it. If the soul lives on after the death of the body, this is because eternal life is given to it as a gift that goes beyond its intrinsic nature.

Nonetheless, Justin shares with Clement the idea that genuine "philosophy" is whatever is true—and therefore goes so far as to claim that Christianity itself is the true philosophy (8). From a philosophical point of view, though, the interest of Justin's *Dialogue* wanes after the initial pages. Most of the text is dedicated to exegesis of the Old Testament, attempting to show that it prefigures and justifies Christian belief. The Jewish character Trypho is mostly a passive straight-man, though he is given an occasional chance to fight back, for instance by suggesting that the doctrine of the virgin birth is plagiarized from myths about Zeus (47). And though the conversation is depicted as a polite one, Justin really shows little respect for the Jewish faith. He includes a rather unedifying diatribe in which the Christian spokesman claims that circumcision and dietary laws are punishments laid upon the Jews for crucifying the Son of God (18). Even in the midst of this disturbing material we do find passages of philosophical interest: the spokesman pauses to comment on the possibility of free will, which must be possessed by the Jews if God is to be just in punishing them for their evil misdeed (141).

This mention of free will and evil brings us back to Irenaeus and his refutation of the Gnostics. You may have noticed that the Gnostic teaching could claim a distinct advantage over the "orthodox" Christian one. By invoking an ignorant secondary God and the baseness of matter, the Gnostics could explain why the world is full of evil and sin, something difficult to explain in a system that recognizes only a single, entirely good First Principle. For Irenaeus and the other Fathers the difficulty is even more, well, difficult. We've already seen Irenaeus insisting on the untrammeled freedom of God, and in coming generations Christians will reject the Neoplatonists' claim that all things proceed from the First Principle necessarily. But if God is free and all-powerful, then why does He allow evil and suffering?

Irenaeus' suggested solution would not prevail in the tradition, though it has found admirers among contemporary philosophers of religion.[8] He begins from the Platonist-sounding assumption that, if souls are created, they must be changeable and imperfect. They begin in a condition like that of children, who need to develop to acquire wisdom and virtue (4.38). The Gnostics say that some are by nature bad and others by nature good. For Irenaeus, by contrast, it is up to each soul to become good. Suffering is the consequence of our inevitable imperfection, but we can strive to perfect ourselves through the exercise of our freedom of choice. Instead of blaming God for not creating us as gods like Himself, we should thank Him for calling us to perfect ourselves and giving us commands we can follow along the way. It's remarkable to see here how the imperfection of mankind is explained through metaphysical necessity, rather than the doctrine of original sin that will be expounded by Augustine. This is a road that Christianity could have taken, but did not. At least, not in the long run. In the short run we find a breathtakingly radical version of Irenaeus' proposal in another apologist, who happens to be the most philosophically interesting early Church Father. So let's continue to look at the origins of Christian philosophy, with the Christian philosophy of Origen.

41

FALL AND RISE
ORIGEN

How do you feel about this whole "all men are created equal" thing? Is it, for example, a truth you hold to be self-evident? Thomas Jefferson did, which is why he led with it in the greatest divorce letter ever written, the American *Declaration of Independence*. But as self-evident truths go, it looks pretty controversial. Before we agree, we will presumably want to understand "men" to refer to all humans, not just adult males. Then there is Jefferson's implication that a divine creator has bestowed the equality in question. That is made explicit in the following clause, which says that it is God who has endowed all of us with inalienable rights, such as the right to pursue life, liberty, and happiness. Self-evident in the late eighteenth century, not so uncontentious nowadays.

Yet even atheists would probably agree that Jefferson was on to something. Most of us believe that all human beings have equal moral standing, and most ethical theories endorsed by today's philosophers reflect that. Followers of Kant want to say that every human should equally be considered an end and not a means. Utilitarians, the heirs of Mill and Bentham, typically think that we should be trying to maximize happiness universally, with each person having an equal claim to that happiness. These sentiments do need to be squared against other, apparently evident truths that push us back in the direction of inequality, for instance, that our loved ones should have more weight in our moral calculations than total strangers do. Still, the equality of every human seems to be a promising starting-point for moral reflection. Equality is not only a starting-point, it is also a goal. We strive to achieve equality in democratic political arrangements, to treat all parties impartially in legal judgments, to eliminate inequality in social and economic conditions.

All of which prompts the following thought: if we humans were indeed created by a just and loving God, then why *weren't* we created equal? It's patently obvious that we come into this world with radically different talents and capacities. Some are naturally intelligent, others are not. Some are gifted athletes, others uncoordinated and clumsy. Some have flowing, silken locks of hair cascading to their shoulders, and then there's me. Even worse is the fact that some people are apparently born *morally* better than others. Certainly, different childhood environments have an impact on our moral character. Yet it does seem that certain people are born with the gifts of instinctive kindness, effortless self-control, and a cheerful outlook on life. Having lived in the American Midwest for several years, I can tell you that most of these people live there. At the other end of the spectrum are the bad seeds, people who have every advantage of privilege and upbringing but find that, like Oscar Wilde, they can resist everything except temptation.

In the ancient world it was, if anything, taken for granted that all men—to say nothing of women—are *not* created equal. Just think of the three classes in Plato's *Republic*, who are distinguished in terms of their inborn tendencies, or of Aristotle's views on natural slavery. Such natural inequalities, including morally significant inequalities, became increasingly difficult to explain as ancient philosophy developed. First the Stoics, then the Platonists and Christians, insisted that the world is the result of providential divine activity. Why does God, despite untrammelled power, fail to arrange the world as we humans strive to arrange our own modest affairs— with equality and justice for all? The difficulty is narrower than the one we have looked at under the rubric of the "problem of evil" in discussing Plotinus. Now we are asking, not why there is anything bad in the universe at all, but more specifically why some people are born without gifts that are naturally given to others.

One answer was given by a group we also mentioned when we looked at Plotinus: the Gnostics. For them, God's plan simply included a division of souls into three types. The best souls, the ones possessed by the Gnostic masters themselves, are permanently righteous and immune to the seductions of the physical world. Such souls are guaranteed to receive salvation. The worst souls cannot achieve salvation, and are lost from the day of their creation. In between are the souls who must struggle towards righteousness. The Gnostic view is bound to seem shocking, not only in its elitism but also in its assumption that God would play favorites in this seemingly unjust manner. It certainly shocked Christian polemicists like Justin Martyr and Clement of Alexandria, who insisted that Christ came to redeem the whole human race, not just a fortunate few. But they did not think through the consequences of this rejection as thoroughly, indeed radically, as another Christian theologian. He was the most philosophically sophisticated and theologically daring of the early Greek Church Fathers. His name was Origenes, known to us in English as Origen.

He was the son of a Christian father who died in the persecutions of the emperor Septimus Severus at the dawn of the third century. At the same time, the wealth of the family was confiscated. But Origen, about 20 years old, had already received an excellent education, which enabled him to support his family as a teacher of grammar, and gave him the tools to exploit the unparalleled intellectual environment of his home city, Alexandria. He followed in the footsteps of Clement by teaching in the city's school for converts to Christianity, and followed him again by drawing on the great Jewish philosopher and biblical exegete Philo of Alexandria. Alexandria was also the center of pagan Platonism, already in the time of Philo and for centuries still after the age of Origen. The pagan Platonists seemed to Origen to be allies, not enemies; he singles out Numenius for special praise. Origen may even have become familiar with them by studying with none other than Ammonius Saccas, the teacher of Plotinus. We know from Porphyry that Ammonius had a student named Origenes, but it is not clear whether this is the same man.[1]

If you had had a chance to sit on the dockside of Alexandria with him, admiring the lighthouse and trading anecdotes about the many philosophers named Ammonius, you might have asked Origen what he considered his greatest achievement. He could, with some justification, have mentioned either one of two massive works that survive today. One responds to a withering critique of Christianity by a Platonist philosopher named Celsus. Here Origen carries on the apologist tradition of Justin and Clement. A second treatise, On Principles, is a tour de force of theological speculation, the high-point of Greek Patristic literature for philosophically minded readers. It survives in quotations of the Greek by later authors, and in a Latin translation by a later admirer and defender, Rufinus, who lived almost two centuries after Origen. Origen also wrote lengthy commentaries on several books of the Bible, which are partially preserved.

But if Origen really wanted to impress you, he would probably have named a work that is now lost: the Hexapla. One of the most astounding feats of philology in the ancient world, this offered a side-by-side comparison of six versions of the Hebrew Bible. In six columns Origen laid out the original Hebrew text, a transliteration of the Hebrew into Greek characters, three attempted Greek translations of the Hebrew, and finally the most widely accepted Greek version, the Septuagint, noting places where this diverged from the Hebrew. Origen was born at the wrong time. He would, I think, have loved to publish the Hexapla on the internet, and do the whole thing with hyperlinks and pop-up windows. As it was, he had to hope scribes would be willing to preserve this massive piece of erudition by copying it out by hand over the coming millennium. They weren't.

Which brings us back to our theme of what an unjust place the world is. Like the earlier Church Fathers, Origen could not accept the elitist doctrine of the Gnostics, which made God as arbitrary in his choices as a scribe deciding which text to preserve. But nor could he see how the world as we see it could be the direct creation of the perfectly just God whose Scripture he so lovingly studied in the Hexapla.

As Sherlock Holmes would say: "once you've eliminated the impossible, whatever remains, no matter how improbable, is the truth." By appealing to divine justice Origen could eliminate the Gnostic theory that God chose to make us unequal. By the evidence of his own eyes he could eliminate the idea that we are all in fact born equal. What remained was the possibility that souls were originally created equal, and only afterwards became unequal as a result of their own choices. A more timid thinker than Origen might have shied away from this radical conclusion. A more timid thinker could thus have avoided repeated condemnation in the coming generations. Origen was denounced by authors as varied as the Byzantine emperor Justinian and the Latin Church Father Jerome—who debated the orthodoxy of Origen with the translator of *On Principles*, Rufinus.[2]

But Origen was anything but timid. He explains in the opening pages of *On Principles* why he takes himself to have great license in devising solutions to theological and philosophical problems.[3] As Christians, Origen and his reader have certain fundamental commitments derived from the clear meaning of Scripture. Origen lists these, but then points out how much remains unresolved. These are the areas that remain open for inquiry. His method is the opposite of the one we found in Irenaeus, who cautioned his readers not to pursue questions that have no answers in revelation. The nature of the soul, the way in which God created the world, whether anything exists without a body—these are just such questions, and Origen will pursue them in *On Principles*.

Although his ideas about the soul are formulated in part as a response to the Gnostics, Origen shares something in common with his opponents. Like them, he sees the salvation of the soul as residing in intellectual fulfillment. Origen's intellectualism is also at play in explaining how souls fell away from God in the first place. When God first created the souls they were all alike. This is not only because of the demands of justice (1.5.3), the theme I've been emphasizing, but also because God Himself is simple and without any diversity. Thus His effects cannot come from Him already possessing variety and diversity (2.9.6). Instead, the souls were all created on an equal footing, as rational beings without bodies but with the power of free choice. Being nothing but minds, they could only exercise this freedom by forming various beliefs. Origen points to the way that desire influences belief. He draws a connection between the Greek word *psyche* or "soul," and the verb *psychesthai*, meaning "to cool down"—because the souls fall away from God when their love for Him grows cold (2.8.3). Here Origen is picking up the theme we found in Clement. We do not just passively find ourselves believing things. Rather, belief always involves the exercise of choice. This is an insight we will meet again in Augustine. We like to imagine that our beliefs are formed rationally, in reaction to the evidence at our disposal. But more commonly we rationalize our beliefs in light of our desires.

For Origen, this is not just a psychological observation but a key to explaining how diversity comes into the world. The souls who chose to adhere most closely to the truth became angels, divided into ranks by their various beliefs. Others became wicked demons. In the middle—like the struggling souls of the Gnostics—are the souls that find themselves in human bodies. Our embodiment is the result of a prior intellectual failure, which was also a failure of will. To undo the damage, God Himself must become embodied in the person of Christ and lead us to salvation. Again, Origen understands this process as an increase in wisdom. He describes God as a teacher who is educating souls on how to improve their status (3.5.8). This pedagogical theme, one we already observed in Clement and will observe again in Augustine, is exactly what we'd expect from Origen, the instructor of new converts. He is also in tune with Irenaeus, who taught that life is a challenge laid down to souls, an opportunity to achieve greater perfection. Unlike Irenaeus, however, Origen boldly suggests that the whole cosmos can be understood as the product of the souls' fall and rise. It is only because of the foolishness of souls that a complex and varied cosmos comes about in the first place, instead of the immaterial community of souls first created by God (2.1.3). Origen further believes, on the basis of certain biblical passages, that eventually all souls—maybe even those of demons—will manage to return to a state of salvation. He indulges in further speculation here, pondering the Stoic doctrine of world-cycles and wondering whether there might be a series of cosmic dramas in which souls first fall away from, and then return to, God (2.3.1).

Characteristically, Origen discusses that possibility without quite committing himself to it wholeheartedly. His willingness to explore ideas in such a tentative way is an appealing feature of his thought, but it can make his actual views difficult to pin down. It doesn't help that our fullest version of On Principles is the Latin one by Rufinus. Since Rufinus' project was to defend Origen against charges of unorthodoxy and even heresy, he quietly corrected passages where Origen strayed into dangerous territory. Meanwhile, later critics of Origen like Justinian tendentiously quote Origen in an effort to make him seem as heretical as possible. Thus passages from On Principles are sometimes preserved in two versions, a Latin one that looks rather banal, and a Greek one that seems flagrantly heretical. Discerning Origen's settled view in such cases—if he even had one—is not easy. For instance, Origen's critics tell us in no uncertain terms that he rejected the doctrine of bodily resurrection, and thought that when the souls achieve salvation they will lose their bodies. This makes Origen sound like a committed Platonist: the soul is fundamentally an immaterial thing, which acquires a casual association to a series of bodies, but can free itself entirely from the physical realm by achieving wisdom. In Rufinus' Latin version, though, Origen is somewhat more circumspect about whether we will ultimately be disembodied.[4]

Be that as it may, *On Principles* is certainly a work deeply influenced by Platonism. So it is rather ironic that Origen's greatest opponent was also a Platonist, named Celsus. The two did not meet in person. Celsus lived in the generations before Origen, and his vicious attack on Christianity came to Origen's attention only when he received a copy from his patron Ambrosius. Celsus had called his diatribe *Logos Alethes*, meaning *True Doctrine* or *True Word*—the word *Logos* in the title is of course a mocking reference to the assertion that Christ is the Word of God. At the request of Ambrosius, Origen wrote a massive refutation which reasserted the truth of the Christian *logos* over that of this pagan upstart.[5] Origen guesses that the irreverent Celsus is an Epicurean (*Against Celsus* 1.8). Apparently he finds it hard to believe that a philosopher this appalling could be anything else! But it's clear that Celsus was a Platonist, and one of those Platonists who really, really didn't like Christians.

Celsus painted adherents of this new faith in the most unflattering of terms, accusing them of deliberate secrecy born out of cowardice and describing them as vermin. The apostles, he said, were a low-born rabble, and Jesus was not the son of a virgin but the illegitimate child of a Roman soldier (1.22). He also had more principled complaints about Christian belief. He disdained their reliance on faith, their habit of discouraging questions and demanding unthinking acceptance of doctrine. Besides, the doctrines they are required to accept are absurd. The virgin birth is scarcely credible (1.28, 32), and the notion that a god could become a man is simply metaphysically impossible. This is one of the places where Celsus' Platonist inclinations become clear, because of his sharp contrast between the divine and the physical, a contrast that no Epicurean would have recognized.

We know all of this thanks to Origen's quotations from Celsus, which are interspersed with lengthy refutations. Celsus made the tactical error of putting many of his attacks into the mouth of a fictional Jewish spokesman, so Origen is to some extent able to turn the debate into one over the meaning of the Scriptures shared by Jew and Christian. Here, we are in something like the territory of Justin's *Dialogue with Trypho*, as Origen shows that the virgin birth and Incarnation are in fact prefigured in the Old Testament. Mercifully, he gives us only one version of the biblical texts he cites, not six. In fact he is perhaps more keen to display his deep knowledge of the pagan tradition than his biblical erudition. Celsus had depicted Christians as ignorant, unquestioning low-lifes, a slander Origen can refute by displaying his own knowledge of philosophy and Hellenic culture. For instance, when Celsus says that the apostles were reprobates before they became followers of

Christ, Origen says: yes, just as were the followers of Socrates before they converted to philosophy (1.3). To Celsus' claim that God cannot inhabit a body, Origen asks, what about the oracle at Delphi (1.70)? Against Celsus' most general point that the Christians demand blind belief in place of reasoned argument, Origen follows the lead of Clement: Hellenic philosophy, or at least the Platonist part of it, is largely in agreement with the Gospels. And no wonder. As Clement had also said, the ideas supposedly "discovered" by Greek thinkers can themselves be traced back to Moses (1.16). There is, then, no opposition between faith and philosophy.

None of this is to say that Origen saw the Bible as just one more philosophical text. To the contrary: he admits, in *Against Celsus* and in his surviving commentaries on Scripture, that the Bible nearly defies correct interpretation at times. It even contains outright historical impossibilities and contradictions, something eagerly pointed out by critics like Celsus and Porphyry. These do not, however, undermine the validity of Scripture. Rather, they are providentially included in the text, to make sure we read it not as a straightforward historical narrative but with higher, allegorical methods of interpretation.[6] The Scripture is designed to help everyone make progress, from the simplest to the most advanced reader. The most basic meaning, what we might call its "literal" sense, is what Origen calls the "bodily" interpretation. When we find contradictions at this level, we are pointed to a so-called "spiritual" interpretation, which involves the sort of symbolic reading pioneered by Philo of Alexandria. To Philo's armory of interpretive weapons Origen adds his own considerable philological skills. For instance, when the Bible says, "In the beginning was the word," Origen catalogues all the different meanings of the Greek word *arche*, or "beginning."[7] It is, as it happens, the very same Greek word used for "principle" in the title of Origen's *On Principles*.

The career of Origen shows us both the power and the limitations of Hellenic philosophy, and in particular Platonism, for the early Christian tradition. On the one hand, Origen's learning could be used to defend the faith, not least by presenting himself as an example of just how sophisticated a Christian can be. On the other hand, all that learning did not keep Origen from being persecuted along with his fellow religionists. He was tortured during the persecution of Decius around 250, and died shortly thereafter. There were also limits to how much Hellenic philosophy a man like Origen could accept. One comes away from his treatise *Against Celsus* realizing that Celsus was a truer Platonist than Origen could ever be. For instance, Celsus assumes that the world's rational design is unchanging, so that it can never contain more or less evil than it does now. Origen instead sees the world as evolving towards a more perfect state, in which all souls are reconciled to God. With Origen and the other Church Fathers history becomes central to the history of philosophy.

No longer is the world a static, unchanging object for us to contemplate. It is rather a stage on which is played out the greatest story ever told. At the center of that story are concrete historical events, especially the birth and crucifixion of Jesus, which give the whole cosmos its meaning and even its intelligibility.

Still, figures like Irenaeus, Clement, and Origen only begin to show us what Christianity will mean for the history of philosophy. In particular, though they do speak of the three Persons of the Trinity and the Incarnation, they are not yet grappling with the complex debates that will rage once Christianity becomes the dominant faith of the empire. The Fathers of the second and third centuries had Gnostics, pagans, and Jews as their primary opponents. In the fourth century the debates will instead pit Christian against Christian. Conflict will rage around the most vexed topic of late ancient Christianity: the Trinity. This is, of course, a theological question, but now we'll see just how philosophically interesting it could become.

THREE FOR THE PRICE OF ONE
THE CAPPADOCIANS

Some things run in families. Musical talent, for example. Consider the Bach family, of Thuringia. They produced not only the renowned Johann Sebastian Bach, but also his children, a good number of whom became significant musicians in their own right. Or more recently, think of the Jackson family, of Gary, Indiana. So deep was their talent pool that they were able to form the *Jackson 5* without even calling on the services of sister Janet. Of course, musical stardom has many things in common with philosophy—the fast cars, the groupies, the constant press attention. But this phenomenon of famous families doesn't seem to be one of them. There are the Schlegel brothers, Friedrich and August, who were major thinkers of German Romanticism. And let's not forget Plato's brothers Glaucon and Adiemantus, who feature in the *Republic*. Okay, Glaucon and Adiemantus weren't necessarily great philosophers. But like the Jacksons, that family did have one heck of a front-man. As far as I can tell though, the greatest philosophical siblings of all time were Christians who hailed from Cappadocia, a region of central Anatolia in modern-day Turkey. Their names were Macrina, Basil, and Gregory.

Actually there were five brothers and five sisters in this Cappadocian family. A decisive influence came from the oldest sibling, Macrina. She helped raise the younger kids, and was partly responsible for bringing her brothers Gregory and Basil to a religious life. When Gregory wrote a dialogue on the soul in imitation of Plato's *Phaedo*, he presented Macrina as a kind of Christian Socrates. She is shown on her deathbed, using arguments to convince Gregory not to grieve at her imminent death.[1] If Gregory gives us anything close to an accurate portrayal of Macrina, she was opinionated and knowledgeable about Hellenic philosophy, able to discourse on fine points of Stoicism, Epicureanism, and medical theory. As usual, though, this female philosopher is known to us only indirectly, through the writings of men—in this case her two brothers.

Of this fraternal pair, Gregory seems to have been more inclined towards philosophy than Basil. Though he had studied at Athens, at Macrina's prompting

Basil became a monk, living in ascetic retreat from the world. He was called away from this vocation to the highly politicized world that was the fourth-century church. In the 360s Basil took up a post in the Cappadocian city of Caesarea, and eventually became bishop there. Much of his life would be devoted to doctrinal battles over Christian theology, as we'll see shortly. For support in this struggle he called on the services of his brother Gregory, who became bishop of a small town called Nyssa. Hence these two Cappadocian thinkers are usually called Basil of Caesarea and Gregory of Nyssa. A third significant Cappadocian philosopher—or rather fourth, counting Macrina—is another Gregory, called Gregory of Nazianzus, because he likewise took up a post as bishop in the small settlement of Nazianzus at Basil's urging.

This Gregory was a dear friend of the family, and often wrote of his longing for the peace offered by a life of retreat with Basil and Macrina. But he was also a well-trained rhetorician who was steeped in previous Christian philosophy. All three Cappadocian fathers were especially influenced by Origen, though they did not follow him indiscriminately, rejecting, for instance, his view that the soul exists before it comes to be in a body. Origen's influence in Cappadocia can perhaps be traced back to yet another Gregory—this name being to Cappadocian thought what the name "Ammonius" is for Neoplatonism. The earlier Gregory Thaumaturgos, meaning "Gregory the wonder-worker," had brought Origenist teachings to the region in the 250s. Drawing on this Origenist tradition and their training in rhetoric and philosophy, the Cappadocians engaged in extensive debate with theological rivals, while also carrying out their daily pastoral duties. Neither of the Gregories took to this life with unmixed enthusiasm. Gregory of Nazianzus in particular had mixed feelings. His resentment at being assigned to such a backwater town by Basil, and his preference for a life of withdrawal, led him to complain bitterly about his calling and to abandon his duties more than once.

Yet he did not shy away from political controversy. His writings in defense of what he took to be orthodoxy became classics, to the point that in the later Byzantine period he was simply called "Gregory the Theologian." He bravely faced the more dangerous side of the controversy as well. During time spent in Constantinople he was showered with stones by rival monks, and then nearly assassinated; the would-be killer had a last-moment change of heart, and Gregory forgave him on the spot.[2] Whatever his misgivings about the perilous, distracting, and contentious life he led as a bishop, we should be grateful that he was forced into a life of active engagement with his Christian community. Many of his surviving writings are orations that were delivered to that community. In one of the most moving he implores his listeners to care for the poor, and in particular for victims of leprosy.[3]

Here Gregory's rhetorical training is on full display, as he tries to bring his audience to feel pity and mercy for the disadvantaged. At one point he speaks of how lepers become so disfigured that they must cry out their own names, so that their former friends will be able to recognize them (10). But Gregory does not only appeal to our emotions; he also calls on the assistance of philosophy. The condition of the lepers, he says, teaches us that things of the body are subject to destruction and suffering, and that only the goods of the soul are invulnerable, a point Stoics and Platonists had been making for a fair few centuries by this stage (19). When Gregory denounces his fellow citizens for their attachment to luxury—floors strewn with flower-petals, slave-boys with modish haircuts serving fine food (17)—he sounds like Epictetus, or any number of authors from the rhetorical movement called the Second Sophistic.

But Epictetus never told us we need to devote our lives to the care of the poor, or that the health of our souls could be secured through tending to those who are diseased in body. As soon as Gregory begins his oration by referring to St Paul's triad of virtues—faith, hope, and love—we realize that we are in a new ethical territory (2). Gregory extols love even above faith and hope, and identifies love of the poor as the purest expression of this virtue. We have here a stark contrast with pagan thinkers, and particularly the pagan Platonists of Gregory's time like the somewhat earlier Iamblichus or the emperor Julian. In fact, like Basil, Gregory made the pilgrimage to the philosophical mecca of Athens, around the same time Julian was there. Yet the fourth century offers no pair of thinkers more opposed than Julian, the anti-Christian emperor, and Gregory the Theologian. Not only did Gregory attack Julian directly in impassioned pro-Christian orations, but he had a completely different understanding of the place of philosophy in the good life. It isn't just that he emphasizes practical action more than Julian and other pagan Platonists. It is also the nature of the action he recommends.

Iamblichus and Julian think the practical side of philosophy means using theurgic ritual to come into contact with the gods. For Gregory, God has already come into contact with us, by sending us His Son. We should humble ourselves just as He did, by going amongst the least fortunate and sharing whatever we have with them (4). Gregory repeatedly invokes Plato's injunction to imitate God insofar as is possible. But his God is a very different one from Plato's, a God who is best imitated by loving one's fellow man without concern for oneself, and gladly choosing the very poverty one tries to alleviate in others. Greek ethics had long revolved around the apparently selfish goal of perfecting oneself. Now Gregory gives us the Christian version of that goal: we help ourselves only by helping others. And by the way, he adds, don't worry about those scaremongers who claim that leprosy might be contagious (28). Those are just silly rumors.

Leprosy was not the only potentially lethal malady found in the eastern Mediterranean at this time. Gregory's nearly averted assassination was the symptom of a chronic social and political disease: a severe case of theological dissent. The careers of both Gregories and of Basil revolved around one of the most bitter and protracted intellectual disputes of the ancient world, a controversy over the Holy Trinity. This dispute threatened the unity of ancient Christianity and vexed political leaders in the highest seats of power. Various emperors tried imposing a solution, negotiating between disputing bishops, and, occasionally, playing them off one against the other, almost always to little avail. The fundamental question was this. Already the earliest Church Fathers, like Origen and the apologists, had recognized that God is Father, Son, and Holy Spirit. Like Jews before them and Muslims after them, the Christians were emphatic that they believed in just one God; yet their God was somehow three.

This problem turned out to need a lot of solving.[4] Although one could wonder about the relation between all members of the Trinity, most attention was directed to the relation of "begetting" between the Father and the Son. If we could understand how this "begetting" works, we might understand better how exactly the Trinity forms a divine unity. In the normal course of events, of course, the relation that a father bears to a son is an asymmetrical one. Fathers beget their sons, whereas sons are begotten by their fathers. For instance, it would be impossible for Joe Keaton to be Buster Keaton's father while also being Buster's son. Yet in the case of God, this is precisely what happens. He is both Father *and* Son. It seems the begetting relation, which we hoped would solve our problem of how God can be both three and one, is just giving rise to further puzzles.

An important early attempt to resolve these puzzles was put forward at the Council of Nicaea, convened by the emperor Constantine in the year 325. Bishops from across the empire assembled and produced a statement of belief, a creed, which would later be seen as a definitive statement of Christian doctrine. But to the extent that consensus was reached, it would not last: Nicaea would be followed by many more councils, which likewise failed to put the dispute to rest. The Nicaean position on the relation of Father to Son was that they are "the same in substance." The broader theological point of this formula was, of course, to ensure that the divine Persons do constitute a unity. The more immediate political point was to put a stop to the malign influence of a theologian named Arius, who leaned towards affirming a significant difference between Father and Son. Nonetheless, the Council wanted to stop short of the heresy known as Sabellianism—named after the third-century theologian Sabellius. This was the view that God is in reality a unity and not a Trinity. For the Persons are in themselves identical, and distinguished from one another only as modes by which the divine unity expresses itself.

Theologians of the fourth century thus presented themselves as steering a course between the two extreme views of Arianism and Sabellianism. Some tried to defuse the controversy by arguing against applying the term *ousia*, the Greek word for substance or essence, to God in the first place. But compromise middle positions were waiting to be occupied. And if ever there was a debate where every possible position was eventually occupied by someone or other, it was the debate over the Trinity. Some theologians proposed modifying the Nicaean formula to say that the Father and Son are "*different* in substance." After the Greek for this expression, modern scholars call this group the "heteroousians." The idea was to concede a real difference in the Persons, albeit that they remain unified by a single divine will. Naturally enough, those who took up this view were accused by opponents of falling into the error of Arius, by effectively affirming three Gods where there should be only one.

Some of these opponents realized they could stake out a ground between this supposedly neo-Arian heteroousian position and the total-identity view of the Sabellians by saying that the Persons are "*similar* in substance." It was this solution that was taken up by the Cappadocians. Of course, they presented their solution not as a correction of the Nicene formula that the persons are the same in substance, but rather as an explanation of the sense in which it is true. Thus Gregory of Nyssa gave the analogy of three humans who share the *same* nature of humanity.[5] As Aristotle himself said in his *Categories*, a universal like "humanity" is itself a sort of substance,[6] which makes it parallel to the single substance of the Godhead. Meanwhile the three individual humans are distinct from one another, yet "similar" in virtue of their same nature, just as the three divine Persons are similar without being fully identical.

Appropriately enough, the debate over these ideas was itself pretty personal. The leading heteroousian intellectual, and the chief target of the Cappadocians' refutations, was a man named Eunomius. In thinking through the implications of his heteroousianism, where Father and Son are said to be the same God and yet "different," Eunomius gave a fairly sophisticated account of how words relate to things. Naturally he was particularly interested in words like "father," "son," and "begotten," but his view can be generalized to all names. Eunomius proposed that a name will reveal the essence or nature of the thing that is named. Names cannot acquire this power by mere convention, but must have some kind of innate correctness. We would not know the begottenness of the divine Son with merely human resources. But now that God has revealed this begottenness, we can say that in the sentence "the Son is begotten by the Father," the word "begotten" gives us a direct insight into the Son's substance.

This is a perfect fit with heteroousian theology, since different words ("begetting" and "begotten") will apply to the Father and to the Son, yielding a difference in substance. Along the way, Eunomius has taken sides in a dispute that goes back at least as far as Plato's *Cratylus*. In that dialogue Plato considers two theories of names, one of which makes names naturally relate to their bearers, as would happen in a case of onomatopoeia.[7] It's not mere chance or custom that makes us use the word "bang" for a loud noise. Loud noises just sound like the word "bang." On the naturalist theory, though, *all* genuine names relate intimately to what they name. Names can even be analyzed, perhaps by means of etymology, to arrive at an understanding of what is named. The Stoics too liked this theory of names. But by late antiquity the dominant position was that of Aristotle, who had said clearly in his work *On Interpretation* that names are conventional (16a). We arbitrarily assign sounds to things, and thereby produce new names that work just fine.

So when Basil of Caesarea comes to refute Eunomius,[8] he needs to reject the naturalist theory of names, and it is only to be expected that he would align himself with the Aristotelian position. This is exactly what he does, though there is some debate about how much he takes directly from philosophical sources, and how much is filtered through previous Christian theological literature. He stakes out a position not unlike the one found in Platonist commentators on Aristotle, according to which thoughts are an intermediary between language and the world. When you hear the word "giraffe," you understand it as referring to a giraffe, but only by way of a thought in your mind, the thought or notion of giraffes. Basil takes this in a skeptical direction by claiming that the names we use can get us only as far as these notions. Never do we find language actually revealing the essence of a thing—it only signifies the way those things are conceptualized in our minds. In the case of the Trinity, this allows him to say that no real difference is being implied when we use one word like "begetting" to refer to the Father, and another word like "begotten" to refer to the Son.

The upshot is that Basil has the anti-Eunomian position he wants, but only by casting doubt on the power of language and thought to get at things in the world. We might take this to show that Eunomius has a big advantage over Basil. Surely, we want to protest, language does refer to the real things, and not only our mental conceptions of them? Surely, too, we can know the essences of these things, if indeed they have essences? Basil's stance seems to land us in a radical skepticism, not just about God but about anything we can name. But Basil's point is somewhat more nuanced than I've made out thus far. Though he does insist that the essences of things remain unknowable to us, he adds that language and our mental conceptions allow us to identify those things and keep track of them. Thus if I say "the tall, strikingly beautiful creature in the enclosure there," I am successfully picking out an object, namely a giraffe. However, the description only leads to identification of the giraffe and the possibility of classing it with other things that share some of its characteristics. Never will I actually achieve a direct grasp of its substance, essence, or being (in Greek, its *ousia*).

Another objection, and one that the Cappadocians would find at least as troubling, is a religious one: their anti-Eunomian theory places God irrevocably beyond the reach of our minds. One might suppose that the Cappadocians would simply bite the bullet here. After all, unlike pagan Platonists, who honored contemplative perfection, didn't they emphasize good actions in this life rather than theoretical understanding? We saw Gregory of Nazianzus persuading his audience to love the poor, and Gregory of Nyssa wrote on the same theme, all in support of a social campaign launched by Basil. As bishop of Caesarea he built a hospice, which offered food and shelter for the indigent. And yet the Cappadocians were also powerfully attracted to a life of seclusion, devoted to the contemplation of God. The tension faced by both Gregories, between pastoral duty and monastic retreat, is one we'll be looking at soon when we discuss the ascetic movement.

So the Cappadocian Fathers insist that we can, rather paradoxically, know this unknowable God. For one thing, as Basil points out, we have a conception of God through His workings, without knowing His substance.[9] For instance, we can say that He is good, because of the goodness of the world he has made. Philosophically, this is on a par with our ability to identify a giraffe through the impressions it makes on us, even if we cannot know its substance. This may still seem unsatisfying. As wonderful as giraffes are, our ultimate happiness does not require our coming to know their substances. With God, things are different. Gregory of Nyssa puts forth a radical response to this dilemma.[10] He admits that God's essence is unknowable, because God is unbounded or infinite. But this means that our desire for Him must also be infinite. The reward we receive through contemplation, and even in the afterlife, is ceaseless progress along an infinite but never-ending path of knowledge. Just as in mathematics a curve may approach a straight line and get indefinitely closer, without ever touching it, so the blessed soul comes ever closer to understanding God completely, without this desire ever being fully satisfied. Some might think this sounds more like the eternal torment of Tantalus than a heavenly reward. But for Gregory, love and desire go hand in hand. Perfect love is love for a beloved object that can never be fully attained, so that the flame of desire is never quenched by the satisfaction of that desire. Thus Gregory remains true to the characteristically Cappadocian conviction that God exceeds our grasp. And the good thing about infinite unknowability is that there is always more to say about it.

43

NAMING THE NAMELESS
THE PSEUDO-DIONYSIUS

Here's another trivia question for you: what do Stephen King and Søren Kier-kegaard have in common? Well, their initials, obviously, and an interest in fear and trembling. But I have in mind something else: their use of pseudonyms. King has written novels under the pen-name of Richard Bachman. Kierkegaard, mean-while, used a variety of pseudonyms in philosophical works like *Fear and Trembling*, supposedly authored by one Johannes de Silentio. Another book by Kierkegaard, entitled *Either/Or*, presents itself as having been written by a scholar named Victor Emerita, who is in turn presenting the work of further authors named A and B. No major philosopher has made more abundant or inventive use of pseudonyms. But as readers, we know that it is Kierkegaard behind all the false names. The same cannot be said for the most important and famous pseudonymous writer of antique philosophy. His works were translated into Syriac, into Arabic, and into Latin. He influenced visionary mystics and rationalist thinkers, making a mark upon medieval philosophy, theology, and even architecture. Yet we have no idea who he was, only who he claimed to be: an associate of the apostles, and a witness to the crucifixion of Christ. He went by the name of Dionysius.

Dionysius the Areopagite was, in the first instance, a minor biblical character. The Book of Acts (chapter 17) mentions him as a man from Athens who was converted to the new faith by St Paul. Perhaps the connection to Athens made this an attractive choice of pseudonym for a Christian Platonist. But whatever his motive, our nameless philosopher ironically took over the identity of a man who is, for us, almost nothing but a name—a convert from the apostolic era. The works of the self-styled Dionysius complete the deception by alluding, almost casually, to his own presence at events from the biblical period. He mentions that he was a witness to the eclipse that occurred when Christ was crucified, and that he enjoyed a vision of Mary along with the apostles James and Peter. One of a series of letters composed by the author is addressed to St John in exile on the island of Patmos.[1]

But of course, neither this letter nor any other philosophical compositions were written by a companion of the apostles named Dionysius. Instead, they were composed several centuries later, in about AD 500. Thus scholars have come to call this author the "Pseudo-Dionysius." The "Pseudo-" was a late addition. Within a generation some were questioning the author's identity and, for good measure, adding that he would seem to be a heretic. But others leapt to defend his apostolic authority. In particular, a man named John of Scythopolis wrote a series of comments explaining the works of Dionysius, along with a prologue which speaks out in favor of Dionysius' authenticity and orthodoxy. The Byzantine theologian Maximus the Confessor, who we'll be looking at in the next chapter, was also an enthusiastic supporter of Dionysius. Thanks to these early adherents, the mask adopted by Dionysius remained firmly in place. Dionysius' stature rose another level when he was, rather amazingly, confused with St Denis, the patron saint of France.

That rather convenient bit of scholarly confusion occurred in the ninth century, when the works of Dionysius were translated into Latin in Carolingian France. In this age the philosophical influence of Dionysius reached a peak, as his works were taken up with unblushing eagerness and great ingenuity by the translator and philosopher John Scotus Eriugena. Eriugena was the greatest philosopher of the early Middle Ages in the Latin West, and took Dionysius as one of his chief inspirations. This may have done Dionysius no favors, given that Eriugena was a radical and controversial thinker. Yet as late as the thirteenth century, no less a thinker than Thomas Aquinas was writing commentaries on Dionysius and quoting him extensively in other works.[2] By this time the works of Dionysius had become standard texts in Christian medieval theology. His influence can be discerned not only in the writings of theologians and philosophers, but even in the design of Gothic churches. Dionysius' theory of angelic hierarchies is represented on the Cathedral of Chartres, and his writings, suffused with images about light, even had an impact on the Gothic use of stained glass. Speaking of hierarchies, that word is another sign of Dionysian influence. He seems to have invented the Greek noun *hierarchia*, from which we get our word "hierarchy."

All of which raises obvious questions: how did this guy get away with it for so long, and how was his deception eventually uncovered? To answer the second question first, it was only at the end of the nineteenth century that two scholars pointed out the fact that Dionysius borrows liberally from the works of Proclus. Yes, that Proclus, the Neoplatonist philosopher. This is how we know that Dionysius wrote his texts around 500—he must have come after Proclus, who died in 485, and

Dionysius is already being mentioned by other authors in the first half of the sixth century, so he wrote his own texts before then. Dionysius made such extensive use of Proclus, and Neoplatonic ideas more generally, that even some contemporaries grew suspicious. If Dionysius had really been an Athenian of the first century AD, he would have been remarkably ahead of his time. But other readers thrilled to Dionysius' ambitious appropriation of Neoplatonism for Christian purposes. Entertainingly, an early remark added to the manuscripts of Dionysius claims that it was Proclus who stole from Dionysius, not the other way around![3]

Those manuscripts of the works of Dionysius preserve five separate texts. First there is a collection of ten letters, culminating in the one supposedly addressed to John. Then there are two works on the notion of hierarchy: one, entitled the *Ecclesiastical Hierarchy*, explains the role of priests, including the purpose and function of the sacraments. The other, the *Celestial Hierarchy*, deals with angels, and applies to the angelic world the Neoplatonic idea that the immaterial world should be structured in ordered ranks. Here we might pause to think of staunch anti-Christian Neoplatonists like Porphyry and, yes, Proclus spinning in their pagan graves as Dionysius rewrites their metaphysics as a structure for Christian theology. But for historians of philosophy, the most exciting texts of the Dionysian collection concern human language and knowledge, and how these fail when we attempt to grasp the nature of God. These two remaining texts are the *Divine Names* and the *Mystical Theology*. Thanks to them, the Pseudo-Dionysius could rightly be honored as the patron saint of negative theology, even if he was not the patron saint of France.

Before getting into the texts themselves, let me say something about this phrase "negative theology." Theologians and philosophers of religion frequently contrast two attitudes concerning the human attempt to grasp God. On the one hand there is positive theology, sometimes called "kataphatic," which comes from the Greek word *kataphasis* meaning "positive assertion." When we say that God is good, or powerful, or compare Him to a lion or a cloud, we are making positive assertions about Him. Positive theology tries to explain how this is possible. Negative theology, meanwhile, is sometimes called "apophatic," because the Greek word for denial is *apophasis*. Negative theologians are more pessimistic about the prospects of naming, describing, and conceiving God. They point out that if God utterly transcends us and the other things God has created, then our language and concepts are unlikely to apply to Him fully, if at all. In their most pessimistic moments, negative theologians may go so far as to say that we are utterly ignorant concerning God and doomed to remain so.

The Pseudo-Dionysius was given to this sort of pessimism, and the unknowability of God was his favorite theme. Imitators followed him for many centuries to come. In his *Mystical Theology*, for instance, Dionysius compares God to darkness beyond all light. As late as the fourteenth century this inspired a mystical author to write a theological text called the *Cloud of Unknowing*. Dionysius doesn't just give us metaphors, though: he argues for God's unnameability and unknowability. For instance, God is simple, so it cannot be the case that our many verbal expressions pick out distinct features of His essence (636C–637A). But his most fundamental rationale is that human cognition is simply inadequate to grasp an object of God's transcendence. Sense-perception cannot grasp things properly understood by the mind; in just the same way, the mind cannot grasp things properly grasped by a higher power, the divine power by which God grasps Himself. This is a power not given to us, at least in this life. Although Dionysius holds out hope that we will be granted a better access to God in Paradise, for now we are stuck with cognitive tools inadequate to the task of understanding our Maker.

The much later philosopher and occasional mystic Ludwig Wittgenstein had some advice that would seem applicable here: "whereof one cannot speak, thereof one must be silent."[4] In the *Mystical Theology* Dionysius more or less follows that advice. He surveys the various sorts of language with which one might try to capture God, and says that some are more clearly inappropriate than others—it is not fully adequate to call God "good" or to call Him a "stone," but it's much easier to see why God is not a stone than why He is not good. We can rise in our understanding of God as we come to see how various expressions are inappropriate for Him—a process that Dionysius compares to making a statue by carving away stone bit by bit. Ultimately, though, we should dispense with *all* verbal description of God, and even with negations (1045D–1048B). If we cannot say that God is good, neither can we say that He is not good. Thus even denials must be denied, a point Dionysius makes in the very last line of the *Mystical Theology*. Having stalemated himself in this game of theological chess, Dionysius does what Wittgenstein would recommend, and puts down his pen. Apparently the first rule of negative theology is, "don't talk about negative theology."

Yet silence is where Dionysius expects us to wind up, not where we begin. Which explains how he could also have written another, even more famous work, the *Divine Names*. In this longer and more complicated text Dionysius moves back and forth between positive and negative theology. His goal is to explain the positive language that is ascribed to God in the Scriptures. Here we have the classic dilemma of the Christian negative theologian—a dilemma that is equally pressing for Jewish and Muslim negative theologians, by the way, as we'll be seeing in the next volume in this series. On the one hand, philosophical considerations show us that human language is inapplicable to God. On the other hand, revealed texts apply human language to God. Dionysius' solution to the dilemma is to explore the extent to which each word applied to God in the Bible is applicable to Him, while also admitting that these words are not really applicable to Him. In fact, his project in the *Divine Names* is somewhat narrower than this: it restricts itself to Scriptural language that seems to be at a conceptual rather than physical level (597B). In the Bible, God is compared to a stone, a cloud, is said to have eyes, a face, and other bodily parts, and so on. Dionysius claims to have written another work on these more physical descriptions of God, but if it ever existed this work is lost.

That leaves us with terms like "good," "love," "powerful," "eternal," "righteous," and so on. It is these terms that form the subject-matter of the *Divine Names*, which moves through the Scriptural language and explains how each expression reveals something about God, while also posing the threat that we will be misled. It is all too easy to think that if an earthly king is good, and God is good, then God and the earthly king somehow share an attribute. But this is not so. Whereas we can experience the goodness of a human king, God is beyond our direct experience, inaccessible to both our sensation and our mind. How, then, are we able to ascribe goodness to God in any sense? Dionysius has a ready answer: he assumes that the things that God makes are somehow revelatory of God's nature, since He is their cause (645A–D). Since God's effects are good, we can say that God is good. At one level this is simply standard Neoplatonic metaphysics, as familiar from authors like Proclus. Proclus has taught us, and taught Dionysius, that effects are contained pre-eminently in their causes. For instance, the unity of each thing is the effect of the perfect unity of the first principle that is truly one. To some extent this is mere common sense: fire, being the cause of heat, is pre-eminently hot.

Dionysius is not entirely happy with this picture, because it would allow us to do what Proclus does with his own metaphysical principles: apply human language and concepts to them in a more or less unproblematic way. But Dionysius is too negative a theologian for that. So he insists that, even if we can make progress towards understanding God as a cause on the basis of His effects, we should not fool ourselves into thinking that we will ever reach Him. Rather, when we call God "good" on the basis that His effects are good, we should remind ourselves that He is beyond any notion of goodness we can conceive. Dionysius marks this point with an influential bit of linguistic trickery: he applies the Greek prefix *hyper-* to each positive term (641A). This prefix was translated into Latin as *super-*. Thus God is not good, but hyper- or super-good. The genius of this, or if you're feeling less charitable, the sneakiness of this, is that it encapsulates both the positive and negative aspects of Dionysian theology in a single term. In one word, he captures the idea that God is so pre-eminently good that He is no longer really "good" in any sense we can understand.

The tension between positive and negative approaches to God is the theme that runs throughout the *Divine Names*. We see it again, for instance, when Dionysius turns to the question of whether the Scripturally sanctioned names apply to God in His entirety. They do, he insists. God is simple, so it is impossible for one name to name one aspect of God and another name some other aspect (641D–644D). Yet he also wants to deny that the names are all synonymous. There is a real diversity of names, but the diversity is caused by our human conceptions, not by the nature of what we are naming. This only stands to reason. After all, we are naming God on the basis of what He has caused, and the things He has caused have many different features. Dionysius uses the analogy of a seal that has made stamps in many bits of wax (644A)—God is single and one, yet has many different effects, by which we name Him. This stress on divine simplicity and unity might cause us to raise an eyebrow, especially given that we were just looking at the Cappadocians. Like them, shouldn't Dionysius be insisting that God is a Trinity, that He is three as well as one? Well yes, and Dionysius is in fact careful to mention the Trinity towards the beginning of his *Divine Names* (592A). But the names he deals with in the rest of the work are names that reveal God as a whole, insofar as they reveal Him at all. When we call God "wise" or "powerful" or "good," this refers to the entire Godhead, not only the Father, the Son, or the Holy Spirit.

Dionysius frequently reminds us that, by revealing something of God, such names tempt us to believe that God is being revealed *fully*. This is why Scripture sometimes calls God by crude physical names, as a kind of warning. No one would really be stupid enough to think that God is literally a stone, or a lion (never mind both a stone and a lion). And of course, Dionysius' final word on the subject of divine names is to use no words at all. In the end, negative theology trumps positive theology, and the highest knowledge of God is a sort of ignorance or unknowing. This is clear in both the *Divine Names* and the *Mystical Theology*, and it might prompt us to wonder: what is the difference between the mystical theologian who has achieved this highest state and an atheist who simply never thinks or knows about God at all? If ignorance is the final destination, it looks like the theologian's fate is the same as the fate of Plotinus' undescended soul and Dorothy in the *Wizard of Oz*, who were already where they wanted to be right at the beginning of their journeys.

But while Dionysius might agree with Dorothy that there is no place like home, he would still say it is worth traveling the yellow-brick road of negative theology. So he must somehow persuade us that the ignorance or emptiness reached once all divine names are transcended is distinct from the ignorance and emptiness of someone who has never given God a moment's thought. This is, of course, a problem that faces all negative theologians. But Dionysius has a distinctively Neoplatonic take on the problem. Under the influence of Proclus, he adopts the idea of procession and return. All of creation is a procession from God, through the ordered ranks partially described in Dionysius' *Celestial Hierarchy*. We start our return from everyday physical names—stone, lion, face, and so on—which are applied to God, but are obviously not applied literally. From there we progress to the sort of terms discussed in Dionysius' *Divine Names*. But we can go even further, leaving behind notions like goodness and power, as we left aside the physical names (1025B).

Thus the end-point is not the ignorance where we started, but the infinity of God Himself. Dionysius calls this unknowing not because it is a lack of knowledge, but because it transcends knowledge. It is, if you will, super-knowledge. With our own reasonably super knowledge about the Neoplatonists, we might compare this to the way that their first principle, the One, mirrors matter, which is non-being and indeterminacy. Both are outside the scale of being, and both are infinite, but for very different reasons. The One is beyond being, matter is below it. If you follow soccer, you might find the following comparison helpful. When a team is playing a game in the pan-European Champions League, it is no longer playing in its national league. But that doesn't mean it has the status of a local club that isn't good enough for the national league. Rather, the club has transcended the English, French, or German league—it is now playing in Europe. The club is beyond the league because it is too good, whereas other teams are not in the league because they are not good enough. So that, in case you were wondering, is what the God of the Pseudo-Dionysius has in common with Bayern Munich.

44

DOUBLE OR NOTHING
MAXIMUS THE CONFESSOR

It's amazing what other people care about. We've all raised an eyebrow at the spectacle of sports fans weeping in despair or screaming with joy over a game we find utterly tedious. Or smiled secretly at a friend's deep emotional attachment to some ridiculous enthusiasm, like model trains, stamp-collecting, or giraffes. In such cases we should no doubt celebrate the variety and richness of people's values. Only to be expected, we might think, in a varied and rich world. But in other cases the incomprehensible passions of other people can be deeply depressing. Think of the many violent conflicts that pit ethnic or religious groups against one another. The animosity between the two groups means everything to the participants; they are willing to die and kill for their tribe. To outsiders this can only seem futile and irrational. Indeed, nearly all such conflicts seem pointless with the benefit of enough distance and perspective.

A good example would be the late ancient dispute over the metaphysical relationship between the divine and human aspects of Jesus Christ. Nowadays I suspect even most devout Christians have given this question no thought whatsoever. From a non-Christian perspective the debate seems even more bewildering. Yet some of the most intelligent citizens of the early Byzantine Empire devoted great effort to disputing the issue. Over the question of Christ's humanity and divinity, and whether these were two different natures or just one nature, councils were convened, political institutions were endangered, and blood was spilled. Some of the blood belonged to the man we'll be discussing in this chapter: the seventh-century thinker Maximus the Confessor. His honorific title "Confessor" refers to his staunch defense of a view that eventually became orthodox in the Byzantine tradition: Christ had two natures, united in a single person. But in his own life he was not celebrated for his orthodoxy. Instead, his enemies literally cut off the hand with which he had written of Christ's two natures, and tore out the tongue with which he had so articulately defended his theology. He died soon after, in the year 662, having joined Socrates in the select group of philosophers who have been violently persecuted for their beliefs.

To understand why anyone would have thought it necessary to mutilate Maximus in this way—and why Maximus would run the risk of being so mutilated—we need to go back a few hundred years, to the fourth century. This was the age of the Cappadocian Fathers, who took part in politicized disputes over fine points of Christian theology. When I looked at them, I concentrated on the question of how the persons of the Trinity relate to one another. We saw that they wanted to steer a course between Arianism, which went too far in the direction of separating the persons of the Trinity, and Sabellianism, which simply identified the persons and held that they are distinct only from our limited human viewpoint. The Cappadocians presented themselves as steering another middle course in another controversy too. In this case, debate raged over the fundamental Christian belief that Jesus of Nazareth was divine—the Son of God become flesh, in order that through His sacrifice, humanity could be redeemed from sin.

This belief brings with it a dilemma much like the one we saw in the case of the Trinity.[1] Just as theologians didn't want to say with the Arians that the Father is utterly distinct from the Son, lest we wind up with two Gods, so they didn't want to compromise the unity of Christ. He was one person, even if He was both man and God. On the other hand, they likewise rejected the Sabellian error of erasing all difference between the persons. So it seemed unacceptable simply to identify Christ's humanity with His divinity. After all, the divine is radically different from the human. If there is no distinction here, then either Christ's humanity is swallowed up in his divinity, or his divinity is entirely humbled and brought down to the level of the human. Neither option looks acceptable. If Christ was only divine, then God did not really take on human nature in order to redeem it. Whereas if he was only human, then his sacrifice was merely the death of some particularly virtuous man, not the Son of God. Besides, Christ was acknowledged as having been immune to sin. How was this possible unless his fallible human nature had somehow been perfected through his divinity?

All parties to the dispute therefore understood that the correct metaphysical understanding would recognize both the divinity and the humanity of Christ. Agreement remained elusive though, when it came to the details. Often, the details were worked out using philosophical distinctions and assumptions. Consider, for instance, the fourth-century theologian Apollinarius. He was especially concerned to safeguard the *unity* of Christ. Towards this end, he invoked the strikingly Platonist rationale that human nature is subject to change, whereas divine nature is unchanging and eternal. But whatever can change can diverge into imperfection. This means that if Christ has human thoughts and a human will, he will inevitably be subject to sin. One way of taking this would be that if Christ is genuinely human, then it is *possible* that he sins—which would be bad enough. But Apollinarius seems to have gone further and said that if Christ had a human will he would *actually* sin, perhaps because he assumed that any genuine capacity must be realized at some point. Looking ahead, we can credit Maximus with being unusually clear-headed on this point. He will distinguish more rigorously between the capacity for thinking or willing something and the actual thinking or willing.

Apollinarius was condemned in the late fourth century, when his attempts to ensure Christ's unity were judged to violate the rule that Christ must be fully human. In sharp contrast was the view of a man named Nestorius, who brings us up to the fifth century. For Nestorius and his followers, Christ not only has two natures, but also two *hypostaseis*. What is a *hypostasis*? Historians of philosophy are most likely to encounter the word in Neoplatonic contexts, as a technical term used for the levels of the Platonist hierarchy, like soul and intellect. In this theological context, though, *hypostasis* means something less elaborate: just an entity that is distinct from other entities. Thus Nestorius' view amounts to splitting Christ into two entities with two natures, one human and one divine. Nestorius received full marks for avoiding the problems of Apollinarianism, but earned only a "must try harder" when it came to the goal of upholding Christ's unity. He and his followers, the Nestorians, did assert that Christ was a single "person," in Greek *prosopon*. But this was seen by critics as a superficial maneuver, a mask of unity concealing a real underlying duality. Indeed, the word *prosopon* means "face" or "visage," and was used to describe the mask-wearing of characters in the Greek theater.

When the Cappadocians took center-stage, they also claimed the middle ground, insisting that Christ is only one *hypostasis*, a single, unified entity, which is nonetheless both divine and human. In explaining this, Gregory of Nyssa (following the lead of Origen) drew on the Stoic theory of physical mixture to envisage a situation in which divinity and human were blended together while retaining their natures. Just as, in a red-hot sword, the metal of the blade is suffused with fire even as the nature of the metal remains distinct from the nature of fire; and as vinegar retains its nature even when mixed into the sea.[2] A similar view was upheld by the influential theologian Cyril of Alexandria. It was, incidentally, on Cyril's watch as lead cleric in Alexandria that the Platonist Hypatia was murdered by a Christian mob (see Chapter 37). Cyril's theology prevailed at the Council of Ephesus in the year 431, which rejected the teachings of Nestorius. But neither this, nor a further council at Chalcedon in 451 that upheld the "one *hypostasis* in two natures" formula, could unite the church. Some communities continued to uphold Apollinarius' "monophysite" theory (the word comes from the Greek for "one nature"), while others preferred the two-nature and two-*hypostasis* view of Nestorius. Still others adhered to the understanding of Christ accepted by the Cappadocians, according to which God was a single person and *hypostasis* out of two natures.

This fracture had deep social and political consequences, and was a potential source of weakness within the Byzantine Empire—that is, the eastern part of the Roman Empire which survived after the fall of the West. In one direction the Byzantines faced constant threats to their security from the "barbarian" tribes that had destabilized the Roman Empire in the first place. In another, they had repeated clashes with the mighty Persian Empire. Then, in the seventh century, the Byzantines were suddenly assaulted by the new and unexpected challenge posed by the armies of Islam. After the death of the Prophet Muhammad in the year 632, Muslim forces achieved an astonishingly rapid series of military conquests. In earlier antiquity Christianity had chased paganism out of the Roman Empire by means of war, coercion, economic incentives, and plain old persuasion. Now Christianity faced the threat of a similar fate at the hands of Islam. All of these pressures made it urgent to eliminate division within the Greek Christian sphere, which made it more appealing than ever to accept a compromise position. A series of Byzantine emperors threw their weight behind one or another solution to the controversy. Perhaps, for instance, both sides might agree to disagree about the number of natures in Christ, and focus on agreeing that Christ is unified by having a single will?

But theologians had, for many generations now, shown that they were too stubborn—or perhaps too conscientious—to be satisfied by verbal formulas that masked genuine differences of doctrine. In other words, they were going to keep causing trouble, barbarian invasions or no. Which finally brings us to our man Maximus.[3] Following his teacher Sophronius, who was both stubborn and conscientious, Maximus wanted to uphold the two-nature theory. Sophronius and Maximus stridently rejected the new one-will idea as a compromise too far. It made no sense to ascribe only one will to a person who has two natures. Maximus carried on the fight after Sophronius died, continuing to insist that having a human nature and a divine nature means having two wills. His opponents fought back, appealing not just to political expediency but also to the point made long ago by Apollinarius: if Christ has two wills, the wills can come into conflict. This means that Christ will inevitably sin, or at least, that He inevitably *could* sin.

Maximus replied with the point I mentioned above: we shouldn't confuse will as a capacity with will in the sense of a decision made by that faculty. Christ's divine will was a separate capacity from his human will, but these two wills always came together to issue a single joint decision, just as Christ's two natures cohered in a single *hypostasis*. And just as the Cappadocians had taught that the divine and human natures are fused without being *confused*—that is, both natures are preserved within a single entity—so Maximus now teaches that the human will of Jesus is preserved, even though it is perfected by the presence of divinity.[4] He reacted similarly to another compromise proposal, namely that Christ has a single "activity." (Here the Greek word I'm translating as "activity" is *energeia*, the source of the English word "energy," which is frequently used as a rather awkward translation for *energeia* in discussions of this debate.)

As with the will, the question is whether Christ's activities or "energies" are of two kinds or only one. The single-activity camp could draw on the authority of the Pseudo-Dionysius, who had spoken of Christ possessing a "theandric" activity, that is, an activity characterized by both divinity and humanity.[5] Maximus greatly admired Dionysius, but nonetheless rejected the single-activity theory just as firmly as he did the single-will theory. His point was much the same as it was in the will case: Christ retained a human capacity for activity, which was perfected by the fusion of His human nature with divine nature. He gave the example of Christ's walking on water. Walking is a natural human act, but Christ's divinity made it possible for him to walk in a supernatural way. So walking on water is a single activity all right, but it must be understood as the simultaneous use of two distinct capacities to act.[6]

If you remember your Aristotle (*On the Soul* 417a), you'll realize that Maximus is echoing the distinction between first and second actuality. Traditionally this distinction is illustrated with Aristotle's own example of learning something, but let's instead think about a coffee-shop loyalty card. Initially it is blank: a state of first potentiality. Then it fills up with stamps, one for each coffee you buy. When the card is full of stamps, it is in a state of first actuality—an actuality that is also a second potentiality or capacity, in this case, the all-important capacity to claim a free cup of coffee. When you redeem the card, that is second actuality. Applying this distinction to Maximus' Christology, we find him saying that Christ has two first actualities, a divine will and a human will. These are capacities to produce a concrete act of willing, which will be a second actuality. Even though the two wills are distinct capacities or first actualities, they always agree, so they coincide at the level of second actuality. This happens when Christ actually wills something—when he, for instance, chooses to turn water into wine instead of coffee. But of course, Maximus does not have beverages percolating through his mind when he discusses all this. Rather, he wants to explain the metaphysical underpinnings of Christ's perfection, his freedom from sin.

After this survey of late ancient Christology and Maximus' metaphysics, you might be feeling that the entire debate was like whole coffee beans: groundless. Their rarefied reflections may seem about as substantial as the froth on a cappucino. (By the way, the word "cappucino" derives, appropriately enough, from the resemblance between the drink and the clothing worn by a certain order of Christian friars. This makes the coffee theme appropriate for discussing Maximus. Perhaps I'll use it again when I get to John Stuart Mill.) Yet for the participants in this debate the issue was anything but trivial. Explaining what Christ was meant explaining how the entire human race had been saved from sin. For us philosophers, the controversy is no less important. Obviously it has huge historical importance, but it is also at root a debate over metaphysics. If you are trying to figure out whether two things are in fact identical—for instance, whether the mind is the same thing as the brain, or whether Christ's humanity is the same thing as his divinity—there's a test you can do. Try to find a property that is possessed by one of the two things and not the other. If you manage this, then you've proven that you are indeed dealing with two separate things, and not just one. This is how philosophers like Plato and Descartes have argued for mind–body dualism. They claimed to discover a feature that the mind has and the body lacks. For instance, Plato argued that the mind is simple and indestructible, a statement that could not be applied to the body.

Exactly this strategy was used in the ancient Christological debate. One thing that seemed certain about the second person of the Trinity, the divine *logos*, was that it could not suffer or be affected. And yet, if there's anything we know about Jesus, it's that he did suffer—he was crucified and died in agony. Here Nestorius and his followers pounced, like the good metaphysicians they were: if God cannot suffer, then there must have been something in Christ other than God, which allowed him to suffer. Cyril of Alexandria wrote a letter of refutation to Nestorius, where he grappled with this difficulty directly.[7] He turned the tables on his opponents by insisting that the whole point of the Incarnation is that God willingly submits His Son to the sufferings of the flesh. The letter concludes with a list of twelve doctrines destructive of the faith. The last item on the list says that if anyone refuses to admit that the Word of God, the second person of the Trinity, suffered by being crucified, then he is to be considered anathema. That means you, Nestorius.

Another example is the apparently bizarre debate over whether the Virgin Mary is to be honored with the phrase *theotokos*, a Greek word meaning "one who gives birth to God." Nestorius disliked this expression because it again seemed indirectly to apply a property to God that God simply cannot have. God is eternal and prior to all things, so how can Mary give birth to Him? Instead, Nestorius proposed that Mary gave birth to Christ insofar as Christ was human. Cyril's response was that Mary did give birth to a man, made of flesh like us. But in so doing she gave birth to God. This is no absurdity, as Nestorius claimed, but rather the whole point: she gave birth to the Word of God made flesh, this being the very meaning of the word "Incarnation." On all these points Maximus agreed with Cyril against Nestorius. He recognized

that Christ had two natures, but added that we should resist the Nestorian temptation to divide everything we say about Christ into two types, one set of statements
that are true because he was God, the other set of statements true because he was a
man. The unification of the two natures makes it possible for both God and man to
suffer, or to be born of a virgin.

Maximus developed these points beyond metaphysics, into the realm of ethics.
Our understanding of the human good is radically transformed by learning that
human nature was divinized in the person of Christ. Of course, normal humans are
not free from sin, or the incarnation of the Word of God, as Christ was. Nonetheless,
we must work towards our own perfection, which means working towards our own
more modest sort of divinity. Maximus was just the latest in a long line of ancient
philosophers to explain how humans can, as Plato put it, "achieve likeness to God
insofar as is possible." But he was also influenced by the more recent Cappadocians
and the Pseudo-Dionysius. From them he took the conviction that God is unknowable in His essence: He can be grasped only through His activities. So even souls who
achieve salvation in the afterlife will be allowed to participate in God's activity,
rather than unifying with the divine essence itself.

What about our life in this world? Here Maximus again responded to earlier
Christian thinkers. Some of them, especially Origen, had defended an intellectualist
vision of the human good, and emphasized the contemplation of God. Maximus
agreed that we should try to contemplate God, but we must do so by means of
grasping His activities, since God Himself transcends the grasp of our limited minds.
Indeed, He suggested that the knowledge of God is what distinguishes Christians
from the Jews, whom he criticized for contenting themselves with the avoidance of
sin. But Maximus recognized too that avoiding sin is no easy feat. We are drawn by
the nature of our bodily existence towards pleasure and the passions, and it requires
strength of will, and not just a clever mind, to subdue these desires to the law of
reason and divinity. Echoing an exegetical tradition that goes back as far as Philo,
Maximus read biblical passages as urging us to fight against the passions. For
instance, the flight of Moses and the Jewish people from Egypt symbolizes, for
Maximus, the need to turn away from the realm of sensation and towards the things
of the mind. He referred to this as a kind of "emptying" of ourselves, removing all
bodily attachments so that nothing but openness to virtue and God remain. This
was an ethical discipline that he not only recommended, but also practiced himself.
And he wasn't the only one.

45

PRACTICE MAKES PERFECT
CHRISTIAN ASCETICISM

Perhaps you've heard about a rather unsettling psychological experiment known as the marshmallow test. A researcher would sit young children in a room and offer them a marshmallow or other treat. The children would be told that if they could restrain themselves from eating the marshmallow until the researcher returned, they would get an additional marshmallow as a reward. Some children ate the marshmallow the second they were alone, while others managed to get through the intervening time, as the effort led them to writhe in their seats, pull their own hair, or loudly lament how slowly the time was passing. The unsettling part—aside from the whole "how do psychologists get away with these mildly sadistic experiments?" issue—is that they checked in with the kids years later, and discovered that those who managed to restrain themselves turned out to do better in life, educationally and in other ways. It's disturbing to think that our fate as adults is already determined by our powers of self-control at a very young age. To be honest, even at my age I would have a bit of difficulty passing the test, at least if the treat on offer were an almond croissant rather than a marshmallow.

I think I'm not alone in this. Most of us fight our inclinations and desires every day, from the moment we resist the urge to stay in bed that little bit longer in the morning, to the moment we decide to forego that one more glass of wine before turning in for the night. It is not just a quotidian challenge, but also a philosophically puzzling phenomenon. Philosophers often call the failure to resist desire *akrasia*, using a Greek word meaning "lack of self-control," sometimes translated "weakness of will." In the strict sense, we are akratic when our desires lead us to act against our judgment about what is in fact best for us to do. This is hard to explain. A naive, but appealingly simple, analysis of human action would go like this: a person considers what is best for them to do, all things considered, reaches a decision, and then acts accordingly. But in cases of *akrasia* we reach such a decision and then ignore it, our judgment overcome by something as humble as a marshmallow.

As the use of the Greek term *akrasia* suggests, this phenomenon was discussed by a number of ancient philosophers, including Plato, Aristotle, and the Stoics. For Socrates as depicted in Plato's early dialogues (especially *Protagoras* 354e–355e), and for the Stoics, *akrasia* in the strict sense is impossible. When we seem to act against our better judgment, this simply means that deep down we are judging, for instance, that it is better to stay in bed than get to work on time, even if we claim to believe otherwise. Aristotle meanwhile takes the view that strong desires can make a judgment temporarily inactive. So for him *akrasia* is possible, but only in a weak sense: one cannot be clear-headed in judging that one should do something even as one is failing to do it.[1] To explain such "clear-eyed *akrasia*" we would need a more complicated moral psychology, such as the one found in Plato's *Republic*. Plato proposes that the soul has three aspects that compete for control: reason, spirit, and desire. When I judge rationally that it's time for bed, but drink more wine anyway, this happens because the desiring part of my soul dominates the rational part.[2]

Plato's was the most influential ancient theory of *akrasia*, but for philosophers who take the theory to its most radical conclusion we must turn to the late antique Christians known as ascetics. The term "asceticism" comes from the Greek *askesis*, which means "practice," and these Christians were indeed putting Plato's theory into practice, pushing themselves to the ultimate limits of self-control. Many pagan Greek thinkers had assumed that truly virtuous people simply lack any vicious desires. For instance, Aristotle believed that the virtuous always *want* to do the right thing. Thus he distinguished virtue from self-control or *enkrateia*, which is the state of character you have if you have bad desires but manage to overcome those desires through rational judgment. By contrast, the Christians assumed that, at least in our fallen sinful state, human life inevitably involves a struggle to defeat temptation. It was the unique prerogative of Christ to be without sin, perhaps even without inclination towards sin. What the ascetics were "practicing" for was a Christ-like state in which desire had been completely defeated by rational judgment, insofar as is possible in this life.

The most famous philosophical treatment of asceticism is not an ancient one but Nietzsche's withering critique of the ascetic impulse in Christianity. You might be familiar with his complaint that asceticism is a denial of life itself, a nihilistic rejection of embodied existence.[3] We can reserve judgment as to whether this is an oversimplification of Nietzsche, but it is certainly an oversimplification of ancient Christian asceticism. In fact the fourth-century ascetics based their way of life around the belief that God Himself had become embodied in this world. This is shown by the career of one of the most famous ascetics, Antony the Great. He is known to us through a biography written by Athanasius, a theologian also known for his controversial writings about the Trinity.[4] Athanasius presents Antony as a fellow critic of the Arians. For Arius and his followers, the divine Son was above all a mediator between God the Father and humanity. Accordingly, the Arians placed the Son on an exalted, but still subordinate level, below the Father. One sign of this was their admission that the divine Son was not co-eternal with the Father—rather, as they put it, there was a time when the Son was not. For critics like Athanasius and Antony, all this amounted to a denial that Jesus Christ was fully God. They insisted that Christ was wholly human and wholly divine, and thus both embodied and perfect. For Antony, asceticism was accordingly a way of imitating God, of striving for a perfect embodied life, not a way of fleeing the body (as Nietzsche would have it).

On these theological foundations Antony built the life immortalized by Athanasius in a biography that would be read and imitated by many generations of Christians, beyond late antiquity and into the medieval age. Some measure of its potential impact is given by Augustine, who tells us of a man who converted to Christianity immediately upon reading it.[5] In the biography we first hear how Antony gave away his family fortune to charity. He reserved only a little for the upkeep of his sister, but then thought better of it and gave even that away, arranging for the sister to live in a community of other ascetics. (Athanasius doesn't tell us how the sister felt about all this.) The existence of that community shows that Antony was not, as sometimes claimed, the first to live a deliberately ascetic life. In fact Athanasius describes him learning from other ascetics. But Antony took things further than most. Others had moved to the outskirts of villages at the edge of the Egyptian desert, subsisting on little food and sleeping on the ground. Antony, though, had himself shut into a tomb, with instructions that a bit of bread should be brought to him every few days.

With such dramatic gestures Antony won fame as one of the so-called "desert fathers," radical ascetics of the fourth century AD whose struggle against desire also earned them the title "athletes of God." Like Antony, many started wealthy but gave away their fortunes. Riches-to-rags stories abound in the ascetic literature.[6] Having chosen poverty, they would reside in conditions of bare survival, devoting their lives to prayer and living in isolated cells or within communities that were forerunners of medieval monasteries. Even more famous than Antony is Symeon the Stylite,[7] who is known for living on the top of a pillar for years at a time, supposedly without food—he had himself tied down so he would not fall off when hunger weakened him. Symeon's pragmatic reason for this lifestyle, elevated in both the literal and the metaphorical sense, was that it would remove him from the visitors who constantly came to interrupt his contemplation. But it had the reverse effect, as he became something of a tourist attraction. So he made the pillar higher. The stories about Symeon are vivid and even graphic, as when he had himself chained to a rock but was then persuaded that his strength of will should be chain enough to keep him there. When he had the chain removed, a swarm of insects was revealed squirming in his chafed flesh, which he had been enduring without complaint. With this sort of memorable detail, it's no wonder that literature about the desert fathers found a wide readership in later antiquity and the medieval age.

The ascetic movement also provided a rare opportunity for women to take starring roles in Christian literature. For there were desert mothers as well. Unfortunately we have no works actually written by female ascetics. Indeed, in all of late antiquity only a handful of Christian women produced surviving writings.[8] The most prominent example is the poetry of the fifth-century Byzantine empress Eudocia, and it doesn't get much less ascetic than being a fifth-century Byzantine empress. Still, collections of sayings by heroes of asceticism—another very popular genre in the centuries to come—frequently included pious remarks ascribed to women like the fourth-century hermit Syncletica. Aristocratic women could also make an impact by sponsoring ascetic communities. An outstanding example was Melania the Elder, who founded such a community in Palestine, and who associated with Rufinus, the translator of Origen. She was also renowned for her learning, reportedly having carefully read the works of Origen and the Cappadocians, reading both day and night, and returning to the key works for repeated study.

For the history of philosophy, the most significant female ascetics were those connected with the Cappadocians. We saw that Macrina, the sister of Basil of Caesarea and Gregory of Nyssa, helped lead her brothers to the path of Christian devotion. She helped many others along this road by founding an ascetic community, as did Melania the Elder. We also saw Gregory present his sister as a keen connoisseur and critic of Hellenic philosophy in his work on the immortality of the soul. This casts her in the Socratic role of a philosopher facing death with arguments, and without fear. Gregory depicts her rather differently in his *Life of Macrina*.[9] Here the emphasis is on her piety, her humility, and her spirituality. After the man she was intended to marry died before they could wed, she dedicated herself to virginity and domestic labor. Though Gregory clearly considers it possible for a woman like Macrina to be a Christian exemplar, he does not drop his assumptions about gender roles. He compliments her for living and working along with the household maids, and in this text gives no hint that she also enjoyed a good old-fashioned Socratic discourse on immortality. Still, there is some continuity between the Macrina of this biography and the Macrina of Gregory's dialogue on the soul, in that the *Life* presents her as a model of measured grief in the face of family deaths. If that doesn't impress you, she is also said to have worked miracles, using nothing but prayer to cure a child of an eye disease and herself of a dangerous tumor.

Similar themes arise in a funeral oration written by the other Cappadocian Gregory, of Nazianzus, for his sister Gorgonia.[10] In this case Gorgonia did marry, but she persuaded her husband to take an oath of chastity with her. (As with Antony's sister, we don't hear how he felt about Gorgonia's vow, except that he went along with it. And this before the invention of the cold shower!) Like Macrina, Gorgonia enjoyed miraculous recovery from injury and illness through prayer. Without casting doubt on the sincerity of these ascetic heroines, we may note that refusing marriage, or marital relations, as in the case of Gorgonia, gave them a chance to escape the strictures of the patriarchal society of late antiquity. The idea that asceticism could restore equality between men and women, lost through sin, is a powerful undercurrent in this literature. In fact Gregory of Nyssa believed that the distinction between male and female gender is itself a result of our sinful state. There was no such distinction in the initial creation of humankind, and it will be eliminated in the hereafter. In this life, meanwhile, outstandingly holy women could wield influence openly, something quite rare in antiquity. They had a significant intellectual impact, even if we learn about it only from men like the Gregories and Augustine, who saw his mother Monica as a paragon of Christian wisdom. Women's use of family wealth to house groups of like-minded ascetics was another way to exert influence.

As all this suggests, despite the image of ancient ascetics as loner hermits the movement had a decidedly political dimension. Melania, Macrina, and other founders wanted their communities to show how humans could live together, devoted to God rather than to competition over wealth and secular power. To some extent even gender inequalities could be eliminated in such groups, though that particular political bombshell was partly defused during the fourth century as it became less acceptable for women and men to join in the same communities. Historians refer to ascetics who lived in communities as "cenobitic," from the Greek *koinos bios*—which means "living in common." They are contrasted to ascetics who lived alone or in relative isolation, who are called "eremitic" from the Greek word *eremos*, meaning "desert." (This is the root of our word "hermit.") One could think of the cenobitic collectives as enactments of the first kind of virtuous city Socrates describes in the *Republic* (372a–d), in which there are no luxuries and all individuals share the same goals. What Socrates' interlocutor Glaucon dismisses as a "city of pigs" was seen more favorably by these late ancient Christians.

As for the more isolated ascetics, a different animal may leap to mind. The countercultural exploits and rough lifestyle of men like Antony and Symeon inevitably brings to mind the Cynics, whose name, as you'll remember, comes from the

Greek for "dog." And like the Cynics, the eremitic ascetics did not lose political relevance by withdrawing from normal civic life. Admittedly they did not, like Diogenes, sit in the midst of the city criticizing passing citizens for their hypocrisy. They didn't need to. An audience sought them out, even in the desert. Symeon on his pillar was a magnet for visitors, who sought his advice on matters ranging from the theological to the mundane. The same is true of Antony, and Athanasius records that the desert father had, at best, mixed feelings about this. Just as Gregory of Nazianzus wished to abandon his pastoral duties to join Macrina in a life of self-restrained retreat, so Antony would sometimes have preferred to be left in peace. But he engaged with his fellow Christians, through advice to visitors and of course by setting an example. We shouldn't underestimate the symbolic power and even the political subversiveness of Antony's decision to abandon his wealth in favor of a lifestyle the ascetics referred to simply as "philosophy."

For the philosophical underpinnings of this philosophical way of life, the key author is Evagrius of Pontus.[11] He hailed from Cappadocia, and was a student of Gregory of Nazianzus. Like other desert fathers, he adopted a hermetic lifestyle to escape temptation. In this case the "escape" was quite literal, since he began to compete as an athlete of God after fleeing from a politically dangerous liaison with a woman in Constantinople. He took up the ascetic life, though it is reported that he returned to Alexandria to dispute with pagan philosophers. In his desert retreat Evagrius wrote extensively about the challenges and tactics of asceticism, in works that were greatly admired by Maximus the Confessor. Not everyone was a fan though. There are clear borrowings from the thought of Origen in Evagrius' writings, so critics of Origen did not hesitate to attack Evagrius too. Indeed, Evagrius sometimes seems to agree with the controversial Origenist claims that all souls existed free from body before they sinned, and that all souls will ultimately achieve salvation.[12]

This link between Origenism and asceticism is no coincidence. For one thing, Origen himself had ascetic leanings. Supposedly, he castrated himself as a teenager to escape the temptations of sex. The church historian Eusebius records that he bravely endured cold and poverty, and went barefoot. (Remind you of anyone?) Even family relationships were sometimes seen as a distraction from piety and prayer: when told that his father had died, Evagrius snapped, "Don't be blasphemous; my father is immortal!"[13] The ascetics had not only religious motives but also a philosophical rationale for their withdrawal from bodily things. Origen described human perfection in highly intellectualist terms, as a process of reaching freedom from the body after many cycles of incarnation. So it's natural that he and his followers would see bodily desire as an obstacle to perfection. Yet like Antony, Origen's admirer Evagrius saw the war against desire as one that must be fought in the here and now, while we are embodied. His writings frequently referred to Plato's three-part soul, and described the ascetic project as the attempt to silence the lower desires, leaving the mind free to contemplate God through prayer. Thus his meditations on the ascetic struggle were really a subtle exploration of how to avoid *akrasia*. He made the struggle personal, by blaming the lower desires on demons that lay constant siege to the ascetic. The demons undermine prayer by introducing unwanted "thoughts," for instance, lustful fantasies that might come to a monk as he tried to pray in his cell, or memories of the ascetic's previous life. He classified these distracting thoughts into eight types: gluttony, avarice, lust, and so on, a list that became the basis for the later tradition of the seven deadly sins.[14]

The talk of demons here is not mere metaphor. Athanasius too described Antony's battles for self-control as a battle against demons, and Evagrius discusses the demons' deceitful tricks in detail. They disguise themselves as angels, they make distracting noises when the ascetic tries to pray, or they temporarily retreat so as to lull the ascetic into false confidence. We might smirk at all this, yet a fairly sophisticated theory of the human soul is implicit in Evagrius' remarks. He sees the imagination as the aspect of the soul that could be targeted by the demons of desire, because imagination is allied with the senses rather than the mind—a psychological analysis that goes back to Aristotle. He also draws on the Stoics, saying that the senses deliver impressions or representations to the mind, which the mind can then choose to follow or reject. These representations constitute the main weapon used by demons. They are trying to distract us from the pure mental apprehension of God. Since God is immaterial, he is not grasped through any impression or representation, but through pure thought, which is the goal of prayer. Evagrius also cites a wise man who claims the brain is a frequent target of demonic attack, apparently because this is a center for the reception of sense images.[15]

For some context, it would be worth turning briefly to a rather different author from around the same period: Nemesius of Emesa. He was a bishop, and possibly another associate of the Cappadocians, who wrote in the late fourth century. He is known to us through his treatise *On the Nature of Man*, a kind of textbook summarizing the teachings of both pagan and Christian philosophers.[16] For modern scholars it is a gold-mine of references to early thinkers whose works may be lost. For a fourth-century audience it was a useful guide to contemporary ideas about anatomy, psychology, free will, and other aspects of human nature. In one section he describes several psychological faculties, including memory and imagination, and explains that they are seated in the brain (§6). But Nemesius is enough of a Platonist to think that the soul also has functions that are exercised without the body—the kind of pure reasoning or contemplation Evagrius too encourages. And though

Nemesius is clearly no ascetic himself, he does mention that a pious man will indulge only the desires that Plato called natural and necessary, meaning those we need to satisfy simply to survive (§18). Antony, Symeon, Macrina, and Evagrius would agree with this. They did not push their asceticism to the point of suicide, but did swear off unnecessary yet pleasant activities such as sex, decent clothes, washing, or food and drink beyond the bare minimum. Marshmallows and almond croissants were definitely off the menu, and not only because they hadn't been invented yet.

Something else Nemesius has in common with the ascetics is the immense historical reach of his writings. His *On the Nature of Man* was translated into Armenian, Syriac, Arabic, and Latin. Collections of sayings about the desert mothers and fathers found their way into all these languages and more. The monastic culture that transmitted the literature of asceticism also became a crucial conduit for mainstream philosophy. The works of Aristotle passed through Christian monasteries of the East, where they were read in Syriac before they were later translated into Arabic. Thus the Syrian monastic communities, which grew out of the ascetic movement, provided a bridge across which philosophy traveled from late antiquity to the Islamic world. I will revisit this story in the next volume of this series. But first we have some unfinished business here with the late antique Christians. We've looked at authors of the Greek tradition pretty thoroughly, but have barely touched on those who wrote in Latin—who include the greatest Christian thinker of antiquity, Augustine.

46

SPREADING THE WORD
THE LATIN CHURCH FATHERS

I suppose that all of us have a few guilty pleasures. I've admitted to a weakness for almond croissants, and this book has provided mounting evidence that I cannot resist a good pun (or indeed, a bad pun). But how many of us are helpless to resist the great works of Latin literature? This was the guilty pleasure of the fourth-century Church Father Jerome. He was raised on a diet, not of almond croissants, but of Latin eloquence, with Cicero and other pagan authors on the menu.[1] As he became more and more serious about his Christianity, this became a matter of increasing spiritual discomfort for Jerome. He flirted with the idea that the Scriptures might offer their own kind of eloquence, but more often he extolled their very lack of polish. These were rough, simple texts, and engaging with them could be seen as a discipline, an ordeal as real as the fasting and abstinence of the desert fathers. Or so claimed Jerome.

And he ought to have known. He was himself something of a desert father, albeit one who retreated to isolation armed with a large library and a squad of scribes to help him with his research. (To borrow a joke: his cave must have been unusually large.) His ascetic practice included not only submitting to the unadorned, even crude prose of the Bible instead of the elegance of Cicero, but also learning to read the Bible in Hebrew. He consulted Jewish scholars and translated the Bible into Latin directly from Hebrew instead of from the Greek Septuagint. In some of the many dozens of letters Jerome wrote to his patrons, friends, and rivals[2] he claimed a nearly unique interpretive privilege on this basis. I have gone to the Hebrew source, he would say, and returned with insights about God's word that have been obscured by translation. We might suppose it obvious that going back to the original language of a text is a good idea, but Jerome's use of Hebrew was controversial. After all, the Greek Septuagint was believed to be a divinely assisted translation. Jerome debated the value of the Hebrew original with no less a personage than Augustine (Letter 112).

In all of this, Jerome was carrying on the work of Origen. Often literally: he drew not only on consultation with Jewish scholars, but also on his extensive acquaintance with the works of Origen. As I have mentioned, Origen's multi-column edition of the Hebrew Bible, the *Hexapla*, has not been preserved for posterity, but Jerome was still able to use it. He gives us a clue into why the *Hexapla* did not survive when he complains about the eye-watering price a copy would demand. This is also relevant to Jerome's feelings of guilt over the pleasures of literature and scholarship.[3] In the ancient world books were luxury items in every sense—expensive to buy, and properly appreciated only by those who had an expensive education. No wonder that Jerome had mixed feelings. He was inspired not only by Origen's scholarship, but also by his ascetic side, and by the example of desert fathers like Antony the Great. Indeed, one of Jerome's own works was a biography of the desert father Paul the Hermit. Jerome's career thus embodies a tension, on the one hand emphasizing the spiritual importance of self-restraint and voluntary poverty, on the other, ennobling the image of the Christian scholar whose education and library were the ancient equivalent of elite private schooling and sports-cars. This helps explain why so many ancient Christian heroes started out wealthy but voluntarily gave up their riches. They pursued a life of poverty, study, and seclusion, but only after they had been educated to an elite level. Usually the better-known Christian ascetics had their cake before they started refusing to eat it.

Why is this tale of ancient Christian neurosis relevant to the history of philosophy? The clue is an author I've already mentioned several times in this chapter: Cicero. We've seen that philosophy was part and parcel of elite education and the canon of classic literature for readers of late antiquity. That's obviously true for the Greek tradition, which looked to Plato as a paragon of both literary and philosophical excellence. But it's also true for readers of Latin. The most significant Church Fathers who wrote in Latin—Tertullian, Lactantius, Ambrose, Jerome, and Augustine—were all well educated and all admired the great Latin stylists, like Ovid, Virgil, and Cicero. How annoying that all these authors were pagans! And how especially annoying that Cicero, often taken as the greatest of the classical Latin authors, also happened to be the primary route through which pagan Hellenic philosophy had reached readers of Latin.

The point is illustrated particularly well by Lactantius. His fame relies on a work called the *Divine Institutes*, written at the dawn of the fourth century in response to the Great Persecution of Christians under the emperor Diocletian.[4] In the *Institutes* he says explicitly that his aim is to use such rhetorical gifts as he has to attack pagan belief and uphold Christianity (1.1). We are here in the territory of apologetics, which we have already explored with the Greek Fathers Clement and Justin Martyr. Clement, though, was far less apologetic about his love for the classical tradition than Lactantius, or after him Jerome. In fact, the *Institutes* of Lactantius slides casually from attacking pagan religion to attacking pagan philosophers, in a way that would have appalled Clement. Even the noble Socrates is not spared, as Lactantius sneers at his dying request to sacrifice a rooster to the god Asclepius (3.20). As for Plato, Lactantius can provoke his audience's scorn by simply mentioning the *Republic*'s idea that women should be shared among men in the ideal state (3.21–2). Sometimes Lactantius' mockery of the philosophers is unintentionally comic, as when he makes fun of the philosophers' belief that people could live on the far side of the earth without falling into the sky (3.24). Australians, hang in there: we're sending help.

Yet Lactantius can't help admiring certain philosophers, in particular Cicero. He loves Cicero above all as the paradigm of Latin eloquence. So although he attacks several passages from Cicero in the course of the *Institutes*, he does so with some degree of respect—he seems to think Cicero should really have known better. And of the various philosophical traditions passed down to him, in part through Cicero's Latin writings, it seems to be Cicero's own preferred school of skepticism that has made the biggest impression on Lactantius. He deftly wields the classical skeptical strategy of emphasizing disagreement amongst his opponents (3.4). He also thinks the skeptics were right when they admitted that perfect knowledge is beyond the capacity of mankind, Stoic claims to the contrary notwithstanding. On the other hand, dogmatic skeptics go too far when they claim we can know *nothing*. That, as Lactantius points out, would be self-defeating, because we would at least know that we know nothing (3.6). Rather, humans can have partial knowledge that falls short of the full understanding we might honor with the name of "wisdom," in Greek, *sophia* and in Lactantius' Latin, *sapientia*.

At best, philosophy done with human resources can be only what its name promises: love of wisdom, but not wisdom itself. For that, we must turn to a source higher than mankind, namely God. Thus Lactantius argues that wisdom is inextricably linked to religion. Interestingly, he seems to assume that the Hellenic philosophy that inspired Cicero was *not* religious. He even says that a pagan would never be able to engage in philosophy and religious ritual at the same time (4.3). For Lactantius, "philosophy" still means Socrates, Plato, Aristotle, and the Hellenistic schools—unsurprising, given that Cicero was such an important source for knowledge of philosophy in Latin. Lactantius seems unaware of Neoplatonism, and especially figures like his contemporary Iamblichus, who fused Platonism with pagan religion. Ironically, though, Lactantius is playing much the same game as Iamblichus. He appeals to a learned audience that still includes many pagans, offering a wisdom built on revealed texts. He tends to quote pagan authorities more than the Bible, even the Hermetic texts so beloved of Iamblichus. This is precisely because he is not preaching to the converted (literally), but aiming his critique of paganism at a broad, literate readership.

At least one Christian reader, Jerome, was more impressed by this critical project of Lactantius than by his positive exposition of Christian doctrines. There's no doubt that the most memorable parts of the *Institutes* are those where he chuckles at the irrationality of pagan belief and pokes holes in philosophical pretentions. But as the work goes on, Lactantius does provide an innovative ethical teaching to replace philosophical theories about virtue. He rejects the Socratic and Stoic notion that virtue is the same thing as knowledge. It is possible, indeed common, for us to know what we should do and lack the *will* to do it (6.5), a point we just considered in the context of the ascetic movement, and one that will be further developed by Augustine. Whereas knowledge is something that comes to us from the outside, through learning, virtue is a state of character that must come from within. Lactantius also objects to the philosophical claim that virtue is the highest good for humankind. Virtue is at best a means to our highest good, namely an immortal life together with God. This makes sense of a passage earlier in the *Institutes*, where Lactantius has argued that one must accept the presence of vice and suffering in the world, since without these virtue would be pointless (3.12). Lactantius would agree with Irenaeus that this life is given to us as a trial and tribulation, so that we can earn salvation the hard way.

Thus virtue, for Lactantius, consists largely in fortitude, in bearing whatever slings and arrows outrageous fortune sends our way. If we are virtuous, we will achieve the promised immortality in the hereafter. For now, a perfect human life in this world will have two aspects, just like the contemplative and practical aspects of happiness in the Aristotelian tradition. But Lactantius gives both aspects a new twist. Instead of rational contemplation, we should dedicate ourselves to worship of God. And instead of a life of heroic practical activity or political engagement, as praised by Aristotle and Cicero, we should help our fellow man. Lactantius places charity at the core of ethics, another idea that will be embraced by Augustine. For Lactantius, charity and all other practical virtues presuppose piety, because we become charitable in order to imitate God and His mercy. He develops his view in part by attacking the radical skeptic philosopher Carneades, who famously came to Rome and gave speeches in praise of justice, and then against justice (see Chapter 16). In the second speech he gave the vivid example of a wise man and a foolish man drowning at sea, with only one plank between them. The wise man would fight for the plank to save his life, justice be damned, because his life is more valuable (5.16). Lactantius first responds, "What is this supposedly wise man doing on a ship?" After all, in the ancient world seafaring was a danger usually faced only to fight wars or make money. More to the point, he adds that the real wise man would fear sin much more than death, sin being any act that harms one's neighbor rather than helping him.

And so it is that, thanks to Lactantius, charity begins at Rome. Like I say, when it comes to puns, I just have no self-control. In this case I should perhaps have tried a bit harder, since neither Lactantius nor the other Latin Church Fathers were actually based in Rome. They came from and lived in various locales in the Western Empire, and even in the East. North Africa in particular produced several theologians, including Lactantius, Tertullian, and Augustine himself. This only stands to reason. In late antiquity the city of Rome was no longer the center of empire. In the fourth century the emperors had relocated to the more easily defended Milan. And by the 380s the emperor Valentinian II wasn't even the most powerful man in Milan. On more than one occasion he had to yield to the bishop of that city: Ambrose.[5] Like his contemporaries the Cappadocians, Ambrose was deeply embroiled in theological controversies, in his case especially with the Arians. Ambrose was reluctantly installed as bishop at the demand of a near-riotous mob, an event that would be regretted in due course by the emperor Valentinian and his mother, Justina, who favored the Arians. In 385, when Valentinian tried to seize a basilica in the city for use by Arians, Ambrose and his supporters faced them down. It wasn't Ambrose's only successful confrontation with imperial authority. Years later another emperor, Theodosius, authorized a massacre of thousands at Thessalonika. Outraged, Ambrose withdrew the sacraments from Theodosius until he performed a humiliating public repentance. Around the same time Ambrose used his deft political skills to prevent pagans from restoring the altar of the goddess Victory near the Senate in Rome. When you're winning battles against Victory herself, you know you're on a roll.

Ambrose is thus frequently cited as the first Christian leader to exert the power of the church as an autonomous political force, which could on occasion thwart emperors or put them firmly in their place. Of course this achievement echoes down the centuries through the medieval age. As a result, Ambrose is better known for his political machinations than his philosophy. Even historians of Christian theology probably think of him in the first instance as a formative influence on Augustine, rather than for his own thought. But like Lactantius, Ambrose contributed significantly to the emerging tradition of Christian ethics. His best-known work, called *De Officiis* or *On Duties*, is a Christian answer to a treatise of the same title by Cicero (that man again!).[6] Indeed, you might think of Ambrose's *On Duties* as a Christian reworking of Cicero, sometimes simply illustrating originally Ciceronian ethical points with examples drawn from the Bible. He tells us how Abraham's willingness to sacrifice his son Isaac at God's command displayed all four classical Greek virtues: wisdom, justice, courage, and temperance (1.25). In one particularly striking juxtaposition of sources, he compares Plato's story of the Ring of Gyges from the *Republic*— which asks whether anyone could resist acting unjustly if they acquired a ring of invisibility—with the virtue of David, who refrained from killing an enemy king who was asleep, even though he could have gotten away with it (3.5, referring to 1 Samuel 26).

As this suggests, Ambrose fully agrees with Greek Church Fathers like Clement of Alexandria that the truths found in Greek philosophy were already proclaimed earlier by Old Testament prophets. Moreover, Ambrose insists that only the Christians have made good on the aspirations of Plato, the Stoics, and other more or less right-minded Hellenic thinkers. He agrees with Plato that our ethical goal should be the subordination of desire to the rule of reason (1.24). But he thinks that all the pagan philosophers still thought too much in terms of what is advantageous to each of us in this life. Even the Stoics, for all their ethical stringency, admitted that one might prefer to be materially comfortable so long as it does not impede the ultimate goal of virtue. For Ambrose, as for Lactantius, even virtue itself is merely a means to the end of eternal life. Thus he condemns wealth and other external goods as being actively *harmful* to the pursuit of our good (2.5), and praises poverty as a path that leads to salvation. It is this difference, Ambrose says, that justifies his decision to write a new *On Duties* to supplant that of the pagan Cicero.

This pattern of using and also criticizing Greek philosophy (which, like my penchant for puns, is becoming increasingly familiar as we go along) goes back to the earliest great Latin Father, Tertullian, who wrote in the second century. He is well known for asking: "What has Athens to do with Jerusalem?"[7] This rhetorical question suggests that he wanted to sweep aside the whole Greek intellectual tradition in favor of the new Christian revelation. And no doubt Tertullian and other Fathers were tempted to toss philosophy aside entirely, following St Paul's warning: "beware lest any man spoil you through philosophy and vain deceit, after the tradition of men."[8] But if we turn to a work Tertullian wrote on the subject of the soul, we see that he is in fact steeped in philosophical knowledge and even well read in medical literature.[9] He finds the medical texts particularly useful because, unusually within the Patristic tradition, he wants to see the soul as a physical substance.

Again, he is taking his lead here from a biblical source: the Book of Genesis, which says that God "breathed life" into Adam (Gen. 2: 7). This leads Tertullian to ally himself with Stoics and medical authors who described the soul as a sort of *pneuma* or breath. A more abstract theological motive is revealed midway through the work, when he criticizes Plato's claim that the soul is un-generated and immaterial. In that case, says Tertullian, why not just call the soul "God" (ch. 24)? A physical account of soul puts it in its rightful place: the soul is created, not divine. Yet Tertullian does not rely only on theological argument or Scriptural citation. He gives powerful philosophical arguments—for instance, that if the soul were immaterial it could not causally influence the body (ch. 6). This, of course, is still a chief argument for physicalist theories in the philosophy of mind today. Tertullian even resists the temptation to grant immateriality to the higher faculties of the soul, such as the intellect. Instead, Tertullian sees intellect as a mere function of a soul that is in itself physical. How else, as he points out, could the intellect be influenced by the senses and learn from them (ch. 18)?

Tertullian seems almost to be criticizing in advance the theory that will, in the coming generations, be defended in Alexandria by Origen. Origen's explanation of sin and the cosmos will revolve around the claim that the soul pre-exists the body. Tertullian wants nothing to do with that idea. He associates it not only with Plato but with the hated Gnostics, whom we saw being refuted by other second-century theologians like Irenaeus and Justin Martyr. Like them, he traces the Gnostic heresy to the influence of Platonist philosophy. This idea that Hellenic thought is a source of heresy helps explain why we so often find Church Fathers expressing hostility towards Plato and other pagan thinkers, even as they reproduce arguments from these same philosophers. Here's a particularly ironic example: Tertullian thinks that Plato was right to argue in the *Phaedo* that the soul was immortal, on the basis that it is simple (ch. 51). Of course, this means for him not that the soul is immaterial, but rather a uniform physical substance. Yet at the beginning of this same work he sarcastically questions whether Socrates was really untroubled when he took the hemlock (ch. 1). Tertullian believes that no one could manage this without faith in God.

If Tertullian could feel this conflicted about the merits of Platonist theories of soul in the second century, how would things be in the fourth century when theologians would be grappling with the arguably heretical theory of Origen? This brings us full circle, back to Jerome. In his biblical scholarship he was influenced by Origen as by no other author. Yet he also became a leading critic of Origenism. A heated dispute broke out between Jerome and his childhood friend Rufinus over the orthodoxy of Origen's works.[10] Each of them produced a Latin translation of Origen's *On Principles*, Jerome trying to bring out its outrageous features, Rufinus trying to minimize them. For Jerome, Origen went too far in the direction of Platonism, depicting the soul as a pre-existing, purely rational entity and thus reducing all human goodness to intellectual perfection. Jerome's contrary position brings together several strands of the Latin Patristic tradition: Tertullian's insistence that soul is created and not eternal, Lactantius' rejection of knowledge as man's highest end, and Ambrose's more moderate Platonic ethics, which implore us to restrain desire by reason but still leave a place for appropriate emotion in the good life.

The so-called "Origenist" debate between Jerome and Rufinus was only one of several heated theological disputes in the fourth century. We've already looked at confrontations over the Holy Trinity and the nature, or natures, of Christ. Next we're going to turn to a man whose career extended into the fifth century but was still shaped by these and other theological debates. This next Church Father displays his own hesitations and psychological frailties as no other ancient author. Yet he spent his later years combating heresy with a sense of unshakable certainty. In the process, he laid down doctrines that would become authoritative for the next thousand years and more. In the next chapter ancient Christian philosophy reaches its peak with the true confessions of Augustine.

LIFE AND TIME
AUGUSTINE'S CONFESSIONS

Walk into any bookstore and you'll find shelves and shelves of autobiographies, with their well-worn narrative themes of personal struggle and redemption, their uneasy combination of retrospective self-critique and carefully crafted self-justification. It is hard for us to imagine that anyone needed to invent the idea of writing that sort of book. But someone did invent it, at the dawn of the fifth century. The author was Augustine, and the book was the *Confessions*. It self-consciously refers to other ancient Christian life-stories. The conversion narrative of the desert father Antony is mentioned in the very same breath as the climactic moment of Augustine's own conversion (8.12.29). Yet, where Antony is a hero who displays superhuman self-control against supernatural enemies—literal demons of temptation—Augustine shows himself to be all too human. His conversion story is told intimately and vividly, and Augustine depicts his own weaknesses with equal vividness. The effect is that the reader can identify with Augustine, can imagine being in his position. Thus, the reader can also imagine following his path to salvation. To use another twentieth-century comparison, Antony was the Superman of ancient Christian literature, an almost otherworldly figure of unattainable virtue. Augustine was Spider-Man, whom we meet as a conflicted adolescent in search of himself, and who remains prone to weakness and self-doubt, just like the rest of us do.

Augustine was not bitten by a radioactive spider, but by the philosophy bug. He read Cicero's dialogue *Hortensius*, now lost, as a young man while studying rhetoric (3.4.7).[1] He was converted, albeit to the cause of philosophy, not yet to the Christian faith. His mother, the long-suffering and pious Monica, longed for Augustine to adopt her religion, but her belief was not shared by Augustine's father. He had other plans for the precocious young man. The family was not wealthy, but money was scraped together to send Augustine for a first-rate education in his home-town of Thagaste and then Carthage, both on the northern African coast. For the time being Augustine would follow his father's dream of riches on earth rather than his mother's dream of riches in heaven. It took a full twelve years after reading the *Hortensius* for Augustine to reach his moment of conversion to Christianity (8.7.17). By that time he was in Milan, where he had been pursuing a career as an up-and-coming rhetorician, earning his keep as a teacher, and wasting his time on such tasks as a panegyric for the emperor Valentinian II (6.6.9).

Those twelve years take up most of the autobiographical part of the *Confessions*. As he writes, Augustine is in his forties, and looking back on his youthful search for a satisfying way to take up Cicero's exhortation to pursue philosophy. He is attracted by astrology, and by a sect called the Manicheans, named after their founding prophet Mani. In the *Confessions* Augustine depicts the Manichean teaching as one that appealed to his naive, youthful impulses. In particular, he associates it with materialism and the Gnostic view of evil as a second principle opposed to God. After his conversion Augustine would go on to write works in refutation of the Manicheans. But as a young rhetoric student in Carthage Augustine was impressed by the Manichean doctrine. Disenchantment set in when he had the chance to meet a Manichean teacher named Faustus, who struck Augustine as having more style than substance (5.3.3, 5.6.11).

Yet it was precisely the Manicheans' conception of substance that Augustine had difficulty shaking off. Again and again in the *Confessions* he explains that he could not help imagining God, and also evil, as physical, material things. He thought of God as a body penetrating the cosmos, as water soaks through a sponge (7.5.7). This is highly reminiscent of the Stoic understanding of God, so it's appropriate that Augustine was liberated from such misconceptions by reading the anti-Stoic philosophy of Plotinus and Porphyry. He came across Latin versions of their writings, translated by a man named Marius Victorinus (7.9.13; on Victorinus see Chapter 52).[2] Thanks to these "books of the Platonists" Augustine was finally able to abandon his materialist assumptions. Plotinus explained to his satisfaction that something could exist without being a body. Just as important, Plotinus' theory that evil is a sort of non-being or privation dispelled the Manichean idea of evil as an autonomous second principle (7.12.18).

This section of the *Confessions* shows Augustine as closer to the attitude of a Clement than a Lactantius: philosophy is not a target for mocking attack, but a useful bridge towards faith. On the other hand, Augustine emphasizes that the Platonist books did *not* teach him the all-important truths about the incarnation and sacrifice of God's son (7.21.27). This is why even the combined forces of Cicero and the Platonists were unable to lead Augustine away from sin and self-interest to a truly "philosophical" way of life. Only the example of Christ could speak to Augustine's will, and not just his intellect. Paradoxically, he needed to will a change in his own will, and this he remained unable to do. It was not for lack of good role-models. In Milan he had not only his mother, who had moved to be with him, but also access to the greatest cleric of his age, Ambrose. Augustine was pushed powerfully towards conversion by hearing Ambrose's sermons (5.14.24). He at first attended these simply to enjoy Ambrose's considerable rhetorical prowess. But in this case there was substance along with the style, and Ambrose's message began to sink in.

Yet, not deep enough. Augustine tells us of his encounter with Ambrose a full three books prior to the story of his eventual conversion. The intervening sections of the *Confessions* provide a powerful illustration of that all-too-familiar human dilemma: knowing what one should do, and refusing to do it. Thanks to the dream-team of Cicero, Plotinus, and Ambrose, Augustine's mind has been converted. He rejects the false teachings of astrology and Manicheanism, accepting the existence of a good, immaterial, supreme God. But he is too tied to the pleasures of the flesh to react accordingly. Augustine compares his situation to that of a man who knows he needs to get out of bed but just can't summon the will to get up (8.5.12). (I have to admit that this example sounds horribly familiar to me, and I'm in good company—it was also used by Marcus Aurelius.[3]) In a more famous passage, Augustine describes himself as praying to God: "make me chaste and temperate, but not yet" (8.7.17). Such conflict within the will is one of the central themes of the *Confessions*, and of Augustine's writings in general. The phenomenon has already been explored earlier in the narrative, with the famous description of a young Augustine stealing fruit from a pear tree with his friends (2.4.9). The irony of the story, with its inevitable reminiscence of the Garden of Eden, is that Augustine did not even want the pears. The theft was an utterly perverse act. He sinned for the sake of being sinful, something Augustine still finds difficult to understand years later as he writes the *Confessions*. The theme of internal conflict reaches a peak in the scenes leading up to Augustine's conversion, in which he is desperate with desire to become a Christian, but unable to make himself do so.

What binds him to his former life is, above all, sexual desire. As a young man he had a mistress of many years, with whom he fathered a son. Rather unfairly, he tries to connect this liaison to the Manichean leanings he had at this time, but neither the young Augustine nor the Manicheans were as debauched as he would like us to believe. In fact, Augustine mentions in passing that he was faithful to the mistress through these years (4.2.2), and the modern reader is less likely to be shocked by the affair than by the casual way the unnamed woman is sent away when a marriage is arranged for Augustine. To be fair, Augustine does tell us that he was terribly upset at the time, though not so upset that he refrained from taking custody of their son. As for the woman's point of view, we are told only that she vowed never to take up with another man (6.15.25). I like to imagine Augustine's mistress getting together with Antony the Great's sister, who we saw being dispossessed and packed off to a nunnery by her brother. They might have shared some choice observations about the noble ascetic impulses of ancient Christianity.

Our understanding of the ascetic movement (Chapter 45) makes it easier for us to understand Augustine's dilemma here. Why, we might be wondering, doesn't he just convert to Christianity and get married? It's not as if all Christians had to become celibate, after all. But the *Confessions* makes clear that Augustine and several of his friends thought of Christian conversion as requiring renunciation of all worldly things, whether this be a career, theatrical and gladiatorial shows, or marriage and sexual relations. In the face of this "all or nothing" choice, Augustine faces an opponent more formidable than any Manichean: himself. His eventual victory comes in a garden, where Augustine has been weeping over his inability to defeat his own desires. He suddenly hears a child's voice from nearby, chanting in Latin: *tolle, lege.* "Take, read." Seizing up his copy of the Bible and opening it at random, he comes upon Paul's letter to the Romans, instructing him to put on Christ and put aside lust (8.12.29).[4] Like Paul himself when he was knocked from his horse, Augustine is finally converted. As I've already mentioned, Augustine alludes to the different parallel of Antony the Great, who was similarly persuaded to give up his riches by reading the Bible.

At this climactic point we are still only in the eighth of the *Confessions'* thirteen books. The autobiographical portion continues on through Book 9, with the story of Augustine's baptism and the death of Monica, following a mystical vision shared by mother and son (9.10.24). It now becomes clear that Augustine is not content to write the first psychologically nuanced autobiography. He wants to write a psychologically nuanced autobiography that ends with a few metaphysical speculations on the nature of memory and time, and for good measure, a bit of Scriptural exegesis. But what does the story of Augustine's life have to do with the philosophy of time, or a commentary on the opening chapters of Genesis?

The temptation is to say that Augustine's was not just any life, and that he cannot tell his story without indulging in that most Augustinian of pursuits, "faith seeking understanding." But it might be truer to say again that Augustine is offering his own story to us only as one particularly vivid example. His path to God is one we are all called to follow, and it raises questions that confront us all. When he looks back on his own life, how does his past manage to live on in his mind? Indeed, is his past anything more than a memory? Furthermore, the story we have just seen is one of Augustine overcoming his separation from God. But even his conversion can bring him to God only partially, precisely because he is a creature, subject to change and imperfection, whereas God is eternal and perfect. Thus Augustine laments at the end of his philosophical analysis that he is "scattered" across time, rather than being fully and eternally present (11.29.39). The same point is made more generally in the final book, which uses the beginning of Genesis to explain how an eternal God can relate to the temporal world He creates. Thus the autobiography is powerfully connected to the closing philosophical section. Or perhaps it would be better to say that the whole *Confessions* is both philosophical and autobiographical. The theme of creation's separation from and return to God is approached in two ways. First, by telling Augustine's life-story, and then by examining what it means that we are able to have life-stories in the first place, because we live in time and not in unchanging eternity.

Even in this section, Augustine retains his habit of acute psychological observation. He asks "what is time?" and then adds, "as long as nobody asks me, then I know" (11.14.17). The puzzles he raises about time were already mentioned by Aristotle and by skeptical philosophers, well known to Augustine thanks to his exposure to Cicero. But there is no ancient text that explores the paradoxical nature of time as thoroughly as the eleventh book of the *Confessions*.[5] The fundamental problem is identified by Augustine when he asks how time can have any length. Past time is already gone, and future time has yet to arrive. That leaves only the present time to exist as having length. But a length of time, like a month, day, minute, or second, cannot be present. Only this instant right *now* can be present, and such an instant seems to have no length (11.25.20). Indeed, although Augustine doesn't mention this, Aristotle had described the present instant—in Greek, *to nun*, which literally means "the now"—as a duration-less division or limit between past and future. So Augustine is, like me when I'm failing to get up in the morning, in good company. He finds common cause with the Stoics too, when he says that if time exists it needs to be some kind of "extension" or "distention" (*distentio*, corresponding to Greek *diastema*). Yet how can this be, if time has no length?

To solve this problem, Augustine turns to the example of a spoken phrase, giving the not very randomly chosen example *deus creator omnium*, "God, creator of all." It takes time to utter these eight Latin syllables, so the sound of the entire phrase is never present as a whole, any more than every minute in an hour could be present all at once. Yet we have no difficulty in hearing this phrase as a unity and understanding it. This can only be because our minds are—at least if we know a bit of Latin—remembering and interpreting the sound as it passes into our ears. We retain the parts of the phrase that have already sounded, and anticipate the syllables yet to come. He also uses the example of hearing a song. The song may go on for minutes, but your mind is capable of putting it all together into one, more or less coherent experience.

Augustine infers that the mind creates temporal extension. A long past time is simply a memory of past events as having taken a long time to happen, and likewise for the expectation of a long future time. This account helps him solve another problem too. It seems that the only things that exist are things that exist now, given that past things no longer exist and future things do not exist yet. But then how can it be true to say, for instance, that Socrates drank hemlock, or that there will be a Buster Keaton movie on TV tomorrow? This is a problem that still fascinates philosophers today. Some, who are called "presentists," agree with Augustine that past and future things do not exist, hence their name. (Disappointing for those who were expecting these to be philosophers who always show up with a nice present.) Other philosophers, who reject presentism, attack the position in part by pressing this question about Socrates and Buster Keaton. What is it that makes past- and future-tense statements true, if neither past nor future things exist in any sense? Already back in the late fourth century, when he existed, Augustine was proposing an answer. Past and future things reside in our memory or expectation, and in that way they do exist presently.

Whether you find this persuasive or not, I hope you'll join me in rejoicing that the *Confessions* is one thing from the past that does still exist. This work is one of Augustine's three masterpieces. It offers us not only one of the great life-stories of antiquity, but also an ideal orientation for Augustine's contributions to the history of philosophy. It takes in all the themes of his career. The flirtation and then break with the Manicheans prefigures a life dominated by polemic, not only against these Manicheans but also against rival Christian sects, the Donatists and Pelagians. Augustine's internal conflict is resolved only with a kind of divine intervention, in the "take and read" scene. This sums up Augustine's stance on human freedom, a stance he developed in large part in his polemic against the Pelagians. According to the Augustinian view, we can succeed in this struggle only thanks to divine assistance. This is so because all of us inherit sin from Adam, a sin which we cannot remove through mere effort. God's grace is needed, which is why His Son had to be sent and sacrificed for us.

The *Confessions* also display the complexity of Augustine's attitude towards pagan culture, and especially the pagan philosophers. That issue will be central to the second of Augustine's masterpieces, the *City of God*. There he will criticize pagan religion and political values, and ask what relationship a committed Christian could have towards the secular political world. In the *City of God* pagan philosophers come in for heavy criticism. Yet throughout his career Augustine also draws on the philosophers, especially the Platonists. Their influence is felt even, or perhaps especially, in Augustine's most ambitious work of theology: *On the Trinity*. Its project, already announced at the end of the *Confessions*, is to understand how humans are images of God and thus characterized by Trinitarian relationships. In explaining this, Augustine develops new and innovative ideas in the philosophy of mind. Both of these other great works of Augustine will be occupying us shortly. But first we're going to be staying with a theme suggested by the last book of the *Confessions*, where Augustine uses his philosophical analysis of time and eternity to interpret the opening verses of Genesis. We'll be turning to two shorter works, *On the Teacher* and *On Christian Teaching*. They may not qualify as milestones on the order of Augustine's three masterpieces, but they will allow us to understand Augustine's views on communication, including the special kind of communication found in Scripture.

48

PAPA DON'T TEACH
AUGUSTINE ON LANGUAGE

There are certain things that fathers are expected to do with their sons, even though mothers can do these same things with their daughters equally well. Playing ball. Going fishing. Going to a football match. Flying a kite. Arguing about borrowing the car. In the ancient world, though, things were a bit different, especially if your dad was Augustine. His idea of a father–son activity was to explore the nature of language together, and to prove after long philosophical debate that all our knowledge derives from God. He wrote up a record of such a dialogue with his son Adeodatus, in a work called *De Magistro*, meaning *On the Teacher*.[1] In the *Confessions* he tells us that it accurately represents Adeodatus' contributions (9.6.14). If this is true, then Adeodatus was a talented lad, one who met a tragic end. His name means "gift of God," but what God gives, He can also take away. Adeodatus was Augustine's son by his mistress, the one sent away when a marriage was arranged for Augustine. He lost the boy too, when Adeodatus died before reaching even twenty years of age.

In his dialogue with the teenaged Adeodatus we see Augustine picking up themes from earlier ancient philosophy and anticipating distinctions still made by philosophers of language today. The most obvious precedent is Plato's theory of recollection. In his dialogue the *Meno*, Plato had Socrates argue that we cannot actually acquire new knowledge through learning. Rather, teachers prompt us to remember forgotten knowledge that is already within our souls. Augustine would not have been able to read the *Meno*, but he did know a summary of the relevant passage from Cicero. In his own dialogue he is going to argue for a similar conclusion: we never gain knowledge from human teachers, but find it in ourselves. On the other hand, he rejects Plato's idea that we are recollecting knowledge from before were born. Instead, it is God Himself who is teaching us from within, though we do not necessarily perceive this when we are learning.

Augustine's path towards this conclusion is also very different from what we find in the *Meno*. Whereas the *Meno* takes the form of an inquiry into virtue, *On the Teacher* investigates language. In particular, it asks how language can lead people to knowledge, if it does so at all. Augustine begins by asking Adeodatus what language is for, and the two agree that we use language to teach others and to remind ourselves (1.1–2). Language is (apparently) able to perform this task because it consists of signs. Not all signs are words. For instance, there are traffic signs, and gestures, like pointing with the finger. But all words are signs. Even such words as "if" and "nothing" are agreed to be signs, even if it is hard to say what they are signs *of* (2.3). The father-and-son team notice that many puzzles arise here. When we are talking, it is not always clear whether we are talking about signs or the things they signify. Augustine gives the example of sophistical arguments, such as: if I get you to say "lion," then a wild beast has just come out of your mouth; or: if you are a man (in Latin *homo*), then you are made of two syllables (8.23). Philosophers would nowadays explain the phenomenon Augustine is highlighting here by distinguishing between "use" and "mention" of a word. If I *use* the word "lion" I am signifying an actual lion. If I only *mention* the word "lion" then I am using this word to refer to the sign, and it is in this sense that I might remark, "'lion' came out of my mouth." The helpful use of quotation-marks was not available to Augustine, though, and he takes seriously the threat that this and other ambiguities pose to the attempt to get clear about how exactly language works. He compares using language to philosophize about language to someone who is scratching an itch in his own fingers, so that he can no longer tell which fingers are itching and which are scratching (5.14).

Nonetheless, the dialogue puts forward an appealing idea about how we might learn. We use signs, which are usually, but not always, linguistic, to teach people about things, and also about other signs. This (again, apparently) leads our listener to gain knowledge of the things we are signifying. Thus I could tell you "giraffes are tall," and you will thereby gain some new knowledge about giraffes, on the off-chance that you didn't already know this important fact. I can also use signs to tell you about other signs, as when I say, "the word 'giraffe' is a noun." Augustine has no quarrel with this second case, where signs teach about signs. But he raises doubts about whether signs can really give us knowledge about things. Certainly this does not happen if I teach you the meaning of a word. Rather, it is the reverse: if I am to teach you what the word "giraffe" signifies, you must already know what a giraffe is. I might, for instance, point and say, "look, that graceful creature with the long neck is a giraffe." In this sort of case I am using a thing to teach you about a sign, not vice versa (10.33). Nor does my pointing at the giraffe—the pointing gesture is also a sign—give you knowledge about giraffes. It only draws your attention to the giraffe, and your sense-perception does the rest.

In fact, Adeodatus and Augustine find that there are puzzles even as to how I could use things to teach about signs. For instance, if I want to show you what the word "dancing" means, I can get up and dance for a minute. But you might conclude that the word "dancing" signifies "dancing for one minute," or "doing a bad imitation of James Brown." You wouldn't necessarily realize that this word refers to dancing in general. This problem of indeterminacy, that is, how we can ever convey to someone the exact meaning of a word, reappeared much later in twentieth-century philosophy of language. A philosopher named Quine raised a puzzle to suggest that all translation is indeterminate.[2] We are to imagine a linguist studying the language of a native tribe. The natives point and say "*gavagai*" when a rabbit runs past. The linguist might infer that *gavagai* means "rabbit," but there are indefinitely many other possibilities. For instance, it might mean "a part of a rabbit," or "I could go for a nice stewed rabbit." Only once he has learned the language can the linguist engage with the natives so as to rule out these possibilities. But it's a puzzle how this is going to be possible, if the linguist cannot get started by learning what individual words mean.

Augustine actually doesn't spend too much time worrying about this problem of whether we can use things to learn the meanings of signs. He perhaps underestimates the difficulty, and assumes that a person of sufficient intelligence will be able to infer what a sign signifies, even if someone else might get the wrong idea (10.32). More difficult, in his view, is the question of how to teach about things using words. Suppose you already know what the words "giraffe" and "tall" mean, and I tell you, "giraffes are tall." At best, my saying this is going to give you a *belief* that giraffes are tall. If you want to *know* that giraffes are tall, just hearing me utter these words is not enough. You must go do some empirical investigation—check out a few giraffes and see if they are tall. But then you'll be learning from your experience of the giraffes that giraffes are tall, not from my statement. In other cases empirical investigation will be irrelevant. I might say to you, "justice is good." Again, even if you know what the words mean, this cannot induce knowledge, even if I try to convince you I am right. Ultimately you must consult your own understanding of justice and goodness to see whether the statement is true or not.

Whether you use sense-experience or consider a more abstract subject within your mind, then, no human teacher will be giving you knowledge. All the teacher can give you is belief, and encouragement to consider things for yourself. Any knowledge you get from this process is not innate, as Plato claimed, but comes from God Himself. It was, after all, God who created the things that we experience through the senses. So when you look at a giraffe to see whether it is tall, you are depending on God's creative act to make it possible for you to gain knowledge. In the more abstract cases, like the one about justice, you are consulting an "inner truth" (12.39), as Augustine puts it. Adeodatus is himself doing that, as he makes up his mind whether Augustine's argument about language is compelling. The inner truth, by whose light we achieve knowledge, is nothing other than God dwelling within us (13.46). So it is God the Father, not Augustine the father, who is in a position to bring Adeodatus to knowledge.

Is language then, like war in the opinion of Edwin Starr, good for absolutely nothing? Well, we have already seen that signs can serve to teach about other signs. But apart from that, they seem only to give us belief. Even in the case where you tell me what you yourself believe, I will not thereby *know* whether you really believe— you might be lying or misspeaking (13.42). For instance, if you say "I love Buster Keaton," I might believe you love Buster Keaton. But maybe you are just trying to persuade me that you have good taste, and secretly you have never even seen one of his movies. (If so, stop reading now and go watch one. The book will still be here when you get back.) The upshot is that signs can only ever bring us to have beliefs about things. But this does not imply that signs are useless: they lead us to examine the things themselves, and to examine our own sense of the truth. Furthermore, a human teacher can use language to dispel misconceptions and errors, by showing their inconsistency or implausibility. This is what Socrates usually did in his conversations, and it is also a common occurrence in the dialogues that Augustine himself wrote early in his career. For Augustine, then, signs in general and language in particular do have an important role to play in bringing us to the truth.

It's worth noting, by the way, that Augustine's argument for all this could be accepted even by an atheist. The atheist will simply reject Augustine's assumption that the truth that dwells within each of us is to be identified with God. But the atheist would not share Augustine's belief that one body of linguistic signs in particular serves to bring us to knowledge: the texts collected in the Bible. The conversion scene from Augustine's *Confessions*—in which he hears a voice telling him "take and read," and then comes across a particularly apt passage of the New Testament—is a vivid example of how signs can lead someone to truth. The Bible Augustine seized on that occasion would have been in Latin. He did know some Greek, but complains in the *Confessions* that he never enjoyed studying it as a child (1.13.20). As for the Hebrew of the Old Testament, this was for Augustine a closed book, if you'll pardon the expression. One might therefore expect him to welcome his contemporary Jerome's project of returning to the Hebrew for a new Latin Bible, and he did point out the usefulness of Latin translations that render the Scriptures in slavishly accurate, "word by word" fashion. On the other hand, he also defended the claims of the Septuagint, the Greek version of the Old Testament.

He discusses these points in a kind of handbook he wrote, entitled *De Doctrina Christiana*, or *On Christian Teaching*.[3] He tells us in its prologue that this work provides general instructions for interpreting the Scriptures, much as you might teach someone to read language in general. For more detailed exegesis of the Bible one can turn, for instance, to his so-called "literal" commentary on Genesis. Here "literal," in Latin, *ad litteram*, means that Augustine avoids allegorical or symbolic interpretation. But in *On Christian Teaching* he does accept the need for such interpretation, at least regarding certain passages. So how do we know which passages should be read allegorically, and which allegorical interpretations to accept? Augustine answers this question with a kind of key to understanding the Bible, which he establishes in the first book of *On Christian Teaching*.

His central claim is that all of Scripture has a single, overarching purpose: to lead its reader to *caritas* (1.36.40). For Augustine this word, usually translated "charity," means a twofold love: towards our neighbor, and towards God. We should also bear love towards ourselves, but Augustine thinks that no one needs to be instructed in that respect. All humans naturally love themselves, as we can see from their instinct for self-preservation (1.24.25). We do, however, need to be taught, indeed constantly reminded and persuaded, to love God and our fellow man. This message is conveyed so clearly and emphatically in the Bible that it can serve as a measuring-stick against which to assess interpretations of any specific passage. If the overall point of the Bible is to lead us to charity, we can be certain that no interpretation inconsistent with charity could be correct. Most obviously, if a passage seems to imply that we should harm our fellow man, then we must resort to allegorical interpretation (e.g. 3.16.24). Of course, there might be more than one allegorical interpretation possible. But so long as these interpretations would promote charity, we can be relaxed about accepting any of them. Augustine even suggests that God predicted that different readers would adopt these various interpretations, so that in a sense all of them could be correct (3.27.38).

Let's try to bring together this work, *On Christian Teaching*, with the theory of learning we found in *On the Teacher*. There we saw Augustine saying that signs cannot give us knowledge but only beliefs. We may then reflect for ourselves, and ultimately turn those beliefs into knowledge thanks to the light of inner truth. Augustine seems to be thinking more or less along the same lines in his handbook on interpreting Scripture. At least, he says in one striking passage that someone who has been confirmed in faith, hope, and charity has no further need of the Scriptures, unless it is to teach others (1.39.43). Furthermore, he again states here that God's assistance is needed to benefit from teaching. And yet, it is worthwhile for one human to teach another—especially if the teaching is based upon the Scriptures— just as it is sensible to administer medicine, even if no one recovers from illness without God willing it (4.16.33).

Something we did not find in *On the Teacher*, though, was the idea that there is really only one thing worth learning. Now, in *On Christian Teaching*, Augustine not only rejects readings of Scripture inconsistent with charity. He seems to dismiss any intellectual activity that fails to help us achieve this aim. This emerges in a sustained discussion of what is and is not worth keeping from pagan writings. Augustine begins with the sentiment that whatever truth has been found by the pagans should be embraced by Christians (2.18.28). But if all truths are equal in this respect, some truths are apparently more equal than others. Detailed knowledge of astronomy, for instance, is to be avoided, because it doesn't help us understand Scripture and might also lead us along the wicked paths of astrology (2.29.46). These were paths Augustine himself traveled as a young man, as we know from the *Confessions*. Overall, Augustine tells his fellow Christians, the right approach to pagan wisdom is the attitude the Israelites took towards Egyptian treasure. They spurned the Egyptians' pagan idols, but happily made off with their gold and other valuables, so as to make better use of them than the Egyptians themselves could (2.40.60). Augustine mentions the Platonists in particular as having provided material worth commandeering for use in Christian teaching.

Here too we can think back to the *Confessions*, which told of how the "books of the Platonists" helped free Augustine from his materialist beliefs. The *Confessions* also illustrate that, for Augustine, the Platonist books are good enough to help interpret the Good Book. He caps his autobiography not only with the philosophical discussion of time we looked at in the last chapter, but also with a detailed reading of the opening verses of Genesis (*Confessions* 12.1.1 and following). At least three of the points he makes here are drawn from his study of Platonist philosophy. First, God is eternal, in Plotinus' sense of not being subject to time, even if Genesis gives the contrary impression by speaking of "days of creation." In fact, time was created along with the physical universe. Second, we can understand the opening sentence of Genesis, "In the beginning God created the heaven and the earth," with the help of Platonist metaphysics. Augustine connects this "heaven" to a phrase found in the Psalms, the "heaven of heaven" (12.13.16). This represents for him an intelligible realm of forms created by God, but still eternal, again in the sense of being above time. Third, Genesis goes on to speak of earth being "without form." This Augustine understands in light of a theory of matter like that of Plotinus, as being utterly formless. Again he opposes this Platonist idea to the more crass, physical imaginings of his own youth, when he was under the sway of the Manicheans (12.6.6).

In keeping with the interpretive theory of *On Christian Doctrine*, here in the *Confessions* Augustine is open to the possibility that other interpretations may be possible. So long as the message that emerges from an interpretation is true, mission accomplished (12.18.27). In fact, Augustine seems to suggest that the Bible necessarily gives rise to multiple interpretations. So concise is its expression, here in Genesis and elsewhere, that it is like a powerful jet of water coming from a confined source. Thus many interpreters may be needed to unfold its entire meaning (12.27.37). But of course, one needs to be careful that one does not defend an interpretation out of pride of ownership, rather than because one's interpretation is true. Reading the Bible should be a cooperative effort carried out by the whole community, not a competition. In a virtuous circle, the charitable attitude taught by Scripture is necessary if we are to take the right attitude towards the very task of interpreting Scripture. Augustine's openness to other interpretations is, of course, itself an example of this correct, charitable attitude.

So how do the Platonist philosophical points that Augustine extracts from the opening of Genesis fit into his overall account of the Bible? In what sense do I become a more charitable person by realizing that matter is formless, or that God is eternal and beyond time? The answer is simple: because it helps me love God. When Augustine came to recognize God as a transcendent creator, who creates formless matter and then fashions a world out of that matter, he left behind the dualist teachings of the Manicheans. This meant accepting that the entire world is itself a kind of sign, pointing towards a Creator who has no opposing principle. This is only one example of Augustine's conviction that even rather advanced metaphysical truths of philosophy are inextricably bound up with issues of morality. To believe in a principle of evil is to fall short of an appreciation of the good, and thus to fall short of goodness.

Augustine therefore sees a powerful link, if not an identity, between the search for knowledge and the search for goodness. So we should not be surprised to discover a parallel between his views on language and his famous teaching on the will. We've seen in this chapter that, for Augustine, language by itself cannot bring us to knowledge. For that we need the involvement of God dwelling within us. Likewise, he believes that we cannot be good without the assistance of God. All humans are born into a state of sin, and no matter how admirable their intentions, they will fall back into sin over and over again if left to their own resources. Even once someone converts to Christianity and receives baptism, every day will still be a struggle against temptation. Augustine makes this point vividly in his *Confessions*—what he confesses is not just youthful weakness and indiscretion, but an ongoing susceptibility to the allure of sin. This brings us to another problem. It is perhaps the greatest problem of Augustine's philosophy, and one that will persist in the subsequent history of Christianity: if only God's help can allow us to avoid evil, can we really say that we retain morally significant freedom?

HELP WANTED
AUGUSTINE ON FREEDOM

Everyone says things they regret. The politician, committing an embarrassing gaffe during a debate. The child, casually letting slip to her babysitter that if her parents were home she would have been in bed a long time ago. Eve saying to Adam, "sure, I know he's a serpent; but I think he makes some good points." But not many people sit down, look over everything they've written, and compose an entire book listing places where they might have chosen their words more carefully. Augustine did. A few years before his death in AD 430 Augustine composed the *Reconsiderations*, in Latin *Retractiones*, which survey his own major writings and single out passages for correction or further comment. This would have been no small task. His writings were staggeringly extensive. An aged Augustine was himself stunned to see, when he counted them up, that he'd written 232 works.[1] But however large the task, Augustine had a good reason to reconsider his words. They had been thrown back at him by opponents, who gleefully seized on passages in Augustine's earlier books. Look, they would say, our view is so reasonable that Augustine himself agreed with it only a few years ago.

One example was a work Augustine finished writing in 391, called *On Free Choice of the Will*. Looking back on it, Augustine admits that he did not always state his ideas about freedom and divine grace as fully as he might have. But he is adamant that his opponents are wrong to see the earlier Augustine as an ally. Opponents were something Augustine never had in short supply. We've already seen him telling the story of his disenchantment with the Manicheans in the *Confessions*, and he went on to write numerous works attacking them. In fact, throughout Augustine's mature career he was always writing attacks on some group or other. This side of Augustine's persona can seem rather unpleasant. As the scholar J. J. O'Donnell said, "a man who could go forty-three years from conversion to his grave without ever a moment when one or another polemical work was not on his plate...must surely be thought to be part of the problem, not part of the solution."[2] But this was an age of polemical dispute, and Augustine was far from unusual in turning his finely honed rhetorical skills to the task of written refutation. Augustine's case was unique in another respect, though. The theological positions he staked out in the course of these debates became fundamental to western Christianity, as we see it in the medieval age, in the Protestant Reformation, and still today.

Apart from the Manicheans, he had two main groups of antagonists: the Donatists and the Pelagians. The Donatists emerged decades before Augustine's birth. They were born out of the anti-Christian persecutions that occurred at the dawn of the fourth century. The emperor Diocletian had commanded Christians to engage in sacrifice to the traditional Roman gods, and to hand over church property and copies of the sacred Scriptures to the pagan authorities. Members of the clergy who complied were denounced by hardliners, leading to a split in the church. The church of the hardliners was named after Donatus, a bishop of Carthage. The "Donatist" movement taught that priests who were guilty of collaboration could no longer perform a legitimate baptism, because they were corrupted by sin. They also believed that Christians may need to be baptized a second time, to cleanse them of sins committed after their initial baptism. The Donatist church was particularly strong in northern Africa, where Augustine was born and where he became a bishop. He devoted a great deal of energy to destroying it. His influence prevailed at a council held at Carthage in 411, which condemned Donatism, and he enthusiastically supported a new imperial edict which (rather ironically, given the origin of the movement) persecuted the Donatists by outlawing their faith and making their property subject to confiscation.

Though Augustine's support for this merciless treatment is not attractive, one can see why he found Donatism pernicious. Not only had it led to schism, but its counsel of perfection threatened to undermine the most basic functions of the church. If the Donatists were right, one would need to know the state of a priest's soul in order to be sure one had been successfully baptized. Worse, even a successful baptism could be only temporary, since it could be undone by sin. Augustine's objection was not only practical, though. Where the Donatists saw the church as a separate community, purified of sin and destined for heaven, Augustine thought that, baptism or no, humans remain prone to sin and constantly in need of God's support to resist that temptation. In the *Confessions* (especially Book 10) he describes his daily struggle against the lure of various pleasures, from food to music to sex. This is not just confession, but a way of making a broader point. Theological conviction and personal experience taught him that the tendency towards sin is an unavoidable part of human life, not something that can be washed away in a single ritual. Baptism is still necessary of course. But rather than signifying the elimination of sinful desires, it signifies an openness to God's help in overcoming those desires.

So, despite his reputation as a grim and demanding moralist, in this debate Augustine was actually leading a fight against moral perfectionism. The same is true of his polemic against the Pelagians.[3] The Pelagians were a group of more recent origin, named after Augustine's contemporary Pelagius (who is, incidentally, the first thinker mentioned in this history of philosophy to hail from Britain). The core of their teaching was that if God commands us to be good, it must be within our power to be good. After all, it makes no sense to command people to do things they are not in a position to do. If I command you to finish reading this chapter, then you have the ability to comply. But if I command you to transform yourself into a giraffe, you'll reject my demand as being not just silly but impossible. Pelagius further argued that in order to be in a position to follow God's command, humans must possess a capacity for free will. It is in everyone's power to come to virtue by exerting this power of choice. His view was taken up by Julian, bishop of the town of Eclanum in southern Italy. Julian became the main opponent and target of Augustine, who wrote a series of increasingly hostile and polemical works against the Pelagian doctrine.

In Augustine's view the Pelagians, like the Donatists, were undermining the whole point of the Christian faith. If, as they claimed, the human will is sovereign and capable of resisting sin all on its own, then why does God need to send His son and allow him to be sacrificed? In fact God doesn't need to do anything at all. He can just wait to see who achieves goodness and who doesn't, through the exercise of free will, and then dispense reward and punishment as appropriate. On the Pelagian view, Christ seems to be sent as a moral teacher who encourages us towards virtue, rather than as the indispensable source of salvation. That's a view we found some of the more intellectualist Church Fathers flirting with, so it is no surprise to see it turning up here in Pelagianism. Against this, Augustine drew above all on the writings of St Paul to set forth what may be his most influential teaching, the doctrine of original sin. You will probably be familiar with the basic idea, which is that the sin of Adam is somehow inherited or shared by all subsequent humans. Only the sacrifice of God's son and, more generally, His gift of divine grace can allow humans to overcome their fallen state. Thus Augustine argued, in direct opposition to the Pelagian view, that we humans do *not* have the capacity to merit salvation on our own. We can only follow God's command to be good if God helps us to do so.

An obvious problem with Augustine's anti-Pelagian position is the difficulty of reconciling it with the possibility of free will. That humans do possess free will, and free will that is morally significant, is a fundamental theme throughout Augustine's writings. His early treatise *On Free Choice of the Will*, the one quoted back at him by Pelagian opponents, could hardly be more emphatic in recognizing the reality of freedom.[4] The work takes the form of a dialogue between Augustine and a friend named Evodius, who had been present at the death of Augustine's mother Monica, and who, like Augustine, went on to be a bishop. At this point in his career the opponents who trouble Augustine are not yet the Pelagians but the Manicheans, who believed that suffering in the world is caused by a principle of evil independent of God. Augustine and Evodius want instead to see suffering as a punishment handed down in accordance with divine justice—without human sin, there would be no suffering.

It's at this stage that free will enters the picture. The two agree that no one can be justly punished for something unless he chooses to do it by his own will. We sin, argues Augustine, when we value things here in the temporal realm rather than that which is eternal (1.15). In other works Augustine restates this idea by saying that all sin can be traced to pride. We are prideful when we bestow on created things the esteem that is due to God alone. Here, in On Free Choice of the Will, Augustine instead puts the point in more Platonic language, echoing Plotinus by contrasting the unchanging eternal realm to the world of bodily, time-bound things. But like Plotinus himself, he depends on arguments that originate with the Stoics. He contends that temporal things should not be valued, because they can be taken away from us, and that control of one's own happiness and one's own will depends on valuing what is not vulnerable in this way. For seasoned historians of philosophy like us, Epictetus leaps inevitably to mind. And the Epictetan flavor of the work is one reason Pelagian opponents could find material here to embarrass the older Augustine. He remarks, for instance, that the virtuous mind cannot be enslaved to desire (1.11), and that virtue can be had merely by willing it (1.13). These remarks fit better with the demanding moral strictures of Stoicism and Pelagianism than the theory of grace Augustine will offer in coming years.

Since Evodius is not a Pelagian, he has a rather different point to press in his dialogue with Augustine (2.1). If it is the power of free will that enables us to sin, then why did God give us this power in the first place? This question sets the agenda for the rest of the work. Augustine's goal will be not so much to vindicate the reality of free will, but to demonstrate that God is not to blame for any evil we see in the created world. And he does owe us an explanation here. Having rejected the Manichean solution of explaining evil and suffering by appealing to a second principle, opposed to God, he must show that all badness can instead be traced ultimately to human choice. Anything bad must be an evil directly willed by humans, or be sent as a just punishment from God for prior evils willed by humans. Hence Evodius' question: why did God give us free will, if it leads to such horrendous results? We saw that in his Confessions Augustine embraced Plotinus' account of evil as deficiency or non-being. He accepted this solution to the "metaphysical problem of evil," the problem of how anything bad can arise in a world that derives solely from a good cause. Here in *On Free Choice of the Will*, by contrast, Augustine is tackling something closer to the modern problem of evil—that is, why a good and omnipotent being would allow evil.

This difficulty arises for him, as it did not for Plotinus, because he assumes that God is a free agent who could have arranged things in a very different way. He could, for instance, have decided not to create free creatures, foreseeing the evil they would do. So why did He create us nevertheless? Augustine's answer is simple: God gives us free will so that we can use it to be good. When we sin, we are misusing this power. But we should no more conclude that the will itself is bad than we would think that our eyes or hands are bad because they can be used to commit evil (2.18). Indeed, it makes no sense to complain that God makes it possible for us to sin. By definition, sin is what God does not want. So if we sin, it must be because we are departing from what God intended us to do with the powers He has granted to us (3.16). Thus the human will is, as Augustine terms it, an "intermediary good." This means it is necessary for goodness, yet can be used for evil. In this the will falls between greater goods that are necessary for good and never used for evil, like virtue, and lesser goods, like the goods of the body. The latter are, as the Stoics said, not even necessary for living a good life (2.19).

But Evodius sees another problem looming (3.2). Even if it was not a mistake for God to give us free will, how was it possible for Him to do so? After all, He knows everything we will do before we do it. How, then, can we be free? If Augustine himself could have seen the future, he would have known that this so-called "problem of divine foreknowledge" would be discussed again and again by philosophers, down through medieval times and into early modernity. But a non-theological version of the problem had already been posed before Augustine. Aristotle's work *On Interpretation* presents the so-called "sea-battle argument," which asked: if it is true now that there will be a sea-battle tomorrow, then is occurrence of the sea-battle inevitable and hence necessary?[5] Augustine is considering more or less the same issue.[6] He adds, however, that God *knows* there will be a sea-battle tomorrow. This changes things in two ways. First, one solution available to Aristotle was to deny that there are present truths about such future events. But that solution is now taken off the table; there must be a present truth, because God already knows it. Second, it may make a difference that we have introduced divine *knowledge* rather than mere truth. For if God really has knowledge of a future sea-battle, then He has total certainty about it. He simply can't be wrong. One might suppose that this certainty yields the necessity of the sea-battle, even if mere truth wouldn't.

Another difference is that Augustine's discussion is narrower than Aristotle's. He is concerned not with all truths about the future, but only God's knowledge of what people are going to *will*. The solution he offers will work only for this case. He tells Evodius that it is incoherent to worry that God's knowledge necessitates anyone to will anything. For no one can will anything if he is necessitated (3.3). Now, this solution looks rather inadequate. Evodius should respond to Augustine by saying, "I am not anxious that God necessitates me to choose *freely*, or to *will* anything. Rather, I am anxious that because God foreknows what I will do, I do not do it by free choice or by will, even if it seems to me that I do." Evodius doesn't press the issue in this way. If he had, Augustine might respond that it is simply obvious that we do exercise will. This shows that we are not being necessitated, by God's knowledge or anything else. Something else Augustine actually does say might help, which is that in general no one makes anything happen by knowing it will happen (3.4). If I tell you that I will introduce another example involving a giraffe pretty soon, then you might thereby know I will do it, but your knowing this doesn't force me to do it. So if the worry is merely that God *causally necessitates* our actions, this worry is misplaced. Again, that response doesn't eliminate the whole problem of divine foreknowledge, but it might be enough to secure Augustine what he is after in this work, namely to show that God is not responsible for our evil choices.

Can Augustine still absolve God of blame later in his career, once he has developed his doctrine of original sin against the Pelagians? According to this doctrine, I cannot be good unless God offers me the assistance of grace. Doesn't that mean that if God decides not to help me, I am condemned to sin? After all, without grace I quite literally cannot choose to be good, or at least cannot be effective in so choosing. At best, I will be in the situation Augustine so memorably describes in his *Confessions*: wanting to convert to virtue and purity but unable to do so because of my lingering sinful desires. Here's a possible solution.[7] Even if I cannot have a good will without God's help, perhaps I can without His help *wish* to have a good will. This wish is what philosophers nowadays call a "second-order desire," meaning a desire about another desire. A standard example is wanting to quit smoking. The simple desire to smoke is a "first-order desire"; the desire to lose this desire to smoke would be second-order. There are also second-order beliefs, as when I believe that my belief that giraffes are tall is a true belief. (See, you were right: I did introduce another example involving a giraffe. It was inevitable.) Now, using this terminology, we can say that even if we can't help having sinful first-order desires for sex, wealth, and so on, we can at least form the second-order desire that these first-order desires go away. As we know from the *Confessions*, that is exactly what Augustine so fervently hoped in the time leading up to his conversion. Already in *On Free Choice of the Will* Augustine speaks of second-order desires. He speaks about the will's ability to apply to itself, that is, to have a will to will something or not to will it (2.19).

Perhaps we can now solve the dilemma faced by Augustine. We can say that it is in my power to will to have a good will, and when I do, God steps in and helps me to have a good will. To put this in terms of the terminology just introduced, my sinful state stops me from having good first-order desires, but I am able to have good second-order desires, which God rewards by changing my first-order desires from bad to good. This would fit well with Augustine's earlier remark that I can be good simply by willing to be good. But the solution presupposes two things, neither of which Augustine can accept once he sets his face against Pelagianism. First, we have assumed that God *must* help whoever wants their first-order desires to change. But grace is a gift, not something to be received on demand. Even if God is merciful and does always help those who ask for grace, He does not have to do so. Besides, as made clear in Augustine's polemic against the Donatists, it isn't as if we can expect God to change our will from sinful to righteous overnight. Rather, the struggle against bad desire and corrupt will is a lifelong one, to be fought one day at a time. Even more problematic is a further assumption of our attempted solution, namely that I can have a good second-order desire on my own, without God's help. Augustine would see this as smuggling in Pelagianism through the back door. Rather, he would say that all human willing, whether first- or second-order, requires God's help if it is to choose the good reliably.

So how can Augustine escape the accusation, pressed by Julian of Eclanum on behalf of the Pelagians, that his God is in fact an unjust monster? This God punishes us for sins we cannot avoid, and our inability to avoid those sins is the result of an original error that was committed not by us, but by Adam. A full response would take us too deep into the realms of Augustine's theology. But a short version of his answer is simply that when somebody wills evil, they are doing exactly what they want. That's the whole point of willing, after all. As Epictetus already pointed out, no one, not even God, can force you to will anything. The fact that you were not in a position to have a better will does not absolve you of the disgrace, the moral failure, and hence the blameworthiness of willing evil. So all we can do is fervently pray for God's assistance, and fervently praise Him for giving us the capacity to will itself. For this capacity can be used to choose rightly, at least if God does assist us. With His help, we can turn away from earthly things and towards unchanging, eternal goods. When we do so our values are transformed, and aligned with those of another community, a heavenly society. This society gives its name to one of Augustine's greatest works: the *City of God*.

50

HEAVEN AND EARTH
AUGUSTINE'S *CITY OF GOD*

B y now you are hopefully getting a sense of how Augustine's writings respond to other, lesser-known Church Fathers. Augustine's love–hate relationship towards Cicero and other Latin stylists is shared by his contemporary Jerome, and Lactantius anticipates the emphasis on the virtue of charity we find in Augustine's interpretive manual *On Christian Teaching*. And the Augustinian position on freedom and sin responds not only to his opponents the Pelagians, but also to an idea put forward by Tertullian. You'll remember that, for Tertullian, the soul is a material substance, a sort of breath. On this basis, he argued that soul is physically transferred to each child by the child's father, a belief known as "traducianism."[1] This explains the weakness of our human souls. Had they been instead created by God, they would be perfect. Against this, Augustine held that God does create each human soul directly. Yet he insisted that all humans share in the sin of their original forefather, Adam. This Augustinian doctrine of original sin can also be understood as an alternative to Origen's theory that originally perfect souls fell as the result of intellectual failure. Augustine agreed with Jerome that this was the wrong way to reconcile divine justice with human imperfection.

Augustine attacks Origen's ideas in what may be his most ambitious single work: the *City of God* (at 11.23).[2] A gargantuan treatise in no fewer than twenty-two books, the *City of God* is in part an attack on paganism, not unlike the attack staged by Lactantius. The immediate occasion of the work came not from Augustine's intellectual context but his historical context. It was written in the wake of one of the most traumatic events to befall the empire during his lifetime: the fall of Rome to the army of the Gothic king Alaric in the year 410. Like a kind-hearted boss, Alaric was actually rather reluctant in giving Rome the sack. He did so to extract concessions and recognition from the empire, not to bring the empire to its knees, so the sacking of the city was more restrained than it might have been. Still, the symbolism of the event was impossible to ignore. Augustine tells us that pagans in this era complaining about dry weather would say, "no rain—it's the Christians' fault!" (2.3).

If Christians could even be blamed when rain didn't fall, they could certainly be blamed when Rome did fall. It was divine payback, the pagans said, for the empire's adoption of Christianity and abandonment of the gods who had protected Rome since its founding.

The *City of God* begins by refuting this accusation, but it certainly doesn't end there. Over the course of the twenty-two books Augustine has time to survey Roman history, to mock pagan belief, to envision what awaits us in the afterlife, indeed to recount the entire story of mankind, beginning with the Garden of Eden. In Book 8 he even provides a concise history of philosophy, beginning with the Pre-Socratics. (Good thing that Augustine lived such a long time ago—that kind of competition I definitely don't need.) Still, his first order of business is to absolve Christianity of responsibility for depriving Rome of its divine defense system. He describes some of the disasters that befell Rome long before Christianity came along, such as the civil wars that led to the fall of the Republic. Cleverly using the pagans' literary hero Homer against them, he also points out that if pagan gods could protect cities, then Troy would not have been burnt down by the Greeks (3.2).

He rebuts the accusation at a more philosophical level too, echoing the value system of the Stoics when he remarks that only a fool would think that defeat in war or the sack of a city is the worst of disasters (4.2). The real calamity is moral depravity, and Rome succumbed to the forces of immorality long before Alaric came along. Again, Augustine is able to turn the pagans' own literature against them here. Aristocratic Romans constantly lamented that the moral fiber of their society unraveled when the Republic gave way to Empire. Augustine gleefully quotes passages from Cicero to this effect (2.21), and reminds us that this transition occurred before Christ was even born, never mind Christianity coming to dominate the empire. Similarly, he alludes to Plato's *Republic* and its critique of tragedy when he is decrying the debauchery of Roman theatrical performances (2.14, 8.13).

This polemic may seem to be of limited interest for us—philosophers being quoted simply to score points in a cultural debate. But in fact we are being subtly introduced to the main theme of the *City of God*, which is crucial for the history of philosophy. Augustine divides his discussion of Rome's failings into two parts, one dealing with earthly concerns like the sacking of cities, the other with the more fundamental questions of virtue and vice. This mirrors another contrast that gives the work its name, the contrast between the city of man and the city of God. The city of God is eternal and its members seek eternal blessedness. The city of man is earthly in its concerns, and its members seek happiness in this life. Augustine traces these two cities back to the dawn of man, and then further still. The pride characteristic of the earthly city began with the fallen angels, while the good angels are the most outstanding citizens of the eternal city. Among the earliest humans, the city of man is associated especially with Cain, who slew his brother Abel. Augustine makes sure to remind us that another fratricide occurred at the founding of Rome, when Romulus killed Remus (15.5).

To tell the rest of this tale of two cities, Augustine devotes a large section of the City of God to a history of mankind, based mostly on the Old Testament. He is not afraid to digress, dwelling on such topics as the practical arrangements on board Noah's Ark (15.27). Unfortunately Augustine doesn't address my main question, which is whether the two giraffes had a special berth with high ceilings. He does, however, ask whether the boat was really big enough to hold all those animals. And what did the carnivorous animals eat? (Augustine suggests chestnuts.) But the overall goal of Augustine's City of God is not to figure out whether goats and sheep were safe from lions and tigers on the Ark. It is to separate sheep and goats in a more figurative sense, by defending the values of the eternal city and exposing the fraudulence of the city of man. To do that, Augustine needs to criticize not just the religious beliefs of pagans but the core values of the society they have built. Along the way he will expose the failure of philosophers who attempted to provide rational support for this pagan culture.

In doing so, he draws inspiration from the pagan historian Varro. He serves as a foil for Augustine throughout much of the City of God. Rather amusingly, given his own prolific writing career, Augustine marvels at Varro's output and wonders whether anyone could read everything that he wrote (6.2). Augustine discusses pagan society first in terms of "human affairs," and then with regard to "divine affairs," an opposition already used by Varro (4.1, 6.3). We already know that Augustine was unimpressed by pagan society when it came to human affairs—the theatrical shows and so on. But he also delivers a penetrating analysis of Roman political history. Why did the Romans expand their realm, subjugating one people after another until their empire stretched from Britain to Mesopotamia? For the sake of glory: the glory that comes through victory, claimed on behalf of some general or emperor, or of Rome itself.

Though Augustine sees the lust for glory as the characteristically Roman sin (5.13), it is only a version of the sin that besets all mankind, the sin of pride. We are prideful when we bestow an esteem on created things that belongs rightfully to God. Augustine remarks that in the earthly city, love of self leads to contempt for God; whereas in the eternal city, love of God leads to contempt of self (14.28). Yet it is not necessarily a sin to love oneself. In fact Augustine thinks we cannot help loving ourselves. We should also love our fellow human beings. But we should love ourselves and other humans as created things, referring this love to God the Creator.

By instead pursuing glory above all else, the Romans have shown that they valued themselves, or their empire, in God's place. That's the bad news for the Romans, and in Augustine's opinion news doesn't get much worse.

But there's good news too, because the single-minded quest for glory can help one to avoid other evils.[3] The outstanding men of Rome, especially in its earlier history, were capable of great self-sacrifice, willing to suffer and even die for the sake of renown. This renown was in the end worthless, and military conquests of no real value either to the conqueror or the conquered (5.17). Yet Augustine gives a kind of grudging respect to the great men of the Roman Republic. What they pursued may have been pointless, but they pursued it with relentless self-discipline, and gained an earthly dominion as their reward. He thus favorably compares the love of glory to the mere love of dominion or political power. Sheer lust for power is compatible with open debauchery and criminality—here he may be thinking of figures like Commodus or Caligula. Those who seek glory instead act well, because they want to be admired (5.19). Augustine's remarks on honor resonate with those of Aristotle, who argued that one should not value honor, but rather value being the sort of person who would *rightfully* be honored.

So glory-lovers make better rulers than lovers of power. But that doesn't mean they make good rulers. Augustine observes that many Roman military campaigns were undertaken mostly to win prestige. Glory-seekers thus initiate needless violence, with horrendous consequences for everyone else concerned. A good ruler would instead look to the true welfare of his people. Predictably, Augustine sees Christian rulers like Constantine as paradigm examples of excellent leadership (5.25). Even though he excludes political rule from the goals of the city of God, he thinks the best political rulers are those who pursue the goal of eternal life. That exemplifies a tension that runs throughout the *City of God*. Augustine dismisses even the most basic physical needs as being of little importance compared to the need to improve one's soul. For instance, at one point he remarks that it is obviously preferable to be enslaved to another human than to one's own desires (19.15). In this same passage he indicates that slavery is unnatural and a result of sin, but gives no sign that it might be a Christian's duty to try to eliminate the practice of slavery, or even to free a single slave if the possibility arises. In such passages Augustine seems disturbingly quietist—so concerned with dismissing the importance of earthly goods that no earthly evil can shock him into recommending political action.

Yet Augustine clearly does think it matters whether people suffer, are enslaved, go hungry. He emphasizes the good results that follow here on earth when political rule is founded in Christian piety. And at the level of the individual, he says that the man who belongs to the city of God will help others and never do harm (19.14).

For such a man loves God and shares God's love of other men. These remarks, of course, fit well with the praise of charity we observed in *On Christian Teaching*. And to some extent Augustine practiced what he preached. He tried to use his position as a bishop for good, and he had ample opportunity to do so, since an ancient bishopric involved not just preaching but significant legal authority. We also find him writing a letter that laments the abduction of free people who are sold as slaves.[4] But it strikes me that he was more interested in crusading against, say, the false theological doctrines of the Pelagians and Donatists than against the violent treatment of women or the practice of slavery. The *City of God* helps to explain this. Here Augustine argues that humans have no hope of stamping out evils in this life. The city of God, unlike the city of man, knows its limits. The rather half-hearted commitment to practical action that results, both at the political and individual level, is reminiscent of what we find in Plotinus. Indeed, Augustine echoes Plotinus' point that those who fight in wars, even wars in a just cause, see themselves as impelled by a regrettable necessity, rather than given a welcome chance to display courage or other virtues (19.7).[5]

This is not to say that the *City of God* was intended as an endorsement of Plotinus' philosophy. Far from it. In fact it contains some of Augustine's most direct criticisms of the Platonists. He admits that the Platonists came closest to articulating the values embraced by citizens of the heavenly city (8.5). But this just makes it more disappointing that they failed in the end. Augustine thinks that Plato, Plotinus, and Porphyry all recognized the reality of a single divine cause, and gives Porphyry in particular extra credit for expressing doubts about the pagan ritual practices of theurgy in the *Letter to Anebo* (10.11; see Chapter 34). Yet the Platonists persisted in accepting a multiplicity of deities. This began with Plato himself, whose dialogue *Timaeus* speaks of lesser gods who assist the divine craftsman in creating the world (12.25). Closer to Augustine's own day, Porphyry lost his nerve and failed to reject theurgy entirely, or to abolish the other divinities and accept the one true God (10.24).

Augustine has already mocked the absurdities of the pagan gods earlier in the *City of God*. He enjoys himself tremendously as he describes the various minor divinities needed for a pagan marriage: one god to lead the bride home, another to keep her faithful to her husband, and the god Priapus, whose responsibilities can't be explained without adding a parental-advisory sticker to the cover of this book. How, Augustine wonders, can the young couple enjoy their wedding-night with this crowd of gods standing around watching (6.9)? More importantly, how can the Platonists lend their intellectual credibility to such absurd religious beliefs? The same goes for Varro, who supplied Augustine not only with historical information but also ample discussion of pagan religion. Varro was too wise a man to accept such beliefs at face value, and was quietly critical of the building of idols and other pagan practices (4.9, see also 4.31). But like Porphyry, who should also have known better, he fell short of the true monotheism championed by the Jews and Christians.

Augustine's criticism of Hellenic philosophy goes deeper than this, though. If he is really to expose the false promises of the city of man, he must show that no earthly realm and no earthly life can lead us to happiness. The Platonists and the Stoics taught that the wise man can achieve blessedness in this life, by freeing himself of emotion and placing no value on earthly things. Augustine uses all his rhetorical powers against these claims in the *City of God*, asking whether it is really credible that someone could be subjected to extreme physical tortures or the ravages of illness and still count himself happy (19.4). Nor should we aspire to the emotionless state of *apatheia* praised by the Stoics.[6] Augustine is frankly appalled by the suggestion that one could fail to grieve over the death of a beloved friend (19.8), a point given added resonance by the tales of grief over the death of a good friend and of his son Adeodatus in the *Confessions*. But what about a life of virtue, identified as the highest good by Aristotle and also by Varro (19.3)? Admirable though virtue may be, in this life it consists an unceasing battle against evil, whether the evils done by others or the evil within oneself. This can hardly be the basis of true happiness.

It seems, then, that the Hellenic philosophical schools offer us no path to supreme blessedness, but only a lesson in withstanding adversity. Augustine has not given up the idea that philosophy should be the pursuit of happiness, but he has abandoned the notion that happiness can be attained in this life. One might imagine a city of men more enlightened than Rome, which would pursue justice and peace instead of glory. But no earthly realm can promise permanent peace and felicity. That reward is given only to those who live in the city of God, and not in this life but in the eternal hereafter. Who among us, then, are the citizens of the eternal city, the ones who will be truly happy? For now, we cannot tell. It is tempting to assume that the earthly representation of this city is the Christian church, but that is not Augustine's view. It would be more like the position of his rivals the Donatists, who saw their church as something like a walled city, separating the righteous few from the sinful multitude. For Augustine, a staunch critic of the Donatists, joining a church cannot exempt one from the empty seductions of the earthly city. In fact, in theory at least, there could already have been citizens of the city of God before the time of Jesus, never mind the institutions of the church, though Augustine thinks that such people would have needed a special revelation of Christ's saving grace (18.47). The upshot is that in this world the two cities are mixed together. Only in the afterlife will we find out who is a sheep and who a goat (see 1.35).

But it seems pretty clear that the pagan philosophers, at least, are goats (maybe that's why they insisted on wearing beards). Augustine accuses even the best of them, the Platonists, of using their powerful intellects for prideful ends. In the *Confessions* Augustine spoke of being helped by Platonists to understand how God could be an immaterial substance. But here, in the *City of God*, he attacks the Platonists' presumption in identifying themselves with such immaterial substances. Humans are not just souls, but souls inhabiting bodies. The Platonists should have marveled at the way that God has fused the soul with the body (22.4). Instead, they marveled at themselves, pridefully claiming the status of an elite few, who alone among humans could free themselves from bodily concerns. Augustine throws this accusation at Porphyry, among others, suggesting that he reserved true intellectual purification for philosophers like himself, while condescendingly allowing lesser humans to participate in the profane practices of theurgy. Nonetheless, Augustine continues to make use of Platonist themes and metaphors. Platonists frequently described themselves as exiles or as prisoners, longing to flee the body and return to the intelligible world. Augustine instead speaks of the city of God itself as a captive here on earth, or as being on a pilgrimage (19.17). Augustine urges us to become, not separate souls freed from evil by individual effort, but members of a human society that gratefully receives an undeserved salvation.

These are just a few examples of the way the *City of God* critically responds to the wisdom of the Greeks, and especially of Plato and his disciples. Augustine is inspired by the Platonists, yet disappointed too. Of all the Greeks, they came closest to recognizing the one true God, but instead they embraced pagan belief. Ironically, they could have understood God more fully had they obeyed the inscription at their own temple in Delphi: "Know thyself." For every human is an image of God, and knowing the nature of oneself is a path to knowing the divine. Augustine traveled this path, and wrote a guidebook for those who were willing to follow him. It is probably the greatest work of ancient Christian philosophy: *On the Trinity*.

ME, MYSELF, AND I
AUGUSTINE ON MIND
AND MEMORY

In the *City of God* Augustine claims that no one can doubt his own existence. If anyone, perhaps a member of the Skeptical Academy, should claim that even this is doubtful, we can reply that it is incoherent to imagine someone thinking he exists and being mistaken about it. After all, no one can be mistaken without existing. Thus, as Augustine puts it, *si fallor, sum*: "if I err, then I exist." Sound familiar? It seems to be a version of the most famous three-word Latin argument in the history of philosophy, *cogito, ergo sum*: "I think, therefore I am." Indeed, when Descartes put forward the argument in his *Meditations*, some of his readers pointed out that the same idea had already appeared in Augustine.[1] But Descartes' use of the argument had at least one advantage over Augustine's: he used it in a very prominent place, as the crucial first step towards dispelling total skepticism. Where did Augustine put it? In the twenty-sixth chapter of the eleventh of the twenty-two books of the absurdly long *City of God*. In the newspaper trade, they call that burying the lead.

In fact, this buried Augustinian treasure isn't even the main point Augustine is making in the twenty-sixth chapter of that eleventh book. It's more a digression, occasioned by his observation that the human mind is an image of the divine Trinity. All of us mirror the threeness of God by existing, knowing we exist, and loving the fact that we exist. Typical Augustine, in more than one way. Not only is a philosophical nugget delivered in a theological wrapping, but it is uncovered through reflection on Augustine's own self. Though Epictetus and Plotinus are worthy candidates for the title, probably no other ancient philosopher was as keen an observer of his own mental life as Augustine. Again and again, he solves theological and philosophical problems by turning inward. His reflections on evil are bound up with an almost obsessive preoccupation with his own struggle against sin. His merciless and detailed self-analysis exposes the gaping divide that separates imperfect, created beings like himself from their Creator. But self-knowledge does not only let us see how different we are from God. Inspired by a verse of Genesis (1: 26–7), which asserts that man is created in God's image, Augustine believes that studying human nature will be a big step in the direction of understanding the divine nature.

That, in a nutshell, is the project of *On the Trinity*, Augustine's most philosophically ambitious work and the culmination of his lifelong quest to understand himself. This quest begins with the realization of the mind's immediate access to itself. So it's no wonder that it was Augustine who first discovered the anti-skeptical argument that would reappear centuries later in Descartes—especially since, like Descartes, he also thought hard about the problem of skepticism. Cicero, one of Augustine's main philosophical sources, had been a Skeptic. Early in his writing career Augustine wrote *Against the Academics*, meaning the Skeptics of the New Academy.[2] Here he didn't yet formulate the argument "if I err, I am" found in the *City of God*, but he identified other types of infallible knowledge, including truths of logic and mathematics. In another earlier work, *On Free Choice of the Will*, he does make the point that no one could be mistaken about whether they exist (2.3). It's telling that, as in the *City of God*, the error argument is presented there as a step towards showing something about God, namely that He exists and is the cause of all other things.

In both cases, it would be a distraction for Augustine to draw too much attention to the error argument. Sure, it's a brilliant argument. Really Augustine deserves to be memorialized in countless T-shirts, mugs, and posters, an honor that has instead gone to Descartes alone. (More than one philosophy student has ruined a first date by turning up in an "I drink, therefore I am" shirt.) But as Augustine also says in *On Free Choice of the Will* (1.11, 2.2), he explores philosophical arguments in order to understand more fully what he already believes as a Christian. Thus Augustine's favorite slogan is a biblical quote (Isaiah 7: 9), which you won't see parodied on too many T-shirts or dorm room walls. *Crede, ut intelligas*: "Believe, so that you may understand." Unlike Descartes, he starts not from skepticism but from faith, and he uses philosophy to explain the articles of that faith. This attitude is compatible with, indeed even demands, lengthy and sustained inquiry into standard philosophical topics like the nature of language, ethics, and metaphysics.

Augustine's treatment of the mind is no exception. Like most Hellenic philosophers, he sees reason or the mind as the highest function of the human soul, while the soul in general is a principle of life. As we can see from early writings Augustine devoted to the topic of soul,[3] he follows the Platonists in particular in thinking that the soul is immaterial, and lives on after the death of the body. One of his early works distinguishes seven grades or faculties of the soul.[4] At the bottom are the functions we share even with plants, like the capacity for growth and nourishment. At the upper end we have two functions of the mind: the desire for truth and its attainment. This inclusion of the desire or love for truth at the most exalted level of the life of soul is a sign of more distinctively Augustinian things to come in *On the Trinity*. As we know from Augustine's *On the Teacher*, he thinks we attain knowledge not through instruction by humans, but by turning towards an inner standard of truth. This again looks rather Platonist, and in fact Augustine speaks in several works of immaterial forms that provide regulative principles (*regulae*) for our knowledge. Of course these are not quite Forms as Plato envisioned them—Augustine treats them instead as ideas in God's mind, following the precedent of several so-called "Middle" Platonists like Philo of Alexandria. This puts the Augustinian soul right where it is for other late ancient Platonists, from Plutarch to Plotinus to Proclus (you don't have to have a name starting with P to be a Platonist, but it helps). As an immaterial substance, the soul has an existence superior to that of the body. But it is inferior to the divine, to which it must look in order to have knowledge. Like Tertullian before him, Augustine insists that the soul is not to be put on a par with God. He doesn't go as far as Tertullian, who identified the soul with physical breath to keep it well below the status of divinity. But he does emphasize that soul changes, for example by undergoing moral progress, whereas God is eternal and thus unchanging.[5]

Nonetheless, there is that line in Genesis telling us that we are created in God's image. In addition, there is the Nicene Creed. You'll remember that the Council of Nicaea established a doctrine on the Trinity that became authoritative for many Christians (see Chapter 42). Augustine was one of them. In line with the Creed, and against the Arians, he asserted the total equality of all three Persons of the Trinity, which together make up a single substance. This means that when he examines his own nature as a human in *On the Trinity*, he is not embarking on a dispassionate inquiry into the nature of the soul, its relation to the body, or the workings of the mind, though all those issues do arise and are given subtle and innovative treatment. Rather, Augustine is believing in order to understand. He is looking for a way in which we humans are trinities, that is, substances which by their very nature unify three aspects or functions, just as God is a unity of three Persons. It would be a bonus if the trinity within us had other features echoing those of the divine Trinity. Ideally, we are looking for an aspect of human nature that not only has a Trinitarian structure, but where all three elements in that structure are equal, as the divine Persons are equal, and where the second element is "begotten" by the first, as the Son is begotten by the Father.

It seems a daunting challenge, but Augustine has no trouble reeling off numerous candidates. After devoting the first books of *On the Trinity* to the Scriptural basis and correct understanding of the Trinitarian doctrine itself, he proceeds to investigate a whole series of trinities found in human nature.[6] The examples involve different kinds of perception, awareness, and cognition. Augustine must look to the soul for good examples, because a trinity of bodies could never fit the bill. The bodies would not be in the same place as one another and thus would not truly be a single substance (8.2). The same problem affects sensory perception. Here Augustine does identify a sort of trinity: there is the external object, the perception of that object, and the mind's focus on that object which binds these two together (11.2). Since the thing that is seen is outside the soul, though, this is the wrong kind of trinity. Suppose, for instance, that you are at the zoo and stop to look at a giraffe. The giraffe is separate from and independent of your power of eyesight, as is proven by the fact that when the giraffe lopes back into its pen you can no longer see it.

Cases like this teach Augustine two lessons. The first is that the trinity we seek must be entirely within ourselves. If any of the three members of the human trinity is outside us, it will be separate and independent, like the giraffe. That would be a major disanalogy with the case of the divine Trinity, so we need to avoid it. The second lesson is that human will or intention binds together the mind with its objects. In the case we just looked at, it is the mind's intention to see the giraffe that produces an act of vision. Bringing these two lessons together, a promising strategy might be to look for a case where the mind wills or intends to know something inside itself. And as luck would have it, this happens all the time: whenever I think about something I know, or imagine something, or remember something. In these cases, I am not relying on something outside of me. If I consider the Pythagorean theorem, imagine a giraffe that is painted blue, or remember the name of my favorite high-school teacher, I am turning my mind's attention to what is already inside it. So in all such cases there are three things. First, the mental content—the theorem, the imaginary blue giraffe, or the teacher's name. Second, the mind's grasping of its own content—its thinking about what it knows, imagines, or remembers. Third, the mind's intention or will to grasp its own content with these mental acts. It is this willing that explains why the mind is entertaining the specific content that it has chosen. For instance, I choose to remember the favorite teacher instead of the teacher who made me stay after school that time, just because I was drawing pictures of blue giraffes instead of paying attention in class.

Augustine, in fact, sees memory as particularly crucial for his project. It is involved even in the other cases of knowing and imagining. When we reflect on previously acquired knowledge we are remembering what we know, and when we imagine new things we are combining images we have experienced before, such as blue and giraffe. So Augustine's fascination with memory is part and parcel of his interest in self-knowledge. Not only does memory turn up prominently in On the Trinity, but Augustine discusses it at length in the tenth book of the Confessions.[7] There he speaks of it as a kind of storehouse or treasury for things we have learned or experienced, with a seemingly limitless storage capacity (*Confessions* 10.8). Somehow, the things we can remember stay hidden within the memory until we will them to come forward. This may be more or less difficult, with some things coming to mind immediately, others hovering just out of reach, as when a word is on the tip of the tongue. But is it really the things themselves that are the objects of memory? After all, I can remember things that are no longer present, and even things that no longer exist.

Augustine concludes from this that, at least in some cases, what the memory produces for us is not the thing we remember but an image of that thing. This helps to explain why remembering something feels so different from really experiencing it. You can remember being angry at your teacher without being angry now, or remember being in intense pain without so much as a twinge of actual pain (10.14–15). Puzzlingly, though, in other cases of remembering we do seem to have the things themselves before our minds. If I recall a number, I would seem to be thinking of the number and not an image of that number. The same would seem to go for the memory itself. It seems absurd to suppose that, when I remember my own memory, I am getting at only an image of that memory (10.15). Which leads Augustine to a puzzle within a puzzle. If memory can remember itself without an image, then it must be able to remember forgetting in the same way. But if this happens directly and not by an image, so that forgetting just is the content of my memory, won't this mean that we are having a mental act that is both a remembering and a forgetting (10.16)? (The puzzle might itself provoke us to remember a similar point in Augustine's *On the Teacher*: the word "nothing" must be a sign, but it is hard to see what it could be a sign of.)

Puzzled though he may be, in the *Confessions* Augustine reaches a firm conclusion that is of great relevance to *On the Trinity*. He is enough of a Platonist to think that he is his own mind, which means that he is his own memory. After all, in remembering his mind he is doing nothing more nor less than getting access to himself. Memory, then, is starting to look like it may offer the trinity we have been looking for. Since the remembered thing or image is within us, we can avoid the problem that arose in the case of seeing, where one element of the trinity was separate from the others. The memory, what it remembers, and the will to remember are all the same thing, namely the mind itself. The three are therefore one substance. Augustine also gets bonus points, because the three seem to be equal to one another, and this trinity even seems to involve a case of internal begetting, just like the divine Trinity. When we recall something, the mind causes an episode of remembering through an act of will, which is tantamount to "begetting" its own content within itself.[8]

Though Augustine's score-sheet is drawn up in accordance with Christian theology, he's incidentally aiming at the most Hellenic of goals: to fulfill that Delphic command, "Know thyself."[9] Unlike philosophers who identified the mind or soul with some kind of body, like fire or air, Augustine thinks self-knowledge means an immaterial mind knowing itself. This might sound like just more Platonism, but to say this would be doing Augustine a disservice. Think of Plotinus' treatment of the perfect self-knowledge possessed by intellect. He argued that such a self-thinking or self-knowing intellect could not be the first principle, as Aristotle had claimed, because it would necessarily fall short of perfect unity by having two aspects. It would be both what thinks and what is thought—both the knower and the known. Augustine goes this one better, by seeing self-knowledge as involving not just duality but trinity. There is not just the mind as subject and object of its own mental act, but also the mind's will, which makes such mental acts possible. This is particularly clear in the cases we've been considering, where the mind remembers some specific content within itself by *choosing* to remember it. Without this intention, which Augustine often calls "love," there would be no act of remembering at all. Even if Augustine is motivated by his theological quest to find a human image of the divine Trinity, the point is a philosophically powerful one.

But Augustine is still not satisfied, because the cases we have been considering also have a fatal flaw. We go from remembering one thing to remembering another, the content of our thought constantly changing (11.8). In a sense, of course, the target of thought never changes, because in each case the mind is thinking about itself. But there is change here nonetheless, and hence a disanalogy to the divine case. To some extent this is unavoidable, since as a created thing the human mind is inevitably subject to change. Yet we can do a little bit better, by leaving aside the acts of thinking and remembering that come and go from moment to moment. These may seem to constitute the whole of our mental life. But, in a bold move, Augustine proposes that the mind never ceases to know, remember, and love itself (10.8, 14.3). Our mental life does not consist only of fleeting thoughts and images, but an enduring self-awareness. He even goes so far as to say that the mind's presence to itself, from moment to moment, is a kind of memory. Thus we can say that you are remembering yourself right now, even if it is more usual to use the word "memory" when we are grasping images of things in the past (14.11).[10]

Obviously, permanent self-awareness, by virtue of its very permanence, offers a better image of the eternal divine Trinity than the other human trinities we have considered. But we shouldn't get carried away, and think that all humans necessarily have an adequate understanding of their own selves. Far from it; even many philosophers, clever though they were, falsely believed that the soul is some sort of body. They made the mistake of adding an extraneous bodily image to the mind's basic awareness of itself. And they were not alone. In fact it is almost impossible for us to free ourselves from physical images when we think of our own minds. Thus we have the most Augustinian of paradoxes: that it should be so difficult for the mind to understand itself, even though the mind cannot help but know itself. This brings us full circle, to the mind's indubitable awareness of itself. Again in *On the Trinity* Augustine makes the point that reminded us of Descartes, that the mind cannot be in doubt about itself (10.10). Nonetheless, the mind's depths, as represented by the seemingly infinite potential of the memory, threaten to elude full exploration. Augustine remarks in the *Confessions* that nothing is closer to the mind than itself, yet still it remains unknown to itself (10.16). There is a parallel here between his ideas about knowledge and his treatment of sin. Just as we cannot fully know ourselves, on the ethical front nothing is more under our control than our own will, yet we remain unable to will the good even when we want to do so. This means that the project of *On the Trinity*, as Augustine himself admits, is doomed to at best partial success. If our own minds are beyond our knowledge and our will, then how much more will God transcend our efforts to understand and love Him as we should?

52

BORN AGAIN
LATIN PLATONISM

The curtain is about to come down on the classical drama that is ancient philosophy. It began in the sixth century BC with Thales. It will end in the sixth century AD or so with the last generations of the Platonist school at Alexandria, and Boethius in the fading Western Empire, after which we are in the medieval period. Actually, you can draw the line earlier or later. We've already examined one thinker who lived into the mid-seventh century, the Byzantine theologian and philosopher Maximus the Confessor. Especially for the Greek-speaking East, we need to think of medieval philosophy as continuous with antique philosophy. In the West, where Latin dominates, there was a greater degree of social collapse. Yet we can still find a degree of continuity, thanks in no small part to a handful of thinkers who preserved ancient philosophy, especially Platonism, in attractively packaged Latin. Here the most important figure is the aforementioned Boethius. But before we get to him I want to consider several other figures, whom we could call the Latin Platonists. Relatively obscure today, they were among the thinkers of antiquity most avidly studied by readers of Latin in the medieval era.

The importation of Hellenic philosophy into Latin was nothing new. Back in the first century BC Cicero and Lucretius had labored to convey the subtleties of the Hellenistic schools to a Latinate readership. Then came Seneca, one of the greatest of the Stoics. But in medieval times Lucretius was not known at all, while Cicero and Seneca exerted influence mostly through Augustine. With these giants lost in the mist of history, medievals had to make do with authors of lesser stature. If you think that two of the indispensable philosophical authors of all time are Calcidius and Martianus Capella, you are probably a monk living in the tenth or eleventh century. In which case you most likely aren't reading this. But knowing about the medieval legacy of the Latin Platonists can be misleading. They weren't trying to save philosophy by setting it down in Latin just before the clock struck midnight and darkness fell. To the contrary, the texts we'll be looking at are erudite and even playful treatments of Greek knowledge, aimed at an elite late antique audience. Accordingly, they are a lot of fun, which helps explain their historical influence.

Along with the misconception that the medievals didn't read books for fun, I'd like to dispel the notion that they refused to read non-Christian authors. There is overt and sincerely held paganism in some of these Latin Platonist works. Even Christian authors like Boethius and his fellow translator Calcidius gave little or no sign of their religious affiliation when they wrote about Hellenic thought. Boethius is a particularly striking case. His philosophical treatises look as if they could have been written by a pagan. Yet he also used philosophical ideas to expound the Trinity. Boethius was following in the footsteps of Marius Victorinus.[1] Augustine tells us that Victorinus began as a bitter opponent of Christianity, perhaps inspired by the anti-Christian polemics of the Platonist philosopher Porphyry. All the more reason to celebrate Victorinus' dramatic conversion to Christianity, which Augustine recounts in the Confessions (8.2.3–5). Within a few pages we see Victorinus go from militant paganism to lukewarm Christianity, which doesn't include attendance at church ("do walls make Christians?" he asks), and finally to enthusiastic adoption of the new faith. As a Christian he had to give up his chair as a teacher of rhetoric under the pagan policies of Julian the Apostate (8.5.10). Victorinus wrote theological works, including commentaries on the Bible and treatments of the Trinity. But his greatest contribution to the history of philosophy was his translation of what Augustine calls the "books of the Platonists," the works by Plotinus and Porphyry which, once rendered into Latin, were a formative influence on Augustine.

As we know, Augustine had studied Greek but far preferred to read Latin. This explains his dependence on Victorinus, and also his extensive use of Varro in works like the City of God. Like Cicero, Varro wrote extensively and informatively about Hellenic philosophy, and he did it in Latin. Augustine speaks also of Apuleius, who qualifies as the earliest Latin Platonist. He wrote in the second century, making him a contemporary of "Middle" Platonists like Numenius, and putting him before the ground-breaking synthesis of the Platonist tradition offered by Plotinus. In the City of God (8.14, 9.8) Apuleius is mocked for his views on the subject of demons. This was a matter of some interest to Apuleius, because the warning voice that spoke to Socrates was identified as a demon. He wrote a philosophical treatise on this subject, in which he followed Plato by making demons intermediaries between the gods and humans.[2] Augustine turns his characteristic wit and sarcasm against all this, whereas Apuleius was cherished by later Latin pagan authors. Especially valued was another work called the Metamorphosis. This features a main character who is turned into an ass, making the Metamorphosis of Apuleius the Midsummer Night's Dream of late antiquity.

Had Augustine read that play, he might well have quoted it with reference to Apuleius and other pagan philosophers: "Lord, what fools these mortals be!" His contemptuous attitude is directed not only at long-dead figures like Apuleius, but also near-contemporaries, which reminds us that paganism was still a going concern in the early fifth century. Indeed, our next two Latin Platonists were pagans who lived at this time. One wrote about a dream, the other about a wedding. Macrobius' *Commentary on the Dream of Scipio* uses Platonist philosophy to expound a text written by Cicero.[3] It appeared at the end of Cicero's *Republic*, which does not survive complete today. As the title indicates, Cicero was taking inspiration from Plato, and the passage being commented upon by Macrobius makes that still more obvious. Plato ended his own *Republic* with a myth, in which a man named Er has a vision of the cosmos and the fate of souls in the afterlife.[4] Cicero accordingly ended his own *Republic* with a cosmic vision, in the form of a dream (he doesn't mention whether the dream came on a midsummer night).

The dreamer is Scipio, grandson of the famous Scipio Africanus who led Rome against Hannibal in the Punic War. In the dream, Scipio Africanus appears to his grandson and shows him a panoramic view of the heavens and earth. The main point of this is to put earthly things in perspective, by revealing to young Scipio the tiny scope of even the Roman Empire in comparison to the cosmos as a whole. Towards the end of the dream Cicero also includes a summary of an argument for the immortality of the soul, taken from Plato's *Phaedrus*. The argument is based on the idea that the soul is the principle of motion and change, both for other things and for itself. Nothing else moves it or causes it to change, for instance, by bringing it into existence. This shows that it is eternal. If you aren't impressed by this argument, you're in good company. Aristotle, for one, dismissed it on the basis that souls are not really self-moving but are moved by things they perceive and desire. But this passage of the *Phaedrus* became one of Plato's best-known arguments. Its popularity is shown by the fact that it turns up here in Cicero.

Given Cicero's overt use of Plato, it's no surprise that an ancient Platonist like Macrobius would be attracted to the *Dream*. His commentary often reads like a discussion of "frequently asked questions" regarding the Ciceronian source. Why do both Cicero and Plato end their works with myths (1.1–2)? What are dreams, and how should we classify the dream Scipio is having (1.3)? What is the overall point Cicero is trying to make with the dream (1.4)? What is the significance of the numbers mentioned in Cicero's cosmology (1.7)? And so on. Along the way, Macrobius gives us plenty of hints as to his own philosophical outlook. He is, of course, keen to emphasize the meeting of minds between Cicero and Plato as read by ancient dogmatic Platonists (he does admit that they differ on a point of cosmological detail, at 1.19). One would never know from Macrobius' *Commentary* that Cicero was actually sympathetic to the Skeptical Academy. Unlike some other ancient Platonists, Macrobius seems to have no allegiance to Aristotle. He mentions him mostly to defend the *Phaedrus* argument about soul's immortality against Aristotle's refutation.

We can be a bit more specific about which kind of ancient Platonism Macrobius adopts. He seems to know both Plotinus and Porphyry well, and unlike Apuleius, inhabits their world-view rather than that of the so-called "Middle" Platonists. Thus Macrobius recognizes a highest God who is ineffable, and who is followed by second and third principles called intellect and soul, just as in Plotinus (1.14). He also accepts Plotinus' views on ethics, holding that the goal for mankind should be a life of intellectual contemplation, withdrawn from things of the body. He justifies the use of myths by both Cicero and Plato by saying that this is an appropriate way for them to present ideas about the soul and its cosmic fate. Nowadays, many readers of the ending myth of the *Republic* find it troubling that Plato depicts the afterlife as a place of reward and punishment, rather than resting his case on the central claim of the rest of the dialogue, namely that virtue is its own reward and vice its own punishment. To say that this does not bother Macrobius would be an understatement. For him, the prospect of reward and punishment is vital, and the key lesson of Cicero's *Dream*.

Yet Macrobius is no less enthusiastic to expand on Cicero's relatively brief remarks about cosmology. He shows off his knowledge of philosophical lore by discussing mathematical aspects of the heavens as discussed in Plato's *Timaeus*. Macrobius is well informed also on such topics as the Milky Way. He cites a number of philosophical theories for this celestial phenomenon (1.12, 1.15), including one from Aristotle's student Theophrastus, that it is a kind of seam where the sky is joined together. He also mentions the opinion of the atomist Democritus, who gets it pretty much right by suggesting that the Milky Way is the light of many stars blurred together. Macrobius fails, however, to mention the widespread view that the Milky Way is a candy bar. His treatment of scientific subjects also extends to the earthly realm. You may remember Lactantius ridiculing the notion that people could live on the far side of a spherical earth, since they would fall off. Macrobius refutes such concerns, pointing out that things fall not in some single "downward" direction, but towards the center of the earth. Otherwise rain would fall sideways at the equator instead of towards the ground (1.22).

So much for the dream; now it's time to go to a wedding. This will quite literally be a match made in heaven, since the groom is the god Mercury, who will wed a human woman named Philology. The story is told by Martianus Capella. I know what you're thinking, but unfortunately the answer is no, he did not invent *a capella* singing. He did, however, invent an extravagant allegory, which goes by the self-explanatory title *The Marriage of Mercury and Philology*.[5] The first section of the book weaves Platonist teachings into a description of the divine wedding ceremony. After an exuberantly pagan opening section, seven "bridesmaids," representing the seven branches of ancient education, give speeches in which they present the arts they symbolize. The edifying narrative is punctuated by distinctly unedifying interludes, in which the gods complain that they are bored, or try to persuade Mercury to call a halt to the speeches so he can get Philology into bed more quickly. It's all presented in torturous Latin festooned with obscure vocabulary, so much so that medieval readers had difficulty making sense of it. What we have here, in other words, is a strong late entry for the title of Ancient Philosophical Work Most Likely to Have Been Written While Under the Influence of Hallucinogenic Drugs. No less a reader than C. S. Lewis said (I know this seems too good to be true, but I am not making it up), "this universe, which has produced the orchid and the giraffe, has produced nothing stranger than Martianus Capella."[6]

Martianus would have loved the idea of a history of philosophy without any gaps. He tries to mention not only every god he can think of, but also every philosopher. Some of them, like Plato and Pythagoras, are deified and made to appear alongside other gods at the wedding (212–13). The possibility of reaching godlike status through learning is perhaps the point of the entire allegory, since we have here a symbol of human learning, Philology, wedding the god Mercury. Alternatively (or additionally), Mercury may represent eloquence, and Martianus' own work is an example of what it symbolically represents: erudition married to literary style. Of course, the idea of attaining godlikeness through philosophy is a well-worn Platonic theme that goes back to Plato himself. But Martianus could draw on more recent ideas to explain how this might be possible. He identifies Mercury as *nous*, using the Greek word for "mind" (92), while Philology seems to represent not humans generally or even the human soul, but more specifically the rational soul.[7] Even her name might be taken to indicate this: "Philology" is a lover of *logos*, of reason and speech. So Martianus was indeed under the influence when he wrote this—the influence of Neoplatonists. Martianus drew, for instance, on Porphyry's now-lost commentary devoted to the sacred pagan writings known as the *Chaldean Oracles*.

Of course, the readers of medieval Christendom cherished Martianus not because of his overt and Platonist-flavored paganism, but in spite of it. However much they may have enjoyed the elaborate narrative frame, the real usefulness of the work for them lay in the speeches of the seven bridesmaids. These speeches covered the disciplines that would later be called the "liberal arts." The seven disciplines were divided into two groups: the so-called "trivium" on linguistic topics, namely grammar, dialectic, and rhetoric, and the mathematical "quadrivium," namely arithmetic, geometry, astronomy, and harmony. Martianus provided medieval authors with a textbook for all seven arts, valuable not only for the information it preserved but also for its relative brevity and introductory character. But none of this would have mattered, had the work not been in Latin. Martianus himself repeatedly draws attention to the fact that he is transmitting Greek learning in a new tongue. Dialectic and Geometry both mention how unusual it is to present their arts in Latin (334, 339, 587), and *nous* is not the only Greek technical term to show up in Martianus' text. The Greek origins of the very names of the arts are also highlighted. Especially significant is the etymology of "Geometry" as "land measurement," which explains why this speech deals at length with what we would call geography.

Though Martianus' *Marriage* was thus highly useful for Latin readers, it is not a translation, and gave medievals no access to the words of Plato himself. For that, they depended entirely on a single, incomplete translation of one dialogue: the *Timaeus*. The translator was Calcidius, who also supplied a commentary that is deeply influenced by Middle and Neo-Platonism.[8] We do not know much about him, our main clue being a preface, which addresses the commentary to a clergyman in Spain named Osius. This suggests a date in the first half of the fourth century, and also that Calcidius was a Christian. Yet, though he does occasionally refer to the Bible, Calcidius makes no effort to Christianize Plato or the Platonists. For the most part he simply ascribes later Platonist ideas directly to Plato. For instance, like Martianus, Calcidius adopts Plotinus' doctrine that the highest God is followed by a second, intellective principle called *nous*.

A more complicated example of his use of Platonist ideas is his treatment of providence.[9] The Middle Platonists drew a distinction between fate and providence. Fate was effectively the sort of divine mastery recognized by the Stoics, which is to say, an immanent principle within the natural world. Fate is a sort of law laid down for the physical cosmos by a more exalted providence, which proceeds from divine, immaterial principles. All things are subject to providence, but only things within the physical, natural world are subject to fate. Now, because human souls have an immaterial part—the part with which they reason and can achieve virtue—humans are not necessarily bound by fate. Insofar as we live in accordance with reason alone and focus on pure contemplation, we effectively exempt ourselves from the law of fate. But as soon as we act within the physical world we submit ourselves to those laws. When Oedipus killed a man who happened to be his father at a crossroads, his action was one performed within the physical realm. Fate governs such actions, in the sense that it apportions reward and punishment in keeping with the laws laid down by providence.

So we can say that it was "fated" that Oedipus would go on to marry his own mother, bring a plague upon his city, and tear his own eyes out. This sounds fairly Stoic, except for the crucial Platonist caveat that Oedipus had a rational soul that was not controlled by fate. If he had chosen in accordance with reason, he could have avoided giving in to his angry impulse at the crossroads, a sure sign that his lower, spirited soul was in charge. These Middle Platonist ideas about providence reappear in Neoplatonists, including Plotinus, Porphyry, and Hierocles.[10] Calcidius brings the theory into Latin, and in the context of a commentary on the *Timaeus* that would be read for many generations to come. One of his allusions to the Bible even brings the Platonist theory of fate together with the Old Testament. He quotes a statement in which God promises that reward and punishment will be sent for the things we do, an indication that fate is a divinely appointed law, triggered by our actions in this world.[11]

The texts I've discussed in this chapter have much in common. Most obviously they are all in Latin, and self-consciously so. Like Cicero before them, they comment on the task of bringing Greek ideas into a new language. The impact of Latin culture too is felt throughout their writings. Macrobius and Martianus Capella knew and used Varro, Cicero, Seneca, Ovid, and Virgil. In fact, Macrobius wrote another work called the *Saturnalia* that presents Virgil as a consummate philosopher (he would be annoyed with me for failing to devote a chapter to the *Aeneid*). Another commonality is that the Latin Platonists frequently drew on the same, relatively narrow range of sources. Plato's *Timaeus* looms larger than other dialogues, though they do refer to favorite passages from elsewhere in Plato, such as that argument for the soul's immortality found in the *Phaedrus*. I mentioned that it was defended by Macrobius, and Calcidius also weaves it into his commentary on the *Timaeus*.[12] As for late antique philosophers, it's striking that the one who seems to have influenced the Latin Platonists most was not a Church Father or even Plotinus, but Porphyry. I've already mentioned Porphyry's impact on Victorinus, Macrobius, and Martianus Capella, but I haven't told you that his commentary on the *Timaeus* was likely an important source for Calcidius. The only Latin Platonist not influenced by Porphyry was Apuleius, which only stands to reason, since Porphyry lived quite a bit later than he did. Our later Latin Platonists, furthermore, adopt Porphyry's interest in Aristotelian logic, without exploring Aristotle much further. Victorinus translated Porphyry's *Isagoge* and Aristotle's *Categories* and *On Interpretation*, which are also the basis for a long portion of Dialectic's speech in Martianus Capella.

In all these respects, our Latin Platonists anticipate what we will find in the last ancient philosopher to be covered in this volume, Boethius. He was an expert on Aristotelian logic and drew heavily on Porphyry. Like Calcidius, he translated Greek philosophy into Latin, and had an enormous impact on medieval culture.[13] (In fact, both Boethius and Macrobius were enthusiastically read and used by Geoffrey Chaucer.) Yet, like Victorinus before him, Boethius did not let his interest in pagan thought stop him from writing about the Trinity. Meanwhile, Martianus Capella's *Marriage* partially anticipates Boethius' greatest work, an allegory, which likewise personifies an intellectual discipline—in this case, Lady Philosophy herself.[14] But the occasion is a less festive one. Boethius composed his *Consolation of Philosophy* while under a death-sentence, and the consolation Lady Philosophy offers him is needed because he faces imminent execution. We've had the marriage; now we end with a funeral.

53

FATE, HOPE, AND CLARITY
BOETHIUS

I find myself reading books about philosophy in some rather strange places. On trains and buses, at the beach, at the department store while family members are trying on clothes—these are just a few of the places I've cuddled up with Plato or Avicenna. In fact, while I was preparing to write this chapter you could have seen me in my kitchen, reading about Boethius while making mashed potatoes. But I draw the line at airplanes. They make me too nervous to work, which I realize is silly. (I know that I'm vanishingly unlikely to die in a plane-crash.) So for me an hour spent in a plane is an hour wasted, at least as far as philosophy goes. In other words, an hour wasted. This makes me all the more impressed when I consider Boethius, who wrote his greatest philosophical work in the certain knowledge that he was indeed about to die. Not while experiencing a plane-crash—that would take some pretty quick writing—but while waiting to be executed at the order of the Ostrogothic king Theoderic, in the year 525 or 526. On the other hand, Boethius got some help that has never been offered to me. While in captivity he was visited by Lady Philosophy herself. His dialogue with her is recorded in the *Consolation of Philosophy*, not only his greatest work but also a work with far-reaching influence on subsequent philosophy and literature.

In the *Consolation* Boethius complains to Lady Philosophy that he has been the victim of political intrigue, and this is true enough. He had occupied a high office under Theoderic, but fell from grace when he came to the defense of a senator named Albinus, who had been accused of treason. The nature of the supposed treason reminds us that we are now at the end of antiquity: the empire is definitively split into two halves, with the western half wobbling but not yet fallen. Theoderic was a Goth who had taken charge of Italy in the 490s, but he was not recognized by the eastern court as a full emperor in the West. Thus, Theoderic had a troubled relationship with Constantinople, and was sensitive to the possibility that his independence might be undermined. This is probably what lay behind the charge of treason against Albinus, who had supposedly communicated with the eastern court. When Boethius spoke out on behalf of Albinus' faithfulness, he fell from favor. He was taken to Pavia, imprisoned, and after an incarceration long enough that he could write his masterpiece, executed.

Because Boethius did live at the very end of antiquity, and because his writings had such a decisive influence on medieval philosophy, he is often thought of as a medieval author. But even if Boethius was in fact ushering in a new age of thought in Christian Europe, with limited access to philosophical literature and disappearing knowledge of Greek, he was not of the medieval age. He was a Roman aristocrat, whose thought-world was still more like that of Cicero than that of Anselm, Abelard, or Aquinas (you don't have to have a name starting with A to be a medieval philosopher, but it helps). Like Cicero, Boethius was a man with a busy public life, who devoted much of his free time to the study and Latin translation of Greek philosophy. Unlike Cicero, however, his attention was devoted almost entirely to Plato and Aristotle. Even more unlike Cicero, Boethius was a Christian who wrote works on Trinitarian theology. In the nineteenth century scholars doubted whether the author of the *Consolation* and the logical works, which have no overt Christian content, could also have produced these theological writings. But these doubts were ill-founded. In fact, even a casual perusal of Boethius' theological works shows that he is putting his knowledge of Aristotelian philosophy to use as he explains God, the Trinity, and the Incarnation.

But let's start where Boethius would probably want us to: his works on Aristotelian logic. In one of these he announced his intention to translate all the works of Plato and Aristotle. If this enormously ambitious project had been brought to fruition, medieval philosophy might have looked very different—Theoderic has a lot to answer for. Before his untimely death Boethius was fairly prolific, but still got only as far as Aristotle's logical works. As we know, the philosophical curriculum in Alexandria began with logic, and Boethius followed this approach too. He produced translations and commentaries—in some cases more than one commentary on a single work—on Porphyry's *Introduction* and most of Aristotle's *Organon*. He also wrote independent treatises, one corresponding to Aristotle's *Topics* but drawing heavily on Cicero's work of the same name. Boethius' focus on logic is not the only thing he shares with the philosophers of Alexandria. He was a near-contemporary of Ammonius, and we often find him making comments about Aristotle that match with the remarks of Ammonius and his pupils. This is probably not because Boethius was in contact with the Alexandrian school, but because he drew on the same sources. Among those sources, the most important was Porphyry. Boethius not only wrote two commentaries on Porphyry's *Introduction*, but also drew heavily on Porphyry's commentaries on Aristotle.

Boethius was a competent, though not terribly innovative, logician. His importance for the history of logic is nonetheless immense, since he became the primary conduit through which Aristotelian logic could reach Latin-reading medieval philosophers.[1] An example of his influence is his decision to discuss a question Porphyry raised, but didn't answer, in his *Introduction*. As you might remember, Porphyry asked what we should say about the status of universals—general features shared by many individuals, such as whiteness or humanity. Boethius' decision to discuss this problem in his commentary ensured that medieval readers would see the metaphysical issue of the status of universals as fundamental in Latin writings about logic.[2] Logic more generally was fundamental for Boethius himself, and he drew on his logical expertise in his works on Christian theology and his *Consolation*. In honor of his interest in the Trinity, I'll give you three examples.

The first has to do with Aristotle's *Categories*. As you'll remember, Aristotle there classifies types of predicates or terms that apply to things. One class of predicates is relation, which would include, for instance, "master" and "slave," or "father" and "son." I don't choose that second example randomly. In a treatise called *On the Trinity*, Boethius realizes that he can exploit the notion of a relation to explain the difference between the Trinitarian Persons, Father, Son, and Holy Spirit. First, though, he is careful to argue that God is an indivisible unity. Unlike created things, like a human who is composed out of both body and soul, God is, as Boethius puts it, nothing but what He is (*id quod est*, 2).[3] Thus, if we say that God is good, we mean not that God is a substance of which goodness is predicated, as white would be predicated of a piece of paper, or as a form like the soul is predicated of a body. Rather, we mean that God is simply goodness itself.

This looks like a good way of securing God's utter simplicity—anything we can say about God will refer to a nature that is identical with God Himself. But that seems to raise problems for the doctrine of the Trinity. If the Father is identical to God, and so is the Son, then won't the Father be identical with the Son, so that we have one and not two Persons? Yes and no, says Boethius. They will indeed be identical, but (now exploiting Aristotle) there is still a relation between them that is sufficient to produce the difference in Persons. The difference doesn't make God into two distinct beings, because adding relations to something doesn't affect what that thing is in itself (5). For instance, I might go stand next to you, so that you bear to me the relation of being to my left; if I then go around the other side, you'll have the relation of being to my right. But you remain unchanged in yourself throughout. (In fact you may not even notice. I'll be very quiet, because I'll probably be reading about philosophy the whole time.) In the same way, God is subject to relations like Fatherhood and Sonhood, without this turning Him into more than one thing.

After all, as Boethius points out, a thing can bear a relation to itself, such as the relation of self-identity. This gives us some idea of what is happening in the Trinity, though not a full understanding, because we never experience something like the Trinitarian relationship among created things.

This mention of created things takes us to another theological work by Boethius, on *Why Things Are Good in Virtue of their Existence.*[4] Here Boethius is going to make use of another weapon from his logical arsenal. This one he borrows from Porphyry: the proper or inseparable accident. Here the idea is that, even if a feature cannot be removed from something in reality, it may be possible to remove it conceptually. The standard example is a human's ability to laugh. Porphyry also gave the example of a scar, which (before the invention of laser surgery) couldn't be taken away from the scarred person. The point is that since such features can at least be removed in our thought, they can't be essential to the thing that has the feature—if the scar on my thumb miraculously disappeared, I would still be me and would still be human.

Thus equipped, let's turn to this theological treatise about why things are good. What Boethius wants to explain here is the fact that "substances that exist, insofar as they exist, are good." Obviously the first thing we might want to figure out is why Boethius would think this is true. One way of explaining it would be that he is accepting the understanding of goodness and evil pioneered by Plotinus, and accepted by Augustine, who is one of Boethius' favorite authors. On this view, evil is just an absence of being, the failure of something to realize its nature to the extent that it could and should. But that means that insofar as anything does exist, it must be good: if it lacked goodness entirely it would simply cease to be. This gives Boethius a problem. He doesn't want to say things are good in their very essence (they are not "substantial goods"). If part of what it is to be me is for me to be good—the way that part of what it is to be me is for me to be rational and alive—then I would be good in exactly the same way as God. For God is good in Himself.

Boethius solves the difficulty by asking us to focus on created things as they would be without any relation to God. We can think about them as they are just in themselves by abstracting away God's existence, as a mathematician abstracts a triangle from matter in order to concentrate on the shape in itself. Without God in the picture, argues Boethius, things could no longer be good by virtue of existing. This shows that substantial goodness does not belong to the nature of these created things in themselves. Like a proper accident, it can be removed in thought, even if not in reality. For goodness is not part of what it is to be, say, a human, a giraffe, or any other created thing—this is one way that they differ from God. If goodness is not intrinsic to them, it must be extrinsic. Our conclusion must be that, while things are indeed good by virtue of their existing, this is only because of a relation to something else, namely their perfectly good cause. Here Boethius seems to show his Platonist leanings. He thinks created things exist through a relation to God, who is goodness itself, like participating in a Platonic Form of Good. Goodness comes to them from outside, bestowed by God rather than belonging to their own natures. But it is still intimately bound up with their existence, because they only exist at all thanks to the will of God, the first good.

Our third and final logical theme is the problem of truths about the future, which seem to make future events inevitable. Aristotle first broached this issue in his *On Interpretation* with the famous example of the sea-battle, and Boethius takes up the question in his commentary on that work. The reading of Aristotle he offers is also found in Greek commentators like Ammonius.[5] According to this reading, Aristotle solves the difficulty by saying that there are only "indefinite" truths about future events. Unfortunately, it again isn't quite clear what Boethius means. He may mean that, according to Aristotle, present statements about the future are going to turn out true or false, but it isn't yet decided which. Thus, if I say "I will watch a Buster Keaton movie tomorrow," then this will certainly wind up being either true or false, but will not become true or false until I actually watch the movie or fail to do so. Alternatively, Boethius might mean that a statement like "I will watch a Buster Keaton movie tomorrow" is right now true, rather than false, but not *necessarily* true. So I could truly say that I will in fact watch the movie, without this meaning that it is inevitable that I watch the movie. After all, the truth I'm asserting here is contingent, because I could easily have decided not to watch a Buster Keaton movie, unwise though that would be. If, on the other hand, I said, "2 + 2 will equal 4 tomorrow," what I am saying will already be *necessarily* true.

A more famous discussion of this issue occurs at the end of that jailhouse classic, the *Consolation of Philosophy*. Here, though, we are dealing with the version of the difficulty discussed by Augustine. Once we admit that God knows future events with certainty, don't we have to conclude that there are indeed present truths about those events, and that the truths are necessary? Boethius arrives at this point only after a long dialogue with his visitor, Lady Philosophy. At first the prisoner Boethius is too distraught to worry about these logical niceties. Lady Philosophy has comforted him with a regime of arguments, first offering him gentle medicines and then more severe ones (1.5). The gentle medicines include getting Boethius to reflect on respects in which he remains fortunate—for instance, his family is still alive, even if he will shortly be killed. Lady Philosophy moves on to show Boethius that there is no point lamenting about the way the wheel of fortune turns. It is in the nature of fortune that the lowly should sometimes be raised up and the powerful cast down. Fortune stays the same only in that it is constantly changing (2.1). Lady Philosophy sounds very like Marcus Aurelius when she dismisses the role of chance in the universe (1.6), or remarks that one should never value anything that can be taken away (2.4).

A more Augustinian note is sounded when Lady Philosophy gives her positive account of happiness. It lies not in virtue and self-mastery, as Epictetus or Marcus might say, but is to be identified with God Himself, which may remind us of Augustine's *City of God*. Still, pagan Hellenic sources are never far from Lady Philosophy's mind. She seems to have read Plato's *Gorgias* closely, as she comforts Boethius by telling him that the wicked of this world only seem to be powerful and happy. In fact, the good alone are powerful and do what they want, whereas the wicked suffer from their own wickedness. What would be good for them, as Plato held, would be corrective punishment (4.3). There's more than a hint of Plotinus mixed into Lady Philosophy's medicine too, perhaps filtered through Augustine. For here we find again the idea that evil itself is nothing (3.12), and therefore that the wicked are simply failing to do anything when they perform evil actions. Seen from the point of view of divine providence, the world contains no evil. Admittedly, it does contain suffering, but even this is sent by providence, either as a test for the good or a punishment for the wicked (4.7).

So far, so optimistic, but it does lead Boethius to that difficulty about providence itself. If God providentially knows everything that will happen, then isn't everything necessary? Lady Philosophy admits that it seems so, because God obviously cannot be wrong about anything. Since it seems that He could not have certainty about things that are in themselves uncertain, there is no possibility that the things He knows be otherwise. Thus, all things that God knows—including future events—are necessary. And God knows everything. Therefore, everything is necessary. Towards a solution, Lady Philosophy points out that if you see something happening presently, that doesn't make what you are seeing necessary. She gives the example of a chariot race (5.4). If the motions of the chariot-drivers are not even necessary while they are occurring, then much less could they be necessary before they occur. Moreover, as they are occurring you can be certain that what you are seeing is happening. This shows that, in a way, certainty is indeed compatible with the absence of necessity.

The problem is that future events don't seem to be like this. From our point of view they are still open or unsettled, in a way that a present event is not. But our point of view is not the same as God's. Appealing to a distinction that was introduced by the Neoplatonist Iamblichus, Boethius has Lady Philosophy say that the way things are known is appropriate not to what is known, but to the knower. Thus events that seem uncertain to us could be certain for God. This is because God does not really know future events *as* future events. He never changes, so that unlike us, He has knowledge that does not alter from moment to moment. Instead, He sees all things—the things that for us are past, present, and future—with a single, simultaneous knowledge. Boethius makes the point in Latin by saying that God's knowledge is not *praevidentia* ("knowing in advance") but *providentia*, which means knowing from a commanding vantage-point, like someone surveying things from a high mountain (5.6).

This idea too is originally Neoplatonic, but Boethius could again have found it in Augustine. God has an unchanging relationship towards things that change in time, and as Plotinus said, a being that lives such an unchanging life can be called "eternal." At first blush, this might seem to make the problem even worse. Now we are saying not only that God knows now what I will do tomorrow, but that He knows *eternally* and *unchangingly* what I will do tomorrow. If the sea-battle argument makes my actions look inevitable, this looks like it could make my actions immutably inevitable. Not quite what we were after. But Lady Philosophy draws the opposite conclusion. God's eternity means He sees every event occurring as if it were present for Him (5.6). His seeing tomorrow's chariot race is just like your seeing today's chariot race. So we should no more think that His foreknowledge implies necessity in a future event than we should think that our ordinary knowledge implies necessity in a present event.

If Boethius too could have known the future, what would he have seen coming for Lady Philosophy? He would probably be pleased with the later unfolding of philosophy in Latin Christendom, since Boethius' own works will play such a central role in that story. This is the tradition that first leaps to mind when one hears the phrase "medieval philosophy": Latin writings from early figures like Alcuin, Eriugena, and Anselm, followed by the rise of scholasticism, which reaches its height with geniuses like Aquinas, Scotus, and Ockham. This Latin tradition will be the subject of a future installment of this series. But in the centuries to come, Lady Philosophy will not only speak Latin. Greek philosophy will continue in the Byzantine world, with less celebrated but fascinating authors like Psellos and Plethon continuing the late antique trend of fusing together Christian theology, Aristotelianism, and Platonism. That too is something we'll examine in another future volume, which will be devoted to Byzantine thought and philosophy in the Renaissance.

But before we continue with Latin- or Greek-speaking Christendom, we will consider a part of Lady Philosophy's future that Boethius certainly wouldn't have seen coming. The wheel of fortune will bring the rise of a new civilization, another vast empire that will play host to some of the most scintillating philosophers of the medieval period. If you asked me to name the greatest and most influential medieval philosopher, I would not pick Aquinas or any other thinker who wrote in Latin. I would instead go with Avicenna, the leading philosopher of the Islamic world. The next book in this series will examine not just Avicenna but the whole history of philosophy in the lands dominated by Islam, from al-Kindī in the ninth century to Mullā Ṣadrā in the seventeenth century, and further still as we follow the story right through to the twentieth century. We'll see that this story takes in not only Muslims, like the figures I just named, but also Christians and the great figures of medieval Jewish philosophy, most notably Maimonides. Texts written in Syriac, Arabic, Persian, and Hebrew will not just transmit and interpret the ideas of late antiquity, but go beyond this inheritance to integrate philosophy into all three Abrahamic faiths. Theologians and the mystics of Sufism and Kabbalah will borrow and further develop the ideas of the philosophers, even as they doubt whether philosophy is really the sole or highest path to truth. I look forward to telling you about philosophy in the Islamic world, in the next volume of the History of Philosophy without any gaps.

NOTES

Preface

1. A second additional chapter deals with Galen, who in the podcast series was instead covered in an interview with James Hankinson. More generally, the interviews can be recommended as adding further depth, and a different perspective, to the material in the book. For instance, you can hear more about ancient political philosophy in the interviews with Tony Long and Dominic O'Meara, and about ancient aesthetics in an episode featuring Anne Sheppard. All the interviews, along with the original podcasts, are available for free online at <www.historyofphilosophy.net>.

Chapter 1

1. *Classical Philosophy*, ch. 13.
2. As usual with Plato, it's hard to tell whether Socrates is meant to be putting this forward as his own view or just one to be considered dialectically.
3. For an introduction to the period see R. M. Errington, *A History of the Hellenistic World, 323–30 BC* (Oxford, 2008).
4. See D. Sedley, "Philosophical Allegiance in the Greco-Roman World," in M. Griffin and J. Barnes (eds.), *Philosophia Togata I: Essays on Philosophy and Roman Society* (Oxford, 1989), 97–119.
5. Diogenes Laertius, *Lives of the Philosophers* 6.54.

Chapter 2

1. Bracketed references to this chapter are to Diogenes Laertius, *Lives of the Philosophers*, 2 vols (Cambridge, Mass., 1925). Unfortunately there is no handy English-language collection of reports on the Cynics, but many are gathered and discussed in W. Desmond, *Cynics* (Stocksfield, 2008). See also G. Boys-Stones and C. J. Rowe, *The Circle of Socrates: Readings in the First-Generation Socratics* (Indianapolis, 2013).
2. *Beyond Good and Evil*, trans. W. Kaufmann (New York, 1966), 38.
3. See P. Adamson, "The Arabic Reception of Greek Philosophy," in F. Sheffield and J. Warren (eds.), *The Routledge Companion to Ancient Philosophy* (London, 2014), 672–88, at 675.
4. *Classical Philosophy*, ch. 38.
5. *Classical Philosophy*, ch. 43.
6. For the ancient tendency to associate women philosophers with domestic issues, see *Classical Philosophy*, ch. 42 and this volume, Chapter 35.

Chapter 3

1. Diogenes Laertius, *Lives of the Philosophers*, tells an anecdote in which Aristippus and Diogenes the Cynic meet one another (2.68), and mentions that the later Cyrenaic Theodorus encountered the Cynic Metrocles (2.102).
2. *Memorabilia* 2.1, 3.8.
3. *Classical Philosophy*, ch. 37.
4. This point has been emphasized by T. Irwin, "Aristippus Against Happiness," *The Monist*, 74 (1991), 55–82.
5. My thanks to Dirk Baltzly for this suggestion.
6. Text 4 in the Appendix of U. Zilioli, *The Cyrenaics* (Durham, NC, 2012), reported by the late ancient author Eusebius. See also Zilioli, Texts 19 and 30.
7. Text 22 in Zilioli, *The Cyrenaics* = Diogenes Laertius, *Lives of the Philosophers* 2.88.
8. See Aristotle, *Nicomachean Ethics* 1172b.
9. See *Classical Philosophy*, ch. 43.
10. Text 32 in Zilioli, *The Cyrenaics* = Sextus Empiricus, *Against the Mathematicians* 7.191.
11. Text 16 in Zilioli, *The Cyrenaics* = Plutarch, *Against Colotes* 1120c.
12. *Classical Philosophy*, ch. 19.
13. A useful overview of developments in later Cyrenaic thinkers is given in A. A. Long, "The Socratic Legacy," in K. Algra *et al.* (eds.), *The Cambridge History of Hellenistic Philosophy* (Cambridge, 1999), 617–41, at 635–9.

Chapter 4

1. Diogenes Laertius, *Lives of the Philosophers* 10. For these texts see also C. Bailey, *Epicurus: The Extant Remains* (Oxford, 1926).
2. For a short introduction to the inscription and references to the edition and commentary of M. F. Smith, see M. Erler, "Epicureanism in the Roman Empire," in J. Warren (ed.), *The Cambridge Companion to Epicureanism* (Cambridge, 2009), 46–64, at 54–9.
3. On this topic see D. Glidden, "Epicurean *Prolepsis*," *Oxford Studies in Ancient Philosophy*, 3 (1985), 175–217.
4. *Classical Philosophy*, ch. 18.
5. The idea was already put forward by the Eleatic philosopher Melissus. See *Classical Philosophy*, ch. 7.
6. See *Classical Philosophy*, ch. 8.
7. See G. Vlastos, "Minimal Parts in Epicurean Atomism," *Isis*, 56 (1965), 121–47.
8. For this much-discussed aspect of ancient atomism see especially D. O'Brien, *Theories of Weight in the Ancient World*, 2 vols. (Paris, 1981 and 1984).

Chapter 5

1. For the contrast between the two schools see J. Warren, "Epicurus and the Pleasures of the Future," *Oxford Studies in Ancient Philosophy*, 21 (2001), 135–79 and T. O'Keefe, "The Cyrenaics on Pleasure, Happiness, and Future-Concern," *Phronesis*, 47 (2002), 395–416.
2. Cicero, *On Moral Ends*, ed. J. Annas, trans. R. Woolf, §1.30. On this topic see J. Brunschwig, "The Cradle Argument in Epicureanism and Stoicism," in M. Schofield and G. Striker (eds.), *The Norms of Nature: Studies in Hellenistic Ethics* (Cambridge, 1986), 113–44.

3. Here I follow the interpretation of R. Woolf, presented in "What Kind of Hedonist was Epicurus?" *Phronesis*, 49 (2004), 303–22, and "Pleasure and Desire," in J. Warren (ed.), *The Cambridge Companion to Epicureanism* (Cambridge, 2009), 158–78. The example below about flying first class is borrowed (okay, stolen) from the latter article, at 160.
4. Cicero, *On Moral Ends* §2.8.
5. On this issue see D. K. O'Connor, "The Invulnerable Pleasures of Epicurean Friendship," *Greek, Roman and Byzantine Studies*, 30 (1989), 165–86; M. Evans, "Can Epicureans Be Friends?" *Ancient Philosophy*, 24 (2004), 407–24; T. O'Keefe, "Is Epicurean Friendship Altruistic?" *Apeiron*, 34 (2001), 269–305.

Chapter 6

1. In his *Death (A Play)*, published in W. Allen, *Without Feathers* (New York [of course: it's Woody Allen], 1975).
2. On whom see V. Tsouna, *The Ethics of Philodemus* (Oxford, 2007).
3. I take the count of 33 from C. Gill, "Psychology," in J. Warren (ed.), *The Cambridge Companion to Epicureanism* (Cambridge, 2009), 125–41, at 138 n. 49. An excellent study of the Epicurean arguments on the topic is J. Warren, *Facing Death: Epicurus and his Critics* (Oxford, 2004). See also S. Rosenbaum, "How To Be Dead and Not Care: A Defense of Epicurus," *American Philosophical Quarterly*, 23 (1986), 217–25, C. P. Segal, *Epicurus on Death and Anxiety* (Princeton, 1990), and V. Tsouna, "Rationality and the Fear of Death in Epicurean Philosophy," *Rhizai*, 3 (2006), 79–117.
4. I will consider medieval Jewish philosophers' responses to the Book of Job in the next volume in this series.
5. On Epicurus' understanding of the gods, see further D. Obbink, "The Atheism of Epicurus," *Greek, Roman and Byzantine Studies*, 30 (1989), 187–223; J. Mansfeld, "Aspects of Epicurean Theology," *Mnemosyne*, 46 (1993), 172–210; D. Konstan, "Epicurus on the Gods," and D. Sedley, "Epicurus' Theological Innatism," both in J. Fish and K. Sanders (eds.), *Epicurus and the Epicurean Tradition* (Cambridge, 2009).
6. Philodemus, *On the Gods* 3.14, cited by D. Obbink, "'All Gods are True' in Epicurus," in D. Frede and A. Laks (eds.), *Traditions of Theology: Studies in Hellenistic Theology, its Background and Aftermath* (Leiden, 2002), 183–222.

Chapter 7

1. Cicero, *To his Brother Quintus* 2.9, Virgil, *Georgics* 2.490–2.
2. A widely available translation is Lucretius, *On the Nature of Things*, trans. R. E. Latham (New York, 1951; rev. edn. 1994). Cited by book and line numbers, which are printed in the margin of this translation.
3. For Lucretius see 1.136–9, 2.260, and for Cicero see this volume, Chapter 17.
4. See *Classical Philosophy*, ch. 8.
5. See S. Greenblatt, *Swerve: How the Renaissance Began* (London, 2011).

Chapter 8

1. See M. Schofield, *The Stoic Idea of the City* (Cambridge, 1991); J. Sellars, "Stoic Cosmopolitanism and Zeno's Republic," *History of Political Thought*, 28 (2007), 1–29.
2. See K. Ierodiakonou, "The Stoic Division of Philosophy," *Phronesis*, 38 (1993), 57–74.

3. For more details see S. Bobzein, "Stoic Syllogistic," *Oxford Studies in Ancient Philosophy*, 14 (1996), 133–92, M. Frede, "Stoic vs. Aristotelian Logic," in M. Frede, *Essays in Ancient Philosophy* (Oxford, 1987), 99–124.
4. *Classical Philosophy*, ch. 30.

Chapter 9

1. See further M. Mignucci, "The Liar Paradox and the Stoics," in K. Ierodiakonou (ed.), *Topics in Stoic Philosophy* (Oxford, 1999), 54–70; S. Bobzien, "Chrysippus and the Epistemic Theory of Vagueness," *Proceedings of the Aristotelian Society*, 102 (2002), 217–38.
2. M. Frede, "Stoics and Skeptics on Clear and Distinct Impressions," in Frede, *Essays in Ancient Philosophy* (Oxford, 1987), 151–78.
3. M. Frede, "The Stoic Notion of a *Lekton*," in S. Everson, *Language* (Cambridge, 1994), 109–28.

Chapter 10

1. Translation from LS 54I.
2. In fact Aristotle presents his god as an alternative immaterial cause to Platonic Forms, and claims that his theory has more explanatory power. See *Metaphysics* 1075b.
3. See P. A. Meijer, *Stoic Theology: Proofs for the Existence of the Cosmic God and of the Traditional Gods* (Delft, 2007).
4. Cicero, *On the Nature of the Gods* 2.63.
5. See further G. Reydams-Schils, *Demiurge and Providence: Stoic and Platonist Readings of Plato's Timaeus* (Turnhout, 1999).
6. A. A. Long, "Soul and Body in Stoicism," *Phronesis*, 27 (1982), 34–57, D. Baltzly, "Stoic Pantheism," *Sophia*, 34 (2003), 3–33.
7. See his *The Gay Science*, §§285 and 341.
8. Marcus Aurelius, *Meditations*, trans. M. Staniforth (London, 1964), 9.28.
9. A hypothesis discussed by R. Sorabji, *Time, Creation and the Continuum* (London, 1983), 184–5.

Chapter 11

1. *Classical Philosophy*, ch. 30.
2. One important difference from modern-day compatibilism, however, is that the early Stoics did not think of this issue in terms of "freedom" (in Greek, *eleutheria*). They sought to reconcile responsibility and the "up to us" with causal determinism, but did not insist that humans are "free" even when causally determined. For this point see S. Bobzien, *Determinism and Freedom in Stoic Philosophy* (Oxford, 1998), 330–1. She argues that it is only with Epictetus that talk of freedom becomes linked to the "up to us."
3. Plotinus, *Enneads* 3.1.5.
4. On this simile see Bobzien, *Determinism and Freedom*, 351–7. She argues that the image was proposed only by the later, "Roman" Stoics and not by Chrysippus.
5. See G. Striker, "Following Nature: a Study in Stoic Ethics," *Oxford Studies in Ancient Philosophy*, 9 (1991), 1–73.
6. *Classical Philosophy*, ch. 26.
7. *Republic* 331c.
8. See M. M. McCabe, "Extend or Identify: Two Stoic Accounts of Altruism," in R. Salles (ed.), *Metaphysics, Soul and Ethics in Ancient Thought* (Oxford, 2005), 413–44.

Chapter 12

1. Piso's story is told in Seneca, *On Anger* 1.18, in Seneca, *Moral Essays*, vol. 1, trans. J. W. Basore (Cambridge, Mass., 1928). References in the main text of this chapter are to this volume.
2. M. Griffin, *Seneca: A Philosopher in Politics* (Oxford, 1992).
3. For an essay connecting one of Seneca's tragedies to his philosophical ideas, see M. Nussbaum, "Serpents in the Soul: A Reading of Seneca's *Medea*," in J. J. Clauss and S. I. Johnston (eds.), *Medea: Essays on Medea in Myth, Literature, Philosophy, and Art* (Princeton, 1997), 219–49.
4. B. Inwood, *Reading Seneca: Stoic Philosophy at Rome* (Oxford, 2005), 12.
5. Seneca, *Natural Questions*, trans. H. M. Hine (Chicago, 1990).
6. Seneca, *Dialogues and Letters* (London, 1997), 56.
7. See J. Cooper, "Posidonius on Emotions," in J. Sihvola and T. Engberg-Pedersen (eds.), *The Emotions in Hellenistic Philosophy* (Dordrecht, 1998), 71–111; R. Sorabji, *Emotion and Peace of Mind* (Oxford, 2000), C. Gill, *The Structured Self in Hellenistic and Roman Thought* (Oxford, 2006), ch. 4.
8. *Classical Philosophy*, ch. 21.
9. For a translation of the *Consolation to Helvia*, see Seneca, *Dialogues and Letters*.

Chapter 13

1. The phrase appears both in his book *Being and Nothingness* (part 4, ch. 2) and his lecture "Existentialism as a Humanism."
2. A. Dihle, *The Theory of the Will in Classical Antiquity* (Berkeley, 1982), M. Frede, *A Free Will: Origins of the Notion in Ancient Thought* (Berkeley, 2011), and C. Kahn, "Discovering the Will: From Aristotle to Augustine," in J. M. Dillon and A. A. Long (eds.), *The Question of Eclecticism* (Berkeley, 1988), 234–59.
3. As argued in A. A. Long, *Epictetus: A Stoic and Socratic Guide to Life* (Oxford, 2002).
4. See C. Gill and R. Hard (eds.), *The Discourses and Handbook of Epictetus* (London, 1995). Cited from section numbers of the translation of the *Discourses*.
5. On this see further T. Brennan, *The Stoic Life: Emotions, Duties, and Fate* (Oxford, 2005), ch. 12.

Chapter 14

1. T. Morris, *If Aristotle Ran General Motors* (New York, 1997).
2. Cited from Marcus Aurelius, *Meditations*, trans. M. Staniforth (London, 1964).
3. M. Beard, "Was He Quite Ordinary?" *London Review of Books*, 23 July 2009.
4. See this volume, Chapter 10.

Chapter 15

1. R. Descartes, *Meditations on First Philosophy*, trans. D. A. Cress (Indianapolis, 1993), 16.
2. Other Pre-Socratics classified as forerunners of skepticism were Xenophanes and Zeno of Elea. See Diogenes Laertius, *Lives of the Philosophers* 9.72.
3. See S. H. Svavarsson, "Pyrrho and Early Pyrrhonism," in R. Bett (ed.), *The Cambridge Companion to Ancient Scepticism* (Cambridge, 2010), 36–57, at 41–53.
4. Here I agree with M. F. Burnyeat, "Idealism and Greek Philosophy: What Descartes Saw and Berkeley Missed," *Philosophical Review*, 90 (1982), 3–40.

5. For the interpretive difficulties of the passage see S. Svavarsson, "Pyrrho's Undecidable Nature," *Oxford Studies in Ancient Philosophy*, 27 (2004), 249–95.

Chapter 16

1. *Classical Philosophy*, ch. 43.
2. Diogenes Laertius, *Lives of the Philosophers* 4.62.
3. See H. Thorsrud, "Arcesilaus and Carneades," in R. Bett (ed.), *The Cambridge Companion to Ancient Scepticism* (Cambridge, 2010), 58–80, and the studies referred to in his n. 17.
4. See further R. Bett, "Carneades' *Pithanon*: A Reappraisal of its Role and Status," *Oxford Studies in Ancient Philosophy*, 7 (1989), 59–94.
5. The Athenians sent a Stoic (Diogenes of Babylon), an Aristotelian (Critolaus), and a Skeptic (Carneades). As pointed out by D. Sedley, "The School, from Zeno to Arius Didymus," in B. Inwood (ed.), *The Cambridge Companion to the Stoics* (Cambridge, 2003), 7–32 at 20 n. 24, the absence of an Epicurean in the embassy probably reflects their lack of political engagement.
6. On whom see C. Brittain, *Philo of Larissa: the Last of the Academic Sceptics* (Oxford, 2001).

Chapter 17

1. The anecdote is recounted in D. Feeney, "Caesar's Body Shook," *London Review of Books*, 22 Sept. 2011.
2. For Cicero's works see the facing-page Latin editions and English translations available in the Loeb series from Harvard University Press. I cite from these in what follows, by section numbers.
3. See J. Barnes, "Antiochus of Ascalon," in M. Griffin and J. Barnes (eds.), *Philosophia Togata I: Essays on Philosophy and Roman Society* (Oxford, 1989), 51–96.
4. J. G. F. Powell, *Cicero the Philosopher* (Oxford, 1995), 98. See further Y. Baraz, *A Written Republic: Cicero's Philosophical Politics* (Princeton, 2012).
5. Seneca, *Epistle* 58.
6. See Powell, *Cicero the Philosopher*, 74.

Chapter 18

1. See G. Striker, "The Ten Tropes of Aenesidemus," in M. Burnyeat (ed.), *The Skeptical Tradition* (Berkeley, 1983), 95–115; J. Annas and J. Barnes, *The Modes of Scepticism* (Cambridge, 1985); R. J. Hankinson, *The Sceptics* (London, 1995), ch. 9; P. Woodruff, "The Pyrrhonian Modes," in R. Bett (ed.), *The Cambridge Companion to Ancient Scepticism* (Cambridge, 2010), 208–31.
2. Citations in the rest of this chapter are to book and section number from J. Annas and J. Barnes (ed. and trans.), *Sextus Empiricus: Outlines of Scepticism* (Cambridge, 2000).
3. Diogenes Laertius, *Lives of the Philosophers* 9.88.
4. For the (appropriately enough, still unresolved) debate see the pieces collected in M. Burnyeat and M. Frede (eds.), *The Original Sceptics* (Indianapolis, 1997).

Chapter 19

1. J. Longrigg, *Greek Medicine from the Heroic to the Hellenistic Age: A Source Book* (London, 1998), §7.2.
2. See V. Nutton, *Ancient Medicine* (London, 2004), ch. 9.

3. Nutton, *Ancient Medicine*, 134–5.
4. *Classical Philosophy*, ch. 11.
5. Nutton, *Ancient Medicine*, 121.
6. Nutton, *Ancient Medicine*, 126.
7. Nutton, *Ancient Medicine*, 132.
8. See the texts gathered in R. Walzer and M. Frede (trans.), *Galen: Three Treatises on the Nature of Science* (Indianapolis, 1985). This includes *On the Sects for Beginners*, to which I refer in what follows.
9. Nutton, *Ancient Medicine*, 149.
10. Nutton, *Ancient Medicine*, 134.
11. For these two works see further in Chapter 20.
12. Nutton, *Ancient Medicine*, 190.

Chapter 20

1. This passage comes from Galen's *On the Differences of Symptoms*, which is included in I. Johnston (trans.), *Galen: On Diseases and Symptoms* (Cambridge, 2006). It's standard to cite Galen's works by referring to the twenty-volume edition produced by C. G. Kühn in the first half of the nineteenth century. In this chapter I will refer to volume and page number of this edition, prefaced by K (for Kühn), because modern editions and translations of Galen normally include the Kühn page references. There is also a series called the *Corpus Medicorum Graecorum* (CMG for short), with many facing-page editions and translations of Galen. These are available online at <http://cmg.bbaw.de>. Facing-page texts of Galen are also available in numerous volumes from the Loeb series published by Harvard University Press. For a handy selection of texts in English see also P. N. Singer (trans.), *Galen: Selected Works* (Oxford, 1997). This contains many of the texts discussed in the present chapter. Finally, there is a series of volumes with English versions of Galen now appearing with Cambridge University Press under the editorship of P. J. van der Eijk.
2. Often abbreviated *PHP* for the Latin title, *De Placitis Hippocratis et Platonis*. In volume 10 of Kühn, volume V 4,1,2 of the CMG.
3. R. Chiaradonna, "Le Traité de Galien *Sur la démonstration* et sa postérité tardo-antique," in R. Chiaradonna and F. Trabattoni (eds.), *Physics and Philosophy of Nature in Greek Neoplatonism* (Leiden, 2009), 43–77.
4. The showmanship involved in Galen's medical demonstrations has a connection to the flourishing of rhetoric at this same period (see Chapter 27). On this topic see M. W. Gleason, "Shock and Awe: The Performance Dimension of Galen's Anatomy Demonstrations," in C. Gill, T. Whitmarsh, and J. Wilkins (eds.), *Galen and the World of Knowledge* (Cambridge, 2009), 85–114; and for Galen's audience, chapter 5 of W. Johnson, *Readers and Reading Culture in the High Roman Empire* (Oxford, 2010).
5. For this see P. Adamson, "Galen on Void," in P. Adamson, R. Hansberger, and J. Wilberding (eds.), *Philosophical Themes in Galen* (London, 2013), 197–211.
6. See D. Leith, "Galen's Refutation of Atomism," in Adamson, Hansberger, and Wilberding, *Philosophical Themes in Galen*, 213–34.
7. R. J. Hankinson, "Galen and the Best of All Possible Worlds," *Classical Quarterly*, 39 (1989), 206–27.
8. A nice example in the *Timaeus* is the human skull, as I discuss in *Classical Philosophy*, ch. 25.
9. For all this see R. J. Hankinson, "Philosophy of Nature," in R. J. Hankinson (ed.), *The Cambridge Companion to Galen* (Cambridge, 2008), 210–41; J. Jouanna, "Galen's Concept of

Nature," in J. Jouanna, *Greek Medicine from Hippocrates to Galen: Selected Papers* (Leiden, 2012), ch. 14.

10. On the topic see further P. J. van der Eijk, "Therapeutics," in Hankinson, *The Cambridge Companion to Galen*, 283–303.

11. Often called QAM for the start of the Latin title *Quod Animi Mores Corporis Temperamenta Sequuntur.*

Chapter 21

1. See Chapter 16.
2. As calculated by R. Goulet, "La Conservation et la transmission des textes philosophiques grecs," in C. D'Ancona (ed.), *The Libraries of the Neoplatonists* (Leiden, 2007).
3. In fact one editor has proposed banning the term completely: L. P. Gerson (ed.), *The Cambridge History of Philosophy in Late Antiquity*, 2 vols. (Cambridge, 2010), 3.
4. *Classical Philosophy*, ch. 43.

Chapter 22

1. Summarized at J. M. Dillon (trans.), *Alcinous: The Handbook of Platonism* (Oxford, 1993), pp. ix–xi.
2. Cicero relates this in the introduction to his translation of the *Timaeus*. See J. M. Dillon, *The Middle Platonists: 80 B.C. to A.D. 220* (Ithaca, NY, 1996), 117.
3. For his teachings see Dillon, *The Middle Platonists*, 115–35, and M. Bonazzi, "Eudorus of Alexandria and Early Imperial Platonism," in R. W. Sharples and R. Sorabji (eds.), *Greek and Roman Philosophy 100 BC–200 AD*, 2 vols. (London, 2007), vol. 2, pp. 365–87.
4. *Classical Philosophy*, ch. 4, and for the Old Academy, ch. 43.
5. Dillon, *The Middle Platonists*, 126–7.
6. On him see Dillon, *The Middle Platonists*, 361–79; M. Frede, "Numenius," *Aufstieg und Niedergang der römischen Welt*, II.36.2 (1987), 1034–75.
7. Porphyry, *Life of Plotinus* 17, in vol. 1 of A. H. Armstrong (trans.), *Plotinus: Enneads*, 7 vols. (Cambridge, Mass., 1966–88).
8. Dillon, *The Middle Platonists*, 370.
9. Dillon, *The Middle Platonists*, 309.
10. Dillon (trans.), *Alcinous: The Handbook of Platonism*, §6.
11. Dillon (trans.), *Alcinous: The Handbook of Platonism*, §32.
12. Dillon, *The Middle Platonists*, 247–58.
13. G. Boys-Stones, "'Middle' Platonists on Fate and Human Autonomy," in Sharples and Sorabji, *Greek and Roman Philosophy 100 BC–200 AD*, vol. 2, pp. 431–47.
14. See H. Tarrant, *Thrasyllan Platonism* (Ithaca, NY, 1993).

Chapter 23

1. *Classical Philosophy*, chs. 3 and 28.
2. G. Boys-Stones, *Post-Hellenistic Philosophy* (Oxford, 2001), 49–59.
3. E. Des Places (ed.), *Numenius: Fragments* (Paris, 1973), fr. 8.
4. See A. Kamesar, "Biblical Interpretation in Philo," in A. Kamesar (ed.), *The Cambridge Companion to Philo* (Cambridge, 2009), 65–91.
5. A good resource is the multi-volume *Cambridge History of Judaism*, of which the first two volumes (Cambridge, 1984 and 1989) take the story up to the age of Philo.

6. Works of Philo are cited from the volumes of the Loeb series, edited by F. H. Colson, G. H. Whitaker, and R. Markus (Cambridge, Mass., 1929–62). For a single-volume collection of Philo's works in English see C. D. Yonge, *The Works of Philo* (Peabody, Mass., 1993, updating Yonge's 1854 translation).
7. i.e. a number equal to the sum of its divisors apart from itself, in this case 1, 2, and 3. The next perfect number, in case you're curious, is 28 (1 + 2 + 4 + 7 + 14), and after that you need to wait a while for the third one to come along.
8. C. Lévy, "Philo's Ethics," in Kamesar (ed.), *The Cambridge Companion to Philo*, 146–71.
9. Dillon, *The Middle Platonists*, 175.
10. Lévy, "Philo's Ethics," 162.

Chapter 24

1. Greek text and English translation F. C. Babbit (trans.), *Plutarch: Moralia*, vol. 5 (Cambridge, Mass., 1936).
2. On whom see J. Opsomer, "M. Annius Ammonius, a Philosophical Profile," in M. Bonazzi and J. Opsomer (eds.), *The Origins of the Platonic System* (Leuven, 2009), 123–86.
3. Respectively in B. Einarson and P. H. De Lacy (trans.), *Plutarch: Moralia*, vol. 14 (Cambridge, Mass., 1967) and H. Cherniss (trans.), *Plutarch: Moralia*, vol. 13, part 2 (Cambridge, Mass., 1976).
4. S. Swain, "Plutarch, Plato, Athens and Rome," in M. Griffin and J. Barnes (eds.), *Philosophia Togata II: Plato and Aristotle at Rome* (Oxford, 1997), 165–87, at 179 and 184.
5. For an assessment of this idea see J. M. Dillon, "'Orthodoxy' and 'Eclecticism': Middle Platonists and Neo-Pythagoreans," in J. M. Dillon and A. A. Long (eds.), *The Question of Eclecticism* (Berkeley, 1987), 103–25.
6. In H. Cherniss (trans.), *Plutarch: Moralia*, vol. 13, part 1 (Cambridge, Mass., 1976).
7. Dillon, *The Middle Platonists*, 237–47.
8. In *Plutarch: Moralia*, vol. 5.
9. On this see L. Van Hoof, *Plutarch's Practical Ethics* (Oxford, 2010).
10. R. Lamberton, *Plutarch* (New Haven, 2001), 109.
11. Van Hoof, *Plutarch's Practical Ethics*, 97.

Chapter 25

1. Bracketed citations in this chapter are *not* to Long and Sedley's reader on Hellenistic philosophy, but rather to the texts translated in R. W. Sharples, *Peripatetic Philosophy 200 BC to AD 200* (Cambridge, 2010).
2. J. Barnes, "Roman Aristotle," in J. Barnes and M. Griffin (eds.), *Philosophia Togata II: Plato and Aristotle at Rome* (Oxford, 1997), 1–69. One point Barnes does not consider is that the antiquated numbering system used in the Aristotelian works suggests that they were indeed more or less out of circulation in the Hellenistic period. See O. Primavesi, "Ein Blick in den Stollen von Skepsis: Vier Kapitel zur frühen Überlieferung des Corpus Aristotelicum," *Philologus*, 151 (2007), 51–77.
3. For discussion and references to further literature see S. Fazzo, "The *Metaphysics* from Aristotle to Alexander of Aphrodisias," *Bulletin of the Institute of Classical Studies*, 55–1 (2012), 51–68.
4. D. Konstan (trans.), *Aspasius: On Aristotle Nicomachean Ethics 1–4, 7–8* (London, 2006).
5. See M. J. Griffin, "What Does Aristotle Categorize? Semantics and the Early Peripatetic Reading of the *Categories*," *Bulletin of the Institute of Classical Studies*, 55–1 (2012), 69–108, at 77.
6. H. B. Gottschalk, "Boethus' Psychology and the Neoplatonists," *Phronesis*, 31 (1986), 243–57.

Chapter 26

1. R. W. Sharples, "Implications of the New Alexander of Aphrodisias Inscription," *Bulletin of the Institute of Classical Studies*, 48 (2005), 47–56.
2. Not that commentary was only a Peripatetic game. We saw how Plutarch and other "Middle" Platonists commented on issues in Plato; another early Platonic commentary that has survived is devoted to Plato's *Theaetetus*, though we do not know its author.
3. The best example is the critical commentary on parts of the *Metaphysics* by the Neoplatonist author Syrianus. See Chapter 35.
4. Cited by section number from R. W. Sharples (trans.), *Alexander of Aphrodisias: On Fate* (London, 1983).
5. There is as yet no English translation, but for one in French see P. Thillet, *Alexandre d'Aphrodise: Traité De la providence* (Lagrasse, 2003).
6. Sharples, *Peripatetic Philosophy*, 87.
7. See R. W. Sharples, *Alexander of Aphrodisias: Supplement to On the Soul* (London, 2004); V. Caston, *Alexander of Aphrodisias: On the Soul Part 1* (Bristol, 2012). These volumes are both from the "Ancient Commentators on Aristotle" series, which includes English versions for many of Alexander's works.

Chapter 27

1. H. E. Butler (trans.), *The Institutio Oratoria of Quintilian*, 4 vols. (Cambridge, Mass., 1920).
2. Augustine, *Confessions* 2.3.
3. A. Luhtala, *Grammar and Philosophy in Late Antiquity* (Amsterdam, 2005), 46.
4. Plutarch, *Platonic Questions* 10.3.
5. On this see T. Suto, *Boethius on Mind, Grammar and Logic* (Leiden, 2012), ch. 4.
6. Luhtala, *Grammar and Philosophy*, 55.
7. G. Anderson, *The Second Sophistic* (London, 1993), 87.
8. In C. D. N. Costa, *Lucian: Selected Dialogues* (Oxford, 2005). My discussion here is indebted to Michael Trapp.
9. Anderson, *The Second Sophistic*, 13.
10. Anderson, *The Second Sophistic*, 23.
11. E. J. Watts, *City and School in Late Antique Athens and Alexandria* (Berkeley, 2006), 17.
12. P. Heather and D. Moncur, *Politics, Philosophy and Empire in the Fourth Century: Select Orations of Themistius* (Liverpool, 2001).
13. Both points suggested by Heather and Moncur, *Politics, Philosophy and Empire*, 18.
14. R. B. Todd (trans.), *Themistius: On Aristotle On the Soul* (London, 1996), with the treatment of the crucial chapter at pp. 122–34. For Alexander and Themistius on intellect see also F. M. Schroeder and R. B. Todd, *Two Greek Aristotelian Commentators on the Intellect* (Toronto, 1990).
15. Heather and Moncur, *Politics, Philosophy and Empire*, 5.

Chapter 28

1. For this and the legend see T. Barton, *Ancient Astrology* (London, 1994), 40.
2. *Classical Philosophy*, ch. 5.
3. Barton, *Ancient Astrology*, 104.
4. On Cicero's treatment of astrology see A. A. Long, "Astrology: Arguments Pro and Contra," in *Science and Speculation: Studies in Hellenistic Theory and Practice*, ed. J. Barnes *et al.*

(Cambridge, 1982), 165–92; A. M. Ioppolo, "L'astrologia nella stoicismo antico," in G. Giannantoni and M. Vegetti (eds.), *La Scienza Ellenistica* (Naples, 1984), 75–91.

5. Barton, *Ancient Astrology*, 92.
6. For more on Aristotle's cosmos see *Classical Philosophy*, ch. 34.
7. G. J. Toomer (trans.), *Ptolemy's Almagest* (London, 1984), §1.1.
8. Long, "Astrology: Arguments Pro and Contra," 170.
9. Barton, *Ancient Astrology*, 53–4.
10. *Confessions* 7.6.
11. Barton, *Ancient Astrology*, 74–6.
12. G. P. Goold (trans.), *Manilius: Astronomica* (Cambridge, Mass., 1977).
13. F. E. Robbins, *Ptolemy: Tetrabiblos* (Cambridge, Mass., 1940). Cited by section number.
14. P. Adamson, "Plotinus on Astrology," *Oxford Studies in Ancient Philosophy*, 35 (2008), 265–91.
15. *Enneads* 3.1.6.

Chapter 29

1. For the works of Plotinus the most widely available English version is by S. MacKenna; but a more reliable translation is that in the seven-volume Loeb series published by Harvard University Press, by A. H. Armstrong. It includes Porphyry's *Life of Plotinus* in the first volume. The treatise, chapter, and section numbers I will cite are standard and found in all editions and translations of Plotinus. The *Life* is also translated in M. Edwards (trans.), *Neoplatonic Saints: The Lives of Plotinus and Proclus by their Students* (Liverpool, 2000).
2. G. Clark, "Philosophic Lives and the Philosophic Life: Porphyry and Iamblichus," in T. Hägg and P. Rousseau, *Greek Biography and Panegyric in Late Antiquity* (Berkeley, 2000), 29–51, at 35.
3. On this problem see J. M. Dillon, "An Ethic for the Late Antique Sage," in L. E. Gerson (ed.), *The Cambridge Companion to Plotinus* (Cambridge, 1996), 315–35, P. Remes, "Plotinus' Ethics of Disinterested Ethics," *Journal of Philosophy*, 44 (2006), 1–23.
4. J. Lacrosse, "Plotinus, Porphyry, and India: A Re-Examination," in P. Vassilopoulou and S. Clark (eds.), *Late Antique Epistemology: Other Ways to Truth* (New York, 2009), 103–17.

Chapter 30

1. *Classical Philosophy*, ch. 21.
2. *Classical Philosophy*, chs. 6, 22, 43.
3. For an argument that Plotinus was the first Platonist to (mis-)interpret the passage this way, see M. Baltes, "Is the Idea of the Good in Plato's *Republic* Beyond Being?," in M. Joyal (ed.), *Studies in Plato and the Platonic Tradition* (Aldershot, 1997), 3–23.
4. Plotinus even says on occasion that Intellect just *is* a number, as is the soul (5.1.5). See further S. Slaveva-Griffin, *Plotinus on Number* (Oxford, 2009).

Chapter 31

1. *Classical Philosophy*, ch. 18.
2. See further E. K. Emilsson, *Plotinus on Sense-Perception* (Cambridge, 1988).
3. For a case that Plotinian eternity is not wholly a-temporal see J. Wilberding, "Eternity in Ancient Philosophy," in Y. Melamed (ed.), *Eternity* (Oxford, forthcoming).
4. I take this point from R. Chiaradonna, "Plotin, la mémoire et la connaissance des intelligibles," *Philosophie antique*, 9 (2009), 5–33.

5. On this idea in Plotinus see E. K. Emilsson, *Plotinus on Intellect* (Oxford, 2007), ch. 1.

6. See e.g. P. Kalligas, "Forms of Individuals in Plotinus: A Re-Examination," *Phronesis*, 42 (1997), 206–27.

Chapter 32

1. For the contemporary debate see M. M. Adams and R. M. Adams (eds), *The Problem of Evil* (Oxford, 1990).

2. For instance, we get into difficulties about whether God could know in advance what actions a creature will freely perform, should He choose to create that creature. The possibility of such so-called "middle knowledge" is discussed in scholastic medieval philosophy.

3. Compare C. Schaefer, "Matter in Plotinus's Normative Ontology," *Phronesis*, 49 (2004), 266–94.

4. An influential study is D. O'Brien, *Plotinus on the Origin of Matter* (Naples, 1991). As we'll see later in this volume, the Plotinian doctrine of evil was already controversial in antiquity. See further J. Opsomer, "Some Problems with Plotinus? Theory of Matter/Evil: An Ancient Debate Continued," *Quaestio*, 7 (2007), 165–89.

5. J.-M. Narbonne, *Plotinus in Dialogue with the Gnostics* (Leiden, 2011), makes a case for wide-reaching implications of this polemic in Plotinus.

Chapter 33

1. Cited by section number from the translation in J. Barnes, *Porphyry: Introduction* (Oxford, 2003).

2. See G. Karamanolis, *Plato and Aristotle in Agreement?* (Oxford, 2005).

3. H. S. Schibli, *Hierocles of Alexandria* (Oxford, 2002), 28.

4. G. Karamanolis, "Porphyry, the first Platonist Commentator of Aristotle," in P. Adamson, H. Baltussen, and M. W. F. Stone (eds.), *Science and Exegesis in Greek, Arabic and Latin*, 2 vols. (London, 2004), vol. 1, pp. 79–113.

5. Collected in R. M. Berchman, *Porphyry Against the Christians* (Leiden, 2005).

6. Cited by book and section number from the translation in G. Clark, *Porphyry: On Abstinence from Killing Animals* (London, 2000). The interpretation that follows is heavily influenced by that of Fay Edwards. On the topic see further R. Sorabji, *Animal Minds, Human Morals: The Origins of the Western Debate* (London, 1993).

7. He takes this comparison from Plato, *Phaedo* 83d. On Porphyry's attitude towards the body see several of the studies in G. Clark, *Body and Gender, Soul and Reason in Late Antiquity* (Farnham, 2011).

Chapter 34

1. For this story see P. Athanassiadi, *Julian: An Intellectual Biography* (London, 1981), 33.

2. J. Dillon and J. Hershbell (trans.), *Iamblichus: On the Pythagorean Way of Life* (Atlanta, Ga., 1991). See further D. O'Meara, *Pythagoras Revived: Mathematics and Philosophy in Late Antiquity* (Oxford, 1989).

3. B. P. Copenhaver, *Hermetica* (Cambridge, 1992).

4. R. Majercik, *The Chaldean Oracles* (Leiden, 1989). See also H. Lewy, *The Chaldean Oracles and Theurgy* (Paris, 1978).

5. See *Classical Philosophy*, ch. 24.

6. J. M. Dillon, "Iamblichus' *Noera Theoria* of Aristotle's Categories," *Syllecta Classica*, 8 (1997), 65–77.
7. C. Steel, *The Changing Self: A Study on the Soul in Later Neoplatonism* (Brussels, 1978); J. M. Dillon, "Iamblichus' Criticisms of Plotinus' Doctrine of the Undescended Soul," in R. Chiaradonna (ed.), *Studi sull'anima in Plotino* (Naples, 2005), 339–51.
8. J. M. Dillon, "Iamblichus' Defence of Theurgy: Some Reflections," *Journal of the Platonic Tradition*, 1 (2007), 30–41.
9. Cited by section number from E. C. Clarke, J. M. Dillon, and J. P. Hershbell (trans.), *Iamblichus: On the Mysteries* (Atlanta, Ga., 2003). The treatise in which Porphyry raised his doubts does not survive, but we have a good idea of its contents thanks to Iamblichus' response.
10. E. R. Dodds, *The Greeks and the Irrational* (Berkeley, 1951), 287.

Chapter 35

1. For studies of several such consolatory works, see H. Baltussen (ed.), *Greek and Roman Consolations* (Swansea, 2013).
2. J. M. Dillon and W. Polleichtner (ed. and trans.), *Iamblichus of Chalcis: The Letters* (Atlanta, Ga., 2009). I cite from their translation of Letter 4 below.
3. See H. S. Schibli, *Hierocles of Alexandria* (Oxford, 2002); P. Adamson, "Freedom, Providence and Fate," in P. Remes and S. Slaveva-Griffin (eds.), *The Routledge Handbook of Neoplatonism* (London, 2014), 437–52.
4. See above, Chapter 26 n. 5.
5. S. Swain, *Economy, Family and Society from Rome to Islam: A Critical Edition, English Translation, and Study of Bryson's "Management of the Estate"* (Cambridge, 2013). This work, like Alexander's *On Providence*, is lost in Greek but survives in Arabic. I cite from the section numbers of Swain's English translation.
6. This point is made forcefully by Swain, *Economy, Family, and Society*, ch. 3, from which I draw the examples that follow.
7. *On Duties* 2.87, quoted at Swain, *Economy, Family, and Society*, 203.
8. For Aristotle on slavery see *Classical Philosophy*, ch. 40.
9. Here I follow Swain, *Economy, Family, and Society*, 267.
10. Epistle 47, in R. M. Gummere (trans.), *Seneca: Epistulae Morales* (Cambridge, Mass., 1979). My translations.
11. A point also made by M. I. Finley, *Ancient Slavery and Modern Ideology* (London, 1980), 121, R. Bradley, "Seneca and Slavery," *Classica et Medievalia*, 37 (1986), 161–72. For a more positive assessment of Seneca's views see M. T. Griffin, *Seneca: A Philosopher in Politics* (Oxford, 1976), 278. On the persistence of slavery after the coming of Christianity see Kyle Harper, *Slavery in the Late Roman World AD 275–425* (Cambridge, 2011).
12. As pointed out by Swain, *Economy, Family, and Society*, 370.
13. M. Schofield, *The Stoic Idea of the City* (Chicago, 1999), 45.
14. See *Classical Philosophy*, ch. 42.
15. For this less optimistic view of the Stoics' attitude see M. Nussbaum, "The Incomplete Feminism of Musonius Rufus, Platonist, Stoic and Roman," in M. Nussbaum and J. Sihvola (eds.), *The Sleep of Reason: Erotic Experience and Sexual Ethics in Ancient Greece and Rome* (Chicago, 2002), 283–326; D. M. Engel, "Women's Role in the Home and the State: Stoic Theory Reconsidered," *Harvard Studies in Classical Philology*, 101 (2003), 267–88.

16. Engel, "Women's Role in the Home and the State," 277.

17. D. O'Meara, *Platonopolis: Platonic Political Philosophy in Late Antiquity* (Oxford, 2005), 85.

18. Letter 1 in Dillon and Polleichtner, *Iamblichus of Chalcis: The Letters*.

19. On this point see O'Meara, *Platonopolis*, ch. 10, and for Eusebius on Constantine, ch. 12.

Chapter 36

1. For details see C. Wildberg, "Proclus' Life and Works," in M. Martijn and P. D'Hoine, *All from One: A Guide to Proclus* (forthcoming).

2. M. Edwards (trans.), *Neoplatonic Saints: The Lives of Plotinus and Proclus by their Students* (Liverpool, 2000).

3. Syrianus, *On Aristotle Metaphysics* 13–14 and 3–4, trans. J. M. Dillon and D. O'Meara (London, 2006 and 2008). For his comments on Platonic dialogues see S. Klitenic Wear, *The Teachings of Syrianus on Plato's Timaeus and Parmenides* (Leiden, 2011).

4. The *Timaeus* commentary is translated in several volumes available from Cambridge University Press. For the *Parmenides* commentary see G. R. Morrow and J. M. Dillon (trans.), *Proclus' Commentary on Plato's Parmenides* (Princeton, 1987).

5. W. O'Neill trans., *Proclus: Alcibiades I* (The Hague, 1965).

6. B. Duvick (trans.), *Proclus: On Plato's Cratylus* (London, 2007). For the *Republic* essays one may consult the French translation, A. J. Festugière (trans.), *Proclus: Commentaire sur la République*, 3 vols. (Paris, 1970).

7. Again, available in French: H. D Saffrey and L. G. Westerink (ed. and trans.), *Proclus: Théologie Platonicienne*, 4 vols. (Paris, 2003).

8. G. R. Morrow (trans.), *Proclus: A Commentary on the First Book of Euclid's Elements* (Princeton, 1970); R. M. van den Berg, *Proclus' Hymns* (Leiden, 2001).

9. Cited in what follows from proposition number of E. R. Dodds, *Proclus: The Elements of Theology* (Oxford, 1933).

10. For a useful guide to the system see R. Chlup, *Proclus: An Introduction* (Cambridge, 2012).

11. On this see C. Steel, "Breathing Thought: Proclus on the Innate Knowledge of the Soul," in J. J. Cleary (ed.), *The Perennial Tradition of Neoplatonism* (Leuven, 1997), 293–309.

12. J. Opsomer and C. Steel (trans.), *Proclus: On the Existence of Evils* (London, 2003). On the topic see further J. Opsomer, "Proclus vs. Plotinus on matter (*De mal. subs.* 30–7)," *Phronesis*, 46 (2001), 154–88.

Chapter 37

1. On his life see P. Athanassiadi, *Julian: An Intellectual Biography* (London, 1981).

2. See E. J. Watts, *City and School in Late Antique Athens and Alexandria* (Berkeley, 2006), 131–8.

3. *Classical Philosophy*, ch. 42.

4. On her see M. Dzielska, *Hypatia of Alexandria* (Cambridge, Mass., 1995).

5. Watts, *City and School*, 192, quoting Damascius, *Life of Isidore* 106a.

6. So argues A. Bernard, "The Alexandrian School: Theon of Alexandria and Hypatia," in L. P. Gerson (ed.), *The Cambridge History of Philosophy in Late Antiquity*, 2 vols. (Cambridge, 2010), vol. 2, pp. 417–36.

7. Translations in H. S. Schibli, *Hierocles of Alexandria* (Oxford, 2002).

8. Watts, *City and School*, 199.

9. J. Opsomer, "Olympiodorus," in Gerson (ed.), *The Cambridge History of Philosophy in Late Antiquity*, vol. 2, pp. 697–710, at 703.

10. For what follows I draw on S. R. P. Gertz, *Death and Immortality in Late Neoplatonism: Studies on the Ancient Commentaries on Plato's Phaedo* (Leiden, 2011).
11. S. Abhel Rappe (trans.), *Damascius' Problems and Solutions Concerning First Principles* (Oxford, 2010).
12. On him see H. Baltussen, *Philosophy and Exegesis in Simplicius* (London, 2008).
13. T. Brennan and C. Brittain (trans.), *Simplicius: On Epictetus Handbook*, 2 vols. (London, 2002). Simplicius wasn't the only Platonist to engage with him; for a study of Plotinus stressing his use of Epictetus, see K. McGroarty, *Plotinus on Eudaimonia: A Commentary on Ennead I.4* (Oxford, 2006).
14. H. Baltussen, "Simplicius of Cilicia," in Gerson (ed.), *The Cambridge History of Philosophy in Late Antiquity*, vol. 2, pp. 711–32, at 719.

Chapter 38

1. M. Share and J. Wilberding (trans.), *Philoponus: Against Proclus on the Eternity of the World*, 4 vols. (London, 2005–10). Cited below by book and section number. For just the work being attacked by Philoponus see H. S. Lang and A. D. Macro (trans.), *Proclus: On the Eternity of the World* (Berkeley, 2001).
2. C. Wildberg (trans.), *Philoponus: Against Aristotle on the Eternity of the World* (London, 1987). Cited below by book and section number.
3. *Against Aristotle*, Prologue.
4. R. Sorabji, *The Philosophy of the Commentators 200–600 AD*, 3 vols. (London, 2004), vol. 2, 8c.
5. S. Gertz, J. M. Dillon, and D. Russell (trans.), *Aeneas of Gaza: Theophrastus with Zacharias of Mytilene: Ammonius* (London, 2012).
6. *Classical Philosophy*, ch. 34.
7. On this see L. Judson, "God or Nature? Philoponus on Generability and Perishability," in R. Sorabji (ed.), *Philoponus and the Rejection of Aristotelian Science* (Ithaca, NY, 1987), 179–96.
8. *Classical Philosophy*, ch. 7.
9. For what follows see R. Sorabji, *The Philosophy of the Commentators*, vol. 2, 22 f.; M. Wolff, "Philoponus and the Rise of Preclassical Dynamics," in Sorabji (ed.), *Philoponus and the Rejection of Aristotelian Science*, 84–120.
10. It should be mentioned that Philoponus was notorious among later Christians for his positions on the two most hotly disputed theological questions of late ancient Christianity, the Trinity and the Incarnation. He was condemned by the "orthodox" for being both a 'Tritheist' (i.e. for dividing God into three substances) and a monophysite (i.e. refusing to distinguish between the human and divine natures of Christ). For more on these controversies see Chapters 42 and 44.

Chapter 39

1. See e.g. R. A. Norris, Jr., "Articulating Identity," in F. Young, L. Aures, and A. Louth (eds.), *The Cambridge History of Early Christian Literature* (Cambridge, 2004), 71–90.
2. M. Ludlow, *The Early Church* (London, 2009), 14.
3. *Apologies*, ed. A. W. F. Blunt (Cambridge, 1911), 1.6; quoted in H. Bettenson, *The Early Christian Church Fathers* (Oxford, 1956), 58.
4. Ludlow, *The Early Church*, 31, quoting Ignatius' *Letter to the Romans*.
5. *Confessions* 7.9.13.

6. A powerful recent exploration of the notion of will in antiquity, which stresses the novel contributions made by Christian thinkers, is M. Frede, *A Free Will: Origins of the Notion in Ancient Thought* (Berkeley, 2011).

7. *Classical Philosophy*, ch. 30.

Chapter 40

1. A. Plantinga, "Reason and Belief in God," in A. Plantinga and D. Wolterstorff (eds.), *Faith and Rationality: Reason and Belief in God* (Notre Dame, Ind., 1983), 16–93, at 74.

2. Extracts translated in R. M. Grant, *Irenaeus of Lyons* (London, 1997). Cited by book and section number.

3. See R. M. Grant, *Gnosticism and Early Christianity* (New York, 1966), M. Edwards, "Gnostics and Valentinians in the Church Fathers," *Journal of Theological Studies*, 40 (1989), 26–47.

4. *Confessions* 11.12.14.

5. Clement of Alexandria, *Stromateis Books 1–3*, trans. J. Ferguson (Washington, DC, 1991). Cited by book and section number.

6. S. R. C. Lilla, *Clement of Alexandria* (Oxford, 1971), 150.

7. Justin Martyr, *Dialogue with Trypho*, trans. T. B. Falls (Washington, DC, 2003). Cited by chapter number.

8. J. Hick, *Evil and the God of Love* (London, 1966).

Chapter 41

1. *Life of Plotinus* 3. For an argument against the identity of Ammonius' student and the Christian theologian, see M. J. Edwards, "Ammonius, Teacher of Origen," *Journal of Ecclesiastial History*, 44 (1993), 169–81.

2. See E. A. Clark, *The Origenist Controversy* (Princeton, 1992).

3. Origen, *On First Principles*, trans. G. W. Butterworth (Gloucester, Mass., 1973), book 1, preface, sections 5–9. Cited below by book, chapter, and section number.

4. On resurrection and universal salvation see M. S. M. Scott, *Journey Back to God: Origen on the Problem of Evil* (Oxford, 2012), chs. 5–6.

5. Cited by book and section number from H. Chadwick (trans.), *Origen: Contra Celsum* [*Against Celsus*] (Cambridge, 1965). For Celsus' attack see J. R. Hoffman (trans.), *Celsus: On the True Doctrine. A Discourse Against the Christians* (Oxford, 1987).

6. See J. W. Trigg, *Origen* (London, 1998), 33.

7. Trigg, *Origen*, 120.

Chapter 42

1. Trans. in W. A. Moore and H. A. Wolfson, *Select Writings and Letters of Gregory, Bishop of Nyssa* (Grand Rapids, Mich., 1954), 430–68. Despite the obvious comparison to the *Phaedo*, the actual philosophical content is not based closely on Plato's dialogue.

2. B. A. Daley, *Gregory of Nazianzus* (London, 2006), 16 and 21.

3. *Oration 14*, trans. in Daley, *Gregory of Nazianzus*, 75–97. Cited by section number.

4. See further L. Ayres, *Nicaea and its Legacy: An Approach to Fourth-Century Trinitarian Theology* (Oxford, 2004).

5. A. Meredith, *Gregory of Nyssa* (London, 1999), 84.

6. *Classical Philosophy*, ch. 30.

7. *Classical Philosophy*, ch. 25.

8. For the following see M. Delcogliano, *Basil of Caesarea's Anti-Eunomian Theory of Names* (Leiden, 2010).
9. Delcogliano, *Basil of Caesarea's Anti-Eunomian Theory*, 191, 217.
10. Meredith, *Gregory of Nyssa*, 107–8.

Chapter 43

1. Letter 10 in C. Luibheid and P. Rorem (trans.), *Pseudo-Dionysius: The Complete Works* (London, 1987). This translation indicates in the margins the sections of the *Patrologia Graeca* edition of Dionysius' works; I cite these in what follows.
2. See F. O'Rourke, *Pseudo-Dionysius and the Metaphysics of Aquinas* (Leiden, 1992).
3. P. Rorem, *Pseudo-Dionysius: A Commentary on the Texts and an Introduction to their Influence* (Oxford, 1993), 14.
4. L. Wittgenstein, *Tractatus Logico-Philosophicus*, trans. C. K. Ogden (London, 1992), §7.

Chapter 44

1. On the history of the debate see e.g. A. Grillmeier, *Christ in Christian Tradition*, 2 vols. (London, 1965), J. Meyendorff, *Byzantine Theology* (New York, 1974), J. McGuckin, *St Cyril of Alexandria: The Christological Controversy* (Leiden, 1994), D. Bathrellos, *The Byzantine Christ* (Oxford, 2004), J. Behr, *The Formation of Christian Theology*, vol. 2: *The Nicene Faith* (New York, 2004).
2. A. Meredith, *Gregory of Nyssa* (London, 1999), 48. See also T. T. Tollefson, *Activity and Participation in Late Antique and Early Christian Thought* (Oxford, 2012), 136.
3. For what follows see A. Louth, *Maximus the Confessor* (London, 1996).
4. Tollefson, *Activity and Participation*, 150.
5. Bathrellos, *The Byzantine Christ*, 63.
6. Tollefson, *Activity and Participation*, 155.
7. *Third Letter to Nestorius*, in J. I. McEnerney (trans.), *Saint Cyril of Alexandria: Letters 1–50* (Washington, DC, 1987). Reprinted in B. D. Ehrman and A. S. Jacobs, *Christianity in Late Antiquity 300–450 C.E.: A Reader* (New York, 2004), 182–8.

Chapter 45

1. *Classical Philosophy*, ch. 38.
2. *Classical Philosophy*, ch. 21.
3. See e.g. Nietzsche's discussion of the ascetic ideal in the *Genealogy of Morals*.
4. Translation in B. D. Ehrman and A. S. Jacobs, *Christianity in Late Antiquity 300–450 C.E.: A Reader* (New York, 2004), 368–77.
5. *Confessions* 8.6.15.
6. On this phenomenon see P. Brown, *Through the Eye of a Needle: Wealth, the Fall of Rome and the Making Christianity in the West 350–550 AD* (Princeton, 2012).
7. See the chapter on him in Theodoret's *Religious History*, translated at Ehrman and Jacobs, *Christianity in Late Antiquity*, 381–7.
8. See S. A. Harvey, "Women and Words: Texts by and About Women," in F. Young, L. Aures, and A. Louth (eds.), *The Cambridge History of Early Christian Literature* (Cambridge, 2004), 382–90. See further E. A. Clark, *Ascetic Piety and Women's Faith: Essays on Late Ancient Christianity* (Lewiston, NY, 1986), M. H. King, *The Desert Mothers* (Toronto, 1989).
9. K. Corrigan (trans.), *Gregory, Bishop of Nyssa: The Life of St Macrina* (Toronto, 1989).

10. Translation in B. A. Daley, *Gregory of Nazianzus* (London, 2006), 63–75.
11. On him see A. M. Casiday, *Evagrius Ponticus* (London, 2006).
12. But for a recent argument against the Origenist reading of Evagrius, see A. Casiday, *Reconstructing the Theology of Evagrius Ponticus* (Cambridge, 2013).
13. Casiday, *Reconstructing the Theology of Evagrius Ponticus*, 25.
14. K. Corrigan, *Evagrius and Gregory: Mind, Soul and Body in the 4th Century* (Farnham, 2009), ch. 5.
15. Casiday, *Evagrius Ponticus*, 73–4.
16. R. W. Sharples and P. J. van der Eijk (trans.), *Nemesius: On the Nature of Man* (Liverpool, 2008). Cited by section number from this translation.

Chapter 46

1. On this issue see H. Hagendahl, *Latin Fathers and the Classics* (Göteborg, 1958).
2. See I. A. Wright (trans.), *Jerome: Select Letters* (London, 1933).
3. For this I draw especially on M. Hale Williams, *The Monk and the Book: Jerome and the Making of Christian Scholarship* (Chicago, 2006). For the expense of the *Hexapla* see p. 153.
4. Lactantius, *Divine Institutes*, trans. A. Bowen and P. Garnsey (Liverpool, 2003); cited by section number. Passages addressing the work to Constantine were added at a later date.
5. On his career see N. B. McLynn, *Ambrose of Milan: Church and Court in a Christian Capital* (Berkeley, 1994).
6. I. J. Davidson (trans.), *Ambrose: De Officiis*, 2 vols. (Oxford, 2001), cited by section number.
7. *De Praescriptione Haereticorum* 7.9.
8. Colossians 2: 8; I quote the King James version.
9. J. H. Waszink (ed.), *Tertullian: De Anima* (Leiden, 2010); English translation E.A. Quain (trans.), *Tertullian: De Anima* (Washington, DC, 1950). Cited by chapter number.
10. See Hale Williams, *The Monk and the Book*, 98, and E. A. Clark, *The Origenist Controversy* (Princeton, 1992).

Chapter 47

1. For translations of the *Confessions* see Augustine, *Confessions*, trans. H. Chadwick (Oxford, 1991), Augustine, *Confessions*, trans. F. J. Sheed (Indianapolis, 1993). Cited by section number. The classic modern study of Augustine's life is P. Brown, *Augustine of Hippo* (Berkeley, 1969).
2. Augustine did know some Greek but admits in the *Confessions* itself that he never enjoyed the study and reading of Greek as he did of Latin (1.13.20).
3. *Meditations* 5.1.
4. The King James Bible version of the astonishingly apt passage reads: "not in rioting and drunkenness, not in chambering and wantonness, not in strife and envying. But put ye on the Lord Jesus Christ, and make not provision for the flesh, to fulfill the lusts thereof" (13: 13–14).
5. See R. Teske, *Paradoxes of Time in St Augustine* (Milwaukee, 1996).

Chapter 48

1. For an English version see P. King (trans.), *Augustine: Against the Academicians and The Teacher* (Indianapolis, 1995). Cited below by section number. For studies see R. A. Markus, "Augustine on Signs," *Phronesis*, 2 (1957), 60–83; M. F. Burnyeat, "Wittgenstein and Augustine De Magistro," *Proceedings of the Aristotelian Society*, suppl. vol. 61 (1987), 1–24;

P. King, "Augustine on the Impossibility of Teaching," *Metaphilosophy*, 29 (1998), 179–95.

2. W. V. O. Quine, *Word and Object* (Cambridge, Mass., 1960), ch. 2.

3. R. P. H. Green (trans.), *Augustine: On Christian Teaching* (Oxford, 2008). On the usefulness of literal translations see 2.13.19, and on the Septuagint 2.15.22. For studies of the work see D. W. H. Arnold and P. Bright (eds.), *De Doctrina Christiana: a Classic of Western Culture* (Notre Dame, Ind., 1995); M. D. Jordan, "Words and Word: Incarnation and Signification in Augustine's *De Doctrina Christiana*," *Augustinian Studies*, 11 (1980), 175–96.

Chapter 49

1. Epistle 224, cited at Kirwan 6. The medieval scholar Isidore of Seville wrote a verse stating, "anyone who claims to have read all your [i.e. Augustine's] works is a liar." This, however, refers to the inaccessibility of Augustine's writings, not their unmanageable extent, as argued by, among others, B. Kent, "Reinventing Augustine's Ethics: The Afterlife of the *City of God*," in J. Wetzel (ed.), *Augustine's City of God: A Critical Guide* (Cambridge, 2012), 225–44, at 228. Still, if anyone does tell you they've read all of Augustine, you have the right to be skeptical.

2. J. J. O'Donnell, *Augustine: A New Biography* (New York, 2005), 110.

3. See G. Bonner, "Augustine and Pelagianism," *Augustinian Studies*, 23 (1992), 33–51, and 24 (1993), 27–47.

4. T. Williams (trans.), *Augustine: On Free Choice of the Will* (Indianapolis, 1993). Cited by section number.

5. See *Classical Philosophy*, ch. 30.

6. See W. L. Craig, "Augustine on Foreknowledge and Free Will," *Augustinian Studies*, 15 (1984), 41–67.

7. Based on E. Stump, "Augustine on Free Will," in E. Stump and N. Kretzmann (eds.), *The Cambridge Companion to Augustine* (Cambridge, 2001), 124–47. On the topic see further J. M. Rist, "Augustine on Free Will and Predestination," *Journal of Theological Studies*, 20 (1969) 420–47; G. O'Daly, "Predestination and Freedom in Augustine's Ethics," in G. Vesey (ed.), *The Philosophy in Christianity* (Cambridge, 1989).

Chapter 50

1. Augustine refers to the doctrine at *On Free Choice of the Will* 3.21.

2. Augustine, *The City of God Against the Pagans*, trans. R. W. Dyson (Cambridge, 1998), cited by section number. For studies of this work and Augustine's political philosophy see R. Dodaro, *Christ and the Just Society in the Thought of Augustine* (Cambridge, 2004); R. W. Dyson, *St Augustine of Hippo: The Christian Transformation of Political Thought* (London, 2005); G. O'Daly, *Augustine's City of God: A Reader's Guide* (Oxford, 1999); J. Von Heyking, *Augustine and Politics as Longing in the World* (Columbia, NY, 2001); J. Wetzel (ed.), *Augustine's City of God: A Critical Guide* (Cambridge, 2012).

3. See further B. Harding, *Augustine and Roman Virtue* (London, 2008).

4. Letter 10.

5. Compare Plotinus, *Enneads* 6.8.5.

6. On this topic see S. Byers, "The Psychology of Compassion: Stoicism in *City of God* 9.5," in Wetzel (ed.), *Augustine's City of God*, 130–48.

Chapter 51

1. For the relation between these two thinkers see S. Menn, *Descartes and Augustine* (Cambridge, 1998).
2. For a translation see Augustine, *Against the Academicians and The Teacher*, trans. P. King (Indianapolis, 1995).
3. *On the Immortality of the Soul* and *On the Quantity of the Soul*, written respectively in 387 and 388.
4. *On the Quantity of the Soul* 70–6, discussed in G. O'Daly, *Augustine's Philosophy of Mind* (Berkeley, 1987), 13–14.
5. See O'Daly, *Augustine's Philosophy of Mind*, 31–4.
6. For English versions see E. Hill (trans.), *Augustine: On the Trinity* (Brooklyn, 1991); S. MacKenna (trans.) and G. B. Matthews (ed.), Augustine, *On the Trinity* (Cambridge, 2002), the latter covering only Books 8–15. Cited by section number.
7. See J. Mourant, *Saint Augustine on Memory* (Villanova, 1980); R. J. Teske, "Platonic Reminiscence and Memory of the Present in St Augustine," *New Scholasticism*, 58 (1984), 220–35; P. E. Hochschild, *Memory in Augustine's Theological Anthropology* (Oxford, 2012).
8. *On the Trinity* 9.12 already makes this point regarding knowledge.
9. Mentioned at *On the Trinity* 10.9.
10. For the self in Augustine see P. Cary, *Augustine's Invention of the Inner Self* (Oxford, 2000), and for this idea of "remembering" what is happening now, R. J. Teske, "Platonic Reminiscence and Memory of the Present in St Augustine," *New Scholasticism*, 58 (1984), 220–35.

Chapter 52

1. For the classic study of Victorinus' place in the Platonist tradition see P. Hadot, *Porphyre et Victorinus* (Paris, 1968).
2. See Plato, *Symposium* 202d–203a. Apuleius also wrote a more general introduction to Plato called *On Plato and his Teaching*.
3. W. H. Stahl (trans.), *Macrobius: Commentary on the Dream of Scipio* (New York, 1952).
4. *Classical Philosophy*, ch. 28.
5. W. H. Stahl, R. Johnson, and E. L. Burge, *Martianus Capella and the Seven Liberal Arts*, 2 vols. (New York, 1971, 1977), with translation of the *Marriage* in volume 2. Cited below by section number.
6. Quoted by Stahl, Johnson, and Burge, vol. 1, p. 21. Also worth quoting is the verdict passed by Stahl on the writing style of the work: "Martianus has been sprung on unsuspecting students of medieval Latin by mischievous teachers as a corrective for the notion that it is easy to read the debased writing of the post-classical period. To inflict a heavy dosage of Martianus even upon a promising graduate student, however, could cause him to abandon thoughts of a career in classical philology" (pp. 33–4).
7. S. Gersh, *Middle Platonism and Neoplatonism: The Latin Tradition*, 2 vols. (Notre Dame, Ind., 1986), vol. 2, p. 639.
8. There is no complete English translation of the *Commentary*, but for studies that quote some parts of the text see J. C. M. van Winden, *Calcidius on Matter* (Leiden, 1959) and J. den Boeft, *Calcidius on Fate* (Leiden, 1970).
9. See den Boeft, *Calcidius on Fate*.

10. I discuss this in P. Adamson, "Freedom, Providence and Fate," in P. Remes and S. Slaveva-Griffin (eds.), *Handbook of Neoplatonism* (London, 2014), 437–52.
11. See den Boeft, *Calcidius on Fate*, 68.
12. See Gersh, *Middle Platonism and Neoplatonism*, vol. 2, p. 479.
13. On the impact of these works in the medieval period see S. Gersh, "The Medieval Legacy from Ancient Platonism," in S. Gersh and M. J. F. M. Hoenen (eds.), *The Platonic Tradition in the Middle Ages* (Berlin, 2002), 3–30.
14. She makes a brief appearance in Martianus too (*Marriage* 96).

Chapter 53

1. For the impact of late ancient logical writings, including those of Boethius, in the medieval era see S. Ebbesen, "Ancient Scholastic Logic as the Source of Medieval Scholastic Logic," in N. Kretzmann, A. Kenny, and J. Pinborg (eds.), *The Cambridge History of Later Medieval Philosophy* (Cambridge, 1982), 101–27.
2. See P. V. Spade (trans.), *Five Texts on the Mediaeval Problem of Universals* (Indianapolis, 1994). This includes Porphyry's *Introduction* and part of Boethius' second commentary on it.
3. I cite from *On the Trinity*, in H. F. Stewart, E. K. Rand, and S. J. Tester (trans.), *Boethius: Theological Tractates and Consolation of Philosophy* (London, 1973), All further references to Boethius' works are to section numbers of this edition, which has Latin and English on facing pages.
4. Text and translation in Stewart, Rand, and Tester, *Boethius: Theological Tractates*. For a useful study of this work see S. MacDonald, "Boethius's Claim that all Substances are Good," *Archiv für Geschichte der Philosophie*, 70 (1988), 245–79.
5. See D. Blank and N. Kretzmann (trans.), *Ammonius and Boethius on Aristotle's On Interpretation 9* (London, 1998), which has not only the texts but also useful introductory material.

FURTHER READING

Further reading is suggested here for each of the main sections of the book, along with recommendations for the topics of specific chapters. References on more specific topics can be found in notes to the chapters of this volume.

Hellenistic Philosophy

K. A. Algra *et al.* (eds.), *The Cambridge History of Hellenistic Philosophy* (Cambridge, 1999).

J. Annas, *Hellenistic Philosophy of Mind* (Berkeley, 1992).

J. Brunschwig, *Papers in Hellenistic Philosophy* (Cambridge, 1994).

M. Burnyeat and M. Schofield (eds.), *Doubt and Dogmatism: Studies in Hellenistic Epistemology* (Oxford, 1980).

C. Gill, *The Structured Self in Hellenistic and Roman Thought* (Oxford, 2006).

M. Griffin and J. Barnes (eds.), *Philosophia Togata I: Essays on Philosophy and Roman Society* (Oxford, 1989).

M. Griffin and J. Barnes (eds.), *Philosophia Togata II: Plato and Aristotle at Rome* (Oxford, 1997).

A. A. Long, *Hellenistic Philosophy* (London, 1974).

A. A. Long and D. Sedley, *The Hellenistic Philosophers* (Cambridge, 1987), vol. 1: translations and commentary, vol. 2: texts.

M. Schofield and G. Striker (eds.), *The Norms of Nature: Studies in Hellenistic Ethics* (Cambridge, 1986).

R. W. Sharples, *Stoics, Epicureans and Sceptics: An Introduction to Hellenistic Philosophy* (London, 1996).

G. Striker, *Essays on Hellenistic Epistemology and Ethics* (Cambridge, 1996).

The Socratic Legacy

G. Boys-Stones and C. J. Rowe, *The Circle of Socrates: Readings in the First-Generation Socratics* (Indianapolis, 2013).

A. A. Long, "Socrates in Hellenistic Philosophy," *Classical Quarterly*, 38 (1988), 150–71.

A. A. Long, "The Socratic Legacy," in K. Algra *et al.* (eds.), *The Cambridge History of Hellenistic Philosophy* (Cambridge, 1999), 617–41.

P. Merlan, "Minor Socratics," *Journal of the History of Philosophy*, 10 (1972), 143–52.

P. A. Vander Waerdt, *The Socratic Movement* (Ithaca, NY, 1994).

Cynics

R. Bracht Branham and M.-O. Goulet-Cazé (eds.), *The Cynics* (London, 1996).

W. Desmond, *Cynics* (Stocksfield, 2008).

D. R. Dudley, *A History of Cynicism from Diogenes to the Sixth Century AD* (London, 1937).

Cyrenaics

T. Irwin, "Aristippus Against Happiness," *The Monist*, 74 (1991), 55–82.
T. O'Keefe, "The Cyrenaics on Pleasure, Happiness, and Future-Concern," *Phronesis*, 47 (2002), 395–416.
V. Tsouna, *The Epistemology of the Cyrenaic School* (Cambridge, 1998).
U. Zilioli, *The Cyrenaics* (Durham, NC, 2012).

Epicurus

C. Bailey, *Epicurus: The Extant Remains* (Oxford, 1926).
J. Fish and K. Sanders (eds.), *Epicurus and the Epicurean Tradition* (Cambridge, 2009).
P. Mitsis, *Epicurus' Ethical Theory: The Pleasures of Invulnerability* (Ithaca, NY, 1988).
T. O'Keefe, *Epicurus on Freedom* (Cambridge, 2005).
T. O'Keefe, *Epicureanism* (Durham, NC, 2010).
J. M. Rist, *Epicurus: An Introduction* (Cambridge, 1972).
J. Warren, *Facing Death: Epicurus and his Critics* (Oxford, 2004).
J. Warren (ed.), *The Cambridge Companion to Epicureanism* (Cambridge, 2009).

Lucretius

K. A. Algra *et al.* (eds.), *Lucretius and his Intellectual Background* (Amsterdam, 1997).
D. Clay, *Lucretius and Epicurus* (Ithaca, NY, 1983).
D. J. Furley, "Lucretius and the Stoics" and "Lucretius the Epicurean: On the History of Man," both in D. J. Furley, *Cosmic Problems* (Cambridge, 1989).
S. Gillespie and P. Hardie (eds.), *The Cambridge Companion to Lucretius* (Cambridge, 2007).
D. Sedley, *Lucretius and the Transformation of Greek Wisdom* (Cambridge, 1998).
M. F. Smith, *Lucretius: On the Nature of Things* (Indianapolis, 2001).

Stoicism

S. Bobzien, *Determinism and Freedom in Stoic Philosophy* (Oxford, 1998).
T. Brennan, *The Stoic Life: Emotions, Duties, and Fate* (Oxford, 2005).
M. Graver, *Stoicism and Emotion* (Chicago, 2007).
K. Ierodiakonou (ed.), *Topics in Stoic Philosophy* (Oxford, 1999).
B. Inwood, *Ethics and Human Action in Early Stoicism* (Oxford, 1985).
B. Inwood, *The Cambridge Companion to the Stoics* (Cambridge, 2003).
A. A. Long, *Problems in Stoicism* (London, 1971).
A. A. Long, *Stoic Studies* (Cambridge, 1996).
J. Rist (ed.), *The Stoics* (Berkeley, 1978).
R. Salles (ed.), *God and Cosmos in Stoicism* (Oxford, 2009).
S. Sambursky, *The Physics of the Stoics* (London, 1959).
J. Sellars, *Stoicism* (Chesham, 2006).
S. Strange and J. Zupko (eds.), *Stoicism: Traditions and Transformations* (Cambridge, 2004).

Seneca

S. Bartsch and D. Wray, *Seneca and the Self* (Cambridge, 2009).

J. M. Cooper and J. F. Procopé (ed. and trans.), *Seneca: Moral and Political Essays* (Cambridge, 1995).

M. Griffin, *Seneca: A Philosopher in Politics* (Oxford, 1992).

B. Inwood, *Reading Seneca: Stoic Philosophy at Rome* (Oxford, 2005).

B. Inwood (trans.), *Seneca: Selected Philosophical Letters* (Oxford, 2007).

Epictetus

C. Gill and R. Hard (eds.), *The Discourses and Handbook of Epictetus* (London, 1995).

A. A. Long, *Epictetus: A Stoic and Socratic Guide to Life* (Oxford, 2002).

T. Scaltsas and A. S. Mason (eds.), *The Philosophy of Epictetus* (Oxford, 2007).

Marcus Aurelius

E. Asmis, "The Stoicism of Marcus Aurelius," *Aufstieg und Niedergang der römischen Welt*, II.36.3 (1989), 2228–52.

Marcus Aurelius, *The Meditations*, trans. G. M. A. Grube (Indianapolis, 1983).

P. Hadot, *The Inner Citadel: The Meditations of Marcus Aurelius*, trans. M. Chase (Cambridge, Mass., 1992).

F. McLynn, *Marcus Aurelius: Warrior, Philosopher, Emperor* (London, 2009).

J. Rist, "Are You a Stoic? The Case of Marcus Aurelius," in B. F. Meyer and E. P. Sanders (eds.), *Self Definition in the Greco-Roman World* (Philadelphia, 1982).

R. B. Rutherford, *The Meditations of Marcus Aurelius* (Oxford, 1989).

J. Sellars, *The Art of Living: The Stoics on the Nature and Function of Philosophy* (Aldershot, 2003).

Skepticism

J. Barnes, *The Toils of Scepticism* (Cambridge, 1990).

R. Bett (ed.), *The Cambridge Companion to Ancient Scepticism* (Cambridge, 2010).

R. J. Hankinson, *The Sceptics* (London, 1995).

D. Sedley, "The Motivation of Greek Skepticism," in *The Skeptical Tradition*, ed. M. Burnyeat (Berkeley, 1983), 9–29.

New (Skeptical) Academy

J. Allen, "Academic Probabilism and Stoic Epistemology," *Classical Quarterly*, 44 (1994), 85–113.

R. Bett, "Carneades' *Pithanon*: A Reappraisal of its Role and Status," *Oxford Studies in Ancient Philosophy*, 7 (1989), 59–94.

C. Brittain, *Philo of Larissa: The Last of the Academic Sceptics* (Oxford, 2001).

Pyrrho

R. Bett, *Pyrrho, his Antecedents and his Legacy* (Oxford, 2000).
T. Brennan, "Pyrrho on the Criterion," *Ancient Philosophy*, 18 (1998), 417–34.
S. Svavarsson, "Pyrrho's Undecidable Nature," *Oxford Studies in Ancient Philosophy*, 27 (2004), 249–95.

Cicero

Y. Baraz, *A Written Republic: Cicero's Philosophical Politics* (Princeton, 2012).
J. Glucker, "Cicero's Philosophical Affiliations," in J. M. Dillon and A. A. Long (eds.), *The Question of Eclecticism* (Berkeley, 1987), 34–69.
B. Inwood and J. Mansfeld (eds.), *Assent and Argument: Studies in Cicero's Academic Books* (Leiden, 1997).
P. MacKendrick, *The Philosophical Books of Cicero* (London, 1989).
J. G. F. Powell, *Cicero the Philosopher* (Oxford, 1995).
R. Woolf, *Cicero: The Philosophy of a Roman Sceptic* (Durham, 2015).

Sextus Empiricus and Pyrrhonism

J. Annas and J. Barnes, *The Modes of Scepticism* (Cambridge, 1985).
J. Annas and J. Barnes (ed. and trans.), *Sextus Empiricus: Outlines of Scepticism* (Cambridge, 2000).
A. Bailey, *Sextus Empiricus and Pyrrhonean Skepticism* (Oxford, 2002).
M. Burnyeat and M. Frede (eds.), *The Original Sceptics* (Indianapolis, 1997).
G. Striker, "The Ten Tropes of Aenesidemus," in M. Burnyeat (ed.), *The Skeptical Tradition* (Berkeley, 1983), 95–115.

Galen and the Ancient Medical Schools

P. Adamson, R. Hansberger, and J. Wilberding (eds.), *Philosophical Themes in Galen* (London, 2013).
J. Barnes and J. Jouanna (eds.), *Galien et la philosophie* (Vandoeuvres, 2003).
L. Edelstein, "The Relation of Ancient Philosophy to Medicine," *Bulletin of the History of Medicine*, 26 (1952), 299–316.
J. Longrigg, *Greek Medicine from the Heroic to the Hellenistic Age: A Source Book* (London, 1998).
V. Nutton, *Ancient Medicine* (London, 2004).
P. N. Singer (trans.), *Galen: Selected Works* (Oxford, 2002).
P. van der Eijk, *Medicine and Philosophy in Classical Antiquity* (Cambridge, 2005).
R. Walzer and M. Frede (trans.), *Galen: Three Treatises on the Nature of Science* (Indianapolis, 1985).

Late Ancient Philosophy

G. Boys-Stones, *Post-Hellenistic Philosophy* (Oxford, 2001).
J. M. Dillon and L. P. Gerson, *Neoplatonic Philosophy: Introductory Readings* (Indianapolis, 2004).
H. Dörrie and M. Baltes, *Der Platonismus in der Antike* (Stuttgart, 1993).
M. Edwards and S. Swain, *Approaching Late Antiquity* (Oxford, 2004).

L. P. Gerson (ed.), *The Cambridge History of Philosophy in Late Antiquity*, 2 vols. (Cambridge, 2010).

P. Remes, *Neoplatonism* (Stocksfield, 2008).

P. Remes and S. Slaveva-Griffin (eds.), *The Routledge Handbook of Neoplatonism* (London, 2014).

M. Schofield (ed.), *Aristotle, Plato and Pythagoreanism in the First Century BC: New Directions for Philosophy* (Cambridge, 2013).

A. Smith, *Philosophy in Late Antiquity* (London, 2004).

R. Sorabji, *The Philosophy of the Commentators, 200–600 AD: A Sourcebook*, 3 vols. (London, 2004).

M. Tuominen, *The Ancient Commentators on Plato and Aristotle* (Stocksfield, 2009).

Middle Platonism

J. M. Dillon (trans.), *Alcinous: The Handbook of Platonism* (Oxford, 1993).

J. M. Dillon, *The Middle Platonists: 80 B.C. to A.D. 220* (Ithaca, NY, 1977; 2nd edn. 1996).

G. Karamanolis, *Plato and Aristotle in Agreement?* (Oxford, 2005).

R. W. Sharples and R. Sorabji (eds.), *Greek and Roman Philosophy 100 BC–200 AD*, 2 vols. (London, 2007).

H. Tarrant, *Thrasyllan Platonism* (Ithaca, NY, 1993).

Philo of Alexandria

A. Kamesar (ed.), *The Cambridge Companion to Philo* (Cambridge, 2009).

J. Mansfeld, "Philosophy in the Service of Scripture: Philo's Exegetical Strategies," in J. M. Dillon and A. A. Long (eds.), *The Question of "Eclecticism"* (Berkeley, 1988), 70–102.

G. Reydams-Schils, "Philo of Alexandria on Stoic and Platonist Psycho-Physiology: The Socratic Higher Ground," *Ancient Philosophy*, 22 (2002), 125–47.

D. T. Runia, *Philo and the Timaeus of Plato* (Leiden, 1986).

S. Sandmel, *Philo of Alexandria: An Introduction* (New York, 1979).

K. Schenck, *A Brief Guide to Philo* (Louisville, Ky., 2005).

H. A. Wolfson, *Philo: Foundations of Religious Philosophy in Judaism, Christianity, and Islam* (Cambridge, Mass., 1948).

Plutarch

F. E. Brenk, J. P. Hershbell, and P. A. Stadter (eds.), *Plutarch: Illinois Classical Studies*, 13 (1988).

J. P. Hershbell, "Plutarch and Stoicism" and "Plutarch and Epicureanism," *Aufstieg und Niedergang der römischen Welt*, II.36.5 (1992), 3336–52 and 3353–83.

C. P. Jones, *Plutarch and Rome* (Oxford, 1971).

R. Lamberton, *Plutarch* (New Haven, 2001).

J. Opsomer, "Plutarch's *De animae procreatione in Timaeo*: Manipulation or Search for Consistency?" in P. Adamson, H. Baltussen, and M. W. F. Stone (eds.), *Philosophy, Science and Exegesis in Greek, Arabic and Latin Commentaries* (London, 2004), vol. 1, pp. 137–62.

L. Van Hoof, *Plutarch's Practical Ethics* (Oxford, 2010).

The Rise of Aristotelianism

A. Alberti and R. W. Sharples (eds.), *Aspasius: The Earliest Extant Commentary on Aristotle's Ethics* (Berlin, 1999).

J. Barnes, "Roman Aristotle," in J. Barnes and M. Griffin (eds.), *Philosophia Togata II: Plato and Aristotle at Rome* (Oxford, 1997), 1–69.

M. Griffin, *Aristotle's Categories in the Early Roman Empire* (Oxford, 2015).

H. B. Gottschalk, "Aristotelian Philosophy in the Roman World," *Aufstieg und Niedergang der römischen Welt*, II.36.2 (1987), 1079–174.

R. W. Sharples, *Peripatetic Philosophy 200 BC to AD 200* (Cambridge, 2010).

R. W. Sharples and R. Sorabji (eds.), *Greek and Roman Philosophy 100 BC–200 AD*, 2 vols. (London, 2007).

Alexander of Aphrodisias

D. Frede, "The Dramatization of Determinism: Alexander of Aphrodisias' *De Fato*," *Phronesis*, 27 (1982), 276–98.

M. Rashed, *Essentialisme: Alexandre d'Aphrodise entre logique, physique et cosmologie* (Berlin, 2007).

R. W. Sharples (trans.), *Alexander of Aphrodisias: On Fate* (London, 1983).

R. W. Sharples, "Alexander of Aphrodisias: Scholasticism and Innovation," *Aufstieg und Niedergang der römischen Welt*, II.36.2 (Berlin, 1987), 1176–243.

M. Tweedale, "Alexander of Aphrodisias' Views on Universals," *Phronesis*, 29 (1984), 279–303.

Rhetoric and Ancient Philosophy

G. Anderson, *The Second Sophistic* (London, 1993).

G. Bowersock, "Philosophy in the Second Sophistic," in G. Clark and T. Rajak (eds.), *Philosophy and Power in the Graeco-Roman World* (Oxford, 2002), 157–70.

M. Heath, "Platonists and the Teaching of Rhetoric in Late Antiquity," in P. Vassilopoulou and S. Clark (eds.), *Late Antique Epistemology* (London, 2009), 143–59.

P. Heather and D. Moncur, *Politics, Philosophy and Empire in the Fourth Century: Select Orations of Themistius* (Liverpool, 2001).

A. Luhtala, *Grammar and Philosophy in Late Antiquity* (Amsterdam, 2005).

I. Sluiter, *Ancient Grammar in Context* (Amsterdan, 1990).

P. Swiggers and A. Wouters (eds.), *Grammatical Theory and Philosophy of Language in Antiquity* (Leuven, 2002).

M. B. Trapp, *Philosophy in the Roman Empire: Ethics, Politics and Society* (Aldershot, 2007).

Astronomy and Astrology

P. Adamson, "Plotinus on Astrology," *Oxford Studies in Ancient Philosophy*, 35 (2008), 265–91.

T. Barton, *Ancient Astrology* (London, 1994).

L. Bouché-Leclercq, *L'Astrologie grecque* (Paris, 1899).

A. A. Long, "Astrology: Arguments Pro and Contra," in *Science and Speculation: Studies in Hellenistic Theory and Practice*, ed. J. Barnes et al. (Cambridge, 1982), 165–92.

O. Neugebauer, *Astronomy and History: Selected Essays* (New York, 1983).

L. Taub, *Ptolemy's Universe* (Chicago, 1993).

Plotinus

A. H. Armstrong (trans.), *Plotinus: Enneads*, 7 vols. (Cambridge, Mass., 1966–88).
L. P. Gerson (ed.), *The Cambridge Companion to Plotinus* (Cambridge, 1996).
L. P. Gerson, *Plotinus* (London, 1998).
D. O'Meara, *Plotinus: An Introduction to the Enneads* (Oxford, 1993).
J. M. Rist, *Plotinus: The Road to Reality* (Cambridge, 1967).

Plotinus on One and Intellect

A. H. Armstrong, "The Background of the Doctrine that the Intelligibles are not Outside the Intellect," in *Les Sources de Plotin* (Geneva, 1960), 393–413.
J. R. Bussanich, *The One and its Relation to Intellect in Plotinus* (Leiden, 1988).
E. K. Emilsson, *Plotinus on Intellect* (Oxford, 2007).
S. Slaveva-Griffin, *Plotinus on Number* (Oxford, 2009).

Plotinus on Soul

H. Blumenthal, *Plotinus' Psychology* (The Hague, 1971).
R. Chiaradonna (ed.), *Studi sull'anima in Plotino* (Naples, 2005).
E. K. Emilsson, "Plotinus on Soul–Body Dualism," in S. Everson (ed.), *Psychology: Companions to Ancient Thought* (Cambridge, 1991).
P. Remes, *Plotinus on Self: The Philosophy of the "We"* (Cambridge, 2007).

Plotinus on Matter and Evil

J.-M. Narbonne, *Plotinus in Dialogue with the Gnostics* (Leiden, 2011).
D. O'Brien, *Plotinus on the Origin of Matter* (Naples, 1991).
D. J. O'Meara, "Evil in Plotinus (*Enn.* I, 8)," in D. J. O'Meara, *The Structure of Being and the Search for the Good* (Aldershot, 1998), §IX.
J. M. Rist, "Plotinus on Matter and Evil," *Phronesis*, 6 (1961), 154–66.

Porphyry

J. Barnes (trans. and comm.), *Porphyry: Introduction* (Oxford, 2003).
G. Clark (trans.), *Porphyry: On Abstinence from Killing Animals* (London, 2000).
S. Ebbesen, "Porphyry's Legacy to Logic," in R. Sorabji (ed.), *Aristotle Transformed* (London, 1990), 141–71.
A. P. Johnson, *Religion and Identity in Porphyry of Tyre* (Cambridge, 2013).
G. Karamanolis and A. Sheppard (eds.), *Studies on Porphyry* (London, 2007).
A. Smith, *Porphyry's Place in the Neoplatonic Tradition: A Study in Post-Plotinian Neoplatonism* (The Hague, 1974).
S. K. Strange (trans.), *Porphyry: On Aristotle's Categories* (London, 1992).

Iamblichus

E. Afonasin, J. M. Dillon, and J. F. Finamore (eds.), *Iamblichus and the Foundations of Late Platonism* (Leiden, 2012).

H. J. Blumenthal and E. G. Clark (eds.), *The Divine Iamblichus* (London, 1993).

H. J. Blumenthal and J. F. Finamore (eds.), *Iamblichus the Philosopher*, special issue of *Syllecta Classica*, 8 (1997).

E. C. Clarke, J. M. Dillon, and J. P. Hershbell (trans.), *Iamblichus: On the Mysteries* (Atlanta, Ga., 2003).

G. Shaw, *Theurgy and the Soul: The Neoplatonism of Iamblichus* (University Park, Pa., 1995).

Proclus

R. Chlup, *Proclus: An Introduction* (Cambridge, 2012).

E. R. Dodds, *Proclus: The Elements of Theology* (Oxford, 1933).

C. Helmig, *Forms and Concepts. Concept Formation in the Platonic Tradition* (Berlin, 2012).

M. Perkams and R. M. Piccione (eds.), *Proklos: Methode, Seelenlehre, Metaphysik* (Leiden, 2006).

L. Siorvanes, *Proclus: Neo-Platonic Philosophy and Science* (New Haven, 1996).

Later Neoplatonism

P. Athanassiadi, *Julian: An Intellectual Biography* (London, 1981).

H. Baltussen, *Philosophy and Exegesis in Simplicius* (London, 2008).

A. Cameron, *The Last Pagans of Rome* (Oxford, 2010).

M. Dzielska, *Hypatia of Alexandria* (Cambridge, Mass., 1995).

C. Steel, *The Changing Self: A Study on the Soul in Later Neoplatonism* (Brussels, 1978).

E. J. Watts, *City and School in Late Antique Athens and Alexandria* (Berkeley, 2006).

Philoponus

F. A. J. de Haas, *John Philoponus' New Definition of Prime Matter: Aspects of its Background in Neoplatonism and the Ancient Commentary Tradition* (Leiden, 1997).

J. F. Phillips, "Neoplatonic Exegeses of Plato's Cosmogony (*Timaeus* 27C–28C)," *Journal of the History of Philosophy*, 35 (1977), 173–97.

R. Sorabji (ed.), *Philoponus and the Rejection of Aristotelian Science* (Ithaca, NY, 1987; new edn. London, 2011).

G. Verbeke, "Some Late Neoplatonic Views on Divine Creation and the Eternity of the World," in *Neoplatonism and Christian Thought*, ed. D. J. O'Meara (Albany, NY, 1982).

Household and State

P. Brown, *The Philosopher and Society in Late Antiquity* (Berkeley, 1978).

P. Garnsey, *Ideas of Slavery from Aristotle to Augustine* (Cambridge, 1996).

D. J. O'Meara, *Platonopolis: Platonic Political Philosophy in Late Antiquity* (Oxford, 2005).

A. Smith (ed.), *The Philosopher and Society in Late Antiquity* (Bristol, 2003).

S. Swain, *Economy, Family and Society from Rome to Islam: A Critical Edition, English Translation, and Study of Bryson's "Management of the Estate"* (Cambridge, 2013).

Philosophy in Christian Antiquity

H. Bettenson, *The Early Christian Church Fathers* (Oxford, 1956).

H. Bettenson, *The Later Christian Church Fathers* (Oxford, 1970).

H. Chadwick, *Early Christian Thought and the Classical Tradition: Studies in Justin, Clement and Origen* (Oxford, 1966).

M. Edwards, *Christians, Gnostics and Philosophers in Late Antiquity* (Farnham, 2012).

G. Evans, *The First Christian Theologians* (Oxford, 2004).

G. Karamanolis, *The Philosophy of Early Christianity* (Stocksfield, 2014).

W. A. Löhr, "Christianity as Philosophy," *Vigiliae Christianae*, 64 (2010), 160–88.

E. Osborne, *The Beginning of Christian Philosophy* (Cambridge, 1981).

C. Stead, *Philosophy in Christian Antiquity* (Cambridge, 1994).

H. A. Wolfson, *The Philosophy of the Church Fathers* (Cambridge, Mass., 1970).

F. Young, L. Aures, and A. Louth (eds.), *Cambridge History of Early Christian Literature* (Cambridge, 2004).

Greek Church Fathers

R. M. Grant, *Greek Apologists of the Second Century* (Philadelphia, 1988).

R. M. Grant, *Irenaeus of Lyons* (London, 1997).

S. R. C. Lilla, *Clement of Alexandria* (Oxford, 1971).

E. Osborne, *Clement of Alexandria* (Cambridge, 2005).

H. B. Timothy, *The Early Christian Apologists and Greek Philosophy* (Assen, 1973).

Origen

G. W. Butterworth (trans.), *Origen: On First Principles* (Gloucester, Mass., 1973).

H. Crouzel, *Origen: The Life and Thought of the First Great Theologian*, trans. A. S. Worrall (San Francisco, 1989).

M. J. Edwards, *Origen against Plato* (Aldershot, 2002).

C. Kannengiesser and W. L. Peterson (eds.), *Origen of Alexandria: His World and His Legacy* (Notre Dame, Ind., 1988).

M. S. M. Scott, *Journey Back to God: Origen on the Problem of Evil* (Oxford, 2012).

J. W. Trigg, *Origen* (London, 1998).

The Cappadocians

B. A. Daley, *Gregory of Nazianzus* (London, 2006).

M. Delcogliano, *Basil of Caesarea's Anti-Eunomian Theory of Names* (Leiden, 2010).

J. McGuckin, *Saint Gregory of Nazianzus: An Intellectual Biography* (Crestwood, NY, 2001).

A. Meredith, *The Cappadocians* (Crestwood, NY, 1996).

A. Meredith, *Gregory of Nyssa* (London, 1999).

J. Zachhuber, *Human Nature in Gregory of Nyssa* (Leiden, 2000).

The Pseudo-Dionysius

S. Gersh, *From Iamblichus to Eriugena: An Investigation of the Prehistory and Evolution of the Pseudo-Dionysian Tradition* (Leiden, 1978).

A. Louth, *Denys the Areopagite* (London, 1989).

C. Luibheid and P. Rorem (trans.), *Pseudo-Dionysius: The Complete Works* (London, 1987).

P. Rorem, *Pseudo-Dionysius: A Commentary on the Texts and an Introduction to their Influence* (Oxford, 1993).

C. Schäfer, *The Philosophy of Dionysius the Areopagite* (Leiden, 2006).

Maximus the Confessor and the Christological Debate

D. Bathrellos, *The Byzantine Christ* (Oxford, 2004).

D. Bradshaw, *Aristotle East and West* (Cambridge, 2007).

A. Louth, *Maximus the Confessor* (London, 1996).

J. Meyendorff, *Byzantine Theology* (New York, 1974).

T. T. Tollefson, *The Christocentric Theology of St Maximus the Confessor* (Oxford, 2008).

M. Törönen, *Union and Distinction in the Thought of St Maximus the Confessor* (Oxford, 2007).

Ancient Christian Asceticism

P. Brown, *Through the Eye of a Needle: Wealth, the Fall of Rome and the Making Christianity in the West 350–550 AD* (Princeton, 2012).

A. M. Casiday, *Evagrius Ponticus* (London, 2006).

E. A. Clark, *Ascetic Piety and Women's Faith: Essays in Late Ancient Christianity* (Lewiston, NY, 1986).

G. Clark, *Body and Gender, Soul and Reason in Late Antiquity* (Farnham, 2011).

S. K. Elm, *"Virgins of God": The Making of Asceticism in Late Antiquity* (Oxford, 1994).

H. Hunt, *Clothed in the Body: Asceticism, the Body and the Spiritual in the Late Antique Era* (Farnham, 2012).

Latin Church Fathers

H. Chadwick, *Early Christian Thought and the Classical Tradition: Studies in Justin, Clement and Origen* (Oxford, 1966).

E. Digeser, *The Making of a Christian Empire: Lactantius and Rome* (London, 2000).

M. Hale Williams, *The Monk and the Book: Jerome and the Making of Christian Scholarship* (Chicago, 2006).

J. Kelly, *Jerome: His Life, Writings, and Controversies* (London, 1975).

N. B. McLynn, *Ambrose of Milan: Church and Court in a Christian Capital* (Berkeley, 1994).

E. K. Osborne, *Tertullian, First Theologian of the West* (Cambridge, 1997).

B. Ramsey, *Ambrose* (London, 1997).

J. Warren Smith, *Christian Grace and Pagan Virtue: The Theological Foundation of Ambrose's Ethics* (Oxford, 2011).

Augustine

P. Brown, *Augustine of Hippo* (Berkeley, 1969).

S. Byers, *Perception, Sensibility, and Moral Motivation in Augustine* (Cambridge, 2012).

H. Chadwick, *Augustine* (New York, 1986).

H. Chadwick (trans.), *Augustine: Confessions* (Oxford, 1991).

C. Kirwan, *Augustine* (London, 1989).

R. A. Markus (ed.), *Augustine: A Collection of Critical Essays* (Garden City, NY, 1972).

J. J. O'Donnell, *Augustine: A New Biography* (New York, 2005).

J. M. Rist, *Augustine* (Cambridge, 1994).

E. Stump and N. Kretzmann (eds.), *The Cambridge Companion to Augustine* (Cambridge, 2001).

M. Vessey (ed.), *A Companion to Augustine* (London, 2012).

Latin Platonism

J. den Boeft, *Calcidius on Fate* (Leiden, 1970).

S. Gersh, *Middle Platonism and Neoplatonism: The Latin Tradition*, 2 vols. (Notre Dame, Ind., 1986).

S. Gersh, "The Medieval Legacy from Ancient Platonism," in *The Platonic Tradition in the Middle Ages*, ed. S. Gersh and M. J. F. M. Hoenen (Berlin, 2002), 3–30.

W. H. Stahl (trans.), *Macrobius: Commentary on the Dream of Scipio* (New York, 1953).

W. H. Stahl, R. Johnson, and E. L. Burge, *Martianus Capella and the Seven Liberal Arts*, 2 vols. (New York, 1971, 1977).

J. C. M. van Winden, *Calcidius on Matter* (Leiden, 1959).

Boethius

M. Gibson (ed.), *Boethius: His Life, Thought and Influence* (Oxford, 1981).

J. Marenbon, *Boethius* (New York, 2003).

J. Marenbon (ed.), *The Cambridge Companion to Boethius* (Cambridge, 2009).

J. C. Relihan (trans.), *Boethius: Consolation of Philosophy* (Indianapolis, 2001).

H. F. Stewart, E. K. Rand, and S. J. Tester (trans.), *Boethius: Theological Tractates and Consolation of Philosophy* (London, 1973).

INDEX